The second edition of this previously well-received handbook will continue to serve as an excellent resource and reference for students, researchers, and especially clinicians.

—*Bruce Hermann, PhD, Matthews Neuropsychology Lab, Department of Neurology, University of Wisconsin—Madison*

This book is a must-have reference for the practicing clinical neuropsychologist and the neuropsychologist-in-training; it will also be of great interest and utility to the clinical psychologist who works in a medical setting or with medically disordered patients. It is clearly and succinctly written by clinicians who have been in the trenches and know what the neuropsychologist needs to know. Each chapter is written by a highly respected expert in his or her field. This is truly an indispensable volume.

—*Deborah Fein, PhD, Board of Trustees Distinguished Professor of Psychology, University of Connecticut, Storrs; Member, Board of Directors, American Academy of Clinical Neuropsychology*

The first edition of *Clinical Neuropsychology: A Pocket Handbook for Assessment* quickly became recognized as an expert reference to the most highly relevant issues in the practice of clinical neuropsychology. Now the second edition affords a modestly reorganized but thoroughly updated presentation from identified authorities in the field that will continue to educate and to support clinical practice in our rapidly evolving profession.

—*Richard C. Delaney, PhD, ABPP/CN, Gaylord Hospital, Wallingford, CT; Yale University School of Medicine, New Haven, CT*

Clinical Neuropsychology

Clinical Neuropsychology

A POCKET HANDBOOK for ASSESSMENT *Second Edition*

Senior Editor
Peter J. Snyder

Associate Editors
Paul D. Nussbaum
Diana L. Robins

American Psychological Association
Washington, DC

Fifth Printing, November 2011

Published by
American Psychological Association
750 First Street, NE
Washington, DC 20002
www.apa.org

To order
APA Order Department
P.O. Box 92984
Washington, DC 20090-2984
Tel: (800) 374-2721
Direct: (202) 336-5510
Fax: (202) 336-5502
TDD/TTY: (202) 336-6123
Online: www.apa.org/books/
E-mail: order@apa.org

In the U.K., Europe, Africa, and the Middle East, copies may be ordered from
American Psychological Association
3 Henrietta Street
Covent Garden, London
WC2E 8LU England

Typeset in Stone Serif by World Composition Services, Inc., Sterling, VA

Printer: Edwards Brothers, Ann Arbor, MI
Cover Designer: Berg Design, Albany, NY
Technical/Production Editor: Genevieve Gill

The statements and opinions published are the responsibility of the authors, and such opinions and statements do not represent official policies, standards, guidelines or ethical mandates of the American Psychological Association. Any information in this book involving legal and ethical issues should not be used as a substitute for obtaining personal legal and/or ethical advice and consultation prior to making decisions regarding individual circumstances.

Library of Congress Cataloging-in-Publication Data

Clinical neuropsychology : a pocket handbook for assessment / Peter J. Snyder, senior editor ; Paul D. Nussbaum and Diana L. Robins, associate editors.—2nd ed.
    p. cm.
    Includes bibliographical references and index.
    ISBN 1-59147-283-0
    1. Neuropsychological tests—Handbooks, manuals, etc. 2. Clinical neuropsychology—Handbooks, manuals, etc. I. Snyder, Peter J., 1964- II. Nussbaum, Paul David. III. Robins, Diana L.

    RC386.6.N48C527 2006
    616.8'0475—dc22   2005005262

British Library Cataloguing-in-Publication Data
A CIP record is available from the British Library.

Printed in the United States of America
Second Edition

To my lovely wife, Amy Laura,
for giving me the two greatest joys of my life—
Molly Rose and Jacob Brendan Eli.

—Peter J. Snyder

To Richard and Mary Nussbaum.

—Paul D. Nussbaum

To Laurie, for her love and support.

—Diana L. Robins

Contents

PART II

Neuropsychology and the Human Life Span

PART IV

Neurological Syndromes

19 Amnesic Syndromes   *463*
Margaret G. O'Connor and Ginette Lafleche

20 Neglect Syndromes   *489*
Mieke Verfaellie and Kenneth M. Heilman

21 The Agnosias   *508*
Russell M. Bauer

Contributors

Russell Addeo, PhD, ABPP/CN
Behavioral Medicine Department
Brooks Rehabilitation
Jacksonville, FL

Daniel N. Allen, PhD
Department of Psychology
University of Nevada, Las Vegas

Peter A. Arnett, PhD
Department of Psychology
Pennsylvania State University
University Park, PA

Russell M. Bauer, PhD, ABPP/CN
Department of Clinical and Health Psychology and
    Neurology
University of Florida
Gainesville, FL

Sue R. Beers, PhD
Associate Professor
Department of Psychiatry
University of Pittsburgh School of Medicine
Western Psychiatric Institute and Clinic
Pittsburgh, PA

Pélagie M. Beeson, PhD
Department of Speech, Language, and Hearing Sciences
Department of Neurology
University of Arizona, Tucson

Arthur L. Benton, PhD, ABPP/CN
Professor Emeritus
Departments of Neurology and Psychology
University of Iowa
Iowa City, IA

Robert M. Bilder, PhD, ABPP/CN
Chief, Medical Psychology-Neuropsychology; and
Professor of Psychiatry and Biobehavioral Sciences and
    Psychology
UCLA Neuropsychiatric Institute and Hospital
Los Angeles, CA

Jennifer J. Bortz, PhD
Mayo Clinic
Scottsdale, AZ

Meryl A. Butters, PhD
Associate Professor of Psychiatry
University of Pittsburgh School of Medicine
Western Psychiatric Institute and Clinic
Pittsburgh, PA

Daniel X. Capruso, PhD, ABPP/CN
Kirby Forensic Psychiatric Center
New York, NY

Ronald A. Cohen, PhD
Department of Psychiatry and Human Behavior
Brown University School of Medicine
The Miriam Hospital
Providence, RI

Ellen Coman, PhD
Halifax Regional Health System
South Boston, VA

David Darby, MBBS, FRACP, PhD
Associate Professor
Centre for Neuroscience
University of Melbourne
Victoria, Australia; and
CogState, Ltd.
Melbourne, Australia

Greig de Zubicaray, PhD
Centre for Magnetic Resonance
University of Queensland
Brisbane, Queensland
Australia

Robert B. Fields, PhD
Assistant Professor of Psychiatry
Drexel University Medical School
UPMC Shadyside Hospital, Senior Care Institute
Pittsburgh, PA

Teri J. Forrest, PhD
Department of Psychology
University of Nevada, Las Vegas

Linda V. Frantom, PhD
Department of Psychology
University of Nevada, Las Vegas

Michael D. Franzen, PhD
Associate Professor of Psychiatry
Drexel University College of Medicine
West Penn Allegheny Health System
Pittsburgh, PA

Leslie J. Gonzalez-Rothi, PhD
Professor, Department of Neurology
University of Florida College of Medicine
Gainesville, FL

Katherine Hammond, PsyD
Private Practice
Pittsburgh, PA

Kerry deS. Hamsher, PhD, ABPP/CN
Neuropsychology Clinic
Milwaukee, WI; and
Clinical Associate Professor of Neurology
University of Wisconsin Medical School
Madison, WI

Brian T. Harel, PhD
Benton Neuropsychology Laboratory
Department of Neurology
University of Iowa Hospitals and Clinics
Iowa City, IA

Kenneth M. Heilman, MD
James E. Rooks, Jr., Distinguished Professor and
    Program Director
Department of Neurology
University of Florida
Gainesville, FL

Grant L. Iverson, PhD
Department of Psychiatry
University of British Columbia
Vancouver, British Columbia, Canada

Melissa A. Jenkins, PhD
Department of Psychiatry and Human Behavior
Brown University School of Medicine
Butler Hospital
Providence, RI

Howard R. Kessler, PhD
Coastal Neurobehavioral Center
Yarmouth, ME

Ginette Lafleche, PhD
Memory Disorders Research Center
Boston University
Boston, MA

John A. Lucas, PhD, ABPP/CN
Associate Professor of Psychology
Department of Psychiatry and Psychology
Mayo Clinic
Jacksonville, FL

Paul F. Malloy, PhD
Department of Psychiatry & Human Behavior
Brown University School of Medicine
Butler Hospital
Providence, RI

Robert L. Mapou, PhD
William Stixrud, PhD & Associates, LLC
Silver Spring, MD

Roy C. Martin, PhD
Director of Neuropsychology Services
Comprehensive Epilepsy Program
Department of Neurology
University of Alabama, Birmingham

Paul Maruff, PhD
Adjunct Professor of Psychology
Alzheimer's Disease Research Group
University of Melbourne
Victoria, Austrialia; and
CogState, Ltd.
Melbourne, Australia

Harry W. McConnell, MD
Brisbane, Australia

Lisa A. Morrow, PhD
Neurobehavioral Toxicology
Western Psychiatric Institute and Clinic
Pittsburgh, PA

Paul D. Nussbaum, PhD
Clinical Neuropsychologist
Adjunct Associate Professor of Neurological Surgery
University of Pittsburgh School of Medicine
Pittsburgh, PA

Margaret G. O'Connor, PhD
Assistant Professor of Neurology
Harvard Medical School
Boston, MA

Ruth O'Hara, PhD
Assistant Professor
Department of Psychiatry and Behavioral Sciences
Stanford University School of Medicine
Stanford, CA

Robert H. Paul, PhD
Department of Psychiatry and Human Behavior
Brown University School of Medicine
The Miriam Hospital
Providence, RI

Laura A. Rabin, PhD
Adjunct Assistant Professor of Psychiatry
Neuropsychology Program and Brain Imaging Laboratory
Department of Psychiatry–DHMC
Dartmouth Medical School
Lebanon, NH

Steven Z. Rapcsak, MD
Department of Neurology
University of Arizona; and
Southern Arizona Veteran's Administration
    Health Care System
Tucson, AZ

Diana L. Robins, PhD
Department of Psychology
Georgia State University
Atlanta, GA

Christopher M. Ryan, PhD
Professor
Department of Psychiatry
University of Pittsburgh School of Medicine
Western Psychiatric Institute and Clinic
Pittsburgh, PA

Stephen M. Sawrie, MD, PhD
Research Assistant Professor
Department of Neurology
University of Alabama at Birmingham School of Medicine

Andrew J. Saykin, PsyD, ABPP/CN
Professor of Psychiatry and Radiology
Director, Neuropsychology Program and
    Brain Imaging Laboratory
Department of Psychiatry–DHMC
Dartmouth Medical School
Lebanon, NH

Thomas F. Scott, MD
Professor of Neurology
Drexel University College of Medicine
West Penn Allegheny Health System
Pittsburgh, PA

Peter J. Snyder, PhD
Professor of Psychology (Neuropsychology)
University of Connecticut (Storrs);
Professeur Associé, Centre de Neuroscience de la Cognition,
    Université du Québec à Montréal; and
    Director and Early Clinical Leader, CNS Clinical Research
    and Development
Pfizer Global Research & Development–Groton Laboratories
Groton, CT

Christopher Starratt, PhD
Department of Psychology
Barry University
Miami Shores, FL

Brett A. Steinberg, PhD
Comprehensive Neuropsychological Services, PC
Cheshire, CT

Gregory P. Strauss, MA
Department of Psychology
University of Nevada, Las Vegas

Rodney A. Swenson, PhD, ABPN
University of North Dakota School of Medicine
MeritCare Neuroscience Clinic
Fargo, ND

Alexander I. Tröster, PhD
Associate Professor
Department of Neurology
University of North Carolina School of Medicine
Chapel Hill, NC

Mieke Verfaellie, PhD
Professor of Psychiatry and Psychology
Memory Disorders Research Center
Boston University School of Medicine
Department of Veterans Affairs Medical Center (151A)
Boston, MA

Robert T. Watson, MD
Professor of Neurology
Department of Neurology
University of Florida College of Medicine
Gainesville, FL

Amy Weinstein, PhD
Department of Neurology
University of Rochester Medical Center
Rochester, NY

Heather A. Wishart, PhD
Assistant Professor of Psychiatry
Neuropsychology Program and Brain Imaging Laboratory
Department of Psychiatry–DHMC
Dartmouth Medical School
Lebanon, NH

Clinical Neuropsychology

toward formal recognition of neuropsychology internships, postdoctoral programs, and board certification requirements all attest to the development of a mature and intellectually rewarding health care specialty.

Over the past 7 to 8 years, we have continued to develop and refine the tools we use to make our diagnoses and treatment decisions. Neuropsychologists are increasingly relying on, and receiving specialized training in the use and interpretation of, functional and anatomic neuroimaging technologies. In addition, with the slow but inevitable expansion of prescription privileges (and the required training on which such privileges depend) for clinical (neuro)psychologists, our field must make a special effort to provide education that integrates psychopharmacological approaches to the treatment of our patients. With this second edition of this handbook, we hope to address (in a small way) how these areas of study are increasingly affecting the manner in which we practice as clinicians. A new chapter has been included to introduce the busy clinician to the range of established and novel neuroimaging technologies that have seen tremendous technological improvements over the past 7 years. In addition, chapters were revised with the intent of adding more specific information related to the neurochemical bases for various disorders, and when appropriate, more information on currently accepted pharmacologic treatment approaches. The reader will also find other new additions, including a chapter on neuro-oncology and one on schizophrenia.

The initial goal that had led to the first edition of this book remains unchanged. That is, we hope to provide a ready reference to assist the busy clinician or doctoral-level trainee selecting from among the many hundreds of tests and assessment techniques that are widely available. A principal aim of this reference book is to help guide the clinician in developing tailored, hypothesis-driven approaches for the assessment of patients with a broad range of common neuropsychological syndromes or neurological disorders. As before, this volume is designed for health care providers who need to make examination strategy decisions rapidly while working in the hospital inpatient unit. For the advanced trainee, we hope that this book will prove particularly useful at times when your clinical supervisors are not readily available themselves. This volume should provide for clinical neuropsychology what already exists for most all other medical or health care specialties: a diagnostic guide that fits into the lab coat pocket (I concede that this book may be a bit heavy for some pockets!). Such manuals "for the house officer" (at least one for each specialty) provide a ready source of information to aid in the differential diagnoses of relevant clinical syndromes. With this edited volume, we attempt to provide a readily available handbook for neuropsychology interns, postdoctoral fellows, and practicing clinicians.

For many interns and fellows who are still in training, their current training site may be their first exposure to working on staff in a hospital setting, because many graduate PhD programs do not include such exposure as part of their training programs. For these students, chapters are included that provide helpful suggestions for the rapid and efficient reading of a patient's medical chart, proper chart noting, understanding a neurologist's notes (and stick figures) detailing his or her neurological findings, and the psychological and behavioral correlates of various types of blood and other laboratory tests. In addition, chapters are included that contain effective approaches to the clinical interview and the bedside neuropsychological exam.

The chapters have been designed to be brief and easily scanned at times when decisions must be made quickly. Although it is exceedingly difficult in an edited volume such as this one, we have attempted to structure all chapters as similarly as possible, to facilitate the efficiency with which any one chapter may be reviewed for pertinent information when the reader is under pressure to make rapid decisions. A few chapters do provide more extensive background information than others because such detail was felt to be necessary given the state of the science in that field. Some areas, of course, owing to the nature of the disorder, do not have clear-cut assessment procedures outlined. As in many clinical investigations, providing areas of potential exploration is more realistic. Each chapter concludes with a short bibliography of primary references for further reading; these references are not meant to be complete but rather to steer the reader toward the relevant literature. Although many tests and measures are suggested for use in the differential diagnoses of specific clinical syndromes, the instructions for their administration and scoring, as well as their normative data, are not provided. In short, the author or authors of each chapter were asked to present their "best advice" for students and trainees for each topic that is covered. Rather than presenting a dry list of relevant tests and normative data, chapter authors have endeavored to provide synopses of relevant concepts, their decision trees for making the differential diagnoses, and the methods by which they rule out competing diagnoses.

The reader should be aware that bibliographic citations for the most common and well-known of assessment tests (e.g., the Wechsler Adult Intelligence Scale) are not provided, because such information is readily available elsewhere. Bibliographic citations are provided, however, for less well-known tests and measures, as well as for specific sets of normative data that are recommended for use in lieu of normative data provided in original test manuals.

It is our hope that this handbook will be of interest to anyone seeking specialty training in psychiatry and neurology, as well as neuropsychology. This book is intended for use by students and clinicians with a strong background in neuropathology, neuroanatomy, and neurophysiology. Additionally, we assume that the readers of this book will have had formal training in clinical psychology, especially in the area of psychopathology, as well as in test theory, design, and measurement. As Lezak (1995) noted in her comprehensive text, "Even to know what constitutes a neuropsychologically adequate review of the patient's mental status requires a broad understanding of brain function and its neuroanatomical principles" (p. 102). I agree with her cautionary statement as much today as I did when I first quoted these words in 1998.

I would like to thank my two coeditors, Paul D. Nussbaum and Diana L. Robins, for their terrific support throughout this project. In addition, I thank several of my current and former students, Jenn Cromer, Robb Pietrzak, Mike Cannizzaro and Brian Harel, who provided enthusiastic and invaluable assistance—especially as my deadline with the publisher drew near! My appreciation also extends to many colleagues at Pfizer Global Research and Development, including Martin Bednar, Wayne Carter, David J. Clark, Diane Jorkasky, and Suhail Nurbhai, for their continual support and encouragement. Finally, I would like to express my sincere gratitude to Susan Reynolds, my acquisitions editor in the Books Department at the American Psychological Association, for her advice and patience throughout this long process.

BIBLIOGRAPHY

Lezak, M. D. (1995). *Neuropsychological assessment* (3rd ed.). New York: Oxford University Press.

PART I

CLINICAL NEUROPSYCHOLOGY: GENERAL ISSUES

Chapter 1

Brian T. Harel, Brett A. Steinberg,
and Peter J. Snyder

The Medical Chart:
Efficient Information-Gathering Strategies and Proper Chart Noting

The medical chart is a repository of clinically and research-oriented information regarding an individual patient. Thus, a patient's medical history and responsiveness to various clinical interventions (i.e., pharmacological, surgical, psychological, rehabilitative), as well as data that may be used in retrospective clinical research studies, are contained within the chart. Having this information in a single, standard format means that it may serve as a vehicle of communication among all health care providers, documenting and coordinating, in a systematic and integrated manner, all care administered to an individual patient. Without this vehicle of communication, the multidisciplinary approach to patient care in a hospital setting would be impossible. Because of this, the medical chart also serves as a record of care should any liability issues arise. With regard to psychiatric issues such as suicide, for example, the medical chart would be checked to ensure that proper assessment and precautionary procedures were followed. More specific to neuropsychologists, the medical chart serves to document the information that led to any diagnosis we might offer, should concerns regarding an evaluation arise.

Another aspect of liability involves the privacy and security of a patient's medical chart. On April 14, 2003, the privacy rule of the Health Insurance Portability and Accountability Act (HIPAA), which was signed into law in August 1996, became active (U.S. Department of Health and Human Services, Office of Civil Rights, 2003). The general goals of this legislation are to protect previously ill Americans who change jobs or residences from losing their health insurance and to provide standards for the electronic transmission of medical information. The second aspect of this legislation has direct relevance for both the privacy and the security of electronically stored medical information. Although a thorough discussion of HIPAA is beyond the scope of this chapter, there are two general points that are directly relevant to our profession. The first is that HIPAA regulations allow patients greater access to, and knowledge of, their own medical records. It is worth noting that psychotherapy notes are now considered protected health information and are more difficult for the patient to gain access to. The second is that the implementation of HIPAA requires psychologists to receive additional training to be in compliance with the privacy rule. The increased emphasis on maintaining privacy and confidentiality, while at the same time allowing for increased patient access to their own records, means that clinicians need to be very careful in both writing and protecting the security of their patient records.

Despite the changes that are taking place as a result of technological advances in the storage and transmission of medical data, and the critical importance that the medical chart plays in coordinating and documenting all facets of patient care, there are relatively few sources of information that describe the basics of proper chart review and chart noting for neuropsychologists who practice in a hospital setting.

I. THE CHART REVIEW

Experienced neuropsychologists, like other hospital-based health care specialists, have developed efficient strategies for obtaining information from the medical chart that is pertinent to their evaluations. The fact that the chart is a repository of information from medical staff across a variety of disciplines (e.g., neurologists, surgeons, physical and occupational therapists [PT/OT], and nurses) requires that the neuropsychologist have a working knowledge of the language and techniques used in other areas of health care. We are not suggesting that neuropsychologists be experts in other fields, but rather that they be capable of conversing with patients' medical care providers and that they have some understanding of the strategies and techniques used in other disciplines (e.g., neurologic diagnosis, patient management techniques, and strategies for providing day-to-day patient care). At the same time, however, neuropsychologists should be aware of the limits of their professional competencies and thus be wary of interpreting data outside of their areas of expertise.

When reviewing the medical chart, it is also important to keep general clinical issues in mind, such as psychosocial and environmental factors, so that treatment recommendations will be optimally effective. To do this, neuropsychologists must be skilled at behavioral and psychological assessment and intervention.

Although it may not be necessary to review all of the sections of the medical chart, it is important to be aware of the various contents should the need arise to find specific data. The following is meant to orient neuropsychologists to a few of the most applicable sections of a typical chart by providing brief descriptions of the pertinent information contained in each section. Not all medical settings will use the same format, however. (It is worthwhile to note that charts are full of medical abbreviations and acronyms. The Appendix at the back of this text provides a listing of the more common abbreviations, and most hospitals publish their own lists of abbreviations that are approved for use in medical charting at that institution.)

A. Sections of the Chart

1. *Referral Information/History and Physical (H&P)* contains referral history, admission history, and results of physical examination.
2. *Admission Data* contains general consent form, initial assessments and evaluations, social work intake/ psychosocial consult.
3. *Pharmacy* contains pharmacy orders.
4. *Treatment* contains admission protocol, treatment orders, physician order sheet.
5. *Progress Notes* contains problem list, progress notes for all disciplines.
6. *Consultations–Medical* contains consultation records for physician, physiatry, psychiatry, neurology, psychology.
7. *Evaluations/Assessments* contains audiology, OT/PT evaluations, pressure sore flowsheet, social work evaluations.
8. *Advance Directives* contains power of attorney and probate papers.
9. *Chemistry/Hematology/Urinalysis/Stool* contains labs.

10. *Microbiology* contains labs.
11. *X-Ray* contains cardiac rhythm sheet, echocardiogram, electrocardiogram (EKG), electromyography (EMG), modified barium swallow results, sleep study, x-ray, and neuroimaging data.
12. *Care Plan/Critical Path* contains individual treatment plan (ITP), patient care plan, and behavior management plans (BMPs).

B. Steps for Reviewing the Chart

As the previous section indicates, the medical chart stores data that can be used to develop a conceptual framework within which the neuropsychological assessment results can be interpreted. For example, review of the chart might reveal information regarding psychoactive medications that could be influencing test performance or affecting the patient's symptoms in a way that might not otherwise be readily apparent. Therefore, we offer several suggested steps to more efficiently direct the neuropsychologist's review of the chart:

1. Clarify the referral question. This will help to guide the review of the medical chart in an organized and efficient manner. If, for example, a patient is referred for evaluation following a stroke, the neuroimaging and PT/OT notes may yield information regarding the arterial territory and functional consequences, respectively, of the vascular event.
2. Read through the initial history and physical examination (H&P), which generally contains the following components (for a more detailed review, see Blumenfeld, 2002):
   a. *Chief complaint (CC)* contains presenting complaint along with brief pertinent background data.
   b. *History of present illness (HPI)* contains complete history of current illness that brought patient to hospital.
   c. *Past medical history (PMH)* contains information about prior medical and surgical problems.
   d. *Review of systems (ROS)* contains brief review of medical systems (e.g., head, eyes, neurologic, and OB/GYN).
   e. *Family history (FHx)* contains a list of immediate relatives and any family illnesses.
   f. *Social and environmental history (SocHx)* contains information about work history, family relationships, and so on.

    g. *Medications and allergies* contains lists of current medications as well as allergies.

    h. *Physical exam* contains information about general appearance, vital signs (temperature, pulse, blood pressure, and respiratory rate), HEENT (head, eyes, ears, nose, and throat), neck, back and spine, lymph nodes, breasts, lungs, heart, abdomen, extremities, nervous system, reproductive system, and skin.

    i. *Results of lab studies* contains data from diagnostic tests (e.g., blood work, tissue biopsy, and radiological tests).

    j. *Assessment and plan* contains brief summary along with diagnosis and suggested interventions.

3. Review reports pertaining to relevant neuroimaging studies (computed tomography [CT], magnetic resonance imaging [MRI], single photon emission computed tomography [SPECT], position emission tomography [PET], and cerebral angiography). Also, read any available electroencephalography (EEG) or neurosurgical reports available in the chart.

4. Review laboratory data for abnormally high or low critical blood or urine test values, for liver function tests, as well as for positive results of drug screen tests. (Chapter 3 of this book provides a review of how such important laboratory studies should be read and interpreted by the neuropsychologist.)

5. Review current medications and dosages as well as whether the patient recently has been taken off or started on a medication that might have a negative impact on neuropsychological functioning.

6. Review prior consultation reports from the medicine, neurology, radiology, neurosurgery, psychiatry, and physiatry services. In particular, it may be useful to focus on the initial and most recent reports so as to have a sense of current functioning as well as progress made to date. (Chapter 2 of this book provides a review of the organization and writing of standard neurological consultation and progress notes. In addition, references are included at the end of the present chapter.)

7. Review progress notes from other relevant disciplines, such as nursing, nutrition, social work, and OT/PT. These notes are useful because they may provide a fairly detailed description of the patient's behavior on admission, level of cooperation with hospital staff, arousability and alertness, as well as any socially inappropriate or

potentially hazardous behaviors. When possible, it is also useful to briefly interview the nursing staff prior to the examination.

8. Note the schedule of appointments, as this is likely to influence the patient's ability to perform optimally during neuropsychological testing. For example, several hours of PT will likely affect a patient's performance on testing that occurs immediately afterward.

II. THE PROGRESS NOTE

The progress note serves as a more immediately accessible summary of the most salient points of the evaluation. Ultimately, a progress note should give the reader (e.g., attending physician) sufficient information regarding the implications of the evaluation so that appropriate care can be provided. Because the progress note functions as a brief summary of the neuropsychological evaluation, it should be written as soon after the evaluation takes place as is reasonably possible. (For maximum usefulness in patient care and in disputes about liability, notes should include the dates and times that they were written.) Although we discuss the general types of information that should be included in the progress note, each facility has its own tradition and culture for writing progress notes.

Initially, we clearly state the reason for the evaluation, including the referral source and question. In much the same way that the referral question directs the review of the medical chart, the referral question should direct the way the note is written (e.g., the language used and specific issues addressed). Behavioral observations and judgments about the validity of the results are then presented. We typically highlight the salient test findings by addressing each functional domain with a one- or two-sentence summary of performance. (To keep this brief, it is important to focus on neurocognitive domains rather than on individual test scores. We may, however, include IQ scores to provide a quantitative frame of reference for the reader's interpretation of other findings.) In addition to the neuropsychological test report data, we include data regarding psychological functioning (e.g., risk of harm to self or others, level of arousal, level of cooperation during examination, and mood and affect). This is followed by a brief summary of our diagnostic impressions and the implications of the results as they relate to the original referral question. If it is appropriate, the prognosis can also be discussed in terms of time since injury or onset of the disease, treatment progress, efficacy of medication(s), and what is currently known about the condition. Furthermore, recommendations that can be readily implemented and are of an immediate nature are included. Finally, as a courtesy, we like to thank the referral source for the opportunity to participate in the patient's care.

Once a progress note is written, it immediately becomes part of that patient's medical record. It is important to remember that this record is regarded as a legal document and that once information is entered into the record, it becomes permanent. For this reason, if an error is made while writing (e.g., a misspelling or an incorrect drug name), it should not simply be scratched out or covered with correction fluid (e.g., White-Out). Instead, the error should be crossed out, the correct word should be printed above or next to it, and the writer's initials should be signed in the same place. If an error is discovered after an entry is complete then a new entry should be entered into the record. This new entry should identify the date, time, and nature of the error that was discovered; it should provide the correct information; and a note should be placed at the location of the old, erroneous note indicating that an error was found and when the revision was added. Finally, it is worth noting that neatly written progress notes are more likely to be useful and to be appreciated by colleagues.

III. THE FUTURE OF MEDICAL RECORDS

Although the electronic storage and transmission of medical charts has engendered concerns regarding privacy and security (as is apparent by the enactment of HIPAA), it also offers considerable possibility. As records become electronic documents, several potential benefits may improve patient care. The first is that information will become accessible more quickly and be available to a greater number of health care professionals. In addition, search engines will allow for a more interactive experience between the medical staff and the medical chart. For instance, algorithms designed to seek out and compare information within the chart will be able to offer "suggestions" as to what type of antidepressant should be used based on information about the patient's current medications, sleep and eating habits, response to a similar class of drugs taken in the past, diagnoses, and so on. In response to the advancement in computer technology, for example, Rollman et al. (2001) evaluated the utility of providing screening and feedback for the initial management of major depression to primary care physicians via electronic medical records. Rollman et al. found that "electronic notification of the depression diagnosis can affect the primary care provider's initial management of major depression" (p. 197). That is, when provided with such electronic notification, the primary care providers were found to respond more rapidly and to manage their patients closely from that point forward. Of course, future research will be needed to determine to what extent this will improve clinical outcomes.

IV. CONCLUSION

This chapter provides a basic overview of how to thoroughly review inpatient medical charts and how to responsibly convey clinical impressions and recommendations through effective chart noting.

BIBLIOGRAPHY

Blumenfeld, H. (2002). *Neuroanatomy through clinical cases*. Sunderland, MA: Sinauer Associates.

Rollman, B. L., Hanusa, B. H., Gilbert, T., Lowe, H. J., Kapoor, W. N., & Schulberg, H. C. (2001). The electronic medical record: A randomized trial of its impact on primary care physicians' initial management of major depression. *Archives of Internal Medicine, 161,* 189–197.

U.S. Department of Health and Human Services, Office for Civil Rights. (2003). *Medical privacy: National standards to protect the privacy of personal health information*. Retrieved April 11, 2003, from http://www.hhs.gov/ocr/hipaa/

CHAPTER 2
Thomas F. Scott

The Neurological Examination

The purpose of this chapter is to acquaint the reader with the elements of a standard neurological examination and their documentation, so that the reader will be able to understand the examination as it is typically documented in patients' charts. The neurological examination is primarily a bedside tool that allows clinicians to localize lesions in the nervous system. Usually it is a combination of multiple findings on the examination that allows this localization, even with single lesions. If the results suggest multiple lesions, the implications of each lesion must be considered both individually and in combinations, and evidence of systemic disease (disease involving more than one organ system) must be taken into account. Thus, the neurological examination must be incorporated into the context of the patient's overall health history and general physical condition.

A standard neurological examination begins with a brief assessment of mental status, followed by testing of cranial nerve function, motor skills, deep tendon reflexes, sensory modalities, and pathological reflexes (generally presented in that order in documentation). In some clinical situations the examination may be abbreviated; in other situations, portions of the examination may be expanded to address a specific complaint.

I. MENTAL STATUS EXAMINATION

The mental status examination is performed and documented as the first part of the neurological examination because it colors the remainder of the testing in terms of reliability. Patients with abnormal affect, for example, may be more likely to show signs of functional (somatoform) illness, and demented or encephalopathic patients may not be able to cooperate fully with the examination. Unfortunately, because of time constraints the reporting of a patient's mental status is often abbreviated, sometimes reduced to a single phrase such as "patient alert and a good historian." Such limited documentation may make changes in mental status difficult to assess during the course of a hospitalization. Ideally, the record also reflects the patient's baseline mental functioning prior to hospitalization.

Level of alertness is noted first as alert, drowsy, stuporous (tending to drift into sleep during testing or arousable only for brief periods), or comatose (with or without spontaneous or purposeful movements). An assigned number on a coma scale is no substitute for a precise description. Next, a comment concerning affect should be made, perhaps in the context of the patient's general behavior and insight during the interview and examination. Orientation is checked in four "spheres": person (self and others), place, time, and purpose. The remainder of the mental status examination varies greatly among clinicians, but several of the following tests are usually performed at the bedside routinely: naming presidents, "serial sevens," registration and memory of three objects at 5 minutes, digit span forward and backward, interpretation of proverbs and similarities, complex figure drawing, spelling *world* forward and backward, and naming five cities. A standardized mental status examination such as the Folstein Mini-Mental State Examination (MMSE) is occasionally used by the neurologist. Determination of probable moderate-to-severe dementia is often made with only a brief neurological examination employing these maneuvers.

More specific bedside testing of higher cortical functions is often added to the mental status examination in patients with evidence of focal lesions. Delineation of aphasias may involve detailed testing but is usually limited to gross observation of speech output, conduction (ability to repeat), and comprehension. Bedside testing should include object naming, awareness of right–left, and testing for visual and sensory neglect (especially important in parietal and thalamic lesions).

II. CRANIAL NERVE EXAMINATION

An abnormality on cranial nerve examination could relate to one or more lesions in the cortex, deep gray matter (e.g., thalamus), or brain stem (including nuclei), or along the course of a cranial nerve through soft and bony tissues. Certain patterns of cranial nerve dysfunction allow clinicians to localize lesions to these areas, and many such patterns are considered to be "classic" findings related to specific anatomic substrates. It is often necessary to combine a cranial nerve finding with other neurological deficits to localize a lesion precisely (see Figure 2.1).

Figure 2.1. Brain stem and cranial nerves.

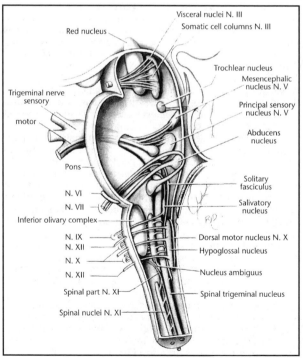

A. Cranial Nerve I

Although the first cranial nerve is often omitted as part of the routine examination, a deficit of smell is often an important clue to a diagnosis. Lesions of the olfactory groove (classically, meningiomas) may present with both psychiatric symptoms related to frontal lobe injury and loss of smell owing to compression of the olfactory nerves. Loss of smell is also common after head trauma, owing to shearing of the branches of the olfactory nerves as they pass through the cribriform plate.

B. Cranial Nerve II

Visual disturbances are listed as part of the cranial nerve examination regardless of the location of the lesion. A visual field disturbance related to hemispheric injury, for example, such as a homonymous hemianopsia, would be noted. Lesions limited to the optic nerve produce monocular visual disturbance. Precise visual acuity is rarely recorded. In patients with near blindness, the distance at which the patient can count fingers is sometimes noted. A funduscopic examination is routinely done and reported as negative if the retina, retinal vessels, and optic discs are free of lesions. Papilledema is a classic finding of increased intracranial pressure owing to tumor, hydrocephalus, or other causes. Visual field neglect, seen frequently contralateral to parietal lesions, is usually noted as part of the mental status examination or under the topic of "higher cortical functions."

When they are intact, many optic nerve functions are summarized by the abbreviation PERRLA (pupils equal, round, and reactive to light and accommodation). The swinging flashlight test may reveal a consensual response despite a relatively poor direct response ipsilaterally, owing to an optic nerve lesion (Marcus-Gunn pupil).

Some classic findings that may be listed under cranial nerve II in the report of the neurological examination are as follows:

1. **The visual field defect homonymous hemianopsia** is a large hemispheric lesion or lesion of lateral geniculate ganglion.
2. **Bitemporal hemianopsia** is a lesion of the pituitary area compressing the chiasm.
3. **Central scotomata** are lesions of the optic nerve, seen classically with optic neuritis.
4. **Superior quadrantanopsia** is a contralateral temporal lobe lesion.

5. **Hollenhorst plaque** is a bright-appearing cholesterol or atheromatous emboli seen on funduscopic examination of the retinal vessels, implying an embolic process.

C. Cranial Nerves III, IV, VI

Cranial nerves that control eye movements are usually largely noted by the abbreviation EOMI (extraocular muscles intact). Palsies of these nerves may be localized to specific nerves or muscles by the experienced examiner, who sometimes uses a red glass lens at bedside. Cranial nerve III and sympathetic fibers are responsible for eye opening, so that a ptosis, with or without Horner's syndrome, is recorded as part of the extraocular muscle test (although the pupil abnormalities associated with these syndromes may be recorded with the visual examination). A classic finding of ocular motility referred to as an **internuclear ophthalmoplegia** (INO) is seen with lacunar infarcts of the medial longitudinal fasciculus (MLF) or with multiple sclerosis plaques in the MLF. Ipsilateral adduction is lost.

D. Cranial Nerve V

Facial sensation is tested to light touch, pinprick, and temperature. If an abnormality respects only one or two divisions of V_1–V_3, this is recorded; it implies a lesion distal to the gasserian ganglion. Distinct splitting of sensory function at the midline face is unusual and may imply a functional disorder. Vibration is not tested, but an examiner may look for splitting of vibratory sensation across the forehead or skull as further evidence of a functional component to a patient's clinical presentation.

E. Cranial Nerve VII

Seventh nerve lesions are referred to as either peripheral or central. In central lesions, located caudal to the seventh nerve nucleus and contralateral to the resulting facial droop, the upper face (periorbital and forehead) is relatively spared. The palpebral fissure may be slightly larger ipsilateral to the face droop. In peripheral lesions weakness is ipsilateral to the lesion of the seventh nucleus or nerve. Other brain-stem signs are seen when the lesion involves the nerve nucleus, and the term **Bell's palsy** is most often reserved for lesions of the nerve distal to the nucleus. Eye closure may be lost in severe cases of peripheral seventh nerve lesions. Hyperacusis is due to loss of seventh nerve influence on the stapes.

F. Cranial Nerve VIII

The eighth nerve consists of an auditory component and a vestibular component. Deafness rarely results from cortical lesions; more often, there is difficulty with sound localization. Common bedside testing involves comparison for gross symmetry with a high-pitched tuning fork or finger rubbing near the ear, and the Weber and Rinne tests (for air conduction compared with bone conduction of sound). Lesions of the vestibular nuclei and of the vestibular portion of the eighth nerve both produce vertigo, nausea, vomiting, and nystagmus.

G. Cranial Nerves IX and X

The examiner records symmetry of palatal elevation and gag reflex, both of which are subserved by these cranial nerves. Hoarseness and dysphagia may be seen with unilateral or bilateral injury to cranial nerve X (vagus); however, lesions of cranial nerve IX may be undetectable clinically.

H. Cranial Nerve XI

Strength of the sternocleidomastoid and trapezius muscles is tested with resistance to head turning and shoulder shrug. The loss of strength is often greater with nuclear or peripheral lesions as opposed to supranuclear injury.

I. Cranial Nerve XII

A unilateral weak tongue deviates toward the side of weakness (and toward the side of the lesion in nuclear or peripheral injury but opposite the side of supranuclear lesions). Nuclear and peripheral lesions are associated with atrophy when chronic.

III. MOTOR SYSTEM EXAMINATION

A. Tone and Power

Normal muscle tone refers to the slight tension present in muscles at rest. Tone may be increased in both pyramidal and extrapyramidal disturbances. Acute central nervous system lesions often produce hypotonia; this evolves over days to produce hypertonicity, referred to as spasticity, which is a velocity-dependent increase in tone, waxing and waning through range of motion. In opposition to these general rules, hypertonicity may be seen acutely in brain-stem lesions (decorticate, decerebrate posturing), and hypotonicity may remain chronically in neuromuscular disease.

Muscle power is manually tested at bedside, with individual muscle groups graded on a scale of 0–5 (0 = *no contraction,* 3 = *movement against gravity,* 5 = *normal*). The neurological history and examination can usually localize weakness to either muscle, the neuromuscular junction, lower motor neuron, or upper motor neuron (see Table 2.1). Proximal predominant weakness or atrophy when symmetrical usually suggests a myopathic condition. Flabby or flaccid weak muscles, often atrophic, are seen in lower motor neuron disorders and are associated with a decrease in deep tendon reflexes (e.g., peripheral neuropathy, spinal muscle atrophy). Upper motor neuron disorders are distinguished by spasticity, increased tone, and increased deep tendon reflexes.

Spasticity may be produced by lesions of the motor cortex, internal capsule, or pyramidal tract within the brain stem or spinal cord. The degree of spasticity may be influenced by the degree of extrapyramidal system involvement. In some neurological disorders, a mixture of upper motor neuron and lower motor neuron dysfunction evolves over time, producing seemingly conflicting upper motor neuron and lower motor neuron findings in the same patient (e.g., amyotrophic lateral sclerosis, vitamin B12 deficiency).

B. Coordination

Equilibrium refers to coordination and balance of the whole body, and when impaired, it is referred to as **truncal ataxia**. This is tested at bedside by observing sitting and standing balance and gait (classically "wide-based" in cases of mild-to-moderate ataxia). The examination is refined with testing of tandem walk (placing one heel directly in front of the opposite toes) and by testing for the Romberg sign, which may produce swaying and truncal movements (eyes are closed after the feet are placed together, arms down).

Limb ataxia (appendicular ataxia) may be present in a single extremity (usually an arm), but it is often seen in an ipsilateral arm and leg pattern, with the patient exhibiting a tendency to fall to that side. When combined with weakness, the term **ataxic hemiparesis** applies (classic for an internal capsule or pontine lacunar stroke when seen as a pure motor syndrome). Limb ataxia is demonstrated by testing finger-to-nose and heel-to-shin movements. Although limb ataxia may be seen in sensory disorders (pseudoathetosis), it is classic for

Table 2.1. Changes in Motor Function

Lesion or disorder	Loss of power	Tone	Atrophy	Fasciculations	Ataxia
Spinomuscular lesion					
a. Anterior horn cell	Focal	Flaccid	Present	Present	Absent
b. Nerve root, plexus, peripheral nerve	Focal or segmental	Flaccid	Present	Occasionally present	Absent
c. Neuromuscular junction	Diffuse	Usually normal	Usually normal	Absent	Absent
d. Muscle	Diffuse	Flaccid	Present but later than in a and b	Absent	Absent
Extrapyramidal lesion	None or mild	Rigid	Absent	Absent	Absent
Corticospinal tract lesion	Generalized, incomplete	Spastic	Absent	Absent	Absent
Cerebellar lesion	None; ataxia may stimulate loss of power	Hypotonic (ataxia)	Absent	Absent	Absent
Psychogenic disorder	Bizarre; no true loss of power; may stimulate any type	Normal or variable; often increased	Absent	Absent	Absent (may simulate ataxia)

Lesion or disorder	Reflexes	Abnormal movements	Pathological associated movements
Spinomuscular lesion a. Anterior horn cell	Decreased or absent	None except for fasciculations	Absent
b. Nerve root, plexus, peripheral nerve	Decreased or absent	None except for fasciculations	Absent
c. Neuromuscular junction	Usually normal	None	Absent
d. Muscle	Decreased	None	Absent
Extrapyramidal lesion	Muscle stretch reflexes normal or variable Superficial reflexes normal or slightly increased No corticospinal tract response	Present	Absent
Corticospinal tract lesion	Muscle stretch reflexes hyperactive Superficial reflexes diminished to absent Corticospinal tract responses	None	Absent
Cerebellar lesion	Muscle stretch reflexes diminished or pendular Superficial reflexes normal No corticospinal tract responses	May be present (intention tremor and ataxia)	Absent
Psychogenic disorder	Muscle stretch reflexes normal or increased (range) Superficial reflexes normal or increased No corticospinal tract responses	May be present	Absent

lesions of the cerebellar system, producing intention tremor (see the following section) and disdiadochokinesia (impairment of rapid alternating movements). Limb ataxia in the absence of weakness implicates a lesion of the cerebellar hemispheres and its projections, whereas truncal ataxia in isolation implicates a lesion of midline cerebellar structures and their projections.

C. Abnormal Movements

1. TREMOR

a. **Essential or physiologic tremor** (usually 8–11 Hz) may be a normal finding demonstrated by having the examinee forcibly extend the arms and digits, although these terms may also be used to denote a pathological idiopathic high-frequency tremor, which is often familial. Essential tremor may be accentuated or attenuated by drugs and disease states. The term **tremulousness** generally refers to transient high-frequency tremor associated with acute illness or anxiety. In severe metabolic disturbances, tremor may coexist with other abnormal movements such as myoclonus (rapid and tense contractions of large muscle groups) and asterixis (intermittent lapses of tone interrupting voluntary movements).

b. **Intention tremor** refers to to-and-fro motions that increase in amplitude as the examinee approaches a target; it is usually demonstrated on finger-to-nose testing in patients with lesions of cerebellar hemispheres and their projections into the brain stem and ventral posterolateral thalami.

c. **Parkinsonian tremor** is usually at lower frequency than essential tremor and is often described as "pill-rolling." Unlike the "action" tremors previously described, tremor in Parkinson's disease is always present at rest (at least intermittently), is variably affected by changes in position, and is associated with stiffness (hence the term cogwheel rigidity) and bradykinesia.

2. BRADYKINESIA, AKINESIA, AND DYSKINESIA

a. **Bradykinesia** is a reduction of normal spontaneous or unconscious semipurposeful movements such as blinking, shifting movements, and facial expressions. Although it is classic for Parkinson's disease, bradykinesia is also seen in other neurodegenerative syndromes, the multistroke state, and depression.

b. **Akinetic mutism** is a condition of extreme lack of movement and interaction, verbal and nonverbal, seen in patients with brain-stem lesions or bilateral hemispheric or deep gray matter lesions. It is also seen in end-stage neurodegenerative disorders. **Catatonic mutism** is a similar condition, seen as a manifestation of severe psychiatric disturbance rather than of structural lesions, and it generally is associated with waxy flexibility or rigidity.

c. **Dyskinesia** is a nonspecific term for complex irregular involuntary movements involving multiple muscle groups. At present most patients with dyskinesia suffer from medication-induced side effects of neuroleptics and anti-Parkinsonian drugs containing L-dopa. **Tardive dyskinesia** refers to neuroleptic-induced choreoathetoid movements primarily of the face, head, shoulders, and upper trunk.

Rapid dyskinetic movements are often termed **choreiform**, and this term may accurately describe the involuntary movements of many patients with tardive dyskinesia as well as with Huntington's disease and Sydenham's chorea. Dystonic movements are slower and associated with increased tone or rigidity (e.g., dystonia musculorum deformans); they may be seen in Parkinson's disease as well as in acute reactions as to neuroleptics. Athetoid movements are intermittent in speed between chorea and dystonia and have a writhing or a more rhythmic quality or both.

3. MISCELLANEOUS ABNORMAL MOVEMENTS

a. **Ballismus** refers to flailing motions of an extremity, usually occurring after stroke involving the subthalamic nucleus.

b. **Tics** refer to rapid movements that are stereotyped and repetitive; these are classic for Tourette's syndrome but may also be seen in mental retardation.

c. **Akathisia**, which may be considered the opposite of bradykinesia, is an increase in the normal spontaneous movements seen in the waking state. Patients with akathisia are fidgety and often pace.

4. DEEP TENDON REFLEXES AND MISCELLANEOUS SIGNS

Deep tendon reflexes are listed by percussion over tendon insertions producing a rapid muscle stretch. These reflexes are mediated by reflex arcs originating in intramuscular organs, which are sensitive to stretching and transmit impulses to alpha motor neurons within the spinal cord, producing a contraction of the percussed muscle. When deep tendon reflexes are increased or hyperactive, reflex spread occurs to other local muscles, and increased speed of reflexes and intensity of muscle contraction occurs. Deep tendon reflexes are generally graded on a 0–4+ (0, +, ++, +++, ++++) basis: 0 implies that reflexes are not elicited; "+" refers to reflexes being present only with Jendrassik's maneuver or other means of accentuating deep tendon reflexes; ++ implies a normal reflex; +++ designates reflexes that appear to be hyperactive but are not necessarily pathological; and ++++ refers to reflexes that are believed strongly to be pathological, or clonus.

a. **Babinski reflex.** Plantar stimulation with a blunt object may produce extension of the great toe and fanning of the other toes, which is believed to be a sign of upper motor neuron disease. Essentially, this sign is synonymous with **plantar response**. Other methods of eliciting an "upgoing toe" involve stimulation of the lateral foot (Chaddock's sign) or pinprick over the dorsum of the foot (Bing's sign).

b. **Cutaneous reflexes** consist of abdominal reflexes, elicited by stimulation of the skin over the four quadrants of the abdomen; cremasteric reflex, elicited by stimulation of the skin over the scrotal area; and anal wink.

c. **Hoffmann's sign** is a sign of hyperreflexia in the upper extremities, elicited by tapping distal digits in the hand and observing for abduction of the thumb.

d. **Frontal release signs** consist of the glabellar tap reflex, the snout reflex, the suck reflex, and the palmomental reflex. These signs indicate usually bilateral frontal lobe disease.

e. Some of the **more common signs of psychogenic neurological dysfunction** are as follows:

Hoover's sign. The examiner places one hand under each heel with the patient in the supine position. The patient is asked to raise one leg; the examiner should feel downward pressure on the opposite leg if voluntary effort is intact.

Astasia-abasia. An unusual lurching gait of psychogenic ataxia.

Hand–face drop test. Used in patients with coma who appear flaccid; if the hand is held over the face and dropped, the patient in psychogenic coma often avoids letting the hand hit the face with subtle motor movements to the side.

Splitting the tuning fork. Patients with psychogenic sensory disturbance beginning at the midline face have a very sharply demarcated loss of sensation to the midface and may also complain of lack of vibratory sensation on the affected side of the forehead, with intact vibratory sensation on the unaffected side of the forehead.

IV. SENSORY EXAMINATION

Like the rest of the neurological examination, the sensory examination is an organized assessment of neuroanatomic structures and systems. It is reserved for last because findings related to cognition and higher cortical functions will color its interpretation. Besides testing the integrity of the peripheral nervous system and spinal cord tracts, tests involving light touch and pinprick may be used to assess the presence of a cortical lesion, such as the test for extinction in parietal lobe lesions (neglect of sensory stimuli contralateral to a parietal lobe lesion when bilateral stimuli are presented). The sensory examination is usually documented simply as a response to five modalities: pinprick, light touch, vibration, position, and temperature. The tools used for these tests consist of a safety pin or other sharp object, a cotton swab, a 128-Hz tuning fork, an ice bag or metal object such as a tuning fork placed over a cooling vent, and calipers, which may be used to test two-point discrimination.

A. Temperature and Pinprick

Perception of sharp versus dull and hot versus cold objects requires integrity of unmyelinated peripheral nerves (which originate as bipolar neurons in the dorsal root ganglia), the spinothalamic tracts of the spinal cord and brain stem, the ventral posterolateral and ventral posteromedial thalami, and thalamic projections to the parietal lobes. Sensation of light touch is transmitted similarly, but it is also likely to be transmitted through the posterior columns. Sensory loss to light touch and pinprick may occur in the distribution of a single nerve, nerve root, plexus pattern, hemicord pattern, transverse cord pattern, or crossed brain-stem pattern, or it may occur somatotropically, corresponding to lesions above the brain stem (e.g., contralateral face-arm-leg). A lesion may be confidently localized to the brain stem when sensory loss occurs on one side of the face and contralateral body. A "stocking-glove" pattern is usually seen in patients with polyneuropathy, often owing to diabetes.

Perception of vibratory and position sense requires integrity of myelinated nerve fibers (originating as bipolar neurons in the dorsal root ganglion), the posterior columns, the medial lemniscus, the ventral posterolateral nucleus of the thalamus, and the cortex. Classically, lesions of the posterior columns are demonstrated by loss of vibratory and position sense out of proportion to loss of other modes (e.g., in vitamin B12 deficiency). Vibratory sensation is best tested with a 128-Hz tuning fork, and position sense is tested by employing small excursions of the distal digits.

B. Examples of Examinations

Following are two examples of the results of neurological examinations as they might appear in a hospital chart either in a typed, dictated form or in a handwritten form. Handwritten notes tend to be replete with commonly used abbreviations, which the neophyte will quickly become acquainted with.

1. EXAMINATION 1

The following represents a normal neurological examination (Figure 2.2 provides an abbreviated and diagrammatic summary of this examination): Patient is alert and oriented times four. Affect appropriate. Names presidents back to Carter easily, registers three out of three complex objects and recalls them at 5 minutes. Proverbs and serial sevens intact. Digit span six or seven numbers forward and backward.

Cranial nerves are intact (pupils equal, round, and reactive to light and accommodation; extraocular muscles intact; face, gag, and palate elevation symmetrical; facial sensation intact in all divisions of cranial nerve V), and fundi are benign. Strength is 5/5 with normal tone and bulk. No pronator drift. Finger-to-nose testing and fine finger movements normal. Gait testing including heel, toe, and tandem walk intact. Heel-to-shin intact.

Deep tendon reflexes are 2+ throughout and symmetrical with downgoing toes. No pathological reflexes.

Sensory exam is intact to vibration, position, light touch, pinprick, and temperature.

2. EXAMINATION 2

The following neurological examination notes could be recorded in a patient with an acute right middle cerebral territory infarct and moderate idiopathic Parkinson's disease: *Mental Status Examination reveals the patient is slightly drowsy. Patient is oriented to place, year, and season but not to month, day of the week, or time of day. Patient does not know how long he has been in the*

Figure 2.2. Chart note for a normal neurological examination: 0 × 4 denotes orientation in four spheres; digits 6# ← → denotes digit span; PERRLA denotes pupils, equal, round, and reactive to light and accommodation; EOMI denotes extraocular muscles intact; V_1–V_3 denotes intact fifth nerve; ∅ drift denotes no pronator drive; F → N denotes finger-to-nose testing; H→ S denotes heel-to-shin testing; and stick figure denotes basic deep tendon reflexes, for example 2+ over the knee means that the knee is normal, whereas 1+ means trace reflexes, and ∅ denotes loss of reflexes.

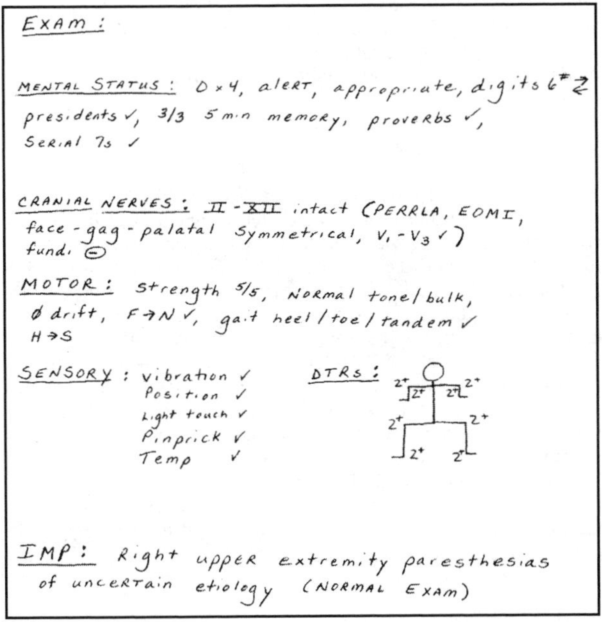
EXAM:

MENTAL STATUS: O × 4, alert, appropriate, digits 6# ⇄
presidents ✓, 3/3 5 min memory, proverbs ✓,
Serial 7s ✓

CRANIAL NERVES: II - XII intact (PERRLA, EOMI,
face - gag - palatal Symmetrical, V_1 - V_3 ✓)
fundi ⊖

MOTOR: strength 5/5, Normal tone/bulk,
∅ drift, F→N ✓, gait heel/toe/tandem ✓
H→S

SENSORY: vibration ✓
Position ✓
Light touch ✓
Pinprick ✓
Temp ✓

DTRs:

IMP: Right upper extremity paresthesias
of uncertain etiology (NORMAL EXAM)

hospital or the reason for hospitalization. Patient refuses to consider the possibility that he might have some left-sided weakness owing to stroke (anosognosia or denial). Patient seems to neglect visually the left field.

Patient can name only one recent president. Patient knows his address and phone number but has trouble naming his four children.

He is unable to register three complex objects. He is unable to perform simple calculations.

On cranial nerve examination, the patient has a left central seventh nerve palsy and some mild tongue deviation on tongue protrusion. Sensory examination of nerves VI through III is not reliable. Patient does not cross the midline with conjugate gaze. Gag intact. Patient is noted to have a snout and glabellar tap.

On motor examination, the patient has increased tone and cogwheel rigidity on the right, and he is flaccid on the left upper extremity. The left lower extremity is remarkable for trace proximal movements to command and proximal and distal withdrawal movements to deep pain. Bilateral Babinskis are present, and deep tendon reflexes are symmetrical and 2+. All sensory modalities are decreased on the left versus neglect on the left. Patient distinguishes different sensory modalities on the right, but reliability is questionable.

V. CONCLUSION

Students of neurology will find a lot of variability in the performance and documentation of the neurological examination as they rotate through ward services. Each physician lends his or her own style to the execution of the examination, although the standard elements of the examination remain. What constitutes an adequate neurological examination differs with the clinical situation. For instance, an internist caring for a patient with a gastrointestinal problem might limit the neurological examination to observance of speech and motor movements and might limit documentation to the phrase "neurologically intact." Of course, a neurology consultant will perform and document a more detailed examination.

Taken together with the history, the neurological examination allows localization of lesions in the nervous system. Localization is needed to formulate rationally a differential diagnosis of neurological disease.

BIBLIOGRAPHY

Adams, R. D., & Victor, M. (1985). *Principles of neurology* (3rd ed.). New York: McGraw-Hill.

Carpenter, M. B. (1985). *Core text of neuroanatomy* (3rd ed.). Baltimore: Williams & Wilkins.

Haerer, A. F. (1992). *DeJong's the neurologic examination* (5th ed.). Philadelphia: Lippincott.

Mancall, E. (1981). *Alpers and Mancall's essentials of the neurologic examination* (2nd ed.). Philadelphia: Davis.

Rowland, L. P. (1995). *Merritt's textbook of neurology* (9th ed.). Baltimore: Williams & Wilkins.

CHAPTER 3

Harry W. McConnell

Laboratory Testing in Neuropsychology

Laboratory tests provide useful clues in the neuropsychological evaluation of a patient. Whether they provide a pathognomic test for a given diagnosis or are used to rule out alternative diagnoses, it is critical for the neuropsychologist to be fluent in their use and abuse in clinical neuropsychology. This chapter focuses on the role of laboratory testing in assisting the neuropsychologist in the diagnosis and treatment monitoring of patients. Although in most institutions it is the psychiatrist or physician who routinely orders such testing, it is also important that the neuropsychologist be aware of and actively participate in the ordering of such tests, because their results may greatly affect the results of neuropsychological testing. The neuropsychologist may also have important input into the ordering of such tests as a result of insight gained from the neuropsychological examination. For example, the neuropsychologist examining a patient with epilepsy must be aware of the antiepileptic drugs (AEDs) that the patient is taking, because a number of AEDs are well-known to affect neuropsychological function. He or she must also be aware of the relevance of the AED blood levels and, possibly, relevant metabolites (e.g., 10,11-epoxide levels in patients taking carbamazepine), because AED toxicity can greatly influence the results of neuropsychological testing. Conversely, the results of cognitive impairment found on testing may be compatible with a pattern seen in AED toxicity and may thus be a reason to check laboratory parameters.

I discuss, first, the general use of some tests and then look at their use in specific psychiatric presentations. Although much of this information may be considered more relevant to the treating psychiatrist than the neuropsychologist, the neuropsychologist, as an active member of the treatment team concerned with the mental status of the patient, should be aware of any factors that may influence the mental state, including not only psychological parameters but also laboratory indices.

I. BLOOD TESTS

A. Hematologic Tests

The main tests to be looked at with respect to neuropsychology are the complete blood count (CBC) and erythrocyte sedimentation rate (ESR). The CBC consists of the red blood cell (RBC), white blood cell (WBC), and platelet counts, as well as the WBC differential (which has to be ordered separately in many laboratories) and the hemoglobin (Hb), hematocrit (Hct), RBC indices (e.g., mean corpusculor volume, MCV; see Table 3.1), and peripheral blood smear. These tests are useful for (a) detection of anemia, polycythemia, infection, or an inflammatory state that might present with an alteration of mental state and (b) monitoring of possible toxic effects of medications (e.g., carbamazepine, clozapine), which can cause bone marrow toxicity and thus may affect these indices. Other hematologic tests of use in neuropsychology include tests for folate and vitamin B12 (deficiency of which may cause marked mental state changes even in the absence of anemia) and of ferritin and total iron-binding capacity (TIBC), which are all of use in the routine evaluation of anemia. Coagulation tests are useful in evaluating liver disease and in monitoring anticoagulation therapy. These tests are outlined in Table 3.1.

B. Endocrinologic Tests

Disturbances of endocrine function may present with virtually any type of mental state change. Table 3.2 summarizes the main endocrinologic tests used in evaluating mental state changes. The most important of these is the testing of thyroid status, which should be done in every patient presenting with psychiatric illness for the first time, because thyroid disorder is an important and common reversible cause of psychiatric illness,

Table 3.1. Hematological Tests of Relevance in Neuropsychology

Test	Comments
White blood cell (WBC) count and differential	Important for evaluating the possibility of (a) infectious diseases, (b) leukemia, and (c) leukopenia from certain psychotropic medications. The WBC differential test is important for evaluating any abnormality of the WBC count, characterizing the individual components of the WBC count.
Red blood cell (RBC) count	Important for evaluating anemia and polycythemia.
Hemoglobin (Hb)	Important for evaluating anemia.
Hematocrit (Hct)	Important for screening, follow-up, and evaluation of anemia and polycythemia.
Mean corpuscular volume (MCV)	Average volume of an RBC; useful in establishing whether an anemia is macrocytic (i.e, increased, such as in alcoholism, folate or B12 deficiency) or microcytic (i.e., decreased, such as in iron deficiency anemia).
Mean corpuscular hemoglobin concentration (MCHC)	Concentration measured in grams per liter of hemoglobin; similar in use to mean corpuscular hemoglobin (MCH) in evaluating anemia.
Red cell distribution width (RDW)	Used in evaluating whether an anemia is a combination of microcytic and macrocytic anemias.
Peripheral blood smear	Characterizes abnormal RBCs, platelets, and WBCs such as the atypical lymphocytes seen in mononucleosis, the hypersegmented neutrophils seen in folate and B12 deficiency, and abnormal RBCs such as in sickle cell disease.
Reticulocyte count	Gives an indication of RBC production and, hence, of bone marrow activity; increased in anemias secondary to blood loss or hemolysis; decreased in anemias secondary to impairment of RBC maturation (e.g., folate, B12, or iron deficiency anemias prior to treatment).

Platelets	May be decreased because of drugs (e.g., valproate, clozapine, phenothiazines) or medical illness, either on its own or along with other cell lines (pancytopenia).
Erythrocyte sedimentation rate (ESR)	Nonspecific index of inflammation; elevated in infectious, neoplastic, and inflammatory (e.g., vasculitis, systemic lupus erythematosus) illness.
Coagulation tests	May be elevated in liver disease of many causes; prothrombin time (PT), international normalized ratio (INR) used to monitor warfarin therapy; partial thromboplastin time (PTT) and activated partial thromboplastin time (APTT) used to monitor heparin therapy.
Folate and vitamin B12 levels	Serum levels of folate and B12 used to screen for deficiency of these important vitamins; deficiency may present with or without concomitant anemia with a variety of mental state changes or neurological sequelae; deficiency may be due to impaired absorption, deficient intake, or medication effects (e.g., antiepileptic drugs); the Schilling test and serum intrinsic factor are useful in evaluating B12 deficiency caused by pernicious anemia; it is important to monitor both B12 and folate because treatment with folate alone may reverse hematological abnormalities (macrocytic anemia) without reversal of neurological deficits; RBC folate is more indicative of overall status than serum levels.
Serum iron (Fe)	Used to evaluate iron deficiency anemia along with total iron-binding capacity (TIBC) and ferritin levels.

Table 3.2. Endocrinologic Tests of Use in Neuropsychology

Test	Comments
Thyroid function tests	Thyroid-stimulating hormone (TSH) is the best screening test; serum triiodothyronine (T3), thyroxine (T4), reverse T3, T3 resin uptake (T3RU), free T4, free thyroxine index (FTI), and antithyroglobulin antibodies and microsomal antibodies are also useful in the evaluation of thyroid illness. Both hypothyroidism and hyperthyroidism may present with psychiatric illness including depression, hypomania, cognitive changes, personality changes, anxiety, delirium, and psychosis. Improvement in mental state often lags behind improvement in biochemical parameters; thyroid testing should also be done to evaluate possible medication-induced thyroid disease (e.g., carbamazepine, lithium).
Thyrotropin-releasing hormone stimulation test	Has been suggested by some as useful in the evaluation of "subclinical" hypothyroidism or in patients with depression.
Plasma cortisol level	Useful in assessment of adrenal function, especially in evaluation of Addison's disease (low cortisol) and Cushing's disease (high cortisol), both of which frequently present with mental status changes.
Dexamethasone supression test (DST)	Measurement of serum cortisol checked at specific times prior to and after the administration of 1 mg of dexamethasone, thought by some to be a biological marker for depression; a normal response, however, does not rule out the possibility of depression, and an abnormal response must similarly be interpreted in the clinical context; may be useful in some ambiguous situations.

Prolactin level	Useful in evaluating patients on antipsychotics with galactorrhea or to evaluate compliance because antipsychotics characteristically increase prolactin; may be of limited use in evaluating nonepileptic seizure-like events (NESLEs) if psychotropics are controlled for and if sample is obtained within 20 minutes of a suspected seizure; a normal value, however, should not be interpreted as representing an NESLE, because there may not be a rise in levels in seizures related to epilepsy. A clear rise in baseline within 20 minutes of a seizure is useful as an indication of suggestion of epilepsy.
Plasma catecholamine levels	Plasma epinephrine and norepinephrine levels are useful in evaluating pheochromocytoma, which may present with paroxysmal anxiety or other mental state changes.
Osmolality, vasopressin level	May be useful in evaluating hyponatremia, which may be secondary to psychogenic polydipsia or to the syndrome of inappropriate secretion of antidiuretic hormone (SIADH), often caused by illness, surgery, or psychotropic medication.
Parathyroid hormone level	Useful in evaluating mental state changes related to hypo- or hypercalcemia or related to changes in phosphorous levels; sometimes occurs after thyroid surgery.
Insulin and C-peptide levels	Useful in the evaluation of paroxysmal hypoglycemia to rule out insulinoma, a rare tumor that may present with paroxysmal anxiety or other mental state changes.

presenting as depression, psychosis, dementia, or essentially any change in mental state. It is critical to be aware of the different thyroid function tests available and their meanings with respect to a given patient, as this is one of the most common causes of neuropsychological impairment and psychiatric presentation from a specific endrocrinologic cause.

C. Biochemical and Immunologic Tests

Disturbances of electrolytes are common in psychiatric patients either as a presenting cause of mental status change (e.g., delirium in hyponatremia) or as secondary to the disease (e.g., hypokalemia in patients with bulimia, related to bingeing) or its treatment (e.g., hyponatremia with carbamazepine). Liver and renal disease may also be a primary cause of presentation (e.g., hepatic or uremic encephalopathy) or, alternatively, secondary to the primary illness (e.g., liver failure in alcoholism) or its treatment (e.g., liver dysfunction secondary to use of AEDs). The serum glucose may give valuable information in cases of suspected diabetes mellitus or hypoglycemia presenting with mental status changes. All these tests, outlined in Table 3.3, are quickly obtained (often within a matter of minutes if requested urgently), are inexpensive, and provide valuable routine laboratory screening and follow-up information in psychiatric populations. The remainder of tests discussed in Table 3.3 are commonly obtained as well in a neuropsychiatric population, but they are generally reserved for more specific clinical situations rather than used for general screening purposes.

II. CEREBROSPINAL FLUID TESTS

The cerebrospinal fluid (CSF) is a valuable adjunct to diagnosis in specific clinical situations. It offers little information in the setting of routine screening of general psychiatric or neurological populations. The CSF bathes the entire central nervous system (CNS) and thus has the potential of offering a unique window into the biochemistry of various neuropsychiatric disorders. It is obtained by means of lumbar puncture for analysis; a small needle is inserted at the level of approximately L3–L4.

The CSF is made up primarily of water and has been termed a "modified tap water"; its study in schizophrenia has been likened to the augurs' examination of animal entrail. Although it is true that 99% of the CSF composition is water and that the many hundreds of studies looking at neurotransmitters and other markers in schizophrenia have not to date produced any

Table 3.3. Biochemical and Immunologic Evaluation Relevant to Neuropsychology

Test	Comments
Electrolytes	Sodium (Na+), potassium (K+), chloride (Cl−), and bicarbonate (HCO3−) are useful screening tests in psychiatric illness and should also be monitored in patients on psychotropics (especially carbamazepine and antidepressants), which may cause hyponatremia; hyponatremia is also seen in various medical illnesses and in syndrome of inappropriate antidiuretic hormone (SIADH) and psychogenic polydipsia; hypokalemia is common in people with bulimia and anorexia related to laxative and diuretic abuse and to bingeing, in which elevations in bicarbonate and decreased chloride may also be seen.
Liver function tests	Useful screening test in psychiatric patients; also should be monitored in patients on psychotropics, which may affect liver function (especially antiepileptic drugs); includes alanine aminotransferase (ALT), alkaline phosphatase (AP), aspartate aminotransferase (AST), gamma-glutamyl transaminase (GGT), and lactate dehydrogenase (LDH), which has five isoenzymes and may be elevated in other medical conditions as well; GGT is the most sensitive of these; bilirubin (total, direct, and indirect) is useful in evaluation of hepatobiliary disease and hemolytic anemia and is ordered separately in some laboratories.
Renal function tests	Blood urea nitrogen (BUN) and creatinine are elevated in renal failure; should be monitored in patients on lithium and amantadine; electrolytes also frequently abnormal in renal failure, especially hyperkalemia; BUN also elevated in dehydration.
Amylase and lipase levels	Used to evaluate pancreatitis and pancreatic carcinoma; should be screened in patients on valproate with any gastrointestinal symptoms; because amylase is also elevated in disease of the salivary glands, lipase levels are helpful to monitor serum lipase levels as well, which are more specific to pancreatic abnormalities; amylase levels are also elevated in patients with bulimia and may be used in this population to monitor compliance concerning binge behaviors.

(Continued)

Table 3.3. Biochemical and Immunologic Evaluation Relevant to Neuropsychology *(Continued)*

Test	Comments
Glucose level	Important in evaluating the possibility of diabetes mellitus or hypoglycemia, which has many causes and may present with a variety of intermittent mental state changes, including delirium and psychosis.
Creatinine phosphokinase (CPK) level	Useful in evaluating possible neuroleptic malignant syndrome (NMS), a severe toxic reaction to antipsychotic medications; also elevated in acute muscle injury, after exercise or intramuscular injections and from muscle disease of many etiologies; CPK isoenzyme MM is used to evaluate skeletal muscle elevations, and the MB fraction is used to evaluate patients with suspected myocardial infarction.
Copper and ceruloplasmin levels	Used to diagnose and evaluate Wilson's disease, an inherited alteration in copper metabolism that presents with personality changes, altered cognition, affective symptoms, or psychosis associated with a movement disorder, usually in adolescents and young adults.
Porphyrins	Porphobilinogen (PBG), aminolevulinic acid (ALA), and other porphyrins and metabolites are used to diagnose porphyria, an inherited metabolic disorder that can present with intermittent psychosis, seizures, and other neuropsychiatric manifestations.
Lupus erythematosus (LE) prep	Used along with other tests, including antinuclear antibodies (ANA), anti-DNA antibodies, lupus anticoagulant, and complement levels in the diagnosis of systemic lupus erythematosus (SLE), which may present with depression, delirium, psychosis, or dementia; phenothiazines, among other drugs, may cause false positive results.

Red blood cell (RBC) transketolase level	Test for the diagnosis of Wernicke's encephalopathy (WE); WE is a medical emergency, commonly occurring in alcoholics (but also in other groups) deficient in thiamine; usually presenting with mental status changes; sometimes associated with ophthalmoplegia, ataxia, or both; because transketolase and thiamine levels take days or weeks to obtain, WE should be diagnosed and treated on clinical grounds in the emergency room, with the tests as confirmatory; glucose should not be given until parenteral thiamine and other B vitamins have been administered.
Rapid plasma reagin test (RPR)	Screening test for syphilis; also used is the venereal disease research laboratories (VDRL) test for screening; important screening test because neurosyphilis presents with many neurological and psychiatric symptoms.
Human immunodeficiency virus (HIV) antibody testing	Screening test for HIV infection, which has been termed the "great masquerader" because it can cause so many different neurological and psychiatric symptoms and thus mimic many many syndromes; pre- and posttest counseling must be given to the individual, and consent must be obtained.
Toxicology screens	Multiple drugs can be screened for at once; useful for suspected drug abuse and for suspected overdoses of an unknown substance; specific drugs may also be requested.
Drug levels	Quantitative values with reference range of therapeutic drugs; in the case of psychotropics, they are particularly useful in assessment of compliance and in patients with a poor response to standard doses; reference ranges for lithium and for the standard antiepileptic drugs (AEDs) may be more useful in guiding dosage but should not be interpreted apart from the individual's response and tolerance of the drug.
Heavy metal screens	Many neuropsychiatric symptoms have been associated with lead, mercury, manganese, arsenic, and aluminum poisoning; these should be tested if a patient with psychiatric presentation has any suggestion of a history of exposure to them.

useful clinical test, the remaining 1% of its composition has the potential to provide vast amounts of information to the clinician.

Although it has been more than a century since the first lumbar puncture, the routine clinical tests performed on the CSF have not changed from the first one performed. The color, pressure, cell count, protein, and glucose levels are measured routinely with every specimen and together give the "CSF profile," indicating more specific diagnoses. In bacterial meningitis, in which the lumbar puncture is most useful, an increase in pressure, WBC count, and protein is seen, as well as a decrease in glucose. The WBC count is usually greater than 1,000/mm3 with a predominance of polymorphonuclear cells. In viral meningitis, there is predominantly monocytic CSF pleocytosis with normal glucose levels and modest elevations in protein. Fungal and tuberculous meningitis are characterized by a predominant lymphocytic pleocytosis with increased protein and decreased glucose levels. Specific staining techniques and cultures along with measurement of antibodies, antigens, or both; other immunologic tests; and the use of the newer polymerase chain reaction (PCR) also help to differentiate the various causes of infection of the CNS. In suspected neurosyphilis, the CSF profile is nonspecific, but the CSF venereal disease research laboratories (VDRL) test is a specific test used for making the diagnosis.

Apart from infections, CSF finds its greatest use in the evaluation of demyelinating disease, especially multiple sclerosis and acute and chronic inflammatory polyradiculoneuropathies. Within psychiatry, examination of the CSF is indicated in acute mental status changes when an infectious or other neurological cause is suspected and neuroimaging has ruled out the possibility of increased intracranial pressure. Lumbar puncture should not be done as a routine screening procedure in psychiatric patients. Its yield is low, and it should only be performed for the specific indications previously discussed.

A. Contraindications

Lumbar puncture is contraindicated in the following circumstances:

- if there is suspicion of increased intracranial pressure with a mass lesion or ventricular obstruction; in such instances, neuroimaging should always be obtained first;
- in the presence of complete spinal subarachnoid block;
- in the presence of significant coagulation defects; and
- if there is evidence of local infection at the site of the lumbar puncture.

In the case of known bacteremia, one should also be extra careful with lumbar puncture because it has been associated with the occurrence of secondary meningitis.

B. Indications

Currently the major indication for lumbar puncture in neurology and psychiatry is to exclude CNS infection. Although many hundreds of studies have been done in psychiatric patients, there is still no recognized indication clinically for the procedure in the field of psychiatry except to exclude neurological illness. However, because meningitis and encephalitis often present with mental status changes, patients with these diseases may see a psychiatrist or neuropsychologist first in the evaluation process.

1. In adults, lumbar puncture is indicated in the evaluation of the following conditions:
    a. suspected infections or postinfectious illness (bacterial, tuberculous, viral, and fungal meningitis; aseptic meningitis, infectious polyneuritis, cysticercosis, toxoplasmosis and rickettsia infections, amebic infections, neurosyphilis, Lyme borreliosis, rubella panencephalitis, subacute sclerosing panencephalitis [SSPE], HIV and herpes simplex encephalitis, encephalitis of uncertain cause);
    b. multiple sclerosis (most useful tests: oligoclonal bands, IgG index, and myelin basic protein);
    c. intracranial hemorrhage (better evaluated in the first instance with neuroimaging; CSF may be diagnostic for subarachnoid hemorrhage even if neuroimaging is negative, however);
    d. meningeal malignancy (pleocytosis, protein, glucose, specific tumor markers);
    e. paraneoplastic syndromes (specific neuronal nuclear and Purkinje cell antibodies are detectable);
    f. pseudotumor cerebri (requires lumbar puncture to diagnose and confirm increased pressure and to exclude meningitis);
    g. normal pressure hydrocephalus (lumbar puncture sometimes is useful in prediction of response to shunting);
    h. amyloid angiopathy (cystatin C, amyloid betaprotein);
    i. neurosarcoidosis (CSF angiotensin converting enzyme);
    j. evaluation of dementia;

    k. stroke (better evaluated in the first instance with neuroimaging; CSF is useful in suspected subarachnoid hemorrhage, when CNS vasculitis is suspected, if septic emboli are suspected, in patients with positive syphilis or HIV serologic studies, and in young patients with unexplained strokes); and

    l. other (systemic lupus erythematosus, hepatic encephalopathy, vitamin B12 deficiency; occasionally in seizures to exclude CNS infection or bleeding, and for intrathecal therapy).

2. In children, lumbar puncture is indicated in the following clinical situations:

    a. suspected meningitis (CSF changes may be less specific and initially normal in children);

    b. other infections (as in adults; most show nonspecific changes except for antibody titers in SSPE, measles, rubella, and progressive rubella panencephalitis);

    c. febrile seizures (only if clinical evidence of meningitis is present, except in infants younger than 12 months, in whom clinical signs may be absent and CSF should be examined);

    d. intracranial hemorrhage in neonates;

    e. pseudotumor cerebri;

    f. lead encephalopathy;

    g. CNS neoplasia (as in adults; best evaluated in the first instance with neuroimaging);

    h. lysosomal storage diseases (measurement of specific glycosphingolipids); and

    i. therapeutic lumbar puncture (intrathecal therapy).

III. URINE TESTS

The most common test of urine used in psychiatric patients is the routine urinalysis and culture to detect infection or renal disease. The test reveals the cell count (increased with infections), the protein (increased in renal disease) and glucose (increased in diabetes mellitus) levels, as well as the specific gravity and microscopic analysis. Urine culture is often needed to establish the cause of infection and the susceptibility of the organism to various antibiotics. Detection of urine infections is important because their presence may exacerbate other changes in mental state and may, in the elderly, even present with delirium and other acute mental state changes. The creatinine clearance test is also checked frequently in psychiatric patients when starting lithium therapy as a sensitive baseline of renal function should the question of renal impairment arise on follow-up. This is particularly important in patients with a history of renal disease. The creatinine clearance is calculated from a 24-hour urine collection using serum values as well.

Other, more specific tests of urine of use in neuropsychiatry include urine toxicology (for suspected drug abuse), trimethylamine (for trimethylaminuria), porphyrin screens (for porphyria), catecholamine and metabolites (for pheochromocytoma), osmolality (for the syndrome of inappropriate antidiuretic hormone [SIADH]), and urine myoglobin (in suspected rhabdomyolysis, such as in neuroleptic malignant syndrome, severe electrical shock, or muscle crush injury).

IV. ELECTROENCEPHALOGRAPHY

Electroencephalography (EEG) is a measure of electrical activity taken from surface electrodes on the scalp. In certain circumstances (e.g., in the evaluation of patients for epilepsy surgery), intracranial electrodes may also be used. Anterior temporal and sphenoidal electrodes may also be helpful in evaluating suspected complex partial seizures. Photic stimulation, sleep, and hyperventilation are all useful activation procedures. Although hundreds of EEG studies have been done in primary psychiatric illness, the abnormalities found are generally nonspecific, and the EEG is used primarily to exclude neurological illness within psychiatry. The EEG is the one test that relates directly to attention and to mental state, however, and therefore it is of particular interest to neuropsychologists.

The EEG is not clinically indicated for general screening of psychiatric patients or for the evaluation of primary psychiatric illness, although it is of some academic interest in these conditions. During electroconvulsive therapy (ECT), EEG monitoring is useful to establish seizure duration and may also be useful in evaluation of patients prior to ECT. The EEG is also useful in suspected drug toxicity and in evaluating suspected lithium toxicity in patients who develop mental symptoms at therapeutic levels, suspected AED toxicity, and suspected intoxication from other psychotropic drugs.

The main indication for an EEG, however, is in the evaluation of suspected epilepsy. It is also useful in the evaluation of episodic behavioral disorders when epilepsy is in the differential diagnosis (e.g., atypical panic attacks, atypical paroxysmal affective or psychotic symptoms, or transient cognitive impairment or inattention in children). Ambulatory or video EEG is often helpful as well in these situations; these tools provide the opportunity for prolonged monitoring and for correlating the EEG findings with the clinical behavior. Sphenoidal or anterior temporal leads are used if a temporal focus is suspected. It should be noted that a normal EEG does not rule out epilepsy, nor does an abnormal EEG rule it in, and the results of an EEG must always be taken within the clinical context. Deep foci, especially frontal, may have normal surface EEG findings even ictally.

Another indication for the EEG in psychiatry is the evaluation of the acute confusional state. In these situations, the EEG is useful for establishing the diagnosis and following the course of delirium. In the assessment of other cognitive impairment, the EEG is useful in the diagnosis of dementia and of cognitive impairment related to depression or to medication effects.

There are also a variety of other illnesses presenting with psychiatric symptoms for which an EEG is indicated, particularly when findings in the history, mental state examination, physical examination, or laboratory tests suggest a neurological or medical basis for the patient's symptoms. Examples include an unusual course of illness (unusual onset, rapid deterioration), a history of known neurological illness such as epilepsy, and atypical mental state findings or focal abnormalities on neurological examination. Table 3.4 shows the primary EEG findings in psychiatric disorders and in neurological illness presenting with psychiatric symptoms.

V. NEUROIMAGING

The main neuroimaging tests of clinical use are computed tomography (CT) and magnetic resonance imaging (MRI). Both types of neuroimaging have distinct advantages and disadvantages. The advantages of MRI over CT are a higher degree of resolution, particularly in evaluating white matter in demyelinating disorders; in searching for the seizure focus in epilepsy when resolution of the hippocampal region in particular is well delineated; and in dementia, infarction, neoplastic disease, vascular malformations, and degenerative disease. It also images the posterior fossa, spinal cord, and brain stem to a much greater degree. It has the other advantage of avoiding radiation and, in patients allergic to iodine, the use of contrast materials to which they might be sensitive. MRI, like CT, may be enhanced by the use of contrast with gadolinium. CT scanning, on the other hand, has the advantage of being much more available, much less expensive, and applicable when MRI is contraindicated because of the presence of ferromagnetic material (e.g., aneurysm clip, pacemaker). It is superior to MRI in a few specific situations: evaluation of meningeal tumors, calcified lesions,

Table 3.4. Primary Electroencephalography (EEG) Findings in Psychiatric and Neurological Illness Presenting With Psychiatric Symptoms

Condition	EEG findings
Schizophrenia	Nonspecific findings; low mean alpha frequency, nonspecific findings in sleep staging.
Depression	Nonspecific changes in waking EEG. Sleep EEGs more useful than awake EEG; decrease in rapid eye movement (REM) latency often seen, especially if delusions and depression are present; also decreases in Stages III and IV and in sleep continuity.
Anxiety disorders	Nonspecific changes in anxiety disorders, often with predominant muscle artifact. Although the EEG changes in panic disorder are also nonspecific, it is worth remembering that panic may also occur as an ictal phenomenon; ambulatory monitoring is helpful to differentiate, especially in cases refractory to traditional treatment and atypical cases.
Delirium	Severity relates to extent of slow wave abnormality. Causes include various medical and neurological conditions: toxic, metabolic, vascular, infectious, postsurgical, traumatic.
Dementia	Nonspecific slowing most common. EEG relates somewhat to degree of impairment. Lag behind cognitive impairment in Alzheimer's disease and EEG changes. Focal EEG changes suggest multi-infarct dementia or normal pressure hydrocephalus. Changes often mild or absent in Pick's disease. Characteristic triphasic complexes in Creutzfeldt-Jakob disease.
Epilepsy	Ictal EEG changes useful in assessing diagnosis and location of focus. Sharp and slow wave activity may also be seen interictally. Interictal changes generally do not correlate with psychiatric symptoms. Ambulatory and video-EEG monitoring often useful.

(Continued)

Table 3.4. Primary Electroencephalography (EEG) Findings in Psychiatric and Neurological Illness Presenting With Psychiatric Symptoms (*Continued*)

Condition	EEG findings
Tumors	Focal slowing may be seen. Psychiatric presentations and EEG findings depend on location and nature of tumor.
Metabolic and toxic conditions	Triphasic waves in hepatic and renal coma. Nonspecific EEG abnormalities in vitamin B12 deficiency, with cognitive impairment and nonspecific slowing in hypothyroidism.
Infections	Herpes encephalitis: temporal sharp complexes. Diffuse slowing in encephalitis of various causes. Focal or generalized slowing or paroxysmal discharges in AIDS. Localized slow waves over area of abscess in localized CNS infection. EEG findings do not generally correlate with psychiatric symptoms.

Note. Source: McConnell, Andrews, Binnie, and Rogers (2003).

acute intracranial hemorrhage, and acute parenchymal infarction. Both types of neuroimaging thus have a valuable place in
clinical practice, and careful consideration should be given to
the type of imaging used on an individual basis. Quantitative
and functional MRI also promise to have an increasing clinical
role in the future.

Other types of neuroimaging that are being used increasingly are single photon emission computed tomography
(SPECT) and positron emission tomography (PET). These offer
a functional image, and although they are still largely research
tools, they are promising technologies. SPECT has the advantage
of being routinely available and being much less expensive,
whereas PET is still largely restricted to research institutes. Both
are most useful clinically in the evaluation of epilepsy and dementia. Neither has a clear indication in primary psychiatric
illness.

VI. USE OF TESTING IN SPECIFIC
PSYCHIATRIC PRESENTATIONS

Laboratory testing must always be considered within the context
of the clinical presentation. The appropriate ordering of tests
depends on an accurate assessment of each individual presentation. Some of the most difficult clinical evaluations in neuropsychology are the evaluation of dementia, atypical affective disorder, and atypical psychosis. Exhibits 3.1 and 3.2 show the
laboratory evaluation of these clinical conditions, which must
be individualized depending on the nature of the presenting
symptoms. In some instances a more detailed assessment than
that noted in the exhibit would be indicated, such as when
there is a family history of a certain metabolic or degenerative
disorder that may present with psychosis or affective disturbance, or when there is an indication from either the history
or the physical examination of other CNS disease.

Other psychiatric presentations may require a different emphasis from those noted in Exhibits 3.1 and 3.2. Although the
tests in Exhibit 3.2 would be appropriate for the evaluation of
atypical anxiety disorder, a history of atypical panic attacks
might warrant the use of ambulatory EEG, because complex
partial seizures may present in this manner. The occurrence of
symptoms seen commonly in seizure disorders with a temporal
lobe focus would indicate further evaluation with EEG. If the
history elucidated the finding of urine changing color, a porphyria screen may be appropriate; if a history of drug abuse
were suspected, a toxicology screen would be important. If the

Exhibit 3.1. Laboratory Evaluation of Dementia

Assessment of dementia in the elderly

Blood tests:
  CBC, ESR, electrolytes, glucose, calcium, phosphorus, TSH, serum B12, RBC folate, RPR

Neuroimaging:
  CT or MRI

Systemic tests:
  Chest X-ray, ECG, urinalysis

Optional tests:
  Lumbar puncture
  EEG
  SPECT
  Antiphospholipid antibodies
  HIV testing
  Toxicology screen
  Heavy metal screening

Assessment of dementia in children and young adults

Preceding tests as in older adults

Blood tests:
  Serum cholestanol (cerebrotendinous xanthomatosis)
  Serum copper and ceruloplasmin (Wilson's disease)
  Serum HIV antibodies (AIDS dementia)
  Serum very long chain fatty acids (adrenoleukodystrophy)
  Serum lactate and pyruvate levels (mitochondrial encephalopathies)
  WBC arylsulfatase A (metachromatic leukodystrophy)
  WBC galactocerebroside beta galactosidase (Krabbe's disease)
  WBC sphingomyelinase (Niemann-Pick disease)
  WBC Gm1 beta-galactosidase (GM1 gangliosidosis)
  WBC hexosaminidase A (GM2 gangliosidosis)
  WBC alpha galactosidase (Fabry's disease)
  WBC alpha-N-acetylglucosaminidase (mucopolysaccharidosis)

Urine:
  Urinary dolichols (ceroid lipofuscinosis)

Other:
  Skin biopsy (polycystic lipomembranous osteodysplasia; pseudoxanthoma elasticum)
  Liver biopsy (Lafora's disease, Niemann-Pick disease)
  Skeletal muscle biopsy (Lafora's disease)
  Brain biopsy (ceroid lipofuscinosis)
  Hand X-rays (polycystic lipomembranous osteodysplasia)
  Nerve conduction studies (neuroacanthocytosis)

Note. CBC = complete blood count; ESR = erythrocyte sedimentation rate; TSH = thyroid-stimulating hormone; RBC = red blood cell; RPR = rapid plasma reagin; CT = computed tomography; MRI = magnetic resonance imaging; ECG = electrocardiogram; EEG = electroencephalography; SPECT = single photon emission computed tomography; WBC = white blood cell. Source: Cummings and Trimble (1995).

Exhibit 3.2. Laboratory Tests to Consider in the
Evaluation of Atypical Psychosis or Affective Disorder

Blood tests:
  CBC, electrolytes, glucose, renal and liver function tests,
    thyroid function tests, serum B12 and RBC folate, RPR,
    calcium and phosphorus, HIV serology in those with risk
    factors, serum cortisol

Systemic tests:
  Chest X-ray
  ECG

Urine tests:
  Urinalysis
  Urine toxicology
  Urine porphyrin screen

Neurophysiological assessment:
  EEG
  Neuroimaging
  CT, MRI, or both

Note. CBC = complete blood count; RBC = red blood cell; RPR =
rapid plasma reagin; ECG = electrocardiogram; EEG = electroencephalography; CT = computed tomography; MRI = magnetic
resonance imaging.

presentation were extremely atypical with an excess of autonomic signs, such as hypertension, associated with episodes of
behavioral disturbance, the clinician should consider measuring
serum and urine catecholamines and metabolites to evaluate
the patient for possible pheochromocytoma, a rare tumor that
may present with such symptoms. It is clearly not practical or
cost efficient (or clinically necessary), however, to screen every
patient with panic attacks, which is one of the most common
psychiatric presentations, for rare tumors. The laboratory
workup must be geared toward the history and physical findings
to avoid the ordering of unnecessary tests.

The age of the patient is also an important consideration
in the laboratory assessment. The evaluation of dementia in
children and young adults, for example, is very different from
that of elderly adults with the same clinical presentation. This
is because different disorders tend to start at different ages, and
the evaluation should be geared toward the possible causes for
the relevant age group. It would be inappropriate, for example,
to screen an older adult presenting with psychosis or dementia
for congenital metabolic illness that presents only in childhood.
The differential diagnosis is not the same in these situations,
and the laboratory evaluation should always be geared around

the differential diagnosis for an individual patient, rather than set protocols for every patient with a given presentation. Protocols do have a use in routine screening of psychiatric patients, such as set laboratory tests ordered on admission to a psychiatric hospital. In these instances, one can be sure that certain common treatable causes of psychiatric illness (e.g., hypothyroidism) will not be missed, but these tests should not replace a full clinical evaluation including a history and physical examination.

VII. CONCLUSION

It is important for the neuropsychologist to be aware of laboratory testing because he or she is one of the principal members of the team involved in the evaluation of the patient's mental state. Both the ordering and interpretation of laboratory tests must be done within the clinical context of the patient, with patient consent and following an appropriate history and mental status, neurological, and physical examination. This chapter has summarized the major laboratory tests of interest to the neuropsychologist. The bibliography contains further readings concerning the specificity, sensitivity, indications, and contraindications for various laboratory tests.

It is critical for all members of the treatment team to be aware of the spectrum of laboratory tests available and to be wary of third-party payer algorithms for the laboratory evaluation of neuropsychological illness. Whereas screening protocols have some use in this population, it is important to consider laboratory tests for individual patients within the context of their presenting symptoms, age, family history, past medical and psychiatric history, and clinical examination and to put this information in the context of a differential diagnosis and management plan for the patient. There have been many brilliant careers wasted looking for specific laboratory tests for primary psychiatric illness, which is best done as a clinical diagnosis based on an extensive patient history, rather than relying on sometimes misleading laboratory tests. The primary role of laboratory tests in neuropsychology is to look for treatable neuropsychiatric causes of a patient's clinical presentation.

BIBLIOGRAPHY

Aminoff, M. J. (1992). *Electrodiagnosis in clinical neurology*. Edinburgh, Scotland: Churchill Livingstone.

Andreasen, N. C. (Ed.). (1989). *Brain imaging: Applications in psychiatry*. Washington, DC: American Psychiatric Press.

Cummings, J. L., & Trimble, M. R. (1995). *Neuropsychiatry and behavioral neurology*. Washington, DC: American Psychiatric Press.

Daniel, D. G., Zigun, J. R., & Weinberger, D. R. (1992). Brain imaging in neuropsychiatry. In S. Yudofsky & R. Hales (Eds.), *Textbook of neuropsychiatry* (pp. 165–186). Washington, DC: American Psychiatric Press.

Fu, C. H. Y., Russell, T., Senior, C., Weinberger, D., & Murray, R. (Eds.). (2003). *Guide to neuroimaging in psychiatry*. London: Routledge.

Jacobs, D. S., Kasten, B. L., Demott, W. R., & Wolfson, W. (1990). *Laboratory test handbook*. Baltimore: Williams & Wilkins.

Lishman, A. (1987). *Organic psychiatry*. Oxford, England: Blackwell Scientific.

Matthews, P. M., & Arnold, D. L. (1991). *Diagnostic tests in neurology*. Edinburgh, Scotland: Churchill Livingstone.

McConnell, H., Andrews, C., Binnie, C. D., & Rogers, T. D. (2003). The EEG in psychiatry. In C. Binnie, R. Cooper, F. Maugiere, J. Osselton, P. Prior, & B. Tedman (Eds.), *Clinical neurophysiology: EEG, paediatric neurophysiology, special techniques and applications* (Vol. 2). London: Elsevier Science.

McConnell, H. W., & Bianchine, J. R. (1994). *Cerebrospinal fluid in neurology and psychiatry*. London: Chapman & Hall.

Peter, J. B. (1994). *Use and interpretation of laboratory tests in neurology*. Santa Monica, CA: Specialty Laboratories.

Rosse, R. B., Giese, A. A., Deutsch, S. I., & Morihisa, J. M. (1989). *Laboratory testing in psychiatry*. Washington, DC: American Psychiatric Press.

Schiller, M. J., Shumway, M., & Batki, S. L. (2000). Utility of routine drug screening in a psychiatric emergency setting. *Psychiatric Services, 51,* 474–478.

Strub, R. L., & Black, F. W. (1993). *The mental status examination in neurology*. Philadelphia: Davis.

Taylor, D., McConnell, H., Duncan, D., & Kerwin, R. (2001). *The South London and Maudsley NHS Trust prescribing guidelines* (6th ed.). London: Martin Dunitz.

Yudofsky, S., & Kim, H. F. (Vol. Eds.). (2004). Neuropsychiatric assessment. In J. M. Oldham & M. B. Riba (Series Eds.), *Review of psychiatry* (Vol. 23). Washington, DC: American Psychiatric Press.

CHAPTER 4

Greig de Zubicaray

Neuroimaging and Clinical Neuropsychological Practice

Neuroimaging technologies have increased in sophistication over the past two decades. They are now applied routinely in clinics and hospitals when there is suspicion of a brain injury or disorder and are therefore more likely to be encountered by clinical neuropsychologists in their day-to-day practice. This chapter provides an overview of some of the more commonly used neuroimaging modalities, including computed tomography (CT), magnetic resonance imaging (MRI), single photon emission computed tomography (SPECT), positron emission tomography (PET), and electroencephalography (EEG), and their applications to some frequently encountered neurological conditions. These technologies vary greatly in terms of their availability, methods of operation, spatial and temporal resolutions, invasiveness, and ability to detect abnormalities of brain structure, metabolism, and function. Often more than one imaging modality will be used to answer a given clinical question. Functional neuroimaging is rapidly becoming a complementary technique to traditional clinical neuropsychological procedures for the evaluation of disorders such as Alzheimer's disease (AD) and epilepsy, because of its simultaneous assessment of cognitive performance and brain function. However, it should not be viewed under any circumstances as a replacement for a more comprehensive neuropsychological assessment. An emerging area of application for neuroimaging is in pharmacology, where it has been used to measure central nervous system (CNS) responses modulated by the administration of drug therapies.

I. COMMON NEUROIMAGING METHODS

Neuroimaging techniques may be broadly classified into two categories: those that examine the integrity of structural features of the CNS, such as tissue and vasculature, and those that reveal its functions. Structural neuroimaging is utilized clinically to detect abnormalities (e.g., lesions) produced by cerebrovascular accidents, head trauma, and tumors, and physiological changes such as atrophy (tissue shrinkage) and metabolic dysfunction that are characteristic features of neurological diseases (e.g., Alzheimer's disease, Parkinson's disease). Although imaging studies that provide information about resting-state CNS metabolism or activity are sometimes referred to as "functional" investigations, the term **functional neuroimaging** is used here in its more common usage to describe methods that provide information about cerebral regions mediating particular sensory, motor, and cognitive processes during task performance. It is important to note that investigations using all of the following techniques are compromised to varying degrees by head movement occurring during image acquisition, and are therefore not always conducted successfully in the clinical setting. In addition, the type of neuroimaging performed on a patient at an institution may be determined more by the availability and cost of a particular method. Table 4.1 provides a summary of the relative spatial resolutions, methods of operation, and general limitations of each of the structural imaging methods. Table 4.2 summarizes similar information concerning the functional imaging techniques.

A. Electroencephalography

The oldest of the neuroimaging techniques in use today, electroencephalography (EEG) measures the bioelectric activity of the brain noninvasively via electrodes placed on the surface of the scalp. Electrode placement is determined according to a consensus-based international standard positioning system. The electrodes detect rhythmic fluctuations in voltage resulting largely from interacting postsynaptic potentials of excitatory and inhibitory cortical neurons. These signals are then amplified, recorded, and filtered to remove artifacts from unwanted bioelectric sources (e.g., from eye movements, heart beats). Different frequencies of varying amplitudes may be identified in the signal

Table 4.1. Structural Neuroimaging Techniques

Modality	Method	Measures	Spatial/temporal resolutions	Limitations
Electro-encephalography (EEG)	Bioelectric activity detected at scalp	Frequency and amplitude Interregional coherence	~2.5 cm at cortical surface/milliseconds	Uncertain localization Unable to detect activity from deep cortical and subcortical structures
Computed tomography (CT)	X-ray attenuation in tissue X-ray attenuation due to intravenously injected radiopaque iodinated contrast agent	Tissue density Selectively enhanced tissue density	2 mm/10s of seconds to minutes	Ionizing radiation (few permitted exposures)
Perfusion CT	X-ray attenuation due to inhaled radiopaque contrast agent	Perfusion (rCBF, rCBV)	3 mm/10s of seconds to minutes	Ionizing radiation (few permitted exposures)
Single photon emission computed tomography (SPECT)	Intravenously injected or inhaled radioactive tracer or ligand	Perfusion (rCBF, rCBV) Neurotransmitter receptor and transporter binding	3 mm/10s of seconds to minutes	Ionizing radiation (few permitted exposures) Uncertain localization Limited slice coverage Indirect measure of neuronal activity

Modality	Contrast mechanism	Measures	Resolution	Limitations
Positron emission tomography (PET)	Intravenously injected radioactive tracer or ligand	Perfusion (rCBF, rCBV) Glucose metabolism Neurotransmitter receptor and transporter binding	3 mm / 10s of seconds to minutes	Ionizing radiation (few permitted exposures) Cyclotron needed to manufacture tracers and ligands
Magnetic resonance imaging (MRI)	Endogenous contrast: T_1- & T_2-weighted Diffusion weighted Diffusion tensor Arterial spin labeling (ASL) Intravenously injected contrast agent: dynamic susceptibility contrast (DSC)	Anatomy (gray matter, white matter, CSF, etc.) Water diffusion in tissue Anisotropic water diffusion in white matter fibers rCBF rCBF, rCBV	< 1 mm / 10s of seconds to minutes 3 mm / 10s of seconds to minutes 3 mm / 10s of seconds to minutes 3 mm / 10s of seconds to minutes 1 mm / 10s of milliseconds	Persons with metal in their bodies (e.g., pacemakers, aneurysm clips) cannot be imaged

Note. rCBF = regional cerebral blood flow; rCBV = regional cerebral blood volume; CSF = cerebrospinal fluid.

Table 4.2. Functional Neuroimaging Techniques

Modality	Method	Measures	Spatial/ temporal resolutions	Limitations
Event-related potentials (ERPs)	Bioelectric activity detected at scalp	Frequency and amplitude Waveform components Interregional coherence/ covariance/ phase synchrony	~2.5 cm/ milliseconds	Uncertain localization Unable to detect activity from deep cortical and subcortical structures
Single photon emission computed tomography (SPECT)	Intravenously injected radioactive tracer	Perfusion (rCBF, rCBV)	3 mm/seconds	Ionizing radiation (few permitted exposures) Uncertain localization Limited slice coverage Indirect measure of neuronal activity Actual temporal resolution determined by hemodynamic responses

Positron emission tomography (PET)	Intravenously injected radioactive tracer	Perfusion (rCBF, rCBV) Glucose metabolism Oxygen utilization	3 mm/seconds	Ionizing radiation (few permitted exposures) Cyclotron needed to manufacture tracers Indirect measure of neuronal activity Actual temporal resolution determined by hemodynamic responses and metabolic rates
Functional magnetic resonance imaging (fMRI)	Endogenous contrast: arterial spin labeling (ASL) Blood oxygen level dependent (BOLD) Intravenously injected contrast agent: Dynamic susceptibility contrast (DSC)	rCBF relative change in de-oxyhaemoglobin rCBF, rCBV	3 mm/ 1 second 1 mm/ 10s of milliseconds 1 mm/ 10s of milliseconds	Persons with metal in their bodies (e.g., pacemakers, aneurysm clips) cannot be imaged Indirect measure of neuronal activity Actual temporal resolution determined by hemodynamic responses

Note. rCBF = regional cerebral blood flow; rCBV = regional cerebral blood volume.

fluctuations, conforming to the delta (0.5 to 3 Hz), theta (4 to 7 Hz), alpha (8 to 12 Hz), beta (13 to 20 Hz), and gamma (21 to 90 Hz) ranges. The distribution of neuronal populations along the cortical surface generates electric fields of potential or *dipoles* that may be used for partial source localization when multiple channels are used for recording (called **quantitative EEG**). This is the basis of topographic mapping of activity with EEG. Fourier transformation is applied to derive the power spectrum from the raw EEG signal, and this is usually interpreted as reflecting the degree of synchrony within local neuronal populations.

Two types of EEG investigations are usually distinguished. These relate to spontaneous or resting state activity and event-related potentials (ERPs) resulting from neural activity evoked in response to a discrete behavioral event. The latter are the basis of functional studies performed with EEG. Functional interrelations between pairs of cortical regions may be investigated via **coherence** and **covariance** measures in resting state and ERP studies. Coherency reflects the degree to which the respective regions' frequencies are correlated, and is often interpreted as a measure of "connectivity" between regions. Covariance measures are restricted to ERP studies and reflect similarities in averaged positive (e.g., P300) or negative (e.g., N200) waveform components across selected regions in the time domain. Measures of phase synchrony between ERPs from distributed cortical regions are used for investigating the dynamic organization of large-scale cortical networks. The use of EEG in clinical settings is widespread. There are virtually no contraindications for its use.

B. Computed Tomography

Computed tomography (CT) is one of the most widely available imaging modalities in the clinical setting and is generally used for structural investigations. It uses ionizing radiation (X-rays) to obtain images of the skull and brain. Image contrast is obtained by directing and focusing (also called **collimating**) multiple X-ray beams through the skull and brain at various angles while an array of detectors determines their varying levels of absorption or attenuation according to different tissue densities. The spatial resolution of CT is therefore directly related to the amount of radiation exposure given during image acquisition, and this is typically much greater than that of a conventional X-ray procedure. In addition, a radiopaque contrast agent or dye may be injected intravenously to enhance certain blood vessels or tissue types. This is a substance (usually iodine) that X-rays are unable to pass through.

A less common type of brain CT involves the inhalation of Xenon (^{13}Xe) gas, used to examine brain perfusion. The passage of this contrast agent through the cerebral vasculature is recorded by measuring the changes in X-ray attenuation, providing time-course information reflecting the changes in blood–Xenon concentration. This procedure can provide measures of regional cerebral blood volume (rCBV) and flow (rCBF), useful for detecting vascular changes.

The technology for CT continues to be developed. Modern multislice helical CT systems are able to scan more rapidly than their axial forebears. There are few contraindications (e.g., pregnancy) for the use of CT despite the use of X-rays, as the risks of exposure to ionizing radiation are considered to be outweighed by the benefits of the clinical information provided by the examination. This, combined with the cost-effectiveness of the procedure compared with other imaging modalities, accounts for its widespread use in the clinical setting. However, there is an increased risk of allergic reaction to contrast agents. Because of its availability and general utility, it is most likely to be among the first imaging investigations performed when there is suspicion of brain injury or disorder.

C. Single Photon Emission Computed Tomography

Single photon emission computed tomography (SPECT) uses intravenously injected radiopharmaceuticals, called **tracers**, that emit gamma ray photons of energy to generate image contrast. Photons emitted by the radioactive tracers interact with electrons in the atoms of the brain tissue and are either absorbed or deflected via a process known as **scattering**. In modern SPECT systems, radiation/photon detection is performed via collimators with multiple Gamma cameras recording the degree of absorption at various angles throughout the brain. The spatial resolution of a SPECT image is determined for the most part by the collimation process, and this is inherently difficult given the uncertain position of the radiation source within the brain.

The information that may be obtained from a SPECT investigation is directly related to the tracer used. Although it has been used primarily for measuring cerebral perfusion (rCBF), recently developed radiopharmaceuticals called **radioligands** allow investigations of cerebral neurotransmitter systems in terms of their receptor density and transporters. Functional imaging is also able to be performed to some extent using maps of rCBF because of the known coupling of hemodynamics and cerebral activity, although the low intrinsic spatial resolution of SPECT limits its utility for studying perfusion in small cerebral structures (Kessler, 2003). The following are some commonly used tracers and their applications:

- Technetium-^{99m}-hexamethyl propylene amine oxime (HMPAO; rCBF)
- Technetium-^{99m}-ethyl cysteinate dimer (ECD; rCBF)
- ^{133}Xe (rCBF)
- ^{123}I-methoxybenzamide (IBZM; dopamine D_2 and D_3 receptor ligand)

SPECT is widely available and like CT has few clinical contraindications other than pregnancy and allergies. Ionizing radiation exposure is slightly greater than that of CT.

D. Positron Emission Tomography

Positron emission tomography (PET) also uses radiopharmaceutical compounds, or tracers, that are either intravenously injected or inhaled in gas form to examine brain perfusion and metabolism. Unlike SPECT, these tracers are labeled with positron-emitting radionuclides. Positrons are the antimatter equivalent of electrons. When a positron collides with an electron, they annihilate each other, producing two gamma ray photons of identical energy that are emitted in opposite directions. The PET system is able to detect these photons by radiation detector elements placed on both sides of the head, allowing localization of the energy emission on a straight line between them. Unlike SPECT, PET offers the ability to measure the concentration of tracers quantitatively. The spatial resolution of PET is limited theoretically by positron range and practically by the spatial resolution of current detector elements.

Because of the short radioactive half lives of the tracers used in PET (on the order of minutes), a machine called a cyclotron—a type of particle accelerator—is necessary to produce them within close proximity of the PET system. This additional expensive infrastructure makes PET one of the less widely available imaging modalities. Like SPECT, PET is able to investigate neurotransmitter receptors and transporters using radioligands. However, there are relatively more radioligands available for PET than SPECT. The application of PET for functional imaging studies is now widespread and generally involves measures of rCBF, oxidative, or glucose metabolism during task performance (Kessler, 2003). Some frequently used tracers and their applications are the following:

- [^{15}O]Water (rCBF)
- 2-[^{18}F]Fluoro-2-deoxy-D-glucose (FDG; glucose metabolism)
- ^{15}O$_2$ (oxygen utilization)
- [^{11}C]Raclopride (dopamine D2 and D3 receptor ligand)
- ^{11}C-Flumazenil (FMZ; benzodiazepine receptor ligand)

Contraindications for clinical PET scanning are similar to those for CT and SPECT given the use of ionizing radiation.

E. Magnetic Resonance Imaging

Magnetic resonance imaging (MRI) uses a combination of strong magnetic fields and short radiofrequency (RF) pulses to create images. An MRI system comprises a large superconducting magnet. When placed within this magnet, the protons of hydrogen nuclei in water molecules contained in brain tissue align with the static magnetic field. Application of an RF pulse at this frequency changes their alignment to a direction perpendicular to the static field, while forcing them to be in phase. Once in phase, an output RF signal can be detected by the MRI system. This signal can be spatially encoded by applying magnetic field gradients along orthogonal directions (anterior–posterior, inferior–superior, and left–right). These short gradient pulses perturb the local field such that the field experienced by one section of tissue is different from another. The state of the tissue magnetization after the RF pulse is an "excited" state and is transitory. There are two processes or contrast mechanisms whereby the signal is lost. These are realignment with the static field (T_1 relaxation) and decay within the perpendicular plane where the spins dephase and cancel each other. This second mechanism actually involves two processes, one that is correctable (T_2 relaxation) and one that is not (T_2^* relaxation). The timing of the RF pulse and sampling of the signal can be manipulated to generate images showing different tissue contrasts according to their respective relaxation times. These **pulse sequences** are generally noninvasive, although an intravenously injected contrast agent is sometimes used that alters the local magnetic field in the tissue of interest.

There are many different pulse sequences that can be applied in clinical MRI investigations of both structure and function (fMRI), and a complete list of these and their respective contrast mechanisms is beyond the scope of the present chapter. A brief overview of the most common ones and some with emerging clinical utility is presented here. Pulse sequences used commonly for clinical applications involve weightings for T_1,

T_2, and T_2^* relaxation. The T_1-weighted structural (volumetric) images show anatomy clearly by exploiting differences in relaxation times. Fat has a short relaxation time, followed by white matter, gray matter, and cerebrospinal fluid (CSF), so on a T_1-weighted image CSF appears dark. With an appropriate T_2-weighting, CSF is bright, gray matter is intermediate (or gray), and white matter is dark. Images with T_2^*-weighting show blood oxygen level dependent (BOLD) contrast (deoxygenated vs. oxygenated blood) and are used for fMRI studies when acquired as a time series.

Two related pulse sequences developed recently that are having increasing clinical application are diffusion weighted imaging (DWI) and diffusion tensor imaging (DTI). These methods measure the phenomenon of water diffusion, or Brownian motion, within brain tissue. In DWI, the global movement of water molecules is quantified by the apparent diffusion coefficient (ADC). In DTI, the directionality of white matter tracts is shown as well as their integrity. This is because in fibrous tissues such as white matter, the diffusion is anisotropic (not isotropic) or orientation dependent in that it is restricted to motion perpendicular to axons along the fiber tracts. Myelin is considered to be the major barrier to diffusion as it encompasses the axons.

Brain perfusion imaging with MRI is generally accomplished using two different contrast mechanisms. Dynamic susceptibility contrast (DSC) involves acquiring a series of images while an intravenously injected contrast agent passes through the cerebral vasculature, changing its magnetization, and is useful for measuring rCBF and rCBV. Arterial spin labeling (ASL) is a more recently developed noninvasive method for measuring rCBF that uses the magnetic properties of endogenous blood water. An RF pulse is used to invert the spins of arterial blood water prior to its entering the brain. These spins are said to be **labeled** or **tagged**. As this water mixes with that of the brain, it results in a reduction of overall magnetization. The difference between a tagged and nontagged image is proportional to the blood flow and can be used to generate a perfusion-weighted image.

Frequently, SPECT, PET, and EEG investigations will be performed in conjunction with MRI. This is usually so that their data can be coregistered or overlaid on the MRI for better visualization and localization of brain anatomy. Compared with SPECT and CT, MRI is currently more expensive and less widely available. There are more contraindications for MRI than other imaging modalities because of the use of high magnetic fields. Magnetizable materials (such as iron) move within the magnetic field and can become lethal, so aneurysm clips, pacemakers, prosthetic devices, and fragments of metal from metal-working become contraindications. In addition, the magnetic field and use of RF pulses introduce some novel problems for patient monitoring that involves cables or wires (e.g., electrocardiograms), although fiber-optic alternatives are being developed rapidly. However, the flexibility of MRI, in conjunction with its high spatial and temporal resolution relative to other imaging modalities, makes it particularly appealing in the clinical setting. It is also more suitable for situations in which serial investigations are required, as CT, SPECT, and PET are all limited by a small number of permitted exposures to ionizing radiation. If current trends in MRI system installation continue, it is likely to be as available as CT in the near future.

II. COMMON CLINICAL APPLICATIONS OF NEUROIMAGING

Neuroimaging modalities are being applied increasingly to provide diagnostic and prognostic information for cerebral disorders. Clinical methods are in a constant state of evolution, with new techniques being applied as soon as they become available. Functional neuroimaging is now being considered clinically useful where a given cerebral region appears structurally normal despite evidence of cognitive impairment, and where the boundaries of normal functioning tissue need to be identified and spared prior to surgical interventions. Comparative studies provide information concerning the relative utility of current techniques in terms of their sensitivity and specificity for detecting cerebral pathological changes associated with a particular disorder, or ability to monitor changes associated with spontaneous recovery or following therapeutic interventions. This is illustrated in the brief summaries of some frequently encountered conditions below.

A. Cerebrovascular Disease

Modern CT imaging has excellent sensitivity and specificity for detecting cerebral hemorrhage. For the detection of early ischemic changes, diffusion weighted MRI is superior to other imaging methods, including other MRI sequences (e.g., T_2-, T_2^*-weighted), and is able to detect an acute infarct within minutes of its occurrence (Barber et al., 1999). On DWI, hyperintense lesions indicate that the diffusional movement of water is restricted in the infarcted area. Prognostic information may be provided by imaging the **ischemic penumbra**, an area of severely hypoperfused but potentially viable tissue that surrounds the focal region of recent infarction (Donnan & Davis, 2002). Survival of the penumbra is the most important determinant of neuropsychological recovery. Perfusion measures provided by CT, PET, SPECT, and MRI have all been used, with PET and MRI measures capable of providing the most detailed information. Analysis of the so-called mismatch between DWI and perfusion-weighted images is now the most commonly used method for identifying the penumbra (Donnan & Davis, 2002). The mismatch refers to the finding of normal diffusion but reduced perfusion in the penumbra around the center of the diffusion abnormality corresponding to the infarct. About 30% of acute infarcts do not show this pattern, because of either completion of the infarction or spontaneous tissue reperfusion (recovery). Another advantage of this method is that repeat examinations may be performed to map the temporal and spatial progression of the penumbra that occurs either naturally or with administration of thrombolytic therapy. Quantitative EEG (qEEG) can be of use in monitoring seizures that occur following cerebrovascular disease, and some preliminary data suggest that it may predict functional recovery (Cuspineda et al., 2003). Serial functional neuroimaging (PET, fMRI) has been used primarily as a research tool to demonstrate cerebral reorganization associated with long-term recovery of function. However, some evidence indicates that it may have prognostic value where ipsilesional activation is still identifiable in the immediate period poststroke (e.g., in motor control; Calautti & Baron, 2003).

B. Traumatic Brain Injury

In the acute stage of traumatic brain injury (TBI), neuroimaging is used primarily to detect hemorrhage (e.g., hematoma), edema (swelling), and ischemic changes. Therefore, the findings are very similar to those in cerebrovascular disease. Diffuse axonal injury resulting from shearing forces may be detected with greater sensitivity than other methods using DWI. In addition, myelin damage may be assessed with DTI, providing information regarding changes in cerebral connectivity (Levin, 2003).

Electroencephalography has an important role in the assessment of posttraumatic epilepsy, primarily due to its capacity to detect interictal epileptiform discharges. Recent qEEG studies also suggest that reduced alpha frequency variability in the acute stage may be related to poorer functional outcome following TBI (e.g., Vespa et al., 2002). Although some functional neuroimaging studies of TBI have been conducted with PET and fMRI, it is worth noting that *any* technique that uses hemodynamic measurements can be confounded by the presence of small ischemic lesions (Hillary et al., 2002). As neuropsychological tests used routinely for TBI assessment become adapted to the neuroimaging environment (e.g., paced serial addition test; Lazeron, Rombouts, de Sonneville, Barkhof, & Scheltens, 2003), it is more likely that these techniques will show greater clinical utility.

C. Epilepsy

Neuroimaging now serves three important roles in the presurgical evaluation of epilepsy: confirming that a seizure disorder exists, localizing the seizure focus, and identifying the boundaries of normal-functioning tissue to be spared during surgical intervention. For some time, scalp EEG has had an undisputed role in confirming the occurrence of interictal epileptiform discharges or "spike" activity, and a lesser role in localizing their focus. Volumetric MRI and FDG-PET provide complementary information regarding the location of interictal dysfunction. Hippocampal sclerosis and focal cortical dysplasias, both common causes of epilepsy, are generally identifiable using a combination of T_1- and T_2-weighted MRI sequences. The addition of FDG-PET provides further information where structural abnormalities are not identifiable with MRI by demonstrating reduced glucose uptake (hypometabolism) in the seizure-related site. Typically, the PET data are overlaid on a T_1-weighted MR image to better delineate the anatomy of the area containing the seizure site and guide surgery. Unilateral hypometabolism also predicts positive neuropsychological outcome postsurgery. The mechanism by which FDG-PET is able to identify seizure foci is still not well understood. Recent use of FMZ-PET suggests it may be a more sensitive method for detecting seizure sites, and unlike FDG-PET, the mechanism by which it is able to localize seizure foci is more direct. Regions of hypometabolism on FMZ-PET correspond to reduced benzodiazepine receptor density and are therefore indicative of local neuronal loss. Attempts to image changes in regional cerebral metabolism and blood flow during seizures have had some success (e.g., ictal PET and SPECT; spike-triggered fMRI) but remain problematic for clinical use for a variety of methodological reasons, notwithstanding the opportunistic nature of seizure onset. Resting-state perfusion measures are generally of limited utility for localizing seizure sites. While typically performed with the sodium amytal ablation procedure (Wada testing), presurgical localization of memory and language function is now also being performed with functional neuro-imaging (Akanuma, Koutroumanidis, Adachi, Alarcon, & Binnie, 2003). Unilateral activation of language- and memory-related cortical regions in fMRI studies accords well with results from Wada testing. In addition, positive correlations between activation asymmetry and neuropsychological outcome post-surgery have been reported, indicating the technique has prognostic value.

D. Alzheimer's Disease

Alzheimer's disease (AD) and mild cognitive impairment (MCI; a risk factor for AD) have been the topics of intense neuroimaging research in recent years. Considerable evidence now indicates that volumetric measures of the medial temporal lobe (MTL) and other cortical structures derived from CT and especially high spatial resolution T_1-weighted MRI sequences are most strongly related to disease severity in AD (e.g., Thompson et al., 2003). These measures also have prognostic value for identifying progression from MCI to AD (Wolf et al., 2003). Volumetric measures provide information about the extent of local and global atrophy in cerebral structures. Measures of perfusion (PET, SPECT, and DSC MRI) and metabolism (FDG-PET) also provide important diagnostic and prognostic information, with MTL and temporoparietal hypoperfusion and hypometabolism most commonly reported in mild AD and MCI (Zakzanis, Graham, & Campbell, 2003). However, a recent analysis of the diagnostic capabilities of these techniques in terms of their cost-effectiveness suggests that a combination of volumetric and DSC perfusion-weighted MRI measures is best, with neither FDG-PET nor SPECT contributing further to the detection of AD (Mc-Mahon, Araki, Sandberg, Neumann, & Gazelle, 2003). The development of novel ligands (e.g., for detecting amyloid plaques) is likely to enhance the clinical utility of PET and perhaps SPECT in the future (Petrella, Coleman, & Doraiswamy, 2003). Findings from qEEG studies indicate that while early AD and MCI are accompanied by an increase in theta and reduction in beta frequency activity, there is considerable overlap with recordings in normal control subjects (Wolf et al., 2003). Memory-based functional neuroimaging techniques have revealed reduced activation in the MTL for both MCI and AD (e.g., Machulda et al., 2003), indicating they may become a useful diagnostic tool where volumetric MRI measurements are normal despite evidence of neuropsychological impairment. Finally, recent application of DTI indicates it may be a sensitive measure of reduced white matter integrity in early AD (Moseley, Bammer, & Illes, 2002). Whether these newer MRI techniques have additional prognostic value awaits further research, although they do appear promising.

III. PHARMACOLOGICAL APPLICATIONS OF NEUROIMAGING

The application of neuroimaging in pharmacological investigations is a relatively recent development. An important use of the technology is to identify neuropharmacological mechanisms or biomarkers of drug interventions in vivo (Frank & Hargreaves, 2003). Neurotransmitter transporter and receptor mapping can be performed directly using radioligands with PET (e.g., [^{11}C]raclopride), and to a lesser extent with SPECT. However, enhancing the affinity of radioligands to bind selectively to specific receptor subtypes (e.g., D_2 vs. D_3 dopamine receptors) targeted by novel drug interventions remains the chief focus for future research. In addition, the cerebral hemodynamic effects of drug delivery can be investigated with MRI sequences such as resting-state DSC and ASL measures of rCBV and rCBF, and BOLD fMRI (Salmeron & Stein, 2002). This technique has been termed **pharmacological MRI**, or **phMRI** for short.

Another application, and one that is of considerable interest to neuropsychologists, is in psychopharmacological investigations. This involves the use of conventional functional neuroimaging techniques (primarily fMRI, PET, and more recently EEG-ERPs) to demonstrate pharmacological modulation of brain function during the performance of cognitive tasks. Typically, these studies are conducted in a blinded, placebo-controlled manner, with activation data from drug and placebo conditions being compared. To date, the modulatory effects of available dopaminergic, cholinergic, and gamma-aminobutyric acid (GABA)-ergic drugs have been studied (e.g., Anderer, Saletu, Semlitsch, & Pascal-Marqui, 2002; Honey et al., 2003; Stephenson et al., 2003; Thiel, 2003). This methodology also offers potential for investigating biomarkers of presymptomatic disease states (e.g., altered cholinergic modulation of memory function in early AD). However, it is worth noting that psychopharmacological neuroimaging with PET and fMRI is complicated by the effects that a drug might have on global and local blood flow and utilization of blood oxygen (Salmeron & Stein, 2002).

IV. CONCLUSION

Neuroimaging techniques are now being used more frequently when there is suspicion of brain injury or disorder. It is therefore important that clinical neuropsychologists be familiar with them. An overview of some of the more common neuroimaging techniques was provided in this chapter, along with brief summaries of their applications to several frequently encountered neurological conditions. In many circumstances, more than one imaging modality is used to provide complementary information (e.g., PET *and* MRI). The clinical application of functional neuroimaging is currently in its infancy. However, given current trends, it can be expected to play an important role in the future. With appropriate training, clinical neuropsychologists are well placed to help determine appropriate task selection and contribute to the interpretation of brain activation maps. The use of neuroimaging in psychopharmacological investigations heralds a new approach to studying neurochemistry and the modulating effects of CNS drug delivery in vivo.

BIBLIOGRAPHY

Akanuma, N., Koutroumanidis, M., Adachi, N., Alarcon, G., & Binnie, C. D. (2003). Presurgical assessment of memory-related brain structures: The Wada test and functional neuroimaging. *Seizure, 12,* 346–358.

Anderer, P., Saletu, B., Semlitsch, H. V., & Pascual-Marqui, R. D. (2002). Perceptual and cognitive event-related potentials in neuropsychopharmacology: Methodological aspects and clinical applications (pharmaco-ERP topography and tomography). *Methods and Findings in Experimental Clinical Pharmacology, 24*(Suppl. C), 121–137.

Barber, P. A., Darby, D. G., Desmond, P. M., Gerraty, R. P., Yang, Q., Li, T., et al. (1999). Identification of major ischemic change. Diffusion-weighted imaging versus computed tomography. *Stroke, 30,* 2059–2065.

Calautti, C., & Baron, J. C. (2003). Functional neuroimaging studies of motor recovery after stroke in adults. *Stroke, 34,* 1553–1566.

Cuspineda, E., Machado, C., Aubert, E., Galan, L., Llopis, F., & Avila, Y. (2003). Predicting outcome in acute stroke: A comparison between QEEG and the Canadian Neurological Scale. *Clinical Electroencephalography, 34,* 1–4.

Donnan, G. A., & Davis, S. M. (2002). Neuroimaging, the ischaemic penumbra, and selection of patients for acute stroke therapy. *Lancet Neurology, 1,* 417–425.

Frank, R., & Hargeaves, R. (2003). Clinical biomarkers in drug discovery and development. *Nature Reviews Drug Discovery, 2,* 566–580.

Hillary, F. G., Steffener, J., Biswal, B. B., Lange, G., DeLuca, J., & Ashburner, J. (2002). Functional magnetic resonance imaging technology and traumatic brain injury rehabilitation: Guidelines for methodological and conceptual pitfalls. *Journal of Head Trauma Rehabilitation, 17,* 411–430.

Honey, G. D., Suckling, J., Zelaya, F., Long, C., Routledge, C., Jackson, S., et al. (2003). Dopaminergic drug effects on physiological connectivity in a human cortico-striato-thalamic system. *Brain, 126,* 1767–1781.

Kessler, R. M. (2003). Imaging methods for evaluating brain function in man. *Neurobiology of Aging, 24*(Suppl. 1), S21–S35.

Lazeron, R. H., Rombouts, S. A., de Sonneville, L., Barkhof, F., & Scheltens, P. (2003). A paced visual serial addition test for fMRI. *Journal of Neurological Science, 213,* 29–34.

Levin, H. S. (2003). Neuroplasticity following non-penetrating traumatic brain injury. *Brain Injury, 17,* 665–674.

Machulda, M. M., Ward, H. A., Borowski, B., Gunter, J. L., Cha, R. H., O'Brien, P. C., et al. (2003). Comparison of memory fMRI response among normal, MCI, and Alzheimer's patients. *Neurology, 61,* 500–506.

McMahon, P. M., Araki, S. S., Sandberg, E. A., Neumann, P. J., & Gazelle, G. S. (2003). Cost-effectiveness of PET in the diagnosis of Alzheimer disease. *Radiology, 228,* 515–522.

Moseley, M., Bammer, R., & Illes, J. (2002). Diffusion-tensor imaging of cognitive performance. *Brain and Cognition, 50,* 396–413.

Petrella, J. R., Coleman, R. E., & Doraiswamy, P. M. (2003). Neuroimaging and early diagnosis of Alzheimer disease: A look to the future. *Radiology, 226,* 315–336.

Salmeron, B. J., & Stein, E. A. (2002). Pharmacological applications of magnetic resonance imaging. *Psychopharmacology Bulletin, 36,* 102–129.

Stephenson, C. M., Suckling, J., Dirckx, S. G., Ooi, C., McKenna, P. J., Bisbrown-Chippendale, R., et al. (2003). GABAergic inhibitory mechanisms for repetition-adaptivity in large-scale brain systems. *Neuroimage, 19,* 1578–1588.

Thiel, C. M. (2003). Cholinergic modulation of learning and memory in the human brain as detected with functional neuroimaging. *Neurobiology of Learning and Memory, 80,* 234–44.

Thompson, P., Hayashi, K. M., de Zubicaray, G. I., Janke, A. L., Rose, S. E., Semple, J., et al. (2003). Dynamics of gray matter loss in Alzheimer's disease. *Journal of Neuroscience, 23,* 994–1005.

Vespa, P. M., Boscardin, W. J., Hovda, D. A., McArthur, D. L., Nuwer, M. R., Martin, N. A., et al. (2002). Early and persistent impaired percent alpha variability on continuous electroencephalography monitoring as predictive of poor outcome after traumatic brain injury. *Journal of Neurosurgery, 97,* 84–92.

Wolf, H., Jelic, V., Gertz, H. J., Nordberg, A., Julin, P., & Wahlund, L. O. (2003). A critical discussion of the role of neuroimaging in mild cognitive impairment. *Acta Neurologica Scandinavica Supplementum, 179,* 52–76.

Zakzanis, K. K., Graham, S. J., & Campbell, Z. (2003). A meta-analysis of structural and functional brain imaging in dementia of the Alzheimer's type: A neuroimaging profile. *Neuropsychological Review, 13,* 1–18.

CHAPTER 5

Howard R. Kessler

The Bedside Neuropsychological Examination

Neuropsychological assessment at the bedside provides a variety of unique challenges in comparison to more extensive assessments performed with outpatients. Hospitalized patients typically present with an acute rather than a chronic or progressive illness. Their acute infirmities are often accompanied by a number of factors that can compromise the examination, including fatigue, depression, medical and postsurgical side effects, and significant sensory or motor changes. They may be referred for assessment for a variety of reasons, including issues relating to capacity (competency) for informed decision making, capacity for independent living versus the need for assisted living, or an elucidation of cognitive strengths and weaknesses for purposes of treatment planning (be they medical, rehabilitative, pharmacological, or other). Perhaps the most difficult and challenging of referral questions is the differential diagnosis among depression (or some other functional etiology), delirium, and dementia. In this climate of escalating health care costs, patient stays continue to shorten, necessitating brevity and economy in the utilization of diagnostic procedures. By virtue of these factors, the neuropsychologist is placed in the unenviable position of having to perform diagnostic procedures rapidly, efficiently, and economically, while ensuring an examination of adequate breadth and depth. The purpose of this chapter is to provide the practitioner both guidelines and a clinical template for performing such an examination at the bedside.

I. DISORDERS OF COMMON REFERRAL POPULATIONS

Patients possessing a number of different conditions may be referred for bedside assessment, each presenting unique barriers to the evaluation. These conditions include the following.

A. Stroke

Patients with middle cerebral artery strokes may suffer from hemiparesis (which limits the use of tests requiring significant motor, visual, or sensory function), may be aphasic (limiting the use of any task requiring language for a response or for comprehension of task demands), or may present with hemi-spatial neglect or hemi-inattention (requiring changes in the manner in which test materials are presented in space). Patients with posterior circulation strokes may suffer from hemianopsia, requiring presentation of test stimuli in the unaffected field. Patients experiencing anterior circulation strokes may be anergic or akinetic, limiting their capacity to respond and to expend sufficient effort during testing. These limitations frequently necessitate major alterations in the test battery, as well as in the mode of stimulus presentation.

B. Traumatic Brain Injury

Patients experiencing the acute effects of traumatic brain injury (TBI) likely suffer from posttraumatic amnesia, and accompanying agitation or inattention may interfere with test administration. Because these patients may perform at an artificially depressed level, formal tests should not be administered until they are sufficiently alert and well oriented in all spheres. These patients may also change or progress rapidly over the course of only a few days, so the examiner must determine the optimal time for formal test administration. This will be dictated largely by the goals stated in the referral question.

C. Dementia

A wide variety of diseases, both systemic and neurological, may result in progressive cognitive decline. A differential diagnosis often needs to be made among various classes of dementia, between delirium and dementia, or between dementia and depression. A variety of systemic diseases, such as brittle hypertension, diabetes, and heart disease, can cause progressive neurological decline, owing to vascular insufficiency. Patients receiving chemotherapy or cranial irradiation can also experience cognitive decline as treatment side effects (see review by Anderson-Hanley, Sherman, Riggs, Agocha, & Compas, 2003). Because the genesis of the disorder is often a crucial diagnostic marker, the clinician may need to go to great lengths to acquire accurate historical information from family members. In the case of the differential diagnosis of dementia, this may not prove to be entirely helpful. For example, the traditional literature on the differential diagnosis of vascular versus Alzheimer's type dementia depended heavily on the "stepwise" decline observed in vascular (or what was previously called multi-infarct) dementia, compared with the gradual decline noted in Alzheimer's disease. However, the newer nomenclature involving "vascular" dementia recognizes the fact that decline can be more gradual, because of chronic vascular insufficiency, which provokes a more gradual course of small vessel ischemic disease, mimicking the course seen in cases of Alzheimer's. This renders it more difficult to identify discrete episodes of onset of cognitive impairment. Depression can also be either a complicating or a clarifying factor in the diagnosis of vascular dementia. On the one hand, patients with depression clearly can appear to suffer from a dementia, despite the fact that their cognitive impairment is functionally determined. On the other hand, however, is the fact that depression is often an early symptom in cases of vascular dementia. This differential diagnosis thus requires an interpretation of qualitative aspects of performance. Both groups may manifest similar overall levels of performance on tests of attention, memory, and executive function. However, the patient with vascular dementia will be more likely to manifest pathognomic signs such as perseveration or confabulation.

D. Delirium

Delirious patients may demonstrate a fluctuating level of consciousness, as well as fluctuating levels of orientation and cognitive capacity. These patients often need to be examined across a number of days, and at various times of the day, for an accurate diagnostic impression to be obtained. This may necessitate the addition to the test battery of a very brief, repeatable measure that may be sensitive to such fluctuating levels of cognition and awareness. Further complicating the diagnosis is the fact that the variability in cognitive functioning that characterizes delirium can often mask the presence of other underlying disease states, such as dementia. The presence of an etiology provoking delirium can often be ascertained by reviewing the medical record for evidence of electrolyte imbalance or medications that might provoke cognitive side effects. Further, the delirious patient will be more likely than, for example, patients with progressive dementia to have some degree of awareness that something is amiss.

E. Postsurgical Deficits

Patients may demonstrate acute neuropsychological deficits immediately after invasive, nonneurological surgery. A determination needs to be made as to whether changes in cognitive function are due to the effects of anesthesia, medications (especially narcotics), or an intraoperative or postoperative event such as stroke during or after coronary artery bypass graft (CABG). This may be an extremely difficult differential diagnosis because of the acuity of these patients, and there is also a high false-positive rate of diagnosis. For example, although CABG may result in stroke, the vast majority of patients demonstrating acute cognitive deficits after such surgery spontaneously remit. The timing of the evaluation is thus crucial in such cases, and it would be prudent to wait at least 24 hours before performing comprehensive neuropsychological testing while monitoring the patient's level of consciousness in the interim.

F. Systemic Illness

Chronic conditions such as diabetes mellitus and hypertension can result in neurological disease (small vessel ischemia), particularly if poorly controlled. Patients with liver or kidney disease may present with symptoms of encephalopathy or delirium, whereas patients undergoing renal dialysis may demonstrate a fluctuating course, depending on where they are in their dialysis schedule. In these patients, it is important to discriminate between transient and relatively permanent impairments. The clinician will need to be sensitive to the presence of comorbidities, which can often be helpful in diagnosis. For example, patients experiencing vascular insufficiency will be far more likely to have cognitive impairment possessing an organic basis if they also present with evidence of peripheral neuropathy.

II. REVIEWING THE MEDICAL RECORD

A. History and Physical Examination

As stated earlier, it is always important to look for comorbid conditions or factors that may have an impact on neuropsychological presentation. This will assist the examiner in identifying the etiology underlying deficient test performance. Conditions provoking vascular insufficiency are one such example, among many. Documented histories of alcohol or drug abuse, neurodevelopmental disorders, seizure disorders, or prior central nervous system insults are all important factors to look for in the record. However, the clinician must also be aware of the fact that such information is often lacking in the clinical record, often necessitating more information gathering from the patient, family members, or the patient's primary care physician.

B. Relevant Laboratory Findings

An examination of particular laboratory test findings can be useful in rendering differential diagnoses of, for example, delirium or acute confusional states. Electrolyte levels, for example sodium or potassium, should be examined. Levels that are grossly outside of the normal range (which can be found in many basic medical textbooks) are often sufficient to provoke delirium. It is important, however, to keep in mind that many of these "normal" levels are for early to middle-aged adults rather than for the elderly. In the elderly, a delirium can be provoked in the presence of a more minor departure in electrolytic levels. Measures of kidney function (e.g., uric acid, blood urea nitrogen [BUN], creatinine), liver function (bilirubin, alkaline phosphatase, LDL cholesterol), and protein status (protein, albumin) should also be reviewed. Abnormal electrolytes, in combination with a disorder with sudden onset or a fluctuating course, would be strongly suggestive of the presence of a delirium.

C. Neuroimaging Results

The three imaging procedures most commonly used in the tertiary care setting are electroencephalography (EEG), computed tomography (CT) scanning, and magnetic resonance imaging (MRI). A variety of newer scanning techniques, as well as more sensitive experimental MRI modeling techniques, are also available but generally are not used in most hospitals. EEG may be useful in identifying the presence of seizure disorders or space-occupying tumors. Most commonly, however, EEG-noted abnormalities are such things as "slowing of the background rhythm" or "diffuse bifrontal slowing." Such findings often possess little diagnostic value to the clinician, nor are they of localizing value to the neurologist. They are often found in Alzheimer's disease and in delirium and are not useful in rendering differential diagnoses between such conditions. Furthermore, approximately 50% of healthy people have abnormal EEGs, so there can be a high false-positive rate. Alternatively, there might be a high false-negative rate when using EEG in cases of seizure disorder, in that the EEG is not a useful measure unless the patient is actively convulsive during the administration of the procedure, showing what is commonly referred to in the report as **clinical correlation**.

CT scanning, though progressing in its utility, nonetheless remains relatively insensitive to disorders affecting subcortical white matter, for example, vascular insufficiency. Similarly, most CT scanning techniques remain insensitive to the effects of concussion. CT scans are useful in identifying the presence of space-occupying lesions (e.g., tumors) or cerebral hemorrhages. MRI scans are more sensitive to white matter disease. T2-weighted images are sensitive to the chronic effects of ischemic demyelination (small vessel occlusive disease), whereas Flair and gadolinium-enhanced scans are sensitive to active white matter disease, for example, as seen in active multiple sclerosis. When reading the interpretations of MRI or CT findings, it is important to note whether the pathology observed represents abnormality or simply normal variation. For example, cortical atrophy is global and nonlocalizing , and can often be noted to be "appropriate for age." Similar statements may be found in the interpretation of white matter lesions. It is important to be able to correlate the MRI or CT abnormalities with clinical findings as well. For example, white matter changes, noted on MRI T2 weighted images, are not uncommon in normal aging. Such findings, in the absence of objective cognitive impairment, should not be used to infer the presence of neurological disease. Furthermore, one pitfall in MRI administration and interpretation is that the examination is often geared toward the referral questions. Hence, an abnormality related to, say, multiple sclerosis, may not be revealed if the referral question is one of concussion or headache.

D. Medications

It is particularly important to account for the effects of a variety of psychoactive medications on test performance. This is particularly crucial in testing elderly patients, in whom poly-pharmacy can present a hindrance to test performance and interpretation. It is also important to look at interactions between drugs and their side effects, within the context of a particular patient's medical condition. For example, patients with hepatic disease may experience heightened side effects of neuroleptics (such as Haldol) because they are metabolized by the liver. Similarly, because benzodiazepines are metabolized by the kidneys, they may provoke increased side effects in patients with renal disease or those undergoing renal dialysis. Anticholinergics, such as amitryptiline (which is often used as a sleep aid or for pain), may have heightened side effects in patients experiencing cardiovascular or cerebrovascular disease, hence provoking increased sedation or memory impairment. Similar findings might be noted in patients taking beta-blockers. This is because both classes of medication may inhibit vascular flow. Side effects found in commonly prescribed medications can be found in Table 5.1 (excerpted from Ellsworth, Witt, Dugdale, & Oliver, 2003).

III. CONDUCTING THE BEDSIDE EXAMINATION

A. Background History and Clinical Interview

The interview and history taking should be a standard part of the bedside assessment. Formats for history taking can be found in many sources and are not reviewed in depth here. (One of the best sources is Strub & Black's [1993] *The Mental Status Examination in Neurology*.) In the case of the bedside assessment, certain background factors are particularly critical and often require that a reliable informant (other than the patient) be identified to provide corroborating information. These factors include the following:

1. GENESIS OF THE DISORDER

A number of questions need to be asked to ascertain information regarding both the onset and progression of a given disorder. For example, was the onset rapid or progressive? Was the onset associated with some medical, psychosocial, or environmental event or stressor? Has the downward progression been relatively linear, or has it occurred in a relatively stepwise or variable fashion? Does the disorder represent a qualitative change in the patient's functioning or an exacerbation of a preexisting condition?

Table 5.1. Side Effects of Commonly Prescribed Medications

Class	Examples of specific drugs Generic (trade name)	Relevant side effects (Common in bold)
Antiarrythmics	Propranolol (Inderal) Nifedipine (Procardia)	**Dizziness, fatigue, lethargy,** depression, drowsiness, hallucinations, insomnia, memory loss, mental changes, strange dreams, anxiety
Anticholinergics	Meclizine (Antivert) Scopolamine (Transderm-Scop)	**Drowsiness,** anxiety, confusion, delirium, delusions, depression, dizziness, excitement, hallucinations, incoherence, irritability, lightheadedness, restlessness, sedation, weakness
Anticonvulsants	Carbamezapine (Tegretol) Valproate (Depakote)	**Drowsiness, sedation,** ataxia, behavioral changes, depression, diplopia, dizziness, **encephalopathy,** fatigue, hallucinations, incoordination, nystagmus, paralysis, paresthesia, tremors
Antihistamines	Hydroxyzine (Vistaril) Cetirizine (Zyrtec) Loratadine (Claritin)	**Drowsiness/somnolence, seizures,** confusion, depression, fatigue, insomnia, nervousness, tremor
Antihypertensives	Enalapril (Vasotec) Lisinopril (Prinivil, Zestril)	**Dizziness, fatigue,** anxiety, insomnia, paresthesia
Antibiotics	Amoxicillin (same) Erythromycin (same)	None
Antiparkinsonians	Carbidopa and levodopa (Sinemet) Amantadine (Symmetrel)	**Agitation, anxiety,** ataxia, **confusion, hand tremor, insomnia,** involuntary choreiform movements, dizziness, fatigue, hallucinations, **nightmares, numbness,** psychosis, **seizures** (Symmetrel), severe depression, **twitching, weakness**

Antipsychotics	Haloperidol (Haldol) Olanzapine (Zyprexa)	Agitation, **akathisia**, amnesia, anxiety, articulation impairment, catatonia, confusion, depression, dizziness, **drowsiness**, euphoria, exacerbation of psychotic symptoms, hostility, insomnia, restlessness, seizures (Haloperidol), somnolence, stuttering, tardive dyskinesia, tremor, vertigo
Acetylcholinesterase inhibitors	Donepezil (Aricept) Galantamine (Reminyl)	Abnormal dreams, depression, dizziness, **fatigue**, **insomnia**, somnolence (Donepezil); syncope (Galantamine)
CNS stimulants	Methylphenidate hydrochloride (Ritalin, Concerta) Amphetamine/ dextroamphetamine (Adderall)	Aggressiveness, akathisia, dizziness, dyskinesia, dysphoria, euphoria, **hyperactivity/restlessness**, insomnia, irritability, libido change, **logorrhea**, overstimulation, psychotic episodes, tics (rare), tremor
Corticosteroids (bronchodilators)	Fluticasone (Flovent) Triamcinolone (Azmacort)	Depression, fatigue, **mood change**, seizures (Triamcinolone), vertigo
Diuretics	Furosemide (Lasix)	Dizziness, paresthesia, restlessness, vertigo
Hormones	Prednisone (Deltasone) Levothyroxine sodium (Synthroid)	Depression, **insomnia**, **mood change**, psychosis, seizures, **tremors**, vertigo
Hypnotics	Zolpidem (Ambien) Temazepam (Restoril)	Amnesia, anxiety, confusion, **daytime sedation/ drowsiness**, dizziness, irritability, **lethargy**, lightheadedness, poor coordination
Narcotic analgesics (opioids)	Oxycodone (Oxycontin) Codeine	Agitation, dizziness, **drowsiness**, restlessness, **sedation**

(Continued)

Table 5.1. Side Effects of Commonly Prescribed Medications *(Continued)*

Class	Examples of specific drugs Generic (trade name)	Relevant side effects (Common in bold)
NSAIDs	Ibuprofen (Advil) Naproxen (Naprosyn) Celecoxib (Celebrex)	Anxiety, confusion, depression, **dizziness, drowsiness**, fatigue, insomnia, tremors
Lipid lowering agents	Atorvastatin (Lipitor) Simvastatin (Zocor)	None (Atorvastatin); dizziness, insomnia, memory loss, tremor, vertigo (Simvastatin)
Oral antidiabetics	Glipizide (Glucotrol) Glyburide (Micronase)	Dizziness, drowsiness, paresthesia
Anxiolytics (benzodiazepines)	Diazepam (Valium) Lorazepam (Ativan) Alprazolam (Xanax)	Anxiety, ataxia, confusion, depression, **dizziness, drowsiness**, fatigue, hallucinations, insomnia, stimulation, tremors, unsteadiness
Mood stabilizers	Lithium Carbonate (Lithium)	Ataxia, clonic movements, confusion, **dizziness, drowsiness, fine hand tremor**, memory loss, restlessness, seizures, slurred speech, twitching
SSRIs	Paroxetine (Paxil) Sertraline (Zoloft)	**Anxiety, dizziness, fatigue, insomnia**, tremor, agitation, delusions, euphoria, hallucinations, myoclonus, psychosis, **sedation**, tremor, twitching
Tricyclic antidepressants	Amitryptiline (Elavil) Nortryptiline (Pamelor)	Anxiety, confusion (elderly), **dizziness, drowsiness**, extrapyramidal symptoms (elderly), fatigue, increased psychiatric symptoms, insomnia, memory impairment, nightmares, panic, seizures, tremors, weakness

Note. CNS = central nervous system; NSAIDs = nonsteroidal antiinflammatory drugs; MAO = monoamine oxidase; SSRIs = selective serotonin reuptake inhibitors. From *Mosby's Medical Drug Reference*, by A. L. Ellsworth, D. M. Witt, D. C. Dugdale, and L. M. Oliver, 2003, St. Louis, MO: Mosby. Copyright 2003 by Elsevier, Inc. Adapted with permission.

2. SELF-CARE

Has the patient been compliant in taking his or her medications? If hypertension or diabetes is present, how stable or brittle has the condition been? If the patient suffers from diabetes, how often has the patient tested his or her blood glucose levels? Has the patient conformed to dietary restrictions? How cognitively and physically active and stimulated was the patient prior to hospital admission? Has there been risk of inadvertent self-harm at home (e.g., from falls or burns)?

3. PRIOR CNS INSULTS

Mild traumatic brain injury (TBI) often goes unnoticed and is rarely found in the patient's medical record. Many physicians, in fact, generally do not address the issue in the standard history. It is important to question the patient regarding the history of such events. It is crucial to look for evidence of not only incidents accompanied by loss of consciousness and anterograde or retrograde amnesia but also more subtle events accompanied by some "alteration" in consciousness. Because whiplash injury can present with cognitive impairment, the history of such episodes must also be ascertained. Additional questions should be posited, looking for a history of things such as near-drowning episodes or a history of toxic exposure. Has the patient experienced episodes of brief interruptions in consciousness (e.g., fugue, or frank loss of consciousness), which may indicate some ongoing or episodic process, such as cerebrovascular disease or seizures? Is there a history of excessive alcohol, drug, or tobacco use, which may contribute to or provoke neurological disease? The literature on alcohol and drug effects on cognition is fairly specific with regard to the effects of various agents. It is important to be aware of the reversibility or permanence of cognitive impairment provoked by these substances. It is also important to note that withdrawal from some substances may provoke temporary alterations in cognition.

4. INSIGHT, SELF-AWARENESS, AND CONCERN

During the course of the clinical interview, it is important to determine the patient's level of awareness of his or her medical state and insight into cognitive and physical limitations. Lack of awareness alone is not necessarily pathognomic of cognitive decline. For example, it is not unusual for a patient to be unaware of medical subtleties because the condition has not been explained adequately to him or her. Poor awareness, in combination with neuropsychological deficits, is, however, helpful in neuropsychological diagnosis. For example, some research suggests that patients with vascular dementia possess better insight than those with Alzheimer's disease, so that the cognitive test profile, in combination with the level of awareness, can be helpful in differential diagnosis. Patients experiencing TBI, various right-hemisphere syndromes, or frontal lobe disorders may present with varying degrees of anosagnosia. Further, when presenting with good awareness, some patients may manifest a rather striking lack of concern (anosodiaphoria). Such a lack of concern, in combination with relatively normal neuropsychological test performance, might be reflective of a psychiatric syndrome such as conversion disorder. However, a lack of concern accompanying noteworthy cognitive impairment will often indicate the presence of a neurobehavioral syndrome. It is also important to look for awareness of excessive complaints or concerns, which may appear in the absence of major cognitive impairment. This may reflect the presence of a primarily psychiatric etiology, such as depression, somatoform disorder, or, in a rare case, malingering.

5. MOOD

A full survey of the patient's mood should routinely be undertaken. This should include investigation of the patient's subjective emotional experience and of particular sources of emotional stress. Neurovegetative symptoms not only need to be surveyed but also need to be confirmed by a chart review (e.g., checking nurses' notes for information on nutritional intake and sleep patterns). (In the case of sleep, it is important to note that temporary alterations in the patient's sleep pattern would not be unusual in the hospital setting, so premorbid information needs to be ascertained as well. Similarly, the quality of hospital food needs to be factored into the judgment of appetite!) Mood also needs to be assessed within the context of the patient's degree of insight, as this relationship has ramifications for the source of the depression (reactive vs. endogenous), which gives the clinician additional information for differential diagnosis. As previously stated, bear in mind also that depression can be an early presenting symptom of neurological disease, not just vascular dementia but, for example, demyelinating diseases such as multiple sclerosis. Mood can exert a significant effect on cognitive functions requiring significant effort (attention, memory, executive functions), particularly in the elderly. The elevated base rate for depression in hospitalized patients, especially the elderly, reflects the necessity for close attention to mood in the neuropsychological assessment. Finally, questions should address the possibility of a psychiatric history, including issues related to both depression and anxiety.

B. Behavioral Observations

Inferences regarding observations of behavior are generally no different from those generated in other types of neuropsychological assessment. In the special circumstance of bedside assessment, the most common concern is with fatigue, which is very common in acutely hospitalized patients, and which may be attributable to a variety of factors, including sleep deprivation, fever or infection, and medication side effects. Fatigue by itself could be sufficient to provoke impaired performance. Whereas most outpatients can be counted on to inform the examiner of subjective feelings of fatigue, inpatients are not necessarily as reliable. Inpatients may also be less likely to push themselves to their absolute level of tolerance because of their infirmities, so they may require more prodding and encouragement from the examiner. There is also a greater possibility that the examination will need to be performed across multiple, brief sessions, which will affect the particular choice and mode of presentation of various test instruments, as well as possibly bias the interpretation of test results.

A second observational factor, which may be more helpful in differential diagnosis, is that of identifying emotional lability (i.e., emotional incontinence, pseudobulbar palsy). Lability possesses a unique quality, separate from a primarily psychological disturbance, in that it is easily provoked and is not necessarily tied directly to an emotional stimulus. Furthermore, it has an impulsive quality, best described as "turning a faucet on, then suddenly off," and tends to be more stereotyped than are more purely emotionally laden expressions. Lability can be helpful in differentiating between depression and an acquired neurological syndrome, as well as in the diagnosis of a specific neurological syndrome, such as stroke. In stroke, the swelling occurring in the brain during the first few months postinjury appears to provoke lability, which may remain in a more subtle form postrecovery. In the case of lability, it is important to determine, typically by eliciting it from the patient, whether the symptom is associated with an underlying emotional experience such as dysthymia.

C. Approach to Assessment

Because of the acuity of the patient's medical status, the principles of bedside assessment differ from those used in less acute environments. Steps need to be taken to ensure both economy and an examination of adequate breadth. The means of accomplishing this will differ based on the patient population. For more comprehensive outpatient assessments, limit testing is an integral part of the examination. It is not unusual to begin by administering more complex tasks; if these are performed adequately, it is unnecessary to administer separate tasks to identify the particular mechanisms involved when the patient has failed (at which time limit testing becomes integral). The luxury of such an approach is often unavailable in bedside assessment, because of significant time constraints as well as limitations imposed by the patient's condition. This makes qualitative and pattern interpretation of results that much more crucial. Furthermore, the classic limit-testing approach is ill suited for certain hospitalized patients, especially the elderly, in whom failure on more complex instruments is far more likely. In such cases, it is often more fruitful to begin with an assessment of basic abilities and move upward toward the more complex. By so doing, less time is wasted, and the emotional effects of failure on the patient are minimized.

It is also important to keep in mind the stated reason for the examination. Prior to the advent of neuroimaging techniques, the neuropsychologist was often asked to provide an opinion as to simply the presence or absence of "brain dysfunction." Today, it is far more important for the neuropsychologist to attempt to provide more definitive information, with regard to not only the presence or absence of dysfunction but also the specific factors and etiologies provoking those findings. As a result, the assessment needs to be sufficiently lengthy so as to provide a comprehensive survey of cognition, within the context of an increasing need for economy. It is not sufficient to simply report whether the test findings reflect abnormality; one must also to provide the referral source with definitive etiological statements that can help to guide subsequent treatment. Clearly, then, the use of the "pathognomic sign approach" becomes somewhat limited, thereby affecting one's choice of test instruments. Finally, the choice of appropriate test instruments needs to take into account the risks of false positives and negatives. If subsequent treatment recommendations are for noninvasive or easily reversible treatments (e.g., medication administration), it is preferable to minimize the risk of false negatives, hence increasing the false-positive risk. Alternatively, if subsequent treatment is more invasive or can lead to more permanent change, false positives can be potentially far more damaging and hence need to be limited in number. Quite frankly, if subsequent treatment is to be particularly invasive or serious, abbreviated assessment probably ought not be performed, unless the condition is straightforward and has been reliably diagnosed or the referral question is more one of rendering prognostic statements or providing rehabilitative recommendations rather than definitive diagnostic statements.

D. Choice of Test Instruments/Test Battery Design

Performing the bedside examination usually requires a good deal of flexibility on the part of the examiner. It is useful to have some instruments in one's armamentarium that are administered to nearly every patient, unless extraordinary circumstances (e.g., aphasia) intervene. This allows for comparisons among patient populations and serves to minimize the possibility of confirmation bias. Although the examiner might want to tailor the examination to the specific referral question being asked, choice of test instruments should not depend, for example, on the working diagnosis. Such "searching for deficits" will invariably result in a large proportion of judgment errors. Those tests that best lend themselves to bedside assessments are those that tap a variety of abilities, possess good normative data, and have demonstrated discriminant validity. Certain abilities should be tested routinely. For example, orientation to time, place, and circumstance may be helpful in differentiating a temporary state such as delirium from a more permanent neurological state. (Comments in the medical chart regarding orientation, e.g., "alert and oriented × 3" should not be trusted unless they are clearly explained. Medical personnel will often write that the patient is "A and O × 3" if the patient is simply alert and reasonably responsive.) It is also useful to have some kind of omnibus test, or standard set of procedures, available; these can often be administered with brevity and yield overall summary scores that are useful in test–retest comparisons. They also may allow time for the administration of more specialized tests to hone in on the abilities that appear to be particularly compromised. The clinician also needs to decide on an appropriate test battery, ideally for use across participants. It may be seductive to choose procedures that have demonstrated utility in identifying the "presence or absence of brain impairment" (e.g., many of the pathological indicators in the Halstead–Reitan Neuropsychological Battery [HRNB]) or tests with established hit rates for defining normality versus impairment). Many practitioners might thus choose those tests from their standard battery that possess the best discriminant validity in that regard. The use of such measures must be balanced against the need to identify not simply impairment but the precise nature and etiology of the disorder. The reader would be advised to include a few such measures (e.g., Trail Making, Digit Span) in the test battery but to rely more heavily on historical data, pattern analysis, and clinical acumen in rendering a final diagnosis.

1. TEST BATTERIES AND OMNIBUS TESTS

Many broad-based batteries and omnibus tests exist for use in neuropsychology, as well as in psychological assessment more generally. Some, for example the HRNB, are poorly tailored for bedside assessment, because of their length and unwieldy test stimuli. Some HRNB subtests, however (such as the Short Form Booklet Category Test, Trail Making, and Seashore Rhythm) can be useful portions of a bedside battery. Other omnibus tests, such as the Wechsler Adult Intelligence Scale—III (WAIS–III) or the Wechsler Memory Scale—III (WMS–III), are geared toward broadly assessing one area of function. These have the advantage of providing detailed information with regard to specific cognitive realms. The advantage inherent in the depth with which omnibus tests tap abilities also represents their downfall in bedside assessment, in that they need to be supplemented significantly with tests of a wide array of other neurobehavioral functions, which renders them almost unwieldy from the perspective of time. The WAIS–III does, however, possess a number of advantages: Because it has been considered to be the "gold standard" for psychological assessment tools for decades, there is a vast array of studies to which to refer in interpreting test findings; it possesses excellent reliability; and it lends itself easily to the use of short forms, either by administering a limited number of subtests or by administering the entire test using short forms of the individual subtests (e.g., the Satz–Mogel short forms). Both approaches provide useful information regarding the prorating of IQ, though Satz–Mogel is potentially more useful in performing pattern analysis. A further technique for obtaining an estimate of IQ is the use of the Wechsler Abbreviated Scale of Intelligence (WASI), though research suggests that this test may not estimate the WAIS–III IQ as well as can be accomplished by simply using the original four subtest versions (Block Design, Matrix Reasoning, Similarities, and Vocabulary) in the actual WAIS–III (Axelrod, 2001). There is also an extensive body of scientific data summarizing the performance of clinical populations on the WAIS–III. Finally, the WAIS–III administration can also be tailored more specifically toward neurological populations, by using the Boston process version (WAIS–R as a Neuropsychological Instrument), and would be particularly useful when short forms are being used in assessment. The WMS–III has excellent norms and allows the examiner to choose those subtests that might be most useful in performing the bedside assessment. This limits the estimation of the summary quotients, but one can nonetheless examine a variety of stages of the memory process. Again, there is a vast body of data examining WMS–III performance in clinical populations.

Alternatively, brief batteries such as the Mattis Dementia Rating Scale (MDRS; Coblentz et al., 1973) or the Neurobehavioral Cognitive Status Examination (NCSE; Kiernan, Mueller, Langston, & VanDyke, 1987) are geared toward brief, broader surveys of multiple functions. When brevity is of the essence, these batteries tend to be more useful than are omnibus tests, because they survey a wide array of functions in a relatively brief time. Their disadvantage, however, is that they do not necessarily do so in sufficient depth, or at a sufficiently complex level, to allow for finer variations in performance. This would pose particular problems when patients are presenting with evidence of more subtle impairment, hence increasing one's false-negative rate. Both can, however, be useful as a foundation for building upward toward a more complex evaluation. Furthermore, the diagnostic utility of the MDRS has been improved with the publication of the Dementia Rating Scale—2 (DRS–2; Mattis, Jurica, & Leitten, 2001), which incorporates not only the body of research using the test but also the Mayo Older Americans Normative Studies (MOANS) scaled scores by age group. The use of age norms should vastly improve the test's diagnostic utility. Both the MDRS and the DRS–2 also allow for eliminating the administration of easier test items if more difficult items have been passed. Clinical experience suggests, however, that the test should be administered in its entirety. This might be particularly useful when using pattern analysis, in particular when assessing the influence of functional factors on test performance. Many of these comments are germane to the use of the NCSE as well. A number of other brief yet comprehensive test batteries have been developed more recently. These include the Kaplan–Baycrest Neurocognitive Assessment (Leach, Kaplan, Rewilak, Richards, & Proulx, 2000), the Repeatable Battery for the Assessment of Neuropsychological Status (RBANS; Randolph, 1998), and the Brief Neuropsychological Cognitive Examination (Tonkonogy, n.d.). All are normed for use with both adults and geriatric patients. The Neuropsychological Assessment Battery is a brand new, comprehensive test battery that includes both a comprehensive examination and a screening module. This has the advantage of tailoring the examination to the bedside patient, and it also lends itself well to follow-up with a more comprehensive examination. It has also been normed for use with both adults and geriatric patients. Recently, the Mini Mental State Examination (MMSE) has been marketed for use by neuropsychologists. This test ought not to be used for diagnostic purposes, however. Rather, it can provide a useful tool for tracking patients over time, regarding especially their baseline level of consciousness, for example, in cases when delirium is suspected.

2. SPECIALIZED TESTS

There is, of course, a wide array of tests available for assessing individual neuropsychological functions. Care needs to be taken in choosing those that are best tailored for, or that lend themselves most easily to, evaluating bedridden patients. In general, tests chosen should be sufficiently brief so as to allow for economy, while still yielding meaningful diagnostic information, by allowing for the assessment of finer gradations in performance. Clinicians can find such tests in many realms of neuropsychological assessment. For example, most neuropsychological assessments of memory incorporate the use of verbal list learning tasks, such as the California Verbal Learning Test, Second Edition (CVLT–II) or the Rey Auditory Verbal Learning Test (RAVLT). Although extremely useful in outpatient assessments, such techniques are likely too difficult for use with hospitalized patients, because of the number of test stimuli involved (16 and 15 words, respectively). Rather, the clinician would be advised to use either the Buschke Selective Reminding procedure or the Hopkins Verbal Learning Test. Both tests have 12 stimuli and also have alternate forms, lending themselves to ease of repeatability. Further, there are also norms for a shortened 6-trial (as opposed to the more traditional 12-trial) version of the Buschke. Using such a test selection strategy may not appear appreciably to affect economy in testing a given function; however, when one considers the use of such a strategy across many tests and abilities, the time saved becomes appreciable. Furthermore, the use of briefer tests helps to minimize the effect imposed by interruptions, which can occur frequently in acute care settings. (It is unlikely that the attending surgeon and his or her residents will want to return later during their walking rounds because the neuropsychologist is busy with the patient!) It is often inadvisable to use tests that are heavily multidimensional in nature (e.g., the Tactual Performance Test [TPT]), because such instruments may result in floor effects, as well as necessitate a great deal more limit testing, thus increasing the time investment. Similarly, tests such as the TPT will be unwieldy to administer at the bedside. Finally, when short forms of some tests are unavailable, it is possible that they can be designed and used with relative reliability. Indeed, what might be most advisable is for clinicians to develop short forms of those tests they use most commonly, to develop a unitary battery for use with inpatients. The advantage of such an approach lies in the familiarity of the battery to the individual clinician. Rather than utilizing an unfamiliar battery, or one that is not necessarily tailored to one's individual needs, the utilization of one's own short forms allows the clinician to extrapolate from a wealth of personal experience with a particular battery approach, hence further improving diagnostic accuracy.

By way of example, I have developed the Neuropsychological Function Examination (NFE; Kessler, 1998a, 1998b). This abbreviated test battery was developed specifically for assessment in the hospitalized inpatient and depends heavily on the use of short forms of previously published, normed, and validated test instruments. I developed two alternate short forms of many tests and performed both normative/alternate forms reliability and validation studies (Kessler, 1998a, 1998b). The battery is brief enough (administered in approximately 60 minutes to normal control participants, 60–90 minutes to hospitalized patients) that it allows for additional testing if needed or if time allows. The memory tests (with delays) are embedded in the middle of the battery to allow for administration in two or three separate testing sessions. The examiner can hence administer these tests, with prescribed interpolated activity, in a separate session, to minimize against the effects of fatigue or to allow for limitations in the amount of time. Two alternate forms were generated for each subtest. Both alternate forms of reliability and validation studies were performed, the latter comparing samples of 10 normal control participants, 10 mildly brain-injured inpatients, and 10 moderately to severely brain-injured inpatients. The participants were matched for age and education. The test battery components are summarized in Exhibit 5.1. Alternate forms reliability coefficients (generated using 56 normal control participants) ranged from –.01 for Orientation to .79 for dominant-hand performance on the Grooved Pegboard. (Nonsignificant correlations, e.g., in Orientation, were generated because of a severe restriction of range, limiting variance and hence the resulting correlation coefficients.) Nineteen of 25 correlations were statistically significant at $p < .01$, with nonsignificant

Exhibit 5.1. The Neuropsychological Function
Examination

Orientation (time, place, circumstance, last three presidents)
WAIS–R subtests (Satz–Mogel)
    Information
    Similarities
    Picture Completion
Boston Naming (10 items)
Writing (6 words, 2 sentences)
Complex-Ideational Comprehension (6 items)
Following Commands (4 items)
Right–Left Orientation (Benton, 10 items)
Praxis (3 items each for buccofacial, transitive limb,
    intransitive limb, modeled after WAB)
Finger Gnosis (Kinsbourne–Warrington, 8 items each hand)
Mathematics Screen (3 items)
Digit Span (WAIS–R)
Buschke Verbal Selective Reminding Procedure (with delayed
    recall and recognition)
Rey (or Taylor) Complex Figure, with immediate and delayed
    recall
Hooper VOT (10 items)
Benton VFD (8 items)
Verbal Fluency (P, W, and Animals or C, L, Fruits)
Trails B
Grooved Pegboard

Note. WAB = Western Aphasia Battery; WAIS–R = Wechsler Adult
Intelligence Test—Revised; VOT = Visual Organization Test;
VFD = Visual Form Discrimination.

correlations likely provoked by either ceiling effects or restriction of range. These latter tests were thus adopted as "screening"
subtests. In the validation study, the following subtests–indices
yielded statistically significant group differences: Orientation,
Picture Completion, Writing, Finger Gnosis, Buschke (Consistent Long-Term Retrieval, Delayed Recall, Recognition), Verbal
Fluency, Trails B Time, and Grooved Pegboard, Dominant Hand
(orthopedic injury cases excluded). In addition, there was a
consistent trend in which control participants performed better
than patients with mild TBI, who performed better than patients
with moderate-severe TBI, on all subtests. Discriminant function
analysis (for normal vs. impaired) yielded correct classification
of all 10 control participants, whereas 17 of 20 TBI patients were
classified as impaired. Three-way classification revealed correct
classification of all control participants, 6 out of 10 mild TBIs
(with 2 classified as normal and 2 as moderate-severe), and 7

out of 10 moderate-severe TBIs (1 classified as normal, 2 as mild), for a total of 23 out of 30 correctly classified. Hence, the utilization of short forms of well-standardized and normed tests, in the hands of the experienced clinician, may possess promise as a bedside assessment tool; I have used them in assessing a number of other clinical populations. Other sample bedside assessment batteries are found in Tables 5.2 and 5.3.

IV. INTERPRETATION OF TEST RESULTS AND RENDERING OF THE FINAL DIAGNOSIS

Because the bedside assessment tends to be briefer than office-based evaluations, qualitative analysis of data, along with an integration of a wide variety of other variables, becomes more crucial to the diagnosis. The general principles for data analysis and interpretation are outlined elsewhere in this volume. In this regard, it is important to determine whether the pattern of test findings makes sense from the point of view of a neurological syndrome or whether they are inconsistent and thus reflective of a process that is not clearly neurogenic. In the case of bedside assessment, special attention needs to be paid to the wide variety of variables mentioned in this chapter. It is important for the clinician to be able to assess neuropsychological test findings in light of working hypotheses regarding the possible source of the patient's deficits; the history, pattern of performance, patient's mood and effort, and comorbid conditions are then integrated to generate a differential diagnosis. On the basis of these variables, the clinician then uses a set of decision trees in making the final diagnosis. Sample decision trees can be found in Exhibit 5.2. Bear in mind that the diagnosis often needs to be tentative, because the patient's status may be quite variable. However, by using the many types of information available, the clinician can usually narrow the differential diagnosis down to one or two prime possibilities, which can then be the focus of attention for other members of the treatment team. Because the differential diagnosis may be tentative, it may be necessary to recommend a reassessment sometime in the future, or to continue to follow the patient through his or her hospital course to further elucidate status. Follow-up evaluations may also be useful in tracking change over time, with special attention to disease progress or recovery and efficacy of medical interventions.

V. CONCLUSION

The bedside neuropsychological examination presents a number of unique challenges to the neuropsychologist, requiring

Table 5.2. Sample Core Bedside Neuropsychological Test Battery for Adults

Type of test	Specific tests
Omnibus	**Cognistat/Neurobehavioral Cognitive Status Examination** or **Brief Neuropsychological Cognitive Examination** or **Kaplan–Baycrest Neurocognitive Assessment** or **Repeatable Battery for the Assessment of Neuropsychological Status**
General Cognitive	WAIS–III Short Form (individual subtests or Satz–Mogel)
Speech-Language	**Boston Naming Test** **Writing–spelling sample** (BDAE Cookie-Theft, WAB Kite, writing to dictation) **Reading sample** (Gray Oral Reading paragraphs, WRAT-3 Reading short form) **Comprehension** (complex ideational material) Brief screening of repetition and ability to follow commands (e.g., Token Test short form) if any of the above language skills are impaired Language-mediated abilities (Benton Left–Right Orientation, WAB Praxis, Kinsbourne–Warrington finger gnosis or HRNB Finger Localization)
Attention-Memory	**Digit Span** **Stroop Neuropsychological Screening Test** Paced Auditory Serial Addition Test (PASAT) Spatial Span (WMS–III) Visual Search tasks, if evidence of hemi-inattention (letter cancellation) **Verbal list learning** (Buschke Verbal Selective Reminding, Hopkins Verbal Learning, with delayed recall and recognition) **Figural recall** (design recall, such as Complex Figure or WMS–III designs, with delayed recall and recognition) Narrative recall (administer if list learning is impaired; Babcock-Levy, WMS–III Logical Memory, with delayed recall and recognition) Visual recognition (administer if figural recall is impaired; CVMT) Recognition Memory Test (Warrington, if recall impaired) Three Words/Three Shapes (Mesulam) for lower functioning patients

(Continued)

Table 5.2. Sample Core Bedside Neuropsychological Test Battery for Adults *(Continued)*

Type of test	Specific tests
Spatial-Construction	**Drawing** (Complex Figure, BVRT-copy, short form) **Construction** (WAIS–III Block Design, Satz–Mogel) Visual discrimination, for patients with poor constructional performance (Benton tests, preferably short-forms with proration of norms) Visual integration (Hooper VOT short form, with proration of norms)
Executive	**Hypothesis testing and concept formation** (Wisconsin Card Sort, 64 cards, or Booklet Category Test, short form) **Verbal reasoning** (WAIS–III Similarities short form, proverb interpretation) **Set Shifting** (Trail Making from HRNB) **Verbal fluency** (abbreviated versions of letter and category, e.g., one or two trials each) Design fluency (Delis-Kaplan or Ruff, useful in lateralizing, or in testing aphasic patients) Motor programming tasks (Luria Contrasting Motor Programmes/Go-No Paradigm, Manual Position Sequencing) Graphomotor programming (mn, ramparts, loops)
Sensorimotor	**Psychomotor speed and coordination** (Grooved Pegboard) Psychomotor speed (Finger Tapping) Strength and effort (Hand dynamometer, useful in differential diagnosis of depression) Mood and Affect **Beck Scales** (Depression, Anxiety) Profile of Mood States (POMS)

Note. Standard tests are in **bold type**; others are optional or for limit testing. WAIS–III = Wechsler Adult Intelligence Scale—III; BDAE = Boston Diagnostic Aphasia Examination; WAB = Western Aphasia Battery; WRAT–3 = Wide Range Achievement Test—3; HRNB = Halstead–Reitan Neuropsychological Battery; WMS–III = Wechsler Memory Scale—III; CVMT = Continuous Visual Memory Test; BVRT = Benton Visual Retention Test; VOT = Visual Organization Test.

Table 5.3. Sample Core Bedside Neuropsychological Test Battery for Geriatric Patients

Type of test	Specific tests
Omnibus	**Mattis Dementia Rating Scale-2 or Brief Neuropsychological Cognitive Examination or Kaplan–Baycrest Neurocognitive Assessment or Repeatable Battery for the Assessment of Neuropsychological Status**
Speech-Language	**Boston Naming Test** **Complex-ideational comprehension** Writing sample (BDAE Cookie-Theft or WAB Kite) Following commands (up to four steps)
Attention-Memory	**Digit Span** (WAIS–III, longer than Mattis version) **3 Words/3 Shapes** (Mesulam) Visual search (Mesulam or other) Stroop Neuropsychological Screening Test Narrative recall (WMS–III Logical Memory or Babcock–Levy, with delay and recognition) Figural recall (WMS–III Visual Reproduction, with delay and recognition)
Spatial-Construction	**Construction** (Clock Test) **Visual Form Discrimination** (Benton VFD, Line Orientation, Facial Recognition, BVRT-copy trial) Visual integration (Hooper VOT)
Executive	**Hypothesis testing and concept formation** (WCST-64) **Set shifting** (Trail Making from HRNB) Verbal reasoning (WAIS–III Similarities short form) Verbal Fluency
Sensorimotor	**Psychomotor speed and coordination** (Grooved Pegboard) **Pathognomonic sign** (synkinesia) Strength-effort (Hand Dynamometer) Psychomotor speed (Finger Tapping) Motor Programming (Luria Manual Position Sequencing)
Sensory	**Pathognomonic sign** (Double Simultaneous Stimulation)
Mood-Affect	**Yesavage Geriatric Depression Survey**

Note. Standard tests are in bold type; others are optional or for limit testing. BDAE = Boston Diagnostic Aphasia Examination; Benton VFD = Visual Form Discrimination; BVRT = Benton Visual Retention Test; HRNB = Halstead–Reitan Neuropsychological Battery; VOT = Visual Organization Test; WAB = Western Aphasia Battery; WAIS–III = Wechsler Adult Intelligence Scale—III; WCST = Wisconsin Card Sorting Test; WMS–III = Wechsler Memory Scale—III.

Exhibit 5.2. Differential Diagnosis of Cognitive Impairment

Factors to consider:
Onset: Acute, chronic
Course: Static, variable, progressive
Insight/awareness: Good, poor, variable, fatigued
Test effort: Good, poor, variable, fatigued
Mood: Euthymic, dysthymic, depressed, variable
Test results pattern: Coherent, variable, uniform impairment

Factor etiology	Surgery	Metabolic	Dementia	Medications	Functional
Onset	Acute	Acute	Chronic	Acute	Acute
Course	Static	Variable	Progressive	Static or variable	Static or progressive
Awareness	Good or poor	Good	Good (V) or poor (AD)	Good	Poor or fatigued
Effort	Good	Variable or poor	Good	Good or fatigued	Poor or fatigued
Mood	Euthymic or dysthymic	Euthymic or variable	Euthymic (AD) or dysthymic (V)	Euthymic or variable	Dysthymic or depressed
Pattern	Coherent	Variable or uniform	Coherent	Coherent or uniform	Coherent or uniform
Look for	CABG, etc.	Metabolic imbalance (Na+, K+, etc.)	Vascular risk or historical decline	Medications with relevant side effects	Stressor or mental health history

Note. AD = Alzheimer's disease; V = vascular disease; CABG = coronary artery bypass graft; Na+ = sodium; K+ = potassium.

the integration of a wide variety of variables not necessarily common to outpatient or broader assessments. This data integration needs to be accomplished with brevity, economy, and efficiency to account for both the patient's unique status and the changing demands of the health care environment.

BIBLIOGRAPHY

Anderson-Hanley, C., Sherman, M. L., Riggs, R., Agocha, V. B., & Compas, B. E. (2003). Neuropsychological effects of treatment for adults with cancer: A meta-analysis and review of the literature. *Journal of the International Neuropsychological Society, 9,* 967–982.

Axelrod, B. N. (2001, October/November). *Rationale for and application of short forms for commonly used neuropsychological measures.* Paper presented at the 21st Annual Meeting of the National Academy of Neuropsychology, San Francisco, CA.

Ellsworth, A. L., Witt, D. M., Dugdale, D. C., & Oliver, L. M. (2003). *Mosby's medical drug reference.* St. Louis, MO: Mosby.

Kessler, H. R. (1998a, February). *Alternate forms reliability and preliminary norms for the Neuropsychological Function Examination, Forms A and B.* Poster session presented at the annual meeting of the American Neuropsychiatric Association, Honolulu, HI.

Kessler, H. R. (1998b, February). *Initial validation of the Neuropsychological Function Examination (NFE) in a traumatic brain injury sample.* Poster session presented at the annual meeting of the American Neuropsychiatric Association, Honolulu, HI.

Strub, R. L., & Black, F. W. (1993). *The mental status examination in neurology* (3rd ed.). Philadelphia: Davis.

Tests and Test Batteries

Coblentz, J. M., Mattis, S., Zingesser, L., Kasoff, S. S., Wisniewski, H. M., & Katzman, R. (1973). Presenile dementia: Clinical aspects and evaluation of cerebrospinal fluid dynamics. *Archives of Neurology, 29,* 299–308.

Kaplan, E., Fein, D., Morris, R., & Delis, D. (1991). *WAIS–R as a neuropsychological instrument.* San Antonio, TX: Psychological Corporation.

Kiernan, R. J., Mueller, J., & Langston, J. (n.d.). *Cognistat: Neurobehavioral Cognitive Status Examination.* Los Angeles: Western Psychological Services.

Kiernan, R. J., Mueller, J., Langston, J. W., & VanDyke, C. (1987). The Neurobehavioral Cognitive Status Examination. *Annals of Internal Medicine, 107,* 481–485.

Leach, L., Kaplan, E., Rewilak, D., Richards, B., & Proulx, G. B. (2000). *Kaplan Baycrest Neurocognitive Assessment.* San Antonio, TX: Psychological Corporation.

Mattis, S., Jurica, P. J., & Leitten, C. L. (2001). *Dementia Rating Scale—2 (DRS–2).* San Antonio, TX: Psychological Corporation.

Randolph, C. (1998). *Repeatable Battery for the Assessment of Neuropsychological Status (RBANS).* San Antonio, TX: Psychological Corporation.

Stern, R. A., & White, T. (2003). *Neuropsychological Assessment Battery (NAB).* Lutz, FL: Psychological Assessment Resources.

Tonkonogy, J. M. (n.d.). *Brief Neuropsychological Cognitive Examination.* Los Angeles: Western Psychological Services.

Detecting Negative Response Bias and Diagnosing Malingering:
The Dissimulation Exam

Perhaps because clinical psychologists are trained to be empathic, the formal evaluation of malingering, or even the suspicion that a patient has put forth less than optimal effort, is frequently initiated only after some red flag is triggered. For example, information derived from the evaluation may not be in agreement with information from the chart review (e.g., the patient presents with dementia after a minor head injury), the situation may include the possibility of external motivation for negatively biasing performance (e.g., cases of evaluation for criminal responsibility), or behavioral observations may indicate less than optimal effort. However, tasks involving clinical intuition and judgment are fraught with error; therefore, it is recommended that subjective determination of negatively biased responding be supplemented with objective indices of response style in most clinical neuropsychological examinations.

An important distinction needs to be made between a patient's behavior and a clinical diagnosis of malingering. That is, to make a diagnosis of malingering, it is necessary both to determine that nonoptimal effort or exaggeration of symptoms has occurred and to ensure that the other diagnostic criteria of malingering are met. The many so-called malingering tests only determine the probability that nonoptimal effort or intentionally poor performance has been exhibited.

I. DEFINITION OF MALINGERING

Malingering is the intentional production of false or greatly exaggerated symptoms for the purpose of attaining some identifiable external reward (American Psychiatric Association, 1994). People may malinger to receive more money in a personal injury lawsuit, to receive workers' compensation or disability benefits, to obtain prescription medications, to avoid prosecution for criminal activities, or to avoid criminal responsibility (i.e., to be held not guilty by reason of insanity).

Within the context of a psychological or neuropsychological examination, malingering is the willful production of poor performance on measures of psychological function for the purpose of obtaining some externally recognized gain or benefit. Malingering is a highly specific diagnostic term. In contrast, **negative response bias** is the production of more pathological or deficient scores than would be expected on the basis of the skill level of the person. Although negative response bias is a necessary condition for the diagnosis of malingering to be made, it can be associated with a variety of clinical situations and conditions. In addition to the motivational situations mentioned previously in connection with malingering, less than optimal performance can be associated with fatigue, disinterest, anxiety states, or depressive conditions. In each of these situations, it is important to obtain some estimate of the degree to which optimal effort was expended.

The concept of malingering as a disorder is not empirically well documented. However, there are several ways in which malingering behavior may develop or become apparent. In the acute phase of treatment, it is possible for malingering to be chosen as a course of action prior to hospitalization. There are individuals who feign illness or injury to receive monetary compensation or material gain. Although the incidence is not known, this variant may represent a minority of the cases. Another form of malingering may occur when individuals admitted to the hospital for a legitimate reason decide to fabricate or magnify their difficulties to forestall discharge, to avoid responsibility, or to gain financial benefit. In factitious disorder, the motivation of the patient is not readily observable or interpretable as an external motivation, as it is in malingering. Instead, for factitious disorder, the motivation may be some subjective value in assuming the role of a sick person.

It is essential to note that malingering behavior does not necessarily occur in the absence of neurologically based impairment. Malingering may occur as an exaggeration of existing deficits or as a behavioral response to an actual, although minor, injury. There are no specific neuroanatomical correlates of malingering. However, the behavior may be more common in situations in which objective documentation is difficult to obtain, for example, in cases of mild head injury, subtle seizure disorders, or low-level neurotoxin exposure. The clinician may only be able to screen for malingering in the hospital setting and then refer for more extensive outpatient evaluation.

II. SUSPICION OF MALINGERING

Pankratz (1988) listed instances in which the suspicion of negative response bias should be raised. We have revised that list as follows:

- consistently giving nearly correct responses to test items;
- a marked discrepancy between obtained scores and scores expected on the basis of premorbid background and medical diagnosis;
- inconsistency between symptoms reported by the patient and symptoms observed by the clinician or other staff;
- bizarre or unlikely answers to test items;
- differences between results on tests of similar constructs that cannot be explained by variable attention, motivation, or medication status, or by psychometric properties of the tests; and
- behavior that is inconsistent with the obtained test results.

In addition to knowing the situations under which malingered deficits may occur, it is useful to know the content areas in which malingered performance can be exhibited. These include the following:

- memory,
- motoric and cognitive skills,
- sensory–perceptual skills,
- academic skill areas such as arithmetic,
- abstract problem-solving skills, and
- fund of information.

Of course, exhibiting behavior that arouses suspicion does not indicate that malingering has taken place. The clinician needs to rule out other possible explanations for the data, such as the following:

1. Is there a medical complication that can explain the discrepancies in the data; for example, does the patient use narcotic medication or have unmedicated orthopedic pain?

2. Does the patient have a psychiatric disorder that can partially explain the test results; for example, can a generalized anxiety disorder in combination with an anoxic episode account for variable attention and low visual–spatial test scores?

3. Is there some personological variable that can account for variable or low effort; for example, is the patient impulsive, sociopathic, or uncooperative?

III. DIAGNOSIS

A. Differential Diagnoses

The diagnostic differentials exist across the entire gamut of clinical possibilities. First, it is necessary to rule out the possibility that the test results represent the actual level of skill impairment. In addition, it is necessary to rule out the interactive effects of cognitive impairment with medication side effects, with psychiatric disorder, and with apathy or lack of motivation.

B. Neuropsychological Examination: An Overview

The basic goal in the evaluation of malingered performance is to decide whether the exhibited performance is possible given the history, medical condition, and psychiatric situation of the patient. Therefore, the first stages of the examination involve obtaining accurate information related to these variables. The chart review, clinical interview and history, and interview of collateral sources are important here. In fact, the most important thing to remember is that the examination for malingered performance is not different from the typical examination, although some specialized instruments and techniques may be included. The main goal is to obtain an accurate interpretation of the assessment results. Because the diagnosis of malingering requires evidence of inconsistency of results, inconsistency of the history with the results, or inconsistencies in the history itself, the interview is an extremely important part of the evaluation.

The clinician must first obtain an adequate history, including information related to academic performance, prior brain insults or injuries, and familial instances of neurological disease. The medical history is frequently well documented in inpatient consultation services, but this should not be taken for granted. In particular, the patient's history should be obtained for the presence of diabetes, hypertension, stroke, or seizure. In cases of alleged mild traumatic brain injury, it is helpful to obtain ambulance crew and emergency department records because circumstances reported at a later time may be inaccurate.

The clinical neuropsychologist's observations of the patient during testing can be informative. The exhibition of attention behavior and normal-appearing effort is not always indicative of adequate motivation, but exaggerated signs of effort combined with very poor scores may be an indication of malingered performance. Analog malingerers (subjects who are given instructions to malinger in the experimental manipulation) report that they may show poor cooperation and general confusion, aggravation and frustration, and slow response times with frequent hesitations during testing (Iverson, 1995).

The testing should be conducted in such a manner that optimal performance is likely. This principle may be difficult to implement in an inpatient hospital setting. However, poor performance should be the result of the patient's effort, not the result of lack of examiner effort to ensure an adequate environment.

Much has been said in the clinical literature regarding inconsistency and its relation to negative response bias. Inconsistency can include a discrepancy between the results expected on the basis of history and the obtained results, a discrepancy between performances separated by time, or a discrepancy between observations by different staff persons. Genuine impairment is diagnosed on the basis of observed inconsistencies, mainly inconsistencies between performance expected on the basis of premorbid estimates and present function, although inconsistencies across time can also be diagnostic of attentional difficulties. There are sometimes explicit guidelines for what constitutes an inconsistency, such as confidence boundaries. The inconsistencies involved in less than optimal effort are sometimes determined on the basis of clinical judgment with all its associated subjectivity. The interpretation of test performance as involving malingered impairment or other forms of negative response bias is made partly on the basis of ruling out other hypothetical reasons for the obtained inconsistency in results.

C. Clinical Model for Assessment

The following is a general overview suggested as a format for evaluating the presence of biased responding. Subsequently, we review various tests that can be used within this assessment.

1. Complete a careful background review.
2. Conduct clinical and collateral interviews.
3. Observe the patient's behavior in more than one situation, for example, with staff and family, in the interview, and during testing.
4. Administer screening procedures for biased effort at the beginning of the examination.
5. a. If screening procedures reveal suspicious performance, conduct a comprehensive examination of level of effort and symptom exaggeration. This assessment should include at least one additional procedure designed to identify biased responding (e.g., digit memory tests such as the Portland Digit Recognition Test, Hiscock and Hiscock procedure, and the Victoria Symptom Validity Test, or other forced-choice procedures).
   b. If screening procedures do not reveal suspicious performance, conduct a comprehensive examination of level of effort only if there are other reasons for clinical suspicion.
6. Examine scores on standard neuropsychological instruments to identify suspicious scores (e.g., Recognition Memory Test scores below 30) or patterns of performance (e.g., average to low average Wechsler Memory Scale—Revised General Memory index with an impaired Attention-Concentration index).
7. If suspicious scores or patterns are observed during testing, return to Step 5a.

D. Suggested Diagnostic Framework for Identifying Malingering

Slick, Sherman, and Iverson (1999) have suggested criteria for classifying levels of suspicion of malingered effort. Although these criteria have not been subjected to a test of external validity, they are offered here as a guiding framework for the interpretation and combination of assessment information regarding less than optimal effort. The first step in using this classification scheme is to rule out other diagnoses such as factitious disorder, somatoform disorder, or psychotic disorder. Then information related to test performance, consistency of information provided, and behavioral observations is combined to arrive at a level of diagnostic certainty. The information to be collated includes whether response bias exists in the test record and whether there are inconsistencies between reported history and

Exhibit 6.1. Diagnostic Categories for Malingering
Neurocognitive Dysfunction (MND)

Definite MND
1. Presence of substantial external incentive
2. Definite negative response bias from forced-choice tests
   or tests of effort
3. Behaviors meeting the criteria are not fully accounted for
   by psychiatric, neurological, or developmental factors.

Probable MND
1. Presence of substantial external incentive
2. Two or more types of evidence (inconsistencies) from
   neuropsychological testing (excluding definite negative
   response bias) *Or*
3. One type of evidence from neuropsychological testing
   and one or more types of evidence from self-report
   inconsistencies. Behaviors meeting the criteria cannot be
   accounted for by psychiatric, neurological, or
   developmental factors.

Possible MND
1. Presence of substantial external incentive
2. Evidence from self-report
3. Behaviors meeting criteria are not accounted for by
   psychiatric, neurological, or developmental factors

documented history, between self-report and known patterns
of brain functioning, between collateral reports and test data,
or between history and test data. In addition, the clinician codes
whether there are inconsistencies between the patient's self-
report and any of the other categories of information. In this
way, the clinician can obtain a classification of possible, probable, or definite malingered cognitive impairment. Exhibit 6.1
provides an overview of the criteria used in this classification
system.

E. Specific Assessment Procedures

There are many specific test procedures designed to detect negative response bias. This section provides an overview of these
procedures as well as general recommendations for their use.
Specific cutoff scores are not provided. This is a growing and
developing area, and the current literature should always be
consulted when making clinical decisions. We are merely pointing the clinician to the relevant literature and potential
procedures.

1. 21-ITEM WORDLIST

The 21-Item Wordlist (Iverson, Franzen, & McCracken, 1991, 1994) takes approximately 5 minutes to administer and score. This test can be used at the beginning of the evaluation as a rapid screen for biased effort. The 21-Item Wordlist consists of 21 words that are presented orally, following which the patient is instructed to recall freely as many words as possible. The patient is then instructed to identify the target words within a two-alternative forced-choice procedure. In analog studies, the rates of detecting experimental malingerers have ranged from 20% to 80%, depending on which cutoff scores were used (Frederick, Sarfaty, Johnston, & Powel, 1994; Iverson & Franzen, 1996; Iverson et al., 1991, 1994). One added benefit of the 21-Item Wordlist is that there is normative information related to the performance of hospitalized substance-abusing patients in comparison to optimal effort (Arnett & Franzen, 1997).

2. REY 15-ITEM MEMORY TEST

The Rey 15-Item Memory Test (Rey, 1964) can be used at the beginning of the examination as a rapid screen. The test consists of 15 items presented in a matrix of three columns by five rows. Patients are told that they will have just 10 seconds to study the items, following which they will have to reproduce the items from memory. The test is quite simple given that the items are arranged in logical, easy-to-remember rows (e.g., numbers, letters, and shapes). The most frequently calculated scores are the total number of correct items and the number of correctly reproduced rows.

Clinicians must know the following about this test. First, there are different methods of administration and scoring. The most widely used administration is to request recall immediately after exposure. Second, the test has limited sensitivity to analog malingering, with variability in detection rates. Third, several different cutoff scores have been recommended. Finally, the test is likely to be even less sensitive if it is administered after other memory procedures because its simplicity will be even more obvious. Arnett, Hammeke, and Schwartz (1995) provided information related to the performance of both neurological patients and malingerers.

3. 16 ITEMS TEST

The 16 Items Test (Paul, Franzen, Fremouw, & Cohen, 1992) can also be used at the beginning of the examination as a rapid screen. It is a modification of the Rey 15-Item Memory Test. Paul et al. (1992) eliminated the geometric designs and added one item to the remaining four sets to make the test simpler and more specific to negative response bias. The test has variable sensitivity but relatively high specificity to negative response bias (Iverson & Franzen, 1996).

4. SYMPTOM VALIDITY TESTING

Symptom validity testing (SVT) is best applied in situations in which more sophisticated procedures or empirically derived cutoff scores are not available. Often it is used in cases involving claimed impairment for a sensory function. Loren Pankratz was the leading proponent of SVT within neuropsychology. Early studies using this method consisted of case reports of individuals who were feigning sensory (Pankratz, Fausti, & Peed, 1975) or memory (Pankratz, 1983) deficits. Patients are exposed to a large number of trials of the stimulus (e.g., sound, tactile sense, or simple memory task) that they claim they cannot experience or remember. Given a two-alternative forced-choice response format, people who are grossly exaggerating their symptoms may score below the probable range of chance, that is, below the confidence interval surrounding random responding (50% correct). SVT is sensitive to blatant exaggeration, but it may not be as sensitive to more subtle or sophisticated approaches to exaggeration. There have been many refinements and extensions of the SVT paradigm to address the issue of low sensitivity. In review articles and chapters, these measures are often classified broadly as forced-choice procedures. Popular refinements include digit memory procedures, word lists, and adaptations of existing tests into two-alternative forced-choice paradigms.

5. HISCOCK AND HISCOCK PROCEDURE

The Hiscock and Hiscock (1989) procedure should be used when a more comprehensive assessment for potential negative response bias in memory is clinically indicated. The shortened version of the test appears to have comparable sensitivity and specificity to the full procedure. Hiscock and Hiscock refined the simple SVT memory procedure to create a digit recognition test. The patient is shown a card with a five-digit number and then, following a delay interval, asked to choose the number in a two-alternative forced-choice task. The test appears to be getting more difficult as the delay interval between digit presentation and recognition response increases from 5 to 10 to 15 seconds. The test contains three blocks of 24 trials for a total of 72 items. In the initial report, Hiscock and Hiscock (1989) demonstrated that a severely demented patient with Alzheimer's disease performed within the probable range of chance, whereas a patient suspected of malingering performed significantly below chance.

The Hiscock and Hiscock procedure has been applied to analog and clinical samples with excellent results. Patients with unequivocal brain damage generally obtain scores greater than 90% correct on the procedure, whereas suspected clinical malingerers and experimental malingerers perform much more poorly (Guilmette, Hart, & Giuliano, 1993; Prigatano & Amin, 1993). High sensitivity and specificity to experimental malingering have been reported in a shortened version (36 vs. 72 items) of the test (Guilmette, Hart, Giuliano, & Leininger, 1994).

6. PORTLAND DIGIT RECOGNITION TEST

The Portland Digit Recognition Test (PDRT; Binder, 1990) is a digit memory procedure that is an extension of the SVT paradigm and a refinement of the Hiscock and Hiscock (1989) procedure. The PDRT should be used when a more comprehensive assessment for potential negative response bias is clinically indicated. Because of the amount of time required to perform the original version, it may have limited use in an acute care hospital. It can also be administered in a shortened version and in a computer version, both of which have shown promise as clinical assessment tools. In this test, patients are presented a string of digits auditorily followed by intervals of interpolated activity (i.e., counting backward). After the interval (5, 15, or 30 seconds), the patient is presented with a two-alternative forced-choice task and instructed to choose the target digits. The PDRT differs from the Hiscock and Hiscock procedure in three ways: (a) The digits are presented auditorily, (b) the delay interval is filled with an interpolating activity, and (c) the third delay interval is 30 seconds as opposed to 15 seconds.

The PDRT takes approximately 45 minutes to administer. The PDRT is sensitive and specific to negative response bias. Blatant exaggeration is identified by below-chance performance. More sophisticated exaggeration is revealed by scores falling below empirically derived cutoffs for people with unequivocal brain damage.

a. Short form

For the short form version, Binder (1993) provided clinical decision rules for discontinuing the PDRT in patients who are showing normal performance. For this abbreviated version, the first 36 easy items are administered. If the patient scores below the cutoff of 19, the entire test is administered. If the patient correctly answers 7 of the first 9 difficult items or 12 of the first 18 difficult items, the test is discontinued.

b. Computerized version

Rose and colleagues (Rose, Hall, & Szalda-Petree, 1995) developed a computerized version of the PDRT. The primary advantage of this version is the ability to compute item response latencies. Differences in response latencies have been shown to be a marker of negative response bias in several studies.

7. VICTORIA SYMPTOM VALIDITY TEST

The Victoria Symptom Validity Test (VSVT; Slick, Hopp, Strauss, Hunter, & Pinch, 1994), a refinement of the Hiscock and Hiscock (1989) procedure, has advantages over both the original Hiscock and Hiscock test and the PDRT in that it is substantially shorter and is computer administered and scored. It can be used in most evaluations in which negative response bias is suspected. The VSVT is a 48-item computer-administered digit memory procedure consisting of three blocks of 18 items, with each block containing 8 easy and 8 difficult items. The primary dependent variables for the test are the total number correct, number of correct easy items, number of correct difficult items, total response time for easy items, and total response time for difficult items. The test takes approximately 15 minutes to administer and is computer scored. The test is sensitive to the negative response bias of experimental malingerers, and nonlitigating persons with closed head injuries are not misclassified on the basis of the cutoff scores.

8. FORCED-CHOICE TEST OF NONVERBAL ABILITY

The Forced-Choice Test of Nonverbal Ability (Frederick & Foster, 1991) should be used when a more comprehensive assessment for potential negative response bias is clinically indicated in the assessment of nonverbal abstraction or general intellectual skills. Frederick and Foster modified the Test of Nonverbal Intelligence by combining the two 50-item forms and eliminating two of the four response choices. Thus, the revised test is a 100-item two-alternative forced-choice procedure. The most obvious score is a comparison to chance. However, the test yields several more sophisticated scores including slope, consistency ratio, and correlation between test performance and item difficulty. These scores appear to be reasonably sensitive and specific to negative response bias (Frederick et al., 1994).

F. Suggestions for Use of General Instruments

Many assessment instruments, especially those developed in the past 10 years, have derived indices that evaluate the level of effort involved in taking the test. Some of these instruments, such as the Halstead–Reitan (Reitan & Wolfson, 1993) or the Luria–Nebraska (Golden, Hammeke, & Purisch, 1980), are lengthy and not suitable for hospital-based practice conducted in a consultation/liaison model. Therefore, they are not reviewed here. The interested reader is referred to the relevant chapter in Franzen (2000).

1. MINNESOTA MULTIPHASIC PERSONALITY INVENTORY—2

The Minnesota Multiphasic Personality Inventory—2 (MMPI–2; Butcher, Dahlstrom, Graham, Tellegen, & Kaemmer, 1989) is best suited for the detection of grossly exaggerated symptoms of psychological dysfunction. To this end, the standard validity scales and several other validity indices are clinically useful. Two careful, thorough, and thoughtful meta-analyses and reviews have provided some guidance for the clinician (Berry, Baer, & Harris, 1991; Rogers, Sewell, & Salekin, 1994). Berry et al. (1991) found that the largest effect sizes were associated with the F scale, the original Dissimulation scale, and the F–K index. Rogers et al. (1994) determined that F, F–K, and the Obvious minus Subtle score demonstrated the greatest effect sizes for both normal control participants and psychiatric comparison groups. On the basis of their review, Rogers et al. offered two sets of cutoff scores for clinical practice.

The following set represents the mean cutoff scores in their meta-analysis and can be used to raise the clinician's index of suspicion regarding possible negative response bias:

a. F-scale raw score greater than 23;

b. F-scale T score greater than 81;

c. F–K index greater than 10; and

d. Obvious minus Subtle score greater than 83.

It is important to note that these scores should be used only to raise one's index of suspicion. The scores are likely to classify falsely a substantial minority of patients with genuine complaints. Extreme elevations on the validity scales and indices are considerably more specific to negative response bias. More conservative cutoff scores suggested by Rogers et al. (1994) are as follows: (a) F-scale raw score greater than 30, (b) F–K index greater than 25, and (c) Obvious minus Subtle score greater than 190. Caution should be exerted here in that less than optimal effort on the MMPI–2 may not directly correspond to less than optimal effort on cognitive measures.

2. PERSONALITY ASSESSMENT INVENTORY

The Personality Assessment Inventory (PAI; Morey, 1991) has seen significant increase in use in the past 10 years. It has some advantages over the MMPI–2 in an inpatient consultation/liaison service in that it is somewhat short (344 items) and the items are written at a lower reading level. There are four validity scales (Inconsistency, Infrequency, Positive Impression Management, and Negative Impression Management). Data so far suggest that the PAI is able to accurately identify response bias. Similar to the MMPI–2, caution regarding the relation between psychological symptoms magnification and less than optimal effort on cognitive measures should be exercised here.

3. WECHSLER MEMORY SCALE—REVISED AND WECHSLER MEMORY SCALE—III

An approach proposed by Mittenberg, Azrin, Millsaps, and Heilbronner (1993) was to compare the Wechsler Memory Scale—Revised (WMS–R; Wechsler, 1987) Attention-Concentration (AC) index score with the General Memory (GM) index score. These researchers operated under the assumption that it is unlikely for someone with normal memory (GM index) to have impaired attention and concentration (AC index). Therefore, large GM–AC discrepancies should be unlikely in genuinely memory-impaired patients, whereas previous research has demonstrated a propensity for analog malingering participants to suppress their performance on attentional tasks such as Digit Span (Bernard, 1990; Iverson & Franzen, 1996). Mittenberg et al. (1993) found that participants instructed to malinger concerning memory suppressed their AC index ($M = 71$) to a greater extent than their GM index ($M = 85$), whereas patients with genuine problems associated with closed head injuries demonstrated the opposite pattern (Mittenberg et al., 1993). These findings were supported by Iverson and Slick (2001) and by Hilsabeck et al. (2003), although Slick, Hinkin, vanGorp, and Satz (2001) warned against confidence in this index when the GM index is above average. These discrepancy scores may be relatively specific to negative response bias. Large GM–AC index score discrepancies may reflect negative response bias. This finding should be followed up by a more careful examination of level of effort.

Glassmire et al. (2003) suggested the Faces subtest of the Wechsler Memory Scale—III (WMS–III) as an index of malingered effort, but more empirical support is needed before this can be enthusiastically recommended. The Digit Span subtest of either the WMS–III or the Wechsler Adult Intelligence Scale—III can be used in looking at the maximum span forward or backward (Iverson & Tulsky, 2003; Mathias, Greve, Bianchini, Houston, & Crouch, 2003).

4. RECOGNITION MEMORY TEST

The Recognition Memory Test (Warrington, 1984) should be used as a within-evaluation assessment of effort. This test appears sufficiently difficult to be unaffected by order of test administration. The Recognition Memory Test consists of two 50-item subtests: Recognition Memory for Words (RMW) and Recognition Memory for Faces (RMF). The test appears to be sensitive to exaggeration in both analog and clinical settings. Iverson and Franzen (1996) found that cutoff scores for both RMW and RMF were sensitive and specific to analog malingering. Millis (1994) demonstrated that litigating patients with mild head injuries scored much lower on both subtests than nonlitigating patients with moderate-to-severe head injuries. Because the subtests are in a two-alternative forced-choice format, patients' scores can be compared with the probable range of chance and with empirically derived cutoff scores. A score of 19 or less on either subtest is significantly below chance ($p < .04$).

5. WISCONSIN CARD SORTING TEST

Researchers have developed indices for evaluating whether optimal effort has been given in the administration of the Wisconsin Card Sorting Test (WCST). Bernard, McGrath, and Houston (1996) developed a discriminant function to classify WCST performance as more similar to that of malingering subjects or clinical subjects. Donders (1999) found the specificity rate to be 5%, whereas Suhr and Boyer (1999) developed a difference formula for classifying performance on the WCST; they provided specificity and sensitivity data for several cutoff scores. Greve and Bianchini (2002) reported high false-positive rates in both of these formulae. Therefore they should never be used in isolation; however, negative findings can probably be interpreted with confidence (high negative predictive value).

IV. CONCLUSION

The recent interest in the detection of malingering is part of the larger clinical concern with establishing whether nonoptimal effort has occurred and determining the validity of the scores obtained from standardized testing. Although this can be a difficult assessment issue, it can be addressed by paying close attention to the history, clinical presentation, and pattern of obtained test scores, as well as by the use of procedures specifically designed to evaluate level of effort and biased responding.

BIBLIOGRAPHY

American Psychiatric Association. (1994). *Diagnostic and statistical manual of mental disorders* (4th ed.). Washington, DC: Author.

Arnett, P. A., & Franzen, M. D. (1997). Performance of substance abusers with memory deficits on measures of malingering. *Archives of Clinical Neuropsychology, 12*, 513–518.

Arnett, P. A., Hammeke, T. A., & Schwartz, L. (1995). Quantitative and qualitative performance on Rey's 15-Item Test in neurologic patients and dissimulators. *The Clinical Neuropsychologist, 9*, 17–26.

Bernard, L. C. (1990). Prospects for faking believable memory deficits on neuropsychological tests and the use of incentives in simulation research. *Journal of Clinical and Experimental Neuropsychology, 12*, 715–728.

Bernard, L. C., McGrath, M. J., & Houston, W. (1996). The differential effects of simulating malingering, closed head injury, and other CNS pathology on the Wisconsin Card Sorting Test: Support for pattern of performance hypothesis. *Archives of Clinical Neuropsychology, 11*, 231–245.

Berry, D. T. R., Baer, R. A., & Harris, M. J. (1991). Detection of malingering on the MMPI: A meta-analysis. *Clinical Psychology Review, 11*, 585–598.

Binder, L. M. (1990). Malingering following minor head trauma. *The Clinical Neuropsychologist, 4*, 25–36.

Binder, L. M. (1993). An abbreviated form of the Portland Digit Recognition Memory Test. *The Clinical Neuropsychologist, 7*, 104–107.

Butcher, J. N., Dahlstrom, W. G., Graham, J. R., Tellegen, A., & Kaemmer, B. (1989). *MMPI–2: Manual for administration and scoring.* Minneapolis: University of Minnesota Press.

Donders, J. (1999) Brief report: Specificity of a malingering formula for the Wisconsin Card Sorting Test. *Journal of Forensic Neuropsychology, 1*, 35–42.

Franzen, M. D. (2000). *Reliability and validity in neuropsychological assessment* (2nd ed.). New York: Kluwer Academic/ Plenum Press.

Frederick, R. I., & Foster, H. G. (1991). Multiple measures of malingering on a forced-choice test of cognitive ability. *Psychological Assessment, 3*, 596–602.

Frederick, R. I., Sarfaty, S. D., Johnston, J. D., & Powel, J. (1994). Validation of a detector of response bias on a forced-choice test of nonverbal ability. *Neuropsychology, 8*, 118–125.

Glassmire, D. M., Bierly, R. A., Wisniewski, A. M., Greene, R. L., Kennedy, J. E., & Date, E. (2003). Using the WMS–III Faces subtest to detect malingered memory impairment. *Journal of Clinical and Experimental Neuropsychology, 25*, 465–481.

Golden, C. J., Hammeke, T. A., & Purisch, A. D. (1980). *The Luria–Nebraska Neuropsychological Test Battery Manual (Revised)*. Los Angeles: Western Psychological Services.

Greve, K. W., & Bianchini, K. J. (2002). Using the Wisconsin Card Sorting Test to detect malingering: An analysis of the specificity of two methods in nonmalingering normal and patient samples. *Journal of Clinical and Experimental Neuropsychology, 24*, 48–54.

Guilmette, T. J., Hart, K. J., & Giuliano, A. J. (1993). Malingering detection: The use of a forced-choice method in identifying organic versus simulated memory impairment. *The Clinical Neuropsychologist, 7*, 59–69.

Guilmette, T. J., Hart, K. J., Giuliano, A. J., & Leininger, B. E. (1994). Detecting simulated memory impairment: Comparison of the Rey Fifteen-Item Test and the Hiscock Forced-Choice procedure. *The Clinical Neuropsychologist, 8*, 283–294.

Hilsabeck, R. C., Thompson, M. D., Irby, J. W., Adams, R. L., Scott, J. G., & Gouvier, W. D. (2003). Partial cross-validation of the Wechsler Memory Scale—Revised (WMS–R) General Memory–Attention/Concentration malingering index in a nonlitigating sample. *Archives of Clinical Neuropsychology, 18*, 71–79.

Hiscock, M., & Hiscock, K. C. (1989). Refining the forced-choice method for the detection of malingering. *Journal of Clinical and Experimental Neuropsychology, 11*, 967–974.

Iverson, G. L. (1995). Qualitative aspects of malingering. *Brain Injury, 9*, 35–40.

Iverson, G. L., & Franzen, M. D. (1996). Using multiple objective memory procedures to detect simulated malingering. *Journal of Clinical and Experimental Neuropsychology, 18*, 38–51.

Iverson, G. L., Franzen, M. D., & McCracken, L. M. (1991). Evaluation of an objective assessment technique for the detection of malingered memory deficits. *Law and Human Behavior, 15*, 667–676.

Iverson, G. L., Franzen, M. D., & McCracken, L. M. (1994). Application of a forced-choice memory procedure designed to detect experimental malingering. *Archives of Clinical Neuropsychology, 9,* 437–450.

Iverson, G. L., & Slick, D. J. (2001). Base rates of the WMS–R malingering index following traumatic head injury. *American Journal of Forensic Psychology, 19,* 5–14.

Iverson, G. L., & Tulsky, D. S. (2003). Detecting malingering on the WAIS–III Unusual Digit Span performance patterns in the normal population and in clinical groups. *Archives of Clinical Neuropsychology, 18,* 1–9.

Mathias, C. W., Greve, K. W., Bianchini, K. J., Houston, R. J., & Crouch, J. A. (2003). Detecting malingered neurocognitive dysfunction using the Reliable Digit Span in traumatic brain injury. *Assessment, 9,* 301–308.

Millis, S. R. (1994). Assessment of motivation and memory with the Recognition Memory Test after financially compensable mild head injury. *Journal of Clinical Neuropsychology, 50,* 601–605.

Mittenberg, W., Azrin, R., Millsaps, C., & Heilbronner, R. (1993). Identification of malingered head injury on the Wechsler Memory Scale—Revised. *Psychological Assessment, 5,* 34–40.

Morey, L. L. C. (1991). *Personality Assessment Inventory.* Odessa, FL: Psychological Assessment Resources.

Pankratz, L. (1983). A new technique for the assessment and modification of feigned memory deficit. *Perceptual and Motor Skills, 57,* 367–372.

Pankratz, L. M. (1988). Malingering on intellectual and neuropsychological measures. In R. Rogers (Ed.), *Clinical assessment of malingering and deception* (pp. 169–192). New York: Guilford Press.

Pankratz, L., Fausti, S. A., & Peed, S. (1975). A forced-choice technique to evaluate deafness in the hysterical or malingering patient. *Journal of Consulting and Clinical Psychology, 43,* 421–422.

Paul, D., Franzen, M. D., Fremouw, W., & Cohen, S. (1992). Standardization and validation of two tests used to detect malingering. *International Journal of Clinical Neuropsychology, 14,* 1–9.

Prigatano, G. P., & Amin, K. (1993). Digit Memory Test: Unequivocal cerebral dysfunction and suspected malingering. *Journal of Clinical and Experimental Neuropsychology, 15,* 537–546.

Reitan, R. M., & Wolfson, D. (1993). *The Halstead–Reitan Neuropsychological Battery: Theory and clinical interpretation.* Tucson, AZ: Neuropsychology Press.

Rey, A. (1964). *L'examen clinique en psychologie* [The Clinical examination in psychology]. Paris: Presses Universitaires de France.

Rogers, R., Sewell, K. W., & Salekin, R. T. (1994). A meta-analysis of malingering on the MMPI–2. *Assessment, 1*, 227–237.

Rose, F. E., Hall, S., & Szalda-Petree, A. D. (1995). Portland Digit Recognition Test—Computerized: Measuring response latency improves the detection of malingering. *The Clinical Neuropsychologist, 9*, 124–134.

Slick, D. J., Hinkin, C. H., vanGorp, W. G., & Satz, P. (2001). Base rate of WMS–R Malingering index in a sample of non-compensation-seeking men infected with HIV-1. *Applied Neuropsychology, 8*, 185–189.

Slick, D., Hopp, G., Strauss, E., Hunter, M., & Pinch, D. (1994). Detecting dissimulation: Profiles of simulated malingerers, traumatic brain-injury patients, and normal controls on a revised version of Hiscock and Hiscock's Forced-Choice Memory Test. *Journal of Clinical and Experimental Neuropsychology, 16*, 472–481.

Slick, D. J., Sherman, E. M. S., & Iverson, G. L. (1999). Diagnostic criteria for malingered neurocognitive dysfunction: Proposed standards for clinical practice and research. *The Clinical Neuropsychologist, 13*, 545–561.

Suhr, J. A., & Boyer, D. (1999). Use of the Wisconsin Card Sorting test in the detection of malingering in a student simulator and patient samples. *Journal of Clinical and Experimental Neuropsychology, 21*, 701–708.

Warrington, E. K. (1984). *Recognition Memory Test*. Windsor, England: NFER-Nelson.

Wechsler, D. (1987). *WMS–R: Wechsler Memory Scale—Revised Manual*. Cleveland, OH: The Psychological Corporation.

Part II

NEUROPSYCHOLOGY AND THE HUMAN LIFE SPAN

CHAPTER 7

Sue R. Beers, Katherine Hammond,
and Christopher M. Ryan

General Assessment Issues for a Pediatric Population

In the two decades since the publication of Fletcher and Taylor's (1984) seminal article emphasizing the behavioral and biological differences between children and adults, the subspecialty of pediatric neuropsychology has reached maturity. With the growing appreciation of the neuropsychological correlates and consequences of diverse medical illnesses (e.g., childhood diabetes) as well as the federal mandate for early intervention services and early childhood education programs, it is not surprising that pediatric referrals are burgeoning at both private practices and hospital clinics. This chapter discusses the scope of disorders that are frequently referred for neuropsychological evaluation for younger patients and particular issues in evaluating children. Appreciating the differences between the child and adult models, we present a general framework to aid clinicians in structuring the pediatric evaluation.

I. UNDERSTANDING BRAIN–BEHAVIOR RELATIONSHIPS IN CHILDREN

The neuropsychological evaluation of children by necessity moves away from the adult model that often emphasizes testing on a single occasion, shifting the focus to the process of change. This construct put forward in Fletcher and Taylor's (1984) article mentioned earlier is particularly important as the field has come to appreciate that brain maturation continues into early adulthood, particularly in the frontal cortex and associated systems, the last areas of the brain to complete development. Subcortical gray matter and limbic system structures as well as the prefrontal cortex continue to show significant myelination, synaptogenesis, and synaptic pruning until approximately the third decade of life. Table 7.1 highlights the salient differences between pediatric and adult neuropsychological assessment.

II. MEDICAL AND NEUROLOGICAL DISORDERS OF CHILDHOOD

Pediatric neuropsychologists are commonly called on to evaluate children with problems ranging from disruptive behavior in the classroom to the neurobehavioral signs and symptoms associated with both neurological and medical conditions. These include the following:

- central nervous system (CNS) disorders (described in Table 7.2);
- medical conditions with possible CNS effects (e.g., sickle cell anemia, childhood systemic lupus);
- learning disabilities and disorders of regulation of attention;
- emotional and behavioral disturbances in conjunction with developmental delays or changes in usual function; and
- unexplained changes in language function, memory, motor function, academic performance, or behavior and personality.

III. ISSUES PARTICULAR TO PEDIATRIC ASSESSMENT

This section provides practical suggestions regarding the comprehensive evaluation of the child. We emphasize issues that the pediatric neuropsychologist might deal with as he or she conceptualizes and synthesizes data into an effective report.

A. Obtaining Background Information

Obtaining the child's social, medical, and educational backgrounds and history of the presenting problem requires an approach that is quite unlike that routinely used with adults.

Table 7.1. Comparison of Pediatric and Adult Neuropsychology

Children	Adults
Immature versus mature system	
Disorder may remain silent	Disorder marked by functional loss
Pace of development differs	Development accomplished
Requires wide range of measurement	Measurement is more focused
Possibility of brain reorganization	
Both plasticity and diathesis have effects	Brain organization fixed
Patterns of recovery differ	Recovery more specific
Course of recovery depends on child and environment	Recovery course less variable
Differences in diagnosis and presentation	
Onset more acute	Insidious onset more common
Symptoms poorly described or nonspecific	Symptoms often specific and well characterized
Behavior changes trigger assessments	Cognitive changes trigger assessments
Developmental delay or learning problems often lead to referral	
Behavioral variability	
Behavior and cognition vary in each child	Adult behaviors/cognition less variable
Children may lack learning history	Educational and vocational baseline known
Attention limits result in multiple sessions	Tolerate longer assessment periods
Environment, temperament, and psychosocial factors have large impact	Cognitive abilities more resistant to transient environmental or psychological effects
Limitations of brain–behavior relationship	
Adult model is inaccurate in children	Adult model developed on large body of research
Undeveloped skills are impossible to measure	Tests measure skills usually developed in normal adults
Focus on strengths and weaknesses	Focus on area of the brain affected

Note. Source: Fletcher and Taylor (1984) and Taylor and Schatschneider (1992).

Table 7.2. Primary and Secondary Disorders of the Central Nervous System (CNS)

Disorder	Example
Primary CNS disorders	Hydrocephalus Meyelomeningocele Epilepsy Brain tumors Traumatic brain injury Meningitis Neurofibromatosis Disorder with genetic etiology (Williams syndrome, Fragile X syndrome, Prader–Willi syndrome, Turner syndrome) Metabolic and degenerative disorders of childhood (e.g., leukodystrophies, mucopolysaccharidoses [MPS] disorders) Environmental neurotoxins (e.g., fetal alcohol syndrome, inorganic lead exposure, inhalant abuse)
Medical disorders with CNS involvement	Prematurity and low birthweight Turner syndrome Phenylketonuria Acute lymphoblastic leukemia Sickle cell disease Diabetes End stage renal disease Pediatric AIDS/HIV infection
Disorders of learning and behavior	Learning disabilities Central auditory processing disorder Attention-deficit/hyperactivity disorder Tourette's disorder Anxiety disorders Autistic spectrum disorders

Children, particularly those under the age of 10, do not relate personal information in the same way as do adults. They often have difficulty identifying and describing salient symptoms or problems in a clear, reliable fashion, and they often have trouble recounting the sequence of events. This is not to say that the child's view of his or her history and present circumstances should be ignored. Although children relate their histories in an idiosyncratic fashion, they often provide details that parents or caretakers have "edited." It is also essential that the clinician meet with the parents or primary caretaker to gather developmental and historical information and then conduct a separate clinical interview with the child. Obtaining medical and psychosocial information requires a much greater reliance on hospital staff, medical records, educational records, and reports from teachers and school psychologists than is usually the case with adult patients.

B. Observing Behavior

A wise mentor once advised, "The neuropsychological evaluation begins the moment that you set your eyes on the patient." For the pediatric neuropsychologist, every aspect of the child's behavior is extremely important. That is, the alert clinician will welcome the family into the office, all the while observing the child's interaction with the parent, his or her social skills, as well as language and motor development. Because it is difficult for some children to complete formal testing, the clinician uses this time as a way to interact with the child to obtain relevant behavioral data to supplement formal test results. Language skills are easily observed in an informal setting. As a rule of thumb, articulation should be commensurate with both expressive and receptive language abilities. For younger children it is important to pay attention to vocabulary skills and naming ability. With older children the clinician should be able to evaluate informally the various aspects of language, including syntax, morphology, phonological comprehension, grammar, semantic knowledge, and pragmatics. Motor skills can also be informally observed, either during the clinical interview or early in the testing session. We observe pencil grasp maturity (an indication of motor control) and any extraneous overflow movements. An assessment can also be conducted of heel-toe movements, tandem gait and balance, and hopping ability.

It is important to evaluate the child's behavior during testing to help establish the validity of the entire assessment. Eliciting and maintaining the typical child's interest and cooperation during an assessment also requires more effort and attention than is usually the case when assessing adults. Sitting for any extended time challenges the patience of many children, and for the child with a developmental disability, attention deficit, or neurological disorder the testing process can lead to inattention, acting out, or even outright refusal. To reduce those problems, the clinician must firmly encourage the resistant child to participate in the evaluation and then work diligently to maintain the child's motivation and cooperation with careful attention to building rapport and consideration of the child's nonverbal cues. The skilled clinician can prevent problems by appreciating the strengths and weaknesses of the child and using as much creativity and flexibility as possible while remaining within standardized procedures. An important skill that experienced clinicians develop over time is that of recognizing when "enough is enough." A skilled clinician carefully monitors the progress of the evaluation and is willing to provide rest breaks or another testing session to preserve the integrity of the data. Although it might seem obvious, we generally ask parents to be sure their child has had a good night's sleep and breakfast or lunch before the test session. For example, testing a child who has been awakened at 4:00 a.m. for the long car ride to the clinic is *not* optimal.

C. Issues in Test Selection and Presentation of Data

An extensive discussion of test selection is beyond the scope of this chapter. Suffice it to say that tests should be chosen within a conceptual framework or hypothesis, as well as with the attributes of the child in mind. With children, test selection is often adjusted "on the spot," as the clinician learns more about the child during the interview process. Until recently, pediatric neuropsychologists had to rely on downward extensions of adult instruments. In addition, normative information was often scant, at best. Fortunately the selection of carefully developed, standardized tests for children has improved. Several of the better instruments provide testing either within (e.g., memory) or across domains and are standardized on the same norm group (e.g., the NEPSY), allowing for more accurate comparisons both within and across abilities. Despite these improvements, at times one must depend on independently developed tests without comparable norm groups. If this is the case, the clinician must use particular care in comparing patterns across test results. As might be expected, the length of the battery is frequently an issue with children. As clinical skills improve, it is often possible to use fewer rather than more instruments. Whatever battery is selected, the clinician must present the results in a way that considers the expertise and interest of the referral source. For more information on this topic, the interested reader is directed to the *1985 Standards for Educational and Psychological Testing* developed jointly by the American Psychological Association, the American Educational Research Association, and the National Council on Measurement in Education (American Psychological Association, 1985).

D. Issues in the Interpretation of Pediatric Test Results

Interpretation of the neuropsychological assessment results is complicated by the fact that the child's CNS is still maturing, and different brain areas may mature at very different rates within any given child. In addition, particularly with children younger than 6 years of age, there are wide but perfectly normal variations in brain maturation. As children mature, this normal range becomes more restricted. Both of these facts mean that it is far more difficult for the neuropsychologist to distinguish developmental *delay* from stable or progressive brain *damage*, and they challenge the ability to make strong inferences about the nature and extent of brain dysfunction in the child. Heterogeneity in brain development, coupled with cultural and experiential differences, further reinforces the view that each child is truly unique, necessitating a cautiously idiographic or "N of 1" approach when interpreting test results. Neuropsychologists make an egregious error when they take a purely nomothetic, or actuarial, approach that simply compares the child's scores with published test norms and identifies performance as falling inside or outside of the "normal" range. Rather, conclusions must be based on a thorough clinical *integration* of age-referenced test scores, qualitative features of performance, behavioral presentation, and historical data gathered during the course of the assessment.

E. Dissemination of Results

Providing useful feedback is a critical part of any assessment, but neuropsychologists are frequently criticized for providing reports that have little relevance to the child's treatment or everyday functioning. Thus, it is important to provide specific recommendations applicable in several settings. When children are involved, providing feedback is frequently a particularly complex and time-consuming process, not only because there are so many diverse parties with a "need to know" but also because each party may expect the evaluation to answer very different questions. Certainly, there should be a common core of information communicated to everyone that includes a general description of the child's cognitive and behavioral strengths and weaknesses. In addition, the physician may want information about etiology or diagnostic rule-outs. Other members of the hospital treatment team may want suggestions that can help with behavioral management. Teachers may want recommendations about educational placement and strategies to enhance classroom performance. Psychiatrists, speech and language therapists, and occupational therapists may need information related to cognitive training. Other psychologists, social workers, and family members may want *all* of this information as well as some discussion of the long-term implications for the child's well-being. Finally, the child also requires sufficient age-appropriate feedback so that he or she can understand expectations and how to participate fully in future treatment recommendations. Both pediatric and general neuropsychological listservs have developed recently and are an excellent avenue to have consultation from many colleagues.

IV. SUGGESTED PROCEDURES FOR THE PEDIATRIC EVALUATION

The remainder of this chapter describes the general steps included in the pediatric neuropsychological evaluation and provides practical information to help the clinician anticipate typical problems encountered when evaluating a child or adolescent in the hospital or outpatient clinic. This information is meant to provide the general foundation to develop the assessment with the assumption that the clinician will consult various texts and recent articles with regard to specific aspects of the disease process that might require modifications of the neuropsychological battery. Of course, consultation or supervision with an experienced clinician is recommended when confronted with a unique or challenging case.

A. Clarification of the Referral Question

Referral requests are frequently vague or ambiguous (e.g., "This child's behavior seems odd to me—what do you think is going on?" or "She's had a recent history of academic decline—why?"). Questions such as these often require a level of clairvoyance that most clinicians do not possess. Since the advent of managed care, third-party payers (i.e., insurance companies) frequently authorize limited time for neuropsychological assessment and require a rationale for the inclusion of *each* instrument. Thus, it is critical to work closely with the referring professional to ensure that the planned assessment actually answers the question of interest. Understanding the rationale for the assessment helps to generate hypotheses regarding the problems that might be manifested by the child during the neuropsychological evaluation that, in turn, guide in the selection of specific neuropsychological tests. The following steps usually occur after receipt of the initial consultation request.

1. **FORMULATE THE QUESTION**

   a. Speak directly with the referring professional if possible.
      i. What behaviors or symptoms have they observed that triggered this request?
      ii. What possible medical or psychosocial conditions could explain the child's problems?
   b. Set primary goals, such as the following:
      i. Describe neuropsychological strengths and weaknesses.
      ii. Clarify diagnostic issues.
      iii. Improve behavioral management.
      iv. Recommend additional evaluations, treatment, or rehabilitation.
      v. Provide specific educational and cognitive retraining recommendations.

2. **DEVELOP THE HYPOTHESES TO GUIDE ASSESSMENT PLANNING**

   a. Consult the neuropsychological literature with respect to current or rule-out diagnoses to guide in planning the battery.
   b. Develop hypotheses that most directly reflect the referral question.
   c. Develop hypotheses that can be tested within the limits of the insurance authorization.

B. Gathering Information

To fully understand the problems a child is experiencing, the clinician needs to consult *multiple* information sources prior to initiating the assessment. Relying on any single source (e.g., medical records *or* parent reports) is likely to provide an incomplete or even biased picture of the child's medical and psychosocial problems. Obtaining as complete a picture as possible about the child's current and previous functioning provides a context in which to interpret the test results and generate treatment or placement recommendations that are reasonable and feasible. For example, when evaluating school-related issues, the clinician can ask parents and children what type of accommodations have been useful in the past and what they would consider to be useful to them now. This collaboration provides the groundwork for recommendations after the evaluation is complete.

Various sources of information are usually available to the clinician. It is important to review current and past medical records to ascertain medical or psychosocial problems that could affect the child's performance, explain the etiology of the child's problem, and help interpret results of the assessment. Admission work-ups and discharge summaries often provide salient information regarding developmental history, medical disorders, accidents, and medications. The clinician should be especially alert to comments about academic or behavioral problems in the classroom and medical or psychosocial problems within the child's extended family. Because performance on neuropsychological tests is affected by practice in the form of previous testing—particularly within the past 6 months—it is important to review the results of any earlier neuropsychological evaluation and modify the selection of tests accordingly.

The process of obtaining information regarding children on an inpatient unit is somewhat different from that associated with outpatient evaluations, offering advantages as well as disadvantages. An inpatient hospitalization provides the clinician with an opportunity to observe the child directly as he or she interacts with peers and adults. However, less time is usually available to gather the information relevant to the evaluation (e.g., school records), and parents are not always available to participate in the evaluation.

The following procedures are recommended prior to formal neuropsychological testing.

1. **FOR INPATIENTS**

   a. Observe the child's interactions with staff.
   b. Contact parents to obtain background information.
   c. Interview key staff regarding the child's behavior and child–family interaction.
   d. Evaluate the child's readiness for formal assessment (e.g., no acute illness, settled into unit, cooperative with other procedures).
   e. Determine feasibility of completing the evaluation and report before discharge.

2. **FOR OUTPATIENTS**

   a. Obtain all relevant records from physician and other health professionals.
   b. Discuss the purpose of the assessment with a family member (usually completed by phone).
   c. Arrange for the responsible parent or child (if age appropriate) to sign appropriate Health Information Portabil-

ity and Accountability Act (HIPAA) compliant release forms at relevant agencies (e.g., counseling centers, physicians, inpatient treatment settings) and arrange for records to be sent. (Note that the details of a HIPAA-compliant request may vary across institutions.)

   d. Provide an opportunity for the child to talk with you about the assessment.
   e. Ask parents to bring school records to the evaluation.

3. PRESENTATION OF THE DEVELOPMENTAL HISTORY

Information about the child's development and academic history is particularly important to a neuropsychological assessment. This section suggests an outline for information gathered from the sources discussed in Section B.

   a. Provide a brief description of current medical, psychosocial, and academic problems.
   b. Describe behavioral symptoms:
      i. mood swings or tantrums,
      ii. staring spells (i.e., an indication of possible seizure activity),
      iii. attention problems,
      iv. relationship difficulties (e.g., "teasing" or frequent fighting with peers), and
      v. sleep problems.
   c. Review pre-, peri-, and postnatal history and subsequent medical history (see Exhibit 7.1).
   d. Review the child's developmental history.

Exhibit 7.1. Developmental History: Key Issues

---

1. Difficulties during gestation/pregnancy
2. Prenatal exposure to toxins or drugs (e.g., nicotine, alcohol, cocaine, etc.)
3. Difficulties during labor and delivery
4. Method of delivery
5. Perinatal events or critical care issues (e.g., hospitalization in Intensive Care Unit)
6. Developmental milestones (see Table 7.3)
7. History of febrile illnesses or seizures
8. History of other major childhood illnesses or toxic exposure (e.g., lead)
9. History of head injuries (with or without unconsciousness) or other neurological problems
10. History of chronic ear infections
11. Educational history

e. Review family history:
    i. Was this child's development different from that of other children in the family?
    ii. Was there a history of psychiatric or neurologic problems (e.g., learning disability; attention deficit disorder) in other family members (e.g., parents, siblings, or extended family)?

4. STRUCTURING THE CLINICAL INTERVIEW

Particular issues regarding the clinical interview are discussed in the first section of this chapter. Many clinicians have an outline for their clinical interview "in their head." However, several of the texts listed at the end of this chapter include samples of pediatric interviews and questionnaires to guide the clinician. The goal of the interview is to

a. ascertain the family's understanding of the need for this assessment;
b. obtain the *parent's view* of child's medical, developmental, social, and academic histories (see Section B.3 and Table 7.3); and
c. obtain the parent's permission and a release of information to contact child's teachers and other relevant professionals; again, check local regulations regarding HIPAA rules and age of consent to sign releases.

After the interview, parents are usually asked to complete instruments to supplement the assessment. These might include the following:

a. developmental history form (e.g., Baron's Pediatric Neuropsychology Questionnaire),
b. standard behavior checklists (e.g., Child Behavior Checklist, Behavior Assessment System for Children, Behavior Regulation Inventory of Executive Function, Stonybrook Parent Symptom Checklist), and
c. personality assessment (Personality Inventory for Children—2nd edition; Minnesota Multiphasic Personality Inventory—Adolescent version).

C. Neuropsychological Testing of the Pediatric Patient

1. INTRODUCING TEST PROCEDURES

Neuropsychological testing differs from other psychological tests in several ways. First, it is often perceived as "fun," at least up to a point. This may stimulate some clinicians to refer to the tests as "games." This should be avoided because, among

Table 7.3. Selected Motor and Language Milestones

Skill	Age 2	Age 3	Age 4	Age 5
Gross motor	Runs well; kicks ball; goes up and down stairs (one step at a time)	Stands on one foot; pedals tricycle; goes up stairs (alternating feet)	Hops on one foot; stands on one foot (5 seconds); goes down stairs (alternating feet)	Stands on one foot (10 seconds); may be able to skip
Fine motor	Builds tower of six cubes; turns book pages singly	Copies circle; copies cross	Copies square; uses scissors; draws persons with two to four parts	Copies triangle; prints some letters; draws person with body
Comprehension	Follows simple commands; identifies body parts; points to common objects	Understands spatial relationships (in, on, under); knows functions of common objects	Follows two-part commands; understands same/different	Follows three-part commands; recalls parts of a story; understands number concepts
Expression	Speaks two- or three-word sentences; labels common objects	Speaks three- to four-word sentences; uses regular plurals; can count three objects; can tell age, sex, and full name	Speaks four- to five-word sentences; can tell story; uses past tense; can count four objects; names one color	Speaks sentences of five or more words; uses future tense; can count 10 or more objects; names four colors

Exhibit 7.2. A Sample Introduction

Following some rapport building and "small talk," testing can be introduced by the following: "*Now I have some interesting things for you to do.* [Depending on the child's level of understanding and motivation] *I'm going to ask you to do things like put pegs in holes as quickly as possible, look at pictures and tell me what's missing or odd about them, put together some jigsaw puzzles, answer general information questions, draw some designs for me, and so on. Some of these are easy and fun. And some of them are hard. Everybody has trouble with some of these tasks. But that's OK. I want to see how you're doing, and I want you just to try your best for me. We're going to be working together for the rest of the morning* [or *part of the afternoon*, etc.]. *Let me know if you need a drink of water, or if you have to go to the bathroom. OK? Do you have any questions? Are you ready?*"

other things, children know that you can stop a game when it is no longer entertaining or when you are tired. Second, neuro-psychological testing usually takes much longer than educational or psychological paper-and-pencil procedures. Thus, testing is facilitated when the clinician provides the child with an age-appropriate introduction to testing that includes the following elements:

a. Indicate who asked for this assessment and, within appropriate limits, why.
b. Tell the child what will happen during the assessment.
c. Inform him or her approximately how long the tests will take.
d. Review the "ground rules," such as level of difficulty (i.e., "Some questions are easy and some are more difficult"), how much feedback will be available, if questions are allowed, and how to request a break from testing.
e. Show the child where the testing will take place. As in other psychological procedures, rapport is facilitated by providing "child-friendly" space. This space should be relatively uncluttered and free of distractors (e.g., toys on display, colorful artwork on the walls).
f. Always show the child where his or her parents will be waiting. (See Exhibit 7.2.)

2. WORKING WITH PARENTS

As noted earlier, it is customary to begin the outpatient clinical interview with parent and child together. After some rapport has been established, ask the family to leave, and work with the child alone. Parents are often reluctant to leave their child and may wish to remain in the testing room. Except for very young children, this is not good clinical practice. A typical response to parent concerns might be "It's very important that I have an opportunity to work with your child alone, without any distractions. Working with Michael is a necessary part of our standardized assessment procedure."

3. MAINTAINING THE CHILD'S COOPERATION

Some children are so engaged by the testing situation that the examiner can administer the entire battery smoothly and efficiently. Unfortunately, other children find the process of being evaluated—or just sitting still for a few hours—so onerous that completing each task becomes a battle. In this case, the clinician maintains control over the testing situation by giving the child the *illusion of control*.

Start the assessment with a task the child is likely to enjoy, perhaps something he or she mentioned during the clinical interview. Avoid discussion with the child while administering a test. If the child asks "Is that right?" after a specific item, provide a reassuring, but nonspecific, response (e.g., "You're really trying" or "Boy, some of these really make you think, don't they? Let's keep on going, and try your best for me"). If the child persistently demands feedback after specific items, an appropriate response might be "We'll talk about it when you return for your feedback session" or "Let's finish this set of questions [tasks] first; then we can talk." It is interesting to note that children often do not ask for more detailed feedback following this initial request, and the clinician should not volunteer additional information *during* the testing session.

If, after completing the test, the child reiterates his or her request for feedback, provide some *brief, but accurate*, feedback (e.g., "You did better on some things than on others, but that's how it is for most kids"). Children often like to provide *you* with feedback, eagerly responding when asked what part of the test they liked best and which part was the most difficult. After completion of the entire session, ask the child if he or she has any questions about anything that occurred during the session. This procedure helps "debrief" the child and allows the clinician to correct any misconceptions about the nature of the assessment or performance. In addition, the ensuing discussion can provide additional insights about how the child thinks and feels.

a. Off-task behaviors during testing.

As the test session continues, the child's attention may wander. This can be prevented to some extent by maintaining a comfortably structured testing situation.

      i. Become well practiced and comfortable with the testing materials before working with any child.

     ii. Move efficiently from one test to another.

    iii. Do not engage in lengthy chats with the child between tests.

    iv. Do not provide an elaborate introduction to each new test.

     v. Improve on-task behavior by implementing a contingency contract (a reward for consistent effortful performance).

    vi. Provide short breaks.

   vii. Keep the session brief.

Perhaps the best way to prevent a child's attention from wandering is to ensure that you are well prepared. This means that the clinician has selected the *minimal number* of tests needed to answer the referral question and has integrated data from both record review and observation of the child during the clinical interview. The testing space must be sufficiently organized so that one can move quickly and effortlessly from one test to another. Although the goal is to complete testing in one session, often with children, especially younger children or very impaired children, a second, or even third, session may be necessary.

b. Early termination.

For any number of reasons, it may not be possible to complete the assessment. In that case, a good rule of thumb is to try to get as much information as possible from a formal assessment as well as from less formal observations. This information is incorporated in the report with clear details about why the assessment was either not completed or never initiated. Finally, recommendations are made to guide future assessment (e.g., evaluate on an outpatient rather than an inpatient basis; delay until the child has recovered from acute illness or trauma). The astute clinician considers terminating the assessment session early when the child passively "refuses" by manifesting minimal effort (e.g., giving "I don't know" responses to questions he or she might be expected to answer), making extremely careless or impulsive responses that are out of character with other behaviors, or becoming directly oppositional.

If the child is so inattentive that he or she cannot focus on task for more than a few minutes, the clinician usually plans to continue the assessment on another day. If the child continues to refuse, one strategy is to change settings to a playroom and interact with the child informally. Although this does not provide standardized results, an observant and creative clinician can gain information regarding the child's general ability level in several areas (e.g., visual–spatial ability can be informally assessed with puzzles, concept formation with guessing games). Finally, prepare a brief report that summarizes behavioral observations, results, and impressions. As customary, this report discusses the extent to which these impressions or conclusions are valid (based on the child's level of cooperation) and makes recommendations that might improve productivity during a later session.

4. TEST SELECTION

Any test used as part of a formal neuropsychological assessment must have representative norms, must span a reasonable age range, and must have good validity and reasonable test–retest reliability. Clinicians necessarily rely on measures with these characteristics to document both cognitive strengths and weaknesses—the first, and perhaps most important, goal for any neuropsychological evaluation. However, as suggested in the following section, clinical interpretation moves beyond the comparison of the child's scores to the published norms to determine whether they fall within the "brain-damaged" range.

How to compose a battery of neuropsychological tests is an art that is not easily taught. Guidelines for test selection might include the following considerations:

a. environment:
   i. medical unit,
   ii. inpatient psychiatric unit, and
   iii. clinic office;
b. clinical training or philosophy of the clinic:
   i. Hastead-Reitan,
   ii. Luria-Nebraska,
   iii. Boston Process Approach, and
   iv. eclectic;
c. clinician's level of experience;
d. referral question;
e. child characteristics:
   i. age,
   ii. cultural background and native language, and
   iii. socioeconomic status; and
f. insurance constraints.

Most clinicians develop a "core" battery that can be used with all patients and then add other tests to this battery when confronted with specific referral questions that may require more information or a different type of information (e.g., a child with traumatic brain injury who had premorbid learning or attention problems). The application of a standard core battery improves diagnostic skills by allowing the clinician to document how different medical and psychiatric disorders influence performance on the same set of neuropsychological tests. In developing this core battery, most clinicians select tests that are readily available and have wide usage, so that another neuropsychologist will be able to evaluate the patient and compare those results with the earlier assessment. This is particularly important for pediatric neuropsychological evaluations because serial assessment is one way to differentiate developmental delays or the effects of state-dependent situations (e.g., acute psychiatric disorder) from permanent brain damage.

There continues to be no consensus as to what specific tests ought to be incorporated into the "ideal" brief battery. Table 7.4 lists useful instruments for a variety of settings. This is not an inclusive list but is meant to provide the names of tests that measure each domain. A recently developed neuropsychological battery appropriate for children ages 3 through 12 years deserves mention. The NEPSY assesses five cognitive domains and is anchored by a norm group that is a representative sample of children within this age range, thus assuring an accurate comparison across domains in the individual child. Another advantage of the NEPSY is that the entire battery need not be administered in compliance with third-party payer procedures that advise against the administration of a "fixed" battery.

D. Interpreting Test Results

Neuropsychological tests are sensitive to brain damage in children, but they are not specific. That is, performance on any single test or series of tests can be influenced by a host of factors, many of which are unrelated to CNS dysfunction. As a consequence, it is sometimes difficult to make strong diagnostic statements about the presence or absence of brain damage or about underlying neuropathology, particularly if the child has been evaluated briefly and at only one point in time. One method favored by clinicians is to use a hypothesis-testing strategy to interpret results and guide in the preparation of the written report. Seven steps delineate this process.

1. Prepare a summary of results organized by domain.
2. Identify cognitive strengths and weaknesses:
   a. place emphasis on domains (e.g., "memory") or subdomains (e.g., "verbal–nonverbal" distinctions) rather than on specific tests,

Table 7.4. Selected Instruments and Brief Descriptions

Age	Instrument and approximate time	Description and comments	Publisher
General Intelligence			
3–adult	Wechsler Intelligence Scales (60 minutes)	Preschool/primary, child, and adult versions. Probably the most recognized intelligence test series. Usually the gold standard for schools.	Psychological Corporation
6–adult	Wechsler Abbreviated Scale of Intelligence (15 minutes)	Developed to provide a short and reliable measure of IQ. Can be supplemented with other Wechsler subtests if necessary.	Psychological Corporation
2.5–adult	Peabody Picture Vocabulary Test, 3rd Edition (10 minutes)	Child identifies the picture that matches the word spoken by the examiner. Often used to obtain an estimate of verbal IQ. Also a measure of receptive semantic knowledge. Alternate forms available.	American Guidance Service
2–adult	Stanford-Binet Intelligence Scale, 4th Edition (60 minutes)	Frequently used with children who have limited cognitive resources. The completely reworked 5th Edition is now available.	Riverside
4–adult	Kaufmann Brief Intelligence Test (15 minutes)	Verbal and nonverbal scales. Excellent for those with limited cognitive resources.	American Guidance Service

(Continued)

Table 7.4. Selected Instruments and Brief Descriptions *(Continued)*

Age	Instrument and approximate time	Description and comments	Publisher
General Intelligence			
6–adult	Test of Nonverbal Intelligence—III (20 minutes)	Similar to Matrix Reasoning on the WAIS-III. Excellent for use with verbal learning disorders, attention problems, and speech and language deficits that impact IQ estimates. Also appropriate for children who have limited command of the English language.	PRO-ED
Academic Achievement			
4–adult	Wechsler Individual Achievement Test, 2nd Edition	Normative sample linked to that of the WISC-III facilitates statistically rigorous identification of IQ/achievement discrepancy important in identifying learning disabilities. A screening form is available.	Psychological Corporation
5–adult	Wide Range Achievement Test, 3rd Edition	Provides a quick screen of academic abilities. Not widely recognized by schools. No measure of reading comprehension.	Wide Range, Inc.
	Language	Children with language deficits should be referred to a Speech and Language specialist for a comprehensive evaluation.	
6–adult	WISC–IV Vocabulary (15 minutes)	Child defines words read aloud. Depends on learning ability, fund of general information, and language development.	Psychological Corporation

5–21	Clinical Evaluation of Language Fundamentals, 4th Edition (30–60 minutes)	Test battery designed to identify language skill deficits in school-aged children, adolescents, and young adults. Includes measures of expressive and receptive speech. Assesses the structural level of the child's language.	Psychological Corporation
2–18	Expressive and Receptive One-Word Vocabulary Tests, 3rd Edition (15 minutes)	Child points to a picture to identify a word read aloud (receptive) or names a picture (expressive). Tests are conormed to provide easy comparison of the two abilities. Tests are usually nonthreatening to very young children and provide a quick estimate of language abilities.	Western Psychological Services
3–12	Token Test for Children (10 minutes)	Child completes five subtests that require completion of increasingly complex tasks using tokens over various shapes and colors. Provides an efficient measure of language comprehension and the ability to follow directions.	Western Psychological Services
5–adult	Boston Naming Test	Assesses word retrieval deficits and ability to benefit from phonemic or semantic cueing. Sensitive to the effects of traumatic brain injury.	Psychological Assessment Resources

(Continued)

Table 7.4. Selected Instruments and Brief Descriptions *(Continued)*

Age	Instrument and approximate time	Description and comments	Publisher
Attention			
6–adult	WISC–IV/WAIS–III Digit Span (5 minutes)	Digits Forward assesses immediate attention; digits Backward provides a measure of working memory. Tables allow for interpretation of these subscores.	Psychological Corporation
6–adult	Continuous Performance Test (15 minutes)	This test is administered by computer to assess attentional dysfunction, vigilance, and impulsivity. Several versions are available.	Multihealth Systems
8–adult	Symbol Digit Modalities Test (5 minutes)	A paper and pencil test that requires the child to pair numbers with symbols. Provides measure of visual scanning, visual tracking, and sustained attention.	Western Psychological Services
Memory and Learning			
5–16	California Verbal Learning Tests—Child Version (40 minutes)	Measures rote learning. Supplemental scores allow assessment of semantic organization and rate of acquisition (i.e., learning curve). Tests recall of 15 categorized words over five trials, a distracter list of 15 similar words, immediate free and cued recall. Delayed free recall, cued recall, and recognition memory are tested.	Psychological Corporation
5–16	Children's Memory Scale (30 minutes)	Includes an assessment of verbal and nonverbal memory in immediate and delay conditions. Conormed on the WISC–III.	Psychological Corporation

5–19	Test of Memory and Learning	An extremely comprehensive measure of attention and memory in immediate and delay conditions. A good instrument for use with head-injured children. Supplemental scores are useful to further characterize memory and learning.	PRO-ED
5–17	Wide Range Assessment of Memory and Learning (45 minutes)	Includes nine subtests measuring verbal and nonverbal memory. Test's factor structure does not support its claim to measure learning. Screening form provides a quick assessment of basic memory skills.	PRO-ED
Visual–Spatial Skills			
3–adult	WPPSI–III/WISC–IV/ WAIS–III/WASI Block Design (15 minutes)	Child arranges colored blocks to replicate a model or printed design. Bonus points for rapid performances. Assesses visuoconstructional ability, visual–spatial perception, and visual analysis and synthesis.	Psychological Corporation
5–adult	Rey Complex Figure (10 minutes)	Child copies a complex geometric figure. Child reproduces a figure immediately after copy and 20 minutes later. Assesses visual–spatial perception, constructional abilities, organization skills, and nonverbal memory. A developmental version is administered and scored somewhat differently than the original figure.	Psychological Assessment Resources

(Continued)

Table 7.4. Selected Instruments and Brief Descriptions *(Continued)*

Age	Instrument and approximate time	Description and comments	Publisher
Visual–Spatial Skills			
5–adult	Hooper Visual Organization Test	Consists of line drawings or familiar objects that are divided into fragments. The child identifies the object. The test assesses visual analysis and synthesis, conceptual organization, and mental rotation abilities. Naming skills are also required.	Western Psychological Services
3–17	Developmental Test of Visual–Motor Integration, 4th Edition (10 minutes)	Assess the coordination of visual perception and fine motor movements. The child copies a developmental sequence of geometric forms. Visual and motor supplements available to document the possible source of deficient overall performance.	PRO-ED
Executive Functioning			
6–adult	Controlled Word Association Test (5 minutes)	Measures access to semantic memory. Children > 8 years complete in three 1-minute trials, naming as many words as possible beginning with three different letters of the alphabet. Younger children name as many animals as possible in 1 min.	Psychological Assessment Resources

Age	Test	Description	Publisher
8–adult	Stroop Color/Word Test (5 minutes)	Measures complex attention and freedom from distractibility. Child reads word and names ink colors. In the Interference Trail, child names the color of ink used to print color words. Words are printed in an incongruous color (e.g., "red" is printed in green ink).	Riverside
6–adult	Trail Making Test (5 minutes)	This test has two versions, depending on the age of the child (9–14 vs. > 14). Often described as a measure of frontal integrity, Reitan considers it to provide a measure of the overall status of the central nervous system.	Reitan Neuro-psychological Laboratories
5–8	Progressive Figures Tests (2 minutes)	This analogue to the Trail Making Test B is administered to younger children.	Reitan Neuro-psychological Laboratories
6.5–adult	Wisconsin Card Sorting Test (15 minutes)	This hypothesis testing task, assesses abstract reasoning, logical analysis, and concept formation. The child is asked to sort 128 cards by a predefined principle (i.e., shape, color, number) that changes without warning.	Psychological Corporation
7–adult	Tower of London (Shallice, 1982) (10 minutes)	This complex reasoning task (aka "Tower of Hanoi" on computer) is used to assess problem solving and procedural memory. The child is given three colored beads that are placed on pegs of different heights. Items are graded in difficulty.	Psychological Assessment Resources

(Continued)

Table 7.4. Selected Instruments and Brief Descriptions *(Continued)*

Age	Instrument and approximate time	Description and comments	Publisher
Executive Functioning			
8–adult	Delis-Kaplan Executive Function System (90 minutes)	Offers advantage of common norm group. Standardized, child-friendly versions of several "traditional" adult neuropsychological instruments. Subtests assess planning, flexibility of thinking, verbal and nonverbal fluency, hypothesis testing, abstract abilities.	Psychological Corporation
Psychomotor Speed and Dexterity			
3–adult	WPPSI–III Animal Pegs; WISC–IV/WAIS–III Coding (3 minutes)	Measures psychomotor speed and attention, visual scanning, and memory. A sensitive indicator of central nervous system dysfunction. Youngest children insert colored pegs into a board according to a key. Older children and adolescents draw various shapes to match target stimuli.	Psychological Corporation
5–adult	Grooved Pegboard (3 minutes)	Measures psychomotor speed and finger dexterity. Child rotates notched pegs to insert into grooved slots with dominant and nondominant hand. Children ages 5–8 complete only first two rows.	Riverside

Personality and Behavior

Age	Instrument	Description	Publisher
3–18	Personality Inventory for Children, Second Edition (30 minutes)	Parent questionnaire that is considered to be the gold standard of personality assessment for younger children. Estimates current problems in adjustment, changes in emotional status and behavior, suggests further areas of evaluation.	Western Psychological Services
14–18	MMPI-A	The adolescent version of the familiar Minnesota Multiphasic Personality Inventory	National Computer Systems
5–18	Behavior Rating Inventory of Executive Function (15 minutes)	Parent and Teacher questionnaire; Adolescent form being developed. Focuses on identifying behaviors associated with executive function deficits. Excellent instrument for evaluating the behavioral effects of traumatic head injury.	Riverside
2.5–18	Behavior Assessment System for Children (30 minutes)	Self, Parent and Teacher rating scales provide a multidimensional approach for measuring behaviors and emotions. Suitable for use in children with learning disability.	American Guidance Service
5–18	Stonybrook Parent Checklist	A qualitative assessment that provides information helpful in describing psychological disorders.	Checkmate Plus, Ltd.
3–17	Conners' Rating Scales—Revised	Self, Parent and Teacher rating scales. The gold standard for assessing attention deficit hyperactivity disorder.	PRO-ED

Note. WAIS-III = Wechsler Adult Intelligence Scale—III; WISC-III and WISC-IV = Wechsler Intelligence Scale for Children, Third and Fourth Editions; WPPSI-III = *Wechsler Preschool and Primary Scale of Intelligence, Third Edition*; WASI = Wechsler Abbreviated Scale of Intelligence; MMPI-A = Minnesota Multiphasic Personality Inventory—Adolescent.

Exhibit 7.3. Possible Explanations for Pattern of
Neuropsychological Test Results

---

1. Poor motivation
2. Inadequate exposure to information or experiences that are
   measured by particular tests (e.g., from impoverished
   environment; frequent school absences)
3. Psychosocial discomfort in testing or social situation
   (e.g., test-taking anxiety; social phobia)
4. Acute physical illness
5. Attention problems
6. Depression, anxiety disorder, oppositional disorders
7. Delay in the maturation of a specific cognitive process
   (e.g., language ability, motor skills)
8. Brain damage (unless otherwise established, the nature
   and type [e.g., focal vs. diffuse] and etiology should be
   discussed in the report)

---

      b. discuss specific test results to emphasize a point that
         has direct relevance to the working hypotheses, and
      c. generate a series of hypotheses to explain the pattern
         of results (see Exhibit 7.3).
3. Evaluate hypotheses systematically, integrating all data.
4. Make a decision about the plausibility of each hy-
    pothesis.
5. List any limitations or problems associated with this as-
    sessment:
      a. omissions of data (e.g., missing school records),
      b. threats to test validity (e.g., hallway noise or interrup-
         tions; child with a cold), and
      c. physical disabilities (e.g., restricted vision; hemipa-
         resis).
6. Present the most reasonable interpretations in the report
    (see Exhibit 7.3):
      a. summarize empirical data to support the interpreta-
         tion and
      b. consider mentioning possible alternative interpreta-
         tions that have been rejected and present reasons
         for rejection.
7. Discuss treatment recommendations and resources.

E. Communicating Results and Recommendations

With the proper authorization, feedback from the neuropsychological evaluation is provided to all parties who will be making
decisions about the child's short- and long-term welfare. The

written report serves as the core material for providing information to the referral source and other professionals involved in the child's care (see Exhibit 7.4). Information provided to parents is most often completed with a follow-up appointment or, if necessary, by telephone. At this time the results and recommendations are presented in a way that optimizes understanding and gives ample opportunity for questions. The feedback process serves to identify effective compensatory strategies as well as serves as the cornerstone for developing new educational and behavioral skills.

The following five steps define the feedback process.

1. Discuss results with referral source:
   a. Complete this step by phone as soon as possible after the evaluation;
   b. problem solve regarding remaining issues or questions; and
   c. plan for providing future clinical services for the child, if applicable.
2. Review results with other members of the medical treatment team, as appropriate.
3. Summarize findings to parents:
   a. Discuss the child's strengths and weaknesses;
   b. educate parents about the diagnostic and treatment implications;
   c. provide information on available resources and recommendations for the involvement of other health professionals, if applicable;
   d. assist parents in preparing for the Individualized

Exhibit 7.4. Pediatric Neuropsychological Evaluation: Report Outline

I. Referral Source
II. Presenting Problem and Background Information
III. Behavioral Observations
IV. Instruments
V. Findings or Results by Domain
a. Intellectual Function   e. Memory and Learning b. Academic Achievement   f. Visual–Spatial Skills c. Speech and Language   g. Motor and Perceptual d. Attention and Executive   Function   Function   h. Behavior and Personality
VI. Summary and Recommendations

Educational Plan meeting if special education is required; and

e. help parents develop a plan to discuss results with their child if questions arise after the feedback session.

4. Provide feedback to teachers or school psychologist, if requested:

a. Consult with parents before discussing the report with the school as certain information may be inappropriate for disclosure (e.g., family psychiatric history),

b. review the child's school placement,

c. discuss strategies to improve the child's classroom performance,

d. review neuropsychological or psychological issues that might be affecting schoolwork,

e. explain the benefits of specific interventions, and

f. be sensitive to the parents' concerns about revealing personal information.

V. CONCLUSION

Like other skills, pediatric neuropsychological assessment improves with specialized training and practice. Exposure to as many different children as possible quickly expands one's knowledge base, develops clinical intuition, and facilitates the generation of recommendations. Although each seasoned practitioner probably has a somewhat different view of how to move from novice to expert status, this chapter highlights an approach that is drawn from collective experiences in a variety of medical, psychiatric, and private practice settings. The recent explosion of books about pediatric neuropsychology can provide the clinician with a wealth of wisdom to accelerate the development of clinical acumen. Although by no means exhaustive, the Bibliography lists several books that may be particularly helpful.

One of the most common errors made by novice neuropsychologists is the tendency to overdiagnose brain damage. Low scores, consistent with brain dysfunction, are interpreted as unequivocal evidence that some insult or disorder has damaged the brain. When making strong statements about the integrity of any patient's CNS, one needs to be cautious, especially if that conclusion is based on a single, brief evaluation of a child. This chapter has emphasized the need to obtain as much information as possible about the child from myriad sources and to integrate that information clinically, with specific attention to functional and behavioral descriptions of neuropsychological deficits. It is this overall pattern and level of functioning considered *within the historical and developmental context*, rather than any single element or test score, that provides the most accurate characterization of the child's neuropsychological status. In other words, the diagnosis of brain damage, when based on neuropsychological test results, is necessarily a diagnosis of exclusion. Before any conclusions can be made that a child's behavior is a direct consequence of structural or functional changes in the CNS, all other possible interpretations of the neuropsychological data must be duly considered and discarded.

BIBLIOGRAPHY

Neuropsychological Issues

American Psychological Association. (1985). *Standards for educational and psychological testing*. Washington, DC: Author.

Baron, I. S. (2004). *Neuropsychological evaluation of the child*. New York: Oxford University Press.

Baron, I. S., Fennell, E. B., & Voelker, K. K. S. (1995). *Pediatric neuropsychology in the medical setting*. New York: Oxford University Press.

Cantwell, D., & Baker, L. (1987). *Developmental speech and language disorders*. New York: Guilford Press.

Feinberg, T. E., & Farah, M. J. (Eds.). (2003). *Behavioral neurology and neuropsychology* (2nd ed.). New York: McGraw-Hill.

Fletcher, J. M., & Taylor, H. G. (1984). Neuropsychological approaches to children: Towards a developmental neuropsychology. *Journal of Clinical Neuropsychology, 6*, 39–56.

Goldstein, G., & Beers, S. R. (Eds.). (2003). *Comprehensive handbook of psychological assessment: Intellectual and neuropsychological assessment*. New York: Wiley.

Goldstein, S., & Reynolds, C. R. (Eds.). (1999). *Handbook of neurodevelopmental and genetic disorders in children*. New York: Guilford Press.

Lyon, G. R. (Ed.). (1994). *Frames of reference for the assessment of learning disabilities: New views on measurement issues*. Baltimore: Paul H. Brooks.

Reynolds, C. R., & Fletcher-Janzen, E. (Eds.). (1997). *Handbook of clinical child neuropsychology* (2nd ed.). New York: Plenum Press.

Shalice, T. (1982). Specific impairments of planning. *Philosophical Transactions of the Royal Society of London, B298*, 199–209.

Spreen, O., Risser, A. H., & Edgell, D. (1995). *Developmental neuropsychology*. New York: Oxford University Press.

Spreen, O., & Strauss, E. (1998). *A compendium of neuropsychological tests* (2nd ed.). New York: Oxford University Press.

Taylor, H. G., & Schatschneider, C. (1992). Child neuropsychological assessment: A test of basic assumptions. *The Clinical Neuropsychologist, 6*, 259–275.

Yeates, K. O., Ris, M. D., & Taylor, H. G. (Eds.). (2000). *Pediatric neuropsychology: Research, theory, and practice*. New York: Guilford Press.

Developmental Considerations

Behrman, R. E., Kliegman, R. M., & Jenson, H. B. (Eds.). (2004). *Nelson textbook of pediatrics* (17th ed.). Philadelphia: Saunders.

Levine, M. D., Carey, W. B., & Crocker, A. C. (Eds.). (1999). *Developmental–behavioral pediatrics* (3rd ed.). Philadelphia: Saunders.

CHAPTER 8

Paul Maruff and David Darby

Age-Related Memory Impairment

Impairment in memory in older people is inferred from self-report, from informant report, or by objective testing. Objective testing typically consists of bedside examination with brief cognitive screening instruments such as the Mini-Mental Status Examination (MMSE), with standardized psychological instruments such as the Weschler Memory Scale (WMS), or with neuropsychological tests of specific memory functions or processes such as the Rey Auditory Verbal Learning Test (RAVLT). Compared with healthy young adults, people over the age of 60 without dementia generally show poorer performance in assessments of memory and other cognitive functions.

I. DEFINITION OF AGE-RELATED MEMORY IMPAIRMENT

The issue intended by terms such as **age-related memory impairment** concerns the extent to which memory performance in an older person with no dementia can be considered abnormal. If an older person's memory functioning is determined to be abnormal, the important issue for the neuropsychologist then becomes, why? The neuropsychologist must consider whether he or she believes the memory impairment to be a consequence of normal aging, a consequence of a concurrent or previous neurological disease or disorder, a secondary consequence of another medical illness or condition, or the first sign of an incipient dementia. Irrespective of how the impairment is detected, or in whom, age-related memory impairment is not a disease itself. Rather, the presence of impairment in memory must be considered in the context of a multidisciplinary diagnostic process.

A. Definitions

A number of classification systems have evolved that seek to characterize or stage the level of memory and cognitive function in older people without dementia. A variety of these are currently in use in different fields of medicine, and consequently, neuropsychologists may be asked to give opinions in relation to these. The different classifications vary in the extent to which they require objective impairment in memory, allow impairment in other aspects of cognition, require that there also be subjective memory impairment, tolerate the presence of a known neurological or medical or psychiatric illness, or tolerate deterioration in activities of daily living. These issues are compared across classifications in Table 8.1 and have been reviewed in detail elsewhere (Collie & Maruff, 2002).

The classification systems listed in Table 8.1 share many important similarities. In fact, differences between the various criteria mainly reflect the context in which the classification systems were developed. It is useful to consider in detail the relative strengths and weaknesses of the classification systems used currently.

1. AGE-ASSOCIATED MEMORY IMPAIRMENT

Age-associated memory impairment (AAMI) is present in individuals age 50 years and above, with normal intellectual function, who complain of memory problems and whose performance on standardized memory tests is one standard deviation below the mean of healthy young adults. Although designed originally to characterize and communicate normal age-related memory impairment, AAMI has also been considered to represent central nervous system (CNS) pathology. However, this classification has been criticized in both applications because it is too restrictive to characterize normal aging, inflates estimates of impairment due to its dependence on normative data from young adults, and allows too much variability in the application of its criteria and has onerous exclusion criteria (Collie & Maruff, 2002).

Table 8.1. Comparison of the Different Systems Used to Classify Impairment in Cognitive Function in Older People With No Dementia

Classification system	Memory impairment	Other cognitive impairment	Cognitive decline	Subjective memory loss	Cognitive tests specified	Neurological condition allowed	Mood condition allowed	Impaired daily living
Age-associated memory impairment	Yes Objective	No	Yes Subjective	Yes	Yes	No	No	N/S
Age-related cognitive decline	Yes Subjective	N/S	Yes Informant Report	N/S	No	N/S	N/S	N/S
Mild cognitive decline (GDS 3)	Yes Objective	N/S	N/S	Yes	Yes	N/S	Yes	Yes
Questionable dementia (CDR 0.5)	Yes Objective	Yes Objective	Yes Objective	N/S	No	N/S	N/S	Yes
Mild cognitive impairment	Yes Objective	No	N/S	Yes	No	No	No	No
Cognitive impairment no dementia	Yes Objective	Yes Objective	No	No	No	No	No	No
Mild neurocognitive disorder	Yes Objective	Yes Objective	Yes Objective	No	No	Yes	N/S	Yes

Note. GDS = Global Deterioration Scale; CDR = Clinical Dementia Rating Scale; N/S = not significant.

2. AGE-RELATED COGNITIVE DECLINE

Although a number of classifications were developed to overcome the limitations of the AAMI criteria (e.g., age-consistent memory impairment and late-life forgetfulness), the most complete and well accepted of these has been age-related cognitive decline (ARCD; American Psychological Association, 1998). The ARCD criteria place no restriction on age, although the definition of *decline* requires evidence or corroboration of subjective reports by a reliable informant. Cognitive impairment is defined as performance of >1 standard deviation below the mean of age and education-matched control data for tests of memory and learning, attention and concentration, executive function, language, and visuospatial function. Exclusion criteria include concurrent medical or psychiatric conditions that could cause change in cognition or the use of psychoactive substances.

The fourth edition of the *Diagnostic and Statistical Manual of Mental Disorders* (*DSM–IV*) of the American Psychiatric Association (1994) includes ARCD (780.9), although not as a diagnostic category or disease. Instead, any patient meeting the criteria for ARCD is recommended to require careful clinical evaluation. For a classification of ARCD, the *DSM–IV* requires that there be an objective impairment in cognitive functioning related to the aging process that is within normal limits for the individual's age. Individuals may have difficulty solving complex problems and remembering appointments or people's names. The impairment cannot be attributed to other medical, psychiatric, or neurological disorders.

3. MILD COGNITIVE DISORDER

The 10th revision of the *International Statistical Classification of Diseases and Related Health Problems* (*ICD–10*) by the World Health Organization (1992) has proposed mild cognitive decline (MCD; F06.7) as a provisional definition under the organic, including symptomatic, mental disorders (F00-F09). The definition of MCD is similar to that of ARCD in the *DSM–IV*. It requires objective evidence of cerebral dysfunction or systemic disease known to cause cerebral dysfunction, a report of cognitive dysfunction by the individual or a reliable informant, and abnormal performance on a test of cognitive function. Like ARCD, the classification is designed to be able to be applied to all adults and not just to older adults. However, studies of this classification applied to older individuals suggest that classification of MCD is unreliable or transient and is satisfied easily by older individuals with high levels of mood symptoms (Collie & Maruff, 2002).

4. QUESTIONABLE DEMENTIA

Whereas constructs such as AAMI and ARCD were designed primarily to identify abnormal aging, other similar classifications consider memory and cognitive abnormalities in individuals without dementia as the mildest manifestation of dementia. Such classifications are generally part of staging systems for dementia (mostly Alzheimer's disease [AD]). For example, the Clinical Dementia Rating Scale (CDR) contains a classification for equivocal dementia (CDR 0.5). However, the classification depends on the assessment of both cognitive function and adaptive behavior. Thus for a CDR of 0.5, any mild memory impairment should be accompanied by normal functions in the individual's home and social life, including their personal care and normal orientation and problem-solving abilities.

The Global Deterioration Scale (GDS) also includes stages termed very mild cognitive decline (GDS 2) and mild cognitive decline (GDS 3), which are defined by the presence of memory and cognitive impairments not severe enough to meet criteria for dementia (Reisberg, Ferris, de Leon, & Crook, 1982). Very mild cognitive decline is equated with normal age-related changes (e.g., AAMI). For example, individuals are classified as GDS 2 if they have specific memory problems such as forgetting where they placed familiar objects or forgetting the names of people they know well. However, they show no objective evidence of memory deficit on clinical interview, and they report no problems in social or employment settings. Mild cognitive decline (GDS 3) is the classification used if impairment in memory or concentration has become obvious on objective assessment and memory problems intrude into more demanding activities of daily living. Patients with this cluster of symptoms may also show increased levels of anxiety.

5. MILD COGNITIVE IMPAIRMENT

Recent research has given rise to the classification of mild cognitive impairment (MCI), and this diagnostic classification now enjoys the greatest clinical use and acceptance in the area of dementia practice and research. Although there have been a number of different definitions of MCI, a recent consensus statement defined MCI as the presence of self-reported memory impairment (preferably corroborated by an informant), an objectively defined memory impairment, normal intellectual function, normal activities of daily living, and no dementia (Petersen, Stevens, et al., 2001). Although Petersen and his group used a cutoff of 1.5 standard deviations below the mean of healthy age-matched normal individuals to classify impairment on any test, the tests are not specified nor is the severity of impairment necessary for classification.

The initial construct of MCI was defined as a transitory stage between normality and AD. However, dissatisfaction with the focus of MCI criteria on memory impairment, and the recognized variability in cognitive impairments that can occur in older people, led to three subclassifications of MCI based on the nature of the cognitive impairments detected. These include MCI amnestic (the original criteria), MCI multiple domains slightly impaired, and MCI single nonmemory domain (Petersen, Doody, et al., 2001). There was also acknowledgment that these different presentations of subtle cognitive impairment may be indicative of different neurodegenerative pathologies. For example, whereas MCI amnestic may describe the prodromal stages of AD, MCI multiple domains slightly impaired may reflect a vascular pathology, and MCI single nonmemory domain may indicate dementia with a more focal presentation such as frontal-temporal dementia. However, these subclassifications have not been validated yet, nor have explicit criteria been presented.

The outcome of a diagnosis of MCI is still not certain. The rate and likelihood of progression from MCI to AD are variable, with prospective studies estimating that between 8% and 55% of people with MCI will convert to AD in 5 years or less. However, almost 25% of individuals with MCI demonstrate cognitive performance that remains impaired, but stable, for 6 to 10 years, whereas some studies show that 25% to 40% of cases of MCI can resolve completely when individuals are reclassified at a later time. These different prognoses could reflect heterogeneity in MCI. However, they could also indicate that the construct itself, or at least the tests on which its classification is based, have some unreliability (Collie, Maruff, & Currie, 2002).

6. COGNITIVE IMPAIRMENT NO DEMENTIA

Cognitive impairment no dementia (CIND) is essentially a label used in research for describing any cognitive impairment in an older person that is not sufficient to satisfy a clinical criteria for dementia (Graham et al., 1997). Therefore, it is a broad classification that can accommodate cognitive impairment related to systemic illness and also to medical or psychiatric conditions. Once classified, the nature of cognitive impairment in CIND can be subclassified by putative etiology (e.g., AD or vascular pathology) or by its association with medical conditions (e.g., diabetes, hypertension). MCI, as defined in the previous section, would be considered a subcategory of CIND.

7. MILD NEUROCOGNITIVE DISORDER

Although not developed specifically to classify memory or cognitive impairment in older people, the *DSM–IV* classification of mild neurocognitive disorder (MND) is relevant to decisions about the nature of memory or cognitive impairment in older people when there is evidence of systemic illness or cerebral dysfunction that is considered to be related to the cognitive impairments detected (American Psychiatric Association, 1994). MND is classified under cognitive disorders not otherwise specified (294.9). In addition to demonstrating a relationship between the memory or cognitive impairment and the systemic illness, this classification system also requires the presence of deficits in at least two domains of cognition, including memory, executive function, attention–speed of information processing, and language. The impairment must be shown on objective tests, be severe enough to interfere with social or occupational function, and represent a decline from some previous level of function, and the cognitive impairment cannot be staged or defined better within the classification system for any other mental disorder.

B. Etiology

The different classification systems shown in Table 8.1 were developed to characterize memory and cognitive impairments across a range of settings. When considered together, however, these classification systems indicate that subtle memory or cognitive impairment in older people without dementia may reflect four broad types of CNS dysfunction. The neuropsychologist should consider each of these areas when abnormal memory or cognitive function is detected on the basis of an assessment of a older person without dementia, although memory or cognitive impairment may reflect more than one type of dysfunction.

1. IMPAIRMENT MAY BE A DIRECT AND NORMAL CONSEQUENCE OF AGING

Cross-sectional studies indicate that performance on many standardized tests of memory and cognition becomes worse with age, even in individuals who remain physically and mentally healthy and in whom any deterioration of sensory function is corrected. The severity of this change is different for various types of cognitive function. For example, average performance on tests of episodic memory may decline by more than a whole standard deviation unit from age 30 to 80. However, a construct called **processing speed** has been shown to account for the majority of variance in age-related changes on a variety of tasks of attention, memory, and executive function (Salthouse, 2001). In these instances, the decline in performance is thought to reflect the normal age-related deterioration of the CNS. However, there is also strong evidence to indicate that cognitive decline with age is not inevitable. For example, some individuals who are over 100 years old show cognitive function that is completely normal.

In addition, prospective serial studies of memory and other cognitive functions in individuals over 60 years of age who remain healthy show little evidence of any decline (e.g., Filit et al., 2002). These data suggest that the presence of memory or cognitive impairment in older people without dementia may be due to the designs of the studies conducted (e.g., cross-sectional rather than longitudinal); the effect of uncontrolled systemic or neurological illnesses, whose prevalence increases with age and which can depress cognitive function; or even the tests used (e.g., older people may be less familiar with computerized tests). It is also possible that the stability of memory (and other cognitive) performance shown in prospective studies reflects the fact that people with true cognitive decline drop out, or are excluded, from ongoing assessments. Although this may affect our ability to make general conclusions about the relationship between age and memory, it does show that at least for a proportion of older people, memory abilities are essentially intact well into the last decade of life. Therefore, the neuropsychologist should not assume that the subtle memory impairment detected in an individual older person is the benign consequence of normal aging.

2. IMPAIRMENT IS THE DIRECT CONSEQUENCE OF AN INJURY, INFECTION, OR DISEASE OF THE BRAIN

Memory and other cognitive impairment can result from direct brain injury or disease. For example, stroke, tumor, infection (e.g., HIV), and metabolic disorders can all present with subtle memory impairment on neuropsychological examination. The incidence of disorders such as cerebrovascular disease, cancer, and metabolic disease (e.g., renal, hepatic, or thyroid disease) increases with age and is consequently highest in individuals over 60 years old. The onset of impairment in memory or cognitive function associated with these different disorders, conditions, or diseases is generally rapid. However, it is not uncommon that individuals with these conditions first seek medical attention because they, or others, observe some new cognitive impairment. The patterns of impairment will vary and give diagnostically useful clues as to the likely underlying possible causes.

3. IMPAIRMENT MAY BE THE INDIRECT CONSEQUENCE OF A MEDICAL CONDITION OR DISEASE

Although disorders of the CNS can affect individuals' memory function and other cognitive abilities, it is also well known that a variety of nonneurological diseases, disorders, or surgical or pharmaceutical interventions, which are also more common in older people, are also associated with subtle impairments in memory and cognitive function. Some of these conditions, such as cancer, alcoholism, or vitamin B12 deficiency, alter cognition through their direct effects on the CNS (see Table 8.2 for possible CNS problems). However, others can affect cognition indirectly, often through unknown mechanisms or as a consequence of their symptoms, like fatigue, depression, or loss of appetite. In some conditions, both direct and indirect mechanisms operate. Table 8.2 includes a list of conditions, diseases, and interventions known to be associated with memory and cognitive impairment in individuals over 60 years old.

4. IMPAIRMENT MAY BE THE EARLIEST MANIFESTATION OF INCIPIENT NEURODEGENERATIVE DISEASE

In the absence of age-related sensory or motor changes, or concomitant medical illness or lifestyle factors, specific impairment in memory can represent the earliest or preclinical stages of dementia (Petersen, Stevens, et al., 2001). This is because AD is the most prevalent form of dementia and is characterized most obviously by amnesia. However, there is also evidence that subtle impairments in other cognitive functions (in addition to or instead of memory) may indicate other types of dementia. For example, subtle difficulties in language functions, such as confrontational naming and comprehension, can indicate the earliest signs of semantic dementia. Subtle impairment in executive functions can be observed in people with frontal-temporal dementia long before they meet criteria for dementia (reviewed in Petersen, Doody, et al., 2001). Given the seriousness of the diagnosis, and the obvious impact that such impairments can have on an individual's ability to live and work independently, the assessment of memory in older people is always conducted with reference to the question of dementia.

Table 8.2. Common Memory Impairments in Older Individuals and Associated Pathologies

Category of memory impairment	Clinical feature	Anatomical lesion	Pathology	Patient information
Primary memory impairment Axial amnesia Korsakoff syndrome	■ Hallmark is rapid rate of forgetting ■ Acquisition of new material is only mildly impaired, but there is marked loss of acquired material over time ■ Recall depends on delay and interpolated material ■ Recognition impaired ■ No ability to form novel associations between different exemplars of categories of stimuli	Hippocampus and entorhinal cortex (usually bilateral)	Amnestic MCI and early Alzheimer's disease Ischemia/infarction (especially left PCA) Encephalitis (herpes simplex, limbic) Hypoxia Temporal lobe surgery Trauma (rarely pure)	Blackboard wiped clean analogy
	Material specific amnesia	Thalamus (dorsomedial nucleus) and hippocampal connections	Thiamine deficiency Infarction Prion disease Rare focal lesions	

Attentional	Focal: Rt posterior parietal Anterior cingulate Frontal lobe regions	Focal lesions including infarction, tumor, focal cortical atrophy, infection	
■ Inefficient and disorganized acquisition ■ Plateau learning ■ Impaired recall ■ Recall aided by cues ■ Recognition usually better than recall	Neuronal systems	Dementia of Lewy body type Parkinson's disease Huntington's disease Progressive supranuclear palsy Cortico-basal ganglionic degeneration Human immunodeficiency virus infection	Distractible, attends partially to stream of information
	Multifocal	Raised intracranial pressure (subdural haematoma, NPH, colloid cyst) Vascular cognitive impairment Encephalitis	
	Psychiatric	Mood disorders Anxiety and compulsive disorders Psychosis Attention deficit disorder	

(Continued)

Table 8.2. Common Memory Impairments in Older Individuals and Associated Pathologies (*Continued*)

Category of memory impairment	Clinical feature	Anatomical lesion	Pathology	Patient information
		Systemic	Drugs and toxins (anticholinergics, sedatives) metabolic, glucose electrolytes, ammonia Organ failure (hepatic, renal, cardiac, respiratory, thyroid) Infections (syphilis, viral cryptococcosis) Inflammation, systemic lupus erythematosis, Whipple's disease, chronic fatigue Nutritional: Vitamin B_{12} deficiency	

Note. MCI = mild cognitive impairment; PCA = posterior cerebral artery; NPH = normal pressure hydrocephalus.

C. Subtypes of Age-Associated Memory Impairment and Possible Neuropathologies

Although the etiology of memory impairment in older people cannot be determined on the basis of neuropsychological assessment alone, some important clues can be derived from careful consideration of the nature of memory impairment. Hypotheses about the etiology of memory impairment can be strengthened by determination of the specific nature of memory problems, their magnitude, whether other cognitive systems are also impaired, and whether there are also impairments in activities of daily living. As this review focuses on memory (as indeed do most criteria used to stage age-related cognitive impairment), we consider profiles of impairment on neuropsychological tests of memory and what these may suggest.

Table 8.2 suggests that the first neuropsychological decision should be to determine whether poor performance on tests of memory represents a phenomenon secondary to attentional impairment. Failure of concentration, sustaining of vigilance, or distractibility can lead to failures that can mimic memory impairment. Demonstration of stable, appropriately attentive abilities is important before conclusions about more focal neuropsychological impairments can be made. Purely quantitative approaches to assessment may fail to detect subtle lapses in attentiveness associated with mild cognitive impairment. The memory impairment typical of attentional dysfunction includes reduced span of immediate recall (e.g., digit span) and inefficient new learning. Attentional disturbances have numerous causes and in severe cases are associated with frank confusion. Focal neurological disorders affecting executive abilities (e.g., frontotemporal dementia or vascular cognitive impairment) can also lead to a similar profile.

If attentional abilities are preserved, the next differentiation is whether there is primary memory failure. This refers to the typical features of a general amnesic syndrome, in which immediate recall (e.g., digit span) is usually normal and information appears to be retained over short periods; but with poor consolidation, there will be susceptibility to interference effects and progressive worsening of recall (even with recognition assistance) over time (so-called rapid rate of forgetting). Novel associations are also difficult to consolidate. Such amnesia is the hallmark of bilateral involvement of the medial (axial) memory circuits involving the hippocampus and thalamus and their connections. Relatively greater impairment of verbal or visual new learning (termed **material specificity**) has some lateralizing significance to language-dominant or -nondominant hemispheres. If there is a primary memory failure, then the extent to which this is accompanied by other cognitive impairment can assist in differentiating focal from multifocal disease. Isolated primary memory impairment is not uncommon and may be a very early prodrome to AD, or may not progress for years, as previously stated.

Impairment of memory may also be related to other cognitive impairments that incidentally impair performance on memory tests. Language disorders, such as semantic dementia, can present with a profile of test results that resembles verbal-specific memory impairment. Relatively poorer confrontational naming results, and preservation of everyday memory function helps differentiate this condition.

II. FUNCTIONAL NEUROANATOMIC CORRELATES OF MEMORY IMPAIRMENT IN OLDER PEOPLE

Table 8.2 shows the anatomical basis for the different types of memory impairment that can be detected in older people with no dementia. This breaks down into two broad associations. First, primary memory impairment characterized by rapid forgetting and the inability to form novel associations while other functions can remain intact reflects disruption to medial temporal and thalamic areas. Second, impairment across a range of cortical (frontal, parietal, and temporal lobes) and subcortical (basal ganglia, caudate, and white matter) areas can give rise to impairments in attention and executive functions that interfere with the ability of individuals to encode new information. Hence, these attentional memory impairments are more important for what they do not indicate rather than being of any localizing value themselves.

III. COMPETING DIAGNOSES

The presence of subtle memory or cognitive impairment in an older person without dementia is not indicative of any specific disease process, injury, or disorder. Therefore, detection of impairment begins a careful search for the cause, and this search is predominantly a process of exclusion. We have already outlined some possible causes in Table 8.2 and consider the differential diagnosis process in the following section. However, the one important and competing issue that the neuropsychologist should consider is that poor performance on memory or cognitive tests by the individual does not necessarily reflect true pathology. Instead, the poor performance reflects individual related factors such as the effects of heightened anxiety, depression, fatigue, or lower motivation; failure to appreciate the requirements of the testing session; sensory or motor impairment; or lack of sufficient language skills or experience to allow optimal performance in the assessment.

Although these factors operate across all aspects of neuropsychological assessment, their effects are accentuated in the assessment of older people without dementia because classification of impairment is mostly based on borderline or subtly abnormal performance. Hence, it is important that the classification of any impairment in an older person be reliable. In a recent study we applied the amnestic MCI criteria to a large group of community-dwelling healthy older people without dementia on three consecutive assessments over 12 months. Whereas 25% of the cohort met the criteria for amnestic MCI on each assessment, only 13% met the criteria on all assessments. Thus, for any single assessment, approximately 50% of MCI classifications were false positive (Collie et al., 2002). This finding may help to explain why some individuals appear to have recovered from their MCI when reclassified on a second occasion. It also illustrates the unreliability in constructs such as MCI.

IV. HISTORY

The history of older individuals presenting for assessment should include the usual demographic, psychosocial, and medical information. Information should also be obtained from individuals about their own perception of their memory and cognitive abilities and any failures or difficulties of which they might be aware. An estimate of when the problem began is also important. Corroboration from a close relative or informant can reveal difficulties where insight may be impaired. The individual should be asked for the reasons as to why he or she sought assessment or referral in the first place and whether the individual has had any assessment of his or her cognitive function performed previously. Previous assessments may be useful for issues of charting decline in cognition or for determining the appropriateness of tests (e.g., it would be inappropriate to give a strategy formation test like the Wisconsin Card Sorting Test if it had been administered recently).

Because subtle impairment in memory and cognitive function can arise from many medical conditions and indeed their pharmacological treatments (e.g., sedatives, anticholinergic medications), as well as being a consequence of surgical procedures that involve either regional or general anesthesia, it is crucial that a thorough medical history be obtained. A list of current medications (including nutritional supplements and other nonregulated medicines) currently used by the individual is a useful starting point for a medical history.

Personal or social events such as death of a spouse, moving to a different house, or a sudden loss of mobility can also give rise to subtle changes in cognition. It is unlikely that changes in cognition are the direct consequence of such events. Instead, these events may merely decrease the adaptive abilities of the individual to cope with the impairment in memory and make it more obvious to other family members or friends. It is possible that reactive depression arising from events such as the death of a spouse can lead to impairment in memory and concentration.

It is also possible that the individual has sought an opinion because he or she is concerned about the risk of developing dementia. This may be the consequence of a friend being diagnosed or recent publicity about neurodegenerative diseases. This type of information can be elicited in discussion about the reasons for individuals seeking professional care.

Psychological symptoms such as dysphoric mood can be indicated by slowing or paucity of speech, flattened affect, or an amotivational state. Alone, these symptoms do not necessarily indicate a psychiatric impairment as they are also characteristic of some neurodegenerative diseases with a predilection for subcortical structures (e.g., Parkinson's disease, Huntington's disease, or progressive supranuclear palsy). Other psychological symptoms such as tangentiality of speech, inappropriateness of thoughts and expression, or bizarre speech or behavior can be important indicators of a late onset psychiatric disorder. Lateralizing signs like hemiplegia, hemianopia, or bradykinesia are obvious with the patient sitting in front of you, but detecting other important signs such as dressing apraxia, lack of care in appearance, or inappropriate clothing may require more careful attention by the neuropsychologist.

V. SENSORY, MOTOR, AND PHYSICAL SYMPTOMS

The presence of subtle sensory or motor impairments, in addition to impairment in memory and cognitive function, is common in older age. These deficits may complicate interpretation of the assessment as described earlier. Specific sensory or motor deficits (referred to as **focal neurological signs**) may suggest contralateral brain disease due to vascular lesions (infarction, hemorrhage, venous occlusion), infection, or neoplasm. Unilateral slowing of pure motor functions (impaired walking arm swing, masklike facial expressions, tremor) may suggest early parkinsonism. Sensory disturbances such as astereognosis, agraphaesthesia, or impaired tactile localization may suggest more rare conditions, such as cortico-basal-ganglionic degeneration (CBGD; an akinetic-rigid syndrome with cortical degeneration). However, sensorimotor lesions only occurring below the neck may indicate spinal cord without brain disease.

Pure motor disturbances of bulbar function (i.e., dysarthria, dysphasia) may suggest focal diseases such as stroke, multiple sclerosis, or motor neuron disease (MND). Peripheral MND features may be associated with frontotemporal dementia and executive disturbances. Hemianopia, though typically caused by infarction, may be simulated by hemispatial neglect or posterior cortical syndromes (such as Balint's syndrome). Extrapyramidal signs would raise the possibility of Parkinson's disease, progressive supranuclear palsy, or Lewy body dementia. Abnormalities of gait may be associated with cerebrovascular disease, Parkinson's disease, and normal pressure hydrocephalus. In general, the neuropsychologist should attempt to clarify with the referring physician the nature and presumed cause of any such deficits.

VI. SEROLOGY AND LABORATORY RESULTS

The usual laboratory evaluations are used to detect a wide variety of conditions usually associated with attentional disturbances. Some of these are regarded as treatable, although the neurological and cognitive disturbances do not always reverse with correction of these metabolic abnormalities. If an initial laboratory screen results in abnormal or equivocal tests, then they are usually repeated or further specific tests are undertaken. Refer to chapter 3 (this volume) for an overview of laboratory testing relevant to clinical neuropsychological practice.

VII. EEG AND NEUROIMAGING

Electroencephalography (EEG) has specific uses to confirm epileptiform changes when epileptic conditions are suspected. EEG was used widely before the advent of modern neuroimaging to suggest both localized and diffuse cerebral dissolution. Even today, EEG remains a useful objective marker of widespread dysfunction typically associated with metabolic or specific organ failure. The characteristic triphasic waves of hepatic failure are one example. If such changes are found, then they can be used to follow improvement with therapy, though it is likely that neuropsychological evaluation is more sensitive to such improvement.

Neuroimaging is particularly useful to exclude primary brain disease, with computed tomography (CT) scanning being the most widely available but less accurate in terms of spatial resolution than magnetic resonance imaging (MRI). MRI is preferred to CT where available, because of the lack of bone artifact that obscures brain structure. The higher resolution of MRI can allow visualization of smaller and multiple strokes that can help explain attentional or multifocal cognitive impairments. The presence of periventricular or more extensive white matter disease (leukoaraiosis) is well shown by MRI but remains controversial as a cause of cognitive impairment (again, attentional disturbances). Very occasionally the ventricular system (which is filled by cerebrospinal fluid [CSF]) dilates, causing hydrocephalus. This may also be associated with attentional disturbances but may also be an "ex vacuo" dilatation due to brain tissue loss rather than obstruction of the CSF pathways.

CT and MRI will effectively exclude brain tumors or large structural lesions. They can also show localized atrophy, which is more helpful than generalized atrophy (which is also not reliably correlated with cognitive deficits). Localized atrophy may also be progressive, for example, affecting the hippocampus within the medial temporal lobe. In the future, such progressive atrophy may help to confirm that isolated amnesia is related to early AD. Other focal atrophy may help confirm the other dementias (e.g., inferolateral temporal lobe atrophy in semantic dementia) or frontal atrophy in frontotemporal dementia. It is important to note that these changes are not always present. They are dependent on shrinkage of cortical tissue and neighboring regions after neuronal death and loss, but this is not universal, sometimes making the neuropsychological examination the only reliable means for such diagnoses.

Other imaging techniques used commonly include single photon emission computed tomography (SPECT) or positron emission tomography (PET). In brief, SPECT is usually ordered to evaluate the regional blood perfusion of the brain. It uses a radio-emitting isotope that can be bound to a carrier molecule sequestered within brain cells that are receiving adequate blood supply. It can provide broad-brush indications of deficits in regional blood perfusion that may suggest typical patterns of more advanced disease (such as Alzheimer's or focal dementias). At best SPECT is usually abnormal, but nonspecific, in mild cognitive impairment.

PET scanning is more expensive and technologically sophisticated. It uses short half-life radio isotopes that emit positrons, which then annihilate with electrons emitting gamma radiation, which can be measured and localized to give three-dimensional maps of brain metabolism. For a more detailed description of this imaging technology, refer to chapter 4 (this volume). At present, PET imaging does not have sufficient specificity to directly assist in diagnosing mild cognitive impairment.

VIII. THE NEUROPSYCHOLOGICAL EXAMINATION

The neuropsychological assessment of an older person relies on a shared understanding of the purpose of the assessment and the ability of the neuropsychologist to inspire confidence and trust in the patient. For older people, establishment of rapport may require more time than in younger people. In assessing older people, it is also important to be aware of any limitations in their sensory and motor functions. Ideally, assessment should be carried out with all sensory impairments corrected as visual or hearing loss can decrease test performance. However, it is not uncommon for people who present for neuropsychological assessment to forget their glasses or hearing aids. Therefore, it is worth stating that reading glasses and hearing aids are required when appointments are made. Some neuropsychological tests designed for older people seek to overcome sensory impairments by using simultaneous spoken and written presentation of stimulus material (e.g., the word learning test from the Consortium to Develop a Registry for Alzheimer's Disease [CERAD] neuropsychological battery) or provide stimulus material specially tailored for people with poor vision.

It is also crucial that patient-related factors such as anxiety, fatigue, or low motivation be considered, as well as the educational and employment history of the patient. Inexperience with testing or assessment, lack of ability in the language used by the neuropsychologist, or concern about the consequences of assessment can all act to depress test performance scores.

IX. KEY NEUROPSYCHOLOGICAL MEASURES

As is evident from the discussion so far, any memory impairments detected in older people must be considered with reference to their other cognitive abilities. Therefore, the neuropsychological assessment of memory must take place within a broader assessment of cognitive abilities, including general intellect, executive function, visuospatial function, attention, language, and motor function.

The clinical assessment of memory should cover immediate retention of information, rate and pattern of learning, efficiency of retrieval or recent and remote information, and the susceptibility to pro- and retroactive inference. Each of these aspects of memory should ideally be evaluated in both verbal and nonverbal modalities. This can be achieved through the use of a standardized test battery or by grouping individual tests. Table 8.3 compares neuropsychological tests that can be used for the assessment of memory in older people. Table 8.3 is not an exhaustive analysis list of memory tests. It presents tests that we have found to be useful in our clinics and for which data from other clinics, laboratories, or studies attest to their validity. The table also provides references to summaries of published normative data for older people for each of the tests included.

There are ever-increasing data suggesting that the performance on various memory tasks is modulated by a number of demographic and social factors that are generally not considered in the normative data. For example, educational level, gender, and language abilities can influence performance on learning tasks. Different cultural backgrounds may also influence performance even within a single country or society (Wong, Strickland, Fletcher-Janzen, Ardila, & Reynolds, 2000).

X. PSYCHIATRIC AND PSYCHOLOGICAL COMORBIDITIES

It is important to understand the psychological health of older people when attempting to interpret their performance on memory and cognitive tests. As stated in Table 8.2, depressive or anxiety disorders in older people can present as impairment on tests of memory. Anxiety and depressive symptoms increase as individuals get older, especially where there is physical illness or frailty (Filit et al., 2002). In some cases, depression in older people can become severe enough to interfere with cognitive function (in particular memory) and appear to be dementia. Therefore, it is important to investigate the presence and severity of depressive or anxiety symptoms in older individuals presenting with memory problems. Another important issue for older people is alcohol abuse. Older individuals complaining of memory loss should be questioned on their alcohol consumption, and abstinence should be recommended.

Table 8.3. Neuropsychological Tests Appropriate for the Assessment of Memory Function in Older People

Memory ability	Neuropsychological test	Brief description	References to normative data for older people
		Verbal information	
Immediate and short term	Digit Span Forward (DSF) from WMS–III	Useful measure of immediate span. Often used to assist inferences about attentional abilities.	Lezak (1995) Spreen and Strauss (1991) Tuokko and Hadjistavropolous (1998)
	Digit Span Backward (DSB) from WMS–III	Used to support inferences about working memory.	Lezak (1995) Spreen and Strauss (1991) Tuokko and Hadjistavropolous (1998)
Word list learning	Selective Reminding Test (SRT)	Inspection of pattern of recall across trials delivers estimates of short-term memory, long term storage, long-term recall. Delayed recall and recognition trials.	Lezak (1995) Tuokko and Hadjistavropolous (1998)

(Continued)

Table 8.3. Neuropsychological Tests Appropriate for the Assessment of Memory Function in Older People *(Continued)*

Memory ability	Neuropsychological test	Brief description	References to normative data for older people
		Verbal information	
	Auditory Verbal Learning Test (AVLT)	Well-validated measure of immediate recall and learning, 15 unrelated words presented over 5 trials and 15 novel words given on interference trial. Supports inferences about learning, recall, recognition as well as providing estimates of primacy and recency effects and vulnerability to interference.	Harris, Ivnik, and Smith (2002) Ivnik et al. (1992) Lezak (1995) Spreen and Strauss (1991) Tuokko and Hadjistavropolous (1998)
	California Verbal Learning Test (CVLT)	Similar to AVLT, but stimuli organized in different semantic categories. This allows quantification of clustering strategy used.	Delis, Kramer, Kaplan, and Ober (1987) Lezak (1995) Spreen and Strauss (1991) Tuokko and Hadjistavropolous (1998)
	Hopkins Verbal Learning Test (HVLT; Brandt, 1991)	Similar to AVLT, but uses only 3 trials and 12 words.	Lezak (1995)

	Test	Description	References
	CERAD Verbal Learning Test	Similar to AVLT but uses on 10 words on three trials with recall and recognition trials.	Lezak (1995)
Prose (story) recall	Logical Memory (WMS-III)	Assesses ability to remember details of a story. Immediate and delayed recall condition.	Tuokko and Hadjistavropolous (1998) Spreen and Strauss (1991) Lezak (1995)
Associative learning	Verbal Paired Associates (WMS-III)	Assess differential learning of high and low frequency associations. Also allows for assessment of delayed recall of word pairs.	Lezak (1995) Spreen and Strauss (1991) Tuokko and Hadjistavropolous (1998)
Immediate recall span	Corsi blocks	Spatial analog to digit span test (and versions now included in WAIS–NI and WMS–III). Forward condition can support inferences about immediate memory or attention, whereas backward span can provide a measure of working memory.	Lezak (1995)
Learning nonverbal information	Benton Visual Retention Test (Benton, 1974)	Memory for geometric designs. Good neuropsychological validity. Supports inferences about learning visual material (although stimuli can be verbally described easily).	Lezak (1995) Spreen and Strauss (1991) Tuokko and Hadjistavropolous (1998)

(Continued)

Table 8.3. Neuropsychological Tests Appropriate for the Assessment of Memory Function in Older People *(Continued)*

Memory ability	Neuropsychological test	Brief description	References to normative data for older people
	Visual information		
	Visual Reproduction Subtest (WMS–III)	Assesses recall of simple figures. Has immediate and delayed recall trial.	Tuokko and Hadjistavropolous (1998) Spreen and Strauss (1991) Lezak (1995)
	Face Memory Test	Assesses recognition memory for 50 faces. Encoding of information ensured by having individuals rating each face as pleasant or unpleasant.	Lezak (1995) Warrington (1996)
	Rey–Osterrieth Complex Figure	Assesses immediate and delayed recall of complex spatial arrangement. Because the individual copies the figure before memory trials, the contribution of constructional and organizational skills to memory recall can be considered.	Lezak (1995) Spreen and Strauss (1991) Tuokko and Hadjistavropolous (1998)

Batteries		
WMS–III	Includes 13 subtests and delivers measures of general memory, attention/concentration, verbal memory and visual memory. Many tests provide both immediate and delayed recall trials. Also includes cued recall or recognition trials.	Lezak (1995) Spreen and Strauss (1991) Tuokko and Hadjistavropolous (1998) Weschler (1995)
Rivermead Behavioural Memory Test	Designed so that tasks resemble everyday situations where memory slips occur (remembering a name, appointment, posting a letter).	Wilson, Cockburn, and Badderly (1992)

Note. WMS–III = Wechsler Memory Scale—III; CERAD = Consortium to Develop a Registry for Alzheimer's Disease; WAIS–NI = Wechsler Adult Intelligence Scale as a Neuropsychological Instrument.

XI. TREATMENTS

There are no currently accepted treatments for age-related cognitive decline. Systemic or medical diseases have their own therapy, with secondary cognitive impairment sometimes resolving, for example, with thyroid hormone replacement for hypothyroidism or steroid therapy for Hashimoto's thyroiditis. Psychiatric conditions, including depression, are treatable, and recognition of the typical patterns of attentional memory impairment may provide further weight for a therapeutic trial of antidepressants. Some primary neurological conditions may also be treated, such as HIV infection with retroviral therapy, but in general, structural damage is usually associated with permanent impairment. Nevertheless, in some conditions, such as vascular cognitive impairment, detection should lead to measures designed to prevent further lesions.

If intrinsic neurodegenerative disease is considered causal, with normal imaging and predominantly mnestic impairment, then it is likely that potentially positive results of trials of therapeutic agents currently in use for AD may be reported by the time that this volume is in print. This may lead to a change in the use of such drugs (e.g., cholinesterase inhibitors, memantine) or other putative disease-modifying agents (e.g., metal chelators, antioxidants, amyloid vaccines) for MCI. If efficacy can be demonstrated, it is clear that earlier detection of decline with earlier instigation of treatment offers the most hope for arrest of decline and reduction of quality of life.

XII. CONCLUSION

As this chapter indicates, the recognition and classification of memory and cognitive impairment in nondemented older individuals presents the neuropsychologist with many challenges. Furthermore, because of the enormous societal and individual burden associated with neurodegenerative diseases generally, and Alzheimer's disease specifically, scientific research into these areas continues to increase rapidly. This research also gives rise to new technologies that may assist in identifying the etiology of memory or cognitive impairment in patients. These include new neuropsychological tests as well as new methods for the application of existing tests. However, they also include genetic, psychopharmcologic, and neuroimaging technologies as well as methods that integrate neuropsychological, clinical, and biological information to assist with diagnosis. In this rapidly changing environment, the neuropsychologist plays an important and central role in identifying and classifying cognitive dysfunction in patients, in integrating their opinion with information from the various neuroscientific investigations, and in communicating this information to patients, their caregivers and other clinicians.

BIBLIOGRAPHY

American Psychiatric Association. (1994). *Diagnostic and statistical manual of mental disorders* (4th ed.). Washington, DC: Author.

American Psychological Association. (1998). Guidelines for the evaluation of dementia and age-related cognitive decline. *American Psychologist, 53,* 1298–1303.

Benton, A. L. (1974). *The Revised Visual Reproduction Test* (4th ed.). New York: Psychological Corporation.

Brandt, J. (1991). The Hopkins Verbal Learning Test: Development of a new memory test with six equivalent forms. *The Clinical Neuropsychologist 5,* 125–142.

Buschke, H. (1973). Selective reminding for analysis of memory and learning. *Journal of Verbal Learning and Verbal Behavior, 12,* 543–550.

Collie, A., & Maruff, P. (2002). An analysis of systems of classifying mild cognitive impairment in older people. *Australian and New Zealand Journal of Psychiatry, 36,* 133–140.

Collie, A., Maruff, P., & Currie, J. (2002). Characterisation of mild cognitive impairment. *Journal of Clinical and Experimental Neuropsychology, 24,* 720–733.

Delis, D. C., Kramer, J. H., Kaplan, E., & Ober, B. A. (1987). *The California Verbal Learning Test.* New York: Psychological Corporation.

Filit, H. M., Butler, R. N., O'Connel, A. W., Albert, M. S., Birren, J. E., Cotman, C. W., et al. (2002). Achieving and maintaining cognitive vitality with aging. *Proceedings of the Mayo Clinic, 77,* 681–696.

Graham, J. E., Rockwood, K., Beattie, B. L., Eastwood, R., Gauthier, S., Tuokko, H., & McDowell, I. (1997). Prevalence and severity of cognitive impairment with and without dementia in an elderly population. *Lancet, 349,* 1793–1796.

Gutierrez, R., Atkinson, J. H., & Grant, I. (1993). Mild neurocognitive disorder: Needed addition to the nosology of cognitive impairment (organic mental) disorders. *Journal of Neuropsychiatry and Clinical Neurosciences, 5,* 161–177.

Harris, M. E., Ivnik, R. J., & Smith, G. E. (2002). Mayo's Older Americans Normative Studies: Expanded AVLT recognition trial norms for ages 57 to 98. *Journal of Clinical and Experimental Neuropsychology, 24,* 214–220.

Ivnik, R. J., Malec, J. F., Tangalos, E. G., Petersen, R. C, Kokmen, E., & Kurland, L. T. (1992). Mayo's Older American Normative Studies: Updated AVLT norms for ages 55 years and older. *Psychological Assessment, 2,* 304–312.

Lezak, M. D. (1995). *Neuropsychological assessment* (3rd ed.). Oxford, England: Oxford University Press.

Petersen, R. C., Doody, R., Kurz, A., Mohs, R. C., Morris, J. C., Rabins, P. V., et al. (2001). Current concepts in mild cognitive impairment. *Archives of Neurology, 58,* 1985–1992.

Petersen, R. C., Stevens, J., Ganguli, M., Tangalos, E. G., Cummings, J., & DeKosky, S. T. (2001). Practice parameter: Early detection of dementia: Mild cognitive impairment. *Neurology, 56,* 1133–1142.

Reisberg, B., Ferris, S. H., de Leon, M. J., & Crook, T. (1982). The Global Deterioration Scale for assessment of primary degenerative dementia. *American Journal of Psychiatry, 139,* 1136–1139.

Salthouse, T. A. (2001). General and specific age-related influences on neuropsychological variables. In F. Boller & S. Cappa (Eds.), *Handbook of neuropsychology: Vol. 6. Aging and dementia.* London: Elsevier.

Spreen, O., & Strauss, E. (1991). *A compendium of neuropsychological tests: Administration norms and commentary* (2nd ed.). New York: Oxford University Press.

Tuokko, H., & Hadjistavropolous, T. (1998). *An assessment guide to geriatric neuropsychology.* Mahwah, NJ: Erlbaum.

Warrington, E. K. (1996). *The Camden Memory Test Battery.* Hove, England: Psychology Press.

Wechsler, D. (1985). *The Wechsler Memory Scale—Revised.* New York: Psychological Corporation.

Wilson, B. A., Cockburn, J., & Badderly, A. D. (1995). *The Rivermead Behavioural Memory Test (RMBT).* Bury St. Edmunds, England: Thames Valley Test Company.

Wong, T. M., Strickland, T. L., Fletcher-Janzen, E., Ardila, A., & Reynolds, C. R. (2000). Theoretical and practical issues in the neuropsychological assessment and treatment of culturally dissimilar patients. In E. Fletcher-Janzen, T. L. Strickland, & C. R. Reynolds (Eds.), *Handbook of cross-cultural neuropsychology* (pp. 3–18). New York: Kluwer Academic/Plenum.

World Health Organization. (1992). *International statistical classification of diseases and related health problems* (10th revision). Geneva, Switzerland: Author.

depressive episode (referred to as late-onset depression) may have a different etiology or presentation from those with an earlier age of onset, LLD is typically defined independent of age of onset, and this is the definition we use here.

LLD frequently manifests as physical symptoms and is often underrecognized, misdiagnosed, and undertreated. Greater severity of LLD aggravates existing medical conditions, predisposes to other serious illnesses, and is associated with functional disability. Major depression is a significant predictor of suicide in older adults, particularly among older men. As a result of its association with significant morbidity and mortality, LLD is a serious public health concern.

LLD appears to be more recurrent and more chronic than is depression in younger patients. The incidence of major depression is much higher in women among younger individuals, whereas this gender difference in incidence is greatly reduced in late life. Although depressed mood is a core symptom of depression, elderly depressed patients exhibit certain symptoms more frequently than younger depressed patients, including hypochondriasis, difficulties with sleep, reduced appetite, and fatigue. These somatic complaints are less useful indicators of depression in elderly people than in young adults, because they are often manifestations of the normal aging process or the comorbid illnesses so common in this population. However, Blazer, Hays, Fillenbaum, and Gold (1997) suggested that when such illnesses are taken into consideration, elderly depressed patients have similar symptom profiles to younger adults. Several measures of depressive symptomatology for older patients, such as the Geriatric Depression Scale, have been developed to exclude questions pertaining to somatic complaints, focusing instead on the worries of older adults and how they interpret their quality of life (O'Hara & Yesavage, 2002).

A key feature of LLD is the presence of complaints regarding decline in cognition in general and memory in particular. Indeed, an increasing number of studies have documented the presence of significant levels of objective cognitive impairment in many of these patients, ranging from mild to more disabling levels of impairment. Cognitive deficits in older adults with depression appear to have significant clinical consequences and have been associated with increased rates of relapse, disability, and poorer response to antidepressant treatment. Some studies have identified deficits in specific cognitive domains (e.g., executive function), and although recent studies suggest that therapeutic approaches to LLD may partially ameliorate the cognitive deficits associated with this disorder, much impairment persists after treatment (Butters et al., 2000). The more consistent observation of cognitive deficits in older depressed patients has led some investigators to suggest that LLD is a distinct syndrome from depression in younger patients, especially in those with late-onset depression (i.e., first onset at or after age 60). Others argue that the cognitive impairments observed in many depressed patients are simply exacerbated with increasing age. These issues remain unanswered, but overall the data suggest that appropriate neuropsychological characterization of patients with LLD may have significant implications for diagnosis, prognosis, and treatment.

B. Neuropsychological Features

In recent years there has been a significant increase in the number of studies investigating neuropsychological functioning in LLD. The following cognitive functions have been observed to be negatively affected in patients with LLD: executive function, psychomotor speed, speed-of-information processing, attention and inhibition, working and verbal memory, expressive language, and visuospatial ability (Butters et al., 2004; Nebes et al., 2000). However, it is important to note that deficits in all these domains are not observed in all studies, and for every study that found a deficit in a particular cognitive domain, at least one investigation has failed to find impairment in that same domain. The inconsistencies among findings most likely reflect the extensive variability among these studies in terms of patient characteristics, methodological approaches, and neuropsychological instruments. A broad range of patient characteristics may negatively affect neuropsychological performance in LLD, including later onset of depression, greater severity of depression, medical comorbidity, and presence of preexisting cognitive impairment (Reynolds, Alexopolous, Katz, & Lebowitz, 2001). Executive function deficits may be particularly related to late-onset depression and vegetative symptoms. Increased age also may be a primary moderator of the relationship between depression and cognition.

To date, only a few longitudinal studies of LLD exist, and the interpretation of their results is limited by small sample sizes and lack of adequate control participants. Though these few studies have shown only modest, if any, cognitive decline over time in LLD, all show that subgroups of patients with more severe cognitive impairment or neuroimaging correlates (e.g., the presence of white matter lesions) were at risk for developing dementia (Jorm, 2001; Nussbaum, 1997). The relationship between depression and the development of dementia is both complex and controversial, and we elaborate on this issue later, in Section IV.A.

Several studies have suggested that certain cognitive impairments in LLD are associated with negative clinical outcomes. Deficits in executive function have been associated with increased relapse and recurrence rates (Alexopoulos et al., 2000). More severe memory problems have been associated with increased risk of dementia and poorer antidepressant response. Similarly, LLD patients with more executive dysfunction have exhibited poorer response to antidepressant treatments (Alexopoulos, 2003). Overall, these studies suggest that patients with LLD who also exhibit executive dysfunction may be at particular risk for negative clinical outcomes.

C. Neurophysiological Correlates

Neuroimaging studies using computed tomography (CT), magnetic resonance imaging (MRI), single photon emission computed tomography (SPECT), and positron emission tomography (PET) have reported a variety of neuropathological features associated with LLD, including impaired dopaminergic and serotonergic function; increased glucocorticoids; reduced hippocampal, caudate, amygdala, and orbitofrontal cortex volume; white matter lesions and hyperintensities; and anterior cingulate deficits (Steffens, Bosworth, Provenzale, & MacFall, 2002). What remains unclear is whether these neuropathological features are correlated rather than causal in their relationship to LLD. Investigations suggest that these neuropathological features underlie the neuropsychological deficits observed in LLD.

1. WHITE MATTER HYPERINTENSITIES

An increasing number of studies have documented the presence of significant numbers of white matter hyperintensities (WMHs) in LLD. WMHs are indicative of ischemic small vessel disease. Increased presence of deep white matter lesions in LLD has been associated with increased mortality (Levy et al., 2003), inability to sustain remission (Taylor et al., 2003), impairments in motivation and concentration (Nebes et al., 2001), and poorer cognitive performance (Nebes et al., 2002). The colocalization of atrophy and white matter lesions, the fact that both relate to advanced age and to factors predisposing to vascular disease, and the similarity of the location of lesions in poststroke depression have led to the hypothesis that LLD constitutes a distinct syndrome, with a vascular component underlying both the depressed mood and the cognitive impairments (Drevets, 1994). Further support for the vascular hypothesis of LLD is that among healthy elderly people the relationship between white matter lesions and depressive symptoms is particularly strong in individuals with the apolipoprotein (ApoE) e4 allele (Nebes et al., 2001). ApoE is a cholesterol carrier that is associated with increased risk of developing Alzheimer's disease.

Some studies have also observed an association between increased subcortical gray matter lesions and significant reductions in orbitofrontal cortex volume (Lee, Ogle, & Sapolsky, 2002). Steffens, Taylor, and Krishnan (2003) found presence of the ApoE e4 allele, increased age, and white matter lesion volume all to be associated with subcortical gray matter lesion volume. These findings implicate cerebrovascular burden in LLD.

2. REDUCED FRONTAL AND HIPPOCAMPAL VOLUME

There is substantial evidence for the existence of structural changes in the brain with depression. Several structural MRI studies have observed reductions in orbitofrontal cortex in LLD (see Ballmaier et al., 2004). In addition, regional cerebral blood flow (rCBF) studies have also observed reduced rCBF in frontal regions of the brain in LLD (Oda et al., 2003). Many suggest that the observed reductions in frontal and prefrontal cortex and metabolism in LLD account for the deficits in executive function and attention that often accompany this disorder.

In addition to prefrontal and orbitofrontal deficits, there is some evidence that the temporal lobes, and hippocampal volume in particular, may also be reduced in LLD. LLD patients with smaller hippocampal volume at baseline appear less likely to achieve remission following antidepressant treatment (Hsieh et al., 2002), and antidepressant treatment may actually protect against hippocampal volume loss (Sheline, Gado, & Kraemer, 2003). Hippocampal atrophy may account for the memory deficits observed in LLD. Indeed, there is a strong association between lower hippocampal volume and later onset of the first episode of depression, suggesting that these patients may be experiencing as yet undeclared Alzheimer's disease (Steffens et al., 2002). Other investigators (Bell-McGinty et al., 2002) have found that the lifetime duration of depression (either as years since first episode or as total number of days spent depressed) is most closely associated with diminished hippocampal volume. One potential explanation for this association is that the reductions in hippocampal volume accrue over time, from depression-associated hypothalamic-pituitary-adrenal (HPA) axis dysfunction.

3. HYPOTHALAMIC-PITUITARY-ADRENAL
AXIS DYSFUNCTION

Neuroendocrinological studies of elderly depressed people reveal a variety of HPA-axis impairments similar to those of younger depressed people (Meyers et al., 1993). Dysfunction may occur at several sites throughout the HPA axis. Increased levels of corticosteroid-releasing factor have been observed in the cerebrospinal fluid of patients with depression. Increased production of adrenocorticotrophic hormone has also been observed, which in turn may contribute to the increased levels of cortisol that are associated with depression. Several recent studies have found increased cortisol levels in nondepressed older adults without dementia to be associated with reduced hippocampal volume and with impaired memory function (e.g., Kalmijn et al., 1998). This has led investigators to suggest that the cognitive deficits observed in LLD, particularly in memory function, may in part be mediated by impairments in the HPA axis that accompany this disorder. Still others suggest that the involvement of cortisol in modulating the serotonin 1A receptors may indicate that HPA-axis impairment plays a more integral role in the development of LLD (Maines, Keck, Smith, & Lakoski, 1999).

4. NEUROTRANSMITTER DEFICITS

Postmortem studies indicate that there is an age-related decrease in serotonin 1A and 2A receptor density and binding potential, suggesting that normal aging alone increases the risk of developing depression. Support for such age-related changes in the serotonergic system comes from additional in vivo studies that have observed that as age increases there are decreases in receptor 2A binding in men and women and decreases in 1A receptor binding in men, although the latter effect was not observed in women (Meltzer et al., 1999). The recent observation that selective serotonin reuptake inhibitors (SSRIs) may enhance cognition in healthy nondepressed adults raises the possibility that impairments in the serotonergic system that contribute to depression may also contribute to the cognitive deficits observed in LLD. Serotonin also has vasoactive properties, and both depression and aging may exert separate, synergistic effects to worsen depression via diminished serotonergic tone and resulting cerebrovasculature dysfunction.

However, the serotonergic system is not the only neurotransmitter system affected by aging. Deficits in the monoaminergic neurotransmitters dopamine and norepinephrine not only have been implicated in depression but also exhibit age-related changes. In addition, dopamine has been implicated in verbal fluency, learning, and attention, and norepinephrine is strongly associated with prefrontal involvement in sustaining and focusing attention. As a result, dual serotonin and norepinephrine reuptake inhibitors may be more effective for improving cognitive deficits in LLD. O'Hara et al. (2005) found that following 8 weeks of treatment, a dual serotonin and norepinephrine reuptake inhibitor resulted in greater improvement in attentional processes in LLD than were seen following treatment with a standard SSRI.

It is important to note that older patients can be more sensitive to antidepressant side effects and that side effects may be more severe. SSRIs appear to have milder side effects than tricyclic antidepressants (TCAs). However, SSRI side effects are still noted more frequently in older patients and include extrapyramidal effects, apathy, anorexia, and possible risk of falls. Older patients respond more slowly to antidepressant medications than younger depressed patients. Although underdosing is a major cause of inadequate response in LLD, we recommend starting with an antidepressant dose of half or less that for younger adults in frail elderly patients, particularly in those with comorbid illnesses. Titration should occur slowly to fully and appropriately assess the side effect–benefit ratio.

D. Theoretical Perspectives

The prominent deficits in executive function and attention in combination with the various neuropathological characteristics of LLD have led to several theories related to the underpinnings of LLD.

1. DEPRESSION–EXECUTIVE DYSFUNCTION SYNDROME

Alexopoulos et al. (2000) proposed the depression–executive dysfunction (DED) syndrome of LLD. They argued that frontostriatal dysfunction contributes both to the development of LLD and to the executive dysfunction that frequently accompanies LLD. In addition to executive dysfunction, Alexopoulos et al. suggested that elderly depressed patients with DED have reduced verbal fluency, impaired naming abilities, paranoia, psychomotor retardation, and loss of interest in activities. They also suggested that patients with DED have poorer treatment response and increased relapse and recurrence rates (Alexopoulos, 2003).

2. REDUCED RESOURCES HYPOTHESIS

The reduced information-processing resources hypothesis proposed by Nebes et al. (2000) and followed by Butters et al. (2004) suggests that processing resources are particularly reduced in older depressed patients and, in turn, mediate neuropsychological impairments in other cognitive domains. Nebes et al. noted that reductions in processing resources appeared to persist following remission of depression and that resource decrements may be a trait marker for LLD.

3. VASCULAR DEPRESSION HYPOTHESIS

Alexopoulos et al. (1997) theorized that a subset of LLD patients may have a distinct syndrome known as **vascular depression**. Vascular depression is characterized by presence of significant cerebrovascular burden as evidenced by subcortical vascular disease, is more likely to occur in LLD patients who have the ApoE e4 allele, is associated with broad-based cognitive impairment, and manifests clinically as loss of motivation and interest but not sad mood, guilt, or worthlessness.

4. HPA-AXIS HYPOTHESES

Several investigators (Lee et al., 2002) have theorized that cumulative exposure to the stress associated with depression results in hypersecretion of cortisol, which in turn results in neuronal death within the hippocampus. Although this explanation may account for the presence of a significant memory deficit in a subgroup of patients with LLD, reduced hippocampal volume has not been associated with the additional cognitive impairments, particularly the executive function deficits that are often observed in this illness.

II. CLINICAL INTERVENTIONS FOR LATE-LIFE DEPRESSION

A. Antidepressant Medications

Although some studies suggest that geriatric depression carries a poorer prognosis than midlife depression, recent literature indicates that when adequately treated, older patients can achieve full response (Reynolds et al., 2001). For patients with geriatric depression, the prognosis is more dependent on medical burden, physical disability, and lack of social support. The timely treatment of depression in elderly people can facilitate partial or complete remission, enhance overall well-being, and minimize cognitive dysfunction. Recent studies investigating the relationship of treatment to cognitive performance in LLD have yielded promising but varied results. However, complexities of depression as a disease, the variability among the methodologies and measures used, and the different antidepressant treatments used all contribute to the variability among studies.

Butters et al. (2000) investigated 45 depressed elderly adults without dementia who achieved remission after 12 weeks with either nortriptyline or paroxetine treatment and observed a modest improvement in cognition following treatment. Among patients with cognitive impairment concomitant with depression, performance on the Mattis Dementia Rating Scale measures of conceptualization and initiation/perseveration rose significantly, when compared with patients with normal cognition during the depressive episode. However, despite the improvement following treatment, the overall level of cognitive functioning in this subgroup remained mildly impaired, especially in the memory and initiation/perseveration domains. Thus, although cognition may improve with treatment for many LLD patients, a proportion of LLD patients show persisting cognitive deficits that are unaffected by improved mood.

Some antidepressant medications may impair cognition, particularly in LLD. TCAs, for example, have anticholinergic properties that may cause cognitive dysfunction, delirium, constipation, dry mouth, blurred vision, and increased intraocular pressure (in cases of preexisting glaucoma). Several reviews suggest that in spite of their efficacy in the treatment of LLD, TCAs have so many undesirable effects that their use in the treatment of elderly patients is limited. But even among the SSRIs, certain antidepressant treatments have been observed to result in impairments in memory and visuospatial ability (O'Hara et al., 2005). In general, antidepressants with anticholinergic, sedative, or orthostatic side effects should not be a first choice for elderly depressed patients, in part because of their negative impact on cognitive functioning.

Some investigators suggest that the presence of WMH may place a patient with LLD at increased risk for development of delirium or cognitive disorders after treatment with TCAs or electroconvulsive therapy (Drevets, 1994). Still others argue that such neuropathological information may identify those at increased risk of poorer treatment response (Kalayam et al., 1999).

B. Psychotherapy

It has been suggested that psychotherapy aimed at depressive ideation and rehabilitation efforts focused on instrumental activities of daily living (IADLs) might improve the outcome of geriatric depression (Alexopoulos et al., 1996). Impairment in IADLs is significantly associated with advanced age, severity of depression, and medical burden. Anxiety and depressive ideation as well as psychomotor retardation and weight loss are also associated with impairment in IADLs. However, there are specific points that make the application of these techniques very difficult. It is not suitable for patients with severe neurocognitive disorder, psychomotor retardation, or sensory impairment (making communication difficult) to enter demanding psychotherapeutic interventions. Severe symptomatology due to general medical condition, like physiological instability, may also restrict the therapeutic maneuvers or significantly delay the process. There is evidence that intensive integrated pharmacotherapy with psychotherapy may be more effective than the usual standard treatment (Unutzer et al., 2002).

C. Electroconvulsive Therapy

Electroconvulsive therapy (ECT) is often recommended for geriatric depression, and in cases in which pharmacotherapies have not provided relief, it is generally considered safe and is preferable to leaving the patient without treatment. The greatest risk is for patients who have had a stroke; ECT is not recommended for such patients until they are at least 6 months poststroke. The coexistence of an "organic" brain disorder might lead to the development of delirium following ECT, which may last for several weeks. There is a significant body of literature documenting cognitive impairments, particularly in memory function following ECT treatment. Although many of these impairments remit, studies suggest that increased age, elevated cortisol levels, and even presence of the ApoE e4 allele may increase the risk for negative cognitive outcomes.

D. Cognitive Augmentation

As a result of the persistent problems with cognitive function in LLD and the association of these deficits with poorer clinical outcomes, some investigators have suggested that both pharmacological and nonpharmacological augmentation strategies may prove useful for ameliorating the cognitive deficits in LLD (Fava, Ruini, & Sonino, 2003). In this regard, pharmacologic augmentation with agents such as the cholinesterase inhibitors might be more helpful in LLD. Trials to investigate such augmentation techniques are ongoing.

Augmentation strategies might also include memory or cognitive training aimed at enhancing cognitive performance. Some investigators have argued that the effortful processing necessary to implement cognitive training strategies may be particularly impaired in depressed elderly patients. Thus, memory training may have limited benefit for this population. However, others (Scogin & Prohaska, 1993) have stated with regard to older adults that "Memory impairment related to depression is potentially amenable to memory training, especially memory training augmented with treatment for depression" (p. 15). Further, although it may be true that some "internal" memory strategies such as categorization, creation of mnemonics, novel interacting images (for more efficient recall of names), and method of loci take practice and effort, "external" memory strategies take less effort, are among the easiest memory techniques to use, can help with organization and self-confidence fairly quickly (decreasing minor memory lapses), and are therefore important for care providers, patients, and families to know about.

External strategies involve the use of physical reminders in one's environment that are prearranged to serve as automatic reminders of what need to be recalled. Three types of physical reminders in particular are recommended (Scogin & Prohaska, 1993):

1. Immediately write things down on a pad, in a "memory" notebook, in a calendar, on a checklist, in an electronic organizer, or on "post-its." Additional external reminders that help with immediate recall also include watches that state the time at the push of a button or "buzz" at preset times, digital voice recorders, and sounding devices.

2. Place reminders in prominent places that are in one's line of sight (e.g., the bathroom mirror, the refrigerator, the back door, next to one's wallet).

3. Associate objects (that we use and lose frequently) with preestablished locations. This helps with objects such as keys, wallets, glasses, and even gifts for family members. The idea here is to first make a list of objects that are frequently misplaced; second, choose a familiar location for each object; and third, practice putting the objects *only* in their designated location.

Specific descriptions of how to teach both external and internal strategies to older adults are included in many books and articles in the literature. A few (but certainly not all) are included here for the reader's use: Crook and Allison's (1992)

How to Remember Names, Hill, Bäckman, and Neely's (2000) *Cognitive Rehabilitation in Old Age*, and Scogin and Prohaska's (1993) *Aiding Older Adults With Memory Complaints*. It is important to note that a comprehensive treatment approach to LLD, combining pharmacological treatments with psychological interventions, and psychological and social support, can achieve a response rate of up to 90% (Gottfries, 2001).

III. NEUROPSYCHOLOGICAL ASSESSMENT OF PATIENTS WITH LATE-LIFE DEPRESSION

A. Clinical Assessment of Depression in Older Adults

For geriatric neuropsychologists, memory problems represent the most common presenting complaint. However, memory problems are not restricted to purely cognitive disorders and commonly exist in LLD. As a result, the most frequent referral questions in geriatric neuropsychology involve clarifying whether cognitive deficits are attributable to dementia, to depression, or to both (Twamley & Bondi, 2004). Given the large number of reports published in recent years characterizing the most common forms of dementia, the ability to discriminate between cases of relatively "pure" depression (i.e., without significant accompanying cognitive impairment) and mild dementia has significantly increased. Moreover, there is a growing literature suggesting that, by and large, cognitive impairments noted in some LLD patients persist into remission. Therefore, patients with both significant cognitive impairment and affective disturbance nearly always have two co-occurring (and sometimes etiologically related) disorders: depression and a neurodegenerative disorder. Given these points, the traditional "depression versus dementia" conundrum has become something of a false dichotomy. Nevertheless, when conducting a neuropsychological evaluation on an older adult, both depression and cognition should be assessed.

Differentiating depression and dementia is complicated by the symptom overlap between them: for example, changes in attention and concentration, memory, behavior, sleep pattern, and energy level (Twamley & Bondi, 2004). The risk of cognitive dysfunction both increases with age and may be greater in LLD (Steffens et al., 2003). As noted earlier (Section B), cognitive impairments in LLD have most consistently been found to affect executive functioning, memory, visuospatial ability, and speed of processing (Butters et al., 2004). At the same time, depression coexists with dementia in 20% to 30% of documented dementia cases (Kaszniak & Scogin, 1995). For this reason, it is important to use measures with established validity and reliability in assessing depression in older adults—and in assessing those who have cognitive impairment in particular.

1. SELF-REPORT CHECKLIST MEASURES

Multiple measures are available for the detection of depression in older adults. The focus of research over the past two decades has centered on the utility of brief self-report checklist measures (Scogin, 1994). There is broad consensus in the literature (Kaszniak & Scogin, 1995; Lichtenberg, 1994; Scogin, 1994) that two measures in particular are clinically useful: the Geriatric Depression Scale (GDS; Yesavage et al., 1983) and the Beck Depression Inventory (BDI/BDI–II; Beck, 1987). Both are brief (5–10 minute administration time) and easily scored.

2. THE GERIATRIC DEPRESSION SCALE

The GDS (Yesavage et al., 1983) was developed with a sample of older adults and is the easiest measure to administer, especially with patients who have cognitive impairments. The long form (30 items) has the best combined sensitivity and specificity for outpatients older than age 55 (e.g., 96% using a cutoff of 10; Olin, Schneider, Eaton, Zemansky, & Pollack, 1992), although a short form (15 items) is also available. One shortcoming is that high-functioning patients often find the yes/no format too limiting. Notably, somatic symptoms are not included on the GDS as they were found not diagnostic of LLD.

3. THE BECK DEPRESSION INVENTORY

The BDI (now BDI–II) was developed on a younger sample but has been used widely with older adults by both researchers and clinicians. However, the rating system is often too complex for use with patients who are cognitively compromised. Items 15–21 involve somatic symptoms that have been found typical of normal aging rather than indicative of geriatric depression per se (Bolla-Wilson & Blecker, 1989). These researchers have suggested only using Items 1–14 with older adults, with a cutoff score of 5. An excellent review of the strengths and weaknesses of the GDS, BDI, and other checklist measures may be found in Scogin (1994, pp. 66–71).

One caveat with regard to the use of these checklist measures is that they only reflect as much as a patient is willing to divulge. Another limitation is that they are reportedly not effective in identifying either dysthymia or a lifetime history of depression (Scogin, 1994). They are best used as guides for further assessment that ideally includes an in-depth clinical interview, use of an interview-based assessment measure, collateral information (including use of an observational rating scale such as the Cornell Scale for Depression in Dementia; Alexopoulos, Abrams, Young, & Shamoian, 1988, described below), or additional testing with actuarial measures such as the Minnesota Multiphasic Personality Inventory—2 (MMPI–2; Butcher, Dahlstrom, Graham, Tellegan, & Kasmmer, 1989) and Millon Clinical Multiaxial Inventory—III (MCMI–III; Millon, 1993) that have validity or specific scales reflecting depressive tendencies.

4. INTERVIEW-BASED MEASURES

Many interview-based measures are available. Two well-known structured measures are based on *DSM–IV* criteria: the Structured Clinical Interview for DSM–IV (SCID) and the Diagnostic Interview Schedule (DIS). Their drawback is that they take longer to administer than is realistic in everyday clinical practice.

One interview-based measure that has been noted in the literature as both economical and useful in estimating severity of depression over time and assessing cognitively impaired or hospitalized patients is the Hamilton Rating Scale for Depression (HRSD; Hamilton, 1967). Although the HRSD has been noted to have better sensitivity and specificity than self-report checklist measures in identifying depression in medical inpatients (Rapp, Smith, & Britt, 1990), this was not true with regard to community-dwelling older adults (Stukenberg, Dura, & Kiecolt-Glaser, 1990). Further, it takes a lot of practice and effort to administer the HRSD reliably (although the 17-item version has interview questions on the form, which helps). It also emphasizes somatic symptoms (which have been found to be more typical of normal aging than diagnostic of LLD). Some clinicians screen initially with one of the checklist measures. If a patient scores above the cutoff, the HRSD can then be used to confirm or provide a quantitative severity rating.

5. COLLATERAL INFORMATION

Collateral information should be included in the assessment process whenever possible. This ideally includes information from family or health care providers relevant to (a) course and history of symptoms; (b) daily functioning; (c) medical, psychiatric, and neurological history; and (d) recent imaging studies. In the case of patients for whom self-report is not feasible because of cognitive impairment or hospitalization, there are observational measures for care providers that target depressive symptoms in particular. One such measure is the Cornell Scale for Depression in Dementia (CSDD; Alexopoulos et al., 1988). The CSDD asks caregivers to rate symptoms in the following areas: mood, behavioral disturbance, somatic signs, cyclic functions, and ideation (suicidality, self-esteem, pessimism, and delusions). A proviso noted in the literature (La Rue, Watson, & Plotkin, 1992) is that lay caregivers such as relatives (and especially relatives who themselves are depressed or anxious) tend to rate patients as having more problems with mood or affect than do professional caregivers such as nursing staff.

6. ACTUARIAL MEASURES

The MMPI–2 (Butcher et al., 1989) has been widely used with older adults and has specific scales and subscales reflecting depressive tendencies: for example, the *D* Scale, Subtle and Obvious measures, Harris–Lingoes Scales, and the Content Scales. These scales facilitate differential diagnostic considerations that the briefer screens cannot provide. However, for cognitively impaired or hospitalized older adults, administration of the MMPI–2 is not realistic (90 minutes is a typical administration time). One alternative is to administer only the first 370 items, which contain Scales 1–10, the Obvious/Subtle Items, and the Harris–Lingoes Scales. In this regard it should be noted that even if the *D* Scale is normal, the Obvious/Subtle Items are important as the "subtle" items reflect the vegetative signs of depression that tend to be endorsed by more mildly depressed individuals, whereas severely depressed patients tend to endorse the "obvious" items.

7. THE MILLON CLINICAL MULTIAXIAL INVENTORY—III

The MCMI–III (Millon, 1993) contains both depression and dysthymia subscales, can be answered in about 30 minutes, and is more easily administered to older patients. However, its strength is with Axis II rather than with Axis I diagnoses. Depending on the older adult in question, administration of the MCMI–III may not be realistic.

B. Clinical Assessment of Cognitive Domains in LLD

Neuropsychological test findings (in moderately to severely depressed older adults with no distinction between early and late onset) have been reported in the geriatric neuropsychological literature (La Rue, 1992, p. 280) as follows: typical presentation: mild memory deficits, mild to moderate visuospatial deficits, and "reduced" abstraction and executive functions; contraindications: mild or questionable depressive symptoms, deficits in receptive language (e.g., comprehension), and severe memory deficit.

In the more recent literature, decrements in LLD have been noted in the following cognitive domains (Butters et al., 2004; Reynolds, 1992; Twamley & Bondi, 2004).

Most often noted:	Executive functions
	Memory
	Processing speed
	Visuospatial skills
Also noted:	Attention
	Expressive language (verbal fluency, naming)

It is interesting to note that a meta-analysis of 22 studies comprising adults age 34 to 72 with major depressive disorder (Zakzanis, Leach, & Kaplan, 1999) found the greatest decrements on tasks assessing the following: delayed recall of episodic memory, verbal fluency, and attention. This is somewhat different from the findings noted previously for LLD.

Keeping all of this in mind, Table 9.1 contains cognitive domains and suggested measures for use in the assessment of individuals with LLD. The list is by no means inclusive—but the measures presented are normed, standardized, reliable, and valid for use with older adults. The list also includes some of the Wechsler Adult Intelligence Scale—III (WAIS–III) subtests and list-learning measures that have been noted (La Rue, 1992; Zakzanis et al., 1999) as informative when assessing LLD patients.

More specifically, on list-learning tests, depressed patients typically show mild to moderate impairment in free recall but a disproportionate improvement on recognition recall with normal or slightly elevated false positives. They also benefit from cuing and show a low intrusion rate (in the normal range). In contrast, Alzheimer's disease patients show a rapid forgetting rate, extremely elevated false-positive errors on recognition testing, and a high rate of intrusions, with particular elevations on cued trials.

Table 9.1. Neuropsychological Assessment of Late Life Depression by Cognitive Domain

Cognitive domain	Tests suggested for clinical use
Attention/ working memory	CVLT–II, Trial I Stroop Color Word Test Trail Making Test: Trails A or Conditions 2 and 3, D-KEFS WAIS–III: Digit Span, Coding WMS–III: Digit Span, Spatial Span
Visuospatial skills	BVRT (Copy) Clock Drawing Judgment of Line Orientation Rey Complex Figure Test-copy WAIS–III or WASI: Block Design, Matrix Reasoning
Language (verbal fluency in particular)	Animal Fluency Boston Naming Test COWAT Token Test
Memory (recall and recognition)	CVLT–II Serial Digit Learning WMS–III: Faces I and II, Family Pictures I and II, Logical Memory I and II BVRT (Memory and Copy)
Executive functions	DKEFS: Tower Test, Trail Making Test, Verbal Fluency Stroop Color Word Test Trails A and B Wisconsin Card Sorting Test (either the standard or 64-card version)
Psychomotor speed	D-KEFS: Trail Making Test (Condition 5) Symbol Digit Modalities WAIS–III: Coding Grooved Pegboard
Mood	Beck Depression Inventory—II Beck Anxiety Inventory Geriatric Depression Scale Hamilton Rating Scale for Depression State Trait Anxiety Inventory

Note. CVLT–II = California Verbal Learning Test, Second Edition; D-KEFS = Delis–Kaplan Executive Functioning System; WAIS–III = Wechsler Adult Intelligence Scale—III; WMS–III = Wechsler Memory Scale—III; BVRT = Benton Visual Retention Test; WASI = Wechsler Abbreviated Scale of Intelligence; COWAT = Controlled Oral Word Association Test.

C. Differential Diagnosis

1. DEMENTIA

As noted earlier, the overlap in symptoms as well as the comorbidity of dementia and depression can make differential diagnosis difficult at best and frequently irrelevant. Nevertheless, the neuropsychological literature (Kaszniak & Christenson, 1994, Kaszniak & Scogin, 1995) has delineated differences in (a) clinical course and history, (b) clinical behavior, and (c) test findings that can help in differential diagnosis of relatively pure cases of depression or dementia. These features continue to be cited in the most recent literature on differential diagnosis (Twamley & Bondi, 2004). The following tables are taken directly from the literature because of their very real utility in differentiating both dementia in general (Table 9.2) and Alzheimer's disease in particular (Table 9.3) from depression.

2. SUBCORTICAL DEMENTIA

A leading source of misdiagnosis in distinguishing between LLD and subcortical dementia is their similar pattern of performance on some cognitive tests: For example, both show a relative sparing on tasks of recognition memory, naming, and visual perception (Welsh-Bohmer, 2001). Further, in cases of subcortical dementia, psychomotor retardation often leads to the misdiagnosis of depression. These realities point to the importance of including measures of mood in any battery of neuropsychological tests administered to an older adult. It should also be noted that subcortical cases manifest depression more often than cortical cases. This may be partly due to the increased insight subcortical patients have about their condition in comparison with AD patients (Huber & Paulson, 1985). It may also be due to what Steffens et al. (2003, p. 1754) described as the "intertwining course" of LLD and cognitive deficits in subcortical ischemic disease (a known risk factor for dementia).

3. ANXIETY AND OTHER PSYCHIATRIC ILLNESSES

About 38% to 58% (Alexopoulos, 1991) of elderly people with major depression also fulfill *DSM–IV* criteria for an anxiety disorder. Many authors have suggested that the presence of anxiety in elderly people should be considered a sign of depression, even in cases that lack true depressive symptomatology (Collins, Katona, & Orrell, 1994). However, it is helpful to screen for anxiety as well as for depression to provide complete information to patients, families, and referring care providers. In this

Table 9.2. Differential Diagnosis of Dementia and Depression

Measure	Depression	Dementia
Clinical course and history	Onset well demarcated	Onset indistinct, insidious
	History short	History long
	Rapidly progressive course	Slow course; early deficits often missed
	Prior psychiatric history or recent crisis uncommon	Prior psychiatric history uncommon
Clinical behavior	Detailed complaints of cognitive dysfunction	Complaints of cognitive loss uncommon
	Put out little effort	Struggle with tasks
	Persistent depression	Apathy with shallow emotions
	Behavior does not reflect cognitive loss	Behavior compatible with cognitive loss
	Rare exacerbation at night	Nocturnal accentuation of dysfunction common
	Common early morning awakening	Variable early morning awakening
	Self-appraisal diminished	Self-appraisal variable
	Intact awareness of deficit	Diminished awareness of deficit
	Mood-congruent delusions	Mood-independent delusions
	Dressing apraxia rare	Dressing apraxia common
	Severe loss of libido	Variable loss of libido
Test findings	Frequent "I don't know" before even trying	Usually will try
	Inconsistent memory loss for recent and remote events	No specific gaps
	Inconsistent performance	Consistently impaired

Table 9.3. Differential Diagnosis of Alzheimer's Disease and Depression

Finding	Depression	Alzheimer's disease
Test findings		
1. Free verbal recall	Variable	Poor
Learning curve	Reduced; U-shaped	Flat
Primacy effect	Reduced	None
Recency effect	Near normal	Impaired
Extra-list errors	Infrequent	Frequent
Don't know errors	Usual	Unusual
Perseveration errors	Uncommon	Common
2. Recognition memory	Relatively intact	Impaired
False-positive errors	Uncommon	Common
3. Semantic organization	Helpful	Unhelpful
4. Prompting	Helpful	Unhelpful
5. Effort in trying tasks	Poor	Good
6. Performance on "automatic" encoding tasks	Intact	Impaired
7. Performance on "effortful" encoding tasks	Impaired	Impaired
8. Performance on tasks of similar difficulty	Variable	Consistent
9. Memory complaint	Extreme	Relatively rare
10. Memory complaint versus memory performance	Overachieves	Underachieves
11. Rate of forgetting	Relatively normal	Rapid
12. Reminders of task directions	Unusual	Needed
Imaging findings		
Cerebral metabolism PET	Bilateral frontal lobe hypometabolism	Bilateral temporoparietal hypometabolism
Cerebral perfusion SPECT	Bilateral frontal lobe hypoperfusion	Bilateral temporoparietal hypoperfusion
MRI	White matter hyperintensities typical in basal ganglia	Cortical atrophy; enlarged sulci; leukoaraiosis
Computerized EEG	Normal	Abnormal

Note. PET = positron emissions tomography; SPECT = single photon emission computed tomography; MRI = magnetic resonance imaging; EEG = electroencephalography.

regard, two checklist measures—the Beck Anxiety Inventory (BAI) and the State–Trait Anxiety Inventory (STAI; Spielberger, Gorush, & Lushene, 1970)—are brief, easy to administer to older adults, and provide a measure of self-perceived anxiety.

4. COMORBID ILLNESSES OR CONDITIONS

There are several potentially lethal diseases that may have depressive or depressive-like symptomatology as their only early manifestations. In most cases it is not true depression but feelings of indifference, apathy, or fatigue instead. Depressed affect is usually absent. Such diseases or conditions include the following: (a) endocrine disorders such as diabetes, hypothyroidism, and hypo/hyperparathyroidism; (b) cancers (especially pancreatic cancer); (c) metabolic disorders such as problems with calcium metabolism; (d) subcortical neurological disorders such as multiple sclerosis (which can exacerbate depression) and early HIV encephalopathy; and (e) menopause. Obviously, the presence of medical conditions that mimic depression must be taken into consideration and ruled out before any psychiatric or cognitive diagnosis can be conferred.

It is also important to be aware of the high prevalence rates of major depression reported in older adults with medical disorders including diabetes, cerebrovascular disease, chronic pulmonary disease, rheumatoid arthritis, and acute myocardial infarction (Watkins et al., 2003). Affective screening is important as depression is often underrecognized—and therefore goes untreated—in these patients.

5. OTHER CONSIDERATIONS

Patients often use alcohol and other substances of abuse to self-medicate their depressive symptoms; this may trigger or exacerbate depression and possibly increase the risk that it will become refractory. It is therefore important to question patients and caregivers regarding substance use history. There are also two brief screens available for use with older adults: the CAGE questionnaire (Fleming, 1995) and the Michigan Alcohol Screening Test (Selzer, 1971).

IV. CONCLUSION

This chapter outlines LLD as a theoretical construct and as a diagnostic entity that has multiple possible neurochemical and functional neurobiological etiologies, and it suggests a variety of treatment options for the clinician. LLD is associated with a number of neuropsychological sequelae, although given the heterogeneity of the disorder and the range of other medical complications seen in elderly people, a specific cognitive profile for LLD remains elusive.

BIBLIOGRAPHY

Alexopoulos, G. S. (1991). Anxiety and depression in the elderly. In C. Salzman & B. Lebowitz (Eds.), *Anxiety in the elderly: Treatment and research* (pp. 63–74). New York: Springer.

Alexopoulos, G. S. (2003). Role of executive function in late-life depression. *Journal of Clinical Psychiatry, 64*(14), 18–23.

Alexopoulos, G. S., Abrams, R. C., Young, R. C., & Shamoian, C. A. (1988). Cornell Scale for Depression in Dementia. *Biological Psychiatry, 23,* 271–284.

Alexopoulos, G. S., Meyers, B. S., Young, R. C., Campbell, S., Silbersweig, D., & Charlson, M. (1997). The "vascular depression" hypothesis. *Archives of General Psychiatry, 54,* 915–922.

Alexopoulos, G. S., Meyers, B. S., Young, R. C., Kalayam, B., Kakuma, T., Gabrielle, M., et al. (2000). Executive dysfunction and long-term outcomes of geriatric depression. *Archives of General Psychiatry, 57,* 285–90.

Alexopoulos, G. S., Vrontou, C., Kakuma, T., Meyers, B. S., Young, R. C., Klausner, E., & Clarkin, J. (1996). Disability in geriatric depression. *American Journal of Psychiatry, 153,* 877–885.

American Psychiatric Association. (1994). *Diagnostic and statistical manual of mental disorders* (4th ed.). Washington, DC: Author.

Ballmaier, M., Toga, A. W., Blanton, R. E., Sowell, E. R., Lavretsky, H., Peterson, J., et al. (2004). Anterior cingulate, gyrus rectus, and orbitofrontal abnormalities in elderly depressed patients: An MRI-based parcellation of the prefrontal cortex. *American Journal of Psychiatry, 161,* 99–108.

Beck, A. T. (1987). *Beck Depression Inventory.* San Antonio, TX: Psychological Corporation.

Bell-McGinty, S., Butters, M. A., Meltzer, C. C., Greer, P., Reynolds, C. F., & Becker, J. T. (2002). Brain morphometric abnormalities in late-life depression: Long-term neurobiologic effects of illness duration. *American Jouranl of Psychiatry, 159*(8), 1424–1427.

Blazer, D. G., Hays, J. C., Fillenbaum, G. G., & Gold, D. T. (1997). Memory complaint as a predictor of cognitive decline: A comparison of African American and White elders. *Journal of Aging and Health, 9,* 171–184.

Bolla-Wilson, K., & Blecker, M. L. (1989). Absence of depression in elderly adults. *Journal of Gerontology: Psychological Sciences, 44,* 53–55.

Butcher, J. N., Dahlstrom, W. G., Graham, J. R., Tellegan, A., & Kasmmer, B. (1989). *Manual for the restandarized Minnesota Multiphasic Personality Inventory: MMPI–2.* Minneapolis: University of Minnesota Press.

Butters, M. A., Becker, J. T., Nebes, R. D., Zmuda, M. D., Mulsant, B. H., Pollock, B. G., & Reynolds, C. F., III. (2000). Changes in cognitive functioning following treatment of late-life depression. *American Journal of Psychiatry, 157,* 1949–1954.

Butters, M. A., Whyte, E., Nebes, R. D., Begley, A. E., Dew, M. A., Mulsant, B. H., et al. (2004). The nature and determinants of neuropsychological functioning in late-life depression. *Archives of General Psychiatry, 61*(6), 587–595.

Collins, E., Katona, C., & Orrell, M. (1994). Diagnosis and management of depression in old age. *Focus on Depression, 2,* 1–5.

Crook, H., & Allison, C. (1992). *How to remember names.* New York: HarperCollins.

Cummings, J. L., & Mendez, M. F. (2003). *Dementia: A behavioral approach* (3rd ed.). Philadelphia: Butterworth Heinemann.

Drevets, W. C. (1994). Geriatric depression: Brain imaging correlates and pharmacologic considerations. *Journal of Clinical Psychiatry, 55*(9), 71–81.

Fava, G. A., Ruini, C., & Sonino, N. (2003). Treatment of recurrent depression: A sequential psychotherapeutic and psychopharmacological approach. *CNS Drugs, 17,* 1109–1117.

Fleming, C. F. (1995). Practical functional assessment of elderly persons: A primary care approach. *Mayo Clinic Proceedings, 70,* 890–911.

Gottfries, C. G. (2001). Late life depression. *European Archives of Psychiatry and Clinical Neurosciences, 251*(Suppl. 6), 57–61.

Hamilton, M. (1967). Development of a rating scale for primary depressive illness. *British Journal of Social and Clinical Psychology, 6,* 278–296.

Hill, C. D., Stoudemire, A., Morris, R., Martino-Saltzman, D., Markwalter, H. R., & Lewison, B. J. (1992). Dysnomia in the differential diagnosis of major depression, depression-related cognitive dysfunction, and dementia. *Journal of Neuropsychiatry and Clinical Neurosciences, 4*(1), 64–69.

Hill, R. D., Bäckman, L., & Neely, A. (2000). *Cognitive rehabilitation in old age.* New York: Oxford University Press.

Hsieh, M. H., McQuoid, D. R., Levy, R. M., Payne, M. E., MacFall, J. R., & Steffens, D. C. (2002). Hippocampal volume and antidepressant response in geriatric depression. *International Journal of Geriatric Psychiatry, 17,* 519–525.

Huber, S. J., & Paulson, G. W. (1985). The concept of subcortical dementia. *American Journal of Psychiatry, 142,* 1312–1316.

Jorm, A. F. (2001). History of depression as a risk factor for dementia: An updated review. *Aust NZJ Psychiatry, 35*(6), 776–781.

Kalayam, B., & Alexopoulos, G. S. (1999). Prefrontal dysfunction and treatment response in geriatric depression. *Archives of General Psychiatry, 56,* 713–718.

Kalmijn, S., Launer, L. J., Stolk, R. P., de Jong, F. H., Pols, H. A., Hofman, A., et al. (1998). A prospective study on cortisol, dehydroepiandrosterone sulfate, and cognitive function in the elderly. *Journal of Clinical Endocrinology and Metabolism, 83,* 3487–3492.

Kaszniak, A. W., & Christenson, G. D. (1994). Differential diagnosis of dementia and depression. In M. Storandt & G. R. VandenBos (Eds.), *Neuropsychological assessment of dementia and depression in older adults: A clinician's guide* (pp. 81–117). Washington, DC: American Psychological Association.

Kaszniak, A. W., & Scogin, F. R. (1995). Assessment of dementia and depression in older adults. *The Clinical Psychologist, 48*(2), 17–23.

La Rue, A. (1992). *Aging and neuropsychological assessment.* New York: Plenum Press.

La Rue, A., Watson, J., & Plotkin, D. A. (1992). Retrospective accounts of dementia symptoms: Are they reliable? *The Gerontologist, 32,* 240–245.

Lee, A. L., Ogle, W. O., & Sapolsky, R. M. (2002). Stress and depression: Possible links to neuron death in the hippocampus. *Bipolar Disorders, 4,* 117–128.

Levy, R. M., Steffens, D. C., McQuoid, D. R., Provenzale, J. M., MacFall, J. R., & Krishnan, K. R. (2003). MRI lesion severity and mortality in geriatric depression. *American Journal of Geriatric Psychiatry, 11,* 678–682.

Lichtenberg, P. A. (1994). *A guide to psychological practice in geriatric long term care.* New York: Haworth Press.

Maines, L. W., Keck, B. J., Smith, J. E., & Lakoski, J. M. (1999). Corticosterone regulation of serotonin transporter and 5-HT1A receptor expression in the aging brain. *Synapse, 32,* 58–66.

Meltzer, C. C., Price, J. C., Mathis, C. A., Greer, P. J., Cantwell, M. N., Houck, P. R., et al. (1999). PET imaging of serotonin type 2A receptors in late-life neuropsychiatric disorders. *American Journal of Psychiatry, 156,* 1871–1878.

Meyers, B. S., Alpert, S., Gabriele, M., Kakuma, T., Kalayam, B., & Alexopoulos, G. S. (1993). State specificity of DST abnormalities in geriatric depression. *Biological Psychiatry, 34,* 108–114.

Millon, T. (1993). *Millon Clinical Multiaxial Inventory* (4th ed.). Minneapolis, MN: National Computer Systems.

Nebes, R. D., Butters, M. A., Mulsant, B. H., Pollock, B. G., Zmuda, M. D., Houck, P. R., & Reynolds, C. F., III. (2000). Decreased working memory and processing speed mediate cognitive impairment in geriatric depression. *Psychological Medicine, 30,* 679–691.

Nebes, R. D., Reynolds, C. F., III, Boada, F., Meltzer, C. C., Fukui, M. B., Saxton, J., et al. (2002). Longitudinal increase in the volume of white matter hyperintensities in late-onset depression. *International Journal of Geriatric Psychiatry, 17,* 526–530.

Nebes, R. D., Vora, I. J., Meltzer, C. C., Fukui, M. B., Williams, R. L., Kamboh, M. I., et al. (2001). Relationship of deep white matter hyperintensities and apolipoprotein E genotype to depressive symptoms in older adults. *American Journal of Psychiatry, 158,* 878–884.

Nussbaum, P. D. (1997). Late-life depression: A neuropsychological perspective. In P. D. Nussbaum (Ed.), *Handbook of neuropsychology and aging* (pp. 260–270). New York: Plenum Press.

Oda, K., Okubo, Y., Ishida, R., Murata, Y., Ohta, K., Matsuda, T., et al. (2003). Regional cerebral blood flow in depressed patients with white matter magnetic resonance hyperintensity. *Biological Psychiatry, 53,* 150–156.

O'Hara, R., Murphy, G. M., Penner, A., Boyle L., Lapp, W., Kraemer, H. C., et al. (2005). Apolipoprotein E genotype impacts the effect of antidepressant therapy on cognitive function in late life depression. Manuscript submitted for publication.

O'Hara, R., & Yesavage, J. A. (2002). The Geriatric Depression Scale: Its development and recent application. In J. Copeland, M. Abou-Saleh, & D. Balzer (Eds.), *Principles and practice of geriatric psychiatry* (2nd ed.). Sussex, England: Wiley.

Olin, J. T., Schneider, L. S., Eaton, E. E., Zemansky, M. F., & Pollack, V. E. (1992). The Geriatric Depression Scale and the Beck Depression Inventory as screening instruments in an older adult outpatient population. *Psychological Assessment, 4,* 190–192.

Rapp, S. R., Smith, S. S., & Britt, M. (1990). Identifying comorbid depression in elderly medical patients: Use of the extracted Hamilton Depression Rating Scale. *Psychological Assessment, 2,* 243–247.

Reynolds, C. F., III. (1992). Treatment of depression in special populations. *Journal of Clinical Psychiatry, 53*(9), 45–53.

Reynolds, C. F., III, Alexopoulos, G. S., Katz, I. R., & Lebowitz, B. D. (2001). Chronic depression in the elderly: Approaches for prevention. *Drugs and Aging, 18,* 507–514.

Scogin, F. R. (1994). Assessment of depression in older adults: A guide for practitioners. In M. Storandt & G. R. VandenBos (Eds.), *Neuropsychological assessment of dementia and depression in older adults: A clinician's guide* (pp. 61–77). Washington, DC: American Psychological Association.

Scogin, F., & Prohaska, M. (1993). *Aiding older adults with memory complaints.* Sarasota, FL: Professional Resource Press.

Selzer, M. L. (1971). The Michigan Alcohol Screening Test: The quest for a new diagnostic instrument. *American Journal of Psychiatry, 127,* 1653–1658.

Sheline, Y. I., Gado, M. H., & Kraemer, H. C. (2003). Untreated depression and hippocampal volume loss. *American Journal of Psychiatry, 160,* 1516–1518.

Spielberger, C., Gorush, R., & Lushene, R. (1970). *STAI Manual for the State–Trait Anxiety Inventory.* Palo Alto, CA: Consulting Psychologists Press.

Steffens, D. C., Bosworth, H. B., Provenzale, J. M., & MacFall, J. R. (2002). Subcortical white matter lesions and functional impairment in geriatric depression. *Depression and Anxiety, 15*(1), 23–28.

Steffens, D. C., Taylor, W. D., & Krishnan, K. R. (2003). Progression of subcortical ischemic disease from vascular depression to vascular dementia. *American Journal of Psychiatry, 160,* 1751–1756.

Stukenberg, K. W., Dura, J. R., & Kiecolt-Glaser, J. K. (1990). Depression screening scale validation in an elderly community-dwelling population. *Psychological Assessment, 2,* 134–138.

Taylor, W. D., Steffens, D. C., MacFall, J. R., McQuoid, D. R., Payne, M. E., Provenzale, J. M., & Krishnan, K. R. (2003). White matter hyperintensity progression and late-life depression outcomes. *Archives of General Psychiatry, 60,* 1090–1096.

Twamley, E. W., & Bondi, M. W. (2004). The differential diagnosis of dementia. In J. H. Ricker (Ed.), *Differential diagnosis in adult neuropsychological assessment* (pp. 276–326). New York: Springer.

Unutzer, J., Katon, W., Callahan, C. M., Williams, J. W., Jr., Hunkeler, E., Harpole, L., et al. (2002). Collaborative care management of late-life depression in the primary care setting. *Journal of the American Medical Association, 288,* 2836–2845.

Watkins, L. L., Schneiderman, N., Blumenthal, J. A., Sheps, D. S., Catellier, D., Taylor, C. B., & Freedland, K. E. (2003). Cognitive and somatic symptoms of depression are associated with medical comorbidity in patients after acute myocardial infarction. *American Heart Journal, 146,* 48–54.

Welsh-Bohmer, K. A. (2001, November). *Diagnosing dementing conditions: Convergence of neuropsychology, imaging, and genetic methodologies.* Workshop presented at National Academy of Neuropsychology, San Francisco, CA.

Yesavage, J. A., Brink, T. L., Rose, T. L., Lum, O., Huang, V., Adey, M.B., & Leirer, V. O. (1983). Development and validation of a geriatric depression screening scale: A preliminary report. *Journal of Psychiatric Research, 17,* 37–49.

Zakzanis, K. K., Leach, L., & Kaplan, E. (1999). *Neuropsychological differential diagnosis.* Lisse, the Netherlands: Swets & Zeitlinger.

CHAPTER 10

Laura A. Rabin, Heather A. Wishart,
Robert B. Fields, and Andrew J. Saykin

The Dementias

The dementias include a broad range of disorders with memory and other cognitive impairment at the core. The neuropsychologist is called on to determine the presence, severity, and possible etiology of dementia and to comment on its likely course and impact on daily functioning. The neuropsychological evaluation is frequently completed alongside other diagnostic studies, such as magnetic resonance imaging and laboratory testing, to evaluate etiology, devise a treatment plan, and help the patient plan for the future. This chapter summarizes general information on dementia and approaches to neuropsychological evaluation and interpretation of test data. For more detailed information the reader is referred to the *Diagnostic and Statistical Manual of Mental Disorders* (4th ed., text revision, *DSM–IV–TR*; American Psychiatric Association, 2000) and recent reviews and books (Albert & Moss, 1988; American Psychiatric Association, 2002; Cummings, Vinters, & Felix, 2002; Doody et al., 2001; Dugue, Neugroschl, Sewell, & Marin, 2003; Growdon & Rossor, 1998; Knopman et al., 2001; Mendez & Cummings, 2003; Olga,

Preparation of this chapter was supported by funding from the National Institute on Aging (R01 AG19771), the Alzheimer's Association (IIRG-99-1653, sponsored by the Hedco Foundation), and the Hitchcock Foundation.

Emery, & Oxman, 2003; Petersen, 2001; Ritchie & Lovestone, 2002; Small et al., 1997).

I. BACKGROUND

A. Definitions and Diagnostic Criteria

The dementias include a group of disorders characterized by memory impairment and one or more additional cognitive deficits. Memory impairment is often prominent as an early symptom. Patients may experience difficulty learning new material or remembering recent conversations or events, and they may misplace valuables, such as keys, or forget to turn off the stove. In more severe dementia, patients also forget previously learned material, including the names of loved ones. Disturbances in spatial abilities, expressive or receptive language, and executive functions (e.g., impaired reasoning ability, poor judgment or insight) are common as well. Examples include underestimating the risks involved in activities (e.g., driving) or exhibiting little or no awareness of memory loss or other cognitive deficits. Patients may also make unrealistic appraisals of their abilities or plan activities that are incongruent with their deficits and prognosis (e.g., preparing to start a new business; American Psychiatric Association, 2002). To receive a diagnosis of dementia, a patient must have cognitive deficits that are sufficiently severe to cause impairment in daily functioning and that represent a change from a previous level of functioning (American Psychiatric Association, 2000). Exhibit 10.1 summarizes the general characteristics of dementias, as outlined in detail for specific dementias in the *DSM–IV–TR*.

Exhibit 10.1. General Characteristics of Dementias

1. Multiple cognitive deficits are present, including the following: (a) memory impairment (new learning or recall) and   (b) one or more of aphasia, apraxia, agnosia, or executive dysfunction.   2. Cognitive deficits significantly impair social or occupational functioning and reflect a significant decline from a previous level of higher functioning.   3. Cognitive deficits are not exclusively present during a delirium.   4. Cognitive deficits cannot be better attributed to another Axis I disorder, such as depression or schizophrenia.

Exhibit 10.2. Etiologies of Dementia

Alzheimer's disease
Vascular dementia
Lewy body dementia
Frontotemporal dementia
Pick's disease
Hydrocephalus
Creutzfeld–Jacob disease
Substance-induced persisting dementia
HIV disease
Head trauma
Parkinson's disease
Huntington's disease
Multiple sclerosis and demyelinating disorders
Other medical conditions

B. Etiologies of Dementia

There are many types of dementia, including Alzheimer's disease (AD), dementia with Lewy bodies, vascular dementia (VaD), dementia due to head trauma, and dementia due to HIV disease, among others. The etiology or possible etiologies of the dementia should be specified when diagnosis is made. The order of onset and relative prominence of the cognitive disturbances and associated symptoms vary with the specific type of dementia. An exhaustive list of dementia etiologies is beyond the scope of this chapter, but the more common etiologies are presented in Exhibit 10.2 (American Psychiatric Association, 2000; Growdon & Rossor, 1998).

In developed countries, the prevalence of dementia is approximately 1.5% at age 65. Prevalence of dementia increases with age, doubling every 4 years after age 65 and reaching approximately 30% at age 80 (Knopman, Boeve, & Petersen, 2003; Ritchie & Lovestone, 2002). AD, VaD, and dementia with Lewy bodies are the most common types of dementia, accounting for approximately 55%, 15%, and 20% of all incidences, respectively (Dugue et al., 2003; McKeith et. al., 1996, 1999). Less prevalent are dementias caused by conditions such as Parkinson's disease and related disorders (e.g., progressive supranuclear palsy), frontal lobe disease (e.g., Pick's disease, frontotemporal dementia), normal pressure hydrocephalus, and chronic alcoholism. These conditions do, however, occur frequently enough to be considered in the differential diagnosis. Far less prevalent are prion diseases. The prevalence rate of Creutzfeldt–Jakob disease (CJD), for example, is 1 in 1 million (Kapur, Abbott, Lowman, & Will, 2003; Roberts, Leigh, Weinberger, & Perry, 1993). Although rare, CJD generates interest because of media attention to the bovine spongiform encephalopathy, or "mad cow," variant (Collinge, 1998). It is important to keep in mind that causes of dementia are not mutually exclusive, and several different pathologies can contribute to a patient's clinical symptoms.

Alzheimer's disease (AD) is a neurodegenerative disorder characterized by progressive cognitive decline and a broad spectrum of brain pathology, including accumulation of fibrillar amyloid-β protein in plaques and vessels, neurofibrillary tangles, and synaptic and neuronal loss (Wegiel, Wisniewski, Reisberg, & Silverman, 2003). Although there are variants of AD, a typical presentation involves (a) an insidious onset, (b) initial symptoms of memory impairment (e.g., deficient consolidation, rapid loss of new information), and (c) a gradually progressive course evolving to include other cognitive functions (Zec, 1993). In contrast, dementia caused by **cerebrovascular disease** is often associated with an abrupt onset (e.g., in the context of a stroke) and a fluctuating or stepwise course, as well as more focal or patchy neurological and neuropsychological deficits (Metter & Wilson, 1993). Early treatment of hypertension and vascular disease can help prevent further progression. The term **vascular dementia (VaD)** actually comprises several heterogeneous syndromes, including cortical (multiinfarct) dementia and noninfarct vascular dementia (Pirttila, Erkinjuntti, & Hachinski, 2003). The relationship between AD and VaD is complex, in part because AD and strokes are both common and coexist frequently, and because evidence suggests that small strokes or risk factors for vascular disease may lead to increased clinical expression of AD (American Psychiatric Association, 2002). Comorbidity of AD and VaD is especially common in the very old (Kalaria & Ballard, 1999).

Dementia with Lewy bodies (DLB) is characterized by hallucinations and delusions occurring early in the disease process, marked day-to-day fluctuations in cognition, repeated falls, syncope, transient loss of consciousness, spontaneous parkinsonism, and neuroleptic sensitivity. Pure DLB involves more prominent attention, executive, and visuospatial impairment, rather than memory deficits, early in its course. In this condition, Lewy bodies, the pathological hallmark of Parkinson's disease usually concentrated in the substantia nigra, are distributed throughout the cortex. The dementia syndrome of DLB is similar to AD, and pathological studies have revealed the presence of Lewy bodies in as many as 20% of AD cases at autopsy. Recent findings indicate that the presence of visual hallucinations and agnosia early in the course of a dementing illness can help distinguish DLB from AD. In addition, as compared with patients with AD, patients with DLB tend to perform better on tests of confrontation naming and verbal memory and worse on tests of executive functioning and visuospatial abilities (Kaufer, 2002; Knopman et al., 2003; McKeith et al., 1996; Patterson & Clarfield, 2003; Walker & Stevens, 2002).

Pick's disease and other **frontal lobe dementias** are fairly rare and are characterized in their early stages by changes in personality, executive dysfunction, deterioration of social skills, emotional blunting, behavioral disinhibition, and language abnormalities. This initial presentation may be mistaken for a psychiatric disorder. Difficulties with memory, apraxia, and additional behavioral disturbances (i.e., apathy or extreme agitation) often appear later in the disease course (American Psychiatric Association, 2000; Knopman et al., 2003). Structural brain imaging of patients with Pick's disease typically reveals prominent frontal or temporal atrophy or both, with relative sparing of the parietal and occipital lobes. The diagnosis is confirmed by an autopsy finding of Pick inclusion bodies; the histopathology of other frontal lobe dementias tends to be more nonspecific. Frontal lobe dementias commonly manifest in individuals between the ages of 50 to 60 but can occur among older individuals (American Psychiatric Association, 2002). Patients with disorders that primarily affect **frontal-subcortical** systems (e.g., brain stem, thalamus, basal ganglia, and associated frontal regions) often display a constellation of symptoms differing from that seen in other types of dementia. These symptoms include bradyphrenia (i.e., slowing of cognitive processes or psychomotor retardation), memory retrieval deficits, executive dysfunction, and deficits in sustained or selective attention and visuospatial skills in the absence of aphasia, apraxia, or agnosia. Such disorders include **Parkinson's disease**, **Huntington's disease**, and **progressive supranuclear palsy**, among others (Assal & Cummings, 2003; Mahurin, Feher, Nance, Levy, & Pirozzolo, 1993).

Normal pressure hydrocephalus (NPH), also known as **nonobstructive or communicating hydrocephalus**, is somewhat of a misnomer, falsely suggesting that intracranial pressure (ICP) is always normal in this condition when in fact there can be elevations in ICP. The terms **nonobstructive** and **communicating** are somewhat more descriptive of the etiology of the condition, which involves an imbalance between production and absorption of cerebrospinal fluid (CSF). Obstructive hydrocephalus, in contrast, involves a blockage of CSF flow and may require surgical removal of the obstruction. NPH is associated with a classic triad of dementia, gait disturbance, and urinary incontinence. Although the disorder is relatively rare, it is important to consider NPH in the diagnostic workup because early detection and treatment may lead to symptomatic improvement (i.e., through serial lumbar punctures or cerebroventricular shunting; Stambrook, Gill, Cardoso, & Moore, 1993).

The most common form of **substance-induced persisting dementia** is caused by alcohol. The **Wernicke–Korsakoff syndrome** consists of two phases. The first is a potentially reversible Wernicke encephalopathy characterized by a confused state, gait ataxia, and eye movement abnormalities. If left untreated with large doses of thiamine, a chronic Korsakoff state follows, characterized by severe anterograde and retrograde amnesia, sensitivity to proactive interference, confabulation, visuospatial and executive deficits, apathy, and disinterest in alcohol. Wernicke–Korsakoff syndrome usually arises in a context of persistent alcohol abuse and poor nutrition. Non-Korsakoff **alcoholic dementia** is characterized by an amnesia comparable to that of Korsakoff's disease but accompanied by behavioral changes and more global and severe intellectual and cognitive impairment (including deficits in conceptualization, problem solving, visuoperception, and motor skills). A more subtle form of alcohol-related cognitive impairment may persist despite abstinence (Parsons, Butters, & Nathan, 1987; Salmon, Butters, & Heindel, 1993; Tarter & Van Thiel, 1985).

The dementia associated with **HIV/AIDS (HIV-D)** includes cognitive, behavioral, and motor dysfunction (for review, see Grant & Martin, 1994). The initial symptoms can be subtle and are often overlooked or misdiagnosed as depression. The typical early changes include the following: (a) reduced attention and concentration (e.g., losing track of conversations, difficulty tracking the plots of books or films), (b) memory problems (e.g., difficulty remembering telephone numbers, appointments, or maintaining medication schedules), (c) motor skill deficits (e.g., poor handwriting, unsteady balance or gait, and a tendency to drop things easily), (d) changes in personality (e.g., apathy, inertia, and irritability), and (e) general slowing of thought processes. Eventually, more widespread deficits develop, including a global dementia often accompanied by vacuolar myelopathy and sensory neuropathies. Higher risk of developing HIV-D is associated with increasing age, decreased CD4 cell count, increased viral load, and in some studies, intravenous drug use. Even in its mild form, cognitive impairment can affect compliance with treatment, functional ability, and survival (McArthur et al., 2003; Price, 2003; Shor-Posner, 2000).

Historically, the term **dementia** referred to a progressive disorder. However, in the current edition of the *DSM–IV–TR* (American Psychiatric Association, 2000), diagnosis is based on the pattern of cognitive findings rather than the reversibility or irreversibility of the condition. Given this change, dementia can technically be diagnosed in young individuals with potential for recovery of function (e.g., people with traumatic brain injury) if they meet the general criteria. Although the degree and nature of the impairment depend on the location and extent of brain injury, posttraumatic amnesia and persisting memory impairments are common features of **dementia due to head trauma**. When it occurs in the context of a single injury, dementia due to head trauma is usually nonprogressive. Repeated head injury, however, may lead to a progressive dementia (American Psychiatric Association, 2000). The term dementia can also be used to describe the cognitive deficits of individuals with **multiple sclerosis (MS)** if the symptoms are severe enough to affect daily functioning and patients otherwise meet criteria. However, MS is often associated with relatively mild deficits without pervasive effects on daily functioning, in which case the term dementia is not appropriate. Furthermore, MS patients may show decreased cognitive functioning during an exacerbation that improves during remission. Practitioners and laypeople alike may still associate the term dementia with progressive cognitive decline in elderly people. The term should therefore be used with caution and with appropriate explanation and context for certain etiologies.

C. Differential Diagnosis of Dementia

Memory impairment is a hallmark of dementia and is required to make a diagnosis. Dementia is distinguished from **amnestic disorder** by the involvement of additional cognitive deficits (e.g., language, visuospatial processing, problem solving). Although dementia and **delirium** both include global cognitive impairment, delirium is characterized by prominent deficits in attention and awareness of the environment, and the symptoms typically develop rapidly and fluctuate in severity (American Psychiatric Association, 2000). Dementia often co-occurs with **depression** or depressive symptoms, but depression alone can cause significant cognitive impairment that is difficult to distinguish from dementia (see chap. 9, this volume). Sometimes, the course of the illness can help with this differential. Cognitive deficits that coincide with the onset of a major depressive episode in a context of previously normal cognition may be more likely due to the depression. In older adults, significant depression-related cognitive impairment can be a harbinger of subsequent dementia (Cummings, 2003). It is therefore important to follow older adults with significant depression-related cognitive impairment even after the depression remits.

Another common differential diagnostic problem is among **dementia**, **mild cognitive impairment (MCI)**, and **normal aging**. Neuropsychological evaluation can be very helpful in distinguishing MCI from dementia, especially when age- and education-appropriate normative data are available (see chap. 8, this volume). **Amnestic MCI** is defined as memory complaints plus a relatively isolated memory deficit on testing with relatively intact intellectual functioning and activities of daily living (Petersen, Stevens, et al., 2001; Saykin & Wishart, 2003). Approximately 15% of patients with amnestic MCI will progress to AD within a year, or up to 40% in 4 years, compared with a 1% to 2% conversion rate in age-matched normal control participants (Peterson, Doody, et al., 2001). It is therefore important to follow patients with neuropsychological testing to track any changes in cognitive functioning (Dugue et al., 2003). In addition to the amnestic subclassification, other variants of MCI have been identified and are currently being investigated empirically, including multiple domain MCI and single nonmemory domain MCI (e.g., language or visuospatial; Busse, Bischkopf, Riedel-Heller, & Angermeyer, 2003; Winblad et al., 2004). When making the diagnosis of MCI, neuropsychologists should qualify the term with an appropriate modifier (e.g., amnestic MCI) to adequately characterize the condition and address issues related to its likely course and outcome (Petersen, Stevens, et al., 2001).

Dementia must also be distinguished from age-related cognitive decline, the mild decline in cognitive functioning that may occur with aging (e.g., loss in efficiency of acquiring new information and mild reductions in processing speed, cognitive flexibility, and working memory). This type of decline is typically nonprogressive and does not lead to functional impairment (Smith & Ivnik, 2003). Finally, cognitive complaints are common in aging and may reflect depression. However, recent research has characterized a group of nondepressed older adults with significant memory complaints who perform normally on neuropsychological testing. These individuals show mild changes in brain structure and activity similar to those seen in patients with MCI or dementia (Saykin et al., 2004). Therefore, cognitive complaints in older adults with no dementia should be taken seriously, and these individuals should be followed over time to determine whether deficits emerge.

D. Associated Problems

Changes in functional capacity, mood, personality, and behavior also occur in dementia and are associated with severity of impairment. Anxiety and depression, for example, may be present at the very early stages of dementia, when compromised learning and problem-solving capacities result in difficulty keeping up with the demands of a job. Suicidal behavior may occur, especially in less impaired individuals, who are more likely to gain insight into their deficits and remain capable of formulating and carrying out a plan of action. As memory and executive functioning worsen, problems may develop in areas such as driving a car and managing medication or finances. Patients with dementia may display increased gullibility, vulnerability, apathy, and disregard for societal norms and expectations. Anxiety is also common at this stage, and some patients manifest overwhelming emotional responses to seemingly minor stressors, such as changes in routine or environment (American Psychiatric Association, 2000, 2002; Cummings, 2003).

When recall of recent events becomes severely impaired, relatively benign confabulations may be replaced by delusions of persecution (e.g., the belief that misplaced possessions have been stolen) or infidelity. Agitation may occur when an individual's memory loss and perceptual distortions result in incorrect comprehension of his or her circumstances (e.g., striking out at a caretaker who is misidentified as an intruder). Threats, combativeness, wandering, and physical violence are also more likely to occur later in the illness and are often associated with frustration, misinterpretations, delusions, or hallucinations. These behaviors pose a particular problem for patients cared for at home, especially by frail spouses, and may necessitate a nursing home or similar long-term care placement. Some patients exhibit a peak period of agitation (or other behavioral disturbance) during the evening hours, referred to as "sundowning." Dementia can also be accompanied by motor disturbances, including gait difficulties, slurred speech, and a variety of abnormal movements. Other neurological symptoms, such as myoclonus and seizures, may occur. Finally, delirium is sometimes superimposed on dementia because the underlying brain disease increases susceptibility to the effects of medications or concurrent medical conditions (American Psychiatric Association, 2000, 2002).

II. NEUROPSYCHOLOGICAL EVALUATION OF DEMENTIA

A. Comprehensive Evaluation

A comprehensive evaluation for dementia should include the following:

- an interview with the patient and a knowledgeable collateral source as well as a review of medical records to obtain patient and family history;
- a thorough medical examination with diagnostic and laboratory testing by a physician trained in geriatric medicine, gero- or neuropsychiatry, or behavioral neurology;
- a screening examination for primary psychiatric disorders (e.g., depression);
- a review of the patient's medication regimen by a professional with expertise in geriatric pharmacology (to rule out cognitive deficits owing to medication effects or interactions);
- an assessment of functional capacities (e.g., by an occupational therapist); and
- comprehensive neuropsychological assessment using tests with appropriate normative data.

Neuropsychological testing of individuals with suspected dementia can be used to accomplish several goals, including providing information about cognitive strengths and weaknesses, establishing a baseline to measure stability or decline over time, assisting in making a diagnosis and treatment recommendations, and assessing the effectiveness of medication/treatment. The assessment typically covers all cognitive and sensorimotor domains, with a focus on memory and other functions required to make the diagnosis. Exhibit 10.3 presents a sample set of instruments used for this type of assessment in the Neuropsychology Program at Dartmouth Medical School. This set of tests requires approximately 3 to 4 hours of face-to-face contact, in addition to the neuropsychological interview, and would be appropriate for assessment of mild cognitive impairment and mild dementia. Modifications are made as needed on the basis of the specific referral question and the patient's individual circumstances. In addition to standardized neuropsychological instruments, several global rating instruments are available, which are useful in establishing diagnoses or providing an index of clinical change over time (Clinical Dementia Rating [CDR]; Berg, 1988; Global Deterioration Scale [GDS]; Reisberg, Ferris, de Leon, & Crook, 1982; Clinician Interview-Based Impression

Exhibit 10.3. Sample Comprehensive Neuropsychological Evaluation

Patient Name _____ Date of Evaluation _____

COMPREHENSIVE EVALUATION: MEMORY DISORDERS/DEMENTIA CLINIC

——— Demographic Questionnaire/Barona Index (Barona, Reynolds, & Chastain, 1984)
——— Dartmouth Lateral Dominance Questionnaire
——— Mini-Mental State Examination (Folstein, Folstein, & McHugh, 1975)
——— Dementia Rating Scale—2 (DRS–2; Jurica, Leitten, & Mattis, 2001)
——— Wechsler Memory Scale—Third Edition (WMS–III), Information and Orientation (Psychological Corporation, 1997)
——— Logical Memory I (WMS–III)
——— Visual Reproduction I (WMS–III)
——— Sensory-Motor Exam: Finger Tapping Test (Reitan & Wolfson, 1993), Graphesthesia (Lezak, 1995)
——— Delis–Kaplan Executive Function Battery (D-KEFS) Trail Making Test (Delis & Kaplan, 2001)
——— Single/Double Simultaneous Stimulation Test (Centofanti & Smith, 1979)
——— Logical Memory II and Recognition (WMS–III)
——— Visual Reproduction II and Recognition (WMS–III)
——— Drawings to Command and Copy (Including Clock-Drawing Test; Mendez, Ala, & Underwood, 1992)
——— California Verbal Learning Test, Second Edition (CVLT–II) Trials 1–5, Interference Trial, Short-Delay Free and Cued Recall (Delis et al., 2000)
——— Digit Span (WMS–III)
——— Block Design from the Wechsler Abbreviated Scale of Intelligence (WASI; Psychological Corporation, 1999)
——— Digit-Symbol/Coding from the Wechsler Adult Intelligence Scale—Third Edition (WAIS–III; Wechsler, 1997)

	CVLT–II Long-Delay Free and Cued Recall and Yes/No Recognition
	Matrix Reasoning (WASI)
	CVLT–II Long-Delay Forced-Choice Recognition
	Vocabulary (WASI)
	Similarities (WASI)
	Beck Depression Inventory—II (Beck, 1996) and/or Hamilton Depression Rating Scale (Hamilton, 1967)
	State–Trait Anxiety Inventory (Spielberger, 1983)
	Praxis from the Boston Diagnostic Aphasia Examination—Third Edition (BDAE; Goodglass, Kaplan, & Barresi, 2001)
	Practical Reasoning/Judgment from Neurobehavioral Cognitive Status Examination (NCSE; Northern California Neurobehavioral Group, Inc., 1988) or Dartmouth Rabin Judgment Questionnaire (Rabin et al., 2005)
	Reading Recognition from the Wide Range Achievement Test—Third Edition (WRAT–3;Wilkinson, 1993)
	Boston Naming Test (BDAE)
	D-KEFS Verbal Fluency
	Comprehension of Complex Ideational Material (BDAE)
	Wisconsin Card Sorting Test (Heaton, Chelune, Talley, Kay, & Curtiss, 1993)
	Squire Memory Self Rating Questionnaire (Squire, Wetzel, & Slater, 1979)
	Activities of Daily Living Scale (Self and Collateral; Saykin et al., 1991)

Additional Tests: _____

[CIBI]; Knopman et al., 1994; Alzheimer's Disease Cooperative Study—Clinical Global Impression of Change [ADCS–CGIC]; Schneider et al., 1997). Also useful as a reference tool is Burns, Lawlor, and Craig's (2001) comprehensive collection of scales used to measure various aspects of cognitive, physical, and affective dysfunction in older adults.

One should begin the assessment with relatively simple measures that provide a general sense of the patient's level of functioning and prevent undue frustration and gradually progress to include more challenging items. More impaired patients may require the replacement of difficult tests with simpler measures (e.g., the 9-item version of the California Verbal Learning Test—II [CVLT–II]; Delis, Kramer, Kaplan, & Ober, 2000). It is, however, important to use measures that are challenging enough to reveal a dementia if present. In the later disease stages, when the patient manifests significant cognitive deficits, it is important to include measures simple enough to demonstrate what the patient can still accomplish. Ideally, an appropriately trained professional such as an occupational therapist would carry out direct assessment of functional abilities in everyday contexts, which may require a home visit. Minimally, everyday functioning should be covered in the interview and through the use of self- and collateral-report questionnaires. The collateral should be someone who has known the patient long enough to have witnessed decline over time, if present. The collateral should also have firsthand knowledge of the patient's current daily functioning in a variety of contexts. Children who live at a distance may not be able to provide sufficient firsthand information, and it may be necessary to access other local sources of information. Sometimes it is helpful to interview the collateral separately from the patient (with the patient's permission) to enable a more open expression of concerns (Duchek et al., 2003).

B. Screening Evaluation

Dementia screening is sometimes more appropriate than a comprehensive evaluation. Shorter screening evaluations are indicated when the patient is unable to tolerate more extensive testing or when the patient's status is changing. A screening evaluation should include at minimum:

- a review of available data (e.g., medical chart);
- patient interview and observations; and
- a dementia screening test, such as the Dementia Rating Scale—2 (DRS-2; Jurica, Leitten, & Mattis, 2001), that

includes measures of orientation, attention, learning and memory, executive function, language and visuospatial ability.

In addition, brief neuropsychological testing should be conducted with a focus on learning and memory, executive functioning, language, and visuospatial abilities, using tests appropriate to the patient's cognitive level. Test selection can be based, in part, on the results of the DRS–2. It may be unnecessary to proceed with more complex memory tests for patients with severe impairment on the memory subtests of the DRS–2. Similarly, for patients exhibiting moderate memory problems on the DRS–2, the Hopkins Verbal Learning Test—Revised (Benedict, Schretlen, Groninger, & Brandt, 1998) or short form of the CVLT–II may be more appropriate than the standard 16-item CVLT–II (Delis et al., 2000). Because the DRS–2 does not include a measure of confrontation naming, a brief test such as an abbreviated form of the Boston Naming Test (Goodglass et al., 2001) may be useful. Exhibit 10.4 presents a sample screening battery. Other brief assessment batteries are commonly used in population based studies (e.g., The Consortium to Establish a Registry for Alzheimer's Disease [CERAD]; Morris, Mohs, Rogers, Fillenbaum, & Heyman, 1988) and clinical trials (e.g., Alzheimer Disease Assessment Scale—Cognitive [ADAS–Cog]; Rosen, Mohs, & Davis, 1984). Depending on the outcome of the screen, the neuropsychologist may recommend a comprehensive follow-up evaluation at a later date when the patient's medical status has stabilized.

C. Interpretation of Test Results

Interpreting neuropsychological test results for dementia involves answering a few basic questions:

- Does impairment exist?
- How severe is the impairment?
- Does the pattern of impairment in the context of the patient's history indicate dementia, and does it suggest the probability of a particular diagnosis? (This will be a clinical diagnosis because many etiologies can only be definitely determined on postmortem neuropathological examination.)
- What are the real-life consequences of this impairment?

Answering the first two questions requires an awareness of expected changes with normal aging along with a consideration of the individual's previous level of functioning and background (e.g., education, vocational history). It also involves the use of

Exhibit 10.4. Sample Brief Neuropsychological Screening Battery

Patient Name _____ Date of Evaluation _____

SCREENING EVALUATION: MEMORY DISORDERS/DEMENTIA CLINIC

___ Mini-Mental State Examination
___ Dementia Rating Scale—2
___ Visual Reproduction I (WMS–III)
___ CVLT-II (Standard or 9-item version) Trials 1–5, Interference Trial, Short-Delay Free and Cued Recall
___ Sensory-Motor Exam (Finger Tapping Test, Graphesthesia)
___ Digit Span (WMS–III)
___ CVLT-II Long-Delay Free and Cued Recall and Yes/No Recognition
___ Visual Reproduction II and Recognition (WMS–III)
___ CVLT-II Long-Delay Forced-Choice Recognition
___ Vocabulary (WASI)
___ Matrix Reasoning (WASI)
___ D-KEFS Trail Making Test
___ Praxis Screen (BDAE)
___ Drawings to Command and Copy (Including Clock-Drawing Test)
___ Boston Naming Test (BDAE)
___ Sentence Comprehension (BDAE)
___ Wisconsin Card Sorting Test (Abbreviated)
___ Beck Depression Inventory—II or Hamilton Depression Rating Scale
___ Activities of Daily Living Scale (Self and Informant)
___ Activities of Daily Living Scale (Self and Collateral)

Additional Tests: _____

Note. WMS–III = Wechsler Memory Scale—III; CVLT-II = California Verbal Learning Test, Second Edition; WASI = Wechsler Abbreviated Scale of Intelligence; BDAE = Boston Diagnostic Aphasia Examination; D-KEFS = Delis-Kaplan Executive Function Scale; NCSE = Neurobehavioral Cognitive Status Examination.

tests that have age- and education-appropriate norms, enabling the neuropsychologist to assess the degree to which an individual's test score departs from expected levels. Ideally, neuropsychologists assessing cognitive changes in older adults would have baseline test data from earlier years to compare with patients' current performance. Because this rarely exists, estimations of premorbid intellectual capacity can be accomplished using demographic variables including educational and occupational histories (e.g., Barona, Reynolds, & Chastain, 1984) and sight-reading vocabulary tests such as the Wide Range Achievement Test—Third Edition (Wilkinson, 1993) or National Adult Reading Test (Blair & Spreen, 1989).

The answer to the third question requires knowledge of the unique features of the different dementias as well as a systematic approach to test interpretation. Adapted from a model proposed by Weintraub (1995), one such approach uses a hierarchical step-by-step method to evaluate the integrity of capacities (e.g., arousal, attention, mood, language) on which the assessment of other capacities (e.g., memory) depends. The following shows the use of this type of interpretation strategy to suggest hypotheses about diagnosis.

Level 1 assessment: *Arousal.* Deficits in arousal suggest the presence of delirium or subcortical dysfunction and limit the usefulness of comprehensive tests of higher level processing such as memory and executive functioning.

Level 2 assessment. This can be divided further into the following:

a. *Attention:* Deficits in attention suggest delirium or subcortical–frontal dysfunction.

b. *Mood and motivation:* Abnormalities in mood or motivation suggest conditions such as depression or dementia owing to vascular or frontal lobe disorders. Depression in older adults can mimic the effects of dementia. For example, psychomotor retardation and decreased motivation can result in individuals with no dementia appearing to have pathophysiologically determined cognitive disturbances in daily functioning and on formal neuropsychological testing. Depression can also cause individuals with no dementia to overreport the severity of cognitive disturbance. It is therefore important to perform a careful mood assessment when conducting a dementia evaluation. Also important to keep in mind, however, is that depression and dementia can coexist (Kaszniak & Christenson, 1994). Finally, consideration should be given to possible secondary gain factors that may influence test performance.

Level 3 assessment: *Language, motor, visuoperceptual, and visuospatial skills.* Focal deficits (e.g., aphasia, visual field deficits, unilateral motor impairment) suggest more circumscribed areas of impairment owing to vascular or other focal disorders (e.g., tumors) and limit the ability to assess higher level functions dependent on these capacities (e.g., verbal memory in a patient with language impairment, visuospatial planning and organization in a patient with motor coordination deficits). If these deficits are detected in advance of ordering testing, the battery should be adjusted accordingly.

Level 4 assessment: *Memory, executive functioning, comportment.* Deficits in these areas are critically important for the differential diagnosis of early dementia, but they cannot be adequately assessed without knowledge of the integrity of other mental functions.

D. Recommendations

The final question—what are the real-life consequences of an impairment?—is often the most difficult to answer. Recommendations regarding real-life consequences of the neuropsychological test deficits generally fall into three categories: (a) need for further assessment, (b) need for treatment, and (c) need for assistance or supervision in specific areas.

1. NEED FOR FURTHER ASSESSMENT

Depending on the outcome of the screening or comprehensive neuropsychological evaluation, recommendations for further assessment may be indicated. These can include the following:

    a. Administer additional neuropsychological testing as noted previously.

    b. Recommend medical or neurological evaluation including neuroimaging where appropriate (e.g., in patients whose neuropsychological presentation suggests a previously unrecognized neurological or medical disorder).

    c. Recommend a psychiatric evaluation (e.g., in patients with depressive or psychotic symptoms or agitation).

    d. Recommend an assessment of specific functional capacities and in-home safety (e.g., to provide caretakers with information about specific self-care skills).

    e. Consider evaluation by a social worker, visiting nurse, or case manager of the patient's living situation and family, community, and fiscal resources.

2. NEED FOR TREATMENT

The results of the neuropsychological evaluation, when considered in the context of other aspects of the comprehensive assessment, may also suggest treatment directions such as the following:

a. Medications or other agents may be indicated to treat the cognitive symptoms of dementia (e.g., cholinesterase inhibitors such as Aricept [donepezil], Razadyne (formerly known as Reminyl) [galantamine hydrobromide], or Exelon [rivastigmine]; or N-methyl-D-asparate [NMDA]-receptor antagonists such as Namenda/Axura/Ebixa [memantine]; also under investigation are Vitamin E and nonsteroidal antiinflamatory drugs [NSAIDs].

b. Psychoactive medication may be indicated to manage symptoms associated with dementia (e.g., psychosis, agitation, depression, anxiety, sleep disturbance).

c. Psychosocial interventions may be helpful, including (a) behavior-oriented treatments that identify the antecedents and consequences of problem behaviors and institute changes in the environment to minimize precipitants or consequences; (b) stimulation-oriented treatments, such as recreational activity, art therapy, and pet therapy, along with other formal and informal means of maximizing pleasurable activities for patients; and (c) emotion-oriented treatments (e.g., supportive psychotherapy, reminiscence therapy, validation therapy, and sensory integration). Though most of these psychosocial treatments have not been subjected to double-blind randomized controlled trials, some are supported by research findings and practice (American Psychiatric Association, 2002).

d. Cognition-oriented treatments (e.g., reality orientation, cognitive retraining, and skills training) focused on specific cognitive deficits may be warranted in patients with sufficiently preserved cognition (American Psychiatric Association, 2002; Small et al., 1997). Books containing memory-enhancing strategies can be recommended for patients with mild cognitive changes, including *The Memory Bible* (Small, 2003), *Total Memory Workout* (Green, 2001), *12 Steps to a Better Memory* (Turkington, 1996), and *The Memory Workbook* (Mason & Kohn, 2001).

e. Environmental changes such as making adjustments to the home environment (e.g., in-home assistance, calendars, message boards, reminder signs, pocket tape re-

corders, beeper/pager systems, and radio frequency devices for locating objects) can be implemented
(American Psychiatric Association, 2002). Safe-return
identification bracelets or global positioning system
(GPS) devices may be useful in patients at risk for getting lost.

3. NEED FOR ASSISTANCE OR SUPERVISION IN SPECIFIC AREAS

Because neuropsychological tests measure general domains
of cognitive functioning (e.g., verbal reasoning) rather than
specific capacities (e.g., the ability to make decisions about medical procedures, to live independently, or to drive safely in one's
neighborhood), recommendations at this level must be undertaken cautiously and often through a direct evaluation. The
neuropsychologist, for example, may recommend a formal driving assessment or in-home evaluation of safety and activities
of daily living. However, because progressive dementias are generally staged according to level of functional impairment,
knowledge about which abilities are typically impaired at different disease stages can help inform statements about functioning.
For example, patients with mild dementia often have problems
balancing checkbooks, preparing complex meals, or managing
complicated medication regimens. Those with moderate impairment may also have difficulties with simpler food preparation,
household cleanup, and chores, and they may require assistance
with aspects of self-care (e.g., reminders to use the bathroom,
help with buttons or shaving). Patients with severe dementia
require considerable assistance with personal care, including
feeding, grooming, and toileting. Those with profound and ter-
minal dementia become oblivious to their surroundings, require
constant care, and may be susceptible to accidents and infectious diseases, which often prove fatal (American Psychiatric
Association, 2002).

Answering more specific questions about a patient's degree
of functional impairment may require a formal assessment of
particular capacities. Published procedures such as those designed to assess capacity to give informed consent or write advance directives (e.g., Hopkins Competency Assessment Test;
Jankofsky, McCarthy, & Folstein, 1992), comply with medication regimen (Fitten, Coleman, Siembieda, Yu, & Ganzell, 1995),
and consent to electroconvulsive therapy (e.g., Competency
Interview Schedule; Bean, Nishisato, Rector, & Glancy, 1994)
offer the clinician help in this area (as do tests of adaptive living
skills such as the Kohlman Evaluation of Living Skills; Kohlman-

Thompson, 1992), but more assessment tools are needed. Although none of these assessment techniques is foolproof, the importance of evaluating specific capacities is underscored by research showing that physicians with expertise in geriatrics demonstrated significant differences in opinion when judging the competency of mildly impaired patients with AD (Marson, McInturff, Hawkins, Bartolucci, & Harrell, 1997).

An important consideration with patients at all levels of dementia is the continued operation of motor vehicles or other equipment (e.g., firearms, heavy machinery) that places the patient and others at risk. The available data suggest that dementia, even when mild, impairs driving performance to some degree, and the risk of accidents increases as the disease progresses (Duchek et al., 2003). This issue raises significant public health concerns, because individuals with dementia (even some with fairly serious impairment) continue to drive. Unfortunately, there is no consensus regarding the threshold level of dementia at which driving should cease. While some clinicians argue that patients with mild dementia benefit from the continued independence and access to services that driving affords, others believe that the risk of accidents is significant even for these mildly impaired individuals. There also is no consensus regarding which neuropsychological assessment tools are best suited for evaluating patients' fitness to drive. However, although the relationship between neuropsychological functioning and driving ability for adults with dementia is complex and requires further elucidation, a recent meta-analysis by Reger et al. (2004) found that measures of visuospatial skills are most helpful in identifying at-risk drivers across different types of driving tests. It is certainly important for neuropsychologists to discuss the risk of driving with all dementia patients and their families, including an exploration of the patient's current driving patterns, any history of becoming lost or involved in traffic accidents, and transportation needs. A social service referral may assist some families with transportation arrangements and costs. Additionally, mildly impaired patients or family members who wish to obtain an independent assessment of driving skills can be referred to an occupational therapist, rehabilitation center, or driving school for a functional assessment using either on-road tests or nonroad evaluations (American Psychiatric Association, 2002; Duchek et al., 2003; Reger et al., 2004).

E. General Considerations

The diagnosis of dementia is often devastating for patients and their families. Neuropsychological test results can assist referring clinicians, patients, and families by documenting areas of impairment and providing explanations of the consequences of these impairments. Test results are most helpful when accompanied by written summaries, personal feedback sessions, and offers of follow-up assistance.

The neuropsychologist can play a strong role in educating the patient and family about the illness, its treatment, and available sources of care and support (e.g., support groups, various types of respite care, long-term care facilities, the Alzheimer's Association). Patients and families often express a desire to further understand the pathophysiology and etiology of the dementing illness. The neuropsychologist can provide useful resources such as articles, books, videotapes, and phone numbers of local or national organizations. Another critical educational process is to help patients recognize current cognitive and behavioral symptoms and anticipate future manifestations. This enables the patient and family to plan for the future and to identify emergent symptoms that warrant medical attention. Individuals with dementia occurring in middle age may have particular difficulty coping with the diagnosis and its impact on their lives. They may seek advice about problems not typically seen with elderly patients, such as relinquishing work responsibilities, obtaining disability benefits, and arranging care for children. It is also helpful for the neuropsychologist to educate the family regarding basic principles of care. Some examples include keeping requests and demands relatively simple, avoiding overly complex tasks that may lead to frustration, being consistent and avoiding unnecessary change, and adjusting expectations in recognition of declines in capacity. The neuropsychologist may also suggest specific behavioral techniques for caregivers to use in dealing with problematic behaviors. Finally, as patients with dementia often lose their ability to make complex medical, legal, and financial decisions, patients and families should be advised about the importance of addressing these issues as early as possible (American Psychiatric Association, 2002).

Ensuring the safety of a cognitively impaired patient becomes a top priority in working with families over time. Therefore, decisions regarding living arrangements should be discussed and reassessed regularly, with consideration of the patient's clinical status and the continued ability of caregivers to supervise the patient and manage his or her care (American Psychiatric Association, 2002). Quality of life is also an important consideration. At present, we lack definitive criteria based on neuropsychological test results to determine when an individual is no longer able to live independently, drive, or make medical and financial decisions. However, through a combination of knowledge of neuropsychiatric disorders, neuropsychological test data, and the application of behavioral and family systems principles, neuropsychologists are equipped to help patients and their families understand, plan for, and cope with the day-to-day consequences of the condition.

III. CONCLUSION

Dementia is a syndrome of generalized and persistent cognitive impairment that (a) represents a deterioration in memory and other cognitive functions from a previous baseline; (b) is of sufficient severity to influence daily functioning; (c) cannot be better explained by a delirium or other disorder; and (d) may be the result of a variety of conditions, some of which are reversible. Familiarity with the base rates and neuropsychiatric characteristics of conditions whose presentation includes cognitive impairment is the first step in the evaluation of possible dementia. The second step is the selection of tests with appropriate norms to sample domains of cognitive processing relevant to both the differential diagnosis of possible dementia and the specific referral question. These domains include arousal, orientation, memory (i.e., learning, rate of forgetting, recall vs. recognition), executive functioning, sensory and motor capacity, attention, language (e.g., naming, fluency, comprehension), and visuospatial processing. The third step is the interpretation of test results in the context of the patient's history and current circumstances. For example, "mildly impaired" test performance probably does not reflect dementia in an elderly individual with limited education who lives independently, manages his or her finances, is able to take public transportation to an appointment, and for whom there is no report of a decline in functioning. Mildly impaired memory test scores in an individual with an advanced education and high baseline level of functioning whose performance on tests of intellectual functioning is in the average-to-above-average range, however, may be evidence of an early stage of dementia. Finally, it should be remembered that the diagnosis of dementia can be very difficult for patients and families. At present, the ability of neuropsychological tests to predict some of the specific real-world consequences of this diagnosis is limited. As a result, is often helpful to consider the neuropsychological evaluation as an opportunity to establish an ongoing relationship with patients, families, and referring clinicians to help them understand and deal with the consequences of the cognitive and behavioral symptoms of dementia. Although it is not often taken, it is a role for which clinical neuropsychologists are uniquely suited.

BIBLIOGRAPHY

Albert, M., & Moss, M. B. (1988). *Geriatric neuropsychiatry*. New York: Guilford Press.

American Psychiatric Association. (2000). *Diagnostic and statistical manual of mental disorders* (4th ed., text revision). Washington, DC: Author.

American Psychiatric Association. (2002). Practice guideline for the treatment of patients with Alzheimer's disease and other dementias of late life. In *Practice guidelines for the treatment of psychiatric disorders: Compendium 2002* (pp. 67–135). Washington, DC: Author.

Assal, F., & Cummings, J. L. (2003). Cortical and frontosubcortical dementias: Differential diagnosis. In V. Olga, B. Emery, & T. E. Oxman (Eds.), *Dementia: Presentations, differential diagnosis, and nosology* (2nd ed., pp. 239–262). Baltimore: Johns Hopkins University Press.

Barona, A., Reynolds, C., & Chastain, R. (1984). A demographically based index of pre-morbid intelligence for the WAIS–R. *Journal of Consulting and Clinical Psychology, 52*, 885–887.

Bean, G., Nishisato, S., Rector, N. A., & Glancy, G. (1994). The psychometric properties of the Competency Interview Schedule. *Canadian Journal of Psychiatry, 39*, 368–376.

Beck, A. T. (1996). *Beck Depression Inventory—II*. San Antonio, TX: Psychological Corporation.

Benedict, R., Schretlen, D., Groninger, L., & Brandt, J. (1998). The Hopkins Verbal Learning Test—Revised: Normative data and analysis of inter-form and test–retest reliability. *The Clinical Neuropsychologist, 12*, 43–55.

Berg, L. (1988). Clinical Dementia Rating (CDR). *Psychopharmacology Bulletin, 24*, 637–639.

Blair, J. R., & Spreen, O. (1989). Predicting pre-morbid IQ: A revision of the National Adult Reading Test. *The Clinical Neuropsychologist, 3*, 129–136.

Burns, A., Lawlor, B., & Craig, S. (2001). *Assessment scales in old age psychiatry*. London: Martin Dunitz Ltd.

Busse, A., Bischkopf, J., Riedel-Heller, S. G., & Angermeyer, M. C. (2003). Subclassifications for mild cognitive impairment: Prevalence and predictive validity. *Psychological Medicine, 33*, 1029–1038.

Centofanti, C. C., & Smith, A. (1979). *The Single and Double Simultaneous Stimulation Test.* Los Angeles: Western Psychological Services.

Collinge, J. (Ed.). (1998). *Human prion diseases: Etiology and clinical features.* Boston: Butterworth-Heinemann.

Cummings, J. L. (2003). Neuropsychiatric symptoms. In R. C. Petersen (Ed.), *Mild cognitive impairment: Aging to Alzheimer's disease* (pp. 41–61). New York: Oxford University Press.

Cummings, J. L., Vinters, H., & Felix, J. (Eds.). (2002). *The neuropsychiatry of Alzheimer's and related dementias.* London: Taylor & Francis.

Delis, D., & Kaplan, E. (2001). *Delis–Kaplan Executive Function Battery.* San Antonio, TX: Psychological Corporation.

Delis, D. C., Kramer, J. H., Kaplan, E., & Ober, B. A. (2000). *The California Verbal Learning Test—Second Edition: Adult version manual.* San Antonio, TX: Psychological Corporation.

Doody, R. S., Stevens, J. C., Beck C., Dubinsky, R. M., Kaye, J. A., Gwyther, L., et al. (2001). Practice parameter: Management of dementia (an evidence-based review): Report of the Quality Standards Subcommittee of the American Academy of Neurology. *Neurology, 56,* 1154–1166.

Duchek, J. M., Carr, D. B., Hunt, L., Roe, C. M., Xiong, C., Shah, K., & Morris, J. C. (2003). Longitudinal driving performance in early-stage dementia of the Alzheimer type. *Journal of the American Geriatrics Society, 18,* 1342–1347.

Dugue, M., Neugroschl, J., Sewell, M., & Marin, D. (2003). Review of dementia. *The Mount Sinai Journal of Medicine, 70,* 45–53.

Fitten, L. J., Coleman, L., Siembieda, D. W., Yu, M., & Ganzell, S. (1995). Assessment of capacity to comply with medication regimens in older patients. *Journal of the American Geriatrics Society, 43,* 361–367.

Folstein, M. F., Folstein, S. E., & McHugh, P. R. (1975). Mini Mental State: A practical method for grading the cognitive state of patients for the clinician. *Journal of Psychiatry Research, 12,* 189–198.

Goodglass, H., Kaplan, E., & Barresi, B. (2001). *Boston Diagnostic Aphasia Examination—Third Edition.* Philadelphia: Lippincott Williams & Wilkins.

Grant, I., & Martin, A. (Eds.). (1994). *Neuropsychology of HIV infection.* New York: Oxford University Press.

Green, C. (2001). *Total memory workout: 8 easy steps to maximum memory fitness.* New York: Bantam Books.

Growdon, J. H., & Rossor, M. N. (Eds.). (1998). *The dementias.* Boston: Butterworth-Heinemann.

Hamilton, M. (1967). Development and rating scale for primary depressive illness. *British Journal of Social and Clinical Psychology, 6,* 278–296.

Heaton, R. K., Chelune, G. J., Talley, J. L., Kay, G. G., & Curtiss, G. (1993). *Wisconsin Card Sorting Test manual: Revised and expanded.* Lutz, FL: Psychological Assessment Resources.

Jankofsky, J. S., McCarthy, R. J., & Folstein, M. F. (1992). The Hopkins Competency Assessment Test: A brief method for evaluating patients' capacity to give informed consent. *Hospital and Community Psychiatry, 43,* 132–136.

Jurica, P., Leitten, C., & Mattis, S. (2001). *Dementia Rating Scale–2.* Lutz, FL: Psychological Assessment Resources.

Kalaria, R. N., & Ballard, C. (1999). Overlap between pathology of Alzheimer's disease and vascular dementia. *Alzheimer Disease and Associated Disorders, 13*(Suppl. 3), 115–123.

Kapur, N., Abbott, P., Lowman, A., & Will, R. G. (2003). The neuropsychological profile associated with variant Creutzfeldt–Jakob disease. *Brain, 126,* 2693–2702.

Kaszniak, A. W., & Christenson, G. D. (1994). Differential diagnosis of dementia and depression. In M. Storandt & G. R. VandenBos (Eds.), *Neuropsychological assessment of dementia and depression in older adults: A clinician's guide* (pp. 81–117). Washington, DC: American Psychological Association.

Kaufer, D. I. (2002). Pharmacologic therapy of dementia with Lewy bodies. *Journal of Geriatric Psychiatry and Neurology, 15,* 224–232.

Kohlman-Thompson, L. (1992). *The Kohlman Evaluation of Living Skills* (3rd ed.). Bethesda, MD: American Occupational Therapy Association.

Knopman, D. S., Boeve, B. F., & Petersen, R. C. (2003). Essentials of proper diagnoses of mild cognitive impairment, dementia, and major subtypes of dementia. *Mayo Clinic Proceedings, 78,* 1290–1308.

Knopman, D. S., Dekosky, S. T., Cummings, J. L., Chui, H., Corey-Bloom, J., Relkin, N., et al. (2001). Practice parameter: Diagnosis of dementia (an evidence-based review): Report of the Quality Standards Subcommittee of the American Academy of Neurology. *Neurology, 56,* 1143–53.

Knopman, D. S., Knapp, M. J., Gracon, S. I., & Davis, C. S. (1994). The Clinician Interview-Based Impression (CIBI): A clinician's global change rating scale in Alzheimer's disease. *Neurology, 44,* 2315–2321.

Lezak, M. D. (1995). *Neuropsychological assessment* (3rd ed.). New York: Oxford University Press.

Mahurin, R. K., Feher, E. P., Nance, M. L., Levy, J. K., & Pirozzolo, F. J. (1993). Cognition in Parkinson's disease and related disorders. In R. W. Parks, R. F. Zec, & R. S. Wilson (Eds.), *Neuropsychology of Alzheimer's disease and other dementias* (pp. 308–349). New York: Oxford University Press.

Marson, D. C., McInturff, B., Hawkins, L., Bartolucci, A., & Harrell, L. E. (1997). Consistency of physician judgments of capacity to consent in mild Alzheimer's disease. *Journal of the American Geriatrics Society, 45,* 453–457.

Mason, D. J., & Kohn, M. L. (2001). *The memory workbook.* Oakland, CA: New Harbinger.

McArthur, J. C., Haughey, N., Gartner, S., Conant, K., Pardo, C., Nath, A., & Sacktor, N. (2003). Human immunodeficiency virus-associated dementia: An evolving disease. *Journal of Neurovirology, 9,* 205–221.

McKeith, I. G., Galasko, D., Kosaka, K., Perry, E. K., Dickson, D. W., & Hansen, L. A. (1996). Consensus guidelines for the clinical and pathologic diagnosis of dementia and Lewy bodies (DLB): Report of the consortium on DLB international workshop. *Neurology, 47,* 1113–1124.

McKeith, I. G., Perry, E. K., & Perry, R. H. (1999). Report of the second dementia with Lewy body international workshop: Diagnosis and treatment. *Neurology, 53,* 902–905.

Mendez, M. F., Ala, T., & Underwood, K. L. (1992). Development and scoring criteria for the Clock Drawing Task in Alzheimer's disease. *Journal of the American Geriatrics Society, 40,* 1095–1099.

Mendez, M. F., & Cummings, J. L. (2003). Dementia: A clinical approach. Boston: Butterworth-Heinemann.

Metter, E. J., & Wilson, R. S. (1993). Vascular dementias. In R. W. Parks, R. F. Zec, & R. S. Wilson (Eds.), *Neuropsychology of Alzheimer's disease and other dementias* (pp. 416–437). New York: Oxford University Press.

Morris, J. C., Mohs, R. C., Rogers, H., Fillenbaum, G., & Heyman, A. (1988). Consortium to establish a registry for Alzheimer's disease (CERAD) clinical and neuropsychological assessment of Alzheimer's disease. *Psychopharmacology Bulletin, 24,* 641–652.

Northern California Neurobehavioral Group, Inc. (1988). *Neurobehavioral Cognitive Status Examination.* Fairfax, CA: Author.

Olga, V., Emery, B., & Oxman, T. E. (Eds.). (2003). *Dementia: Presentations, differential diagnosis, and nosology* (2nd ed.). Baltimore: Johns Hopkins University Press.

Parsons, O. A., Butters, N., & Nathan, P. E. (Eds.). (1987). *Neuropsychology of alcoholism: Implications for diagnosis and treatment.* New York: Guilford Press.

Patterson, C. J., & Clarfield, A. M. (2003). Diagnostic procedures for dementia. In V. Olga, B. Emery, & T. E. Oxman (Eds.), *Dementia: Presentations, differential diagnosis, and nosology* (2nd ed., pp. 61–85). Baltimore: Johns Hopkins University Press.

Petersen, R. C. (2001). Mild cognitive impairment: Transition from aging to Alzheimer's disease. In K. Iqbal, S. S. Sisodia, & B. Winblad (Eds.), *Alzheimer's disease: Advances in etiology, pathogenesis, and therapeutics* (pp. 141–151). New York: Wiley.

Petersen, R. C., Doody, R., Kurz, A., Mohs, R. C., Morris, J. C., Rabins, P. V., et al. (2001). Current concepts in mild cognitive impairment. *Archives of Neurology, 58,* 1985–1992.

Petersen, R. C., Stevens, J. C., Ganguli, M., Tangalos, E. G., Cummings, J. L., & DeKosky, S. T. (2001). Practice parameter: Early detection of dementia: Mild cognitive impairment (an evidence-based review): Report of the Quality Standards Subcommittee of the American Academy of Neurology. *Neurology, 56,* 1133–1142.

Pirttila, T., Erkinjuntti, T., & Hachinski, V. (2003). Vascular dementias and Alzheimer's disease. In V. Olga, B. Emery, & T. E. Oxman (Eds.), *Dementia: Presentations, differential diagnosis, and nosology* (2nd ed., pp. 306–335). Baltimore: Johns Hopkins University Press.

Price, R. W. (Ed.). (2003). *Acquired immunodeficiency syndrome dementia complex* (2nd ed.). Baltimore: Johns Hopkins University Press.

Psychological Corporation. (1997). *Wechsler Memory Scale—Third Edition, WMS–III technical manual.* San Antonio, TX: Author.

Psychological Corporation. (1999). *Wechsler Abbreviated Scale of Intelligence manual.* San Antonio, TX: Author.

Rabin, L. A., Borgos, M. B., Saykin, A. J., Root, M. D., Wishart, H. A., Flashman, L. A., et al. (2005). Judgment in older adults with AD, MCI, and cognitive complaints: Development and preliminary psychometric evaluation of the Dartmouth Rabin Judgment Questionnaire. *Proceedings of the 33rd Annual Meeting of the International Neuropsychological Society Meeting, 13.*

Reger, M. A., Welsh, R. K., Stennis Watson, G., Cholerton, B., Baker, L. D., & Craft, S. (2004). The relationship between neuropsychological functioning and driving ability in dementia: A meta-analysis. *Neuropsychology, 18,* 85–93.

Reisberg, B., Ferris, S. H., de Leon, M. J., & Crook, T. (1982). The Global Deterioration Scale (GDS) for assessment of primary degenerative dementia. *American Journal of Psychiatry, 139,* 1136–1139.

Reitan, R. M., & Wolfson, D. (1993). *The Halstead–Reitan Neuropsychological Test Battery: Theory and clinical interpretation* (2nd ed.). Tucson, AZ: Neuropsychology Press.

Ritchie, K., & Lovestone, S. (2002). The dementias. *The Lancet, 360,* 1759–1766.

Roberts, G. W., Leigh, P. N., Weinberger, D. R., & Perry, R. (1993). *Neuropsychiatric disorders.* London: Wolfe Publishing/ Mosby.

Rosen, W. G., Mohs, R. C., & Davis, K. L. (1984). A new rating scale for Alzheimer's disease. *American Journal of Psychiatry, 141,* 1356–1364.

Salmon, D. P., Butters, N., & Heindel, W. C. (1993). Alcoholic dementia and related disorders. In R. W. Parks, R. F. Zec, & R. S. Wilson (Eds.), *Neuropsychology of Alzheimer's disease and other dementias* (pp. 186–209). New York: Oxford University Press.

Saykin, A. J., Janssen, R. S., Sprehn, G. C., Spira, T., Kaplan, J., & O'Connor, B. (1991). Longitudinal evaluation of neuropsychological function in homosexual men with HIV infection: 18-month follow-up. *Journal of Neuropsychiatry and Clinical Neuroscience, 3,* 286–298.

Saykin, A. J, & Wishart, H. A. (2003). Mild cognitive impairment: Conceptual issues and Structural and functional brain correlates. *Seminars in Clinical Neuropsychiatry, 8,* 12–30.

Saykin, A. J., Wishart, H. A., Rabin, L. A., Santulli, R. B., Flashman, L. A., West, J. D., & Mamourian, A. C. (2005). *Regional brain atrophy in older adults with cognitive complaints and amnesic MCI.* Manuscript submitted for publication.

Schneider, L. S., Olin, J. T., Doody, R. S., Clark, C. M., Morris, J. C., Reisberg, B., et al. (1997). Validity and reliability of the Alzheimer's Disease Cooperative Study—Clinical Global Impression of Change. *Alzheimer Disease and Associated Disorders, 11,* S22–S32.

Shor-Posner, G., (2000). Cognitive function in HIV-1-infected drug users. *Journal of Acquired Immune Deficiency Syndromes, 25,* S70–S73.

Small, G. (2003). *The memory bible: An innovative strategy for keeping your brain young.* New York: Hyperion.

Small, G. W., Rabins, P. V., Barry, P. P., Buckholtz, N. S., De-Kosky, S. T., Ferris, S. H., et al. (1997). Diagnosis and treatment of Alzheimer's disease and related disorders: Consensus statement of the American Association for Geriatric Psychiatry, the Alzheimer's Association, and the American Geriatrics Society. *Journal of the American Medical Association, 278,* 1363–1371.

Smith, G. E., & Ivnik, R. J. (2003). Normative neuropsychology. In R. C. Petersen (Ed.), *Mild cognitive impairment: Aging to Alzheimer's disease* (pp. 63–88). New York: Oxford University Press.

Spielberger, C. D. (1983). *State–Trait Anxiety Inventory.* San Francisco: Consulting Psychologists Press.

Squire, L. R., Wetzel, C. D., & Slater, P. C. (1979). Memory complaint after electroconvulsive therapy: Assessment with a new self-rating instrument. *Biological Psychology, 14,* 791–801.

Stambrook, M., Gill, D. D., Cardoso, E. R., & Moore, A. D. (1993). Communicating (normal-pressure) hydrocephalus. In R. W. Parks, R. F. Zec, & R. S. Wilson (Eds.), *Neuropsychology of Alzheimer's disease and other dementias* (pp. 283–307). New York: Oxford University Press.

Tarter, R. E., & Van Thiel, D. H. (Eds.). (1985). *Dementia associated with alcoholism.* New York: Plenum.

Turkington, C. A. (1996). *12 steps to a better memory.* New York: Arco.

Walker, Z., & Stevens, T. (2002). Dementia with Lewy bodies: Clinical characteristics and diagnostic criteria. *Journal of Geriatric Psychiatry and Neurology, 15,* 188–194.

Wechsler, D. (1997). *Wechsler Adult Intelligence Scale—Third Edition.* San Antonio, TX: Psychological Corporation.

Wegiel, J., Wisniewski, T., Reisberg, B., & Silverman, W. (2003). The neuropathology of Alzheimer dementia. In V. Olga, B. Emery, & T. E. Oxman (Eds.), *Dementia: Presentations, differential diagnosis, and nosology* (2nd ed., pp. 89–120). Baltimore: Johns Hopkins University Press.

Weintraub, S. (1995). Examining mental state. In M. A. Samuels & S. Feske (Eds.), *Office practice of neurology* (pp. 698–705). New York: Churchill Livingstone.

Wilkinson, G. S. (1993). *The Wide Range Achievement Test—Third Edition (WRAT–III) administration manual.* Wilmington, DE: Wide Range Incorporated.

Winblad, B., Palmer, K., Kivipelto, M., Jelic, V., Fratiglioni, L., Wahlund, L.-O., et al. (2004). Mild cognitive impairment–beyond controversies, towards a consensus: Report of the international working group on mild cognitive impairment. *Journal of Internal Medicine, 256,* 240–246.

Zec, R. F. (1993). Neuropsychological functioning in Alzheimer's disease. In R. W. Parks, R. F. Zec, & R. S. Wilson (Eds.), *Neuropsychology of Alzheimer's disease and other dementias* (pp. 3–80). New York: Oxford University Press.

PART III

NEUROLOGICAL DISORDERS

CHAPTER 11

Alexander I. Tröster and Peter A. Arnett

Assessment of Movement and Demyelinating Disorders

The pathophysiologies, signs, and symptoms of movement and demyelinating disorders are distinct. However, because their neuropsychological profiles overlap, the most common movement and demyelinating disorders are considered within one chapter. At this time there is no "diagnostic" test (neuropsychological or otherwise) for the conditions outlined in this chapter, and neuropsychologists are rarely asked to make differential diagnoses among movement and demyelinating disorders. Many differences in neuropsychological profiles associated with various disorders are based on group studies that do not reveal the diagnostic sensitivity and specificity of neuropsychological test profiles. Consequently, it is advisable to report whether neuropsychological evaluation results are or are not consistent with a particular condition. Neuropsychologists are, however, asked to assist in differential diagnosis when there is a suspicion of a psychogenic movement disorder, or, in individuals with dementia, whether the dementia is associated with the movement/demyelinating disorder, depression, or some other neurological condition such as Alzheimer's disease. Referrals also are often made to obtain a baseline neuropsychological evaluation, enabling one with repeat evaluation to determine if a dementia is evolving, if a particular drug treatment is associated with cognitive and behavioral change, or if an individual is likely to require assistance with activities of daily living. More recently, with the reemergence of neurosurgical treatments for movement disorders, neuropsychologists are increasingly being asked to determine possible cognitive and behavioral contraindications to surgical intervention and to document cognitive and behavioral changes as a result of such treatments.

I. MOVEMENT DISORDERS

A. Definitions and Description of the Disorders

1. DEFINITIONS

a. Abnormal Movements

Extrapyramidal movement disorders (invariably affecting the basal ganglia) are of two broad types: **akinetic** (involving paucity of voluntary movement) and **hyperkinetic** (involving excessive, involuntary movements). Terms pertaining to **paucity of movement** include the following:

(a) **Akinesia** is loss or reduction of voluntary movement.

(b) **Hypokinesia** is slowing in the *initiation* of movements.

(c) **Bradykinesia** is slowing in the *execution* of movements.

Abnormalities involving **excessive movements** include the following:

(a) **Tremors** are rhythmic, repetitive, oscillating movements of a body part. **Resting tremor** is one occurring at rest; **action (kinetic or intention) tremor** occurs during movement; and **postural tremor** is observed when the affected body part is voluntarily held against gravity.

(b) **Chorea**, or choreiform movements, are asynchronous, irregular, and appear to semipurposively move from one body part to another.

(c) **Ballismus** is an irregular, unilateral, choreiform movement, typically affecting an upper limb. The limb appears to move in a "flinging" fashion.

(d) **Dystonia** is characterized by prolonged muscle contraction, often painful, causing abnormal posture, twisting, or repetitive movements.

(e) **Tics** are repetitive, sudden, transient, stereotyped movements, with a limited distribution. When prolonged, tics are described as dystonic.

(f) **Athetosis** refers to peripheral dystonic movements that look like "writhing" movements, typically iatrogenic in origin.

(g) **Dyskinesia** strictly refers to any involuntary movement; most often used to describe complex, choreiform, dystonic movements of iatrogenic origin. Not only seen after chronic neuroleptic treatment, dyskinesias can develop as a side effect of dopaminergic agonist treatment for parkinsonism.

(h) **Myoclonus** refers to brief, repetitive, shocklike muscle contractions of central nervous system (CNS) origin, typically affecting the same muscles. It can be of cortical or subcortical origin. When of subcortical origin, myoclonic movement is generalized; when of cortical origin, myoclonus is typically focal or multifocal.

(i) **Fasciculation** is visible as "twitches" beneath the skin; caused by random, repetitive contractions of groups of muscle fibers.

b. Parkinsonism

Parkinson's disease (PD) and parkinsonism are not synonymous. PD refers to a specific disease. **Parkinsonism**, however, refers to a syndrome consisting of four motor signs: tremor, rigidity, akinesia, and postural abnormalities. This syndrome is seen in PD but can also be a manifestation of numerous other conditions (see Table 11.1), including those that are neurodegenerative, vascular, metabolic, toxic, infectious, or even psychogenic (Tröster, Fields, & Koller, 2000).

2. DESCRIPTION OF DISORDERS AND EVOLUTION OF DISEASE STATES

a. Parkinson's disease

Age-adjusted prevalence estimates of PD in the United States range from 98 to 175 per 100,000, and annual incidence is estimated at 11 per 100,000, reaching a peak of 93 per 100,000 among those age 70 to 79 years. All four signs of parkinsonism rarely emerge simultaneously, and typically PD has a unilateral onset. Some have suggested that PD involves a long prodrome, and this, coupled with the fact that PD can first present with nonmotor symptoms, makes early diagnosis difficult. Although several sets of diagnostic criteria exist, none is uniformly accepted. Diagnostic accuracy for PD (verified at autopsy) is approximately 75%.

Although PD most often becomes symptomatic during the sixth decade of life, juvenile and young-onset forms occur. Early in PD, cognitive abnormalities (including conceptual reasoning, memory, attention, and visuospatial) are ascribed to a dysexecutive syndrome attributable to frontostriatal dysfunction. A recent study estimated that 36% of newly diagnosed patients have

Table 11.1. Conditions That Can Produce Parkinsonism

Type of condition	Condition or disorder
Structural	Hydrocephalus; chronic subdural hematoma; arteriovenous malformation; tumor
Vascular	Multiple infarcts; amyloid angiopathy; Binswanger's disease; basal ganglia infarct
Toxins	Manganese; mercury; carbon monoxide; carbon disulfide; cyanide; MPTP (1-methyl-4-phynyl-1,2,3,6-tetrahydropiridine)
Drugs	Lithium; neuroleptics
Infectious	Creutzfeld–Jakob disease; viral encephalitis; syphilis; encephalitis lethargica (Von Economo's disease); HIV; sarcoid, toxoplasmosis, cryptococcosis
Neurodegenerative	Parkinson's disease; olivopontocerebellar atrophy; Shy–Drager Syndrome; progressive supranuclear palsy; striatonigral degeneration; corticobasal ganglionic degeneration; Parkinson–ALS–dementia complex of Guam; pallido-ponto-nigral-degeneration; dentato-rubro-pallido-luysian atrophy; Alzheimer's disease; diffuse Lewy body disease (also called Lewy-body variant of Alzheimer's disease and Lewy body dementia); Huntington's disease; Pick's disease; Fahr's disease (familial, idiopathic basal ganglia calcification); multiple sclerosis; neurocanthocytosis
Inherited metabolic	Wilson's disease; Gaucher's disease; Hallervorden-Spatz disease; GM1 gangliosidosis
Traumatic	Dementia pugilistica
Psychogenic	Conversion and factitious disorders; malingering

Note. From "Parkinson's Disease and Parkinsonism," by W. C. Koller and B. B. Megaffin, in C. E. Coffey and J. L. Cummings (Eds.), *Textbook of Geriatric Neuropsychiatry*, 1994, Washington, DC: American Psychiatric Press. Copyright 1994 by the American Psychiatric Association. Adapted with permission.

cognitive deficits detectable on formal testing (Foltynie, Brayne, Robbins, & Barker, 2004). Dementia evolves only in a minority of patients, with the most commonly reported prevalence estimates falling into the 20% to 50% range (Tröster & Woods, 2003). Though heterogeneous, and probably better referred to as the "dementias of Parkinson's disease," the dementia is typically of the "subcortical" type and characterized by predominant impairments in attention and executive functions, visuospatial disturbance, and memory. Language and praxis are typically relatively preserved.

b. Parkinson-plus syndromes

The conditions from which PD is most difficult to differentiate perhaps is a class of disorders known as **parkinson-plus syndromes**. Parkinson-plus syndromes include **progressive supranuclear palsy** (PSP; also known as Steele–Richardson–Olszewski syndrome), the **multiple system atrophies** (Wenning, Colosimo, Geser, & Poewe, 2004; previously called olivopontocerebellar atrophy [OPCA], striatonigral degeneration [SND], and Shy–Drager syndrome [SDS] but more recently referred to as multiple system atrophy of the parkinsonian [MSA-P] and cerebellar [MSA-C] types), and **corticobasal degeneration** (CBD). The inclusion of CBD among parkinson-plus conditions is warranted by virtue of the typical clinical features but may be debated on neuropathological grounds because CBD is recognized as a tauopathy, unlike PD and MSA, which are α-synucleinopathies.

Progressive supranuclear palsy (Steele–Richardson–Olszewski syndrome). Prevalence in the United States was thought to be about 1.5 per 100,000, though more recent studies fairly consistently reveal an age-adjusted prevalence of about 5 per 100,000. Unlike PD, symptoms typically are symmetric at onset, resting tremor is minimal, and gait disturbance (postural imbalance) is an early sign. Dysarthria may also appear earlier than in PD. Symptoms typically respond poorly to dopaminergic medications. Later combinations of signs of PSP are more characteristic of the disease: prominent vertical gaze palsy, disproportionate axial versus limb rigidity, prominence of gait disturbance, facial spasticity, and impairment of saccadic eye movements. Age at onset is narrower than in PD, with few cases (about 5%) having onset before age 50. The typical onset, as in PD, is in the sixth decade of life. Progression of the disease is more rapid than in PD, with immobility occurring a median of 6 years after diagnosis. Unfortunately, underdiagnosis of the condition often results in formal diagnosis only about 3.5 years after symptom onset. No uniform set of diagnostic criteria exists, but research criteria have been proposed (Litvan et al., 1996). A recent study evaluating four sets of criteria vis-à-vis autopsy-proven cases found criteria to have sensitivity ranging from 13% to 55%, and specificity from 93% to 100%, when raters were provided with clinical information from the patients' first visit. When applied to information from the patients' last visits, the four sets of criteria had sensitivity ranging from 34% to 89% and specificity ranging from 74% to 98%. Some have suggested cognition to be unaffected in PSP, and overdiagnosis of dementia to be attributable to patients' bradyphrenia, emotional changes, and visual dysfunction. There is no consensus about prevalence of dementia in PSP, and in different patient series dementia was reported to occur in 50% to 80% of cases. The dementia is of the subcortical type, with pronounced executive dysfunction (Grafman, Litvan, & Stark, 1995). Episodic memory impairment may be comparable to that in PD, but executive and attentional deficits may be present earlier and progress more rapidly in PSP than PD. The executive behavioral deficits have been linked to magnetic resonance imaging (MRI)-visualized frontal lobe pathology.

Multiple system atrophies. Multiple system atrophies (MSAs) refers to progressive neurodegenerative conditions that involve a variable combination of extrapyramidal (parkinsonian) and pyramidal motor signs, cerebellar ataxia, and autonomic dysfunction. Diagnostic accuracy is poor (25%–50%), and although probabilistic diagnostic criteria have been proposed, they remain to be prospectively evaluated. Two predominant motor presentations are recognized: MSA-P (80% of cases) and MSA-C (20% of cases), probably corresponding closely to SND and OPCA. Prevalence estimates range from 2 to 5 per 100,000 (Wenning et al., 2004), and incidence is estimated at 3 per 100,000 among people age 50 to 99 years. Cognitive impairments include deficits in attention, executive function, verbal fluency, and memory (Dujardin, Defebvre, Krystkowiak, Degreef, & Destee, 2003; Monza et al., 1998). Though similarities in the cognitive profiles of PD and MSA outweigh differences, attention and verbal fluency may be more impaired in MSA than PD when the groups are equated for overall severity of cognitive deficits.

Corticobasal degeneration. Corticobasal degeneration (CBD) has an insidious onset late in adulthood and is slowly progressive. Its prevalence and incidence have not been reported, and this is probably in large part a reflection of poor diagnostic accuracy. The initial presentation is typically asymmetric, occasionally "alien limb" syndrome is evident, and both cortical and subcortical deficits (of which apraxia is a key cortical feature) are evident. The patient's most typical initial complaint involves clumsiness, stiffness, and jerkiness of an arm and, less frequently, clumsiness of a leg. The most common early movement problems are akinesia and rigidity. Dementia was thought to occur rarely, and if so, late in the disease, but this may be incorrect, and the observed frequency of cognitive deficits in CBD may be a function of whether case series are drawn from movement disorder or dementia centers. Cognitive deficits are increasingly appreciated as being a part of CBD (Graham, Bak, & Hodges, 2003), and CBD can present neurobehaviorally resembling frontotemporal dementia and primary progressive aphasia. Typical cognitive deficits include apraxia, phonological rather than semantic deficits, poor episodic memory, and executive dysfunction. When aphasia is present, it is most often of the nonfluent type. Because the clinical features of CBD can be produced by conditions other than CBD, and pathologically confirmed CBD can have heterogeneous clinical presentations, it has been proposed that **corticobasal syndrome** (CBS) be the term applied to conditions characterized by the core motor and cortical features of CBD regardless of etiology, whereas CBD be reserved for neuropathologically distinct CBD regardless of clinical presentation.

c. Wilson's disease

Wilson's disease (WD) is a disorder of copper metabolism. Inherited via an autosomal recessive gene on chromosome 13, the disease can become symptomatic between ages 5 and 50, although most cases present between 8 and 16 years of age. Prevalence is estimated at 3 per 100,000. Presentation is highly variable but most often involves liver disease (more often in females than males) or neurological signs and symptoms (more often in males). Kayser–Fleischer (copper corneal) rings are not specific to WD and do not occur in all cases of WD. Neurological signs and symptoms most commonly include dysarthria and poor coordination, but patients can also have postural abnormalities, dystonia, chorea, and the full parkinsonian syndrome. Treatments aimed at restriction of copper intake and enhanced copper elimination are thought to be very effective in reversing hepatic, renal, and cerebral dysfunction. However, even in treated patients, deficits can be seen in reaction time, attention, executive function, and memory along with emotional issues such as impulsiveness, irritability, apathy, and disinhibition (Portala, Levander, Westermark, Ekselius, & von Knorring, 2001).

d. Huntington's disease

A disorder inherited in autosomal dominant manner, Huntington's disease (HD) symptoms typically emerge in the mid-30s to mid-40s. Initial manifestations of HD include personality change, adventitious movements, and the gradual emergence of chorea and cognitive impairment, progressing to dementia. In the juvenile form (onset before age 20), resting tremor and rigidity may predominate. Prevalence is estimated at 5 to 7 per 100,000. The course of the disease spans 10 to 30 years, and death is usually attributable to complications of HD (e.g., pneumonia). The characteristic subcortical dementia associated with HD has been well characterized. Commonly, deficits are observed in memory (encoding and retrieval), working memory and complex (divided and selective) attention, executive functions, and aspects of visuoconstructional performance. There is a slowness of thought and word retrieval, though aphasia and apraxia are not evident (Zakzanis, 1998). Cognitive and behavioral measures have been helpful in predicting functional capacity, especially in instrumental activities of daily living (i.e., in those skills required to remain independent within the community; Hamilton et al., 2003).

3. VARIANTS OF DISORDERS

Postencephalitic parkinsonism, drug (1-methyl-4-phynyl-1,2,3,6-tetrahydropiridine [MPTP])-induced parkinsonism, and Parkinson-dementia complex of Guam are rarely encountered. Cognitive deficits in MPTP parkinsonism resemble those seen in PD.

4. NEUROPATHOLOGICAL CORRELATES

a. Parkinson's disease

Idiopathic PD is characterized by pigmented cell loss in the substantia nigra (especially the ventrolateral aspect), presence of Lewy bodies in the substantia nigra, locus caeruleus, substantia innominata, and dorsal vagal nucleus. Dopamine is reduced in nigrostriatal system structures (putamen more than caudate) and projections to the frontal cortex and limbic system. There is loss of noradrenergic cells in the locus caeruleus, and serotonergic cell loss in the raphe and dorsal vagal nuclei. Nucleus basalis cell loss is also observed and is associated with cholinergic depletion.

b. Progressive supranuclear palsy

Four pathological findings are consistently evident in PSP: astrocytic gliosis, loss of nerve cells, neurofibrillary tangle (NFT) presence, and granulovacuolar nerve cell degeneration. Unlike PD, PSP involves the entire substantia nigra. The NFTs are different from those observed in Alzheimer's disease (AD). Other loci of pathology include globus pallidus, subthalamic nucleus, dentate nucleus, red nucleus, periaqueductal gray, and the pontine tegmentum. Cholinergic depletion is evident in the nucleus basalis and laterodorsal tegmental nucleus, but cortical cholinergic loss is mild. Dopamine is comparably reduced in the caudate, putamen, and substantia nigra.

c. Multiple system atrophies

Cell loss and gliosis are evident in the striatum (especially putamen), substantia nigra, inferior olives, pons, and cerebellum. Lewy bodies, except for incidental ones, are absent, but oligodendroglial cytoplasmic inclusions are widespread. Sporadic OPCA-associated lesions most often affect substantia nigra, striatum, and less commonly locus caeruleus and dentate nucleus. There might be increased putaminal iron deposition in SND.

d. Corticobasal degeneration

No accepted set of neuropathologic criteria for CBD diagnosis exists. Although "ballooned neurons" are almost always found in CBD, they also occur in Pick's disease and other neurodegenerative conditions. In CBD they are observed in cortex (most often in an asymmetric, frontoparietal distribution), substantia nigra, and with greater variability among gray matter structures such as subthalamic nucleus, globus pallidus, dentate nucleus, locus caeruleus, and lateral thalamus. Neuronal loss and gliosis are also evident in the structures previously outlined, and there is depigmentation of the substantia nigra.

e. Wilson's disease

In the hepatolenticular degeneration of WD, there is striking red pigmentation of the basal ganglia. Spongy degeneration and astrocytosis can be observed in the putamen and frontal cortex. Basal ganglia may show neuronal loss and axonal degeneration. Degenerative changes are less evident in dentate and substantia nigra.

f. Huntington's disease

Early changes are limited to subcortical structures, but at autopsy cortical and caudate atrophy are prominent. There is loss of especially the medium-sized spiny neurons and their gamma-aminobutyric acid (GABA)-ergic efferents in the caudate and putamen. The consequent atrophy of striatopallidal and striatonigral fiber bundles is thought responsible for the movement abnormalities in HD. Reactive gliosis is observed in affected areas.

B. Functional Neuroanatomical Correlates

Although the traditional model of frontal-basal ganglionic connectivity positing five segregated, parallel loops needs updating given recent findings (Saint-Cyr, 2003), the basic model remains a useful heuristic for understanding neurobehavioral dysfunction in movement disorders. The five circuits are named according to their function or site of frontal origin: the **motor circuit**, originating in the supplementary motor area; the **oculomotor circuit**, originating in the frontal eye field; and the **lateral orbitofrontal**, **anterior cingulate**, and **dorsolateral prefrontal** circuits. The first two circuits are important in motor function, whereas the latter three circuits are important in cognition and behavior. Behavioral deficits associated with pathology of the three circuits are as follows:

- **dorsolateral:** poor organizational and memory search strategies, stimulus-boundedness, impaired cognitive flexibility, dissociations in verbal and manual behavior;
- **orbitofrontal:** personality change, mood disorders, environmental dependency, and obsessive-compulsiveness; and
- **anterior cingulate:** impaired motivation and ineffective response inhibition.

Several points bear emphasizing about functional correlates of frontosubcortical circuit dysfunction. First, in neurodegenerative conditions, cognitive and behavioral syndromes are likely to be complex because multiple circuits are often disrupted. Second, although broad statements about anatomic–functional correlates can be advanced, details are less well worked out and controversial. For example, there is little debate that patients with PD often demonstrate executive dysfunction. What remains debated is the extent to which executive deficits account for other (e.g., memory) deficits. Third, some have proposed that circuits are open and interconnected. Even if closed, the circuits have open components, allowing for the possibility that cognitive dysfunction reflects disruption of afferent or efferent connections between the open component and another structure.

A simplified illustration of the key pathophysiology in PD is presented in Figure 11.1. In PD, diminished dopaminergic innervation of the striatum (especially the putamen) results in decreased activity of inhibitory projections from the striatum to the substantia nigra (pars reticulata) and internal globus pallidus. These structures' consequently increased inhibitory effect on the external globus pallidus, together with increased activity in the inhibitory projections from the striatum to the external globus pallidus, lead to a decrease in the inhibitory effect exerted by the external globus pallidus's projections on the subthalamic nucleus. The subthalamic nucleus's overactive excitatory projections to the internal globus pallidus/substantia nigra (pars reticulata), together with the already diminished inhibition of the internal globus pallidus/substantia nigra pars reticulata by striatal projections, lead to excessive inhibition of the ventrolateral thalamus. This, in turn, leads to a diminution of the excitatory thalamic influence on motor cortex.

In HD, there is a preferential loss of inhibitory, GABAergic projections from the striatum (especially caudate) to the external globus pallidus. The external globus pallidus's inhibitory control over the subthalamic nucleus is thus enhanced. Increased inhibition of the subthalamic nucleus in turn results in reduction of this structure's excitatory influences on substantia nigra pars reticulata and internal globus pallidus. The internal globus pallidus and substantia nigra pars reticulata thus have a diminished inhibitory influence on thalamus, which in turn leads to overactivation of excitatory projections from thalamus to motor cortex.

C. Competing Diagnoses

Neuropsychologists are rarely asked to distinguish among movement disorders; neuropsychological tests lack the needed specificity, although they can help in differential diagnosis. Rather, referral questions often center on whether a suspected dementia is associated with the movement disorder, AD, or depression. Occasionally, referrals are to seek confirmation that a patient is experiencing delirium or that neuropsychological evaluation supports (or not) a diagnosis of psychogenic movement disorder.

1. PARKINSON'S DISEASE VERSUS ALZHEIMER'S DISEASE VERSUS DEMENTIA WITH LEWY BODIES

Often the differential between AD and PD is made easily: In typical PD and AD, the dementias conform to patterns of

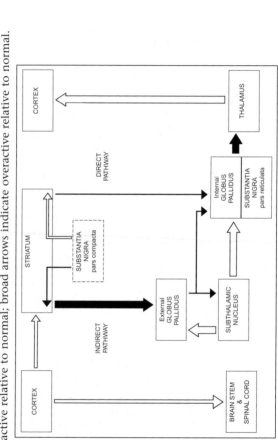

Figure 11.1. Frontostriatal circuit dysfunction in Parkinson's disease (from Tröster & Fields, in press). Solid arrows indicate inhibitory influence; open arrows indicate excitatory influence; narrow arrows indicate underactive relative to normal; broad arrows indicate overactive relative to normal.

"subcortical" and "cortical" dysfunction, respectively. The issue becomes more difficult when the patient presents with extrapyramidal signs and a mixture of cortical and subcortical cognitive dysfunction. It is possible, then, that the patient has one in the spectrum of Lewy body diseases or CBD. Several factors make neuropsychological evaluation and differentiation of AD, Parkinson's disease with dementia (PDD), and dementia with Lewy bodies (DLB) difficult. First, it is unclear whether PDD is an entity distinct from DLB. Currently, if cognitive or behavioral deficits emerge before or within 1 year of onset of the extrapyramidal movement disorder, a diagnosis of DLB is made, whereas if cognitive deficits emerge more than 1 year after the movement disorder, a diagnosis of PDD is made. This diagnostic distinction is somewhat arbitrary. Second, the majority of cases of DLB (about 80%) also have pathologic features of AD, most often plaques (McKeith et al., 2003). Despite these challenges, some consistent, if not sizable, differences in the neuropsychological profiles of AD and DLB have emerged. Specifically, DLB is associated with greater impairments in verbal fluency, attention, and visuoperceptual functions than AD, whereas AD presents with more severe memory deficits (Aarsland et al., 2003). In contrast, studies attempting to differentiate PDD and DLB have met with less consistent success. While some have reported greater attentional, executive, and verbal fluency impairments in DLB than PDD (e.g., Downes et al., 1998), others have failed to find any differences in attention or other functions (e.g., Noe et al., 2004). Cognitive deficits in CBD are variable, but typically language and memory are better preserved in CBD than AD (Pillon et al., 1995). Two hallmarks of CBD are a pronounced, early apraxia and the alien hand sign, which typically develops within 1 to 2 years of disease onset. Cognitive impairment patterns reflect asymmetric, cortical, and subcortical pathology. Occasionally CBD can present as frontotemporal dementia and primary progressive aphasia. A preliminary comparison of cognitive deficits in AD, PD, PDD, DLB and CBD is provided in Table 11.2.

2. DEMENTIA VERSUS DEPRESSIVE DEMENTIA IN PARKINSON'S DISEASE

Depression is common in PD, with lifetime prevalence estimated to be about 40% (for reviews, see McDonald, Richard, & DeLong, 2003; Tröster & Letsch, 2004). Depression is a risk factor not only for PD itself but also for dementia in PD. Depression, probably of at least moderate severity, exacerbates executive and memory deficits. Because depression probably affects the severity rather than the pattern of cognitive impairment in PD,

Table 11.2. Patterns of Cognitive Impairments in Movement Disorders and Alzheimer's Disease

Area of cognitive impairment	PD	PD + Dementia	DLBD	CBGD	AD
Attention	0/-	-/-	-	-/-	-
Problem-solving/conceptualization/ cognitive flexibility	-	-			-/-
Speech (e.g., dysarthria)	-	-	-/-	-	0
Language					
Visual confrontation naming	0/-	-	-/-	-	-/-
Letter fluency	0/-	-	-/-	-/-?	0/-
Category fluency	-	-/-	-/-	-?	-
Word knowledge	0/-	0/-	?	0	-
Anterograde memory					
Encoding	0/-	-	-	0/-	-/-
Storage	0	0/-	-	0/-	0/-
Retrieval	-	-	-/-	-/-?	-
Proactive interference	0	-	0/-	0/-?	-
Retrograde memory	0	-	?	0/-?	-
Praxis	0	0/-	-	-	0
Alien-hand sign	0	0	0	-	0
Visuoperceptual functions	-	-/-	-	0/-?	-
Visuoconstructional functions	0/-	-	-	?	-/-

Note. PD = Parkinson's disease; DLBD = diffuse Lewy body disease, CBGD = corticobasal ganglionic degeneration; AD = Alzheimer's disease; 0 = unimpaired; - = mild-to-moderate impairment; — = moderate-severe impairment; ? = unknown or to-be-confirmed.

it becomes difficult to determine from a single assessment the extent to which a dementia in a PD patient with depression reflects PD as opposed to depression. The implication, however, is important. Cognitive impairment due to depression is likely to resolve with successful treatment of the depression, whereas the cognitive impairment of PD does not. Thus, we recommend that etiologic determination be deferred until adequate depression treatment has been undertaken. Repeat assessment is then likely to reveal the etiology of the cognitive impairment in the depressed PD patient.

3. PSYCHOGENIC MOVEMENT DISORDERS

Neuropsychological evaluation cannot adequately differentiate *psychogenic* from *organic* movement disorders. Even neurological criteria lack specificity, and as many as 6% to 30% of cases diagnosed as psychogenic are ultimately found to have an organic movement disorder. Misdiagnosis of an organic as a psychogenic movement disorder is more likely than the converse. A neuropsychological profile consistent with, for example, PD is more helpful in directing one *away* from a psychogenic diagnosis than a normal evaluation is in directing one *to* a psychogenic diagnosis. Use of personality inventories (e.g., the Minnesota Multiphasic Personality Inventory, or MMPI) is fraught with difficulty, as both organic and psychogenic movement disorders are likely to show "1–3" elevations, and proposed "correction" factors have not been evaluated in movement disorders. If a psychogenic movement disorder is suspected, it is imperative that the nature of the psychological condition be identified (e.g., factitious, somatoform, or malingering).

D. Medical History and Laboratory Data

The patient's history should always be scrutinized for recreational and medicinal drug use. Because several movement disorders are heritable, family history should always be investigated. In young individuals with movement abnormalities (e.g., chorea), especially when recreational intravenous drug use history is present, questioning about HIV-risk factors or diagnosis is indicated.

1. **Parkinson's disease** Laboratory tests are typically not used in the diagnosis of PD. At times, if an infectious condition is suspected as a cause of parkinsonism, cerebrospinal fluid (CSF) studies are undertaken. Laboratory tests are more likely to be done in juvenile onset or young-onset parkinsonism to rule out metabolic, toxic,

and inherited conditions. In suspected toxic etiology, urine is typically screened for heavy metals (e.g., mercury, manganese) and recreational drugs (e.g., cocaine, narcotics). For metabolic conditions, urinalysis will likely screen for dolichols, amino acids, oligosacharides, and organic acids.

2. **Progressive supranuclear palsy:** Biochemistry, urinalysis, and hematology are normal. CSF findings are not specific.

3. **Multiple system atrophies:** In autosomal dominant OPCA, the genotype can be determined by genetic linkage and polymerase chain reaction (PCR) methods. Electromyography (EMG) and nerve conduction velocity studies are typically used when OPCA is associated with amyotrophy and lower motor neuron involvement.

Autonomic dysfunction tests are used especially in SDS and might include tests such as blood pressure response to standing up or head tilt, heart rate response to standing, sphincter EMG, urodynamic studies, and gastrointestinal swallow and emptying studies. Laboratory tests are generally not helpful in diagnosis of SND.

4. **Corticobasal degeneration:** Biochemistry, hematology, and urinalysis are normal.

5. **Wilson's disease:** Family history should be investigated. Prior liver disease and gastrointestinal symptoms may be noted in the history. Serum ceruloplasmin (reduced), urinalysis for copper (typically increased to 100–1,000 µg per 24-hour sample), slit-lamp examination for Kayser–Fleischer rings, and measurement of copper content of a liver biopsy (the most important in diagnosis) are helpful.

6. **Huntington's disease:** Given the discovery that CAG trinucleotide repeats are expanded in HD, DNA analysis is confirmatory when the number of repeats is 40 or greater. Family history of the disorder must be present. Biochemistry, urinalysis, hematology are normal.

E. EEG and Neuroimaging Correlates

Electroencephalography (EEG) studies in movement disorders are generally unhelpful. Abnormal findings are nonspecific. EEG is helpful if Creutzfeldt–Jakob's disease is suspected as a cause of parkinsonism: It shows characteristic generalized slowing and pseudoperiodic sharp wave activity.

Neuroimaging studies vary in their helpfulness. If hydrocephalus, tumors, hematoma, infarcts, basal ganglia calcification, or infections are suspected as causing parkinsonism, computed tomography (CT) or MRI is helpful in demonstrating this. Imaging studies are also recommended when parkinsonism is accompanied by rapid cognitive deterioration. In PD, PSP, and HD, both MRI and CT are normal early in the course of these diseases. MRI reveals narrowing of the high signal region between substantia nigra and the red nucleus in some PD patients. PSP, later in the disease, is likely to be associated with increased signal in the periaqueductal region, dilation of the cerebral aqueduct, and reduction of midbrain diameter. In intermediate to advanced HD, atrophy of the caudate and putamen, and decreased pallidal signal, might be evident on T1-weighted MRI. Putaminal signal loss on MRI might indicate that SND is more likely than PD. Cerebellar and brainstem atrophy are observed in MSA but not PD. MRI is often helpful in Wilson's disease: T2-weighted MRI may reveal the characteristic "face of the giant panda" sign (i.e., hypointensity of superior colliculus, preserved signal from lateral substantia nigra pars reticulata, and high signal intensity in the tegmentum with exception of the red nucleus). MRI will likely also reveal cerebral atrophy, ventricular dilation, and lenticular signal hyperintensity.

Numerous functional imaging studies using positron emission tomography (PET) or single photon emission computed tomography (SPECT) have been carried out in movement disorders (Brooks, 2000). Their clinical use, however, remains to be more rigorously demonstrated. PET-visualized glucose hypometabolism in the frontal and striatal regions is more likely to be observed early in SND and PSP than PD. Unilateral temporo-parietal-occipital hypometabolism is observed on PET in CBD, but this can also be seen in cases of asymmetric AD. The diffuse cortical and striatal hypometabolism seen on PET in HD is likely nonspecific.

F. Areas of Emphasis Within the Neuropsychological Evaluation

Clinicians partial to the use of fixed batteries (e.g., Halstead–Reitan Battery) always administer the same test battery, and thus the following comments are directed to clinicians selecting tests for use in flexible batteries. Clinicians administering lengthy, fixed batteries need to be particularly cognizant of fatigue effects common in PD, as well as the fluctuation of symptoms (on–off phenomenon) to which some PD patients are prone. Ideally, PD patients should be evaluated during the "on" phase, permitting them to perform optimally. A lengthy neuropsychological test battery administered during both on and off phases is likely to yield a pattern of strengths and weaknesses that is difficult to interpret meaningfully.

Regardless of the type of movement disorder, the neuropsychological profile will often resemble one that might be expected from frontosubcortical dysfunction, and if a dementia is present, the profile is expected to conform to one associated with subcortical dementias. Because most of the movement disorders discussed in this chapter are associated with progressive cognitive dysfunction, it is important to obtain estimates of premorbid functioning. Although a cognitive screening examination might not yield useful information early in the course of diseases: it is worthwhile to obtain a baseline on a screening measure: This will facilitate monitoring of cognitive function once the patient can no longer cooperate with a lengthy neuropsychological test battery. Although a Mini-Mental State Examination score of 23 and below has good sensitivity (98%) and adequate specificity (77%) in detecting dementia among PD patients with *Diagnostic and Statistical Manual of Mental Disorders* (4th ed. [*DSM–IV*]; American Psychiatric Association, 1994) diagnosed dementia, it is not sensitive to milder cognitive impairment, probably because the instrument deemphasizes executive functions.

Some clinicians will advocate use of an intelligence test. Although the Wechsler Adult Intelligence Scale—III (WAIS–III) and predecessors have several strengths, one has to consider the time it takes to administer in relation to the information it yields. It might be preferable to administer a subset of tests (or the Wechsler Abbreviated Scale of Intelligence [WASI]) to derive an IQ estimate, and to estimate from this if a decline from a previously higher level of intelligence has likely occurred. The WASI's inclusion of Matrix reasoning is quite helpful for movement disorders. Subtests that are timed and have significant motor demands are less likely to yield useful information in a patient with profound motor impairments.

Because many movement disorders are associated with a frontosubcortical cognitive dysfunction pattern, emphasis is placed on the evaluation of attention and executive functions (e.g., conceptual flexibility, abstraction, planning, monitoring of behavior). Because visuo-perceptual-spatial dysfunction is often observed early in PD and HD, these functions are also thoroughly evaluated. Priority is given to memory tests that permit differentiation of recall and recognition deficits. Language tests sensitive to word search inefficiency (e.g., verbal fluency, visual confrontation naming) are given more emphasis than repetition and comprehension tests. Because mood disturbance is common, assessment of depression and anxiety is imperative. Because symptoms of PD overlap with those of depression and anxiety, an interview should be done to supplement and clarify data from self-report questionnaires and scales such as the Beck Depression Inventory—II (BDI–II) or Beck Anxiety Inventory (BAI). Quality of life is evaluated in an increasing number of patients because the aim of treatment is not simply to reduce parkinsonian symptoms but to improve the patient's quality of life.

G. Neuropsychological Measures Helpful in Differential Diagnosis

Table 11.3 lists some tests that may be helpful in evaluating movement disorders. This listing should not be viewed as prescriptive or exhaustive; rather test selection must be based on the referral question and the patient's ability to cooperate with the tests.

Although measures are less likely to be helpful in differential diagnosis among movement disorders, several measures are helpful in differentiating between PD with dementia and HD on the one hand, and CBD and AD on the other hand. In particular, measures of language (fluency and visual confrontation naming), praxis, attention, and memory are helpful in this regard. The sensitivity and specificity of different patterns of performance among these patient groups remain to be empirically demonstrated.

With respect to verbal fluency, letter fluency (e.g., Controlled Oral Word Association Test [COWAT]) and semantic category fluency (e.g., the Animal Naming Test from the Boston Diagnostic Aphasia Examination) tasks are helpful. Verbal fluency may be preserved early in PD. Patients with movement disorders and dementia are likely to perform particularly poorly on letter fluency tasks, whereas patients with AD perform especially poorly on semantic fluency. The patient with PD has only mild if any difficulty with visual confrontation naming (e.g., Boston Naming Test), and even PDD and HD involve lesser deficits than does AD. Excellent normative data applicable to elderly people are available for naming and fluency tests (e.g., Heaton, Miller, Taylor, & Grant, 2004).

Among attention tests, the Trailmaking and Stroop tests may be helpful in differentiating AD, PDD, and DLB, with DLB

Table 11.3. Commonly Used Neuropsychological Tests by Cognitive Domain Assessed

Cognitive domain	Test
Premorbid estimates	Barona Demographic Equations; North American Adult Reading Test; Wechsler Test of Adult Reading; Wide Range Achievement Test
Neuropsychological screening	Mattis Dementia Rating Scale; Mini Mental Status Examination; Repeatable Battery for the Assessment of Neuropsychological Status
Intelligence	Kaufman Brief Intelligence Test; Raven's Progressive Matrices; Wechsler Abbreviated Scale of Intelligence; Wechsler Adult Intelligence Scale (recent editions)
Attention and working memory	Auditory Consonant Trigrams; Brief Test of Attention; Continuous Performance Tests; Digit and Visual Spans; Paced Auditory Serial Addition Test; Stroop Test[a]
Executive function	Cognitive Estimation Test; Delis-Kaplan Executive Function Scale; Halstead Category Test; Trailmaking Test[a]; Wisconsin Card Sorting Test; Tower of Toronto; Tower of London
Memory	Benton Visual Retention Test; California Verbal Learning Test; Rey Auditory Verbal Learning Test; Selective Reminding Test; Rey Complex Figure Test[a]; Wechsler Memory Scale (recent editions)[a]
Language	Boston Naming Test; Controlled Oral Word Association Test; Sentence Repetition; Token Test; Complex Ideational Material
Visuoperception	Benton Facial Recognition Test; Benton Judgment of Line Orientation; Hooper Visual Organization Test
Motor and sensory perception	Finger Tapping[a]; Grooved Pegboard[a]; Hand Dynamometer[a]; Sensory–Perceptual Examination

Mood State and Personality	Beck Anxiety Inventory; Beck Depression Inventory; Hamilton Depression Scale or Inventory; The Neuropsychiatric Inventory; Minnesota Multiphasic Personality Inventory (recent editions); Profile of Mood States; State–Trait Anxiety Inventory; Maudsley Obsessional–Compulsive Inventory; Yale–Brown Obsessive Compulsive Scale; Hospital Anxiety and Depression Scale; Montgomery–Åsberg Depression Rating Scale
Quality of life, coping, and stressors	Parkinson's Disease Questionnaire; Medical Outcomes Study 36-Item short form; Sickness Impact Profile; Coping Responses Inventory; Ways of Coping Questionnaire; Life Stressors and Social Resources Inventory

[a] Test may not be appropriate for patients with marked motor impairment.

demonstrating greatest impairment. Norms for elderly people for these test are available (e.g., Heaton et al., 2004; Moering, Schinka, Mortimer, & Graves, 2004). On memory tests such as the Wechsler Memory Scale—III (WMS–III), only preliminary data from small samples have been published to characterize performance in AD, PD, and HD. Consistent with its predecessor, patients with AD earn lower memory index scores than HD and PD patients. The Working Memory Index in AD is relatively preserved, and retention and retrieval auditory composite scores reveal the expected lack of benefit from provision of a recognition format and rapid forgetting. Patients with PD and HD, unlike those with AD, show relatively intact "retrieval" auditory process scores. Whether the WMS–R finding of much more rapid forgetting on Logical Memory and Visual Reproduction subtests in AD than movement disorders, and the proclivity of AD patients to make intrusion errors on Visual Reproduction, extends to the WMS–III remains to be demonstrated.

Subgroups of PD patients demonstrating patterns of cortical and subcortical dementia on the California Verbal Learning Test (CVLT; and presumably the newer CVLT–II) exist (Massman, Delis, Butters, Levin, & Salmon, 1990), but the PD patient without dementia is likely to demonstrate only mild, if any, impairment on recall and to perform fairly normally on recognition. Whereas semantic encoding is diminished, serial encoding is preserved, and normal serial position effects are seen. A similar pattern is seen in HD. The patient with AD, however, is likely to demonstrate equally impaired recall and recognition and to make many intrusion and perseveration errors. Clinicians using the Auditory Verbal Learning Test (AVLT) will similarly find that PD is associated with preserved recognition and will find the norms for elderly people provided by Harris, Ivnik, and Smith (2002) helpful.

In terms of apraxia, PD and PDD patients are likely to perform normally. AD and CBD both will show impairments, but CBD patients will especially so and early in the disease. One test useful for apraxia screening is the apraxia test from the Western Aphasia Battery.

Clinicians will often seek a Wisconsin Card Sorting Test (WCST) short form for administration to individuals with movement disorders or dementia. Two short forms have been found to be sensitive to AD, HD, and PD with and without dementia: Nelson's (1976) short form and a version with traditional administration and scoring methods but using only 64 cards, now published as the WCST-64.

Among cognitive screening examinations, the Dementia Rating Scale (both DRS and DRS–2) can be helpful because performance patterns of AD, HD, PD, PDD, and DLB have been characterized on this test. Compared with AD, patients with HD perform significantly more poorly on the Initiation/Perseveration test, and PD patients perform more poorly on the Construction test. Patients with PDD and DLB perform more poorly on Initiation/Perseveration and Construction subtests than AD patients, whereas AD patients perform significantly more poorly on the Memory test compared with the other groups (Aarsland et al., 2003). When depressed, PD patients' performance deteriorates, especially on the Initiation/Perseveration and Memory subtests.

Care needs to be taken in assessing mood state because symptoms of depression and anxiety overlap with those of PD and to some extent HD. Thus, depression and anxiety disorders may be overestimated using traditional cutoffs on self-report scales such as the BDI and BAI, although these scales can still be validly used with PD patients (Higginson, Fields, Koller, & Tröster, 2001; Levin, Llabre, & Weiner, 1988). Table 11.4 provides empirically validated cutoffs for some depression scales commonly used in PD.

H. Psychiatric Morbidity in Movement Disorders

Depression is common among individuals with HD and PD. In HD, it is estimated that 30% of individuals experience major depressive episodes, 5% experience dysthymia, and many more experience episodes of dysphoria (Cummings, 1995). Suicide prevalence is considerably greater in HD than in the general population (approximately a four- to sixfold increase) and in other neurological disorders frequently accompanied by depression. Individuals with HD and depression, and those HD patients over age 50 years, appear especially vulnerable. Other psychiatric morbidity in HD includes personality changes, which frequently are evident many years before diagnosis. Such changes might include irritability, lability, social disinhibition, and apathy. HD patients with intermittent explosive disorder and antisocial personality disorder appear more prone to aggressive outbursts. Estimates of psychosis range from about 5% to 25%. The psychosis often resembles that observed in schizophrenia.

Estimates of the prevalence of depression in PD vary greatly and range between 7% and 90%. The preponderance

Table 11.4. Self-Report and Rating Scales With Empirically Modified Cutoff Scores to Detect Depression in Parkinson's Disease

Scale (Reference)	No. of items, maximum score, traditional cutoff	PD cutoffs recommended by	Recommended cutoff to distinguish depressed vs. non-depressed PD (sensitivity/specificity)	Recommended screening cutoff for PD (sensitivity/specificity)	Recommended diagnostic cutoff for PD (sensitivity/specificity)
Beck Depression Inventory	21 items; Maximum = 63 10 = mild 12 = moderate 30 = severe	Leentjens, Verhey, Luijckz, and Troost (2000)	13/14 (0.67/0.88)	8/9 (0.92/0.59)	16/17 (0.42/0.98)
Hamilton Rating Scale for Depression (17-item)	17 items; Maximum = 50 8 = mild 14 = moderate 19 = severe 23 = very severe	Leentjens, Verhey, Lousberg, Spitsbergen, and Wilmink (2000)	13/14 (0.88/0.89)	11/12 (0.94/0.75)	16/17 (0.75/0.98)
		Naarding, Leentjens, Van Kooten, and Verhey (2002)	12/13 (0.80/0.92)	9/10 (0.95/0.98)	15/16 (0.99/0.93)

| Montgomery-Åsberg Depression Rating Scale | 10 items; Maximum = 60
15 = mild
25 = moderate
31 = severe
44 = very severe | Leentjens, Verhey, et al. (2000) | 14/15 (0.88/0.89) | 14/15 (0.88/0.89) | 17/18 (0.63/0.94) |

Note. From *Therapy of Parkinson's Disease* (3rd ed.), by R. Pahwa, K. E. Lyons, and W. Koller (Eds.), 2004, New York: Marcel Dekker Ltd. Copyright 2004 by Marcel Dekker Ltd. Adapted with permission.

of estimates indicates that about 30% to 40% of individuals with PD will experience depression (Tröster & Letsch, 2004). Half of this number of patients will meet criteria for major depression and the other half for dysthymia. Anxiety symptoms are a prominent feature among PD patients with depression. Diagnosis of depression in PD is difficult, given that symptoms such as fatigue, psychomotor slowing, and appetite changes occur in PD without depression. Depression may also occur in about 70% of CBD patients, though in CBD there is also a notable prevalence of apathy, irritability, and agitation.

Psychosis characterized by paranoid delusions, hallucinations, and confusion is estimated to occur in 20% to 30% of patients. Psychosis often relates to treatment with dopamimetics. Although anticholinergics on their own rarely produce acute confusional states, elderly PD patients are particularly vulnerable to acute confusional states when treated with a combination of anticholinergics and dopaminomimetics. Patients with DLB in particular appear sensitive to neuroleptic-induced hallucinations. Overall, it appears that depression and hallucinations are more common in DLB than AD, but delusions are more common in AD.

I. Treatment Effects on Cognition and Behavior

Symptomatic treatments (dopaminergic agents and surgical interventions such as ablation and deep brain stimulation) are available for PD. CBD responds poorly to dopaminergic medications. There are no treatments at present for HD. Dopamine-depleting agents and neuroleptics, which lessen choreiform movements but do not improve other symptoms, are usually only used in patients with the most severe and disabling movement disorder because of their side effects. Tables 11.5 and 11.6 list the more common medications and surgical interventions used in PD along with their cognitive and behavioral effects.

II. DEMYELINATING DISORDERS

A. Definitions and Description of the Disorders

1. DESCRIPTION OF DISORDERS AND EVOLUTION OF DISEASE STATES

Demyelinating conditions include **multiple sclerosis** (MS), **concentric sclerosis** (or **Balo's disease**, a variant of MS characterized by rings of demyelination in cerebral white matter), **Schilder's disease** (a variant of MS involving diffuse sclerosis

Table 11.5. Possible Neurobehavioral Effects of Medications Commonly Used in the Treatment of Parkinson's Disease (PD)

Drug category	Generic name(s)	Trade name(s)	Possible neurobehavioral adverse effects in PD	Possible neurobehavioral therapeutic effects in PD
Dopamine replacement	levodopa + carbidopa	Sinemet Atamet	Hallucinations, delusions, euphoria, confusion, depression, anxiety, agitation, nightmares; hedonistic homeostatic dysregulation syndrome (Giovannoni et al., 2000); cognitive ("frontal") effects vary by disease stage	May improve working memory early in disease (Costa et al., 2003); may improve dysphoria
Combined dopamine replacement and COMT inhibitor	levodopa + carbidopa + entacapone	Stalevo	Depression, psychosis, but generally unstudied due to novelty of drug	
Dopamine agonists ergot alkaloids	bromocriptine	Parlodel	As for levodopa, possibly more severe; minimal effect on cognition (Cooper et al., 1993; Piccirlli et al., 1986; Weddell & Weiser, 1995)	
	pergolide	Permax	As for levodopa, possibly more severe somnolence; minimal cognitive effect (Stern et al., 1984)	

(Continued)

Table 11.5. Possible Neurobehavioral Effects of Medications Commonly Used in the Treatment of Parkinson's Disease (PD) (*Continued*)

Drug category	Generic name(s)	Trade name(s)	Possible neurobehavioral adverse effects in PD	Possible neurobehavioral therapeutic effects in PD
non-ergot alkaloids	pramipexole	Mirapex	Similar to levodopa; fatigue, somnolence	
	ropinirole	Requip	Similar to levodopa; fatigue, somnolence	
COMT inhibitors	entacapone	Comtan	Hallucinations	
	tolcapone	Tasmar		Possible attention and memory improvement when used as adjunct to levodopa (Gasparini et al., 1997)
MAO inhibitors	selegiline	Eldepryl Deprenyl	Rare confusion or hallucinations	Small, uncontrolled studies suggest possible cognitive benefits (Hietanen, 1991; Finali et al., 1994) but not confirmed in large prospective study (Kieburtz et al., 1994)
Anticholinergics	trihexyphenidyl biperiden benztropine	Artane Akineton Cogentin	Sedation, delirium, memory impairment, executive dysfunction (Bedard et al., 1999; Koller, 1984; Meco et al., 1984; Reid et al., 1992)	
Antiglutamatergics	amantadine	Symmetrel		

Table 11.6. Possible Neurobehavioral Effects of Modern Surgical Interventions for Parkinson's Disease (PD)

Procedure type	Target	Possible adverse effects in PD	Possible beneficial effects in PD
Ablation	Globus pallidus interna (GPi)	Confusion Depression Hypomania Cognitive impairment (especially after bilateral procedure)	Reduction in obsessive–compulsive symptoms
	Ventralintermediate nucleus of thalamus (Vim)	Confusion Rare cognitive impairment	Reduction in depressive and obsessive symptoms
	Subthalamic nucleus (STN; modern target)	Not reported	Not reported
Deep brain stimulation	GPi	Rare cognitive dysfunction Hypomania Depression	Mildly improved *performance* on some memory tests (probably not a true memory improvement); reduced anxiety and depressive symptoms
	Vim		Reduction in depressive symptoms Mild naming improvement

(Continued)

Table 11.6. Possible Neurobehavioral Effects of Modern Surgical Interventions for Parkinson's Disease (PD) (Continued)

Procedure type	Target	Possible adverse effects in PD	Possible beneficial effects in PD
	STN	Apathy Depression (including suicidality), (Hypo)mania Psychosis Euphoria/mirth Hypersexuality Dopamine dysregulation syndrome Cognitive impairment	Reduction in depressive and anxiety symptoms
Transplantation	Putamen and/or caudate	Psychosis Depression Cognitive dysfunction	Transient memory improvement

Note. From "Neuropsychiatric Complications of Medical and Surgical Therapies for Parkinson's Disease," by D. J. Burns and A. I. Tröster, 2004, *Journal of Geriatric Psychiatry and Neurology, 17*, pp. 172–180. Copyright 2004 by Sage Publications, Inc. Reprinted with permission of the authors and Sage Publications, Inc.

characterized by a monophasic course, affecting younger patients), **Devic's disease** (a variant of MS characterized by a single spinal, typically cervical, demyelinating lesion, accompanied by signs of demyelination in the optic pathway), **central pontine myelinolysis**, and **Marchiafava–Bignami disease** (which involves primary degeneration of the corpus callosum). Other, very rare, conditions include **acute disseminated encephalomyelitis** (usually occurring in relation to acute hemorrhagic leucoencephalitis) and **acute hemorrhagic leucoencephalitis**, which is characterized by sudden onset of severe neurological disturbance, rapid progression, and frequently death. MS is by far the most common among these conditions, and the only condition that has been adequately studied from a neuropsychological perspective. Consequently, this review focuses on MS.

The incidence and prevalence of MS vary geographically, with few cases near the equator and larger numbers of cases in northern and southern latitudes (from about 60 to 300 per 100,000). Thus, although there are estimated to be between 250,000 and 350,000 people with MS in the United States, residents north of latitude 40° N are about three times as likely to have MS as are residents of southern U.S. regions. This differential geographic pattern suggests an environmental contribution to the disease. A significant genetic contribution to MS is suggested by the 30% to 40% concordance in identical twins but only 1% to 13% in fraternal twins.

The disease is about twice as likely to affect women as men and has its onset typically in the 30s. It is likely that MS is acquired before puberty, but actual disease onset occurs in most patients (about two thirds) between the ages of 20 and 40. Onset before age 15 is rare; late onset after age 40 is commonly characterized by quicker progression and greater morbidity. Average life expectancy following disease onset is estimated at 30+ years, but variability is great. Typically, MS runs its course over one or more decades; rarely does death from MS-related complications ensue within months of disease onset. Two severity outcome definitions of MS have been identified. In the **benign** outcome, patients remain fully functional 15 years post disease onset. In the **malignant** outcome, there is a rapidly progressing course that leads to significant disability or death relatively soon after disease onset. Most patients fall in between these two extremes.

Initial symptoms vary greatly, but the most common symptoms at MS onset are muscle weakness, paresthesias, gait/balance problems, and visual disturbances. Visual anomalies are characterized by diplopia, loss of visual acuity, blurry vision, and visual field defects. Other common symptoms include urinary disturbance, fatigue, problems with balance, and paresthesias (usually numbness and tingling in the limbs, trunk, or face). Significant cognitive difficulties and problems with depression are common symptoms as well. The mode of symptom onset in MS is typically acute or subacute. Many MS symptoms are transient and unpredictable. For example, visual disturbances and paresthesias may last for seconds or hours. Because of the short-lived and sometimes bizarre nature of the symptoms, it is not uncommon for patients in the early stages before formal diagnosis to be labeled with hysteric/somatization disorders.

The diagnosis of MS was typically based on Poser and colleagues' criteria (Poser et al., 1983) up until the recent publication of revised (McDonald et al., 2001) guidelines. The latter guidelines are now considered the gold standard for the diagnosis of MS. A key difference from the Poser criteria is that the McDonald criteria involve the systematic integration of MRI data with clinical and paraclinical diagnostic methods. MRI data were not considered in a systematic way under the old diagnostic system. Another key addition is that the revised criteria provide guidelines for diagnosing MS presentations involving an insidious progression in which clear attacks and remissions are absent. Outcomes in this new diagnostic system include "MS," "not MS," and "possible MS." The last group is considered at risk for MS but falls short of the diagnostic criteria for making a diagnosis.

To meet criteria using the revised guidelines, patients must have had two or more discrete attacks of the disease lasting at least 24 hours. These attacks, or episodes of neurological change, should also implicate the presence of lesions in at least two different sites in the central white matter. In addition, at least 30 days should separate the onset of each attack. Thus, lesions should be separated in both time and space. Regarding the use of lesions detected by MRI, specific criteria for defining these lesions as abnormal and characteristic of MS are laid out elsewhere (McDonald et al., 2001). Although MRI data are now considered preferable to other paraclinical tests, additional tests are considered useful in the absence of clear-cut MRI findings or atypical clinical presentations. In particular, the presence of oligoclonal immunoglobulin (IgG) bands in the CSF different from those in the serum, or elevated IgG, can be used. In addition, visual evoked potentials (VEPs) can be used to supplement the clinical examination to reveal evidence of additional lesions. When the presentation of MS involves insidious progression, abnormal CSF findings that reflect inflammation and abnormal immune functioning are necessary. In addition, evidence for lesions being separated in space, established by MRI or abnormal VEP, is considered essential. Finally, lesions should be separated in time as reflected by the onset of new MRI lesions or increased level of disability over the course of at least 1 year.

Attacks, relapses, or exacerbations that imply new disease activity are common. Previously, MS was classified by two major disease-course types: relapsing–remitting and chronic progressive. However, this system has been updated (Lublin & Reingold, 1996) and now includes four course types. **Relapsing–remitting** is the most common type, affecting over half of all patients, and is characterized by clearly defined disease relapses. Recovery can be complete or with sequelae and residual deficit. A defining feature of the relapsing–remitting type is that there is no progression of disease between relapses. The next most common type of MS is **secondary progressive**. This disease type is first characterized by a relapsing–remitting course, then progression. If there are relapses once the disease evolves to secondary progressive, this progression is evident even between relapses. However, relapses and remissions may or may not occur. Next most common is the **primary progressive** type, and this involves an unremitting disease progression from disease onset for most patients. However, there is occasional stabilization and even improvement in functioning for others, but no clear relapses. Finally, **progressive relapsing** is the least common type of MS and involves disease progression from onset that is punctuated by acute relapses from which patients may or may not fully recover. The term **chronic-progressive** formerly encompassed all progressive types.

After the first episode of symptoms for the relapsing–remitting type of MS, complete remission typically ensues. Subsequent episodes are unpredictable, occurring weeks to years later, and associated symptoms remit less completely or not at all. Relapses themselves may last days to weeks, more rarely hours or months.

Approximately 45% to 65% of people with MS experience cognitive impairment, but most (about 80%) patients with deficits are relatively mildly affected. However, even mild cognitive problems in MS have been shown to impede everyday activities (e.g., work, homemaking, personal-care activities, and social activities; Higginson, Arnett, & Voss, 2000). About 20% to 30% of MS patients experience cognitive impairment severe and extensive enough to qualify for the diagnosis of dementia. Dementia in MS is characterized by a "subcortical dementia" pattern of cognitive impairments, at least if one looks at groups of patients. As Beatty (1996) pointed out, there is, however, considerable heterogeneity among individuals' cognitive impairments, and only 10% to 15% of people with MS might exhibit all of the cognitive deficits associated with subcortical dementia.

2. NEUROPATHOLOGIC CORRELATES

MS is a demyelinating disease of the CNS thought to be caused by an autoimmune process, a slow-acting virus, or a delayed reaction to a common virus (Brassington & Marsh, 1998). Demyelination occurs in the form of multiple discrete plaques at demyelinated sites that are formed, in part, by proliferating astrocytes. The plaques appear as ill-defined, pale, pink-yellow lesions in the unfixed brain. Myelin sheaths within plaques are either destroyed or swollen and fragmented. Neural conduction is facilitated by myelin because an intact nerve is enclosed in myelin sheaths separated by gaps from which the nerve impulse jumps. Affected areas thus interfere with or block neural transmission by limiting this saltatory conduction process. Axons and cell bodies of neurons often remain intact. The size of plaques varies from about 1.0 mm to several centimeters.

Symptoms from demyelination in MS typically reflect functions associated with affected areas. Plaques can occur in the brain, spinal cord, or both areas. The location of plaques is highly variable between patients. Within the cerebrum, plaques near the lateral and third ventricles are most common. The frontal lobes are the next most commonly affected, even when the size of the frontal lobes relative to the rest of brain is taken into account. Plaques in other major lobes of the brain are also frequently observed. In addition, plaques are commonly seen in the optic nerves, chiasm, or tracts, as well as the corpus callosum, brain stem, and cerebellum. Plaques are also found in white matter regions of the thalamus, hypothalamus, and basal ganglia. The majority of plaques (about 75%) are observed in the white matter, but some occur in the gray matter and in the juncture between the gray and white matter. Some remyelination occurs with acute MS plaques.

B. Functional Neuroanatomical Correlates

Because lesion size and distribution are highly variable in MS, there is no one pattern of cognitive dysfunction that might be considered "typical." Early in the course of MS (typically suspected but unconfirmed MS), neurobehavioral deficits might be a manifestation of a single lesion (and cognitive deficits will depend on the lesion's location). Early in confirmed MS, the neurobehavioral deficit pattern is often consistent with multifocal lesions. Deficits consistent with diffuse pathology (e.g., a "subcortical dementia") typically develop later in the disease, although such a pattern of deficits may be present early. Conversely, a patient who has had MS for some time might be quite intact cognitively. It should be noted that disease type (course) and disease duration are not good predictors of cognitive deficits in patients. However, there is evidence from recent longitudinal work that patients with cognitive deficits are at greater risk for cognitive decline over time than patients with minimal cognitive difficulties on initial testing (Kujala, Portin, & Ruutiainen, 1997). Generally, cognitive deficits tend to be proportional to MRI-visualized total lesion load, as well as cortical and callosal atrophy. Some studies have reported an association between the location of lesions on MRI and particular patterns of dysfunction, such as primarily frontal lesion patterns associated with executive task dysfunction.

The few functional MRI (fMRI) studies on cognitive functioning in MS suggest that contrary to most expectations, MS patients display *greater* increases in brain activation (as measured by fMRI) compared with non-MS control participants when performing complex cognitive tasks (Hillary et al., 2003). This counterintuitive finding has been replicated in other neurological conditions as well, including traumatic brain injury and HIV. This increased activation has often been interpreted as reflecting compensatory activation required to perform the same mental operations as non-brain-damaged persons.

C. Competing Diagnoses

Competing neurological diagnoses include the variants of MS, acute disseminated encephalomyelitis, and leukoencephalitis, in which neuropsychology is not helpful given a literature limited to case studies. Sometimes the most difficult differential diagnosis is a conversion reaction, given the often strange nature and course of symptoms in MS. The MMPI is probably not very helpful in making this differential, because Scales 1, 3, and 8 are elevated (to a lesser extent Scale 2) because of endorsement of "true" neurological symptoms. Even correction attempts have not been useful, and experimental MMPI scales designed to separate "organic" from "pseudo-neurological" patients have very poor sensitivity and specificity in MS (ranging from about 40%–60%).

D. Medical History and Laboratory Data

Medical history is typically noncontributory. In the patient with isolated "visual" symptoms, it is wise to inquire about possible recent infections or vaccinations. History of systemic disease is helpful in differentiating MS from lupus erythamatosus. No test in itself is diagnostic of MS, and multiple, corroborating laboratory data need to be interpreted carefully. Presence of abnormal oligoclonal bands in the CSF and abnormal IgG synthesis rates are most helpful observations toward diagnosis. During the active phase of the disease, CSF examination shows evidence of an inflammatory reaction (increased number of lymphocytes and macrophages) and an elevated protein level.

E. EEG and Neuroimaging Correlates

Nonspecific MRI findings characteristically seen in MS include white matter lesions that are larger than 6 mm in diameter, occur below the tentorium, and occur close to the ventricles in a poorly demarcated pattern. It is estimated that 80% of patients with MS (excluding those with monosymptomatic disease) have abnormal MRIs. Figures 11.2 and 11.3 illustrate, respectively, typical and atypical demyelination patterns in MS. MRI data are now considered preferable to other paraclinical tests (like those reflecting CSF abnormalities) in the diagnostic process (McDonald et al., 2001).

Evoked potential (EP) studies have lower sensitivity than MRI and CSF studies. EP abnormalities are seen in 20% to 80% of patients, and visual EPs are helpful in confirming the neural basis of vague symptoms. EP studies serve no useful diagnostic purpose in the patient with known optic neuritis or spinal cord lesions.

F. Areas of Emphasis Within the Neuropsychological Evaluation

The most informative investigation regarding typical patterns of cognitive impairment in MS remains the seminal study by Rao, Leo, Bernardin, and Unverzagt (1991) comparing 100 community-based MS patients with 100 matched healthy control participants on an extensive neuropsychological battery. Subsequent studies have generally supported their findings and suggest that memory and complex attention/speeded information processing are the cognitive domains most affected in MS. Regarding memory, problems encoding and retrieving both verbal and visual information are most common. These are typi-

Figure 11.2. A T-2 weighted magnetic resonance imaging (MRI) scan from a 38-year-old male presenting with symptoms of optic neuritis. Several areas of increased signal intensity in the periventricular white matter, typical of multiple sclerosis, are visible.

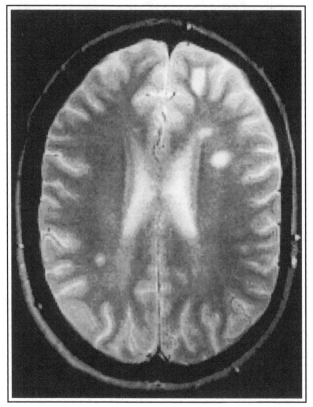

Figure 11.3. A T-1 weighted, postcontrast (gadolinium DTPA) magnetic resonance imaging scan from a 35-year-old female presenting with complaints of left-sided numbness. A peripherally enhancing lesion, which at biopsy was found to represent an area of demyelination consistent with an atypical multiple sclerosis plaque, is visible.

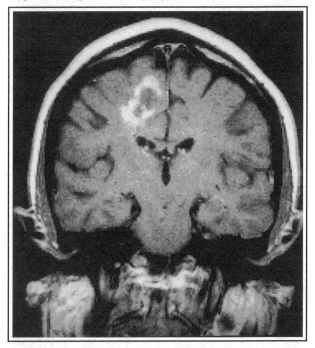

cally manifested as immediate and delayed-recall memory deficits on neuropsychological testing. About 30% of patients have substantial problems, another 30% have moderate problems, and the remaining 40% have mild or no problems with this type of memory (Brassington & Marsh, 1998). Working memory, the ability to maintain and manipulate information "online," is also commonly impaired in MS. Delayed-recall deficits are usually a function of deficient immediate recall, not forgetting.

The learning curve across repeated trials is similar in slope in MS patients compared with control participants but is lower in magnitude. Percentage retention, recognition, and incidental memory following a delay and remote memory are usually intact in MS. Clinically, memory problems are often manifested as complaints of difficulty remembering conversations, appointments, work tasks, and so on.

Perhaps just as common as memory deficits in MS are those involving complex attention and speeded information processing. It can be difficult to separate speeded information processing from attentional functioning because the latter is necessary for performing any speeded cognitive task. In clinical evaluations, it is also important to be cognizant of the possibility that memory problems in MS may, in part, be a function of deficits in these domains. MS patients typically show their greatest difficulty on tasks requiring rapid and complex information processing, such as those requiring swift application of working memory operations, attentional switching, or rapid visual scanning. About 20% to 25% of MS patients have substantial difficulty in this cognitive domain. Simple attention span is usually intact, but mild impairments are sometimes found. Clinically, complex attention/speeded information-processing problems are commonly manifested as difficulty tracking and keeping up with and focusing on details of conversations, work tasks, television programs, and so on. The next most common cognitive domain typically affected in MS is executive functioning. Deficits in cognitive flexibility, concept formation, verbal abstraction, problem solving, and planning are commonly found. Approximately 15% to 20% of individuals with MS show substantial difficulties in this cognitive domain. These problems may manifest clinically as difficulty planning day-to-day activities (e.g., job tasks, meals, grocery shopping), verbal disinhibition and tangential speech, as well as problems organizing ideas and shifting appropriately from one topic to another in conversation.

Verbal–linguistic skills are variably affected in MS. Aphasias are only seen in rare cases in MS, but mild confrontation naming difficulties are sometimes seen. Similarly, alexia, agraphia, and apraxia are rare. In contrast, speech abnormalities such as dysarthria and hypophonia are common in MS. Also, deficits in verbal fluency are common. Because fluency tasks require rapid production of information, patients' poor performance on them may also be an indicator of the memory retrieval difficulties that are common to MS (Fischer et al., 1994). In addition, the slowed speech common to MS should be considered as a possible contributor to patients' verbal fluency, as well as deficits in information-processing speed. About 20% to 25% of patients have substantial problems on verbal fluency tasks. Fluency problems may manifest clinically as word-finding problems that impair the flow of patients' conversations.

Visuospatial deficits occur with reasonable frequency in MS, with 10% to 20% of patients showing substantial difficulty with higher order visuospatial skills involving angle matching or face recognition. It is unclear whether higher order visual deficits are a function of primary visual disturbances involving blurred vision and diplopia (Rao et al., 1991). Clinical manifestations may involve accounts of running into things frequently while walking (e.g., doorways) or driving (e.g., hitting curbs) because of visual miscalculations.

Although intellectual functioning is affected significantly in about 20% of patients, most patients score within the broad normal range on general measures of intelligence. Little systematic research on changes in academic skills in MS has been conducted, but these are assumed to be intact in most patients.

Because MS is characterized by heterogeneous cognitive findings, a test battery sampling multiple areas of cognitive functions is helpful. The battery should be kept relatively brief (2–3 hours) given the fatigability of individuals with MS, especially in light of recent data suggesting that patients' performance deteriorates more significantly than that of non-MS patients over the course of a demanding neuropsychological evaluation (Krupp & Elkins, 2000).

An efficient way of approaching neuropsychological testing in MS is to conduct a brief screening evaluation to determine whether further testing is warranted. MS patients impaired in one domain of cognitive functioning are not necessarily impaired in others (Rao et al., 1991). Thus, neuropsychological assessments that evaluate the major areas of cognitive functioning typically impaired in MS are critical because performance on a test in one domain provides little information about the likelihood of deficits in other domains. Rao and colleagues have developed the Brief Repeatable Battery of Neuropsychological Tests in Multiple Sclerosis (Rao, Cognitive Function Study Group, & National Multiple Sclerosis Society, 1990), comprised of tests most sensitive to cognitive impairments typically seen in MS; most tests also include alternate forms to allow for repeat testing. This battery includes a six-trial version of the Verbal Selective Reminding Test, 10/36 Spatial Recall, Oral Symbol

Digit Modalities Test, the Paced Auditory Serial Addition Test (PASAT), and Word List Generation (verbal fluency). Comprehensive norms for the Brief Repeatable Battery of Neuropsychological Tests (BRB) are available (Boringa et al., 2001). The BRB takes about 20 to 30 minutes to administer.

A slightly more extensive consensus battery was recently suggested that includes most of the BRB tests in addition to measures of emotional functioning and fatigue. This battery, known as the Minimal Assessment of Cognitive Function in MS (MACFIMS; Benedict et al., 2002), is designed to take approximately 90 minutes. It includes the 2-second and 3-second PASAT, Word List Generation (COWA), Oral Symbol Digit, CVLT-II, and the Brief Visuospatial Memory Test–Revised (BVMT-R). Additionally, the battery includes a measure of executive functioning, the Delis–Kaplan Executive Function Scale Sorting Test, and a measure of visuospatial skill, the Judgment of Line Orientation. It should be noted that the latter test, in addition to other visuo-perceptual-spatial tests, is difficult to interpret in patients with double vision or optic neuritis. The battery also includes optional measures designed to measure depression and fatigue, in addition to premorbid functioning. Measurement of depression is important because depression is common in MS, and because some recent research has shown an association between depression and cognitive dysfunction in MS (Arnett, Higginson, Voss, & Randolph, 2002).

A comprehensive neuropsychological battery has recently been suggested as well (Arnett, 2003). This approach recommends many of the same tests suggested in the BRB and the MACFIMS but expands on them. Measures of global intelligence, academic functioning, confrontation naming, and working memory are added, in addition to a slightly more extensive evaluation of long-term memory and executive functioning. All of these suggested approaches to neuropsychological assessment in MS survey the major domains of cognitive functioning typically affected in the disease and differ primarily in their comprehensiveness. Selection of one battery versus another depends on the goals for the evaluation, in addition to the setting in which the evaluation takes place.

Measures of motor speed and intelligence are probably more helpful in the early disease course so as to establish a baseline. Discrepancies between Verbal and Performance IQs (the latter being lower) can be misleading, as interpretation of this finding is complicated by motor and sensory deficits commonly observed in MS.

G. Neuropsychological Measures Helpful in Differential Diagnosis

Differential diagnosis is rarely requested in cases of MS. Rather, characterization of cognitive deficits, their potential impact on social and occupational functioning, and the assessment of change over time are common reasons for neuropsychological referral. Neurologists experienced in MS make judicious, appropriate use of neuropsychology, requesting evaluations only when clinical examination or cognitive screening indicates probable cognitive dysfunction.

Tests of learning and memory often reveal poor recall and better recognition. Evidence of encoding deficiencies is equivocal, although encoding is frequently normal. Sensitivity to proactive interference is typically normal. Remote memory might be affected, and if so, patients perform better on recognition than free-recall tasks of remote memory. Paul, Blanco, Hames, and Beatty (1997) have shown that some aspects of autobiographical memory are deficient in MS, in particular, personal semantic memories based on the Autobiographical Memory Interview and famous faces based on the Famous Faces test. Briefer tests (e.g., the Presidents test) have typically been found to be less sensitive to remote memory dysfunction in MS.

H. Psychiatric Morbidity in Multiple Sclerosis

Although anxiety and depression symptoms are common among MS patients, careful interview is needed to clarify whether the symptoms reflect a mood disturbance or a somatic manifestation of MS. Raising the screening cutoff on the BDI has also been suggested to ensure that self-reported symptoms exceeding what might be expected when neurovegetative symptoms of depression overlap with MS symptoms can be accounted for. A recent survey indicated that MS patients had approximately a 50% lifetime risk for depression (Sadovnick et al., 1996). This lifetime risk is much higher than in the general population but is also higher compared with many other neurological disorders and chronic illnesses. One study has reported a suicide rate 7.5 times higher in MS patients than the general population, but this large figure requires replication.

Depression has been shown to be treatable through brief and even telephone-based cognitive–behavioral therapy (Mohr et al., 2000) as well as group therapy. Also, cognitive–behavioral stress management training has been shown to reduce emotional distress in MS (Fischer et al., 1994). Nonetheless, depression has historically been undertreated in MS, despite the fact that it is unlikely to remit spontaneously. Successful treatment of depression is associated with greater adherence to immuno-therapy.

There is no consensus regarding the nature of depression in MS. Some investigators have suggested that neurovegetative symptoms of depression are not valid indicators of depression because of their overlap with MS symptoms (e.g., sleep distur-bance, fatigue, sexual dysfunction), whereas others have pro-vided evidence to the contrary. This debate suggests that caution is warranted in interpreting neurovegetative symptoms of de-pression as depression symptoms in any individual MS patient.

The cause of depression in MS is unknown, but high levels of perceived stress, low levels of social support, and disease exacerbation/pharmacological treatment have been shown to be associated with increased depression and emotional distress. A genetic interpretation of the relationship between depression and MS has been ruled out because of studies showing that unipolar major depression is not more common in first-degree relatives of depressed MS patients compared with first-degree relatives of nondepressed MS patients. Nonetheless, a biological contribution to depression in MS has been suggested by emerg-ing evidence of an association between depression and both neuroanatomical and functional neuroimaging parameters. De-pression is associated with reduced quality of life and the use of generally less effective (emotion-focused) coping strategies in MS. Patients with a history of depression, either before or after MS onset, appear to be at increased risk for future depressive and manic states.

Although it was initially assumed that there was no rela-tionship between depression and greater cognitive impairment in MS, more recent work has suggested an association. In particular, some studies have found that complex attention and information-processing speed (Arnett et al., 2002), and perhaps executive deficits, are associated with depression in MS. These associations are most likely to be seen when depression symp-toms uncontaminated by MS symptomatology (e.g., neurovege-tative symptoms) are excluded from the measurement of depres-sion and the focus is on mood and negative evaluative depression symptoms (Arnett, Higginson, & Randolph, 2001). Surprisingly, the severity of neurological disability has typically not been found to be associated with depression in MS.

Anxiety is possibly more common than depression in MS but has been infrequently studied. Data are limited, but the point prevalence of clinically significant anxiety is thought to be about 25%; the lifetime prevalence is unknown. The cause of anxiety in MS unknown, but it is prominent in the early stages of the disease when diagnosis and prognosis are most uncertain. Decline in distress is associated with more definitive diagnostic statements by treatment professionals. There are no published studies treating specific anxiety disorders in MS. Comorbidity of anxiety and depression in MS is more associated with thoughts of self-harm, social dysfunction, and somatic complaints than either alone (Feinstein, O'Connor, Gray, & Feinstein, 1999). The only other emotional disorder occurring with any significant frequency in MS is bipolar disorder. Point prevalence is estimated at 0% to 2% and lifetime prevalence 13% to 16%. There are no published treatment studies of bipolar disorder in MS. Its cause is unknown.

III. CONCLUSION

This chapter reviewed the pathophysiology, clinical correlates, psychiatric comorbidities, and neuropsychological sequelae of both movement and demyelinating disorders. These two sets of neurological diseases were considered together because their neuropsychological profiles overlap considerably. Many of the movement and demyelinating disorders discussed, despite their different pathophysiologies and heterogeneous neuropsychological deficits, share features of a *subcortical* pattern of impairment, meaning mood disturbances, slowness of thought, inattention, impoverished recall and word retrieval, and executive dysfunction.

BIBLIOGRAPHY

Aarsland, D., Litvan, I., Salmon, D., Galasko, D., Wentzel-Larsen, T., & Larsen, J. P. (2003). Performance on the Dementia Rating Scale in Parkinson's disease with dementia and dementia with Lewy bodies: Comparison with progressive supranuclear palsy and Alzheimer's disease. *Journal of Neurology, Neurosurgery, and Psychiatry, 74*, 1215–1220.

American Psychiatric Association. (1994). *Diagnostic and statistical manual of mental disorders* (4th ed.). Washington, DC: Author.

Arnett, P. A. (2003). Neuropsychological presentation and treatment of demyelinating disorders. In U. K. P. Halligan & J. Marshall (Eds.), *Handbook of clinical neuropsychology* (pp. 528–543). Oxford, England: Oxford University Press.

Arnett, P. A., Higginson, C. I., & Randolph, J. J. . (2001). Depression in multiple sclerosis: Relationship to planning ability. *Journal of the International Neuropsychological Society, 7,* 665–674.

Arnett, P. A., Higginson, C. I., Voss, W. D., & Randolph, J. J. (2002). Relationship between coping, depression, and cognitive dysfunction in multiple sclerosis. *The Clinical Neuropsychologist, 16,* 341–355.

Beatty, W. W. (1996). Multiple sclerosis. In O. A. Parsons, R. L. Adams, J. L. Culbertson, & S. J. Nixon (Eds.), *Neuropsychology for clinical practice: Etiology, assessment, and treatment of common neurological disorders* (pp. 225–242). Washington, DC: American Psychological Association.

Bedard, M. A., Pillon, B., Dubois, B., Duchesne, N., Masson, H., & Agid, Y. (1999). Acute and long-term administration of anticholinergics in Parkinson's disease: Specific effects on the subcortico-frontal syndrome. *Brain and Cognition, 40,* 289–313.

Benedict, R. H. B., Fischer, J. S., Archibald, C. J., Arnett, P. A., Beatty, W. W., Bobholz, J., et al. (2002). Minimal neuropsychological assessment of MS patients: A consensus approach. *The Clinical Neuropsychologist, 16,* 381–397.

Boringa, J. B., Lazeron, R. H. C., Reuling, I. E. W., Ader, H. J., Pfennings, L., & Lindeboom, J., (2001). The Brief Repeatable Battery of Neuropsychological Tests: Normative values allow application in multiple sclerosis clinical practice. *Multiple Sclerosis, 7,* 263–267.

Brassington, J. C., & Marsh, N. V. (1998). Neuropsychological aspects of multiple sclerosis. *Neuropsychology Review, 8,* 43–77.

Brooks, D. J. (2000). PET studies and motor complications in Parkinson's disease. *Trends in Neurosciences, 23*(Suppl. 10), S101–S108.

Burns, D. J., & Tröster, A. I. (2004). Neuropsychiatric complications of medical and surgical therapies for Parkinson's disease. *Journal of Geriatric Psychiatry and Neurology, 17,* 172–180.

Cooper, J. A., Sagar, H. J., & Sullivan, E. V. (1993). Short-term memory and temporal ordering in early Parkinson's disease: Effects of disease chronicity and medication. *Neuropsychologia, 31,* 933–949.

Costa, A., Peppe, A., Dell'Agnello, G., Carlesimo, G. A., Murri, L., Bonuccelli, U., et al. (2003). Dopaminergic modulation of visual-spatial working memory in Parkinson's disease. *Dementia and Geriatric Cognitive Disorders, 15*(2), 55–66.

Cummings, J. L. (1995). Behavioral and psychiatric symptoms associated with Huntington's disease. *Advances in Neurology, 65,* 179–186.

Downes, J. J., Priestley, N. M., Doran, M., Ferran, J., Ghadiali, E., & Cooper, P. (1998). Intellectual, mnemonic, and frontal functions in dementia with Lewy bodies: A comparison with early and advanced Parkinson's disease. *Behavioural Neurology, 11*(3), 173–183.

Dujardin, K., Defebvre, L., Krystkowiak, P., Degreef, J. F., & Destee, A. (2003). Executive function differences in multiple system atrophy and Parkinson's disease. *Parkinsonism and Related Disorders, 9,* 205–211.

Feinstein, A., O'Connor, P., Gray, T., & Feinstein, K. (1999). The effects of anxiety on psychiatric morbidity in patients with multiple sclerosis. *Multiple Sclerosis, 5,* 323–326.

Finali, G., Piccirilli, M., & Piccinin, G. L. (1994). Neuropsychological correlates of I-deprenyl therapy in idiopathic parkinsonism. *Progress in Neuro-Psychopharmacology and Biological Psychiatry, 18,* 115–128.

Fischer, J. S., Foley, F. W., Aikens, J. E., Ericson, D. G., Rao, S. M., & Shindell, S. (1994). What do we *really* know about cognitive dysfunction, affective disorders, and stress in multiple sclerosis? A practitioner's guide. *Journal of Neurological Rehabilitation, 8*(3), 151–164.

Foltynie, T., Brayne, C. E., Robbins, T. W., & Barker, R. A. (2004). The cognitive ability of an incident cohort of Parkinson's patients in the UK. The CamPaIGN study. *Brain, 127* (Pt. 3), 550–560.

Gasparini, M., Fabrizio, E., Bonifati, V., & Meco, G. (1997). Cognitive improvement during tolcapone treatment in Parkinson's disease. *Journal of Neural Transmission, 104*(8–9), 887–894.

Giovannoni, G., O'Sullivan, J. D., Turner, K., Manson, A. J., & Lees, A. J. (2000). Hedonistic homeostatic dysregulation in patients with Parkinson's disease on dopamine replacement therapies. *Journal of Neurology, Neurosurgery, and Psychiatry, 68,* 423–428.

Grafman, J., Litvan, I., & Stark, M. (1995). Neuropsychological features of progressive supranuclear palsy. *Brain and Cognition, 28,* 311–320.

Graham, N. L., Bak, T. H., & Hodges, J. R. (2003). Corticobasal degeneration as a cognitive disorder. *Movement Disorders, 18,* 1224–1232.

Hamilton, J. M., Salmon, D. P., Corey-Bloom, J., Gamst, A., Paulsen, J. S., Jerkins, S., et al. (2003). Behavioural abnormalities contribute to functional decline in Huntington's disease. *Journal of Neurology, Neurosurgery and Psychiatry, 74,* 120–122.

Harris, M. E., Ivnik, R. J., & Smith, G. E. (2002). Mayo's Older Americans Normative Studies: Expanded AVLT Recognition Trial norms for ages 57 to 98. *Journal of Clinical and Experimental Neuropsychology, 24,* 214–220.

Heaton, R. K., Miller, W. S., Taylor, M. J., & Grant, I. (2004). *Revised comprehensive norms for an expanded Halstead–Reitan battery: Demographically adjusted neuropsychological norms for African American and Caucasian adults.* Lutz, FL: Psychological Assessment Resources.

Hietanen, M. H. (1991). Selegiline and cognitive function in Parkinson's disease. *Acta Neurologica Scandanavica, 84,* 407–410.

Higginson, C. I., Arnett, P. A., & Voss, W. D. (2000). The ecological validity of clinical tests of memory and attention in multiple sclerosis. *Archives of Clinical Neuropsychology, 15,* 185–204.

Higginson, C. I., Fields, J. A., Koller, W. C., & Tröster, A. I. (2001). Questionnaire assessment potentially overestimates anxiety in Parkinson's disease. *Journal of Clinical Psychology in Medical Settings, 8*(2), 95–99.

Hillary, F. G., Chiaravalloti, N. D., Ricker, J. H., Steffener, J., Bly, B. M., Lange, G., et al. (2003). An investigation of working memory rehearsal in multiple sclerosis using fMRI. *Journal of Clinical and Experimental Neuropsychology, 25,* 965–978.

Kieburtz, K., McDermott, M., Como, P., Growdon, J., Brady, J., Carter, J., et al. (1994). The effect of deprenyl and tocopherol on cognitive performance in early untreated Parkinson's disease. *Neurology, 44,* 1756–1759.

Koller, W. C. (1984). Disturbance of recent memory function in parkinsonian patients on anticholinergic therapy. *Cortex, 20,* 307–311.

Koller, W. C., & Megaffin, B. B (1994). Parkinson's disease and parkinsonism. In C. E. Coffey & J. L. Cummings (Eds.), *Textbook of geriatric neuropsychiatry* (pp. 433–456). Washington, DC: American Psychiatric Press.

Krupp, L. B., & Elkins, L. E. (2000). Fatigue and declines in cognitive functioning in multiple sclerosis. *Neurology, 55,* 934–939.

Kujala, P., Portin, R., & Ruutiainen, J. (1997). The progress of cognitive decline in multiple sclerosis: A controlled 3-year follow-up. *Brain, 120,* 289–297.

Leentjens, A. F., Verhey, F. R., Lousberg, R., Spitsbergen, H., & Wilmink, F. W. (2000). The validity of the Hamilton and Montgomery–Asberg depression rating scales as screening and diagnostic tools for depression in Parkinson's disease. *International Journal of Geriatric Psychiatry, 15,* 644–649.

Leentjens, A. F. G., Verhey, F. R. J., Luijckx, G.-J., & Troost, J. (2000). The validity of the Beck Depression Inventory as a screening and diagnostic instrument for depression in patients with Parkinson's disease. *Movement Disorders, 15,* 1221–1224.

Levin, B. E., Llabre, M. M., & Weiner, W. J. (1988). Parkinson's disease and depression: Psychometric properties of the Beck Depression Inventory. *Journal of Neurology, Neurosurgery, and Psychiatry, 51,* 1401–1404.

Litvan, I., Agid, Y., Calne, D., Campbell, G., Dubois, B., Duvoisin, R. C., et al. (1996). Clinical research criteria for the diagnosis of progressive supranuclear palsy (Steele–Richardson–Olszewski syndrome): Report of the NINDS–PSP international workshop. *Neurology, 47*(1), 1–9.

Lublin, F. D., & Reingold, S. C. (1996). Defining the clinical course of multiple sclerosis: Results of an international survey. *Neurology, 46,* 907–911.

Massman, P. J., Delis, D. C., Butters, N., Levin, B. E., & Salmon, D. P. (1990). Are all subcortical dementias alike? Verbal learning and memory in Parkinson's and Huntington's disease patients. *Journal of Clinical and Experimental Neuropsychology, 12,* 729–744.

McDonald, W. I., Compston, A., Edan, G., Goodkin, D., Hartung, H.-P., Lublin, F. D., et al. (2001). Recommended diagnostic criteria for multiple sclerosis: Guidelines from the international panel on the diagnosis of multiple sclerosis. *Annals of Neurology, 50,* 121–127.

McDonald, W. M., Richard, I. H., & DeLong, M. R. (2003). Prevalence, etiology, and treatment of depression in Parkinson's disease. *Biological Psychiatry, 54,* 363–375.

McKeith, I. G., Burn, D. J., Ballard, C. G., Collerton, D., Jaros, E., Morris, C. M., et al. (2003). Dementia with Lewy bodies. *Seminars in Clinical Neuropsychiatry, 8*(1), 46–57.

Meco, G., Casacchia, M., Lazzari, R., Franzese, A., Castellana, F., Carta, A., et al. (1984). Mental impairment in Parkinson's disease. The role of anitcholinergic drugs. *Acta Psychiatrica Belgique, 84*(4), 325–335.

Moering, R. G., Schinka, J. A., Mortimer, J. A., & Graves, A. B. (2004). Normative data for elderly African Americans for the Stroop Color and Word Test. *Archives of Clinical Neuropsychology, 19*(1), 61–71.

Mohr, D. C., Likosky, W., Bertagnolli, A., Goodkin, D. E., Van Der Wende, J., Dwyer, P., & Dick, L. P. (2000). Telephone-administered cognitive–behavioral therapy for the treatment of depressive symptoms in multiple sclerosis. *Journal of Consulting and Clinical Psychology, 68,* 356–361.

Monza, D., Soliveri, P., Radice, D., Fetoni, V., Testa, D., Caffarra, P., et al. (1998). Cognitive dysfunction and impaired organization of complex motility in degenerative parkinsonian syndromes. *Archives of Neurology, 55,* 372–378.

Naarding, P., Leentjens, A. F., Van Kooten, F., & Verhey, F. R. (2002). Disease-specific properties of the Hamilton Rating Scale for depression in patients with stroke, Alzheimer's dementia, and Parkinson's disease. *Journal of Neuropsychiatry and Clinical Neurosciences, 14,* 329–334.

Nelson, H. E. (1976). A modified card sorting test sensitive to frontal load deficits. *Cortex, 12,* 313–324.

Noe, E., Marder, K., Bell, K. L., Jacobs, D. M., Manly, J. J., & Stern, Y. (2004). Comparison of dementia with Lewy bodies to Alzheimer's disease and Parkinson's disease with dementia. *Movement Disorders, 19,* 60–67.

Paul, R. H., Blanco, C. R., Hames, K. A., & Beatty, W. W. (1997). Autobiographical memory in multiple sclerosis. *Journal of the International Neuropsychological Society, 3,* 246–251.

Pahwa, R., Lyons, K. E., & Koller, W. C. (Eds.). (2004). *Evaluation and treatment of anxiety and depression in Parkinson's disease.* New York: Marcel Dekker.

Piccirilli, M., Piccinin, G. L., D'Alessandro, P., Finali, G., Piccolini, C., Scarcella, M. G., et al. (1986). Cognitive performaces in Parkinsonians before and after bromocriptine therapy. *Acta Neurological (Napoli), 8*(3), 167–172.

Pillon, B., Blin, J., Vidailhet, M., Deweer, B., Sirigu, A., Dubois, B., et al. (1995). The neuropsychological pattern of corticobasal degeneration: Comparison with progressive supranuclear palsy and Alzheimer's disease. *Neurology, 45,* 1477–1483.

Portala, K., Levander, S., Westermark, K., Ekselius, L., & von Knorring, L. (2001). Pattern of neuropsychological deficits in patients with treated Wilson's disease. *European Archives of Psychiatry and Clinical Neuroscience, 251,* 262–286.

Poser, C. M., Paty, D. W., Scheinberg, L., McDonald, I. W., Davis, F. A., Ebers, G. C., et al. (1983). New diagnostic criteria for multiple sclerosis: guidelines for research protocols. *Annals of Neurology, 13,* 227–231.

Rao, S. M., Cognitive Function Study Group, & National Multiple Sclerosis Society. (1990). *Manual for the Brief Repeatable*

Battery of Neuropsychological Tests in Multiple Sclerosis. New York: National Multiple Sclerosis Society.

Rao, S. M., Leo, G. J., Bernardin, L., & Unverzagt, F. (1991). Cognitive dysfunction in multiple sclerosis: 1. Frequency, patterns, and prediction. *Neurology, 41,* 685–691.

Reid, W. G., Broe, G. A., Morris, J. G., Hely, M. A., et al. (1992). The role of cholinergic definciency in neuropsychological deficits in idiopathic Parkinson's disease. *Dementia, 3,* 114–120.

Sadovnick, A. D., Remick, R. A., Allen, J., Swartz, E., Yee, I. M. L., Eisen, K., et al. (1996). Depression and multiple sclerosis. *Neurology, 46,* 628–632.

Saint-Cyr, J. A. (2003). Frontal-striatal circuit functions: Context, sequence, and consequence. *Journal of the International Neuropsychological Society, 9,* 103–127.

Stern, Y., Mayeux, R., Ilson, J., Fahn, S., & Cote, L. (1984). Pergolide therapy for Parkinson's disease: Neurobehavioral changes. *Neurology, 34*(2), 201–204.

Tröster, A. I., & Fields, J. A. (2003). The role of neuropsychological evaluation in the neurosurgical treatment of movement disorders. In D. Tarsy, J. L. Vitek, & A. M. Lozano (Eds.), *Surgical treatment of Parkinson's disease and other movement disorders* (pp. 213–240). Totowa, NJ: Humana Press.

Tröster, A. I., & Fields, J. A. (in press). Parkinson's disease, progressive supranuclear palsy, corticobasal ganglionic degeneration and related disorders of the frontostriatal system. In J. E. Morgan & J. H. Ricker (Eds.), *Comprehensive textbook of clinical neuropsychology.* London: Taylor & Francis.

Tröster, A. I., Fields, J. A., & Koller, W. C. (2000). Parkinson's disease and parkinsonism. In C. E. Coffey & J. L. Cummings (Eds.), *Textbook of geriatric neuropsychiatry* (2nd ed., pp. 559–600). Washington, DC: American Psychiatric Press.

Tröster, A. I., & Letsch, E. A. (2004). Evaluation and treatment of anxiety and depression in Parkinson's disease. In R. Pahwa, K. E. Lyons, & W. C. Koller (Eds.), *Therapy of Parkinson's disease* (3rd ed., pp. 423–445). New York: Marcel Dekker.

Tröster, A. I., & Woods, S. P. (2003). Neuropsychological aspects of Parkinson's disease and parkinsonian syndromes. In R. Pahwa, K. E. Lyons, & W. C. Koller (Eds.), *Handbook of Parkinson's disease* (3rd ed., pp. 127–157). New York: Marcel Dekker.

Weddell, R. A., & Weiser, R. (1995). A double-blind cross-over placebo-controlled trial of the effects of bromocriptine on psychomotor function, cognition, and mood in de novo

patients with Parkinson's disease. *Behavioural Pharmacology,*
6, 81–91.

Wenning, G. K., Colosimo, C., Geser, F., & Poewe, W. (2004).
Multiple system atrophy. *Lancet Neurology, 3,* 93–103.

Zakzanis, K. K. (1998). The subcortical dementia of Huntington's
disease. *Journal of Clinical and Experimental Neuropsychology,*
20, 565–578.

CHAPTER 12
Amy Weinstein and Rodney A. Swenson

Cerebrovascular Disease

Cerebrovascular disease is defined as any pathological process involving blood vessels in the brain. The vascular pathology can include lesions of the vessel wall, occlusion of the vessel, rupture of the vessel, or malformation. This chapter focuses on the cerebrovascular conditions most frequently encountered by a neuropsychologist. The role of the neuropsychologist when working with this patient population is to determine changes in cognitive and emotional behavior post cerebrovascular accident (CVA). Accordingly, the neuropsychologist gathers data, often at repeated intervals, to monitor the degree and course of impairment, subsequent recovery, and prognosis and to assist in establishing suitable rehabilitation programs in collaboration with a rehabilitation team.

I. CLASSIFICATION OF CEREBROVASCULAR DISEASE

A. Cerebrovascular Accident

The CVA, or stroke, is the most common type of cerebrovascular disease. Approximately one-half million people per year in the United States are expected to suffer from strokes of various causes. During the development of a stroke, a specific part of the brain does not receive adequate nutrients, specifically oxygen and glucose, owing to disrupted blood supply. After several minutes of deprived blood supply without adequate collateral blood circulation, **infarction** (areas of damaged or dead tissue) occurs. If blood supply is restored within an appropriate time limit, brain tissue remains viable and function recovers. If **ischemia** from tissue starvation owing to insufficient blood flow obstruction occurs but the ischemic tissue has sufficient collateral supply, functional impairments are temporary, with eventual recovery.

B. Evolution of Disease Expression

Factors that influence the type, extent, and symptoms of a stroke include size of blood vessels (small capillaries vs. large major arteries), degree of blood vessel weakness and capacity for compensation by surrounding vessels, preexisting lesions and degree of recovery, location of lesion, and rate of symptom development.

C. Types of Cerebrovascular Disorders

Mechanisms that account for brain tissue starvation include (a) obstruction of blood vessels, which causes disrupted or deficient blood flow to the brain, and (b) hemorrhage, or arterial rupture, which causes bleeding within the brain tissue itself.

1. OBSTRUCTIVE ISCHEMIC STROKES

Blockage of a blood vessel can occur when a clot travels from its origin and becomes lodged along the way in the cerebral artery. This can occur rapidly, over hours or days, or episodically, depending on the mechanism of obstruction.

a. Cerebral thrombosis

Obstruction of blood flow can be due to buildup of **atherosclerotic plaques**, which are fat deposits within the artery walls. Obstruction of blood flow to the brain results from accumulation of clots of coagulated blood and plugs of tissue and plaques that remain at the point of formation and narrow the vessel openings, thereby restricting passage of blood flow. This type of stroke can evolve over hours or days. Because thrombotic strokes tend to evolve from plaques in the internal carotid artery and vertebral basilar arteries, regions fed by the middle cerebral artery and vertebral basilar artery are most affected.

b. Cerebral embolism

An **embolus** is either a plug of thrombus material or a fatty deposit broken away from blood vessel walls or a plug of foreign matter such as clumps of bacteria or obstructive gas bubbles. Obstruction of blood flow can be due to a blood clot, air bubble, fat plug, or small mass of cells traveling from another vessel and lodged into a smaller one, restricting circulation and causing sudden onset of symptoms.

c. Cerebral atherosclerosis

Obstruction of blood flow can occur when narrowing of the vessel results from thickening and hardening of the arteries.

d. Cerebral vasculitis

Inflammation or vasospasm (spasmodic constriction of blood vessels) can cause narrowing of the vessels and restriction of blood supply.

2. HEMORRHAGIC STROKES

This type of stroke results from massive bleeding into brain tissue. Causes of cerebral hemorrhage include hypertension, congenital cerebral artery defects, toxins, and blood disorders. Onset is abrupt, with poor prognosis when loss of consciousness is beyond 2 days.

a. Spontaneous intracranial hemorrhage secondary to ruptured aneurysm

Aneurysms are balloonlike expansions from blood vessels caused by congenital defects, hypertension, arteriosclerosis, embolisms, or infections. The weakened vessel walls make them prone to rupture.

b. Intracranial hemorrhage from arteriovenous malformation

An arteriovenous malformation is a congenital collection of abnormal blood vessels with abnormal blood flow that tend to be weak and susceptible to vessel leakage.

c. Subarachnoid hemorrhage

Bleeding under arachnoid matter can cause damage to brain tissue from pressure effects and irritation.

3. LACUNAR STROKES

This type of vascular insufficiency results when small branches of the cerebral arteries become occluded. The softened infarcted tissue leaves multiple small lacunae. The resulting infarcts are so minuscule that there may be no obvious clinical symptoms, although location is a critical determinant of symptom presentation. Computed tomography (CT) and arteriography tend to have negative findings.

4. TRANSIENT ISCHEMIC ATTACKS

Usually caused by transient focal ischemia, transient ischemic attacks (TIAs) are linked to atherosclerotic thrombosis. These brief events last from a few minutes to a number of hours and typically reverse themselves. TIAs are more commonly associated with atherosclerosis and hypertension, particularly in males. They can involve any cerebral or cerebellar artery. The individual attack may resolve abruptly or gradually.

5. MULTI-INFARCT STATES

Several conditions can lead to multi-infarct states, including small vessel ischemic changes, which are often associated with atherosclerosis, diabetes, and hypertension. Small vessel changes also can be the result of cranial radiation, which has been demonstrated to affect the intimal walls of blood vessels and subsequently lead to small vessel changes. Any disorder that can lead to a hypercoagulable state can be a setup for multi-infarct states. It is not atypical for patients with these syndromes to present "acutely," but care should be taken during history taking; many times a stepwise deterioration can be evident in the behavioral history.

II. FUNCTIONAL NEUROANATOMIC CORRELATES

A. Distribution of Blood Supply to the Brain

Blood supply to the brain is transported by two carotid arteries and two vertebral arteries, with both vessels entering on each side of the body.

1. INTERNAL CAROTID ARTERIES

These arteries enter the skull at the base of the brain and branch out to form two major arteries and a number of smaller arteries.

a. Major branches

Major branches (anterior cerebral artery and middle cerebral artery) irrigate the anterior and middle regions of the cortex. The anterior cerebral artery has branches that supply the orbital

frontal lobes, medial frontal lobes, cingulate gyrus, anterior fornix, parts of the corpus callosum, and the posterior parietal
region. The middle cerebral artery is the greatest blood supplier
of the cerebral hemispheres. Its branches supply internal nuclear
masses; orbitofrontal, precentral, and anterior regions; plus anterior temporal, posterior temporal, and posterior parietal
branches.

b. Minor branches

Minor branches (ophthalmic artery, anterior choroidal artery, posterior communicating artery, and anterior communicating artery) irrigate various subcortical regions. The posterior
communicating artery joins the middle cerebral artery and the
posterior cerebral artery on each side, and the anterior communicating artery joins the anterior and middle cerebral arteries.

2. VERTEBRAL ARTERIES

The vertebral arteries enter at the base of the brain and
join to form the basilar artery, which gives off smaller arteries
and then branches into the posterior cerebral artery. The vertebral arteries supply the spinal cord, brain stem (medulla, pons,
midbrain), cerebellum, and posterior diencephalon.

a. Major branches

These arteries (basilar artery and posterior cerebral artery)
supply parts of the temporal and occipital lobes. The posterior
cerebral artery, which branches off from the vertebral system,
supplies the lower surface of the temporal lobe and large areas
of the occipital lobe and visual cortex.

b. Minor branches

Interconnection of all these arteries (anterior inferior cerebellar artery and posterior inferior cerebellar artery) form the
circle of Willis. If blockage of a vertebral or carotid artery occurs
on one side, this circular connection helps compensate the half
of the brain that has lost its blood supply.

3. NEUROPATHOLOGICAL AND NEUROPSYCHOLOGICAL SYMPTOM CORRELATES

Interruption of blood supply to specific brain regions is
often associated with characteristic neuropsychological signs
and symptoms. The distribution of the major anterior, middle,
and posterior cerebral arteries irrigates both cortical and subcor-

tical regions. Table 12.1 provides a review of arterial blood supply to functional–anatomic divisions of brain regions considered of primary importance from a neuropsychological perspective.

III. DIAGNOSES TO RULE OUT

Compared with CVAs, other causes of cognitive impairment such as tumors, progressive dementing diseases (e.g., Alzheimer's disease, Pick's disease, and Lewy body disease), and movement disorders presenting with dementia (e.g., Parkinson's disease and Huntington's disease) typically present with a slow, progressive course. Multi-infarct dementia of vascular origin can be misdiagnosed as an Alzheimer's-type dementia because symptoms can vary depending on the location of the small strokes and symptom progression. Often, multi-infarct states present in a stepwise fashion as opposed to the more insidious decline that is seen in Alzheimer's disease. Also, it is often the case that "acute" presentations of multi-infarct events are magnified by changes in the person's environmental structure. Therefore, a careful history is important in delineating all the factors that lead to behavioral changes.

Diagnostic clues from medical history should include medical risk factors for cerebrovascular disease such as hypertension, atherosclerosis in other parts of the body, coronary heart disease, atrial fibrillation, previous CVA or TIA, carotid bruit, rheumatic heart disease, diabetes, smoking, excessive alcohol use, and use of birth control pills.

IV. RELEVANT LABORATORY, NEURORADIOLOGICAL, AND ELECTROPHYSIOLOGICAL STUDIES

Other prominent neurological conditions that may be mistaken for vascular dementia include infectious processes, metabolic encephalopathies, toxic conditions, and nutritional deficiencies. Medical studies are critical to rule out or account for conditions that contribute to physical and behavioral changes.

Neuropsychologists should be familiar with relevant laboratory, neuroradiological, and electrophysiological studies to assist in diagnosis, neuropsychological test interpretation, and treatment recommendations. The neuropsychologist, of course, is not qualified to interpret these tests but should be knowledgeable about the typical laboratory values associated with these medical tests and able to discuss these test results with the

Table 12.1. Arterial Blood Supply to Functional–Anatomic Divisions of the Brain Relevant to Neuropsychology

Function	Impairment	Brain structure	Blood supply
Sensorimotor	Paralysis of contralateral face, arm, and leg	Primary motor area, precentral gyrus	Middle cerebral artery, anterior cerebral artery
	Sensory impairment over face, arm, and leg	Primary sensory area, postcentral gyrus	Middle cerebral artery, anterior cerebral artery
Language	Broca's aphasia	Inferior frontal gyrus in dominant hemisphere	Middle cerebral artery
	Wernicke's aphasia	Superior temporal gyrus in dominant hemisphere	Middle cerebral artery
Visual perception	Homonymous hemianopia	Optic radiation deep in temporal convolution	Middle cerebral artery, posterior cerebral artery
	Visual integration, spatial neglect, visual agnosia	Parietal–occipital lobe, nondominant hemisphere	Middle cerebral artery
	Constructional apraxia, dressing apraxia	Parietal lobe, nondominant hemisphere	Middle cerebral artery
	Gerstmann's syndrome (agraphia, acalculia, alexia, finger agnosia, right-left confusion)	Angular gyrus of the dominant hemisphere	Middle cerebral artery
Movement	Ideomotor and ideational apraxia	Left temporal, parietal, occipital area	Middle cerebral artery, posterior cerebral artery

Memory	Short-term and long-term memory impairment	Hippocampus, medial temporal lobes, frontal lobes, basal forebrain, medial thalamus	Medial cerebral, posterior cerebral, anterior choroidal, and posterior communicating arteries
	Working memory impairment	Dorsolateral frontal lobes	Anterior cerebral artery
Frontal-executive	Impairment in set maintenance, problem solving, planning, self-evaluation, ability to modify behavior	Dorsolateral frontal	Middle cerebral artery
	Impairment in inhibition, emotional regulation	Orbital frontal	Anterior cerebral artery
	Akinesia, bradykinesia, dyskinesia	Basal ganglia, putamen, globus pallidus, caudate nucleus, amygdaloid	Anterior choroidal artery, middle cerebral artery

physicians involved in the acute workup of the patient. Knowledge of these results might influence interpretation of the neuro-psychological assessment if the tests are done at an early stage (see chap. 3, this volume). For example, diagnosis of vascular dementia is inappropriate if a patient is acutely hyponatremic, is suffering from oxygen deprivation, or has uremic poisoning because of kidney failure.

- **Routine laboratory tests.** Routine laboratory studies typically include a complete blood count (CBC) Panel 20, electrolytes, and blood-clotting-factor studies.
- **Cardiac tests.** In acute myocardial infarction (MI), cardiac enzyme levels are often requested. In infectious endocarditis, blood cultures are typically taken. Other important tests that are beneficial to consider include an electrocardiogram (EKG) to rule out possible MI or arrhythmia, a chest X-ray to rule out cardiomegaly or infection, and oxygen saturation levels or blood gases.
- **Other relevant laboratory tests.** If rheumatologic or inflammatory disease is considered, the physician typically orders erythrocyte sedimentation rate (ESR) and fluorescent antinuclear antibody (FANA) tests. In coagulopathies, more advanced studies such as protein C and protein S, as well as anticardiolipin and venereal disease resource laboratory (VDRL) studies are typically ordered. In systemic cancer, guaiac stools are often considered. Some stroke-related symptoms are due to illicit drug use; therefore, a drug screen, particularly aimed at cocaine and amphetamines, is helpful.
- **Computed tomography.** In general, when a patient presents with symptoms of a stroke, a head CT scan is done to rule out a hemorrhage, infarct, or mass lesion. It is important to appreciate that CT scans do not always show evidence of a stroke initially because the densities on CT scans of newly acquired stroke are often similar to those of normal brain tissue. Typically, 3 to 4 days after a stroke has completed, a lesion is appreciable on CT scan.
- **Magnetic resonance imaging.** Occasionally, magnetic resonance imaging (MRI) is indicated; this type of imaging is more capable than CT of detecting small vessel, subcortical strokes. MRI scans can also be particularly helpful in patients with a newly acquired stroke because, unlike the CT scan, it enables disclosure of preexisting underlying periventricular white matter disease. Detecting the presence of coexisting white matter lesions has

obvious implications for neuropsychological interpretation, prognosis, and recovery.

- *Other diagnostic tests.* Carotid ultrasound is of value in determining whether obstructed carotid arteries could be a source of embolus. This procedure also serves as a general screen for vascular disease. An echocardiogram or transesophageal echocardiogram, which provides better images of the heart as it pumps blood through the valves and chambers, is sometimes performed if a cardiac source is suspected.

V. STANDARD NEUROPSYCHOLOGICAL ASSESSMENT

Table 12.2 provides an introductory review of tests recommended for basic neuropsychological assessment of patients with CVA. In addition to Table 12.2, the following Web sites can be helpful in finding standard instruments for use in post-stroke assessment.

- http://www.oqp.med.va.gov/
  Appendix B of this site provides an extensive listing of instruments and their uses in assessment of poststroke patients. Disability ratings, outcome measures, functional rehabilitation assessment, and quality-of-life measures are included along with supporting references.
- http://www.strokecenter.org/
  This site offers prehospital stroke assessment tools, acute assessment scales, functional assessment measures, and several measures designed to measure outcome of treatment interventions.

VI. ALTERNATIVE NEUROPSYCHOLOGICAL TESTING

Administration and valid interpretation of standardized neuropsychological tests are often quite difficult in this patient population. The following section provides some hints for alternative neuropsychological testing approaches when standardized neuropsychological testing is ineffective.

Hemiparesis, visual field cuts, weakness, aphasia, and a host of other acquired behavioral syndromes in patients with stroke often tax the neuropsychologist to the point that individually customized neuropsychological assessment is often the rule and

Table 12.2. CVA-Related Neuropsychological Disorders and Tests of Assessment

Function or impairment	Suggested neuropsychological tests	References[a]
Aphasia		
Broca's aphasia Wernicke's aphasia Transcortical motor aphasia Global aphasia Transcortical sensory aphasia Conduction aphasia	Boston Diagnostic Aphasia Examination Multilingual Aphasia Examination Western Aphasia Battery	Goodglass and Kaplan (1983a, 1983b) Benton and Hamsher (1989) Kertesz (1979)
Comprehension	Token Test	Boller and Vignolo (1966)
Naming	Boston Naming Test	Kaplan, Goodglass, and Weintraub (1983)
Vocabulary	Peabody Picture Vocabulary Test	Dunn and Dunn (1981)
Verbal fluency	Controlled Oral Word Association Test	Benton and Hamsher (1976, 1989); Spreen and Strauss (1991)
Reading	National Adult Reading Test	Nelson, Nelson, and O'Connell (1978)
Writing	Boston Diagnostic Aphasia Examination: Cookie Theft Picture	Goodglass and Kaplan (1983a, 1983b)

Visual perception		
Homonymous hemianopia	Double Simultaneous Stimulation Test	Walsh (1987)
Visual organization and integration	Hooper Visual Organization Test	Hooper (1958); Hooper Organization Test Manual (1983)
Visual motor construction	Wechsler Adult Intelligence Scale—Revised: Block Design, Object Assembly	Wechsler (1994, 1955, 1981) Benton, Hamsher, et al. (1983) Benton and Van Allen (1968)
Visual recognition	Visual Form Discrimination Test	Benton, Hamsher, et al. (1983)
Face recognition	Test of Face Recognition	
Attention		
Auditory attention	Wechsler Adult Intelligence Scale—Revised: Digit Span	Wechsler (1994, 1955, 1981)
	Paced Auditory Serial Addition Test	Gronwell (1977); Gronwell and Sampson (1974)
	Verbal and Nonverbal Cancellation	Mesulam (1985, 1988) Schenkenberg et al. (1980)
Visual attention and spatial neglect	Line Bisection Test Symbol Digit Modalities Test	Smith (1982)

(Continued)

Table 12.2. CVA-Related Neuropsychological Disorders and Tests of Assessment *(Continued)*

Function or impairment	Suggested neuropsychological tests	References[a]
Movement		
Ideomotor and ideational apraxia	Boston Diagnostic Aphasia Examination: Apraxia Test	Goodglass and Kaplan (1983)
Memory		
Short-term, long-term, and working memory	Wechsler Memory Scale—Revised California Verbal Learning Test	Wechsler (1945, 1987) Delis, Kramer, Kaplan, and Ober (1987)
	Buschke Selective Reminding Test Hopkins Verbal Learning Test Rey Auditory Verbal Learning Test Rey-Osterreith Complex Figure Benton Visual Retention Test	Buschke and Fuld (1974) Brandt (1991) Rey (1964); Taylor (1959) Osterreith (1944) Benton (1974)
Frontal-executive		
Set maintenance and set shifting	Trail Making Test	Army Individual Test Battery (1944)
Problem solving		
Conceptualization		
Response inhibition	Wisconsin Card Sorting Test Stroop Interference Test	Berg (1948); Grant and Berg (1948); Stroop (1935); Jensen and Rohwer (1966)

Note. CVA = cerebrovascular accident.
[a] Neuropsychological test references cited here can be found in *Neuropsychological Assessment* (3rd ed.), by M. D. Lezak, 1995, New York: Oxford University Press.

not the exception. The addition of creative testing beyond the limits of standardized tests can also be helpful in designing rehabilitation strategies that might aid the patient. The following sections provide specific examples of alternative neuropsychological testing approaches that may be used when standardized neuropsychological testing is ineffective.

A. Visual Neglect

In the acute assessment of a patient with right-hemisphere stroke who has visual neglect, it is not helpful for the neuropsychologist to administer numerous visuospatial tests that the patient will continually fail. Rather, it is important for the neuropsychologist to minimize the problem of neglect when attempting to assess higher cortical visual–perceptual functions by using methods of remediation or compensation. If such a patient is failing miserably on the Block Design test, for example, it is helpful to limit presentation of the blocks to the "good" right visual field. Line bisection is another difficult test for patients with right parietal dysfunction; therefore, after left hemineglect has been identified, one can structure the task by writing letters at the end of each line to be bisected. Having the patient read the letters out loud ensures that he or she attends to the entire line before bisecting it. Likewise, vertical alignment of the picture arrangement stimulus cards can overcome the barrier of visual inattention.

B. Aphasia

Patients with aphasic syndromes often perform poorly on a variety of tests simply because they are given verbal instructions that are not understood because of underlying comprehension deficits. Comprehension problems can be minimized by examiner demonstrations and use of nonverbal gesturing and facial expression to enhance communication. Expressive problems can often be overcome by multiple-choice or yes–no recognition testing in which the patient does not have to provide a complex verbal response.

C. Hemiparesis

Most neuropsychologists agree that it is of little value to test motor speed, such as finger-tapping performance, in patients with severe hemiparesis. Although patients with left-hemisphere stroke who have severe right hemiparesis often are also clumsy and slow with their left hand, functional evaluation of the left hand for assessing performance on nonspeed tests would be of benefit.

VII. THE NEUROLOGICAL EXAMINATION

The neurological examination provides critical information regarding simple sensorimotor function that should be carefully reviewed by the neuropsychologist. Physical symptoms that may directly affect the neuropsychological evaluation include numbness, weakness, or paralysis of face, arm, or leg; sudden blurring, decreased vision, or double vision in one or both eyes; difficulty speaking owing to dysarthria; and dizziness, loss of balance, or loss of coordination. It is critical for the neuropsychologist to appreciate the contribution of basic sensorimotor system disturbance when assessing higher cognitive function to guide test selection and enhance accuracy of test interpretation. Poor performance on a measure of word production, for example, may be due to dysarthric speech rather than impaired semantic fluency. Neuropsychological testing in the assessment of cardiovascular disease should include attention to the following issues.

A. Timing of the Evaluation

The first thing to consider when evaluating a patient with a newly acquired stroke is the timing of the evaluation. A stroke is an evolving situation, and findings during the acute stage could definitively change in the ensuing months. Therefore, the neuropsychologist must consider the typical neurobehavioral recovery course of the stroke and point of measurement. Regardless of whether a stroke has stabilized or is evolving, a neuropsychological evaluation is critical in assisting both initial and long-term diagnostic and rehabilitative treatment planning.

B. Identifying Strengths and Weaknesses

An important perspective to take at this stage is one of identifying strengths as well as weaknesses. The purpose of the neuropsychological evaluation is not only to look at what areas of deficit are prevalent but also to identify remaining cognitive strengths that can be exploited in the rehabilitative compensatory process.

C. Test Administration and Interpretation

1. THE QUALITATIVE APPROACH

It is often necessary to adjust standardized administration procedures when evaluating stroke patients to elicit behavior and account for major deficits. It is important to look beyond final scores as a criterion for determining the degree of brain damage because the cognitive processes used by patients as they struggle to perform neuropsychological tests are frequently more revealing than the final quantitative outcome on a test. Fine-tuned analysis of patients' qualitative behavior can measure improvement that final scores cannot convey. For example, on the Picture Arrangement subtest of the Wechsler Adult Intelligence Scale—Revised (WAIS–R), a patient with a right-hemisphere stroke may perform poorly. When tested months later, the patient may continue to obtain similarly poor scores, yet instead of misarranging all of the cards as he did earlier, he now only misarranges one of four cards. This finding indicates improvement, despite an unchanged final score. The qualitative approach is important for neuropsychologists to consider when trying to document improvement as well as to provide justification for ongoing rehabilitation.

2. ECOLOGICAL VALIDITY

Neuropsychologists have to be concerned about the ecological validity of their tests. For example, if one is finding significant problems on measures of apraxia during a neuropsychological evaluation, it is important to discuss these findings with the physical and occupational therapists working with the patient to see how this deficit is affecting the patient in real-life situations.

3. ENVIRONMENTAL CONDITIONS

Environmental conditions during testing can have a notable influence on examination and rehabilitation of cognition and behavior. The neuropsychologist should always be aware that patients can show an amplification of cognitive abnormalities in unfamiliar environments with distractions and overstimulation.

4. FUNCTIONAL SIGNIFICANCE

Direct and clear communication of test results is important when working with professionals from other disciplines involved in the treatment of patients as well as with patients and family members. Whereas the training of neuropsychologists emphasizes identifying and understanding the complex cognitive processes involved in a behavior, attempts to translate these processes into functional activities often remain obtuse. It is critical to present neuropsychological data in a format that has functional meaning and significance, so that impressions and recommendations can be used by staff and family to enhance recovery.

D. Determining Patient Competency

The neuropsychologist is often faced with addressing issues of competency in stroke patients. It is important when determining competency to consider what phase of recovery the patient is in, because competency status may change rather dramatically as recovery progresses. A detailed analysis of the patient's available behavioral responses helps to clarify his or her potential for independence and self-care. Some patients with aphasia, for example, have relatively unimpaired reasoning and judgment, yet impoverished expressive language renders them unable to communicate their ideas effectively.

VIII. TREATMENT ISSUES

Emotional and medical concerns should be taken into account when devising a rehabilitation strategy for patients with vascular disorders.

A. Treatment of Emotional Behaviors

It is important for the neuropsychologist to monitor emotional behavior continually to provide needed psychotherapeutic intervention, as well as to assist the physician or therapist in appropriately treating the behavior. The neuropsychologist should not underestimate the powerful influence of emotional factors in shaping a patient's ultimate recovery. Individual as well as family education and psychotherapy can be helpful in motivating patients to achieve their highest level of functional outcome.

Behavioral techniques such as distraction are often helpful in controlling emotional lability and can prevent the need for antidepressant drugs, which may further compromise cognitive abilities. Monitoring of neurovegetative signs and degree of participation in therapies may provide clues to whether psychopharmacological intervention is warranted. In some cases, medications to assist in emotional regulation or reduce symptoms of anxiety and depression can serve to facilitate the recovery process by enabling active participation in rehabilitation.

B. Medication

Drugs are often used to treat conditions that either accompany or result from cerebrovascular disease. **Anticoagulants** are drugs used to dissolve clots or prevent further clotting; **hypertensive** drugs are used to control blood pressure; and **steroid** drugs are used to reduce cerebral edema, or swelling. Familiarity with use of these and other medications in patients undergoing neuropsychological evaluation is important, because side effects can confound test performance and interpretation. The book *Neurotoxic Side Effects of Prescription Drugs* by John C. M. Brust (1996) is a helpful resource that can familiarize neuropsychologists with medication side effects from drugs frequently prescribed to patients with CVA.

C. Cognitive Rehabilitation

Cognitive rehabilitation is a therapeutic intervention based on assessment and understanding of the patient's brain-behavioral deficits. Cognitive rehabilitation may be directed toward numerous areas of cognition, including concentration, selective and divided attention, vigilance, speed of information processing, perception, verbal and visual memory, verbal comprehension and communication, reasoning, problem solving, judgment, initiation, planning, and self-monitoring.

Interventions can have an assortment of approaches, including strengthening or reestablishing previously learned behavior, use of compensatory cognitive mechanisms to establish new cognitive performance, and use of environmental compensatory mechanisms to establish new behavior through external means. Of equal importance is helping people adapt to their cognitive disability, despite problems in modifying or compensating for cognitive impairments. The goal of rehabilitation is to improve patients' overall quality of life and achieve functions that are relevant to patients' daily life. Every neuropsychologist working with CVA patients in an inpatient setting should be familiar with basic rehabilitative techniques.

1. VISUAL–PERCEPTUAL DEFICITS

For patients with right hemisphere stroke, therapy designed to assist in orienting to the intact left visual field is helpful. It is important to distinguish among inattention, neglect, and a field cut in these patients (see chap. 20, this volume). Simple techniques such as making a brightly colored line on the left side of the page when the patient is reading may help the patient to orient to his or her left side, thereby enabling him or her to read a complete line. The neuropsychologist should work hand in hand with the occupational therapist in the rehabilitation of these types of disorders.

2. SPEECH AND LANGUAGE DEFICITS

Typically, speech pathologists are involved not only in the evaluation of speech and language disturbances but also in their treatment. The neuropsychologist should be able to assist the speech pathologist with treatment efforts by helping to differentiate the nature of the language disturbance and identifying other cognitive disturbances, such as diminished initiation and impaired memory, that may contribute to overall language performance. For example, on the Token Test, which is a measure of verbal comprehension, impaired memory rather than aphasia may be the cause of compromised performance on the more complex multistep commands. By simplifying memory demands or training the patient in mnemonics, preserved aspects of language can be enhanced.

3. MEMORY DEFICITS

Memory disorders are variably amenable to rehabilitation strategies depending on the nature of the impairment (e.g., encoding vs. retrieval deficits). Schacter's method of vanishing cues (Schacter & Glisky, 1986), which exploits implicit memory processing, can be helpful for teaching some procedural aspects of memory, but experience has shown this to be limited and quite time consuming. For the patient who demonstrates significant retrieval problems, however, use of compensatory strategies such as a notebook and memory log can be helpful.

4. EXECUTIVE FUNCTION DEFICITS

Rehabilitation of any kind is difficult unless patients have adequate attention and awareness regarding their deficits. Executive system dysfunction can lead to serious impediment of the ability to organize, sequence, plan, benefit from feedback, and carry over treatment information. Effective evaluation and rehabilitation of executive system function is necessary in all patients with stroke disorder (see chap. 25, this volume). Adding structure to a patient's environment to make it more predictable and reduce distractions can significantly improve cognitive function and emotional adjustment. Sohlberg and Mateer (1989a) provided helpful executive system rehabilitation techniques.

Comprehensive articles and textbooks are available to instruct the practitioner in more inclusive implementation of cognitive rehabilitation techniques in clinical practice (see Cicerone et al., 2000; Sohlberg & Mateer, 1989a). Cicerone et al., after reviewing the literature, provide a valuable appraisal of evidence-based interventions for specific stroke patients with specific types of cognitive deficits.

In addition, over the last several years, there have been significant developments in the area of virtual reality technology and driving assessment in many rehabilitation centers. The interface of neuropsychological testing data with virtual world simulation can be helpful with determination of cessation of or returning to driving privileges and other behavioral applications (Lengenfelder, Schultheis, Al-Shihabi, Mourant, & DeLuca, 2002; Rizzo & Buckwalter, 1997; Wald, Liu, Hirsekorn, & Taylar, 2000).

IX. PSYCHIATRIC COMORBIDITY ASSOCIATED WITH STROKE

Psychological and psychiatric comorbidity often result from an acquired neurological disease. The neuropsychological examination may assist in differentiating the amplification of preexisting emotional behaviors from newly acquired primary brain-based or secondary reactive emotions (see Heilman, Bowers, & Valenstein, 1993; Starkstein & Robinson, 1992).

A. Preexisting Emotional Illness

The possibility of a preexisting psychiatric condition with subsequent poststroke amplification requires close evaluation and monitoring because inadequate coping skills and diminished emotional reserve may contribute to poor adjustment. Careful review of medical history and clinical interview with family members are critical to establishing a positive psychiatric history.

B. Emotional Adjustment to Illness

An appreciation for the normal grieving process, as a reaction to the profound loss occurring with a stroke, is important. It is not uncommon for patients, as well as their families, to experience depressive symptoms as they begin to adjust to the condition. Experiencing the various stages of grieving is considered appropriate and even healthy because it will enable the patient and family ultimately to cope better. Early intervention with antidepressant medication is contraindicated unless depressed mood is excessively prolonged and extreme.

C. Caregiver Burden

Instruments to assess caregiver burden have been developed, such as the Sense of Competence Questionnaire (SCQ), that provide reliable and valid data for assessing the burden of caregiving as experienced by partners of stroke patients (Scholte op Reimer, de Haan, Pijnenborg, Limburg, & VandenBos, 1998).

Instruments such as these can often be good "ice-breakers" with families in helping them start to address the changes associated with their stroke partner that they often would not share in follow-up visits.

D. Emotional Changes Resulting From Brain Lesions

The contribution of the cortex to emotional processing is to interpret and analyze emotional information and express and regulate affective behavior. As a result of a CVA, and depending on the location of a neocortical injury, the patient may suffer an injury to the functional neuroanatomic circuitry that shapes emotional processing and responding. These issues should be well understood by the family and caregivers.

1. HEMISPHERIC DIFFERENCES

Studies of change in mood and emotional experience as a result of brain lesions have suggested that patients with left-hemisphere damage with frontal and caudate involvement are more often depressed or anxious, whereas those with right-hemisphere damage tend to be indifferent or euphoric. Patients with right-hemisphere lesions may have difficulty with emotional facial expression and emotional vocal prosody; hence they can appear indifferent. Depression should not automatically be assumed in patients demonstrating flattened facial and prosodic emotional expression related to frontal lobe and right hemisphere lesions. In many of these patients, internal emotional experience and mood state are discrepant with outward emotional expression. Furthermore, voluntary and involuntary expression of humor can also be misleading, because patients may demonstrate laughter in response to a joke but not when commanded to show facial and prosodic emotional affect (e.g., happy, sad, angry).

2. RIGHT HEMISPHERE

The right hemisphere contains a "vocabulary" of nonverbal affective signals (facial expressions, prosody, and gestures). Patients with right-hemisphere damage, therefore, are frequently unable to discern the emotional meaning of facial, vocal, and gestural expression of emotion, as well as to engage in similar emotional expression.

3. FRONTAL AND SUBCORTICAL REGIONS

Portions of the frontal lobe are intimately bound to subcortical, primarily limbic structures. Hence, damage to frontal convexity and orbital poles can result in flattened affect, apathy, loss of social control, and overly emotional behavior. With lesions involving frontal/subcortical/basal ganglia regions, obsessive–compulsive symptoms including ruminative, checking, and perseverative behavior may also be present and might profoundly interfere with the rehabilitation process.

4. CORTICOBULBAR MOTOR PATHWAYS

Lesions that interrupt the corticobulbar motor pathways bilaterally release reflex mechanisms for facial expression from cortical control. Emotional lability (i.e., involuntary laughing or crying) results in symptoms of inappropriate emotional expression with appropriate emotional experience. Again, it is important not to interpret this stereotypical excess of emotional expression as representative of mood state.

X. CONCLUSION

This chapter provides an overview of the wide range of causes and types of CVAs, blood supply to anatomic–functional divisions of the brain, issues related to assessment of cognitive and emotional disorders resulting from CVAs, and general cognitive rehabilitative interventions. This topic encompasses a broad range of behavioral disorders that can accompany damage to the brain by way of the vascular system. Additional, more detailed and specific information beyond the scope of this review can be found in the publications listed in the bibliography and Web sites listed in the body of this chapter.

BIBLIOGRAPHY

Adams, G. F., & Victor, M. (1989). *Principles of neurology* (4th ed.). New York: McGraw-Hill.

Bornstein, R. A., & Brown, G. G. (1991). *Neurobehavioral aspects of cerebrovascular disease*. New York: Oxford University Press.

Brandstater, M. E. (1990). An overview of stroke rehabilitation. *Stroke, 21*(Suppl. II), II-40–II-42.

Brust, J. C. (1996). *Neurotoxic side effects of prescription drugs*. Stoneham, MA: Butterworth-Heinemann.

Cicerone, K. D., Dahlerg, C., Kalmer, K., Langenbahn, D. M., Malec, J. F., Bergquist, T. F., et al. (2000). Evidence-based cognitive rehabilitation: Recommendations for clinical practice. *Archives of Physical Medicine and Rehabilitation, 81*, 1596–1615.

Goodglass, H., & Kaplan, E. (1983). *Assessment of aphasia and related disorders* (2nd ed.). Philadelphia: Lea & Febiger. (Distributed by Psychological Assessment Resources, Odessa, FL)

Heilman, K. M., Bowers, D., & Valenstein, E. (1993). Emotional disorders associated with neurological diseases. In K. M. Heilman & E. Valenstein (Eds.), *Clinical neuropsychology* (3rd ed., pp. 461–497). New York: Oxford University Press.

Lengenfelder, J., Schultheis, M. T., Al-Shihabi, T., Mourant R., & DeLuca, J. (2002). Divided attention and driving: A pilot study using virtual reality technology. *Journal of Heart Trauma Rehabilitation, 17*(1), 26–37.

Lezak, M. D. (1995). *Neuropsychological assessment* (3rd ed.). New York: Oxford University Press.

Rizzo, A. A., & Buckwalter, J. G. (1997). Virtual reality and cognitive assessment and rehabilitation: The state of the art. In G. Riva (Ed.), *Studies in Health Technology and Informatics: Vol. 44. Virtual reality in neuro-psycho-physiology: Cognitive, clinical and methodological issues in assessment and treatment* (pp. 123–145). Amsterdam, the Netherlands: IOS Press.

Ross, E. D. (1985). Modulation of affect and nonverbal communication by the right hemisphere. In M. M. Mesulam (Ed.), *Principles of behavioral neurology* (pp. 239–258). Philadelphia: Davis.

Schacter, D. L., & Glisky, E. L. (1986). Memory remediation: Restoration, alleviation and the acquisition of domain specific knowledge. In B. P. Uzell & Y. Gross (Eds.), *Clinical neuropsychology of intervention* (pp. 257–282). Boston: Martinus Nijhoff.

Scholte op Reimer, W. J., de Haan, R. J., Pijnenborg, J. M., Limburg, M., & VandenBos, G. A. (1998). Assessment of burden in partners of stroke patients with the sense of competence questionnaire. *Stroke, 29*, 373–379.

Sohlberg, M. M., & Mateer, C. A. (1989a). *Introduction to cognitive rehabilitation: Theory and practice*. New York: Guilford Press.

Sohlberg, M. M., & Mateer, C. A. (1989b). Training use of compensatory memory books: A three stage behavioral approach. *Journal of Clinical and Experimental Neuropsychology, 11*, 871–891.

Starkstein, S. E., & Robinson, R. G. (1992). Neuropsychiatric aspects of cerebral vascular disorders. In S. C. Yudofsky & R. E. Hayes (Eds.), *Textbook of neuropsychiatry* (2nd ed., pp. 449–472). Washington, DC: American Psychiatric Press.

Wald, J., Liu, L., Hirsekorn, L., & Taylar, S. (2000). The use of virtual reality in assessment of driving performance in persons with brain injury. In J. D. Westwood, H. M. Hoffman,

G. T. Mogel, D. Stredney, & R. A. Robb (Eds.), *Studies in health technology and informatics: Vol. 70. Medicine meets virtual reality: 2000 envisioning healing: Interactive technology and the patient–practioner dialogue* (pp. 65–67). Amsterdam, the Netherlands: IOS Press.

CHAPTER 13

Roy C. Martin, Jennifer J. Bortz,
and Peter J. Snyder

Epilepsy and Nonepileptic Seizure Disorders

Epilepsy is a common neurological disorder characterized by
recurrent seizures. **Seizures** are defined as paroxysmal events
produced by abnormal electrical discharges of the brain and
may manifest as sudden, brief attacks that may alter motor
activity, consciousness, or sensory experiences. Convulsive seizures are the most common type of paroxysmal event, but any
recurrent seizure pattern is considered "epilepsy." Many forms
of epilepsy have been linked to viral, fungal, or parasitic infections of the central nervous system; known metabolic disturbances; the ingestion of toxic agents; brain lesions; tumors or
congenital defects; or cerebral trauma. Although the direct
causes of seizures are not always readily observable, with the
advent of sophisticated histological, neuroimaging, and biochemical techniques, it is becoming increasingly possible to
diagnose the causes of seizure disorders that have, in the past,
been difficult to identify (e.g., microscopic brain lesions). Because it can result from a myriad of differing insults to the
nervous system, ranging from identifiable structural pathology
including space-occupying lesions (e.g., brain tumors, vascular
malformations) to pathological processes of unknown etiology
that are indiscernible by current neurodiagnostic techniques,
epilepsy is best thought of as a class of symptoms rather than
a "disease" per se. Exhibit 13.1 contains a glossary of terms used
in this chapter.

Exhibit 13.1. Glossary of Terms

Clonic: alternating contraction and relaxation of muscles

Convulsion: paroxysms of involuntary muscular contractions, relaxations, or both

Epileptogenic focus: a discrete area of the brain wherein the electrical discharges that give rise to seizure activity originate

Gliosis: a proliferation of neuroglial tissue (largely nonnervous, supporting tissue of the brain and spinal cord) in the central nervous system

Ictus: the period of time during which an epileptic seizure occurs

Paroxysm: a sudden, periodic attack or recurrence of symptoms; a sudden spasm or convulsion of any kind

Seizure: a recurrent paroxysmal event that is characteristic of epilepsy; may or may not include impairments of consciousness or convulsions

Tonic: increased muscle tone sustained over a given length of time, such as during a seizure

Uncus: a hook-shaped anterior portion of the hippocampal gyrus, within the temporal lobe of the brain

---

This chapter also describes **nonepileptic seizures,** which are behavioral–paroxysmal events that resemble epileptic seizures but are most often behavioral and emotional manifestations of psychological distress, conflict, or trauma. Broadly considered, any such spell that is not produced by an electrophysiologically based event (e.g., syncope) could be regarded as a nonepileptic seizure. However, this chapter uses the term **nonepileptic psychogenic events** (NEPE) to refer to psychologically based spells that have no identifiable electrographical or neurological correlate. The section on nonepileptic seizures is intended to provide an overview of NEPE diagnostic and treatment issues. For a comprehensive review of this topic, the reader is referred to *Nonepileptic Seizures* (Rowan & Gates, 2000).

I. EPILEPSY

A. Prevalence

Approximately 2% of the population will have at least one seizure sometime during their lives. The prevalence of epilepsy is approximately 1% within the United States (i.e., 2.3 million cases). Peak incidence occurs in early childhood and then in late adulthood (over the age of 75). Incidence rates for epilepsy range from 40 to 70 new cases per 100,000 per year.

B. Medically Refractory Seizure Disorders

From 30% to 45% of patients with epilepsy are medically refractory to conventional antiepileptic pharmacotherapy; at any time in the United States, about 240,000 patients may be candidates for brain surgery to alleviate their seizures (Surgery for Epilepsy, National Institute of Health, 1990). Recurrence risk in people having a single first seizure of idiopathic/cryptogenic etiology ranges from 30% to 50%, whereas the recurrence rate for symptomatic first seizures tends to be over 50% (Hirtz et al., 2003). Recent practice parameter guidelines, established by the American Academy of Neurology and Child Neurology Society, recommend an individualized assessment approach prior to treatment after the first unprovoked seizure, with a balanced consideration of the risks for another seizure weighed against the risks associated with chronic antiepileptic medication use (Hirtz et al., 2003).

When noninvasive treatments (e.g., antiepileptic medication) have not been successful in controlling a seizure disorder, surgical removal of the discharging tissue is often considered. Patients may be suitable candidates for surgical intervention if the epileptogenic discharge originates in a localized area of the brain and if the seizures are of such severity and frequency that they seriously interfere with the patient's quality of life. The prognosis for such surgical intervention, with regard to reducing the frequency and severity of seizures, depends largely on the size and location of the discharging foci. The incidence of unsuccessful alleviation of seizures increases in patients with multiple or bilateral epileptogenic foci and in cases of incomplete resection of the discharging tissue.

C. Classification of Seizures and Epilepsy Syndromes

Over the past several decades, consensus efforts have resulted in formal classification and terminology systems for seizures and epilepsy syndromes (Commission on Classification and Terminology of the International League Against Epilepsy [ILAE], 1981, 1989). These classification systems have led to advancements in the diagnosis and treatment of the epilepsies. The classification of seizures must first determine whether the event is epileptogenic (originating from the central nervous system)

Exhibit 13.2. Abbreviated Classification of
Epileptic Seizures

I. Generalized Seizures (convulsive or nonconvulsive)
    A. Absence seizures (petit mal)
    B. Myoclonic seizures
    C. Clonic seizures
    D. Tonic seizures
    E. Tonic-clonic seizures (grand mal)
    F. Atonic seizures
II. Partial Seizures
    A. Simple Partial Seizures
        1. With motor symptoms
        2. With somatosensory or special sensory symptoms
        3. With autonomic symptoms
        4. With psychic symptoms
    B. Complex-Partial Seizures
        1. Beginning as simple-partial seizures and progressing
           to impairment of consciousness
           a. With no other features
           b. With features as in II.A.1–4
           c. With automatisms
        2. With impairment of consciousness at onset
           (psychomotor)
           a. With no other features
           b. With features as in II.A.1–4
           c. With automatisms
    C. Partial Seizures Evolving to Secondary Generalized
       Seizures

Note. Adapted and abbreviated from "Proposal for Revised Clinical and Electroencephalographic Classification of Epileptic Seizures," by the Commission on Classification and Terminology of the International League Against Epilepsy, 1981, *Epilepsia, 22*, pp. 489–501. In the public domain.

or not. This can be accomplished through clinical observation, medical examination, and laboratory tests. Electroencephologram (EEG) is the most critical of diagnostic procedures to the identification of seizures.

Seizures are classified into two broad types based on the clinical features of the event and the electrographic pattern revealed by the EEG. Generalized seizures and partial seizures are the two major seizure classifications. Exhibit 13.2 lists the two seizure types and major subtypes. Below are descriptions of these seizure types.

1. TYPES OF SEIZURES

a. Generalized seizures

Approximately one third of all patients with epilepsy suffer from generalized seizure disorders, including a variety of generalized motor and "absence" seizure types. In primary generalized seizures, in which the seizure does not begin as a partial seizure (see the following section), the paroxysmal discharges typically arise from deep structures located in the base and middle of the brain (brain stem or thalamus). Unlike many patients with partial seizures, patients with generalized seizures do not experience any psychic or sensory disturbances at the start of the seizure (aura), and there are no focal motor behaviors elicited by the seizure (e.g., automatic motor movements of limbs on only one side of the body).

Generalized motor seizures are divided into subtypes (e.g., tonic, clonic) depending on the motor sequence observed during the seizure event (see Exhibit 13.2), and collectively they represent the most common of the primary generalized epilepsies. There is some evidence pointing to a genetic basis for some of the subtypes of this group of seizure disorders.

Typical absence (petit mal) seizures usually occur in childhood, between the ages of 4 and 12, and only rarely persist into adulthood. These seizures are associated with a brief (5- to 30-second) staring spell and a highly characteristic EEG pattern.

b. Simple- and complex-partial seizures

Of the 2% of the population with epilepsy, two thirds have simple- or complex-partial seizure disorders. Partial seizures begin in one part of the brain and may or may not spread to other regions; they usually consist of specific motor, sensory, or psychic alterations. The psychic changes are often accompanied by stereotyped automatic movements (leading to the term psychomotor) such as lip smacking, chewing, or eye blinking. These seizures often originate from one or both of the temporal lobes (usually from the hippocampus or amygdala, structures that are buried within the temporal lobes), and they are often accompanied by emotional changes that are quite variable from one person to another. The most common of these emotional changes is fear, but sadness, pleasure, or deja vu feelings are frequently reported as well. Hallucinations or misperceptions are also common ictal phenomena of simple- and complex-partial seizures. These sensory experiences can be auditory, tactile, visual, or olfactory.

In **simple-partial epilepsy**, there is no alteration in consciousness as a result of the seizure discharge. In **complex-**

partial epilepsy, impaired consciousness results directly from the seizure discharge. Although both simple-partial and complex-partial seizures typically result from a localizable seizure focus, the electrical discharge may spread to other cortical areas and trigger discharges from other possible epileptogenic foci, resulting in secondarily generalized seizures. Often the specific ictal motor and sensory phenomena exhibited by individual patients correspond to the cerebral localization, or focus, of the epileptic discharge, and the progression of symptoms may indicate the degree of spread of abnormal electrocerebral activity during a seizure. Should this electrocerebral activity spread widely enough, it will be associated with readily apparent alterations in consciousness (complex-partial seizures).

2. EPILEPSY SYNDROMES

Classification of epilepsy syndromes considers a broad array of potential factors including not only seizure type but also factors such as clinical history of the epilepsy (e.g., age at seizure onset, history of febrile illness), family history of seizures, etiology, and neurological status (Commission on Classification and Terminology, 1989). Epilepsy syndromes can be broadly classified by two factors: whether the epilepsy is of localized or generalized nature by EEG and clinical signs and whether the etiology is known (idiopathic/cypogenic or symptomatic; Commission on Classification and Terminology, 1989). The most likely epilepsy syndrome encountered by the neuropsychologist will be that of temporal lobe epilepsy. Because temporal lobe epilepsy is the largest single type of seizure disorder, and because it is most frequently associated with cognitive, emotional, personality, and behavioral alterations (both during and between seizures), most of the following sections concentrate primarily on this type of epilepsy.

3. TEMPORAL LOBE EPILEPSY

Of the approximately 2% of the population with epilepsy, 40% to 60% have simple-partial or complex-partial seizures (with or without secondary generalization) of temporal lobe origin. Glaser (1978) estimated that seizures of temporal lobe origin are found in approximately 25% of children and 50% of adults with epilepsy.

Many investigators have reported specific cognitive deficits, such as memory disturbances, that differentiate patients with **temporal lobe epilepsy** (TLE) from those with other types of epilepsy (Jones-Gotman, 1991). The duration of the disorder in years has been shown to be positively correlated with the degree of neurocognitive dysfunction (Strauss, Hunter, & Wada, 1995). Recent work on the neurodevelopmental impact of childhood-onset temporal lobe epilepsy has strongly supported the presence of widespread neurocognitive dysfunction as well as diffuse brain structure abnormalities (Hermann et al., 2002).

Patients with TLE often present with the following:

- febrile seizures in infancy (Berg, Levy, Novotny, & Shinnar, 1996) and early onset in childhood;
- mesial temporal sclerosis on neuroimaging, although more widespread brain abnormalities can be present;
- early anoxic episodes in childhood,
- family history of epilepsy, and
- resistance to antiepileptic medication.

D. Multidisciplinary Approach to Diagnosis

A variety of diagnostic techniques are routinely used to infer the location of epileptogenic foci, ranging from **structural brain-imaging techniques** (e.g., computed tomography [CT], magnetic resonance imaging [MRI]) to the **imaging of brain function** as represented by changes in metabolism or electrical activity (e.g., measurements of regional cerebral blood flow with positron emission tomography [PET], single photon emission tomography [SPECT], MRI spectroscopy, functional MRI [fMRI], EEG, or magnetoencephalography [MEG]). All of these techniques are highly complex, and no single diagnostic approach, in isolation, provides definitive data that can be used to guide surgical decisions. The proper diagnostic evaluation of patients whose seizures are not easily controlled by medications requires the collective efforts of a multidisciplinary team, all members of which are typically on staff at an epilepsy center. At the very least, these teams consist of a neurologist, neurosurgeon, neuropsychologist, social worker, and neurological nurses.

E. The Neuropsychological Examination

1. PURPOSE OF EXAM

The neuropsychological examination serves four functions. First, it provides standardized assessment of a broad range of cognitive functions that allows for the determination of a patient's cognitive strengths and weaknesses. Second, it can be useful in determining the lateralization and localization of dysfunctional epileptogenic brain regions that may not be observable with standard (structural) neuroimaging techniques and for which EEG data are equivocal. Such data have been shown to add modest predictive value to both seizure laterality determination (Moser et al., 2000) and prediction of seizure outcome after anterior temporal lobectomy (ATL; Sawrie et al., 1998).

Because many patients with epilepsy present with temporal or frontotemporal epileptogenic foci or both, they are at risk for developing iatrogenic impairments in speech and memory functions following surgical treatment. To diminish this risk, cortical and subcortical regions that are crucial for cognition, in particular, for speech and memory, must be identified presurgically. Third, the neuropsychological examination has proved its value with the subset of patients who have left temporal lobe epileptogenic foci and whose seizure disorders are of childhood origin (Hermann et al., 2002). For these patients, atypical patterns of cortical organization have been found to occur more often than in the general population. These features are broadly seen as reflecting either intra- or interhemispheric cortical reorganization (Jokeit & Markowitsch, 1999; Strauss, Wada, & Goldwater, 1992). The former kind would be reflected in speech representation beyond the conventional, or usual, perisylvian zones of the left hemisphere; the latter are reflected in right hemisphere dominance for speech. For such individuals, the possibility of anomalous functional topography for speech and other higher cognitive functions can make the usual diagnostic rules, based on studies of adult-onset brain lesions, only partly applicable or even frankly misleading. Finally, the neuropsychological examination is useful in the presurgical identification of surgical candidates who are likely to suffer debilitating functional impairments following surgery (Bell & Davies, 1998).

An overview of the methods by which the neuropsychological examination contributes to the comprehensive preoperative evaluation of epilepsy patients is detailed in the following sections. It is important to remember that in most epilepsy surgery programs, the presurgical neuropsychological evaluation typically occurs prior to invasive electrophysiological procedures (e.g., depth EEG, cortical grid mapping). Hence, any neuropsychological test battery must be designed not merely to detect unilateral mesiotemporal or lateral temporal lobe dysfunction but also to aid in the detection of focal dysfunction throughout the neocortex.

2. STEP-BY-STEP GUIDE

Test battery selection must be determined not by isolating the neurocognitive functions that are typically subsumed by the neocortical region that contains the epileptogenic focus, but rather by the range of adaptive behaviors potentially affected by surgery. Multiple levels of each function must be examined, and both intact and impaired functions must be appraised to determine potential adverse/iatrogenic effects of surgery. For any patient, the type and extent of behavioral and cognitive impairments that are expected to result from surgical intervention contribute to the determination of both surgical candidacy and type and extent of surgical resection.

Standard, "off-the-shelf" neuropsychological test batteries, such as the Halstead–Reitan Neuropsychological Battery (HRB), do not reliably differentiate among patients with TLE, schizophrenia, bipolar disorder, and "brain damage." That is, although the HRB might be sensitive to the detection of central nervous system dysfunction in a general sense, it lacks the diagnostic specificity required for use in the comprehensive evaluation of medically refractory epilepsy patients. Several suggestions are offered in the following sections to aid in the construction of a useful neuropsychological examination battery.

a. Patient history and clinical interview

In taking a patient's developmental, family, medical, social, and occupational histories, one must pay careful attention to identifying possible precipitating or etiologic factors. Important factors potentially affecting cognition in epilepsy patients include the age at first seizure occurrence, age of onset of chronic seizures, etiology of seizures, seizure frequency and type, and occurrence of febrile convulsions in infancy. This information will aid in the interpretation of late achievement of developmental milestones, childhood learning disorders, employment history with various levels of occupational complexity, and social functional level. The clinical interview with both the patient and the family forms an integral part of the neuropsychological evaluation, therefore, and the information provided often leads to a more focused assessment that may target specific areas of deficit in greater detail.

Finally, it is important for the neuropsychologist to obtain an accurate history of current antiepileptic drug (AED) therapy, as well as of the timing and duration of prior AED mono- or polytherapy trials. The problem of behavioral toxicity—that is, impairment of cognitive functions secondary to AED treatment in the absence of frank neurotoxic side effects—is an important issue to consider when evaluating the data obtained from a neuropsychological examination (Meador, 2001). For example, the speed of access to information in short-term memory storage is sensitive to phenobarbital concentration, whereas the speed of access to information held in long-term memory storage is much less affected. Several excellent reviews of neuropsychological side effects of both the older and the "new generation" AEDs have been published (see McConnell & Duncan, 1998).

b. Observation of ictal semiology

When interviewing the patient, it is important to observe his or her facial morphology carefully. Facial asymmetries may be noticeable in 50% to 80% of patients with TLE, in comparison with about 30% of matched control participants. It is also important to note any obvious speech disturbances, especially during a seizure event. When the seizure discharge involves the language areas located within the perisylvian region of the dominant hemisphere for speech, there is typically a transient epileptic aphasia during and immediately postictus. Rarely, this transient epileptic aphasia is due to seizure activity in the supplementary motor area.

If the opportunity to observe the patient during a seizure presents itself, it is important to observe the occurrence of any motoric automatisms. For example, *forced* (versive) turning of the head and eyes and dystonic posturing of a limb at seizure onset are reliably contralateral to the side of the epileptogenic focus; therefore, this behavioral observation provides a good indicator of laterality of the focus in patients with focal onset of seizure activity.

The presence of peri-ictal auras just prior to seizure onset, which may be reported by the patient or family, is often indicative of TLE. Compared with patients with extratemporal foci, those with TLE have reported a higher incidence of visceral, psychic (e.g., fear), cognitive (i.e., déjà vu), and olfactory–gustatory auras and automatic behaviors (Gloor, Olivier, Quesney, Andermann, & Horowitz, 1982).

c. Upper-extremity motor examination

This portion of the evaluation is useful in discerning lateralized dysfunction of the prefrontal cortex; it also may be helpful in distinguishing patients with TLE from those with other types of seizure disorders. For example, although patients with complex-partial seizures and a unilateral temporal lobe epileptogenic focus often show a clear deficit in motor performance as measured by finger-tapping and pointing tasks, patients with focal involvement of the caudal aspect of the primary motor strip also show a profound defect on measures of fine motor praxis with the contralateral upper extremity. **Recommended tests and measures include (a) the Rapid Finger Oscillation**

Test, (b) the Purdue Pegboard Test, and (c) the Grooved Pegboard Test.

d. Sensory–perceptual examination

The typical sensory–perceptual examination involves the separate assessment of visual–perceptual functions and simple audition, an informal visual fields examination, and a tactile sensory examination. The use of visual-searching procedures to evaluate the relative efficiency with which a patient searches or attends to left versus right visual space may lead to the observation of a visual field cut or hemineglect, both of which have clear localizing significance. Likewise, various deficits in auditory processing (e.g., for environmental sounds, rhythmic pattern discrimination) are suggestive of focal involvement of primary or tertiary auditory centers or both in or near the superior temporal gyri of one or both hemispheres. In addition, the careful analysis of tactile sensory–perceptual deficits (typically involving double simultaneous stimulation of the face and upper extremities) may lead to evidence suggestive of focal dysfunction of unilateral primary sensory areas. **Recommended tests and measures include (a) single and double simultaneous tactile stimulation, (b) informal tests of visual fields and audition, and (c) the Mesulam and Weintraub Visual Scanning Task.**

e. Attentional controls, concentration, and "executive" functions

The evaluation of these important neurobehavioral domains may require a diverse set of procedures, such as design fluency and continuous-performance tests (Jones-Gotman, 1991). Many of these tests are now computer administered to provide for the accurate measurement of various psychophysical variables, such as reaction time. Deficits in the maintenance of sustained concentration, focused attention, divided attentional controls, and both response inhibition and the production of frequent perseverative errors all may lead to the suggestion of focal frontal lobe involvement (Jones-Gotman, 1991). Furthermore, the pattern of performance across this range of tests often leads to the prediction of left versus right and medial versus lateral frontal lobe involvement. However, the potential for eliciting false localizing signs is quite high, and both false-positive and false-negative diagnostic errors are frequently made. For example, poor performance on several of these measures may be secondary to anticonvulsant toxicity. As is usually the case, such diagnostic impressions require independent corroborative evidence from other sources. **Recommended tests and measures include (a) the Trail Making Test, Parts A and B, (b) the Ruff Figural Fluency Test, (c) the Working Memory Index of the Wechsler Memory Scale—III (WMS–III), (d) the Benton Serial Digit Learning Test, (e) the Wisconsin Card Sorting Test, (f) Competing Programs and Go/No-Go tasks, and (g) the Delis–Kaplan Executive Function System (Delis, Kaplan, & Kramer, 2001).**

f. Speech and language examination

Expressive speech functions may be assessed by a myriad of techniques including controlled oral word production, confrontation naming, sentence repetition, and rapid rote reading (with and without distractors). A common interictal "memory" impairment in patients with left TLE, but not those with right TLE, is the presence of dysnomia. In addition, patients with left temporal or frontotemporal foci often show a clear deficit in the fluidity of speech production, as well as a transient aphasia secondary to ictal events with focal onset in the perisylvian region. **Recommended tests and measures include (a) single-letter and category-level verbal fluency tests and (b) the Boston Naming Test.**

Receptive language functions may be assessed by various techniques, ranging from speech–sounds discrimination tests to dichotic-listening procedures. Specific deficits in the areas of word reading, reading comprehension, and the appropriate use of syntax and grammar all are diagnostically significant. Zaidel (1985) argued that the right hemisphere in a normal population has limited but measurable competence for comprehending both spoken and written language, but that it is generally impoverished in its ability to produce meaningful verbal expression. Such preclinical research findings, along with the demonstration of specific functions known to be primarily mediated by the right hemisphere (e.g., modulation of prosodic speech, appropriate interpretation of emotional tone in speech), have specific implications with regard to the determination of the extent of any planned surgical resection in the right frontotemporal and temporoparietal regions. **Recommended tests and measures include an informal assessment of prosody of speech as well as the following subtests of the Boston Diagnostic Aphasia Examination (BDAE): (a) Commands, (b) Passive Subject–Object Discrimination, (c) Complex Ideational Material, and (d) Reading Sentences and Paragraphs.**

g. Examination of mnestic functions

The neural networks underlying memory encoding, storage, and retrieval are complex and well integrated, branching to many areas of the brain that only recently have been recognized as important in memory function. A common theme running throughout the research in this area is the paramount importance of the hippocampi and adjacent parahippocampal gyri (at least in humans) for the encoding and retrieval of new learning. Jasper (1962, p. 387) correctly noted that the amnesia that is a common characteristic of temporal lobe ictal automatisms seems "most likely due to a functional or paralytic blockade of the normal functions of the hippocampus and related neuronal systems which seem essential to mechanisms for the recording of immediate experience." This finding is crucial in the diagnostic workup of patients in whom epilepsy surgery is being considered, because in many instances, both hippocampi (and adjacent neocortex) do not contribute equally to the overall integrity of the complex neural network for memory. Rather, a preponderance of such patients have a unilateral distribution of memory patency owing to an early, lateralized brain injury. Thus, if the only remaining functional hippocampus is epileptogenic, removal of this structure may eliminate the seizure activity but would be akin to a bilateral hippocampectomy, with disastrous results for memory functioning.

In addition to guarding against such a tragic neuropsychological syndrome, a comprehensive memory examination is useful in assisting in the localization of focal neurological dysfunction and, perhaps, the epileptogenic focus. Clear impairment in short-term recall for verbal information, with relatively intact verbal-reasoning abilities (e.g., no significant verbal IQ–performance IQ [VIQ–PIQ] split), is highly suggestive of focal left temporal lobe dysfunction. Unfortunately, for reasons discussed later, we do not currently have comparable neuropsychological measures for the reliable detection of focal right temporal lobe dysfunction.

h. Verbal memory examination procedures

The impairment in the encoding, storage, and recall of verbal information may be measured through story narratives or with serial list learning procedures. In the former task, the patient is afforded the benefit of processing information that is embedded in a salient social context, whereas in the latter type of task, the patient must remember a list of words that may not share any obvious contextual relationship. Impaired performance across these broad sets of measures is often observed in patients with left temporal lobe epilepsy. Furthermore, the use of certain types of verbal memory measures (e.g., paired-associate learning paradigms) might afford greater diagnostic specificity than other types (e.g., story learning; Loring, 1994). Two types of verbal memory tests (i.e., paired-associate learning and story learning) appear to correlate reasonably well with histopathological disturbances in the left CA1 and CA3 hippocampal subfields, as well as in the parahippocampal gyrus. **Recommended tests and measures include (a) two subtests of the WMS–III: Verbal Paired Associates and Logical Memory I and II, and (b) the California Verbal Learning Test—Second Edition (CVLT–II).**

i. Examination of memory for visually presented information

The assessment of visual (nonverbal) memory is typically conducted by observing the immediate and delayed recall production of novel graphic designs. Several clinical studies have shown that patients with right TLE perform significantly worse than those with left TLE in their recall of fairly complex line drawings and that those with right TLE are more impaired than patients with right frontal epileptogenic foci in their ability to recall very simple drawings after a 30-minute delay (although other studies have failed to show such group differences). In addition, patients with right TLE (but not left TLE) sometimes (but not always) show impairments on tests of immediate recall for human faces, an observation that highlights the role of the right inferotemporal cortex in higher order visual processing for the faces of conspecifics.

Despite these encouraging clinical findings, there have been numerous conflicting studies showing that most current tests of visual memory suffer from significant problems of face validity. Although the tests appear to measure one's ability to rely on nonverbal mediation for the encoding and later recall of novel stimuli, virtually all of these tests allow for verbal mediation as well. Essentially, none of the widely used visual memory tests have been shown to have a satisfactory degree of construct validity and reliability (Barr & Bozeman Epilepsy Consortium, 1995). The search for nonverbalizable graphic designs for use in constructing memory tests with greater construct validity and reliability remains elusive. It is equally important to develop a new generation of "true" visual memory tests that are equivalent to matched verbal memory measures in terms of task difficulty. **Recommended tests and measures include (a) the Visual Reproduction I and II subtests of the WMS–III, (b) the Rey–Osterreith Complex Figure Test, (c) the Denman Facial Recognition Memory Test (Denman, 1984), and (d) the Biber Figure Learning Test.**

j. Intellectual–conceptual measures

In general, standard measures of verbal–conceptual compared with visual–performance intellectual functioning (e.g., VIQ–PIQ differences on the revised Wechsler Adult Intelligence Scale [WAIS–III]) are poor indicators of left versus right temporal lobe epilepsy, although an early age of seizure onset is associated with lower IQ scores across all domains. Hermann et al. (1995) found that only the Vocabulary subtest (and none of the other 10 subtests) reliably discriminated between patients with left versus right TLE. Performance across virtually all measures of intellectual functioning is linearly related to seizure frequency. Patients with an early age of seizure onset, long duration of epilepsy, and a high seizure frequency demonstrate significantly greater cognitive dysfunction in comparison to those with a later age of seizure onset, a shorter duration of epilepsy, and a lower seizure frequency. Although several investigators have reported a negative correlation between the presence of epilepsy and intelligence in children, Ellenberg, Hirtz, and Nelson (1986) studied children both before and after the onset of seizures and found that the occurrence of seizures is not causally related to lower IQs. They claimed that the lower IQs commonly observed in epileptic children are accounted for by other, associated neurological deficits.

Finally, a complete neuropsychological evaluation of patients with epilepsy requires the selection of independent measures of reasoning and judgment to supplement intelligence testing (e.g., the Wisconsin Card Sorting Test), because patients with extratemporal dysfunction demonstrate great difficulty on untimed, trial-and-error tasks in which they are required to use feedback from their previous response to guide their next choice. **Recommended tests and measures include (a) the WAIS–III or Wechsler Intelligence Scale for Children—III (WISC–III) and (b) the Wisconsin Card Sorting Test.**

k. Role of the intracarotid amobarbital procedure in the presurgical evaluation of epilepsy patients

The intracarotid amobarbital procedure (IAP; also called the "Wada test") is used in the context of presurgical evaluation to help determine the following issues: (a) seizure lateralization,

(b) prediction of seizure outcome after surgery, (c) determination of language lateralization, and (d) prediction of memory outcome following surgery (see review by Simkins-Bullock, 2000). For patients who are candidates for surgical intervention, the accurate determination of hemispheric dominance for speech is extremely important, and the IAP currently provides the least ambiguous method for accomplishing this, although recent studies using fMRI and MEG techniques suggest that these techniques may be valid alternatives.

In a well-known study, Milner (1975) found that in patients with evidence of early damage to the left cerebral hemisphere, 81% of right-handed and 30% of left- or mixed-handed individuals demonstrated left-hemisphere speech dominance, whereas 51% of left-handed patients with early damage to the left cerebral hemisphere lateralized speech function to the contralateral side. Milner (1975) also reported evidence of mixed speech dominance (MSD) in 15% of the left- or mixed-handed patients in her series ($N = 122$).

The preceding finding regarding the prevalence of MSD in an epileptic population is inconclusive, however, for three reasons. First, several other investigators have reported very different estimates of MSD in their samples (see review by Snyder, Novelly, & Harris, 1990). Second, there is little agreement among researchers at centers that perform the IAP as to what the criteria should be for determining the presence of speech production from the "minor" hemisphere. Finally, it may be that MSD can never be determined with certainty using the IAP as long as there is no definitive method for determining complete unilateral anesthetization of the perioperccular speech zones (Snyder et al., 1990). In short, although the IAP provides the most definitive method of determining unilateral speech dominance in epilepsy surgery candidates, its usefulness in the determination of MSD remains unresolved.

The assessment of memory functions in the awake, fully conscious patient often leads to false lateralizing signs, depending on whether the epileptogenic lesion is situated more laterally or mesially in the temporal lobe, because the mesial temporal structures are essentially not material specific for new learning (Helmstaedter, Grunwald, Lehnertz, Gleißner, & Elger, 1997). Rather, it is the left versus right overlying temporal neurocortex that appears to be material specific for the encoding of new verbal versus visual information, respectively. For this reason, among others, the IAP has long been known to be extremely important for the reliable determination of unilateral hemispheric patency for mnestic functions (see historical review by Snyder & Harris, 1997). Accordingly, the IAP has become a key part of the neuropsychologist's repertoire within epilepsy centers (Loring, Meador, Lee, & King, 1992; Snyder et al., 1990). Essentially, if IAP results indicate that the suspected epileptogenic focus cannot be resected without significant risk of global amnesia, there is no justification for continuing with presurgical evaluation.

l. Determining cognitive and behavioral effects of surgical intervention

One of the most critical aspects of neuropsychological assessment is to estimate the risks of epilepsy surgery, especially anterior temporal lobectomy, on cognitive function. Numerous studies have documented postoperative decline in verbal memory and retrieval-based language abilities in a substantial proportion of patients undergoing left anterior temporal lobectomy, whereas risk to visual memory function is noted in many patients undergoing right anterior temporal lobectomy (see review by Bell & Davies, 1998). Determining the extent of this cognitive change following surgery has traditionally relied on unstandardized criteria that fail to account for methodological artifacts in a test–retest situation (i.e., practice effect, regression-to-the-mean; Chelune, Naugle, Luders, Sedlak, & Awad, 1993; McSweeney, Naugle, Chelune, & Luders, 1993). These, in turn, may lead to under- or overestimates of the extent of individual or group-based cognitive change reported in the literature. Recent studies have provided statistical methods for determining reliable cognitive change after epilepsy surgery at both an individual patient level and a group level. These standardized regression equations and reliable change formulas have been calculated for several common neuropsychological tests (e.g., WMS–III, CVLT) and help control for interindividual differences on clinical and demographic variables such as baseline performance level, age, education, and seizure duration (Hermann et al., 1996; Martin et al., 2002; Sawrie, Chelune, Naugle, & Luders, 1996). These empirically derived methods produce standardized change scores that use a common metric (z score change), allowing direct comparison across different tests.

m. Psychiatric morbidity in epilepsy

Increasing attention in the medical community has been devoted to psychiatric issues facing people with epilepsy. The incidence of psychiatric disorders in epilepsy is considerable and generally thought to be higher than in nonclinical populations, other neurological groups, and nonneurological clinical groups (Torta & Keller, 1999).

When evaluating psychiatric function in the person with epilepsy, the examiner should consider several potential risk factors, including neurobiologic variables (e.g., etiology, seizure type, duration of epilepsy), psychosocial factors (e.g., fear of seizures, sense of self-control, social support), and iatrogenic factors (e.g., medication type and number; Wiegartz, Seidenberg, Woodard, Gidal, & Hermann, 1999). It is important to consider the temporal relation with the emergence of the psychiatric symptom to the timing of seizure occurrence. Of particular note is differentiating among interictal psychosis, postictal psychosis, and ictal psychosis, because symptom expression may be related to seizure type, localization of epilepsy, or frequency of seizures (Lancman, 1999).

It is often felt that patients with TLE show a poorer response to medical treatments and a higher incidence of psychiatric difficulties than do patients with other types of epilepsy. In fact, a centuries-old historical association has been described between TLE and hysteria (Glaser, 1978). Flor-Henry (1969) found that in TLE, psychotic disturbances were significantly increased in patients in whom the epileptogenic foci were lateralized to the dominant hemisphere for speech. He also found a significant correlation between left temporal lobe seizure foci and schizophrenic syndromes, and between right-sided foci and bipolar syndromes (Flor-Henry, 1969). Although a number of database studies of patients with TLE at various surgery programs have supported the position that psychoses that are not attributable solely to peri-ictal behavioral and sensory disturbances are prevalent among these patients, other empirical studies have not confirmed this relationship.

In 1977, Bear and Fedio reviewed research that indicated a long interval of approximately 15 years between seizure onset in TLE and the observation of a "schizophrenialike psychosis," which occurs in some patients. This finding suggests that the psychiatric disorder is a secondary and atypical effect of the major underlying neurological process. Bear and Fedio (1977) noted that there is no compelling reason why any type of psychosis should accurately describe the behavioral sequelae of a neurological process at a specific locus in the brain. This may be why standard personality tests, such as the Thematic Apperception Test and the Rorschach Inkblot Test, which are based on psychodynamic principles and normed on psychiatric populations, have yielded inconsistent results in categorizing patients with TLE. For this reason, actuarial-inventory procedures such as the Minnesota Multiphasic Personality Inventory—2 (MMPI–2) are recommended. Trimble (1983), however, noted that although many comparative studies with the MMPI have been conducted, many of them have failed to differentiate among groups of patients with various seizure types and epileptogenic foci. These findings imply that even if epileptic patients suffer from an increased prevalence of psychopathology, it may be attributable to other factors (e.g., anoxic events, head injury, related developmental disturbances) that are only indirectly associated with epilepsy.

n. Psychosocial adjustment and quality-of-life issues

In recent years, greater attention has been paid to the formal evaluation of the role that epilepsy plays in a patient's psychosocial development as well as in the quality of interpersonal relationships and social adjustment. It has now become the "standard of care" to monitor quality of life in a broad sense that is not limited to the reduction of seizure frequency and severity prior to and following surgical intervention (Gilliam, 2002). Accordingly, several inventories that measure the quality of life of epilepsy patients across a wide range of indices have been developed in recent years (Perrine et al., 1995). **Recommended tests and measures include (a) the MMPI–2 (the first 400 items, to provide basic scale scores), (b) the Spielberger State–Trait Anxiety Inventory, (c) the Beck Depression Inventory, and (d) the Quality of Life in Epilepsy Inventory, 31-item version.**

F. Psychosocial Issues for Patients With Epilepsy

1. SOCIAL STIGMA

Most people with epilepsy are able to enjoy interesting and happy lives as active members of the societies in which they live. Still, some people with epilepsy show a broad range of alterations in personality and in emotional, cognitive, intellectual, sensory, and motor functioning as a result of their seizure disorders. In addition, some face further problems in coping with epilepsy in their homes and communities: All patients with epilepsy are at risk of experiencing social stigma, prejudice, or even hostility, which typically result from a lack of information and understanding (Schachter, 2002). This lack of understanding varies across racial and cultural groups, with some cultures persisting to this day in viewing epilepsy as infectious, "dirty," or caused by pernicious supernatural influences. Although Western cultures no longer subscribe to this belief system, people with epilepsy continue to encounter negative attitudes in many areas here, ranging from immediate family and school environments to the job market.

2. EPILEPSY AND THE LAW

The law in most Western societies serves both to discriminate against and to protect people with epilepsy. For example, people with uncontrolled epilepsy are prohibited from operating motor vehicles. Although this regulation is entirely reasonable and prudent from a public safety perspective, it is a hard restriction to accept for someone whose social life and employment opportunities are disrupted as a result. There are considerable differences among states concerning legal restrictions. Patients with epilepsy have also been discriminated against in their attempts to procure health and life insurance policies, although there has been moderate improvement in this legal area over the past few decades.

Special services for patients with epilepsy, including financial assistance, housing, education for handicapped children, and legal assistance services, have recently become more widely available. In the United States, the single most active resource center and organization for people with epilepsy and their families is the Epilepsy Foundation, Inc. (4351 Garden City Drive, Landover, MD 20785). This organization maintains a library that is open to any interested person (people with epilepsy and their families, students, and health care providers) as well as a toll-free telephone number for information (1-800-332-1000) and a Web site (www.epilepsyfoundation.org).

II. NONEPILEPTIC SEIZURES

A. Epidemiology

1. INCIDENCE

The incidence of nonepileptic psychogenic events (NEPE) is approximately 5% to 20% in outpatient settings and up to 40% in comprehensive epilepsy centers (Gates & Mercer, 1995).

2. RISK FACTORS

Nonepileptic psychogenic events are more common in young adults, in women (3:1 ratio), and in patients with histories of sexual or other forms of physical abuse (Alper, Devinsky, Perrine, Vazquez, & Luciano, 1993). No clear relationship has been found between educational level, intellectual ability, personality profiles, or neuropsychological status and NEPE;

Exhibit 13.3. Historical and Current Terminology for
Nonepileptic Seizures

Nonepileptic events
Nonepileptic attacks
Nonepileptic seizures
Nonelectrical seizures
Pseudoseizures
Pseudoepileptic seizures
Psychogenic seizures
The Sacred Disease (Hippocrates)
Hysteroepilepsy (Charcot)
Hysterical epilepsy (Freud)

however, certain aspects of the neuropsychological evaluation
may identify risk factors that can assist in differential diagnosis
and treatment of NEPE.

B. Terminology

The terms used to refer to NEPE are as varied and confusing as the
disorder itself. Far from simplifying communication between
professionals and patients, terms for NEPE that include the word
epilepsy or *seizure* often foster confusion regarding the disorder
and its important distinction from epileptic seizures (see Exhibit
13.3). To minimize this problem, the descriptive term *episodic
stress reaction* has been found useful in many clinical discussions
with patients who have NEPE and their families.

C. Differential Diagnosis

1. NEPE VERSUS EPILEPSY

The primary imitator of epilepsy is NEPE, and vice versa.
Health professionals, whether neurologists or primary care physicians, in the outpatient setting often find it difficult to differentiate epileptic from nonepileptic seizures, primarily because of
the high degree of overlap between the phenomenology of these
two disorders. Patients' subjective experience and clinical behavior are frequently quite similar, if not indistinguishable. Patients who present with either epileptic seizures (ES) or NEPE
may show the following symptoms:

- alterations in consciousness and periods of unrespon-
  siveness;

- motor and sensory symptoms (e.g., motor automatisms);
- postictal confusion;
- spells that appear to arise during sleep;
- self-injury during ictal or behavioral events;
- similar types of cognitive and mood disturbances, including memory impairment; and
- attention and concentration deficits, slowed thinking, and emotional lability.

The psychiatric sequelae of ES and NEPE can both be quite severe and result in significant functional disability. Additional overlap between ES and NEPE lies in the fact that a significant number of patients with NEPE have concomitant histories of neurological insult, electrographic seizures, and other nonspecific EEG abnormalities. Moreover, the reported incidence of epilepsy in patients with NEPE has ranged from 10% to 80%, and from 5.9% to 40% of patients with well-documented epilepsy have coexisting NEPE (see review by Ramsay, Cohen, & Brown, 1993), although more recent studies have pointed to the lower end of that estimate (Benbadis, Agrawal, & Tatum, 2001).

Frontal lobe epilepsy is perhaps the most difficult seizure disorder to differentiate from NEPE. Ictal discharges originating deep in the frontal lobes may not be detected by conventional surface EEG, resulting in a completely normal record throughout a clinical spell. Ictal behaviors are often bizarre and less stereotyped than those associated with more common forms of epilepsy (e.g., screaming, pelvic thrusting, asymmetrical tonic posturing, desynchronous or cycling movements). Thus, a combination of atypical ictal behavior and the absence of EEG abnormality places patients with frontal lobe epilepsy at particularly high risk for being misclassified as having NEPE or other primary psychiatric conditions.

In many cases, admission to an inpatient video-EEG seizure-monitoring unit is the only means by which documentation of NEPE can be accomplished. This setting allows for online correlation of behavioral events or clinical spells through simultaneous video and EEG recordings. The diagnosis remains one of exclusion, however, requiring thorough investigation of organic causes. Physical and psychiatric disorders that should be excluded prior to NEPE diagnosis are listed in Exhibit 13.4 and are briefly described later in this section.

2. NEPE VERSUS OTHER PAROXYSMAL DISORDERS

Although the greatest overlap in clinical signs and symptoms occurs between NEPE and ES, other organic disorders can convincingly mimic epilepsy. As shown in Exhibit 13.4,

Exhibit 13.4. Common Physiological and Psychiatric Disorders That Mimic Nonepileptic Seizures

Physiological
Epilepsy
Orthostatic hypotension
Cardiac arrhythmias
Syncope
Migraine
Transient ischemic attacks
Paroxysmal movement disorders
Sleep disorders
Hypoglycemia
Hyperventilation
Psychiatric
Somatoform disorders
Conversion disorder
Somatization disorder
Dissociative disorders
Panic disorders
Affective disorders
Posttraumatic stress disorder
Psychotic disorders
Factitious disorder with physical symptoms
Malingering

symptoms similar to NEPE may result from many other paroxysmal disorders besides epilepsy, including cardiovascular events (e.g., orthostatic hypotension), cerebrovascular episodes, paroxysmal movement disorders (e.g., benign essential myoclonus), sleep disorders (e.g., hypnagogic myoclonic jerks), acute and chronic hyperventilation, and hypoglycemia.

3. PSYCHIATRIC DISORDERS

The psychological characteristics associated with NEPE can be quite varied, making presenting signs, symptoms, and course of the disorder difficult to integrate into formal classification schemes, although recent attempts have been published (see Selwa et al., 2000). Features of NEPE can meet diagnostic criteria for multiple psychiatric diagnoses (see Exhibit 13.4), although NEPE most commonly holds true to its historical classification as a conversion disorder.

NEPE is the second most frequent symptom profile among conversion disorders, occurring in approximately 15% of patients with that disorder (Toone, 1990). Several other psychiatric conditions, however, are commonly associated with NEPE (for a review, see Gates, 1998). In one study, Bowman and Marland

(1996) formally determined psychiatric diagnoses of 45 adult patients with NEPE seen in a tertiary-care video-EEG facility. Application of standardized instruments and the revised third edition of the *Diagnostic and Statistical Manual of Mental Disorders* (*DSM–III–R*; American Psychiatric Association, 1987) diagnostic criteria revealed the following patient distribution: 89% somatoform disorders, 91% dissociative disorders, 64% affective disorders, 62% personality disorders, and 49% posttraumatic stress disorder. Forty-seven percent of patients met criteria for other types of anxiety disorders. Of note, a high lifetime rate of other conversion symptoms was documented in 18 patients observed to demonstrate ictal conversion symptoms, suggesting that NEPE is likely one of many conversion symptoms manifested in the course of the disorder. In rare cases, patients present with a factitious disorder in which symptoms are intentionally produced to maintain a sick role (Gates, 1998). Factitious disorders are differentiated from malingering, in which material gains motivate simulation or exaggeration of symptoms.

D. Neuropsychological Correlates

Probably because of the heterogeneity of this patient population and the vast overlap of signs and symptoms, there have been no consistent differences that reliably separate patients with NEPE from those with well-defined epilepsy on formal tests of neuropsychological functioning. In light of the difficulties in identifying consistent quantitative differences between NEPE and ES groups, Bortz and colleagues (Bortz, Prigatano, Blum, & Fisher, 1995) investigated the question of whether qualitative characteristics of patients' performance on a recognition memory task could differentiate NEPE and ES groups. In responses to the CVLT, patients with NEPE (compared with those with ES) produced a negative response bias on the Recognition Memory subtest, characterized by (a) a tendency to recognize explicitly fewer target words and (b) generation of relatively few false-positive responses. A CVLT response bias cutoff score below 0 (i.e., a negative response bias) showed a sensitivity of 61% and a specificity of 91% in the correct classification of patients with nonepileptic seizure (NES). An important caveat to these data, however, is that they found a similar response pattern in patients with frontal lobe epilepsy. Moreover, this tendency appears to be distinct from that seen in patients with frontal lobe lesions, who show the expected leniency, or positive response bias (Bortz, Wong, Blum, Prigatano, & Fisher, 1997). Replication and extension of these findings may prove useful in identifying differential response patterns in these patients.

It is notable that the nature and length of the neuropsychological examination afford a unique opportunity to establish a meaningful working alliance with patients presenting with a complex psychological disturbance. It is not uncommon that abuse and trauma histories are elicited during the evaluation, even though patients are routinely asked about such risk factors in other clinical settings and may have denied such experiences. This history has frequently been revealed during attempts to clarify the reason for unexpectedly low WAIS–R Information and Vocabulary scores that are inconsistent with psychosocial history and achievement or other test scores. Histories of academic underachievement, truancy, and frequent or extended absences from school may raise a red flag of significant emotional distress during childhood or adolescence. Obtaining a detailed history of these problems is crucial because patients with long-standing ES may have similar patterns of test performance owing to academic difficulties, school absences, and attention or memory deficits secondary to their seizure disorder.

E. Personality Assessment

Numerous studies have examined usefulness of MMPI profiles in the differential diagnosis of NEPE. Wilkus and colleagues published several papers concerning a series of decision rules used to differentiate NEPE from ES (see Wilkus & Dodrill, 1989). Empirical application of these criteria by other investigators has yielded varying degrees of specificity and sensitivity, with considerable overlap between ES and NEPE groups (see review in Rowan & Gates, 2000). Mason, Mercer, Risse, and Gates (1996) reported a 60% correct classification rate for NEPE and 30% incorrect classification for ES using a set of decision rules revised for the MMPI–II. The sizable error rate led these authors to question the predictive value of previously established MMPI decision rules.

Although the reliability of various categorization rules remains controversial, MMPI somatization profiles have assisted in identifying key NEPE risk factors. For example, Connell and Wilner (1996) found that a higher mean Scale 3 elevation, combined with earlier onset of seizures, differentiated groups of patients with NEPE versus those with ES; in their study, the highest diagnostic hit rate was derived from Scale 3 for NEPE and from age at onset for ES (90% and 83%, respectively). Other investigators have identified Scale 3 elevations, either in isolation or in conjunction with other variables, as differentially characteristic of NEPE (e.g., Snyder et al., 1997). In all, it appears that MMPI findings play an important role in identifying risk factors associated with NEPE and that differential diagnosis can be significantly enhanced by clinical exploration of these factors (i.e., stress and emotional conflict issues) and integration with other diagnostic information. MMPI data are also valuable in treatment planning for patients with both NEPE and ES.

F. Provocative Testing Procedures

Placebo induction, or provocative testing procedures, are often used to support a diagnosis of NEPE. The goal of these procedures is to evoke a behavioral spell identical to the patient's spontaneous episodes. Clinical techniques include photic stimulation, hyperventilation, tactile compression, injection of physiologic saline or other chemical placebos, placement of epidural patches soaked in alcohol, and hypnotic suggestion. Although such tests may provide useful diagnostic information, consideration of several risks and caveats is warranted (Lancman, Lambrakis, & Steinhardt, 2001).

A major risk associated with these procedures is the potential threat to the therapeutic alliance established between patients and clinicians. Specifically, techniques in which patients are directly given false information, or in which they may later perceive that they have been misled or manipulated, could potentially cause additional distress and resentment in an already emotionally fragile patient. Rather, when an induction is deemed appropriate, permission should be obtained from the patient to try a procedure that may produce a clinical spell similar to those occurring spontaneously. Consent allows the patient to be an active participant in, rather than a subjugated object or victim of, the diagnostic process.

If the induction attempt is successful, then patients and family members are asked to rate the degree to which the induced spell resembled a typical seizure. Induced spells that are highly similar to typical events are considered supportive of the NEPE diagnosis. However, a positive clinical finding (i.e., elicitation of a subjectively and behaviorally typical spell in the absence of concomitant EEG abnormalities) does not confirm a diagnosis of NEPE; careful consideration of several additional factors is required. One factor is the fact that the base rate of the frequency of a positive induction in patients with well-documented ES has not yet been sufficiently explored. Second, the possibility of a mixed disorder remains; patients with more than one type of spell may have both NEPE and underlying ES (Gates, 1998). Third, patients with either type of disorder may be unaware of what their typical spells are like, and they may not be able to estimate reliably the degree of similarity between an induced and a spontaneous spell or seizure. With the patient's consent, it is often helpful to review videotaped spells with someone who has witnessed these events to have him or her assess the extent to which the spell resembles previous events.

G. Patient Education and Treatment

Patients with known or suspected risk factors for NEPE are told of this possibility early in the diagnostic process. This "inoculation technique" gives patients additional time to gather and process relevant information in a manner intended to promote understanding and acceptance of psychological aspects of the disorder (Carton, Thompson, & Duncan, 2003). In this way, treatment of NEPE begins early by (a) presenting the diagnosis in a therapeutic manner, (b) dispelling misconceptions and addressing personal and social stigma concerning the diagnosis, and (c) providing educational information for patients and families.

In presenting the diagnosis, the clinician must fully consider the emotional fragility of most patients with NES. NES is a manifestation of relatively primitive and ineffective coping mechanisms. The contribution of enmeshed or otherwise dysfunctional interpersonal relationships to the disorder is often complex. Fear of abandonment, including loss of the physician–patient relationship, can be overwhelming to these patients. As described by others in the literature (e.g., Gates & Mercer, 1995), we recommend presenting the diagnosis of NEPE to patients and their families in a "good news" format, intended to convey a genuine sense of accomplishment in the collaboration required to make the diagnosis, the desire to form a strong therapeutic working alliance, and optimism about therapeutic outcome. Several points are emphasized to the patient and family, including (a) the importance of arriving at an accurate diagnosis; (b) the opportunity to plan for successful treatment; (c) the chance to discontinue antiepileptic drugs and eliminate related side effects; and (d) the likelihood that memory, attention, and other cognitive and affective problems will improve with remission of the disorder. For higher functioning patients, the possibility of being able to drive, to resume daily activities, and to return to school or work serves as a primary reinforcer for therapeutic intervention.

Understanding and acceptance of the diagnosis is frequently enhanced by review of the diagnostic process and discussion of educational information with family members. In select cases, family participation in the therapeutic process can significantly enhance treatment efficacy.

H. Prognosis

Literature regarding prognosis and outcome following diagnosis of NEPE is limited. Of the few outcome studies that have been conducted, NEPE remission occurs in only 50% or less of patients (Reuber et al., 2003; Selwa et al., 2000). Favorable prognostic factors that have been identified include female gender, an independent lifestyle, higher intelligence, normal EEG findings, paroxysmal behavioral characteristics (i.e., catatonic behavior), and no prior history of psychotherapy. Unfavorable prognostic factors include a long-term, chronic history of NEPE or other psychiatric disorders, family history of epilepsy, unemployment, and evidence of coexisting epilepsy.

III. CONCLUSION

This chapter is divided into two major sections. In the first section, we have presented the definition, classification, and epidemiology of epilepsy, as well as a description of how this common central nervous system condition is managed clinically. We further provided a step-by-step guide to the neuropsychological examination of epilepsy patients. In the second section, we provided a review of the diagnosis of NEPE, or pseudoseizures, including guidance for the assessment and treatment of patients with suspected NEPE.

BIBLIOGRAPHY

Alper, K., Devinsky, O., Perrine, K., Vazquez, B., & Luciano, D. (1993). Nonepileptic seizures and childhood sexual and physical abuse. *Neurology, 43,* 1950–1953.

American Psychiatric Association. (1987). *Diagnostic and statistical manual of mental disorders* (3rd ed., rev.). Washington, DC: Author.

Barr, W. B., & Bozeman Epilepsy Consortium. (1995). The right temporal lobe and memory: A critical reexamination. *Journal of the International Neuropsychological Society, 1,* 139–149.

Bear, D. M., & Fedio, P. (1977). Quantitative analysis of interictal behavior in temporal lobe epilepsy. *Archives of Neurology, 34,* 454–467.

Bell, B. D., & Davies, K. G. (1998). Anterior temporal lobectomy, hippocampal sclerosis, and memory: Recent neuropsychological findings. *Neuropsychology Review, 8,* 25–41.

Benbadis, S. R., Agrawal, V., & Tatum, W. O. (2001). How many patients with psychogenic nonepileptic seizures also have epilepsy? *Neurology, 57,* 915–917.

Berg, A. T., Levy, S. R., Novotny, E. J., & Shinnar, S. (1996). Predictors of intractable epilepsy in childhood: A case-control study. *Epilepsia, 37,* 24–30.

Bortz, J. J., Prigatano, G. P., Blum, D., & Fisher, R. S. (1995). Differential response characteristics in nonepileptic and epileptic seizure patients on a test of verbal learning and memory. *Neurology, 45,* 2029–2035.

Bortz, J. J., Wong, J., Blum, D., Prigatano, G. P., & Fisher, R. S. (1997). Differential verbal learning and memory characteristics in frontal lobe epilepsy. *Journal of the International Neuropsychological Society, 3*(1), 73–74.

Bowman, E. S., & Marland, O. M. (1996). Psychodynamics and psychiatric diagnoses of pseudoseizure subjects. *American Journal of Psychiatry, 153,* 57–63.

Carton, S., Thompson, P. J., & Duncan, J. S. (2003). Non-epileptic seizures: Patient's understanding and reaction to the diagnosis and impact on outcome. *Seizure, 12,* 287–294.

Chelune, G. J., Naugle, R. I., Luders, H., Sedlak, J., & Awad, I. A. (1993). Individual change after epilepsy surgery: Practice effects and base-rate information. *Neuropsychology, 7,* 41–52.

Commission on Classification and Terminology of the International League Against Epilepsy. (1981). Proposal for revised clinical and electroencephalographic classification of epileptic seizures. *Epilepsia, 22,* 489–501.

Commission on Classification and Terminology of the International League Against Epilepsy. (1989). Proposal for revised classification of epilepsies and epileptic syndromes. *Epilepsia, 30,* 389–399.

Connell, B. E., & Wilner, A. M. (1996). MMPI–2 distinguishes intractable epilepsy from pseudoseizures: A replication. *Epilepsia, 37*(5), 19.

Delis, D. C., Kaplan, E., &. Kramer, J. H. (2001). *Delis–Kaplan executive function system: Technical manual.* New York: Psychological Corporation.

Denman, S. B. (1984). *Denman Neuropsychology Memory Scale.* Charleston, SC: Sidney B. Denman.

Ellenberg, J. H., Hirtz, D. G., & Nelson, K. B. (1986). Do seizures in children cause intellectual deterioration? *New England Journal of Medicine, 314,* 1085–1088.

Flor-Henry, P. (1969). Schizophrenic-like reactions and affective psychoses associated with temporal lobe epilepsy: Etiological factors. *American Journal of Psychiatry, 126,* 400–403.

Gates, J. R. (1998). Diagnosis and treatment of nonepileptic seizures. In H. W. McConnell & P. J. Snyder (Eds.), *Psychiatric comorbidity in epilepsy* (pp. 187–204). Washington, DC: American Psychiatric Press.

Gates, J. R., & Mercer, K. (1995). Nonepileptic events. *Seminars in Neurology, 15,* 167–174.

Gilliam, F. G. (2002). Optimizing health outcome in active epilepsy. *Neurology, 58*(Suppl. 5), S9–S19.

Glaser, G. H. (1978). Epilepsy, hysteria, and "possession": A historical essay. *Journal of Nervous and Mental Disease, 166,* 268–274.

Gloor, P., Olivier, A., Quesney, L. F., Andermann, F., & Horowitz, S. (1982). The role of the limbic system in experiential phenomena of temporal lobe epilepsy. *Annals of Neurology, 12,* 129–144.

Gowers, W. R. (1881). *Epilepsy and other chronic convulsive diseases.* London: Churchill.

Helmstaedter, C., Grunwald, T., Lehnertz, K., Gleißner, U., & Elger, C. E. (1997). Differential involvement of left temporolateral and temporomesial structures in verbal declarative learning and memory: Evidence from temporal lobe epilepsy. *Brain and Cognition, 35,* 110–131.

Hermann, B. P., Gold, J., Pusakulich, R., Wyler, A. R., Randolph, C., Rankin, G., & Hoy, W. (1995). Wechsler Adult Intelligence Scale—Revised in the evaluation of anterior temporal lobectomy candidates. *Epilepsia, 36,* 480–487.

Hermann, B., Seidenberg, M., Bell, B., Rutecki, P., Sheth, R., Ruggles, K., et al. (2002). The neurodevelopmental impact of childhood-onset temporal lobe epilepsy on brain structure and function. *Epilepsia, 43,* 1062–1071.

Hermann, B. P., Seidenberg, M., Schoenfeld, J., Peterson, J., Leveroni, C., & Wyler, A. R. (1996). Empirical techniques for determining the reliability, magnitude, and pattern of neuropsychological change following epilepsy surgery. *Epilepsia, 37,* 942–950.

Hirtz, D., Berg, A., Bettis, D., Camfield, C., Camfield, P., Crumrine, P., et al. (2003). Practice parameter: Treatment of the child with a first unprovoked seizure: Report of the Quality Standards Subcommittee of the American Academy of

Neurology and the Practice Committee of the Child Neurology Society. *Neurology, 60,* 166–175.

Jasper, H. H. (1962). Mechanisms of epileptic automatism. *Epilepsia, 3,* 381–390.

Jokeit, H., & Markowitsch, J. H. (1999). Aging limits plasticity of episodic memory functions in response to left temporal lobe damage in patients with epilepsy. In H. Stefan, F. Andermann, P. Chauvel, & S. Sharvon (Eds.), *Advances in neurology* (Vol. 81, pp. 251–258). Philadelphia: Lippincott Williams & Wilkins.

Jones-Gotman, M. (1991). Localization of lesions by neuropsychological testing. *Epilepsia, 32*(Suppl. 5), S41–S52.

Lancman, M. E. (1999). Psychosis and peri-ictal confusional states. *Neurology, 53*(Suppl. 2), 33–38.

Lancman, M. E., Lambrakis, C. C., & Steinhardt, M. I. (2001). Psychogenic pseudoseizures. In A. B. Ettinger & A. M. Kanner (Eds.), *Psychiatric issues in epilepsy* (pp. 341–354). New York: Lippincott Williams & Wilkins.

Loring, D. (1994). Neuroanatomic substrates of clinical memory measures [Symposium II: Hippocampus, memory and epilepsy]. *Epilepsia, 35*(Suppl. 8), 79.

Loring, D. W., Meador, K. J., Lee, G. P., & King, D. W. (1992). *Amobarbital effects and lateralized brain function: The Wada Test.* New York: Springer-Verlag.

Mason, S. L., Mercer, K., Risse, G. L., & Gates, J. R. (1996). Clinical utility of the MMPI–II in the diagnosis of non-epileptic seizures (NES). *Epilepsia, 37*(Suppl. 5), 18.

Martin, R., Sawrie, S., Gilliam, F., Mackey, M., Faught, E., Knowlton, R., & Kuzniecky, R. (2002). Determining reliable cognitive change after epilepsy surgery: Development of reliable change indices and standardized regression-based change norms for the WMS–III and WAIS–III. *Epilepsia, 43,* 1551–1558.

McConnell, H. W., & Duncan, D. (1998). Behavioral effects of antiepileptic drugs. In H. W. McConnell & P. J. Snyder (Eds.), *Psychiatric comorbidity in epilepsy* (pp. 245–361). Washington, DC: American Psychiatric Association.

McSweeney, A. J., Naugle, R. I., Chelune, G. J., & Luders, H. (1993). "T scores for change": An illustration of a regression approach to depicting change in clinical neuropsychology. *The Clinical Neuropsychologist, 7,* 300–312.

Meador, K. J. (2001). Cognitive effects of epilepsy and of antiepileptic medications. In E. Wyllie (Ed.), *The treatment of epilepsy: Principles and practice* (3rd ed., pp. 1215–1225). Philadelphia: Lippincott Williams & Wilkins.

Milner, B. (1975). Psychological aspects of focal epilepsy and its neurosurgical management. In D. P. Purpura, J. K. Penry,

& R. D. Walter (Eds.), *Advances in neurology* (Vol. 8, pp. 299–321). New York: Raven Press.

Moser, D. J., Bauer, R. M., Gilmore, R. L., Dede, D. E., Fennell, E. B., Algina, J. J., et al. (2000). Electroencephalographic, volumetric, and neuropsychological indicators of seizure focus lateralization in temporal lobe epilepsy. *Archives of Neurology, 57,* 707–712.

Perrine, K., Hermann, B. P., Meador, K. J., Vickrey, B. G., Cramer, J. A., Hays, R. D., & Devinsky, O. (1995). The relationship of neuropsychological functioning to quality of life in epilepsy. *Archives of Neurology, 52,* 997–1003.

Ramsay, R. E., Cohen, A., & Brown, M. C. (1993). Coexisting epilepsy and non-epileptic seizures. In A. J. Rowan & J. R. Gates (Eds.), *Nonepileptic seizures* (pp. 47–54). Stoneham, MA: Butterworth-Heinemann.

Reuber, M., Pukrop, R., Bauer, J., Helmstaedter, C., Tessendorf, N., & Elger, C. (2003). Outcome in psychogenic nonepileptic seizures: 1 to 10-year follow-up in 164 patients. *Annals of Neurology, 53,* 305–311.

Reynolds, E. H., Elwes, R. D. C., & Shorvon, S. D. (1983). Why does epilepsy become intractable? Prevention of chronic epilepsy. *Lancet, II,* 952–954.

Rowan, A. J., & Gates, J. R. (Eds.). (2000). *Nonepileptic seizures* (2nd ed.). Stoneham, MA: Butterworth-Heinemann.

Sawrie, S., Chelune, G., Naugle, R., & Luders, H. (1996). Empirical methods for assessing meaningful neuropsychological change following epilepsy surgery. *Journal of the International Neuropsychological Society, 2,* 556–564.

Sawrie, S., Martin, R., Gilliam, F., Roth, D., Faught, E., & Kuzniecky, R. (1998). Contribution of neuropsycholgical data to the prediction of temporal lobe epilepsy surgery outcome. *Epilepsia, 39,* 319–325.

Schachter S. C. (2002). Introduction: Stigma and epilepsy [Special issue: "Stigma and Epilepsy in the 21st Century: Time to Heal"]. *Epilepsy & Behavior, 3,* 1–2.

Scheibel, M. E., Crandall, P. H., & Scheibel, A. B. (1974). The hippocampal-dentate complex in temporal lobe epilepsy: A Golgi study. *Epilepsia, 15,* 55–80.

Selwa, L. M., Geyer, J., Nikakhtar, N., Brown, M. B., Schuh, L. A., & Drury, I. (2000). Nonepileptic seizure outcome varies by type spell and duration of illness. *Epilepsia, 41,* 1330–1334.

Simkins-Bullock, J. (2000). Beyond speech lateralization: A review of the variability, reliability, and validity of the intracarotid amobarbital procedure and its nonlanguage uses in epilepsy surgery candidates. *Neuropsychology Review, 10,* 41–74.

Snyder, P. J., & Harris, L. J. (1997). The intracarotid amobarbital procedure: An historical perspective. *Brain and Cognition, 33,* 18–32.

Snyder, P. J., Martin, R. C., Ceravolo, N., Turrentine, L., Franzen, M. D., Valeriano, J., et al. (1997). Neuropsychological and clinical indicators for rapid identification of patients with nonepileptic seizures [Abstract]. *Epilepsia, 38*(Suppl. 8), 170.

Snyder, P. J., Novelly, R. A., & Harris, L. J. (1990). Mixed speech dominance in the intracarotid sodium Amytal procedure: Validity and criteria. *Journal of Clinical and Experimental Neuropsychology, 12,* 629–642.

Spencer, S. S., Spencer, D. D., Williamson, P. D., & Mattson, R. H. (1983). Sexual automatisms in complex partial seizures. *Neurology, 33,* 527–533.

Strauss, E., Hunter, M., & Wada, J. (1995). Risk factors for cognitive impairment in epilepsy. *Neuropsychology, 9,* 457–463.

Strauss, E., Wada, J., & Goldwater, B. (1992). Sex differences in interhemispheric reorganization of speech. *Neuropsychologia, 30,* 353–359.

Surgery for Epilepsy, National Institute of Health. (1990). Consensus conference: Surgery for epilepsy. *Journal of the American Medical Association, 264,* 729–733.

Tinuper, P., Provini, F., Marini, C., Cerullo, A., Plazzi, G., Avoni, P., & Baruzzi, A. (1996). Partial epilepsy of long duration: Changing semiology with age. *Epilepsia, 37,* 162–164.

Toone, B. K. (1990). Disorders of hysterical conversion. In C. Bass (Ed.), *Somatization: Physical symptoms and psychological illness* (pp. 207–234). London: Blackwell.

Torta, R., & Keller, R. (1999). Behavioral, psychotic, and anxiety disorders in epilepsy: etiology, clinical features, and therapeutic implications. *Epilepsia, 40*(Suppl. 10), 2–20.

Trimble, M. R. (1983). Personality disturbances in epilepsy. *Neurology, 33,* 1332–1334.

Wiegartz, P., Seidenberg, M., Woodard, A., Gidal, B., & Hermann, B. (1999). Co-morbid psychiatric disorder in chronic epilepsy: Recognition and etiology of depression. *Neurology, 53*(Suppl. 2), 3–8.

Wilkus, R., & Dodrill, C. B. (1989). Factors affecting the outcome of MMPI and neuropsychological assessments of psychogenic and epileptic seizure patients. *Epilepsia, 30,* 339–347.

Wyllie, E. (1995). Developmental aspects of seizure semiology: Problems in identifying localized-onset seizures in infants and children. *Epilepsia, 36,* 1170–1172.

Zaidel, E. (1985). Language in the right hemisphere. In D. F. Benson & E. Zaidel (Eds.), *The dual brain: Hemispheric specialization in humans* (pp. 205–231). New York: Guilford Press.

CHAPTER 14
John A. Lucas and Russell Addeo

Traumatic Brain Injury and Postconcussion Syndrome

Traumatic injuries represent the leading cause of death and disability in young adults in the United States and other industrialized countries. When traumatic injury to the head is sufficient to cause alterations in consciousness, neurological impairment, or cognitive deficits, an underlying injury to the brain is assumed.

The clinical assessment of patients with traumatic brain injury (TBI) should focus on two main goals: evaluating the nature of the injury and understanding the full extent of its effects. To achieve these goals, the clinician must carefully construct a history of the injury, including information regarding (a) the nature of the event; (b) the status of consciousness before, during, and after the event; (c) the amount of time that has passed since the injury; and (d) the clinical course of symptoms. This information should be gathered from several sources, including the patient, family members, and medical records. The nature of the injury will guide the choice of test measures administered and will allow consideration of the types of questions that should be answered by the assessment. Once the full extent of cognitive and noncognitive changes is determined, the neuropsychologist can help inform and guide subsequent interventions.

TBI may result in focal, multifocal, or diffuse cerebral dysfunction and often involves structures and systems beyond the site of initial impact. If focal lesions are present, they typically exist within the context of more generalized, nonspecific damage to the brain. Moreover, preexisting conditions, psychological sequelae, and other factors may obscure or exacerbate cognitive symptoms following TBI. Knowledge of both the mechanisms underlying TBI and the nonorganic factors that may contribute to postinjury cognitive disorders is therefore essential for competent neuropsychological assessment of these patients.

I. CLASSIFICATION

Brain injury resulting from head trauma is a dynamic process, not only evolving over the minutes, hours, and days following the injury but in some cases continuing over the course of weeks and months. Neuropsychological results may vary depending on the time of the assessment, the nature and location of the trauma, the estimated severity of the injury, and the extent of secondary effects, such as metabolic alterations, interruption of blood flow, and cerebral swelling.

A. Open Versus Closed Head Injury

Head injuries may be broadly classified as either open or closed, depending on whether the integrity of the skull has been breached. The term **open head injury** most often refers to trauma in which the skull is crushed or penetrated by a foreign object. The majority of fatalities following head trauma are seen in patients with open head injury. In **closed head injuries** (also called blunt or nonpenetrating injuries), the skull remains relatively intact. Impact injuries that involve skull fractures are technically considered open head injuries; however, their clinical presentation is typically more consistent with that of closed head injuries.

The neuropathological effects of head injury typically occur as a result of two processes. The **primary injury** is the damage to the brain caused by the penetrating object or impact forces at the time of trauma. Although the primary injury itself is usually focal and limited in duration, it sets in motion a series of physiological and metabolic processes that produce **secondary effects.** These effects can be as damaging to brain tissue as the primary injury, if not more so. Some secondary effects invariably occur (e.g., edema), whereas others may or may not develop, depending on the nature, location, and extent of the primary injury. The more common consequences of primary injury and potential secondary effects are reviewed in the following sections.

1. PENETRATING HEAD INJURIES

The majority of penetrating brain injuries are missile injuries caused by bullets. As a bullet travels, air is compressed in front of it, leading to an explosive effect on entering the body. When the missile is of low velocity (i.e., less than 1,000 ft/s), brain damage is typically restricted to the missile track, and the victim may remain conscious. With higher velocity missiles, however, damage typically extends well beyond the missile track, and victims are usually rendered unconscious.

a. Primary injury
1. destruction of brain tissue at the site of entry and along the path of object,
2. intracranial bleeding due to damaged blood vessels, and
3. meningeal and cerebral laceration.

b. Potential secondary effects
1. destruction of brain tissue during surgical removal of foreign object and during cleansing (i.e., debridement);
2. ischemia (i.e., interruption of blood flow to tissue);
3. edema (i.e., reactive swelling of brain tissue); note that both ischemia and edema are much worse if the brain is penetrated by a high-velocity missile;
4. brain infection (e.g., meningitis, abscess); and
5. posttraumatic epilepsy.

2. CLOSED HEAD INJURIES

Brain damage caused by closed head injuries also occurs in two stages. The primary injury (i.e., the damage incurred at the time of impact) sets in motion a series of physiological processes that may produce secondary effects.

a. Primary injury

1. Brain contusions and lacerations:
   a. Bruising is typically seen at the site of impact and is often referred to as a **coup** lesion. In addition, pressure during impact often causes the brain to rebound and hit the skull opposite the initial blow, typically resulting in a larger contusion, referred to as a **contrecoup** lesion.
   b. Contusions and lacerations are also commonly seen on the inferior surface of brain, owing to the action of the brain rubbing against the base of the skull.

The orbitofrontal and anterior temporal lobe regions are the most common sites of contusion and lacerations, independent of where the head was struck.

2. Diffuse axonal damage often results from shearing of axons and white matter tracts.

3. Disruption of vasculature, including epidural hematomas, subdural hematomas, subarachnoid hemorrhages, or intracranial bleeding, may represent either primary or secondary effects of closed head injury.

   a. Epidural hematomas, fed under arterial pressure, cause acute and rapid compression of the brain and brainstem and can lead to death if not treated surgically.

   b. Subdural hematomas and subarachnoid hemorrhages are caused by bleeding from vessels surrounding the dura of the brain. These vascular complications can cause compression and possible ischemia.

   c. Intracranial bleeding occurs when blood vessels within the brain parenchyma are damaged.

b. Potential secondary effects of closed head injury

1. ischemia;
2. edema;
3. increased intracranial pressure and herniation;
4. hypoxia;
5. obstructive hydrocephalus;
6. posttraumatic epilepsy;
7. diaschesis: disruption of neuronal activity in regions connected to the affected brain region; and
8. metabolic and neurotransmitter changes associated with damage to neurons, the brain's response to injury, and the healing process.

3. SKULL FRACTURES

Closed head injuries with skull fractures may present with additional primary and secondary features, including the following:

a. Primary injury

1. cranial nerve damage and related palsies,
2. damage to vasculature entering or leaving base of skull, and
3. pituitary stalk damage (if basilar skull is fractured near the sella).

b. **Potential secondary effects**

1. collection of air in the cranial cavity (i.e., aerocele),
2. infection,
3. cerebrospinal fluid leakage, and
4. endocrine/hormonal dysfunction (if pituitary stalk is damaged).

B. Measurement of Severity of TBI

Several indices may be used to gauge the severity of TBI, including (a) the length and depth of altered consciousness and (b) the presence and extent of posttraumatic amnesia.

1. ALTERED CONSCIOUSNESS

At the moment of impact, victims of TBI typically demonstrate immediate loss of consciousness (LOC), suppression of reflexes, and brief changes in cardiopulmonary functions. Although most vital signs return to normal and stabilize within a few seconds, the victim may remain unconscious (i.e., comatose). The depth of LOC and the amount of time it takes a patient to regain consciousness are often used as an indication of the severity of the brain injury. Patients often cannot provide reliable information regarding the length of their own LOC. Independent collateral information from a witness to the injury, police reports, or emergency medical records should therefore be sought.

a. Length of LOC

Several LOC grading systems have been published, but no one system has achieved consensus among medical professionals. The classification system developed by the Mild Traumatic Brain Injury Committee (MTBIC) of the Head Injury Interdisciplinary Special Interest Group of the American Congress of Rehabilitation Medicine (1993) grades TBI severity as follows:

1. mild injury: LOC for 30 minutes or less and
2. moderate-to-severe injury: LOC longer than 30 minutes.

b. Depth of coma

Depth of coma is also commonly used to measure TBI severity. The Glasgow Coma Scale (GCS; Teasdale & Jennett, 1974) assesses verbal responses, eye-opening behavior, and best motor responses, resulting in a total score ranging from 3 to 15 points (see Table 14.1). The GCS is often performed at the scene of the injury or in the emergency room and can be repeated throughout recovery to gauge changes in arousal and depth of coma.

Table 14.1. Glasgow Coma Scale

Response	Score
Verbal response	
None	1
Incomprehensible sounds	2
Inappropriate words	3
Confused	4
Oriented	5
Eye opening	
None	1
To pain	2
To speech	3
Spontaneously	4
Best motor response	
None	1
Abnormal extension	2
Abnormal flexion	3
Withdraws	4
Localizes	5
Obeys	6

Note. Source: Teasdale and Jennett (1974).

The GCS classifies TBI as follows:

1. mild injury: at least 13 points,
2. moderate injury: 9 to 12 points, and
3. severe injury: 8 or fewer points.

The GCS is sensitive to moderate and severe head injuries and is useful for predicting neurobehavioral outcome (i.e., the higher the score, the better the prognosis). Sensitivity at the milder end of the spectrum is limited, prompting the development of the extended Glasgow Coma Scale (GSC-E; Nell, Yates, & Kruger, 2000). The GSC-E provides information useful in characterizing mild grades of concussion, as defined by the American Academy of Neurology (presented later in this chapter).

2. POSTTRAUMATIC AMNESIA

Posttraumatic amnesia (PTA) refers to a disturbance of memory for events that occur immediately following a head injury. This is caused by the interruption of mechanisms responsible for ongoing encoding and memory storage. Length of PTA is typically more accurate than length of coma in predicting recovery of function, with longer periods of PTA associated with more severe brain injuries and poorer recovery of function. Both coma and PTA, however, provide separate sources of information to predict outcome and therefore should both be evaluated.

Length of PTA may be elicited by asking the patient to describe his or her first memories after the accident. It is important, however, to distinguish between episodic and semantic memories of the injury. "Memories" that are based on information provided to the patient after full return to alert consciousness are semantic memories, not true episodic memories, and should not be used to estimate length of PTA. PTA should be based only on the patient's actual memory of the events themselves, not what they were later told about the events. Review of records from rescue personnel, emergency department, and subsequent hospitalization may help determine length of PTA.

A typical PTA grading system is as follows:

a. mild injury: PTA less than 1 hour,
b. moderate injury: PTA for 1 to 24 hours, and
c. severe injury: PTA longer than 24 hours.

Others have supplemented the previously discussed criteria to include finer scaling at the extremes. These include very mild (PTA less than 5 minutes), very severe (PTA for 1–4 weeks), and extremely severe injuries (PTA longer than 4 weeks).

The Galveston Orientation and Amnesia Test (GOAT; Levin, O'Donnell, & Grossman, 1979) is a mental status examination commonly used to assess the extent and severity of amnesia during the acute recovery phase of TBI. The GOAT comprises 10 questions, 8 of which assess orientation to person, place, and time. The remaining 2 questions ask the patient to describe the first memory recalled *after* the injury (i.e., to detect PTA) and the last memory recalled *prior to* the injury (to detect retrograde amnesia). The GOAT is scored on a scale of 0–100 and may be administered repeatedly during recovery. Higher scores reflect better functioning:

a. normal: 76–100 points,
b. borderline: 66–75 points, and
c. impaired: 65 or fewer points.

C. Concussion

The Congress of Neurological Surgeons defines concussion as "a clinical syndrome characterized by the immediate and transient post-traumatic impairment of neural function such as alteration of consciousness, disturbance of vision or equilibrium, etc." (Johnston, McCrory, Mohtadi, & Meeuwisse, 2001, p. 150). Concussion is often used synonymously with mild TBI (mTBI) and can occur with or without complete LOC or PTA. Some of the more frequently observed behavioral features of patients during acute concussion include vacant stare, delayed responding, inability to focus attention, disorientation, confusion, slurred or incoherent speech, motor incoordination, excessive emotionality, or forgetfulness.

Following recovery from acute cerebral concussion, a wide variety of subjective cognitive, somatic, and psychological symptoms may be observed. These symptoms are often reported in stages rather than all at once.

1. EARLY SYMPTOMS OF CONCUSSION

Early symptoms typically develop within 24 hours of an injury, or shortly after a comatose patient regains consciousness. These symptoms include the following:

- a. headache,
- b. dizziness,
- c. vomiting,
- d. nausea,
- e. drowsiness, and
- f. blurred vision.

Nausea, vomiting, drowsiness, and blurred vision are typically short-lived complaints, whereas headache and dizziness may persist for weeks or longer.

2. LATE SYMPTOMS OF CONCUSSION

The onset of some behavioral symptoms may be delayed for several days to weeks after TBI. These include the following:

- a. irritability,
- b. anxiety,
- c. depression,
- d. poor memory,
- e. impaired concentration,
- f. insomnia,
- g. fatigue, and
- h. visual and auditory complaints.

3. CONCUSSION GRADING SCHEMES

In recent years, there has been increased interest in grading the severity of concussion symptoms. This interest has arisen primarily from the desire to more formally evaluate and manage the relatively high incidence of sports-related concussions suffered by amateur and professional athletes. There are currently at least 25 published sports-related concussion severity scales (Johnston et al., 2001); however, a recent symposium on sports-related concussion failed to endorse any single grading scheme because of the absence of scientifically validated return-to-play guidelines (Aubry et al., 2002). Four of the more commonly used grading schemes are presented in Table 14.2 for comparison purposes.

4. POSTCONCUSSION SYNDROME

Postconcussion syndrome (PCS) is defined as a collection of physical, cognitive, and affective symptoms commonly reported following a concussion. Nearly 15% of patients with mild head injury continue to complain of postconcussion symptoms 1 year after their injury. Until recently, the prevailing model of concussion depicted a transitory alteration of consciousness without any associated pathological changes in the brain. Because of this view, organic bases for postconcussion complaints of longer duration were dismissed in favor of psychological or motivational explanations. Recent studies, however, demonstrate that the structural and metabolic changes that take place in the brain following mild head injury may contribute to the persistence of some cognitive sequelae.

The exact nature of PCS remains controversial. The proportion of patients with mild head injury who complain of PCS 1 year after injury more than triples if litigation is involved. Data such as these are often used to highlight the potential role of nonorganic factors in PCS. These and other diagnostic issues pertaining to patients with persistent PCS are presented later in this chapter.

5. SECOND IMPACT SYNDROME

A rare but catastrophic complication of concussion can occur when an individual suffers repeated head injuries over a relatively brief time interval. This phenomenon, called **second impact syndrome**, is observed in contact sports such as boxing, football, and ice hockey, as well as in noncontact sports such as equestrian events. Second impact syndrome occurs when an individual sustains a second head injury while still symptomatic from an earlier concussion. Even if the second injury is mild, the victim can demonstrate rapid deterioration from an alert, conscious state to coma and possibly death, all within minutes to hours following the trauma.

Autopsy studies indicate that second impact syndrome is associated with autonomic dysregulation of blood vessel diameter. The resulting rise in cerebral blood volume causes increased intracranial pressure, diminished cerebral perfusion, and increased risk of fatal brain herniation.

Table 14.2. Frequently Used Concussion Grading Schemes

	Concussion severity grading guidelines			
	American Academy of Neurology (1997)	Cantu (1986)	Colorado Medical Society (1991)	Congress of Neurological Surgeons (1966)
Grade 1 Mild	Confusion < 15 minutes No LOC	PTA < 30 minutes No LOC	Confusion No PTA No LOC	Transient neurological sx No LOC
Grade 2 Moderate	Confusion ≥ 15 minutes No LOC	PTA > 30 minutes LOC < 5 minutes	Confusion Any PTA No LOC	LOC with complete recovery in < 5 minutes
Grade 3 Severe	Any LOC	PTA > 24 hours LOC > 5 minutes	Any LOC	LOC ≥ 5 minutes

Note. LOC = loss of consciousness; PTA = posttraumatic amnesia; sx = symptoms.

II. NEUROANATOMICAL CORRELATES OF TBI AND CONCUSSION

A. Pathophysiological Changes

Studies indicate that even mild head injury can cause structural damage to the brain. Subsequent to head trauma, diffuse damage may be seen in long, large-caliber neuronal fibers. Previously, it was believed that damage was caused by axonal tearing; however, it now appears that compression or stretching of axons is the actual mechanism of injury. Axonal compression or stretching creates a focal abnormality on the surface membrane of the axon that, within 3 hours after the injury, is sufficient to impair axoplasmic transport. This leads to accumulation of organelles and axoplasm at the site of the abnormality, resulting in swelling (i.e., edema). The swollen axon then separates. The proximal section remains attached to the cell body, and the distal segment collapses and undergoes phagocytosis by nearby glial cells. Axonal swellings may persist unchanged or the axons may attempt to regenerate. In the regenerative process, sprouting and growth cone formation are observed at or near the site of the swelling. Over the course of several weeks, the sprouts elongate, extend through the parenchyma, and enter the myelin sheaths of the detached distal axonal segments that have previously collapsed. If axons do not regenerate, reactive deafferentation (i.e., death of "downstream" neurons owing to lack of synaptic input) is observed within 60 days of the injury.

B. Neurochemical Changes

Cells that are not mechanically damaged as a result of TBI are nonetheless exposed to significant metabolic and neurochemical changes. The cascade of changes following head injury begins with a sharp, transient increase in concentrations of acetylcholine and excitatory amino acids such as glutamate. The acute release of glutamate causes widespread neuronal depolarization and ionic flux of potassium across the membrane into the extracellular space. Within 2 minutes of a mild injury, the concentration of extracellular potassium increases 2-fold; 10-fold increases are observed following moderate. Changes in potassium concentration cause increased glycolysis, which, in turn, results in accumulation of lactic acid within the cells. This leads to a state of metabolic depression (i.e., decreased metabolism and cerebral blood flow). In animals, the presence and severity of metabolic depression correlate strongly with behavioral changes.

III. NEURODIAGNOSTIC DATA

Increasingly sophisticated techniques of neural, metabolic, and electrophysiological imaging have permitted improved identification of cerebral abnormalities following TBI, even when damage is subtle.

A. Computed Tomography and Magnetic Resonance Imaging

Gross brain pathology associated with moderate to severe head trauma is typically well visualized on both computed tomography (CT) and magnetic resonance imaging (MRI) scans. Although structural imaging studies of mTBI patients are often negative, MRI typically identifies abnormalities more readily than CT. Mild orbitofrontal and temporal lobe contusions, for example, are commonly missed by CT scanning because of bone artifact. In addition, CT is poor in visualizing diffuse axonal injury and trauma-induced lesions in the basal ganglia. One advantage that CT holds over MRI is the ability to detect hemorrhage soon after injury. At 3 weeks postinjury, however, MRI may detect residual hemorrhage that may be missed by CT. Quantitative MRI techniques have recently been developed and are especially useful in understanding TBI. This methodology measures the volume of brain structures and allows comparison to normative data or to a patient's prior brain scan, thus improving sensitivity to cerebral abnormalities and volumetric changes beyond what is possible with unassisted visual inspection.

B. Electroencephalography

Electroencephalographic (EEG) studies indicate that posttraumatic epilepsy is common following penetrating brain injuries, with incident estimates approaching 50% (e.g., Grafman & Salazar, 1996). The overall risk of posttraumatic epilepsy following closed head injury is comparatively low (2%–5%), with a higher incidence associated with more severe injury (11%), skull fracture (15%), and hematoma (31%).

Nonspecific, nonepileptic EEG abnormalities may be detected following mTBI. The EEG tends to be most abnormal when performed soon after the injury and when there is alteration of consciousness associated with the injury. In approximately 10% of patients with cerebral concussion, slight diffuse EEG abnormalities may persist beyond 3 months.

C. Brainstem Auditory Evoked Potentials

Abnormal brainstem auditory evoked potentials (BAEPs) are most often found in patients with more severe TBI; however, approximately 10% to 20% of patients with mTBI also demonstrate abnormal BAEPs. Abnormalities are more prevalent in patients who suffer long periods of unconsciousness, but they do not appear to be related to performance on neurocognitive measures.

D. Functional Imaging

In general, TBI patients demonstrate reduced cerebral blood flow and widespread abnormalities in cerebral glucose metabolism beyond any structural abnormalities identified on CT or MRI. These metabolic abnormalities tend to be most severe closer to the time of injury; improvements correlate with clinical recovery. Evidence of metabolic depression can be found in some mTBI patients as long as 6 months postinjury. Methods of determining functional status of brain activity include positron emission tomography (PET), single photon emission computed tomography (SPECT), functional magnetic resonance imaging (fMRI), and diffusion tensor imaging (DTI). Although it is beyond the scope of this chapter to review all of these procedures in detail, each provides images of regional brain activation that can be compared across or within individuals. These methods show exciting promise in understanding the mechanisms underlying brain dysfunction and evaluating subtle cerebral pathology associated with mTBI. At present, however, functional imaging of TBI patients tends to be more common in research than clinical settings.

IV. NEUROPSYCHOLOGICAL ASSESSMENT

A decision-making model of assessment of TBI patients is presented in Figure 14.1. With the exception of brief screening measures (e.g., Mini-Mental State Examination, GOAT, Standardized Assessment of Concussion) or informal bedside testing to monitor recovery or guide early rehabilitation therapies, formal neuropsychological assessment of TBI patients should be deferred until after the postacute stage of injury. Most TBI patients will be unable to tolerate the demands of extensive neuropsychological testing during the initial stages of recovery. Moreover, the dynamic nature of symptoms in the acute and postacute phases would render comprehensive neuropsychological assessment

Figure 14.1. Decision making in neuropsychological assessment of TBI patients. TBI = traumatic brain injury; MMSE = Mini-Mental State Examination; GOAT = Galveston Orientation and Amnesia Test; PTA = posttraumatic amnesia; LOC = loss of consciousness; GCS = Glasgow Coma Scale; BDI–2 = Beck Depression Inventory—II; MMPI–2 = Minnesota Multiphasic Personality Inventory—2; STAI = State–Trait Anxiety Inventory; STAXI = State–Trait Anger Expression Inventory; PCS = postconcussion syndrome.

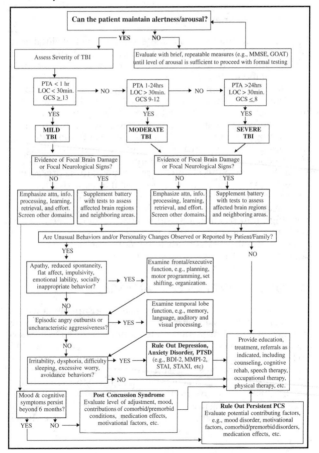

invalid for most diagnostic and long-term planning purposes. A 6-week waiting period is usually adequate; however, the exact time frame may vary depending on the severity of the injury and the purpose of the assessment.

A. Assessing Moderate and Severe TBI

Patients with moderate and severe TBI can display the full spectrum of impairment across all cognitive domains. Very severely injured individuals are likely to show general impairment of all cognitive abilities; however, less severely impaired patients demonstrate unique patterns of preserved and impaired abilities consistent with the focal (or multifocal) nature of brain damage incurred. A complete assessment should therefore screen for deficits in all cognitive and sensory–perceptual domains. Deficits identified on the screening examination can then be pursued with more detailed assessment.

1. STRUCTURAL DAMAGE

The presence of structural damage, such as skull fractures, contusions, hemorrhages, or pressure effects (e.g., hematomas, edema, obstructive hydrocephalus), can often guide the choice of measures administered. Specifically, cognitive domains associated with the damaged area, surrounding brain regions, and potential contrecoup involvement should be thoroughly examined.

2. FOCAL NEUROLOGICAL DEFICITS

Special attention must always be paid to the presence of any focal neurological deficits, such as motor, sensory, or language impairment (e.g., hemiplegia, hemianopia, anosmia, aphasia), because they may

a. provide information regarding focal brain dysfunction,
b. guide more detailed assessment of affected brain regions, and
c. dictate modifications of test administration (e.g., ensuring placement of visual stimuli in the intact hemispace of a patient with an homonymous hemianopia or visual neglect).

3. COMMON COGNITIVE DEFICITS

Certain cognitive deficits are relatively common following moderate and severe closed head injuries. The high incidence of orbitofrontal and anterior temporal lobe contusions associated with these injuries typically produce the following deficits:

a. attention deficits and distractibility,
b. slowed cognitive processing and behavioral responding,
c. impaired learning and retrieval of new information,
d. deficits in auditory or visual processing, and
e. executive dysfunction (e.g., initiation deficits, poor planning and organization, impaired motor programming, perseveration, anosagnosia, impulsivity).

B. Assessing mTBI

The most common cognitive sequelae of mTBI are diffuse reductions in attention and information processing, most likely owing to diffuse axonal injury. Test batteries should therefore include measures with sufficient sensitivity to detect these changes (see Table 14.3). The majority of mTBI patients improve to within normal limits on most neuropsychological measures within 30 days; however, a subset of patients may continue to demonstrate impairment beyond this time.

1. REACTION TIME AND PROCESSING SPEED

Reaction time (RT) tests measure the time it takes a patient to respond to presented stimuli. **Simple RT** is typically measured by asking patients to look at a blank screen and press a keypad as soon as a stimulus is presented. A variation of this paradigm is the **choice RT** test, in which both target stimuli and foils are presented in random order and the patient must respond only when the target stimulus is detected. Choice RT is one way of measuring **selective attention**, which is defined as the capacity to focus on certain stimuli while ignoring or suppressing awareness of competing, distracting stimuli (Lezak, 1995).

Given the rapid and precise requirements for measurement, RT tests are typically administered via computer. Most of the commercially available continuous performance tests (CPT) include simple and choice RT paradigms as well as more complex measures of attention. Test stimuli, presentation rates, and length of the test vary depending on the instrument used, and most paradigms can be customized to measure variables of interest. Although CPTs were originally developed for use with children, their popularity in adult assessment has grown. Normative data for adults, however, are somewhat limited and typically based on standard administration paradigms.

Commonly used paper-and-pencil measures of processing speed include Part A of the Halstead–Reitan Trail Making Test, the Digit Symbol subtest of the Wechsler Adult Intelligence Scale—III (WAIS–III), the Symbol–Digit Modalities Test (Smith,

Table 14.3. Common Neuropsychological Measures Used to Evaluate Cognitive Dysfunction in Mild Traumatic Brain Injury

Domain	Measure
Reaction time	Continuous Performance Tests
Processing speed	Trail Making Test, Part A WAIS–III Digit Symbol Symbol–Digit Modalities Test Stroop Word Reading Stroop Color Naming
Vigilance	Digit Vigilance Test Visual Search and Attention Test WAIS–III Symbol Search Ruff 2 & 7 Selective Attention Test
Divided attention	Stroop Color–Word Interference Trail Making Test, Part B
Working memory	Digit Span Backward WAIS–III Letter-Number Sequencing WAIS–III Arithmetic WMS–III Spatial Span Paced Auditory Serial Addition Test (PASAT) Auditory Consonant Trigrams (ACT)
Retrieval	Boston Naming Test (Spontaneous vs. Phonemic Cue) Semantic Category Fluency California Verbal Learning Test–2 (Free Recall vs. Cued Recall & Recognition)

Note. WAIS–III = Wechsler Adult Intelligence Scale—III; WMS–III = Wechsler Memory Scale—III.

1982), and the Word Reading and Color Naming trials of the Stroop paradigm (Stroop, 1935).

2. VIGILANCE

Vigilance refers to the ability to sustain selective attention. Typically, stimuli are presented sequentially over time, and the patient is required to indicate when a target is perceived. This can be evaluated with CPT or by any number of paper-and-pencil measures. Cancellation tests, such as the Digit Vigilance Test (Lewis & Rennick, 1979), Visual Search and Attention Test (Trennery, Crosson, DeBoe, & Leber, 1990), and Ruff 2 & 7 Selective Attention Test (Ruff, Niemann, Allen, Farrow, & Wylie, 1992), are common measures of vigilance. Patients are instructed to scan rows of letters, numbers, or symbols and cross out specified targets. WAIS–III Symbol Search also measures vigilance by requiring patients to search for targets among a group of symbols. In general, vigilance tests are typically scored for time to completion and accuracy.

3. DIVIDED ATTENTION

The ability to divide one's attention between two or more concurrent tasks places significantly greater demand on information-processing capacity than tests of selective or sustained attention. Reaction time paradigms can be used to measure divided attention by requiring patients to perform an unrelated task (e.g., counting backward) while responding to target stimuli. Other commonly used measures of divided attention include the interference trial of the Stroop paradigm and Part B of the Halstead–Reitan Trail Making Test.

4. WORKING MEMORY

Working memory is defined as the temporary storage of information in an active state, wherein the information can be manipulated as needed. Common measures of working memory require patients to repeat digits backward, tap blocks in reverse sequence, or perform mental calculations. The Digit Span, Letter-Number Sequencing, and Arithmetic subtests of the WAIS–III are commonly used to evaluate working memory ability. Other measures of working memory include the Spatial Span subtest of the Wechsler Memory Scale—III, Auditory Consonant Trigrams (Brown, 1958; Stuss, Stethem, & Poirier, 1987), and the Paced Auditory Serial Addition Test (PASAT; Gronwall, 1977).

5. RETRIEVAL

Some TBI patients may experience retrieval deficits in the form of word-finding problems or difficulty accessing previously stored information. These deficits may be observed on tests of memory, confrontation naming, semantic category fluency, or semantic knowledge. Patients who demonstrate significantly improved performances with cuing or recognition testing may have primary retrieval deficits.

6. SYMPTOM VALIDITY TESTS

Patients who present with cognitive complaints may have conscious or unconscious motivations to perform poorly on neuropsychological tests. Given the complex presentation of TBI cases, understanding the patient's effort and motivation during testing is essential to interpretation of test results. This is important in all cases of TBI, but particularly for cases in which litigation or other nonorganic factors may influence performance.

Effort and motivation are commonly evaluated by means of symptom validity tests (SVTs). Most SVTs are simple, forced-choice memory techniques, such as (a) Portland Digit Recognition (Binder, 1993), (b) Hiscock Forced-Choice Procedure (Hiscock & Hiscock, 1989), (c) Forced-Choice Recognition Trial of the California Verbal Learning Test (CVLT–2; Delis, Kramer, Kaplan, & Ober, 2000), (d) Test of Memory Malingering (TOMM), (e) Computerized Assessment of Response Bias (CARB; Allen, Conder, Green, & Cox, 1999), and Word Memory Test (WMT; Green, Allen, & Astner, 2001). Severely impaired but well-motivated patients with neurological disease perform well on these measures. Patients who perform below expectation on SVTs may be motivated to perform at levels significantly lower than their actual ability, thus calling into question the validity of their cognitive test results. A more detailed discussion of SVTs and detection of poor effort on neuropsychological tests can be found elsewhere in this volume.

C. Assessing Sports-Related Concussion

Some have estimated that there are about 300,000 sports-related concussions every year in the United States. Concussions occur in nearly all contact sports at all levels of play, from intramural activities at schools to professional athletics. Assessment and management of concussion is important to prevent further injury and potentially cumulative neuropsychological deficits. The American Academy of Neurology's Quality Standards Subcommittee (1997) has provided practice parameters for the management of concussions in sports.

Although patients with sports-related concussion may be assessed clinically following the general model previously described for evaluation of mTBI, several test batteries and evaluation programs have recently been developed for the specific purpose of diagnosing and managing sports-related injuries. Most of these evaluation programs establish baseline levels of performance prior to play to provide comparison data in the event that an athlete later suffers a concussion. Data collected at baseline typically include demographic characteristics, medical history, history of developmental disorders, and rating scales of physiologic symptoms commonly experienced following concussion. Neuropsychological evaluation typically involves quick screening of cognitive domains most sensitive to concussion, such as information-processing efficiency, attention, and memory.

Paper-and-pencil and computerized methods are both currently available for the cognitive assessment of sports-related concussion; however, computerized assessments have gained immense popularity owing to their ease of use and speed of test administration and scoring. Most computerized programs offer multiple alternative forms to minimize practice effects and facilitate detection of reliable cognitive change during recovery from concussion. They also provide normative data to identify athletes with possible developmental disorders or athletes who may purposefully perform poorly at baseline to give the false appearance of rapid recovery on posttrauma testing.

1. STANDARDIZED ASSESSMENT OF CONCUSSION

One of the more widely used paper-and-pencil protocols is the Standardized Assessment of Concussion (SAC). The SAC screens for problems with orientation, immediate memory, concentration, and delayed memory. The measures take approximately 5 minutes to administer and are sensitive to the immediate effects of concussion, even in the absence of LOC or PTA. An electronic version of the SAC (eSAC) has recently been developed that can be administered on a personal, handheld computer. The eSAC is currently available only as a companion product to the Concussion Resolution Index (described in the following section).

2. CONCUSSION RESOLUTION INDEX

The Concussion Resolution Index (CRI; Erlanger et al., 2003) is an Internet-based computer program that assesses attention, working memory, learning capacity, and RT. The assessment takes approximately 25 minutes to administer, including completion of questionnaires related to medical history, physiologic symptoms, and so on. Normative data are currently available from over 400 adolescent and adult athletes. The CRI can interface with the eSAC (described in the previous section), so that the athletic trainer can provide a sideline assessment, if needed, and later synchronize those data with the athlete's CRI baseline.

3. IMMEDIATE POSTCONCUSSION ASSESSMENT AND COGNITIVE TESTING

The Immediate Postconcussion Assessment and Cognitive Testing (ImPACT; Lovell et al., 2003; Maroon et al., 2000) is a *Windows*-based computer program that assesses attention, working memory, RT, nonverbal problem solving, and response variability. It takes approximately 20 minutes to administer and also includes documentation of demographics, medical history, and physiologic symptoms. Normative data are available from over 900 adolescents and young adults on the neuropsychological screen. Separate norms are available for athletes with a history of Special Education. Norms for the ImPACT Postconcussion Symptoms Scale are available from over 2,300 high school and university students.

4. COGSPORT

CogSport is a stand-alone computer software program that measures RT to evaluate attention, working memory, new learning, incidental memory, adaptive problem solving, and spatial abilities (Collie, Darby, & Maruff, 2001). It was developed and normed in Australia, and it has recently been made available in the United States (www.cogstate.com).

5. AUTOMATED NEUROPSYCHOLOGICAL ASSESSMENT METRIC

The Automated Neuropsychological Assessment Metric (ANAM) is a computerized neurocognitive battery developed by the U.S. Army for baseline screening and serial assessment of Armed Forces personnel. It has been used for a variety of purposes, including assessing drug reactions and posturanium exposure. Although the ANAM was not developed specifically to assess concussion-related cognitive impairments, it has been used clinically with mTBI patients.

V. ASSESSMENT OF NONCOGNITIVE SYMPTOMS

In addition to cognitive deficits, assessment of TBI patients should include evaluation of noncognitive sequelae, such as the patient's level of awareness, physiologic symptom constellation, psychiatric symptoms, and psychosocial factors. Assessment of awareness and physiologic symptoms are discussed briefly in this section. Assessment of psychiatric and psychosocial sequelae is discussed in the following section.

A. Assessing Awareness

In cases of moderate and severe brain injury, patients may demonstrate unawareness or denial of changes in their cognitive, physical, or behavioral functioning (Prigitano & Schacter, 1991).

Relative unawareness of deficits has been associated with poor rehabilitation outcome and poor vocational success. One common method of assessing awareness in patients with moderate and severe TBI is the use of rating scales such as the Patient Competency Rating Scale (Fordyce & Roueche, 1986) or the Awareness Questionnaire (Sherer, Hart, & Nick, 2003). Typically, both the patient and a collateral informant (ideally, a family member) rate the patient's level of functioning across a variety of domains, such as the ability to prepare a meal, control emotion, attend to personal hygiene, and so on. The two sets of ratings are compared, and the discrepancies provide a measure of awareness. Discrepancies on measures of awareness may also provide an indication of the reliability of patients' self-reports regarding the nature of their injuries and their symptoms.

Assessment of awareness is typically not indicated in mTBI because patients are generally well aware of their deficits. In some cases, however, patients with mTBI may not fully recognize cognitive impairments until they have tried to resume previous activities or roles. Other mTBI patients may become overly vigilant to changes in their cognitive ability and may overreport the extent and severity of their perceived deficits. In such cases, discrepancies between patient and informant ratings on awareness measures may be significant in the opposite direction of that observed in patients with moderate-to-severe TBI.

B. Assessing Physiological Complaints and Symptoms

It is helpful to assess the frequency and severity of common physiological symptoms and complaints with formal symptom rating scales. Measures such as the Postconcussion Symptom Checklist (Gouvier, Cubic, Jones, Brantley, & Cutlip, 1992) and Postconcussion Symptoms Scale (Lovell & Collins, 1998) ask patients to rate the presence and severity of symptoms such as headache, nausea, visual disturbance, insomnia, and so on. It is important to note, however, that self-reported cognitive symptoms are only modestly associated with objective cognitive deficits on formal neuropsychological testing, and in some cases may be more strongly related to the patient's level of psychological distress.

VI. PSYCHIATRIC AND PSYCHOSOCIAL SEQUELAE

The emotional impact of head injury can often be devastating to victims and their families. Alterations of personality, mood, and behavior may be organically based, reactive to the trauma and its sequelae, or both.

A. Psychiatric and Psychosocial Sequelae of Moderate and Severe TBI

Psychiatric symptoms following moderate and severe TBI are usually of organic etiology. This does not exclude the possibility of additional reactive symptoms; however, such reactions are typically less prominent than organically based changes. Approximately two thirds of patients with moderate and severe TBI continue to demonstrate personality changes up to 10 years posttrauma. Although the severity of some of these changes lessens over time, the symptoms continue to be viewed by family members as significant.

1. PERSONALITY CHANGES

Alterations of personality following moderate and severe closed head injury typically reflect damage to frontal or temporal lobe regions, resulting in exaggerated, muted, or poorly regulated affect.

a. Frontal lobe personality changes

When the frontal lobe is injured, personality may change in one of two ways. Patients may become more activated and excitable than before the injury, or they may demonstrate markedly reduced activation.

1. Excitability can be manifested as (a) impulsivity, (b) emotional lability or mood swings, (c) socially inappropriate behaviors, or (d) immature behavior.
2. Symptoms of reduced activation include (a) apathy, (b) decreased spontaneity or abulia, (c) lack of interest, or (d) emotional blunting.

b. Temporal lobe personality changes

Damage to temporal lobe limbic structures following TBI is typically associated with episodic emotional dyscontrol, including the following:

1. episodic hyperirritability,
2. angry and aggressive outbursts, and
3. sudden onset of dysphoric mood states.

2. PSYCHIATRIC DISORDERS

Psychiatric diagnoses are more common in patients with moderate and severe head injuries than in the population at large. Some of the more frequent disorders are as follows:

 a. mania,
 b. paranoia,
 c. psychosis with predominantly negative symptoms (e.g., flattened affect, suspiciousness, social withdrawal), and
 d. depression with or without anxiety.

B. Psychiatric and Psychosocial Sequelae of mTBI

Fatigue, cognitive inefficiency, irritability, and physical discomfort owing to mTBI are often sufficient to produce dysphoric mood. Patients with mTBI may find that tasks that were once automatic require greater effort and concentration, and that the ability to perform or track multiple tasks simultaneously is limited, if not absent. Adjustment reactions to these cognitive changes are common and may develop into clinical syndromes of depression and anxiety if not addressed early. Without proper education about the natural evolution of mild brain trauma, patients may lose self-confidence, worry excessively about the long-term consequences of the injury, and become distressed by their own irritability and low frustration tolerance.

Other sources of stress that may contribute to dysphoric mood states include (a) diminished occupational performance and reduced sense of self-efficacy, (b) alteration of appearance from the injury, (c) role changes within the family or in other interpersonal relationships because of the injury, and (d) stressful interactions with insurance, medical, or legal professionals. It is important to identify any and all potential stressors and psychological symptoms, because these may exacerbate cognitive symptoms and contribute to the persistence of cognitive complaints beyond physiologic recovery of mild head injury.

VII. PERSISTENT POSTCONCUSSION SYNDROME

Approximately 10% of patients with mTBI will complain of postconcussion symptoms (PCS) more than a year following their initial injury. The etiology of persistent postconcussive complaints in patients with no obvious neuroimaging abnormalities is often difficult to determine. This difficulty arises in part because the majority of postconcussive complaints are non-specific in nature. In addition to potential organic etiologies, the role of other contributing factors, including comorbid and preexisting symptoms, substance abuse, developmental disorders, medication effects, psychological sequelae, and motivational factors must be considered when evaluating patients with persistent PCS.

A. Evaluating Nonspecific Symptoms

The majority of symptoms associated with PCS are nonspecific in nature (e.g., headache, dizziness, fatigue) and are readily endorsed by patients with other medical disorders, as well as by medically healthy individuals (Lees-Haley & Brown, 1993). Consequently, all potential sources of these symptoms should be ruled out, including the following.

1. COMORBID MEDICAL CONDITIONS

Other injuries and complications sustained at the time of the head injury, such as neck or back injuries, orthopedic injuries, and related pain syndromes, are important to assess. In general, studies indicate that individuals with significant additional peripheral injuries are more prone to develop persistent postconcussion symptoms.

2. PREEXISTING MEDICAL CONDITIONS

A variety of medical conditions may contribute to the development and persistence of nonspecific cognitive and physiological symptoms. Some of the more common preexisting conditions include the following:

    a. hypertension,
    b. diabetes,
    c. hypoglycemia,
    d. thyroid dysfunction,
    e. psychiatric disorder,
    f. pain disorders,
    g. previous concussion or brain injury, and
    h. sleep disorders.

3. SUBSTANCE ABUSE

The relationship between substance abuse and TBI is well documented. The physical and cognitive sequelae of abuse and withdrawal may confound the postinjury symptom picture of patients with a dual diagnosis of substance abuse and TBI. A review of symptoms and cognitive deficits typically associated with substance abuse can be found elsewhere in this volume.

4. DEVELOPMENTAL DISORDERS

A history of learning disability or attention deficit disorder should be ruled out, as these may result in subtle impairment of attention or new learning.

5. MEDICATION SIDE EFFECTS

Irritability, agitation, anxiety, drowsiness, dizziness, nausea, inattention, and memory complaints are common side effects of numerous medications. The examiner should be especially aware of any narcotic analgesic or anticholinergic medication use, as these preparations may be associated with changes in mental status.

B. Genetic Factors

Recent research has demonstrated a link between genetic phenotypes and outcome following brain injury. For example, possession of the e4 allele of apolipoprotein E (ApoE) adversely affects rehabilitation outcome. Investigations of the genetic aspects of TBI are currently in an early stage of development but hold promise for our future understanding of individual differences in outcome following head injury.

C. Psychological Factors

Adjustment disorders with depressed or anxious mood (or both) are common following TBI and may contribute to complaints of fatigue, irritability, insomnia, poor concentration, and impaired memory. Some have suggested that a history of childhood sexual or physical abuse may also predispose patients to develop mood disorders, somatic complaints, or cognitive complaints following head injury.

D. Motivational Factors

The question of secondary gain invariably arises when patients complain of persistent postconcussive symptoms. In one study, poor test performance was attributed to motivational factors in approximately half of study participants with PCS beyond 6 months postinjury (Youngjohn, Burrows, & Erdal, 1995). Assessment of patients who are planning or currently involved in litigation, or seeking compensation in some manner regarding the injury, warrant special attention with regard to motivation and effort.

The rewards of financial compensation following head injury are not the only potential motivations for persistent cognitive complaints and poor neuropsychological test performance. Brain injuries may elicit behaviors from others that serve to reinforce disability. It is therefore important to identify potential secondary gain derived from changes in the nature of interpersonal relationships at home or in the work environment.

Motivational factors may be conscious or unconscious. Although identification of possible motivational factors does not necessarily rule out organic cerebral dysfunction, understanding these factors can help the neuropsychologist discern a more accurate representation of the patient's true cognitive abilities. Careful observation of test behaviors and consistency of effort put forth by the patient throughout the assessment often provides clues to the role of motivational factors in test performance. Formal measures of motivation during testing were reviewed briefly earlier in this chapter and are discussed in greater detail elsewhere in this volume.

VIII. CONCLUSION

The neuropsychological sequelae of TBI vary greatly with the nature of the trauma, location and severity of brain involvement, and extent of secondary effects. Comprehensive assessment of TBI patients should begin with careful characterization of the circumstances and severity of the injury, with special efforts being made to obtain information from collateral sources, such as witnesses to the injury or emergency medical records. Neurodiagnostic data and information about focal neurological deficits are also important and may help inform and guide the evaluation. Patients with moderate or severe TBI commonly demonstrate diffuse cognitive dysfunction, with an overlay of more prominent focal or multifocal deficits. Patients with milder TBI and concussion tend to demonstrate selective impairments of information-processing speed and efficiency, often observed on measures of attention, executive function, learning, and retrieval. In addition to cognitive assessment, the evaluation of noncognitive features such as awareness of deficits, physiological symptoms, mood, personality change, and motivational factors is necessary to fully characterize the patient's level of functioning and to assist in treatment planning.

BIBLIOGRAPHY

Allen, L. M., Conder, R. L., Green, P., & Cox, D. R. (1999). *Computerized assessment of response bias.* Durham, NC: CogniSyst.

American Academy of Neurology, Quality Standards Subcommittee. (1997). Practice parameter: The management of concussion in sports [Summary statement]. *Neurology, 48,* 581–585.

Aubry, M., Cantu, R., Dvorak, J., Graf-Baumann, T., Johnston, K., Kelly, J., et al. (The Concussion in Sport Group). (2002). Summary and agreement statement of the First International

Conference on Concussion in Sport, Vienna 2001. *British Journal of Sports Medicine, 36*(1), 6–10.

Binder, L. M. (1993). An abbreviated form of the Portland Digit Recognition Test. *The Clinical Neuropsychologist, 7,* 104–107.

Brown, J. (1958). Some tests of the decay theory of immediate memory. *Quarterly Journal of Experimental Psychology, 10,* 12–21.

Cantu, R. C. (1986). Guidelines for return to contact sports after cerebral concussion. *Physical Sportsmedicine, 14,* 75–83.

Collie, A., Darby, D. G., & Maruff, P. (2001). Computerised cognitive assessment of athletes with sports related head injury. *British Journal of Sports Medicine, 35,* 297–302.

Colorado Medical Society. (1991). *Report of the Sports Medicine Committee: Guidelines for the management of concussion in sports.* Denver, CO: Author.

Congress of Neurological Surgeons. (1966). Committee on Head Injury Nomenclature: Glossary of head injury. *Clinical Neurosurgery, 12,* 386–394.

Delis, D. C., Kramer, J. H., Kaplan, E., & Ober, B. A. (2000). *California Verbal Learning Test* (2nd ed). San Antonio, TX: Psychological Corporation.

Erlanger, D. M., Feldman, D., Kutner, K., Kaushik, T., Kroger, H., Festa, J., et al. (2003). Development and validation of a Web-based neuropsychological test protocol for sports-related return-to-play decision-making. *Archives of Clinical Neuropsychology, 18,* 293–316.

Fordyce, D. J., & Roueche, J. R. (1986). Changes in perspectives of disability among patients, staff, and relatives during rehabilitation of brain injury. *Rehabilitation Psychology, 31,* 217–229.

Gouvier, W., Cubic, B., Jones, G, Brantley, P., & Cutlip, Q. (1992). Post-concussion symptoms and daily stress in normal and head injured college populations. *Archives of Clinical Neuropsychology, 7,* 193–211.

Grafman, J., & Salazar, A. (1996). Traumatic brain injury. In B. S. Fogel, R. B. Schiffer, & S. M. Rao (Eds.), *Neuropsychiatry* (pp. 935–946). Baltimore: Williams & Wilkins.

Green, P., Allen, L. M., & Astner, K. (2001). *The Word Memory Test.* Durham, NC: CogniSyst.

Gronwall, D. M. A. (1977). The Paced Serial Addition Task: A measure of recovery from concussion. *Perceptual and Motor Skills, 44,* 367–373.

Hiscock, M., & Hiscock, C. K. (1989). Refining the forced-choice method for the detection of malingering. *Journal of Clinical and Experimental Neuropsychology, 11,* 967–974.

Johnston, K. M., McCrory, P., Mohtadi, N. G., & Meeuwisse, W. (2001). Evidence-based review of sports-related concussion: Clinical science. *Clinical Journal of Sport Medicine, 11,* 150–159.

Kaplan, E. F., Goodglass, H., & Weintraub, S. (1983). *The Boston Naming Test* (2nd ed.). Philadelphia: Lea & Febinger.

Lees-Haley, P. R., & Brown, R. S. (1993). Neuropsychological complaint base rates of 170 personal injury claimants. *Archives of Clinical Neuropsychology, 8,* 203–209.

Levin, H. S., O'Donnell, V. M., & Grossman, R. G. (1979). The Galveston Orientation and Amnesia Test: A practical scale to assess cognition after head injury. *Journal of Nervous and Mental Disease, 167,* 675–684.

Lewis, R. F., & Rennick, P. M. (1979). *Manual for the Repeatable Cognitive–Perceptual–Motor Battery.* Clinton Township, MI: Ronald F. Lewis.

Lezak, M. D. (1995). *Neuropsychological assessment* (3rd ed.). New York: Oxford University Press.

Lovell, M. R., & Collins, M. W. (1998). Neuropsychological assessment of the college football player. *Journal of Head Trauma Rehabilitation, 13,* 9–26.

Lovell, M. R., Collins, M. W., Iverson, G. L., Field, M., Maroon, J. C., Cantu, R., et al. (2003). Recovery from mild concussion in high school athletes. *Journal of Neurosurgery, 98,* 296–301.

Maroon, J. C., Lovell, M. R., Norwig, J., Podell, K., Powell, J. W., & Hartl, R. (2000). Cerebral concussion in athletes: Evaluation and neuropsychological testing, *Neurosurgery, 47,* 559–671.

McCrea, M., Kelly, J. P., Randolph, C., Cisler, R., & Berger, L. (2002). Immediate neurocognitive effects of concussion. *Neurosurgery, 50,* 1032–1040.

Mild Traumatic Brain Injury Committee of the Head Injury Interdisciplinary Special Interest Group of the American Congress of Rehabilitation Medicine. (1993). Definition of mild traumatic brain injury. *Journal of Head Trauma Rehabilitation, 8,* 86–87.

Nell, V., Yates, D. W., & Kruger, J. (2000). An extended Glasgow Coma Scale (GCS-E) with enhanced sensitivity to mild brain injury. *Archives of Physical Medicine and Rehabilitation, 81,* 614–617.

Prigatano, G. P., & Schacter, D. L. (1991). *Awareness of deficit after brain injury: Clinical and theoretical issues.* New York: Oxford University Press.

Ruff, R. M., Niemann, H., Allen, C. C., Farrow, C. E., & Wylie, T. (1992). The Ruff 2 & 7 Selective Attention Test: A neuropsychological application. *Perceptual and Motor Skills, 75,* 1311–1319.

Sherer, M., Hart, T., & Nick, T. G. (2003). Measurement of impaired self-awareness after traumatic brain injury: A comparison of the patient competency rating scale and the awareness questionnaire. *Brain Injury, 17,* 25–37.

Smith, A. (1982). *Symbol Digit Modalities Test (SDMT): Manual* (Revised). Los Angeles: Western Psychological Services.

Stroop, J. R. (1935). Studies of interference in serial verbal reactions. *Journal of Experimental Psychology, 18,* 643–662.

Stuss, D. T., Stethem, L. L., & Poirier, C. A. (1987). Comparison of three tests of attention and rapid information processing across six age groups. *The Clinical Neuropsychologist, 1,* 139–152.

Teasdale, G., & Jennett, B. (1974). Assessment of coma and impairment of consciousness: A practical scale. *Lancet, 2,* 81–84.

Trennery, M. R., Crosson, B., DeBoe, J., & Leber, W. R. (1990). *Visual Search and Attention Test.* Odessa, FL: Psychological Assessment Resources.

Youngjohn, J. R., Burrows, L., & Erdal, K. (1995). Brain damage or compensation neurosis? The controversial post-concussion syndrome. *The Clinical Neuropsychologist, 9,* 112–123.

CHAPTER 15

Lisa A. Morrow

Neurotoxicology

In the United States there are over 60,000 chemicals in commercial use, many of which, such as lead, pesticides, and solvents, are known hazards to the human nervous system (Goetz, 1985). The clinical presentation of adverse cognitive and behavioral changes will depend on the type of exposure, as well as individual characteristics, although there is no specific pattern of cognitive deficits associated with individual chemicals (Hartman, 1995). That is, the neuropsychological impairments are generally diffuse, with deficits reported for memory, attention, visuospatial ability, motor speed, problem solving, and mental flexibility. Advances in neuroimaging have recently been suggested to be especially useful in assessing patients with a history of neurotoxic exposure (Haut et al., 2000; Morrow, Steinhauer, & Ryan, 1994). This chapter discusses parameters of exposure, the most frequently encountered neurotoxins, documentation of exposure, as well as neuropsychological and neurophysiological assessment techniques.

I. PARAMETERS OF EXPOSURE

There are four primary routes of absorption into the human body: inhalation, ingestion, dermal, and injection. The most common route of entry is through inhalation. Risk of exposure will be reduced with the use of protective equipment such as respirators, gloves, proper clothing, and fume hoods, but these measures do not always preclude a toxic exposure.

A. Acute Effects

Acute effects are distinguishable from chronic effects for most agents. For example, acute lead toxicity will produce gastrointestinal symptoms, whereas chronic exposure will result in central nervous system (CNS) and peripheral nervous system (PNS) changes, as well as disruption of hemoglobin synthesis. In the clinical setting, a patient will typically present with acute effects from a high dose of a chemical, usually in the context of an accidental spill or leak, or in cases of voluntary abuse (e.g., glue sniffing). Symptoms from an acute exposure may be confined to minor respiratory irritation or more severe neurological effects that range from incoordination to dizziness to convulsions, coma, and death. Research studies have suggested that an acute overexposure, as opposed to low-level chronic exposure, may place one at greater risk for increased neuropsychological deficits over time (Morrow, Steinhauer, & Condray, 1998; Pierce, Pecker, Tozer, Owen, & So, 1998).

B. Chronic Effects

Chronic effects are seen in people with a history of exposure over an extended time period. Typically, symptoms will not appear for years, but with the onset of neurobehavioral changes (e.g., memory impairment, motor slowing), deficits may be permanent and irreversible. There is some evidence that prior occupational exposure to neurotoxic chemicals may place one at greater risk for more progressive cognitive decline with aging (Schwartz et al., 2000) or development of dementia-type illnesses (e.g., Alzheimer's disease) in later life (Kukull et al., 1995).

II. FREQUENTLY ENCOUNTERED NEUROTOXINS

A. Heavy Metals

Lead and mercury are probably the most common heavy metal neurotoxins seen in clinical practice. Initial signs of **adult lead poisoning** are gastrointestinal symptoms, motor neuropathy, and generalized cognitive impairment. With very high lead levels, patients may display the classic "wrist drop." The most common way to establish lead concentration is to measure lead

in whole blood. For adults, current recommended levels are
< 25 µg/dl of blood. Initial presenting signs of **lead poisoning
in children** are changes in mental status, gait disturbance, and
onset of seizures. For children, the current recommended levels
are < 10 µg/dl of blood. Children will have higher lead levels
than adults in similar exposure situations, and lack of iron and
minerals in the diet and use of alcohol may increase lead absorption. General signs of encephalopathy (memory loss, irrational
behavior) may accompany both acute and chronic lead toxicity.
Common sources of lead exposure are shown in Table 15.1.

Symptoms of **mercury poisoning** were highlighted by the
"mad hatters" syndrome in workers employed in the early 20th
century in the felt-hat industry. Exposure to **inorganic mercury**
produces coarse tremor (hatter's shakes), salivation, motor
weakness, pain, vomiting, diarrhea, and renal failure. Personality changes—increased emotional tension and irritability (ere-
thism)—may begin before the motor changes. **Organic mercury**
exposure is associated with ataxia, dysarthria, neuropathy, deafness, excessive sweating and salivation, tremor, mental slowing,
and visual constriction. People exposed to mercury may also
report a metallic taste in the mouth, and a brown line may be
noticeable on the teeth. Neuropsychological effects may be the
first signs of mercury poisoning. Studies of people exposed to
mercury have documented changes across a number of cognitive
domains (memory, abstraction, visuospatial ability), and it has
been suggested that mercury levels be under 25 µg/m³ to avoid
neurotoxic effects (see Table 15.1 for the most common sources
of mercury exposure).

B. Organic Solvents

People with a history of acute or chronic solvent exposure (see
Table 15.1 for common sources) report a range of somatic and
neurobehavioral symptoms. The most common acute symptoms are headaches, nausea, dizziness, decreased attention and
concentration, and a general feeling of intoxication. Patients
with long-term chronic exposure often describe symptoms during exposure but remittance on exposure termination lasting a
few days or more. However, with continued chronic exposure,
symptoms such as headaches and dizziness may not diminish,
and patients may report the onset of memory and personality
changes. Many people with chronic solvent effects also state
that their symptoms seem to increase when they are in the
vicinity of noxious odors (e.g., gasoline). Threshold limit values
have been established for many individual solvents (Proctor,

Table 15.1. Common Sources of Exposure for Various Neurotoxins

Lead	Mercury	Organic solvents	Pesticides and insecticides	Carbon monoxide
Automobile manufacture, repair	Dentistry	Paints	Farming	Steel mills
Industrial and commercial painting	Farming	Varnishes	Landscaping	Coal mines
	Metal and electrical work	Glues	Contaminated food	Charcoal grills
Dentistry	Painting	Cleaning agents		Poorly ventilated appliances (furnace)
Brick making	Photography	Plastics		Car exhaust
Plumbing	Taxidermy	Textiles		Fire fighting
Explosives (lead-encased bullets)	Alcohol brewing	Pharmaceuticals		
Refinishing wood	Food (grain treated with fungicide)	Agricultural products		
Pottery				
Photography				
Chinese herbal medicines				

Hughes, & Fischman, 1988). Because of the short half-life of solvents (24–48 hours), it is very difficult to estimate body burden. Also, because solvents are highly lipophilic, there may be individual differences in absorption and clearance rates depending on the amount of fat tissue. If blood or urine samples are not taken within several hours of exposure, or if air sampling measures are not done or available from the workplace, the clinical interview (see next section) becomes the primary source for estimating duration, frequency, and dose of exposure. Prominent neuropsychological deficits are changes in memory, attention, mental flexibility, and psychomotor speed. Emotional changes are also common (e.g., depression), although studies show there is typically no correlation between psychiatric symptoms and neuropsychological performance (Morrow et al., 2000; Morrow, Ryan, Hodgson, & Robin, 1990).

C. Pesticides and Insecticides

Billions of pounds of pesticides are used each year worldwide (see Table 15.1 for common sources). Organophosphates are one of the most widely used pesticides, and the toxic CNS effects are produced by inhibiting acetylcholinesterase, thereby increasing acytelcholine levels. Acute neurotoxic effects of organophosphate poisoning include a "garlic" breath odor, salivation, lacrimation, excessive sweating, intestinal cramps, vomiting, fatigue, ataxia, bulbar signs, muscular fasiculations, and respiratory distress. Symptoms typically occur soon after exposure but may be delayed up to 12 hours. Poisoning is verified when serum cholinesterase levels are reduced by 10% to 50%. However, symptoms may occur with only a 30% drop when the exposure is quite rapid, or with chronic low-level exposure over time there may be a drop to 70% with no symptoms. Neuropathy may also occur, often with a delay, following organophosphate poisoning. CNS effects such as choreo-athetosis have also been reported. The toxicity of pesticides is complicated by the fact that many have various chemical stabilizers and may be mixed with other chemical agents, such as solvents. Although applicators have a high risk of exposure, risk of poisoning may be even higher in a nonoccupational setting (e.g., spraying in the home or office). As with other neurotoxins, moderate to severe cognitive and psychiatric changes have been reported following acute and chronic exposure. Reductions in motor speed and coordination are prominent neuropsychological findings, along with reductions in memory and visuoperception (Farahat et al.,

2003). Emotional disturbances, particularly anxiety, have been reported in people with pesticide poisoning.

D. Carbon Monoxide

Carbon monoxide (CO) is generated when organic compounds, such as wood and gas, are not completely burned (see Table 15.1 for sources). CO is rapidly absorbed in the lungs and has an affinity for hemoglobin that is 210 to 240 times greater than oxygen. The resulting carboxyhemoglobin (COHb) impairs oxygen transport to tissue and produces hypoxia. Cigarette smokers have higher levels of COHb (average 10%–15%) than nonsmokers (average 1%). Methylene chloride—a primary ingredient in paint remover—is metabolized to CO, and elevated COHb levels may persist longer from this type of exposure than from CO exposure alone. With exposure to CO at 4,000 parts per million (ppm) or higher, dizziness and weakness may be the only symptoms prior to lapsing into coma. With exposure to 500 to 1,000 ppm, headache, dizziness, weakness, and mental confusion will occur, and possibly hallucination. Levels of COHb exceeding 60% are usually fatal, whereas levels between 30% and 40% are associated with collapse and syncope. At around 25%, there may be headache, nausea, and cardiac changes. Symptoms are usually absent with levels below 15%. Body burden for CO may vary depending on factors such as exertion, circulation, and presence or absence of anemia. Although most reports suggest that patients with CO poisoning will have only transient neurobehavioral changes, there is evidence for a delayed neuropsychiatric sequelae following CO toxicity. That is, patients may manifest no symptoms for days or weeks following the exposure but then show a rapid change in cognitive function (e.g., aphasia, memory decline) and fairly severe psychiatric symptoms (e.g., psychosis; Smith & Brandon, 1970). White matter hyperintensities have been shown to be increased following CO poisoning and associated with cognitive impairments (Parkinson et al., 2002). Neuropsychological deficits have also been reported following long-term low-level chronic exposure to CO (Ryan, 1990).

III. DOCUMENTING EXPOSURE

When a patient is initially evaluated for a possible neurotoxic exposure, background information should be obtained from the patient as well as collaterals (e.g., spouse, coworker). This interview, which is outlined next, should gather as much information as possible concerning symptom onset, the work environment, and use of protective clothing. If the toxin is known, biological measures (e.g., heavy metal screen, COHb levels) should be assessed as soon as possible. Company records, if available, should be gathered, as well as the material safety data sheet (MSDS) for each suspected chemical. Finally, if the patient complains of changes in mental status, a neuropsychological evaluation is recommended as well as functional neuro-imaging or neurophysiological assessment. Because many chemicals may also involve the peripheral nervous systems, these tests may also prove helpful.

A. Interview

The most important information will likely be obtained from the clinical interview. Interviews with coworkers and family members may help to verify symptoms. The following is a list of questions we ask all patients who come to our clinic with a history of neurotoxic exposure. Whereas the majority of patients are exposed in the workplace, exposures can occur in the home as well (e.g., CO exposure), and questions should be modified to the environment where the exposure took place. Coexposures from hobbies (e.g., furniture stripping) should also be queried.

1. What type of work do you do and what are the work requirements?
2. What is your work setting like (e.g., work space, ventilation)?
3. What protective equipment do you wear and how often do you wear it (e.g., gloves—latex or cloth; respirator—mask, cartridge, airline; special clothing)?
4. What chemical(s) do you work with?
5. How long have you worked with each of these chemicals?
6. What type of contact did you, or do you, have with the chemicals (air, skin, ingestion)?
7. How often would you estimate that you come into contact with chemicals on the job (<5%, 5%–15%, >30%)?
8. How many days (or hours) has it been since you were last exposed to chemicals?
9. Was there ever any incident or accident when you were suddenly exposed to a large amount of chemical? If so, did you seek treatment?
10. What problems did you *first* notice following your exposure? Ascertain changes to physical well-being (e.g.,

headaches, fatigue), cognitive function (e.g., memory loss, concentration), and behavior (e.g., depression, anxiety).
11. What problems do you *now* have?

B. Estimating Body Burden

For many patients it will be difficult or impossible to establish **body burden**—the amount of chemical in tissue or blood. With the exception of some heavy metals, most chemicals are excreted from the body in a relatively short time. For example, solvents have a half-life of only 24 to 48 hours, and the half-life elimination of CO is approximately 5 hours when breathing air and around 90 minutes with administration of pure oxygen. Therefore, for most chemical exposures, unless urine or blood measures are taken very shortly after a tissue exposure, estimating body burden will be problematic. In rare instances, air monitoring may have been done at the worksite, and information regarding time-weighted averages or the level of exposure in terms of parts per million may be available. In many instances it is also difficult to determine the exact chemical, or mixture of chemicals, the patient was exposed to and what tests should be done. Often patients do not present for a neuropsychological evaluation until weeks or months following an exposure and may not know the chemical(s) they were exposed to. Patients who report a possible exposure should always be evaluated by a physician with training and expertise in occupational and environmental medicine.

C. Material Safety Data Sheet

All work sites are required to have an MSDS for any hazardous chemical on the property and to make this available to workers. MSDSs are not uniform and may look quite different, depending on the manufacturer. However, certain information is required to be contained in the MSDS.

- names used to identify the substance, including trade names and chemical names;
- a list of the hazardous substances and the chemical and physical properties of the chemical;
- fire and explosion data and the reactivity of the chemical;
- conditions to be avoided, as well as the general requirements for health protection (e.g., ventilation, respirators);
- adverse health effects that cover both acute (e.g., muscle weakness, drowsiness) and chronic (e.g., infertility,

cancer) effects for different exposure routes (e.g., inhalation, ingestion); and

- first-aid measures to treat overexposure.

IV. NEUROPSYCHOLOGICAL CHANGES ASSOCIATED WITH EXPOSURE

To a large extent, the neuropsychological profile of people with acute and chronic neurotoxic exposure is very similar, although as noted earlier, the presenting physical symptoms may be somewhat distinctive for different chemical agents. Generally, there is no specific pattern of impairment on cognitive tests, because most neurotoxic exposures will mimic an encephalopathy. As with most incidents of general CNS damage, prominent presenting symptoms are changes in personality and memory and attentional deficits (Morrow et al., 1990; Morrow, Kamis, & Hodgson, 1993; Morrow, Robin, Hodgson, & Kamis, 1992). Often patients report difficulty reading and "getting the right word out," but documented deficits in language function (e.g., frank aphasia) are usually absent. We find that because many of these patients are not profoundly impaired, and often have an estimated premorbid IQ that is average or above average, a battery utilizing sophisticated information-processing tests (Morrow, Stein, Bagovich, Condray, & Scott, 2001) or complex reaction time (Osterberg, Orbaek, Karlson, Bergendorf, & Seger, 2000) may provide the best measure of changes in neuropsychological function. The neuropsychological exam should be heavily weighted toward tests of learning, memory, attention, and concentration. Motor speed may also be reduced—from either CNS damage or peripheral neuropathy—and tests assessing reaction time should be included. Tests such as the Mini-Mental Status Examination or the Cognitive Evaluation Examination should be avoided because they will not be sensitive to subtle neuropsychological changes. Several batteries have been developed specifically for use with exposed patients. With the exception of a battery for use with acute CO exposure, the neuropsychological test batteries were developed for use in large-scale epidemiological studies or clinical assessment of patients with some type of neurotoxic exposure. For the most part, the majority of tests within the batteries are standard neuropsychological tests. A brief description of the most widely used batteries is outlined below, and the tests included in each battery are presented in Table 15.2.

Table 15.2. Neuropsychological Test Batteries

Neurobehavioral Core Test Battery (NCTB)	Neurobehavioral Evaluation System (NES)	Pittsburgh Occupational Exposures Test (POET) Battery	Carbon Monoxide Neuropsychological Screening Battery
Pursuit Aiming	Finger Tapping	Verbal Paired Associative Learning and Delayed Recall	General Orientation
Simple Reaction Time	Hand–Eye Coordination	Symbol–Digit Associative Learning and Delayed Recall	Digit Span
Digit Symbol	Simple Reaction Time	Incidental Memory	Trail Making Test
Benton Visual Retention—Recognition	Continuous Performance Test	Recurring Words	Aphasia Screening
Digit Span	Symbol–Digit Substitution	Wechsler Memory Scale	WAIS Digit Symbol
Santa Ana Dexterity	Pattern Memory	Visual Reproductions	WAIS Block Design
Profile of Mood States	Digit Span	Immediate and Delayed Recall	
	Serial Digit Learning	Embedded Figures Test	
	Paired Associate Learning and Delayed Recall	Grooved Pegboard	
	Visual Retention	Trail Making Test	
	Pattern Comparison	WAIS–R Digit Span	
	Vocabulary Test	WAIS–R Digit Symbol	
	Profile of Mood States	WAIS–R Information	
		WAIS–R Similarities	
		WAIS–R Picture Completion	
		WAIS–R Block Design	

Note. WAIS = Wechsler Adult Intelligence Scale.

A. World Health Organization Neurobehavioral Core Test Battery

The World Health Organization Neurobehavioral Core Test Battery (NCTB; Johnson, 1990) was conceived as a quick and economical battery of tests to identify neurotoxic effects. It is targeted for industrial and nonindustrial countries and is very brief: six tests focusing on visuospatial and visuomotor function and a brief self-report measure of mood state. Studies suggest that many of the individual tests can discriminate between exposed and nonexposed persons, but testing done in several European countries has shown a wide variation in test performance among the groups tested, suggesting limited use without appropriate normative data.

A computerized version of the NCTB has been developed with the addition of a visual learning test. The computerized battery, the Milan Automated Neurobehavioral System (MANS), has shown fairly good correlation with the paper-and-pencil version and was able to discriminate between people exposed to heavy metals and nonexposed controls (Cassitto, Gilioli, & Camerino, 1989).

B. Neurobehavioral Evaluation System

Now in its third revision, the Neurobehavioral Evaluation System (NES; Baker, Letz, & Fidler, 1985) was initially developed for use in epidemiological field studies of active workers at risk for developing neurobehavioral complications from workplace exposure. It is a computerized battery, with minimal interaction between the examiner and the participant. The battery includes more attention and memory tests than the NCTB, and it has been shown to be sensitive to neurobehavioral changes associated with neurotoxic exposure. The NES has also been translated into several languages. However, because the NES allows one to select certain tests and to tailor the administration on the basis of certain test situations (e.g., repeated testings), normative data must be collected for individual applications.

C. Pittsburgh Occupational Exposures Test Battery

The Pittsburgh Occupational Exposures Test Battery (POET; Ryan, Morrow, Bromet, & Parkinson, 1987) requires about 90 minutes to administer and was developed to be used primarily as a clinical assessment for individual patients with a history of neurotoxic exposure. It is heavily weighted to assessing learning, memory, attention, and mental flexibility. Normative data for 182 nonexposed blue-collar workers was collected, and factor analysis of the data revealed five cognitive domains: Learning and Memory, Attention and Mental Flexibility, Visuospatial Ability, Motor Speed and Eye–Hand Coordination, and General Intelligence. Means and standard deviations for men ages 21 to 59 have been published (Ryan et al., 1987). In addition, coefficients for age and education were derived for each test so predicted test scores could be determined and compared with established cutoffs for impairment. Published studies have shown that the POET battery is effective in discriminating exposed from nonexposed workers in both clinical and occupational settings (Morrow et al., 2001; Morrow, Steinhauer, Condray, & Hodgson, 1997).

D. Carbon Monoxide Neuropsychological Screening Battery

Messier and Meyers (1991) developed a brief battery of six cognitive tests to assist with evaluating patients who present to an emergency room with CO poisoning. A study comparing patients before and after treatment with hyperbaric oxygen and matched control participants who were tested twice found the test battery discriminated patients from control participants. Following treatment, the patients had improved test scores that exceeded expected practice effects. Use of a quick cognitive screening battery to detect subtle symptoms of acute CO poisoning may be particularly beneficial when deciding whether to implement hyperbaric oxygen treatment.

E. Recommended Tests for Use With Exposed Patients

The tests, or test battery, of choice for assessing exposed patients will depend on several issues, such as whether the person is presenting for a clinical evaluation or if testing is to be repeated over the workshift. The NES is probably the battery of choice if repeated testing is to be done (e.g., beginning and end of a workshift) and time is limited. The POET battery is probably best suited for clinical assessments, especially if the patient works in an environment in which he or she is exposed to harmful chemicals. We routinely use the POET battery in our clinic and supplement the battery with additional standard tests. Additional tests we find most useful are ones that assess complex information processing, divided attention, and working memory, such as the Paced Serial Addition Test (Gronwall, 1977) or the Four-Word Short-Term Memory Test (Morrow & Ryan, 2003). Subtests from the Wechsler Memory Scale—III, such as Mental Control and Orientation, are less likely to detect subtle neuropsychological changes in exposed patients. An assessment of psychiatric symptomatology should always be included. We typically use the Beck Depression Inventory—II, the Symptom Checklist 90—Revised, and the Millon Clinical Multiaxial Inventory (MCMI). The MCMI is particularly useful because it provides information for both Axis I and Axis II disorders and is much shorter than the Minnesota Multiphasic Personality Inventory (MMPI). Finally, as with any disorder that may produce cognitive and psychiatric changes, one must consider possible symptom enhancement. That is, there may be gains— primary or secondary—to patients if they are diagnosed with a cognitive impairment. There are a number of paper-and-pencil tests that have been developed to try to determine if a patient is malingering or exaggerating symptoms, although the tests are typically validated by asking control participants to "fake bad" (Rogers, 1988).

V. NEUROPHYSIOLOGICAL AND NEUROIMAGING TECHNIQUES IN EXPOSED CASES

To document quantifiable CNS damage in exposed patients, functional imaging techniques—including positron emission tomography (PET), single photon emission computed tomography (SPECT), and functional magnetic resonance imaging (fMRI)—may be particularly well suited for people with solvent and pesticide exposure. Several studies have noted decreased blood flow to both cortical and subcortical areas in solvent-exposed patients. Patients with neurotoxic exposure show a high rate of abnormality on SPECT, with the most common areas of decreased function seen in the temporal lobes, frontal lobes, basal ganglia, and thalamus. Magnetic resonance imaging (MRI) and computed tomography (CT) are less likely to show changes in patients with solvent and pesticide poisoning, although they will show the white matter changes associated with CO poisoning (lesions of the globus pallidus) and toluene abuse.

Psychophysiological measures (e.g., event-related potentials [ERPs], cardiac and pupil reactivity) have had limited use with exposed patients, but studies suggest these may be particularly sensitive to neurotoxic exposure (Morrow et al., 1994).

That is, impairment on neuropsychological tests may not be noted until deficits are clinically significant, but subclinical levels of impairment may be seen on ERPs. Work in our laboratory has shown that the P300 component of the ERP is significantly delayed in people with a history of solvent exposure (Morrow, Steinhauer, & Hodgson, 1992; Steinhauer, Morrow, Condray, & Dougherty, 1997). Both cardiac and pupillary measures have also shown abnormalities in this patient population (Morrow & Steinhauer, 1995) as well as other measures of autonomic nervous system function (Steinhauer, Morrow, Condray, & Scott, 2001). These measures may also be helpful in assessing cognitive function unconfounded by patient motivation.

VI. CONCLUSION

Patients with complaints of neuropsychological and psychiatric changes should always be interviewed regarding a possible exposure to neurotoxins. A neurotoxic exposure can occur in the home or workplace, and symptoms may have an abrupt or a delayed onset, depending on the chemical agent. The neuropsychological evaluation should be more than a brief screening and should focus on complex tests of learning and memory, attention, information processing, mental flexibility, and emotional function. Neurophysiological assessment and neuroimaging are also recommended, particularly if cognitive and physical symptoms do not subside.

BIBLIOGRAPHY

Baker, E. L., Letz, R., & Fidler, A. (1985). A computer-administered neurobehavioral evaluation system for occupational and environmental epidemiology. *Journal of Occupational Medicine, 27,* 206–212.

Cassitto, M. G., Gilioli, R., & Camerino, D. (1989). Experiences with the Milan Automated Neurobehavioral System (MANS) in occupational neurotoxic exposure. *Neurotoxicology and Teratology, 11,* 571–574.

Farahat, T. M., Abdelrasoul, G. M., Amr, M. M., Shebl, M. M., Farahat, F. M., & Anger, W. K. (2003). Neurobehavioral effects among workers occupationally exposed to organophosphorous pesticides. *Occupational and Envrironmental Medicine, 60,* 279–286.

Goetz, C. G. (1985). *Neurotoxins in clinical practice.* New York: Spectrum.

Gronwall, D. M. A. (1977). Paced Auditory Serial Addition Task: A measure of recovery from concussion. *Perceptual and Motor Skills, 44,* 367–373.

Hartman, D. E. (1995). *Neuropsychological toxicology* (2nd ed.). New York: Plenum Press.

Haut, M. W., Leach, S., Kuwabara, H., Lombardo, L. J., Whyte, S., Callahan, T., et al. (2000). Verbal working memory and solvent exposure: A positron emission tomography study. *Neuropsychology, 14,* 551–558.

Johnson, B. L. (Ed.). (1990). *Advances in neurobehavioral toxicology: Applications in environmental and occupational health.* Chelsea, MI: Lewis.

Kukull, W. A., Larson, E. B., Bowen, J. D., McCormick, W. C., Teri, L., Pfanschmidt, M. L., et al. (1995). Solvent exposure as a risk factor for Alzheimer's disease: A case-control study. *American Journal of Epidemiology, 141,* 1059–1071.

Messier, L. D., & Myers, R. A. M. (1991). A neuropsychological screening battery for emergency assessment of carbon-monoxide-poisoned patients. *Journal of Clinical Psychology, 47,* 675–684.

Morrow, L. A., Gibson, C., Bagovich, G. R., Stein, L., Condray, R., & Scott, A. (2000). Increased incidence of anxiety and depressive disorders in persons with organic solvent exposure. *Psychosomatic Medicine, 62,* 746–750.

Morrow, L. A., Kamis, H., & Hodgson, M. J. (1993). Psychiatric symptomatology in persons with organic solvent exposure. *Journal of Consulting and Clinical Psychology, 61,* 171–174.

Morrow, L. A., Robin, N., Hodgson, M. J., & Kamis, H. (1992). Assessment of attention and memory efficiency in persons with solvent neurotoxicity. *Neuropsychologia, 30,* 911–922.

Morrow, L. A., & Ryan, C. M. (2003). Normative data for a working memory test: The four word short-term memory test. *The Clinical Neuropsychologist, 16,* 373–280.

Morrow, L. A., Ryan, C. M., Hodgson, M. J., & Robin, N. (1990). Alterations in cognitive and psychological functioning after organic solvent exposure. *Journal of Occupational Medicine, 32,* 444–450.

Morrow, L. A., Stein, L., Bagovich, G. R., Condray, R., & Scott, A. (2001). Neuropsychological assessment, depression and past exposure to organic solvents. *Applied Neuropsychology, 8,* 65–73.

Morrow, L. A., & Steinhauer, S. R. (1995). Alterations in heart rate and pupillary response in persons with organic solvent exposure. *Biological Psychiatry, 37,* 721–730.

Morrow, L. A., Steinhauer, S. R., & Condray, R. (1998). Predictors of improvement in P300 latency in solvent-exposed adults. *Neuropsychiatry, Neuropsychology and Behavioral Neurology, 11,* 146–150.

Morrow, L. A., Steinhauer, S. R., Condray, R., & Hodgson, M. J. (1997). Neuropsychological performance of journeymen painters under acute solvent exposure and exposure free conditions. *Journal of the International Neuropsychological Society, 3,* 269–275.

Morrow, L. A., Steinhauer, S. R., & Hodgson, M. J. (1992). Delay in P300 latency in patients with organic solvent exposure. *Archives of Neurology, 49,* 315–320.

Morrow, L. A., Steinhauer, S. R., & Ryan, C. M. (1994). The utility of psychophysiological measures in assessing the correlates and consequences of organic solvent exposure. *Toxicology and Industrial Health, 10,* 537–544.

Osterberg, K., Orbaek, P., Karlson, B., Bergendorf, U., & Seger, L. (2000). A comparison of neuropsychological tests for the assessment of chronic toxic encephalopathy. *American Journal of Industrial Medicine, 38,* 666–680.

Parkinson, R. B., Hopkins, R. O., Cleavinger, H. B., Weaver, L. K., Victoroff, J., Foley, J. F., & Bigler, E. D. (2002). White matter hyperintensities and neuropsychological outcome following carbon monoxide poisoning. *Neurology, 58,* 1525–1532.

Pierce, C. H., Pecker, C. E., Tozer, T. N., Owen, D. J., & So, Y. (1998). Modeling the acute neurotoxicity of styrene. *Journal of Occupational and Environmental Medicine, 40,* 230–240.

Proctor, N. H., Hughes, J. P., & Fischman, M. L. (1988). *Chemical hazards of the workplace* (2nd ed.). Philadelphia: Lippincott Williams & Wilkins.

Rogers, R. (Ed.). (1988). *Clinical assessment of malingering and deception.* New York: Guilford Press.

Ryan, C. M. (1990). Memory disturbance following chronic low-level carbon monoxide exposure. *Archives of Clinical Neuropsychology, 5,* 59–67.

Ryan, C. M., Morrow, L. A., Bromet, E. J., & Parkinson, D. K. (1987). Assessment of neuropsychological dysfunction in the workplace: Normative data from the Pittsburgh Occupational Exposures Test Battery. *Journal of Clinical and Experimental Neuropsychology, 6,* 665–679.

Schwartz, B. S., Stewart, W. F., Bolla, K. I., Simon, D., Bandeen-Roche, K., Gordon, B., et al. (2000). Past adult lead exposure is associated with longitudinal decline in cognitive functioning. *Neurology, 55,* 1144–1150.

Smith, J. S., & Brandon, S. (1970). Acute carbon-monoxide poisoning: 3 years experience in a defined population. *Postgraduate Medical Journal, 46,* 65–70.

Steinhauer, S. R., Morrow, L. A., Condray, R., & Dougherty, G. (1997). Event-related potentials in workers with ongoing occupational exposure. *Biological Psychiatry, 42,* 854–858.

Steinhauer, S. R., Morrow, L. A., Condray, R., & Scott, A. (2001). Respiratory sinus arrhythmia in persons with organic solvent exposure: Comparisons with anxiety patients and controls. *Archives of Environmental Health, 56,* 175–180.

Chapter 16
Robert M. Bilder

Schizophrenia

Schizophrenia is a highly prevalent disorder, affecting some 1% of the population worldwide. This syndrome is one of the leading causes of disability among young adults. It is now recognized that substantial proportions of this disability and limitations in the potential for rehabilitation are mediated by pervasive and severe neuropsychological deficits. For several decades, pharmacological treatment with "conventional" antipsychotics (e.g., chlorpromazine, haloperidol, and fluphenazine) has done a good job of ameliorating the "positive" symptoms of schizophrenia (e.g., delusions, hallucinations), but these treatments provide at best partial normalization of neuropsychological deficits. "Atypical" antipsychotic agents (e.g., clozapine, risperidone, olanzapine, ziprasidone, quetiapine, and aripiprazole) may have comparable efficacy on positive symptoms and minimize some of the adverse effects associated with conventional treatments. There is a new spirit of therapeutic optimism that some of these agents yield cognitive benefits, and major efforts are underway to find new treatments for the cognitive deficits of schizophrenia. With these advances comes increased clinical and research interest in characterizing the cognitive deficits of schizophrenia and determining how these deficits may benefit from treatment. In the clinical assessment of schizophrenia, understanding the cognitive features of the syndrome may thus be particularly helpful in making appropriate treatment and rehabilitative, educational, and vocational plans.

I. DIAGNOSIS

The diagnosis of schizophrenia (according to the *Diagnostic and Statistical Manual of Mental Disorders,* 4th ed., text revision [*DSM–IV–TR*]; American Psychiatric Association, 2000) is based on clinical observation of characteristic symptoms (two or more from the following list):

- delusions,
- hallucinations,
- disorganized speech,
- grossly disorganized or catatonic behavior, and
- negative symptoms (e.g., affective flattening, alogia, or avolition).

There must also be a significant deterioration in work, interpersonal relations, or self-care compared with premorbid levels, and symptoms must have persisted for at least 6 months. The diagnosis also requires a series of rule-outs (see Section VI this chapter. Although specific consideration of neuropsychological deficits has been considered for revisions of the *DSM–IV–TR* criteria, so far the diagnosis is based exclusively on direct clinical observation of the patient and observations gleaned from collateral sources. From the neuropsychological perspective, it may be noted that there is usually little correlation between delusions and hallucinations and the neuropsychological profile. In contrast, prominent disorganization and negative symptoms have shown moderate correlations with neuropsychological impairment. It is also particularly useful for neuropsychological assessment to consider carefully the nature of deterioration and the degree to which this deterioration includes cognitive dysfunction as a mediator of the impairments in work, educational achievement, and social functioning.

II. DEVELOPMENTAL PROCESS AND ETIOLOGY

The etiology of schizophrenia is unknown. It is generally presumed that schizophrenia has a neurodevelopmental origin, but no specific etiology has yet been confirmed. There is a known genetic risk; for the monozygotic twin of an individual with schizophrenia the risk is about 50%, and for any first-degree family members of an individual with schizophrenia there is approximately a 10% likelihood of developing the syndrome.

There are also more subtle deficits in neurocognitive functioning, even among the nonschizophrenic family members of people with schizophrenia. The nature of the genetic contribution
remains unclear. There is consensus that polygenic contributions are most likely, and genetic linkage studies have yielded
multiple candidate genes.

The age of onset for schizophrenia is modally in late adolescence or early adulthood, but there is a broad spectrum of onset
ages from early childhood throughout the senium, with some
debate about whether early-onset and late-onset cases may comprise etiologically distinct syndromes. Some clinical signs of
illness may be apparent from birth. One series of studies showed
that infants who would later develop schizophrenia can be distinguished from their siblings who do not develop schizophrenia by examining behavior on home movies of first birthday
parties. Other data suggest there may be increasing social or
cognitive deficit in early adolescence, before any other signs of
the syndrome appear. The findings are sometimes difficult to
interpret, however, because the onset of psychotic symptoms
varies markedly, with some patients showing a gradual onset
of social isolation and dysfunction without any overt psychotic
symptoms and others showing an abrupt "break" from appar-
ently normal behavior to florid psychosis. In a study of "first-
episode" patients, for example, it was found that the average
duration from the first appearance of overt psychotic symptoms
to the time at which patients were hospitalized for treatment
was over 1 year, and more subtle signs of behavioral change
were often detected years previously (Bilder et al., 2000). There
does appear to be an association of earlier onset with greater
severity of neuropsychological deficits, and the pattern of deficits in early-onset cases is more likely to include deficits in verbal
abilities (Bilder et al., 1991).

III. SCHIZOPHRENIA "SUBTYPES"

The *DSM–IV–TR* subtypes of schizophrenia include the paranoid
type, disorganized type, catatonic type, undifferentiated type,
and residual type. There are also multiple course descriptors
that note whether the course is continuous, episodic (recurrent
episodes with or without residual symptoms), or single episode.
For reasons that remain unclear, the catatonic type of schizophrenia is less frequently observed today compared with the
era before the widespread use of antipsychotic drugs. Older literature generally suggested that cognitive deficits are less severe
in the paranoid type compared with other subtypes. There are

relations of illness course characteristics with cognitive deficit. Typically, early onset, continuous, or recurrent illnesses with residual symptoms have more severe cognitive deficit compared with later onset, single episode, or recurrent episodic illnesses without residual symptoms.

In the 1980s a distinction was made between Type I and Type II schizophrenia. The **Type I** syndrome was putatively characterized by more positive and fewer negative symptoms, good response to treatment, and relatively normal-appearing brain structure and cognitive function. The **Type II** syndrome was thought to be marked by more negative symptoms, poor treatment response, abnormal brain morphology, and more severe neurocognitive deficits. Although these broad distinctions are not without merit, it has become clear that there is enormous variability and that clear distinctions do not mark these two syndromes. A stronger case has been made for the distinction between **deficit** and **nondeficit** schizophrenia (Carpenter, Arango, Buchanan, & Kirkpatrick, 1999), and although it is clear that individuals with the deficit syndrome have more severe neurocognitive deficits, the pattern of deficits may not be distinctive.

IV. NEUROPATHOLOGICAL–NEUROCHEMICAL CORRELATES OF EACH VARIANT

Although there is persuasive evidence that schizophrenia is marked by pathological changes in brain structure and a diversity of neurochemical abnormalities that have been identified, none have yet proved to be either diagnostic or clearly related to neurocognitive profile or prognosis. In general, modest correlations have been observed between neurocognitive deficits and generalized markers of cerebral pathology, as observed in enlargement of the ventricular system, reduction in overall brain volume, or, more specifically, the reduction in cortical gray matter or specific subcortical and limbic regions. These correlations are not sufficiently robust to be useful in the assessment of individual cases. There is hope that future treatments may benefit from a pharmacogenomic approach. This would become possible if genetically meaningful subpopulations could be identified, each of which might benefit from specific drugs. For example, research suggests that a subgroup of patients may have a mutation in the promoter region of a gene coding for the alpha-7 subunit of the nicotinic acetylcholine receptor; this may be associated with specific neurocognitive deficits, abnormalities of hippocampal structure, and specific electrophysiological abnormalities considered a reflection of deficient sensory "gating" (Freedman et al., 2003). This could lead to new therapeutic approaches targeting those patients who would most benefit from nicotinic receptor modulation. Research is underway using similar strategies to identify new discrete phenotypes and the genes to which they may correspond, in hopes that new specific treatments will be discovered.

V. FUNCTIONAL NEUROANATOMIC CORRELATES

Considerable interest in schizophrenia research has centered on attempts to identify the pathological substrate(s) of the syndrome, and both functional neuroimaging and neuropsychological assessment have been prominent in these efforts. Multiple studies have focused on dysfunction of frontal lobe systems and their prominent projections to basal ganglia and temporolimbic targets. It has been difficult to determine unequivocally whether these dysfunctions are more likely attributable to specific regional deficiencies in key frontal, limbic, diencephalic, or striatal function, or whether a widespread neurochemical dysfunction (e.g., in the broad populations of brain cells that rely on N-methyl-D-asparate [NMDA] receptor function) may best account for these observations. Regardless of the cause, it is clear that people with schizophrenia tend to show marked deficits on functional measures usually associated with the integrity of these regions (e.g., deficits of executive and learning–memory functions are prominent), and functional neuroimaging experiments have repeatedly shown that patients either fail to appropriately activate relevant frontal and limbic regions or show excessive activation in these regions (which has been interpreted as inefficiency of the relevant neural networks).

Neuropsychologists should be cautious in drawing any conclusions about possible neuroanatomical substrates of functional deficits in schizophrenia, and similarly, avoid drawing functional conclusions if neuropathology has been documented in a particular case of schizophrenia, because the pathology is likely to be neurodevelopmental in origin and thus inferences based on evidence from "classic" lesion studies may be misleading. For example, although hippocampal volume deficits may be prominent in schizophrenia, there is little evidence that these volume reductions are linked to memory deficits, as might be suspected from the study of patients who have a history of normal development and then have focal lesions to the hippocampal region. Instead, it is suspected that the volume reductions in the mesiotemporal lobe may reflect altered connectivity between frontal and limbic regions, and thus the overall integrity of this integrated system may be compromised, affecting attentional or executive functions. In general, however, evidence of frank neuroanatomical compromise will not be apparent on routine clinical examination, because the deficits are usually subtle (e.g., volume reductions of 5% or even smaller), so neuroradiological reports will most often be negative or comment only on the appearance of the ventricular system or cortical cerebrospinal fluid (CSF) spaces being slightly enlarged with respect to expectations for age. If focal lesions are noted in frontotemporal or limbic regions, this may suggest that schizophrenia is not the most appropriate diagnosis, and every effort should be made to rule out other possibly treatable diseases.

VI. COMPETING DIAGNOSES

Because the diagnosis of schizophrenia is still based on clinical observation of characteristic psychopathological symptoms and their course, the neuropsychological exam is usually not critical to differential diagnosis. It is crucial, however, to rule out other possible causes of psychosis, and particularly in the initial diagnosis neuropsychological assessment may play an important role. Key rule-outs include psychotic disorder due to a general medical condition, delirium, and dementia. History is usually the key to making these determinations, and thus the neuropsychological examination of a patient for whom the diagnosis of schizophrenia is suspected must incorporate appropriate consideration of other medical disorders, including results of laboratory tests and physical examination. Neuropsychologists should consider the "typical" presentation and increase suspicion of psychosis explained by other medical conditions if the presentation deviates substantially from these expectations.

Although there is great variability, the "typical" presentation (a) involves generalized cognitive deficit with most striking deficits in memory, executive, and attentional functions but does not include focal or strongly lateralizing signs on the neuropsychological or neurological exam; (b) is more likely to involve a period of decline prior to onset of psychosis, and less frequently includes history of acute onset, without any deterioration in social, occupational, or vocational functioning; (c) may include auditory hallucinations along with hallucinations in other modalities, but hallucinations limited to visual, olfactory, gustatory or somatic modalities are rare; and (d) involves age of onset in late adolescence or early adulthood, with onset in early child-hood and late life being relatively uncommon.

VII. DIAGNOSTIC CLUES FROM MEDICAL HISTORY

Medical history is usually only of value in the negative, that is, by ruling out other medical causes of psychosis and schizophrenia-like symptoms. At the same time, it should be noted that the history of individuals who will go on to develop schizophrenia is often marked by subtle delays in neurodevelopmental mile-stones, including motor, language, and social skills develop-ment. Subtle generalized cognitive deficits may be noted, and academic problems are common. Some research has suggested that there are associations of schizophrenia with obstetric com-plications or maternal influenza infection (particularly during the second trimester of gestation), but these findings are seldom of use in individual case diagnosis or prognosis, and it is likely that only a small proportion of all cases may have neurodeve-lopmental disturbances caused by viral pathology. Great care should be exercised in the initial diagnosis of schizophrenia, however, to rule out possible associations with a broad range of systemic illnesses, because diseases affecting a diversity of organ systems can yield psychotic symptoms that may masquer-ade as schizophrenia. Diagnostic errors occur frequently in cases in which psychosis is caused by toxic–metabolic encephalopa-thies (including psychoses associated with drug or alcohol abuse) and delirium.

VIII. SENSORY, MOTOR, AND OTHER PHYSICAL SYMPTOMS

Schizophrenia may involve a broad range of subtle deficits in sensory and motor functioning. Formal testing typically reveals "soft" sensory abnormalities; for example, on tests of double-simultaneous stimulation in auditory, visual, or tactile modal-ities, extinctions are often found, although these tend not to aggregate strongly to indicate lateralized deficits. Olfactory sen-sitivity, and particularly olfactory discrimination ability, may be compromised. Tests of motor speed and dexterity uniformly reveal slowing and discoordination, although these deficits are usually comparable in magnitude to the degree of generalized cognitive deficit observed on other formal tests of memory and executive function.

IX. EEG AND NEUROIMAGING CORRELATES

There are no pathognomonic signs of schizophrenia on electro-encephalography (EEG) or neuroimaging, but there are clear abnormalities. Decreased magnitude of the P300 event-related potential is among the most consistent findings in schizophrenia research, and the frontal P300 may be particularly robust as a marker of genetic vulnerability to schizophrenia (Turetsky, Cannon, & Gur, 2000). Structural neuroimaging consistently has revealed increased ventricular size and increased sulcal CSF volumes, widespread decreases in the volumes of cortical gray matter, and decreases in the volume of the hippocampal formation, particularly in its anterior and middle lateral aspects (Narr et al., 2004). Several studies using diffusion tensor imaging (DTI) suggest that there may be decreases in fractional anisotropy consistent with abnormalities in white matter structure. Functional magnetic resonance imaging (fMRI) has revealed both decreased activations in response to cognitive challenges, suggesting failure of patients to marshal appropriate neural systems, and increases in activation thought to reflect inefficiency of neural systems and thus a need for excess recruitment.

Positron emission tomography (PET) imaging examining overall patterns of regional cerebral blood flow or cerebral metabolic rates during rest or cognitive activations has paralleled the findings from fMRI. PET imaging using specific ligands has suggested that there may be increased release of dopamine from presynaptic terminals in response to stimulant medications. Unfortunately, none of these methods has yet led to enhanced diagnosis or treatment of schizophrenia.

X. NEUROPSYCHOLOGICAL EXAMINATION

The neuropsychological examination of an individual with schizophrenia is usually most important for characterization rather than differential diagnostic purposes. The characterization of cognitive strengths and weaknesses may be particularly important for treatment and vocational planning. Because the average age of onset for schizophrenia is in late adolescence or early adulthood, assessment of an individual with schizophrenia of relatively recent onset often must consider educational planning as well. Given these goals, a broad assessment is typically warranted, which takes into consideration general intellectual abilities and academic skills, along with more specific neuropsychological abilities that are frequently found to be impaired

Exhibit 16.1. MATRICS Neurocognitive Domains and Candidate Tests

Working Memory
Brief Assessment of Cognition in Schizophrenia
(BACS)–Digit Sequencing
Wechsler Memory Scale—III Spatial Span
Wechsler Adult Intelligence Scale—III (WAIS–III) Letter-
Number Sequencing
University of Maryland Letter–Number Span
Spatial Delayed Response Task

Attention/Vigilance
3–7 Continuous Performance Test (3-7 CPT)
Continuous Performance Test—Identical Pairs (CPT–IP)

Verbal Learning and Memory
Neuropsychological Assessment Battery (NAB)—Daily
Living Memory
Hopkins Verbal Learning Test (HVLT)—Revised

Visual Learning and Memory
NAB–Shape Learning
Brief Visuospatial Memory Test (BVMT)—Revised

Speed of Processing
Category Fluency
Trail Making A
WAIS–III Digit Symbol-Coding
BACS Symbol Coding

Reasoning and Problem Solving
WAIS–III Block Design
BACS Tower of London
NAB Mazes

Social Cognition
Mayer-Salovey-Caruso Emotional Intelligence Test—
Managing Emotions
Mayer-Salovey-Caruso Emotional Intelligence Test—
Perceiving Emotions

(such as learning–memory, executive, attentional, visuospatial, and psychomotor abilities; see Exhibit 16.1).

The first aim of neuropsychological assessment in schizophrenia, as in assessment of other disorders, is to gain the fullest appreciation of the goals and current understanding of the patient, the family if involved, and the referral source. It is critical to determine the extent to which patient and caregivers are familiar with the disorder, its typical course, and its typical consequences. History taking may most fruitfully adopt the perspective of schizophrenia as a neurodevelopmental disorder, and frequently findings include early signs of developmental delay in motor, cognitive, social, or academic skills. It is not uncommon, however, for subtle deficits to go unnoticed by family members, and indeed a period of 1 to 2 years frequently elapses between the initial overt signs of psychosis and the time at which patients first come to clinical attention. It is also important to recognize that schizophrenia is a highly heritable disorder, with risk in first-degree family members that is approximately 10-fold that for unrelated individuals. Thus a comprehensive family history is often useful both in modulating clinical confidence in the diagnosis itself and in gaining understanding of the family network within which the patient may continue to live and draw support.

It should also be recognized that the overt signs of schizophrenia may not be apparent in family members despite the presence of cognitive impairment. Studies of cognition in the undiagnosed first-degree family members of people with schizophrenia reveal cognitive deficits that are intermediate between affected (diagnosed) and unrelated individuals.

The neuropsychological examination results themselves are most likely to show a pattern of generalized impairment across multiple cognitive domains, with most prominent deficits in verbal learning and memory, executive functions, and attentional functions, and relative sparing of basic reading–writing skills, vocabulary, and general information. On average, deficits range from one to two standard deviations below the appropriate norms for healthy individuals from similar sociocultural backgrounds. We have found that virtually all patients, including those with the least severe general cognitive deficits, tend to have relative weaknesses on tests of learning and memory, whereas patients with more severe global deficits tend to have additional relative impairments of executive functions (Bilder et al., 2000). More severe deficits in learning–memory, vigilance, and executive function have also been linked to poorer performance on a variety of social, vocational, and rehabilitative outcome measures (Green, 1996; Green, Kern, Braff, & Mintz, 2000).

A significant challenge for assessment and effective use of neuropsychological results is posed by difficulties that patients and their families may have in accepting the gravity of the usual prognosis. It is typical for individuals and their loved ones to be overwhelmed by a recent diagnosis of this lifelong and disabling disorder, and particularly given the efficacy of current treatments against the most florid symptoms of the syndrome, they may feel, after initial treatment and resolution of these symptoms, that there is no need for continued treatment and no need to proceed conservatively with respect to reengaging in stressful activities. A strong psychoeducational approach should therefore be advocated to increase patient and family understanding of the risks of relapse following medication discontinuation (which are severe and well documented, with more than 50% of patients likely to relapse within the first year of discontinuation, a rate approximately threefold higher than those who remain in treatment), and the likely effects of stress on relapse (which are probably moderate, although documentation of this is less robust).

XI. KEY NEUROPSYCHOLOGICAL MEASURES IMPORTANT TO DIFFERENTIAL DIAGNOSIS

As noted earlier, the neuropsychological examination is often less critical to differential diagnosis of schizophrenia than it is for characterization of deficits and formulating treatment plans. In general, a broad neuropsychological battery that includes measures of general ability and provides adequate measurement of memory, attention, and executive functions will be most informative with respect to clinical decision making. Measures of basic academic achievement are often important to help make decisions about appropriate educational plans and to determine which basic skills for independent living are available and which may require support. It is usually critical to go beyond the psychometric assessment of cognition and achievement to evaluate other features important to the capacity for independent living, and some scales have been developed recently to determine what impact deficits in cognitive functioning may have on activities of daily living and social–vocational adjustment (e.g., Clinical Global Impression of Cognition in Schizophrenia [CGI-CogS]; Bilder, Ventura, & Cienfuegos, 2004).

To the extent that differential diagnosis is important, the neuropsychological exam should include measures that can help rule out other focal disturbances of brain function. To the extent that this is important, more detailed assessment of lateralized sensory and motor functions is appropriate, and more detailed language examination may help rule out variants of aphasia that may masquerade as "formal thought disorder" (e.g., jargonaphasia or the "word salad" seen in Wernicke's aphasia).

The National Institute of Mental Health recently awarded a contract to the University of California, Los Angeles (Steven Marder, principal investigator; Michael F. Green, coprincipal investigator) to help, among other things, generate a consensus neurocognitive test battery that could be useful for clinical trials of drugs that may benefit cognition in schizophrenia. This project, titled "Measurement and Treatment Research to Improve Cognition in Schizophrenia" (MATRICS), has progressed through several stages, the first of which was to develop a consensus about the cognitive domains that would be important to measure, and then to determine which tests would be best to assess those domains. A study is currently underway to determine the psychometric properties of some of the leading candidate tests for each of the domains. The seven domains and 20 tests selected as candidates for this psychometric study are listed in Exhibit 16.1.

The ultimate goal of the MATRICS psychometric study is to narrow the range of candidate tests down to a single test for each domain, so that the total duration of the battery for assessing treatment effects can be limited to less than 90 minutes in duration. Whereas this battery or similar alternatives would not be adequate to provide the kind of assessment that would be helpful in either differential diagnosis of schizophrenia or treatment planning, it would provide a good summary of current cognitive functioning in an individual with an established diagnosis of schizophrenia and should serve well its intended goal—namely, to help clinicians document the effects of treatments (both psychopharmacological and rehabilitative or psychotherapeutic). Other instruments developed for brief, repeated assessment of multiple cognitive domains may offer similar value (e.g., the Repeatable Battery for Assessment of Neuropsychological Status [RBANS]; Randolph, Tierney, Mohr, & Chase, 1998). One brief battery has been assembled specifically for the assessment of cognition in schizophrenia (Battery for the Assessment of Cognition in Schizophrenia [BACS]; Keefe et al., 2004), and fully computerized batteries are available that provide similar series of tests for evaluating treatment effects in schizophrenia (Sharma & Bilder, 2004).

XII. PSYCHOLOGICAL/PSYCHIATRIC COMORBIDITY

It is interesting that many comorbid psychological conditions considered by some scientists to be prevalent in schizophrenia are typically ruled out by the current psychiatric nosology as manifest in the *DSM–IV–TR*. For example, depression, anxiety including prominent obsessive–compulsive or phobic components, and multiple personality disorders are unlikely to be diagnosed if the symptoms are "better accounted for" by the diagnosis of schizophrenia. Some specific personality disorders (schizoid, schizotypal, or paranoid) may presage the initial diagnosis of schizophrenia, but it remains unclear whether these are predisposing factors. It also remains unclear whether individuals who have the diagnosis of schizophrenia and who have comorbid mental disorder syndromes differ substantially from individuals who do not have these comorbid syndromes. Some have suggested that depression, obsessive–compulsive disorder, and panic disorders in schizophrenia are not only common but also important and independently treatable syndromes (Bermanzohn et al., 2000).

A major problem in schizophrenia is posed by comorbid substance use disorders. Smoking is extremely prevalent in schizophrenia, is associated with smoking-related health disorders, and thus may be an important component of the overall reduced life expectancy associated with this disorder (acknowledging that the rate of suicide is also elevated in schizophrenia and contributes to decreased life expectancy). Alcohol and drug use disorders also frequently complicate the diagnosis and management of people with schizophrenia.

XIII. TREATMENT ALTERNATIVES

The medical management of schizophrenia almost always involves the use of antipsychotic drugs. Many patients continue to receive what are widely referred to as **conventional antipsychotic drugs** or **neuroleptic drugs** (including haloperidol and fluphenazine). These drugs tend to have high potency as antagonists at the D2 dopamine receptor, and D2 receptor occupancy in the basal ganglia is often >80% at therapeutic doses. In the last decade, the so-called "atypical" antipsychotic drugs (clozapine, risperidone, olanzapine, ziprasidone, quetiapine, and aripiprazole) have seen increased utilization. These agents are called atypical primarily because they have lower liability for extrapyramidal side effects (primarily parkinsonian symptoms) compared with conventional agents. The atypical agents also have been proposed to have different mechanisms of action (i.e., due to their activity at serotonin, histamine, adrenergic, or cholinergic receptors), but so far the precise mechanisms of action responsible for antipsychotic efficacy remains unclear, and some suggest that variations in D2 dopamine binding may provide adequate explanation of all antipsychotic drug efficacy (Kapur & Remington, 2001).

Regardless of mechanism of action, research reports have suggested that there are cognitive benefits of treatment with atypical compared with conventional antipsychotic drugs. Recent evidence suggests, however, that this benefit may be relatively modest, particularly when the atypical antipsychotic drugs are compared with lower doses of conventional agents (i.e., average improvement of only about .25 standard deviation units, with respect to initial deficits that are about 1.5 standard deviation units below healthy comparison groups). There is no clear evidence of distinct cognitive advantages for one particular atypical agent compared with another, but so far few studies have focused on this possibility.

Multiple new avenues for adjunctive treatment specifically to enhance cognitive functioning in schizophrenia are under development. Some of the promising strategies include glycinergic modulation (i.e., addition of glycine, d-cycloserine, d-serine, or other agents capable of enhancing transmission in the NMDA receptor system) and cholinergic modulation (i.e., either by using cholinesterase inhibition or by modulating nicotinic cholinergic transmission). Other procognitive strategies are also being examined, including other forms of dopamine modulation (either by stabilizing DA neurotransmission using partial agonists such as aripiprazole or by using D1 receptor agonists), and some agents for which the mechanism of action remains obscure (e.g., modafinil, used for the indication of narcolepsy).

Nonpharmacological treatments are also being actively pursued, with some researchers using cognitive–behavioral psychotherapy and others applying more specific cognitive remediation strategies similar to those used for patients following known neurological insults. So far, however, there is no widely accepted treatment path for enhancing cognitive function in people diagnosed with schizophrenia, and individual design of treatment programs remains extremely difficult and largely limited by lack of adequate resources. The neuropsychological exam may benefit, however, from routinely checking several features of the current treatment algorithm for a given patient. First, it is well demonstrated that high levels of anticholinergic activity may have prominent adverse effects on learning–memory functions, and patients with schizophrenia, particularly those treated with conventional antipsychotic drugs, may receive anticholinergic treatments for control of parkinsonian signs.

Improvements in cognitive function can sometimes be affected by reducing the antiparkinsonian treatments (usually requiring a parallel dose reduction in the antipsychotic agent). Some patients may also be receiving higher doses of conventional antipsychotic drugs than are warranted on clinical grounds (the tendency in some practices is to increase the dose if symptoms do not respond well, and this is sometimes done despite lack of significant improvement in symptom control). Many patients, particularly those with "treatment-refractory" symptoms, also receive multiple different antipsychotic agents, or multiple antipsychotic agents in conjunction with mood stabilizers. Although some of these treatment regimens may be beneficial, their efficacy remains largely untested, and our clinical experience is that some patients show some improvement in cognitive function simply through simplification (elimination or reduction) of current pharmacological treatments. Of course, such treatment recommendations must be suggested and implemented only with greatest caution and attention to the possible adverse impact of psychotic symptom relapse, along with consideration of the possibility for suicide or other adverse consequences.

XIV. CONCLUSION

This chapter presents an overview of the diagnosis, possible etiologies, and epidemiology of schizophrenia. Approaches to the classification of the range of clinical presentations for this disease are described, as are the neuroimaging and other neurological correlates. The chapter also discusses recent attempts to improve on the neuropsychological assessment of patients with schizophrenia (e.g., the MATRICS initiative) and the range of currently available treatment options.

BIBLIOGRAPHY

American Psychiatric Association. (2000). *Diagnostic and statistical manual of mental disorders* (4th ed., text revision). Washington, DC: Author.

Bermanzohn, P. C., Porto, L., Arlow, P. B., Pollack, S., Stronger, R., & Siris, S. G. (2000). Hierarchical diagnosis in chronic schizophrenia: A clinical study of co-occurring syndromes. *Schizophrenia Bulletin, 26,* 517–525.

Bilder, R. M., Goldman, R. S., Robinson, D., Reiter, G., Bell, L., Bates, J. A., et al. (2000). Neuropsychology of first-episode schizophrenia: Initial characterization and clinical correlates. *American Journal of Psychiatry, 157,* 549–559.

Bilder, R. M., Lipschutz-Broch, L., Reiter, G., Mayerhoff, D., & Lieberman, J. A. (1991). Neuropsychological deficits in the early course of first episode schizophrenia. *Schizophrenia Research, 5,* 198–199.

Bilder, R. M., Ventura, J., & Cienfuegos, A. (2004). *Clinical Global Impression of Schizophrenia (CGI-CogS).* Unpublished manuscript.

Carpenter, W. T., Jr., Arango, C., Buchanan, R. W., & Kirkpatrick, B. (1999). Deficit psychopathology and a paradigm shift in schizophrenia research. *Biological Psychiatry, 46,* 352–360.

Freedman, R., Olincy, A., Ross, R. G., Waldo, M. C., Stevens, K. E., Adler, L. E., et al. (2003). The genetics of sensory gating deficits in schizophrenia. *Current Psychiatry Reports, 5,* 155–161.

Green, M. F. (1996). What are the functional consequences of neurocognitive deficits in schizophrenia? *American Journal of Psychiatry, 153,* 321–330.

Green, M. F., Kern, R. S., Braff, D. L., & Mintz, J. (2000). Neurocognitive deficits and functional outcome in schizophrenia: Are we measuring the "right stuff"? *Schizophrenia Bulletin, 26,* 119–136.

Kapur, S., & Remington, G. (2001). Dopamine D(2) receptors and their role in atypical antipsychotic action: Still necessary and may even be sufficient. *Biological Psychiatry, 50,* 873–883.

Keefe, R. S. E., Goldberg, T. E., Harvey, P. D., Gold, J. M., Poe, M., & Coughenour, L. (2004). The Brief Assessment of Cognition in Schizophrenia: Reliability, sensitivity, and comparison with a standard neurocognitive battery. *Schizophrenia Research, 68,* 283–297.

Narr, K. L., Thompson, P. M., Szeszko, P. R., Robinson, D. G., Jang, S., Woods, R. P., et al. (2004). Regional specificity of hippocampal volume reductions in first episode schizophrenia. *Neuroimage, 21,* 1563–1575.

Randolph, C., Tierney, M. C., Mohr, E., & Chase, T. N. (1998). The Repeatable Battery for the Assessment of Neuropsychological Status (RBANS): Preliminary clinical validity. *Journal of Clinical and Experimental Neuropsychology, 20,* 310–319.

Sharma, T., & Bilder, R. (2004). Standardisation and cross validation study of Cogtest—An automated neurocognitive battery for use in clinical trials. *European Neuropsychopharmacology : The Journal of the European College of Neuropsychopharmacology, 14*(Suppl. 3), S386.

CHAPTER 17

Stephen M. Sawrie

The Neuropsychology of Adult Neuro-Oncology

Intracranial neoplasms are classified broadly into two categories: (a) primary brain tumors, comprising cellular elements from the central nervous system (CNS), and (b) secondary, or metastatic, tumors, which arise from a non-CNS primary site. The overwhelming majority of metastatic tumors come from primary sites in the lung, breast, skin (melanoma), kidney, and colon. Primary brain tumors are classified by their predominant cellular constituent on light microscopy. The majority of primary brain tumors are of glial cell origin, including astrocytomas, oligodendrogliomas, ependymomas, and glioblastoma multiforme (GBM). Meningiomas arise from the meningothelial cells of the arachnoid, whereas neuroblastomas and medulloblastomas arise from neuronal elements. Germ cells give rise to the germinoma, teratoma, and craniopharyngioma, whereas the pituitary adenoma can arise from any of the endocrine cells in the pituitary gland. Finally, CNS lymphocytes and histiocytes can give rise to primary CNS lymphoma, a growing category in the era of HIV and organ transplantation.

I. EPIDEMIOLOGY

According to data derived from the National Cancer Institute's Surveillance, Epidemiology, and End Results program, there are approximately 18,000 cases of newly diagnosed primary brain tumors each year (Ries et al., 2003). This number has risen slowly over the past decade, primarily because of the aging population. The annual incidence for all malignant brain tumors in 2000 was 6.6 per 100,000 person per year. Men were higher at 8.0 than women at 5.4 across all races, and Caucasians were higher at 7.2 than Blacks at 4.1 across gender. Mortality rate in 2000 was 4.5 per 100,000 person across all races. However, mortality for people older than 65 years old was 18.0 compared with 2.7 for those under the age of 65. Five-year relative survival rates for all malignant tumor types across all ages from 1992 to 1999 was 32.8%. Survival rose to 61.8% for people under the age of 45 and fell to as low as 4.1% for those older than 75 years. The GBM and astrocytoma were most common, comprising a total of 62% of all primary brain tumors. Five-year survival rates were 6% and 34%, respectively.

II. GRADING AND CLASSIFICATION

Grading is based on the histopathologic features of a tumor biopsy sample, typically viewed under light microscopy. Several systems have been proposed to grade primary intracranial neoplasms. In 1949 Kernohan, Mabon, Svien, and Adson proposed a system that graded tumors based on histopathologic dedifferentiation rather than tumor type. In 1981 a new system was published (the St. Anne–Mayo system) that graded tumors based on the presence of four histopathologic features: nuclear atypia, mitotic figures, vascular/endothelial proliferation, and necrosis (Daumas-Duport & Szikla, 1981). The World Health Organization (WHO) published a classification and grading system in 1993 that was most recently revised in 2000. In this latest revision, the nomenclature for tumor diagnosis corresponds to histopathologic grade, classifying tumors by their biologic potential (Smirniotopoulos, 1999). Table 17.1 compares these three grading systems for astrocytic tumors.

The WHO Grade I juvenile pilocytic astrocytoma is generally considered a benign neoplasm and does not contain any of the four St. Anne–Mayo histopathologic features. The WHO Grade II astrocytoma may contain one of the four St. Anne–Mayo features, usually nuclear atypia, and can therefore be graded as I or II by the Kernohan and St. Anne–Mayo systems. The anaplastic astrocytoma (AA) contains two abnormal histologic features (usually atypia and mitosis), warranting a Grade III from WHO and St. Anne–Mayo, and Grade II–III by

Table 17.1. Comparison of Grading Schemes for Astrocytic Tumors

WHO designation	WHO grade	Kecnohan grade	St. Anne–Mayo grade	St. Anne–Mayo criteria
Pilocytic astrocytoma	I	I	Excluded	—
Astrocytoma	II	I, II	1	No criteria fulfilled
			2	One criterion: usually nuclear atypia
Anaplastic (malignant) astroctoma	III	II, III	3	Two criteria: usually nuclear atypia and mitosis
Glioblastoma	IV	III, IV	4	Three or four criteria: usually the above and necrosis and/or endothelial proliferation

Note. WHO = World Health Organization.

Kernohan. The GBM is almost universally graded as IV and is characterized histopathologically by at least three of the four St. Anne–Mayo criteria. Oligodendrogliomas and meningiomas are graded similarly based on the presence or absence of the anaplastic features mentioned earlier.

The gliomas, which comprise approximately 50% of all CNS tumors and up to 80% of all CNS malignancies, are often categorized as either low or high grade. High-grade gliomas (HGG) are WHO Grade III or IV and consist of the AA, anaplastic oligodendroglioma (AO), the anaplastic mixed glioma, and the GBM. Grade III and IV meningiomas are sometimes included in this category for research and clinical purposes. Low-grade gliomas (LGG) are WHO Grade I and II and consist of the juvenile pilocytic astrocytoma, the astrocytoma, the oligodendroglioma, and the low-grade mixed glioma. For research purposes, the Grade I and II meningiomas, pineal tumors, and pituitary adenomas are sometimes included in this group.

III. HISTORY AND NEUROLOGICAL EXAMINATION

The majority of patients with brain tumors seen by neuropsychologists have already been diagnosed, and therefore the records sent with the patient will include a detailed history and physical examination. To fully make use of these records, however, the neuropsychologist should be familiar with the significance of specific historical and physical findings. Furthermore, there may be the rare instance in which a patient is referred to the neuropsychologist for an evaluation of symptoms from an as yet undiagnosed brain tumor. For instance, a patient with an undiagnosed frontal lobe glioma might be referred for evaluation of possible depression and attentional complaints in the context of new-onset headaches. It would not be unreasonable to initially treat this patient for depression and tension headache. However, findings from a thorough neuropsychological evaluation might raise the possibility of neuroimaging in this patient. Knowledge of the clusters of signs and symptoms common in patients with brain tumors can guide the neuropsychologist in alerting the referral source to the potential need for further diagnostic workup.

A. The Current Complaint

A detailed history is one of the most valuable components in the initial workup of the patient with a brain tumor. Because over 80% of primary brain tumors comprise nonfunctional tissue (e.g., gliomas, meningiomas), most symptoms are caused by compression and resultant edema, giving rise to the so-called **space-occupying lesion**. However, certain tumors, particularly the pituitary adenoma, can give rise to specific symptoms secondary to the nature of the tissue composing the tumor. Because the presenting symptoms of a brain tumor can be subtle, it is appropriate to further characterize the current complaint. A good mnemonic for this is OPQRST, which stands for Onset, Palliative–Provocative features, Quality, Radiation, Severity, and Timing. Consider the initial complaint of headaches, which is the most common initial complaint from the patient with a brain tumor. Any new-onset headache should always include the possibility of some type of intracranial lesion in the initial differential diagnosis. A headache secondary to a space-occupying lesion is characteristically worse following any type of valsalva maneuver that could increase intracranial pressure (ICP). The pain is often described qualitatively in terms of "tightness" and "pressure," much like a tension headache, and is most often generalized. Head pain secondary to a brain tumor does not typically radiate. For instance, radiation to behind the eye is often more indicative of a cluster headache. Severity will vary but in most cases is severe enough to be the reason why the patient sought medical attention in the first place. Having the patient rate the pain on a scale from 0 to 10 with well-defined endpoints will allow the clinician to follow severity over time (e.g., headaches secondary to brain tumors often respond to steroids, and tracking severity can often provide a good clinical estimate of treatment effectiveness). Finally, the timing of the headache is diagnostic, with headaches secondary to a brain tumor characteristically being worse upon awakening in the morning.

Other presenting symptoms that are common with space-occupying lesions include new-onset seizures, syncopal episodes, nausea and vomiting, and dizziness. These symptoms require the same level of detailed exploration. Tumors comprising functional tissue, such as the pituitary adenoma (PA), can cause symptoms secondary to their specific endocrine functions. The prolactin-producing PA can cause amenorrhea and galactorrhea in premenopausal women, and impotence and loss of libido in men. The PA that secretes thyroid-stimulating hormone can cause symptoms of hyperthyroidism such as anxiety, tremors, diaphoresis, palpitations, and heat intolerance. The growth-hormone-producing PA can result in signs of acromegaly such as frontal bossing, thickened skin, skin tags, macroglossia, and macrognathia. The most common symptom is back pain, often secondary to kyphosis. Signs and symptoms of the corticotropin-secreting PA are consistent with Cushing's syndrome and include central adiposity, hypertension, abdominal stria, hirsutism, and glucose intolerance.

B. Possible Cognitive Symptoms

Cognitive symptoms secondary to brain tumors are quite variable and clearly depend on the location of the lesion. Frontal tumors can be cognitively silent, producing only psychiatric or personality changes. Disinhibition and apathy have both been described with frontal tumors. Executive dysfunction and higher order attentional difficulties can accompany frontal lobe tumors. Dominant temporal lobe tumors can cause an expressive aphasia, particularly if they are more anteriorly located. Episodic memory loss can also signal a dominant temporal lobe lesion. Parietal tumors, particularly those in the right hemisphere, can cause visuospatial dysfunction. Tumors near the

motor strip or its descending fibers can cause either focal paralysis or increased tone, whereas sensory strip lesions can cause
pain, temperature, and proprioceptive loss, as well as higher
order sensory deficits such as graphesthesias. Tumors in the
occipital lobe or anywhere along the occipital tract will cause
a visual disturbance. Bitemporal hemianopsia is characteristic
of a sellar mass that impinges on the optic chiasm. Disturbance
of primary occipital cortex typically results in a contralateral
homonymous hemianopsia, often with macular sparing. Disturbance of secondary or tertiary visual cortex can result in a variety
of agnosias.

C. The Neurological Examination

A normal neurological examination is the most common finding in patients with brain tumors. However, there are specific
neurological findings that either individually or together should
raise the suspicion of an intracranial mass. Perhaps the most
common exam finding is papilledema, indicative of increased
intracranial pressure. This finding alone should move intracranial mass to the top of the differential diagnosis. An asymmetry
in visual acuity is also of concern. Visual fields will be disrupted
for tumors affecting the optic tract. Meningiomas occasionally
impinge on the optic nerve, causing a monocular decline in
ipsilateral vision, whereas parietal, temporal, and occipital tumors might affect the optic tracts caudal to the chiasm, causing
a contralateral hemianopsia. Failure of bilateral simultaneous
stimulation in the context of normal unilateral visual fields is
consistent with a neglect syndrome, which often localizes to
the right parietal lobe. Opthalmoplegias can be indicative of a
brainstem tumor. A unilateral decline in audition can sometimes
signal an acoustic neuroma. In the motor examination it is
important to recognize any asymmetries in bulk, tone, and
strength. Increased deep tendon reflexes are indicative of an
upper motor neuron lesion, and in the context of increased
tone, decreased bulk, and decreased strength might be indicative
of an intracranial mass disrupting motor cortex or descending
fibers. A thorough sensory examination is particularly important
in the context of sensory complaints such as numbness, tingling,
or paresthesias. Typically, sensory deficits secondary to an intracranial space-occupying lesion are less well localized than a
spinal cord lesion. Deficits in higher order sensation, such as
graphesthesia, two-point discrimination, and stereognosis, can
be elicited from the patient with a tumor affecting sensory
association cortex. An ataxic gait or poor finger-to-nose can be

indicative of cerebellar compression or herniation secondary to mass effect or hydrocephalus.

IV. LABORATORY STUDIES

A thorough history and physical examination usually provide more valuable information than laboratory studies for the patient with an intracranial lesion and often lead directly to neuroimaging. However, sellar masses that interrupt the hypothalamic-pituitary axis can produce abnormal serum results. A chemistry profile will reveal electrolyte or glucose abnormalities common with these tumors. Prolactin, luteinizing hormone (LH), follicle-stimulating hormone (FSH), adrenocorticotrophic hormone (ACTH), cortisol, thyroid-stimulating hormone (TSH), and free thyroxine (FT4) should be considered if a pituitary adenoma or other sellar mass is suspected. A complete blood count (CBC) with differential can help rule out an infectious process such as an abscess. Coagulation studies such as prothrombin time (PT), international normalized ratio (INR), and partial thromboplastin time (PTT) can be helpful in ruling out hypercoagulable syndromes secondary to malignancy. A lumbar puncture is almost always contraindicated in the presence of a space-occupying lesion as it can induce herniation secondary to increased ICP.

V. NEUROIMAGING AND NEUROPATHOLOGY

A. Metastatic Lesions

The T1-weighted magnetic resonance imaging (MRI) with contrast is the diagnostic study of choice if one suspects a metastatic tumor. These lesions are characteristically located at the gray-white junction because of the density of blood vessels at this location. Postcontrast studies will demonstrate a ring enhancement surrounding the tumor. Often there will be multiple lesions. Biopsy will reveal the tissue of origin from the primary tumor.

B. Juvenile Pilocytic Astrocytoma

The Grade I juvenile pilocytic astrocytoma (JPA) is also well demarcated on imaging, with smooth borders. It is hypointense on T1 but enhances with contrast. It is hyperintense on T2-weighted imaging. Its histology is interesting. On a touch prep it is easy to see the extremely long cellular elements that are characteristic of a JPA. On high-power light microscopy, one can also find the characteristic elongated eosinophilic inclusions known as Rosenthal fibers.

C. Low-Grade Astrocytoma and Oligodendroglioma

The low-grade astrocytoma is hypointense on T1, but unlike the JPA does not enhance with contrast (see Figure 17.1). However, it is hyperintense on T2-weighted imaging. Characteristic histological features include pleomorphic nuclei, long fibrillary processes, and an absence of mitotic figures, necrosis, or vascular proliferation.

The low-grade oligodendroglioma is hypointense on TI and will not enhance with contrast. However, calcifications can be found in up to 50% of cases on computed tomography (CT). Light microscopy reveals the characteristic "fried egg" appearance comprised of small cells with a round nucleolus and clear cytoplasm.

D. Anaplastic Astrocytoma and Oligodendroglioma

The Grade III AA or oligodendroglioma can have a similar radiographic profile to the LGG. It can be well circumscribed, is hypointense on T1, does not usually enhance with contrast, but is hyperintense on T2-weighted imaging. However, histological features will include pleomorphism and increased cellularity with vascular proliferation, mitotic figures, and nuclear atypia.

E. Glioblastoma Multiforme

The Grade IV GBM often has a distinct radiographic appearance. The mass is typically quite large with a hypointense heterogeneity on T1. Contrast will often produce a variable ring enhancement due to vascular proliferation (see Figure 17.2). T2-weighted imaging typically reveals an even larger lesion due to the vast amount of edema. Midline shift is common. The histology is similar to the AA with the additional features of necrosis, even greater vascular proliferation, and sheets of tumor cells crowded along necrotic borders ("pseudopalisading").

F. Magnetoencephalography: Mapping of Functional Tissue

Magnetoencephalography (MEG) is a relatively new imaging modality that is being used in surgical treatment planning

Figure 17.1. T1-weighted magnetic resonance imaging (MRI) with contrast of patient with a Grade II astrocytoma. Notice how the tumor is hypointense and does not enhance with contrast. Mass effect is evident by the smaller size of the temporal horn of the right lateral ventricle. Circles represent coregistered magnetic sources localized from visual stimulation in the left visual field. Notice the location of the tumor relative to the magnetoencephalography (MEG)-localized right primary visual cortex.

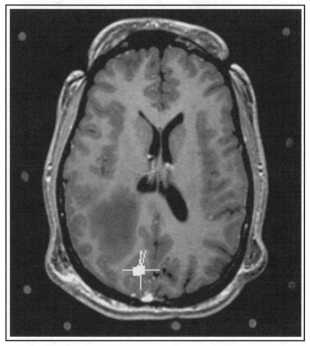

to localize functional tissue near a tumor based on magnetic flux recorded at the surface of the skull during repeated epochs of stimulus presentation. Figure 17.1 demonstrates localization of primary visual cortex in a patient with a Grade II astrocytoma. Figure 17.2 demonstrates the localization of magnetic sources secondary to somatosensory stimulation coregistered

Figure 17.2. T1-weighted magnetic resonance imaging (MRI) with contrast of patient with a glioblastoma multiforme (GBM). Notice the hypointense heterogeneity surrounded by variable ring enhancement. Circles represent coregistered magnetic sources localized from somatosensory stimulation of the left lip and the fifth digit of the left hand. Notice the location of the tumor relative to the magnetoencephalography (MEG)-localized sensory cortex.

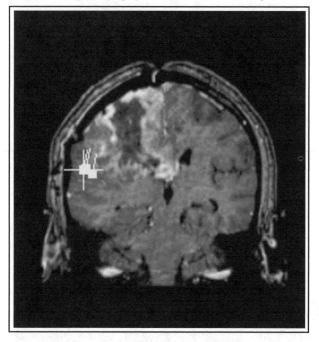

to an MRI of a patient with a GBM. These images can be used by the neurosurgeon to minimize resection of functional tissue while maximizing resection of tumor.

VI. OVERVIEW OF TREATMENT OPTIONS

According to the National Comprehensive Cancer Network Practice Guidelines in Oncology (v.1.2002), maximal safe resection is the initial treatment of choice for both LGG and HGG when possible. If resection is not possible, a stereotactic biopsy is usually performed to histologically grade the tumor. For patients with an LGG who undergo a full resection, radiation therapy (RT) versus close observation is recommended if older than 45 years of age, whereas close observation is recommended for younger patients. In the event of a subtotal resection or stereotactic biopsy, RT is recommended for control of symptoms. If asymptomatic, the patient and treating physician must decide between radiation or close observation. Highly conformal partial brain (rather than whole brain) RT is now considered standard of care when radiation is indicated. A lower dose of 50.4 Gy was established by Shaw, Arusell, et al. (2002) RT for LGG does not prolong overall survival but does increase disease-free survival at 5 years (Karim et al., 2002). The treatment algorithm is the same for patients with an AA or AO, except adjuvant treatment includes a regimen of procarbazine, CCNU, and vincristine (also known as PCV). The treatment of GBM may or may not include surgery, depending on patient factors such as age and comorbid medical conditions. Chemotherapy typically follows. Medical management commonly includes antiepileptics for seizure control and corticosteroids for treatment of peritumoral vasogenic edema.

VII. NEUROPSYCHOLOGICAL EVALUATION

A. The Referral Question

The nature of the neuropsychological evaluation for patients with a primary brain tumor depends largely on the referral question from the physician. Common referral issues in this setting are included in Exhibit 17.1. Because of the varied nature

Exhibit 17.1. Common Referral Issues for Patients With Primary Brain Tumor

1. Evaluate possible cognitive decline secondary to radiation therapy
2. Evaluate possible cognitive decline secondary to tumor recurrence
3. Evaluate possible neurotoxicity secondary to chemotherapy
4. Characterize cognitive status for rehabilitation program
5. Predict survival in high-grade glioma patient based on current cognitive status
6. Evaluate quality of life and psychiatric status for possible psychosocial/psychiatric intervention

of the referral issues, there is no "typical" neuropsychological battery for the evaluation of a patient with a primary brain tumor. For instance, the evaluation of cognitive status to guide a rehabilitation program will be somewhat comprehensive, whereas the evaluation to detect cognitive decline secondary to possible recurrence will likely be much more focused. Tumor location will also affect the selection of tests for a neuropsychological battery. A tumor involving the frontal lobe will emphasize executive function, whereas a tumor that encroaches on the dominant temporal lobe will emphasize tests of language and memory function. Figure 17.3 presents an algorithm based on recent studies of cognition and quality of life (QOL) in patients with primary brain tumors that is meant to guide the development of a test battery to best address the pertinent issues in each patient as a function of histological grade, time of diagnosis (recent vs. remote), surgical intervention, and adjuvant treatments such as RT and chemotherapy.

B. Evaluation of the Patient With Low-Grade Glioma

The nature of the evaluation of the patient with an LGG is influenced by the location of the lesion, recent versus remote diagnosis, surgical intervention versus close observation, and adjuvant therapy (e.g., radiation). Given these factors, there are four common issues that can be addressed in a neuropsychological evaluation.

1. REHABILITATION

If the patient has been newly diagnosed with an LGG, a comprehensive neuropsychological evaluation at this point can guide future rehabilitation of functional deficits secondary to the tumor, particularly if the lesion is in the dominant temporal lobe. This is based on a study by Hahn et al. (2003) demonstrating that patients with dominant-hemisphere primary brain tumors experience significantly greater dysfunction in memory, verbal fluency, verbal learning, and mood than their nondominant-hemisphere counterparts. Hahn et al. reasoned that these cognitive and emotional deficits could serve as the basis for tailored rehabilitation programs. Furthermore, a neuropsychological evaluation of the patient with a left-hemisphere tumor might reveal the need for medical interventions such as antidepressant therapy.

2. RECURRENCE

A baseline evaluation at the time of diagnosis is also important for the early detection of recurrence based on follow-up

Figure 17.3. Algorithm to guide the development of a test battery in the evaluation of the patient with a glioma. dx = diagnosis; RT = radiation therapy; AA/AO = anaplastic astrocytoma/anaplastic oligodendroglioma; GBM = glioblastoma multiforme; QOL = quality of life; PCV = procarbazine, CCNU, and vincristine.

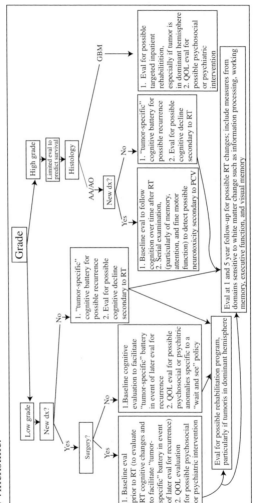

neuropsychological evaluations. Armstrong, Goldstein, Shera, Ledakis, and Tallent (2003) found that overall performance on an individualized follow-up evaluation based on a "tumor-specific" model could signal up to a fivefold increase in the probability of recurrence. In this study, patients underwent a comprehensive neuropsychological evaluation at the time of diagnosis that covered the domains of attention, information processing, motor control, verbal short-term memory, verbal associative and long-term memory, visuospatial short-term memory, visual associative and long-term memory, visuospatial perceptual processing, language, intellectual–conceptual function, and personality–mood status. From this baseline evaluation, Armstrong et al. used two rules to select up to five tests for a tumor-specific follow-up evaluation: (a) Each test must have a theoretical structure–function relationship relative to the patient's tumor location and (b) the patient must have demonstrated at least a one standard deviation impairment on the test relative to overall baseline performance (all baseline scores were standardized to z scores). The patient's performance on each of the tests comprising this tumor-specific model was then standardized to a z score, and an average of the z scores gave an overall indicator of follow-up performance. In their analysis, a decline of one standard deviation on this overall tumor-specific index was associated with a 400% increased chance of recurrence. This model, although somewhat unwieldy, can provide empirically based functional information to the referring physician regarding the possibility of tumor recurrence.

3. COGNITIVE EFFECTS OF RADIATION THERAPY

Whether or not conformal RT causes deleterious cognitive effects is still unresolved, with results appearing to differ on the basis of study design (cross-sectional vs. longitudinal) and duration of the study. In a cross-sectional, retrospective study by Surma-aho et al. (2001), the group receiving RT demonstrated significantly worse performance on an estimate of Wechsler Adult Intelligence Scale (WAIS) Performance IQ, Modified Benton Visual Retention (MBVR) first reproduction, and MBVR percentage forgotten. These findings remained significant after controlling for tumor grade, extent of resection, tumor progression, and RT type (whole vs. partial brain). In another cross-sectional study, Postma et al. (2002) found that cerebral atrophy predicted performance on measures of graphomotor speed, information processing, and memory, whereas white matter changes predicted performance in attention, information processing, and memory in 21 patients with LGG, 20 of whom had also undergone RT. In a 1996 longitudinal study by Vigliani, Sichez, Poisson, and Delattre, a sample of 17 patients with LGG who had undergone RT demonstrated significant decline on only 1 of 12 cognitive measures at 6 months post-RT and on none of the tests from Month 12 to 48, suggesting that the risk of cognitive decline secondary to radiation is low, at least up to 4 years following treatment. These results were essentially replicated in a recent 2-year longitudinal study of 17 patients with LGG who had undergone conformal RT (Torres et al., 2003). However, in a recently completed 6-year longitudinal study of patients with LGG who underwent RT (Armstrong et al., 2002), patients demonstrated a significant decline after Year 5 on the Continuous Performance Test and on four measures from the Biber Figure Learning Test (total, postinterference retrieval, delayed recall, and retention after delay). This suggested that (a) the cognitive effects of RT did not appear for at least 5 years following treatment, (b) these late effects were primarily in the areas of sustained visual attention and visual memory, and (c) previous longitudinal studies simply had not followed patients long enough to detect these late declines. Furthermore, when performance scores were standardized to z scores, it was found that between 20% and 67% of the sample demonstrated impairment of at least one standard deviation, depending on the measure. It is therefore my opinion that there is enough empirical evidence to warrant a baseline evaluation at time of diagnosis to facilitate a possible later evaluation of cognitive effects secondary to RT. The baseline evaluation should be comprehensive, with emphasis on the domains of visual attention and memory.

4. QUALITY OF LIFE

Quality of life (QOL) is becoming an increasingly important area of evaluation in patients with primary brain tumors (Weitzner, Meyers, & Byrne, 1996). This is particularly relevant for patients with LGG who often live for many years after the initial diagnosis. The current model of QOL is multidimensional, patient oriented, and disease specific. For this reason, I recommend the inclusion of the Functional Assessment of Cancer Therapy Scale—General (FACT–G; Cella et al., 1993) with the Brain subscale (FACT–BR; Weitzner et al., 1995). The 28-item FACT–G assesses the domains of physical, social, emotional, and functional well-being, as well as satisfaction with the treatment relationship. The FACT–BR includes the 28 items of the FACT–G, as well as an additional 20 items specific to patients with brain tumors. Inclusion of this scale in a neuropsychological battery can elicit specific concerns that patients with brain tumors are experiencing. In combination with a mood index such as the Profile of Mood States, this information can be used to direct the patient toward specific psychosocial and psychiatric interventions or services. It should be noted that a QOL/mood assessment is particularly important in the patient with a biopsy-proven LGG. One study found that patients with biopsy-proven LGG demonstrated significantly lower scores on measures of vitality, motor function, bladder control, and psychomotor function than patient with suspected LGG (i.e., those patients with imaging evidence consistent with LGG who opted to forgo surgery or stereotactic biopsy; Reijneveld, Sitskoorn, Klein, Nuyen, & Taphoorn, 2001).

C. Evaluation of the Patient With High-Grade Glioma

Many of the issues discussed in the evaluation of the patient with LGG also apply to the patient with HGG. For instance, a thorough QOL evaluation is equally important in patients with HGG versus LGG. The evaluation of cognitive effects secondary to radiation is less important given the shorter survival times of patients with GBM (although this may appear as a referral question for the patient with AA). Similarly, serial evaluation for possible recurrence becomes less important in the context of survival that is measured in months rather than years. However, tailored rehabilitation programs for patients with HGG are gaining popularity, and a thorough neuropsychological evaluation can provide vital information for individualized program development. More specific to the patient with HGG is the evaluation for neurotoxicity. Patients with LGG typically do not receive chemotherapy, and if they do it is usually in the context of tumor progression or recurrence. However, the current standard of care for patients with an AA or AO includes a regimen of PCV, which occasionally causes certain neurotoxic side effects that can be monitored in serial neurocognitive assessments.

1. REHABILITATION

Despite the variable nature of the functional deficits secondary to a malignant primary brain tumor, these impairments are similar to those commonly treated in general cancer rehabilitation programs (Marciniak, Sliwa, Spill, Heinemann, & Semik, 1996). In a study of 132 patients with primary and secondary brain tumors, gross cognition and motor function were measured at baseline and following an inpatient rehabilitation program using the FIM™ (Marciniak, Sliwa, Heinemann, & Semik, 2001). Mean cognitive and motor scores were equivalent across all tumor types at baseline and increased significantly by the end of the rehabilitation program. Furthermore, there was no difference between the LGG and HGG patients at baseline or in terms of change over time. This study suggests that patients with HGG benefit as much from an intensive inpatient rehabilitation program as their LGG counterparts. A thorough baseline neuropsychological evaluation can detect weaknesses that need to be addressed in rehabilitation, as well as strengths on which the rehabilitation team can capitalize.

2. PREDICTING SURVIVAL

Whereas detecting recurrence is less important in the patient with HGG, there is evidence to suggest that neurocognitive performance at time of diagnosis can be helpful in predicting survival. In a multivariate analysis of cognitive and clinical variables in patients with HGG, Meyers, Hess, Yung, and Levin (2000) found that a combination of clinical variables and performance on the Hopkins Verbal Learning Test, Digit Span, and Digit Symbol accounted for 49% of the variance in survival, which was significantly better than the 34% accounted for by the clinical variables of age, histology, diagnosis-to-treatment interval, and Karnofsky Performance Status (Karnofsky & Burchenal, 1949). Performance on these measures or ones similar to them might assist the patient and treating physician in evaluating the risks and benefits of participation in clinical trials or other novel treatments.

3. NEUROTOXICITY

As noted, the standard of care for patients with an AA or AO includes a regimen of PCV. A standard administration consists of CCNU 110 mg/m^2 on Day 1, procarbazine 60 mg/m^2 beginning on Day 8 for 14 consecutive days, and vincristine 1.4 mg/m^2 on Days 8 and 29 (Levin et al., 1980). A more aggressive approach is sometimes used, which increases the doses of procarbazine (75 mg/m^2) and CCNU (130 mg/m^2; Cairncross et al., 1994). Postma et al. (1998) found significant neurotoxic side effects in 4 of 26 patients with either AA or oligodendroglioma treated with the aggressive administration of PCV. Neuropsychological effects included memory disturbance, apathy, personality changes, and ataxia. Some of these signs and symptoms were reversible when administration was moved to a more standard dosing. However, some neurological deficits continued for months after discontinuation in three or four patients. Focal, serial neurocognitive assessment during aggressive administration of PCV can alert the treating physician to subtle developing neurotoxicity.

D. Clinical Trials

The field of neuro-oncology is replete with clinical trials, and it is not uncommon for a neuropsychologist to be asked to provide cognitive outcomes data in a new investigation. For instance, Meyers, Weitzner, Valentine, and Levin (1998) used a broad array of neuropsychological tests as primary outcomes measures in a study of the neurobehavioral and neurological effects of methylphenidate in patients with primary brain tumors. Shaw, Rosdahl, et al. (2002) presented data on the effect of donepezil on cognitive and QOL functioning in patients with primary brain tumors. Virtually every new chemotherapeutic clinical trial in patients with brain tumors will assess some aspect of cognition and QOL in outcomes analysis. These studies provide further opportunity for the neuropsychologist to participate in the care of patients with brain tumors.

VIII. CONCLUSION

Neuropsychological evaluation of patients with primary brain tumors has become increasingly prevalent over the past decade, particularly for patients with LGG who may live for years after initial diagnosis and treatment. Neuropsychologists should be aware of the common initial complaints of a patient with a primary intracranial lesion, as well as characteristics of neuro-imaging and the neurological exam. The neuropsychological evaluation can guide rehabilitation strategies, detect recurrence, predict survival, characterize cognitive change secondary to adjuvant treatments, characterize QOL, and inform potential psychosocial or psychiatric interventions. Finally, clinical trials of new cancer agents commonly require cognitive or QOL assessment in their comprehensive outcomes analysis, providing the neuropsychologist with the opportunity to contribute to the establishment of the standard of care for patients with brain tumors.

BIBLIOGRAPHY

Armstrong, C. L., Goldstein, B., Shera, D., Ledakis, G. E., & Tallent, E. M. (2003). The predictive value of longitudinal neuropsychologic assessment in the early detection of brain tumor recurrence. *Cancer, 97,* 649–656.

Armstrong, C. L., Hunter, J. V., Ledakis, G. E., Cohen, B., Tallent, E. M., Goldstein, B. H., et al. (2002). Late cognitive and radiographic changes related to radiotherapy: Initial prospective findings. *Neurology, 59,* 40–48.

Cairncross, G., Macdonald, D., Ludwin, S., Lee, D., Cascino, T., Buckner, J., et al. (1994). Chemotherapy for anaplastic oligodendroglioma: National Cancer Institute of Canada clinical trials group. *Journal of Clinical Oncology, 12,* 2013–2021.

Cella, D. F., Tulsky, D. S., Gray, G., Sarafian, B., Linn, E., Bonomi, A., et al. (1993). The Functional Assessment of Cancer Therapy scale: Development and validation of the general measure. *Journal of Clinical Oncology, 11,* 570–579.

Daumas-Duport, C., & Szikla, G. (1981). Délimitation et configuration spatiale des gliomas cerebraux [Definition of limits and 3D configuration of cerebral gliomas: Histological data, therapeutic incidences]. *Neurochirurgie, 27,* 273–284.

Hahn, C. A., Dunn, R. H., Logue, P. E., King, J. H., Edwards, C. L., & Halperin, E. C. (2003). Prospective study of neuropsychologic testing and quality-of-life assessment of adults with primary malignant brain tumors. *International Journal of Radiation Oncology, Biology, Physics, 55,* 992–999.

Karim, A. B., Afra, D., Cornu, P., Bleehan, N., Schraub, S., De Witte, O., et al. (2002). Randomized trial on the efficacy of radiotherapy for cerebral low-grade glioma in the adult: European Organization for Research and Treatment of Cancer Study 22845 with the Medical Research Council Study BRO4: An interim analysis. *International Journal of Radiation Oncology, Biology, Physics, 52,* 316–324.

Karnofsky, D. A., & Burchenal, J. H. (1949). The clinical evaluation of chemotherapeutic agents in cancer. In C. M. Macleod (Ed.), *Evaluation of chemotherapeutic agents* (pp. 191–205). New York: Columbia University Press.

Kernohan, J. W., Mabon, R. F., Svien, H. J., & Adson, A. W. (1949). A simplified classification of gliomas. *Mayo Clinic Proceedings, 24,* 71.

Levin, V. A., Edwards, M. S., Wright, D. C., Seager, M. L., Schimberg, T. P., Townsend, J. J., et al. (1980). Modified procarbazine, CCNU, and vincristine (PCV 3) combination chemotherapy in the treatment of malignant brain tumors. *Cancer Treatment Reports, 64,* 237–244.

Marciniak, C. M., Sliwa, J. A., Heinemann, A. W., & Semik, P. E. (2001). Functional outcomes of persons with brain tumors after inpatient rehabilitation. *Archives of Physical Medicine and Rehabilitation, 82*, 457–463.

Marciniak, C. M., Sliwa, J. A., Spill, G., Heinemann, A. W., & Semik, P. E. (1996). Functional outcome following rehabilitation of the cancer patient. *Archives of Physical Medicine and Rehabilitation, 77*, 54–57.

Meyers, C. A., Hess, K. R., Yung, W. K., & Levin, V. A. (2000). Cognitive function as a predictor of survival in patients with recurrent malignant glioma. *Journal of Clinical Oncology, 18*, 646–650.

Meyers, C. A., Weitzner, M. A., Valentine, A. D., & Levin, V. A. (1998). Methylphenidate therapy improves cognition, mood, and function of brain tumor patients. *Journal of Clinical Oncology, 16*, 2522–2527.

Postma, T. J., Klein, M., Verstappen, C. C., Bromberg, J. E., Swennen, M., Langendijk, J. A., et al. (2002). Radiotherapy-induced cerebral abnormalities in patients with low-grade glioma. *Neurology, 59*, 121–123.

Postma, T. J., van Groeningen, C. J., Witjes, R. J., Weerts, J. G., Kralendonk, J. H., & Heimans, J. J. (1998). Neurotoxicity of combination chemotherapy with procarbazine, CCNU and vincristine (PCV) for recurrent glioma. *Journal of Neurooncology, 38*, 69–75.

Reijneveld, J. C., Sitskoorn, M. M., Klein, M., Nuyen, J., & Taphoorn, M. J. (2001). Cognitive status and quality of life in patients with suspected versus proven low-grade gliomas. *Neurology, 56*, 618–623.

Ries, L. A. G., Eisner, M. P., Kosary, C. L., Miller, B. A., Clegg, L., Mariotto, A., et al. (Eds.). (2003). *SEER Cancer Statistics Review, 1975–2000*. Bethesda, MD: National Cancer Institute.

Shaw, E., Arusell, R., Scheithauer, B., O'Fallon, J., O'Neill, B., Dinapoli, R., et al. (2002). Prospective randomized trial of low- versus high-dose radiation therapy in adults with supratentorial low-grade glioma: Initial report of a North Central Cancer Treatment Group/Radiation Therapy Oncology Group/Eastern Cooperative Oncology Group study. *Journal of Clinical Oncology, 20*, 2267–2276.

Shaw, E., Rosdahl, R., Culbreth, M., Enevold, G., Naughton, M., Lovato, J., et al. (2002, November). *Phase II study of donepezil (Aricept) in cognitively impaired brain tumor patients*. Paper presented at the meeting of the Society of Neuro-Oncology, San Diego, CA.

Smirniotopoulos, J. G. (1999). The new WHO classification of brain tumors. *Neuroimaging Clinics of North America, 9*, 595–613.

Surma-aho, O., Niemela, M., Vilkki, J., Kouri, M., Brander, A., Salonen, O., et al. (2001). Adverse long-term effects of brain radiotherapy in adult low-grade glioma patients. *Neurology, 56*, 1285–1290.

Torres, I. J., Mundt, A. J., Sweeney, P. J., Llanes-Macy, S., Dunaway, L., Castillo, M., et al. (2003). A longitudinal neuropsychological study of partial brain radiation in adults with brain tumors. *Neurology, 60*, 1113–1118.

Vigliani, M. C., Sichez, N., Poisson, M., & Delattre, J. Y. (1996). A prospective study of cognitive functions following conventional radiotherapy for supratentorial gliomas in young adults: 4-year results. *International Journal of Radiation Oncology, Biology, Physics, 35*, 527–533.

Weitzner, M. A., Meyers, C. A., & Byrne, K. (1996). Psychosocial functioning and quality of life in patients with primary brain tumors. *Journal of Neurosurgery, 84*(1), 29–34.

Weitzner, M. A., Meyers, C. A., Gelke, C. K., Byrne, K. S., Cella, D. F., & Levin, V. A. (1995). The Functional Assessment of Cancer Therapy (FACT) scale: Development of a brain subscale and revalidation of the general version (FACT–G) in patients with primary brain tumors. *Cancer, 75*, 1151–1161.

Chapter 18

Pélagie M. Beeson and Steven Z. Rapcsak

The Aphasias

Aphasia is an acquired language impairment that results from neurological damage to the language areas of the brain, which are typically located in the left hemisphere. Also referred to as **dysphasia**, aphasia is characterized by impaired word selection, language production, and language comprehension. Incorrect word choice and sound substitution errors are common features of aphasic speech and are referred to as paraphasic errors, or **paraphasias**. Language comprehension deficits are present to some extent in all aphasias, but a subtle impairment may become apparent only when the patient is tested with syntactically complex sentences. Because aphasia is a central language impairment, it affects not only spoken language but also the comprehension and production of written language (i.e., reading and writing). Reading impairment is referred to as **alexia**, and writing disorders are labeled **agraphia** (or *acquired* alexia and agraphia to distinguish them from developmental disorders of reading and writing). The specific characteristics of aphasia and its accompanying deficits reflect the site and extent of neurological damage, as well as individual differences in brain organization. Various aphasia syndromes are characterized by identifiable constellations of language symptoms and provide a useful framework for the diagnostic evaluation of patients with aphasia.

Figure 18.1. Schematic drawing of the left hemisphere of the brain.

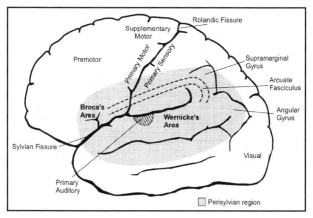

I. ETIOLOGY

The most common cause of acute aphasia is ischemic stroke (embolic or thrombotic) in the distribution of the left middle cerebral artery, which provides the main blood supply to the perisylvian cortical language areas (Figure 18.1). Other causes of acute aphasia include cerebral hemorrhage (hypertensive, or following the rupture of an aneurysm or arteriovenous malformation) and traumatic brain injury. In contrast, slowly progressive aphasia typically occurs with brain tumors and cortical degenerative disorders (e.g., aphasia associated with dementia of the Alzheimer's type or primary progressive aphasia). Transient aphasia may be associated with transient ischemic attacks (TIAs), migraine, and seizures.

Aphasia most often results from left-hemisphere lesions because about 95% of right-handed individuals and about 70% of left-handed individuals are left-hemisphere dominant for language. However, aphasia can occur following right-hemisphere damage in left-handed individuals; and, in rare cases, right-hemisphere damage in a right-handed individual results in what is called **crossed aphasia**.

II. FUNCTIONAL NEUROANATOMIC CORRELATES OF APHASIA

A. Perisylvian Versus Extrasylvian Lesions

Aphasia is most often caused by damage to the perisylvian language areas of the left hemisphere (see Figure 18.1). The perisylvian language zone includes Broca's area, which is involved in the motor programming of speech; Wernicke's area, which is critical for the auditory comprehension of spoken words; and the supramarginal gyrus and the underlying arcuate fasciculus, which links Broca's and Wernicke's areas and is thought to play an important role in repetition. Aphasia may also be caused by lesions that do not directly damage the perisylvian language areas but isolate them from brain regions involved in semantic processing and the production of volitional speech. The extrasylvian aphasias are referred to as **transcortical aphasias**.

B. Fluency

Aphasic speech production can be classified as either fluent or nonfluent.

- **Fluent aphasias** are characterized by plentiful verbal output consisting of well-articulated, easily produced utterances of relatively normal length and prosody (i.e., variations of pitch, loudness, rhythm). Fluent aphasias are associated with posterior (post-Rolandic) lesions that spare anterior (pre-Rolandic) cortical regions critical for motor control for speech.
- **Nonfluent aphasias** are characterized by sparse, effortful utterances of short phrase length and disrupted prosody. Nonfluent aphasias are associated with anterior, or pre-Rolandic, lesions that compromise motor and premotor cortical regions involved in speech production.

C. Auditory Comprehension

Auditory processing is defective in most aphasic patients, although the severity of the impairment varies with aphasia type. Anterior lesions result in relatively mild auditory comprehension impairments, whereas posterior lesions (especially if they involve Wernicke's area) result in significant impairment of auditory processing.

D. Repetition

Aphasia types differ with regard to the preservation of repetition ability.

- Repetition of spoken utterances requires an intact perisylvian region: posterior regions (Wernicke's area) for auditory processing, anterior regions (Broca's area) for speech production, and the critical connecting fiber tract (arcuate fasciculus). Therefore, lesions anywhere in the perisylvian region are likely to disrupt repetition.
- Extrasylvian lesions are characterized by preserved repetition despite severe reduction of spontaneous speech (transcortical motor aphasia), severe comprehension disturbance (transcortical sensory aphasia), or both (mixed transcortical aphasia).

E. Naming

All individuals with aphasia exhibit naming impairment, or **anomia**, usually in combination with other language deficits. However, naming impairment can also occur in relative isolation in patients with anomic aphasia. Because of its ubiquitous nature, anomia is considered the least useful localizing sign in aphasia.

III. ASSESSMENT OF APHASIA

The initial assessment of aphasia can be performed informally, as in the context of a bedside evaluation. A 15- to 30-minute interview that includes conversational interaction, as well as some structured tasks, is typically adequate to discern the presence or absence of aphasia, provide an estimate of the aphasia severity, establish a profile, and document the relative strengths and weaknesses of the patient (Exhibit 18.1). A more formal, in-depth assessment of aphasia is necessary for other purposes, such as designing a treatment plan, prognosticating recovery, and answering research questions.

A. Medical Chart Review

In addition to obtaining information about the patient's current and past medical history, the following information should be obtained, if possible:

- **handedness:** to anticipate possible exceptions to left-hemisphere dominance for language and to guide the assessment of writing in cases of hemiparesis (i.e., to determine whether writing will be assessed with the dominant or nondominant hand);

Exhibit 18.1. Key Questions to Consider When Examining for Aphasia

Is it aphasia?		
▪ Is the patient awake and alert with the intention to communicate?	Y	N
If not, assessment will be invalid.		
▪ Is there evidence of word retrieval difficulty (anomia)?	Y	N
Example: _____		
▪ Are there paraphasic errors?	Y	N
phonemic semantic neologistic		
Example: _____		
▪ Is there evidence of comprehension difficulty?	Y	N
Example: _____		
▪ Is the language impairment present across all modalities?	Y	N
spoken language auditory comprehension		
writing reading		
What is the aphasia profile? (Use decision tree in Figure 18.2.)		
▪ Is the verbal output fluent or nonfluent?	_____	
▪ Is auditory comprehension significantly impaired?	Y	N
▪ Is repetition significantly impaired?	Y	N
What is the communication status?		
▪ How severe is the communication impairment?		
mild moderate severe		
▪ Is the patient using compensatory strategies to achieve communication?	Y	N
gesture _____ writing _____		
drawing _____ other _____		

- **education and occupation:** to shape assumptions regarding premorbid language, reading, and writing abilities; and
- **vision and hearing status:** to determine the need for eyeglasses or sound amplification during testing.

B. Bedside Evaluation

To assess aphasia properly, one must ensure that the patient is awake, alert, and able to engage in interaction with the intent to communicate. If the patient has diminished responsiveness or is inattentive and uncooperative, the assessment for aphasia should be delayed because the performance of an obtunded, delirious, or confused patient will not provide a valid basis for language assessment. General measures of mental status, such as the Mini-Mental State Examination, are not appropriate for individuals with aphasia because of the dependence of these tests on language comprehension and production.

Bedside assessment should concentrate on four language tasks: production of conversational speech, auditory comprehension, repetition, and naming. A brief assessment of reading and writing should also be performed. Throughout the evaluation, the examiner should seek to discover the patient's successful communication strategies, as well as to reveal deficits. Particularly when the impairment is obvious and severe, the examiner should discern what level of assistance results in successful communication and how communication breakdowns are best repaired.

1. ASSESSMENT OF CONVERSATIONAL SPEECH

Begin the evaluation by conversing with the patient. While establishing rapport, listen for evidence of language impairment. Having reviewed the medical chart for background information, ask biographical questions that allow observation of the patient's ability to communicate. Ask open-ended questions to elicit a sample of connected speech. Picture description can also be used to elicit spontaneous speech. Obtain enough information to address the following questions:

a. Is there evidence of word-retrieval difficulty?

1. Are there word-finding pauses, hesitations, or self-corrections?
2. Does the patient show circumlocution, which means talking around the topic because of inability to retrieve specific words?

   (a) semantic circumlocution: "Hand me that thing over there, that thing for my nose, that wiper, you know, that . . ." [facial tissue] or
   (b) empty circumlocution: "It's for this one and that one, and one and two and three, and then boom, boom, boom . . . and I wish I could tell you." [target unknown].
3. Are there paraphasic errors?
   (a) verbal or semantic paraphasia: an incorrect word that may be related to the intended word in meaning (e.g., *he* for *she*),
   (b) literal or phonemic paraphasia: error of sound selection (e.g., *boap* for *boat*), or
   (c) neologism: a novel utterance that bears no obvious relationship to the intended word in sound or meaning (e.g., *kleeza* for *table*).

b. Is the output fluent or nonfluent?

1. Fluent aphasia is characterized by the following:
   (a) utterance length that is typically greater than four words and may approximate a normal range of five to eight or more words;
   (b) relatively normal speech prosody (i.e., pitch, loudness, and timing variations), although fluent utterances may be interrupted by occasional hesitations, word-finding pauses, and revised utterances;
   (c) articulation that is relatively facile and produced without struggle; and
   (d) conversational speech that is lacking in informational content and may sound "empty" because of a paucity of content words (e.g., nouns and action verbs) and an excess of grammatical functors (e.g., articles, prepositions, conjunctions) and indefinite words (e.g., "thing").
2. Nonfluent aphasia is characterized by the following:
   (a) reduced utterance length of typically less than four words; may be primarily single words;
   (b) halting speech lacking normal prosodic variations of pitch, loudness, and timing;
   (c) effortful articulation, although reactive or automatic responses may be surprisingly well articulated, such as "hello" or "fine" or "I don't know"; and
   (d) reduced grammatical complexity, with utterances consisting mostly of nouns and lacking function

words, resulting in agrammatic, or "telegraphic," speech.

2. ASSESSMENT OF AUDITORY COMPREHENSION

Auditory comprehension is typically impaired to some extent in all aphasias. A patient's ability to respond in a natural conversational exchange should be observed, but it is also important to evaluate responses to auditory–verbal information on more structured tasks. Response modalities may need to be adapted so that other impairments do not cause response interference (e.g., unreliable "yes" or "no" responses may require pointing to notecards printed with *yes* and *no* or + and –).

a. Sample tasks

1. word recognition ("Where's the phone?" "Show me the chair."),
2. commands of increasing complexity for the patient to carry out,
   (a) simple commands ("Make a fist."),
   (b) multistep complex commands ("Point to the window, the door, and then the pen."), and
3. yes/no questions of increasing complexity ("Do you live in Tucson?" "Do you close your umbrella when it starts to rain?").

b. Take note of the following:

1. At what point does auditory comprehension break down: single words, short commands, complex commands?
2. How does the patient respond to auditory comprehension difficulties? Are there requests for clarification or repetition? Is there a lack of awareness of the deficit?
3. If comprehension problems are mild, they may become evident only in difficult listening situations that require divided attention or under conditions of fatigue.

3. ASSESSMENT OF REPETITION

Although the ability to repeat spoken utterances has little communicative value, repetition tasks provide an assessment of speech input and output processes and have diagnostic value for aphasia classification and lesion localization. If repetition is severely impaired, and even single words are not repeated, emotionally laden words or phrases may evoke better responses (e.g., *money, I love you*).

a. Sample tasks

1. repetition of single words (e.g., *dog, apple, baseball*),
2. Short phrases (e.g., *a cup of coffee, salt and pepper, go for a walk*), and
3. Sentences of increasing length (e.g., *The telephone is ringing. He saw a very good movie. I had cereal, toast, and juice for breakfast.*).

b. Take note of the following:

1. Is repetition better or worse than spontaneous speech?
2. Does repetition break down at the single-word level or only at the sentence level?
3. Do repetition attempts result in the production of paraphasic errors?

4. ASSESSMENT OF NAMING

Although word-finding difficulties in spontaneous speech may suggest anomia, formal testing of confrontation naming allows direct assessment of the patient's ability to retrieve specific words. The extent of naming difficulty is a good general measure of aphasia severity. Select common objects in the room for naming, and if no errors are made, probe naming of less common objects. Individuals with aphasia typically exhibit a word frequency effect, in that more frequently used content words (e.g., *shirt*) are retrieved more easily than less frequent words (e.g., *collar*). Naming can also be assessed in response to questions, but they should probe relatively common knowledge and not be dependent on higher education or extensive vocabulary. Aphasia typically results in impaired confrontation naming regardless of the modality of presentation (visual, auditory, or tactile). Naming deficits confined to a single modality suggests recognition impairment or agnosia (see Section V).

a. Sample tasks

1. naming common objects: cup, watch, table, pencil;
2. naming of less common items: fingernail, collar, eraser;
3. responding to questions (What do you use to tell time? What color is an apple?);
4. naming to definition (What do you call the African animal with the long neck?); and
5. generative naming (Name all the animals you can think of in 1 minute. Name all the words you can think of that begin with the letter *S* in 1 minute).

b. Take note of the following:

1. What is the nature of the naming errors?
2. Are there paraphasic responses? What type?
3. Can the patient produce the word if given the first sound, that is, with phonemic cuing?
4. Is there any evidence of modality-specific impairment, such as naming difficulty when shown an object, but improved naming when allowed to hold the object?
5. Is there awareness of errors? Are there attempts to self-correct? Are those attempts successful?
6. Is the patient able to generate at least 12 to 15 animal names in 1 minute?

5. ASSESSMENT OF READING AND WRITING

A bedside evaluation of reading and writing is brief by necessity. Inquire whether the patient has attempted to read or write and what difficulties were experienced. Reading and writing abilities are generally impaired in aphasia. If reading and writing are spared, the patient may not have aphasia but rather a selective impairment affecting speech input or output processes (see Section V). If aphasia is mild, and the patient is not fatigued, a more extensive exploration of reading and writing may be performed to assess the type and severity of alexia and agraphia.

a. Sample tasks

1. Read aloud single words or sentences.
2. Carry out written commands.
3. Write single words to dictation. Include nouns, verbs, and functors. Also include words with regular (e.g., *bake*) and irregular (e.g., *choir*) spellings
4. Write a sentence or paragraph.

b. Take note of the following:

1. Is the patient able to read aloud? What kinds of reading errors (paralexias) are produced in oral reading? Are they visually similar to the target? Is the patient sounding out the word so that some errors are phonologically plausible? Are there more errors on words with irregular versus regular spelling? Is the patient spelling out the word letter by letter?
2. Does the patient comprehend written words? Sentences?
3. What is the nature of the spelling errors? Are they phonologically plausible (e.g., *kwire* for choir), suggesting

reliance on a phonological spelling strategy? Are they semantically related to the target (e.g., *apple* for orange)?
4. Are there motor difficulties that interfere with writing? If paralysis precludes use of the dominant hand, can writing be accomplished with the nondominant hand? Does the patient have difficulty forming legible letters even when using a nonparalyzed limb (i.e., apraxic agraphia)?

6. PRAGMATIC ASSESSMENT OF COMMUNICATION ABILITY

There can be considerable variation in communicative success by individuals with similar language impairments. Throughout the examination process, take note of the communication strategies used by the patient. First, note whether the patient is aware of the communication deficit. If so, what attempts are made to repair communication failures? Does the patient supplement spoken utterances with gesture or with attempts to write or draw? In the case of unintelligible or perseverative utterances, does the patient convey information through tone of voice and prosodic variations? What are the most successful communication modalities and strategies for this patient?

IV. CLASSIC APHASIA SYNDROMES

The performance profile that emerges from the brief language assessment can be used to assign patients to one of eight classic aphasia syndromes. Classification is achieved by a series of binary decisions regarding fluency, auditory comprehension, and verbal repetition as shown in Figure 18.2. Various aphasia syndromes have been used for over a century to communicate the profile of a patient. However, not all patients exemplify a classic aphasia type; in such cases, patients may be distinguished by their divergence from a given syndrome.

Although it is important to assess reading and writing abilities, performance in those modalities does not predict aphasia type. Oral reading performance often is similar to spoken language, and written language deficits may mimic the agrammatic or paragrammatic elements of spoken language. However, there is considerable variability within a given aphasia type regarding reading and writing ability. For that reason, a description of reading and writing abilities is not included in the following summaries of the clinical characteristics that constitute the classic aphasia syndromes.

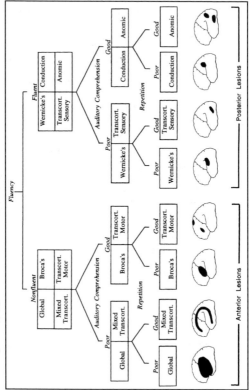

Figure 18.2. Decision tree for classification of aphasia on the basis of fluency, auditory comprehension, and repetition abilities. A schematic drawing of each of the associated lesion locations is shown for each of the eight classic aphasia types. Transcort. = transcortical.

A. Fluent Aphasias

Anomic aphasia is a fluent aphasia in which there is good auditory comprehension and repetition.

- **Conversational speech** is fluent, with normal utterance length and grammatically well-formed sentences. Word-finding difficulty in spontaneous speech may be evidenced by occasional pauses and circumlocutions.
- **Auditory comprehension** is good for everyday conversation, but there may be some difficulty with complex syntax or in difficult listening situations, such as those that require divided attention.
- **Repetition** is generally preserved even for full-length sentences.
- **Naming** impairment, in the absence of other significant language deficits, is the hallmark of this aphasia type.
- **Lesion location.** Lesions in *acute* anomic aphasia are usually located outside the perisylvian language zone and involve the angular gyrus or the inferior temporal region. Moderate and mild aphasias of various types caused by perisylvian lesions may evolve to *chronic* anomic aphasia. Generalized effects of head trauma, Alzheimer's disease, and increased intracranial pressure associated with brain tumor can also result in anomia; therefore, except in cases of acute anomic aphasia, anomia has limited localizing value.
- **Accompanying deficits.** Anomic aphasia often exists without significant concomitant neurological deficits, but when caused by lesions of the angular gyrus, it may be associated with the Gerstmann syndrome (finger agnosia, acalculia, agraphia, left-right confusion) and limb apraxia. Significant impairment of reading and spelling may accompany anomia because of damage to left posterior temporo-parieto-occipital regions.
- **Prognosis.** Acute anomic aphasia frequently resolves to minimal language impairment in the form of occasional word-finding difficulty. Anomic aphasia is the most common evolutionary endpoint for mild-to-moderate aphasia of all types.

Conduction aphasia is a fluent aphasia in which there is good comprehension but poor repetition.

- **Conversational speech** is fluent with relatively normal utterance length but is marred by paraphasias. Phonemic paraphasic errors predominate, and self-correction attempts may result in increasingly closer phonological approximations of the desired word, referred to as *conduit d'approche*. Rate of speech may be slowed by word-finding problems and attempts to self-monitor, but the overall prosodic pattern is akin to normal. Despite word-finding difficulties and paraphasias, spontaneous speech is much more meaningful than in Wernicke's aphasia.

- **Auditory comprehension** is relatively good for casual conversation. Single-word comprehension is well preserved, but patients may have difficulty with complex syntax or multistep commands.
- **Repetition** impairment is the hallmark of conduction aphasia, despite relatively good spontaneous speech. Paraphasias tend to be particularly prominent during repetition tasks. In severe cases, patients may not be able to repeat even single words. In milder cases, single-word repetition is possible, but phrase or sentence repetition is impaired. Repetition of unfamiliar or meaningless items is especially difficult. In some cases, attempts at sentence repetition may result in semantic restatements rather than verbatim repetition (e.g., "He's gone" for "He is not coming back").
- **Naming** is always impaired. Paraphasic errors are not uncommon and are typically phonemic.
- **Lesion location**. Conduction aphasia results from posterior perisylvian lesions affecting primarily the supramarginal gyrus in the parietal lobe and the underlying white matter (arcuate fasciculus).
- **Associated deficits**. Conduction aphasia is not associated with significant motor deficit, but cortical sensory loss affecting the right side of the body may be present. Limb and buccofacial apraxia are not uncommon.
- **Prognosis**. Conduction aphasia may persist or may evolve into anomic aphasia.

Transcortical sensory aphasia (TcSA) is a fluent aphasia with impaired comprehension and preserved repetition.

- **Conversational speech** is fluent with relatively normal utterance length, but semantic paraphasias, word-finding difficulties, and circumlocutions are common. Verbal output may sound similar to that of Wernicke's aphasia in that utterances may be semantically empty because of a lack of content words and overuse of functors and imprecise words, but output is generally not as voluble as in Wernicke's aphasia.

- **Auditory comprehension** is significantly impaired, although usually not to the extent seen in Wernicke's aphasia.
- **Repetition** is surprisingly preserved, sometimes even for long complex utterances and unfamiliar words. Patients repeat words and sentences without evidence of comprehension and may spontaneously correct minor grammatical violations. At times, repetition cannot be inhibited (echolalia).
- **Naming** is severely impaired.
- **Lesion location.** TcSA most commonly results from extrasylvian lesions involving the temporo-parietal-occipital region, typically located posterior and deep to Wernicke's area. This posterior region is in the watershed zone between the posterior and middle cerebral artery territories. In a smaller number of cases, TcSA follows lesions of the parieto-occipital convexity. Preservation of Wernicke's area and connections to anterior motor speech regions allow for repetition to be spared in TcSA. Alzheimer's disease can also result in a TcSA profile.
- **Accompanying deficits.** TcSA may be accompanied by right hemianopia and right hemisensory loss.
- **Prognosis.** TcSA due to stroke may evolve to anomic aphasia. TcSA associated with dementing disease may progress to Wernicke's aphasia over time and ultimately to global aphasia.

Wernicke's aphasia is a fluent aphasia with poor auditory comprehension and repetition.

- **Conversational speech** is fluent, easily articulated speech of relatively normal utterance length. Abundant semantic and phonemic paraphasias are present, as well as some neologisms. Speech may be completely meaningless to the listener, sometimes referred to as **jargon aphasia**. Utterances may be empty because of a lack of content words (nouns, verbs), an excess of grammatical words (e.g., articles, prepositions), and overuse of imprecise words (*it*, *thing*). Word retrieval failures may result in circumlocutions. Utterances may violate the rules of syntax and grammar, resulting in paragrammatic speech (e.g., "We need the thing in the over the house"). Verbal output may be excessive and rapid, with an apparent lack of inhibition of the flow of speech, referred to as "press of speech" or **logorrhea**.
- **Auditory comprehension** is severely impaired, often even at the single-word level. Difficulty with complex

syntax or multistep commands is always present. Poor self-monitoring of their own speech may make patients surprisingly unaware of their inability to produce meaningful speech and result in failure to attempt self-correction.

- **Repetition** is significantly defective; patients may not be able to repeat even single words. Repetition is similar to spontaneous speech in that it contains phonemic and semantic paraphasias.
- **Naming** attempts are often paraphasic, and severe anomia is the rule.
- **Lesion localization**. Wernicke's aphasia is typically associated with large posterior perisylvian lesions encompassing the posterior superior temporal gyrus (Wernicke's area) and often extending superiorly into the inferior parietal region. A common cause is embolic occlusion of the inferior division of the left middle cerebral artery.
- **Accompanying deficits**. Right visual field defect sometimes accompanies Wernicke's aphasia. Lack of awareness of the language deficit (i.e., anosagnosia) is common in the acute stage.
- **Prognosis**. If auditory comprehension improves over time, the profile becomes more consistent with conduction aphasia. Other cases may evolve in the direction of TcSA. A particularly good recovery could result in residual anomic aphasia.

B. Nonfluent Aphasias

Transcortical motor aphasia (TcMA) is a nonfluent aphasia characterized by relatively good auditory comprehension and preserved repetition.

- **Conversational speech** is nonfluent, but unlike patients with Broca's aphasia, who try to communicate, patients with TcMA are generally abulic and make little attempt to produce speech spontaneously. In the acute stage, patients may be mute. When utterances are produced, usually after a long delay, they tend to be of reduced length (typically less than four words) and grammatical complexity. Articulation is generally preserved.
- **Auditory comprehension** is good for most conversational interaction, but there may be difficulty with complex syntax or multistep commands. Accurate assessment of auditory comprehension is problematic in some cases

because of prominent akinesia (i.e., the failure to initiate voluntary movement) and the tendency to perseverate.

- **Repetition** is preserved in striking contrast to the virtual absence of spontaneous conversational speech.
- **Naming** can be relatively preserved. Unlike most other aphasias, in TcMA confrontation naming may be better than spontaneous speech production. Generative naming, however, is a particularly difficult task for patients with TcMA.
- **Lesion location.** Lesions producing TcMA involve extrasylvian regions of the left frontal lobe. In some cases the lesions are mesial, in the distribution of the anterior cerebral artery, encompassing the supplementary motor area (SMA) and the cingulate gyrus, which play an important role in the initiation of speech. TcMA has also been described following dorsolateral frontal lesions located anterior or superior to Broca's area. These lesions are often in the watershed zone between the middle and anterior cerebral artery territories.
- **Associated deficits.** Mesial frontal lesions may be associated with contralateral leg weakness and urinary incontinence. Dorsolateral frontal lesions in the watershed territory may be associated with predominantly proximal weakness of the right extremities, at times sparing the face.
- **Prognosis.** TcMA may essentially resolve, or it may persist as relatively mild anomic aphasia.

Broca's aphasia is a nonfluent aphasia in which there is relatively good comprehension and poor repetition.

- **Conversational speech** is nonfluent, with slow, halting speech production. Articulatory impairment is common. Utterances are of reduced length (typically less than four words) with simplified grammar, referred to as **agrammatism.** Nouns predominate, with some verbs and adjectives but very few functors. Words often lack morphological endings, such as *-ing*, *-es*, *-ed*.
- **Auditory comprehension** is relatively good for conversational speech, but there is considerable difficulty with complex syntax or multistep commands. Especially difficult are semantically reversible or passive sentences in which word order cues alone are not sufficient for correct comprehension (e.g., "The girl was pushed by the boy").
- **Repetition** is limited to single words and short phrases, typically commensurate with the length of spontaneous utterances.

- **Naming** is always impaired to some degree, especially for low-frequency words. Motor speech production deficits may interfere with intelligibility.
- **Lesion location.** Lesions restricted to Broca's area cause only transient disruption of speech production and fluency. Persistent Broca's aphasia results from much larger perisylvian lesions encompassing the entire territory of the superior division of the middle cerebral artery. The lesions typically include not only Broca's area proper but also both banks of the Rolandic fissure (including the motor and sensory regions for the face), the insula, anterior parietal lobe, and subcortical regions deep to these areas. Persistent Broca's aphasia characteristically evolves from global aphasia over several months.
- **Associated deficits.** Right hemiparesis is common, affecting the face and the arm more than the leg. Motor programming deficits including buccofacial apraxia, apraxia of speech, and apraxia of the nonparalyzed left limb are frequently observed.
- **Prognosis.** Variable recovery occurs in Broca's aphasia; patients in whom the cause is vascular have the best chance of some recovery of language.

Mixed transcortical aphasia (MTcA), also called the **isolation syndrome**, is a nonfluent aphasia with poor comprehension but relatively preserved repetition.

- **Conversational speech** is similar to that found in global aphasia, in that meaningful verbal expression is severely limited or is absent altogether. Stereotyped utterances are common, as is echolalia, the inappropriate, and somewhat irrepressible, repetition of what others say.
- **Auditory comprehension** is markedly impaired, often even at the single-word level.
- **Repetition** of phrases and complete sentences is preserved, although repetition typically occurs without comprehension.
- **Naming** is significantly impaired.
- **Lesion location.** MTcA is seen in association with diffuse or multifocal lesions that result in anatomic isolation of the perisylvian language zone from surrounding cortical areas. MTcA may follow carotid artery occlusion, producing a confluent arc of infarction in the watershed region along the periphery of the middle cerebral artery vascular territory. MTcA has also been described in cortical dementia and following carbon monoxide poisoning.

- **Accompanying deficits.** Right-sided weakness or sensory loss may be present in cases of MTcA caused by stroke.
- **Prognosis.** Variable recovery occurs in MTcA; patients in whom the cause is vascular have the best chance of some recovery of language.

Global aphasia is a severe nonfluent aphasia with poor auditory comprehension and poor repetition.

- **Conversational speech** is nonfluent with slow, halting speech production. Utterances may be restricted to single words or phrases that are perseverative, such as *I can see.* Articulatory impairment is common. Some meaning may be conveyed by inflectional variations imposed on otherwise meaningless utterances (e.g., *nokeydoe, nokeydoe*).
- **Auditory comprehension** is reduced to the extent that even single-word comprehension is significantly compromised. Comprehension is markedly impaired at the phrase or sentence level.
- **Repetition** is defective, and even single words may not be repeated accurately.
- **Naming** is severely impaired.
- **Lesion localization.** Lesions in global aphasia are extensive and typically involve the entire left perisylvian language zone. A common cause is embolic occlusion of the main stem of the middle cerebral artery.
- **Accompanying deficits** include right hemiparesis, right hemisensory loss, and right homonymous hemianopia.
- **Prognosis.** Global aphasia may evolve to Broca's aphasia or may persist as global aphasia.

V. OTHER APHASIA SYNDROMES

A. Subcortical Aphasias

Many cortical lesions extend to subcortical regions, but aphasia can also result from deep lesions that appear to spare the cerebral cortex. Subcortical aphasias include thalamic aphasia and aphasia associated with damage to the basal ganglia and surrounding white matter pathways (i.e., nonthalamic subcortical aphasia). Although not fully understood, it appears that subcortical lesions result in cortical dysfunction caused by the disruption of normal white matter connections.

1. **Thalamic aphasia** reflects a pattern of language performance distinct from the cortical aphasias. In general, it is characterized by fluent utterances (but may have

reduced spontaneous output), anomia, verbal paraphasias, mild-to-moderate impairment of auditory comprehension, and preserved repetition. Prognosis for thalamic aphasia is typically good, with resolution to mild anomic aphasia.

2. **Nonthalamic subcortical aphasia** is the term sometimes used to refer to aphasia associated with damage to the basal ganglia or white matter pathways with preservation of the thalamus and language cortex. The resulting aphasia profile can be quite variable. In some cases, spoken output is nonfluent and agrammatic, whereas others produce fluent paraphasic utterances. Speech production problems have also been noted, including reduced articulatory precision, prosodic disturbance, and even hypophonia. The variation in symptoms is thought to relate to lesion location within the striato-capsular region and the extent of involvement of surrounding white matter.

B. Aphasia Associated With Cortical Degenerative Disease

Language impairment is one of the symptoms of generalized cognitive decline associated with dementia. In the case of Alzheimer's disease, language deterioration typically follows a progressive course that begins with anomic aphasia, proceeds to transcortical sensory aphasia and then Wernicke's aphasia, and ultimately becomes global aphasia. In some patients, progressive language deterioration occurs without significant dementia and is referred to as **primary progressive aphasia** (PPA). The relatively selective impairment of language seen in PPA reflects a subtype of asymmetrical cortical degeneration, or focal cortical atrophy. The resultant behavioral profile is variable (presumably reflecting the region of cortical atrophy) and can manifest as any of the cortical aphasia syndromes. Two general patterns of progressive aphasia have been characterized.

1. **Semantic dementia** reflects a progressive loss of semantic knowledge that results in fluent, anomic language. Grammatical competence remains strong, and repetition is preserved. However, auditory comprehension becomes degraded as the disease progresses. Semantic dementia has been associated with cortical atrophy in the left anterior and inferior temporal lobes.

2. **Progressive nonfluent aphasia** is characterized by nonfluent, agrammatic language with word-finding

difficulties and phonemic paraphasias. Repetition is impaired, and auditory comprehension may be affected as well. Apraxia of speech also may be noted. This syndrome is associated with brain atrophy in the left inferior frontal lobe.

VI. DISTINGUISHING APHASIA FROM OTHER DISORDERS

Aphasia needs to be distinguished from other disorders that impair communication. The following disorders are distinct from aphasia.

A. Input Problems

1. **Pure word deafness** refers to a selective impairment of speech input processing. Patients with pure word deafness cannot comprehend or repeat spoken language, but their spontaneous speech production and naming are intact, and they can read and write without difficulty. In some cases, recognition of environmental sounds is also preserved. Pure word deafness is a rare syndrome that usually results from bilateral damage to the auditory cortex of the temporal lobes. A unilateral deep left temporal lobe lesion may also result in pure word deafness by disconnecting Wernicke's area from auditory input.

2. **Pure alexia**, or alexia without agraphia, refers to an acquired reading impairment that occurs in the absence of significant aphasia. Language production and auditory comprehension are preserved. Patients can also write, although they are frequently unable to read what they have written. In cases of pure alexia, reading is accomplished by serial identification of the letters of a word, so that it is referred to as **letter-by-letter reading**. The syndrome is typically seen following damage to the left inferior-occipital region within the territory of the posterior cerebral artery. Such lesions often result in dense right hemianopia. However, pure alexia also occurs without a visual field cut when damage to white matter tracts disconnects the flow of visual information to the cortical regions responsible for processing written words.

3. **Agnosia** refers to recognition failure affecting a single sensory modality (i.e., visual, tactile, auditory). Patients with agnosia may be unable to name objects presented

in a particular sensory modality, but naming is possible when the same object is presented in a different modality. For instance, a patient with visual agnosia may not be able to recognize and name an object on visual presentation, but the name of the object is easily retrieved when the individual is provided with nonvisual input (e.g., given the object to feel or asked to name it in response to a spoken definition). By contrast, naming impairments associated with aphasia persist regardless of the modality of presentation.

B. Production Problems

1. **Apraxia of speech** is a disturbance of motor programming for the positioning and movement of the articulators for speech production. It can exist in the absence of muscle weakness and buccofacial apraxia, that is, without a disturbance of motor control for nonspeech movements of the articulators.
2. **Dysarthria** refers to a group of motor speech disorders caused by weakness, slowness, or incoordination of speech musculature resulting in imprecise articulation. Dysarthria can co-occur with aphasia, but it should be regarded as an impairment of speech rather than language.
3. **Mutism** is the term applied to the complete inability to produce speech caused by a wide range of neurological and nonneurological disorders. Mute patients do not talk, but they should not be considered aphasic when it can be demonstrated that auditory and reading comprehension are preserved, and successful written communication is possible.

VII. KEY NEUROPSYCHOLOGICAL TESTS

Numerous standardized tests are available for the assessment of aphasia. Most of these measures are not designed for bedside administration and are best reserved for clinical administration during the nonacute stage. Following is a sampling of tests commonly used by speech-language pathologists and clinical neuropsychologists.

A. Examining for Aphasia

1. **Selected standardized aphasia tests**
   ▪ Boston Diagnostic Aphasia Examination, Third Edition (Goodglass, 2001)

- Western Aphasia Battery (Kertesz, 1982)
- Aphasia Diagnostic Profiles (Helm-Estabrooks, 1992)
2. **Naming**
- Boston Naming Test (Kaplan, Goodglass, & Weintraub, 2001)
3. **Auditory comprehension**
- Token Test of the Multilingual Aphasia Examination (Benton, deHamsher, & Siven, 1994)

B. Determining the Status of Cognitive Processes

A clear understanding of the nature of the aphasic language impairment is gained by careful examination of cognitive processes necessary for language. Some tests and informal assessment measures are designed to allow for isolation of the specific component processes involved in spoken or written language.

- Psycholinguistic Assessment of Language Processing in Aphasia (PALPA; Kay, Lesser, & Coltheart, 1992)

C. Assessing the Impact of Aphasia

The tests referenced above primarily assess language impairment. Other assessment tools were designed to examine the disability that results from the aphasia, that is, the consequences of the impairment at a more functional level. Examples of such measures include the following:

- ASHA Functional Assessment of Communication Skills for Adults (Frattali, Thompson, Holland, Wohl, & Ferketic, 1995) and
- Communication Activities of Daily Living, Second Edition (Holland, Fromm, & Frattali, 1999).

VIII. CONCLUSION

This chapter provides an introduction to differential diagnosis of aphasia. We reviewed the assessment and interpretation of behavioral characteristics, with an emphasis on the inpatient bedside examination. The social consequences of aphasia can be tremendous, affecting employment, economic status, social roles, and overall sense of well-being. It is difficult to quantify such variables (and their change over time), particularly when the language impairments limit information exchange regarding the impact of the deficit. Appropriate measures for these social consequences, or handicaps, are limited; however, clinicians should not overlook such critical issues.

BIBLIOGRAPHY

References for Standardized Tests

Benton, A. L., deHamsher, K. S., & Siven, A. B. (1994). *Multilingual Aphasia Examination*. Iowa City, IA: AJA Associates.

Fratalli, C. M., Thompson, C. K., Holland, A. L., Wohl, C. B., & Ferketic, M. M. (1995). *ASHA Functional Assessment of Communication Skills for Adults*. Bethesda, MD: American Speech-Language-Hearing Association.

Goodglass, H. (2001). *Boston Diagnostic Aphasia Examination* (3rd ed.). Philadelphia: Lippincott Williams & Wilkins.

Helm-Estabrooks, N. (1992). *Aphasia Diagnostic Profiles*. Chicago: Riverside.

Holland, A. L., Fromm, D., & Frattali, C. (1999). *Communication activities of daily living* (2nd ed.). Austin, TX: PRO-ED.

Kaplan, E., Goodglass, H., & Weintraub, S. (2001). *The Boston Naming Test*. Philadelphia: Lippincott Williams & Wilkins.

Kay, J., Lesser, R., & Coltheart, M. (1992). *Psycholinguistic Assessment of Language Processing in Aphasia*. East Sussex, England: Erlbaum.

Kertesz, A. (1982). *Western Aphasia Battery*. San Antonio, TX: Psychological Corporation.

Sources of Additional Information

Benson, D. F., & Ardila, A. (1996). *Aphasia: A clinical perspective*. New York: Oxford University Press.

Chapey, R. (Ed.). (2001). *Language intervention strategies in adult aphasia* (4th ed.). Baltimore: Lippincott Williams & Wilkins.

Duffy, J. R. (1995). *Motor speech disorders: Substrates, differential diagnosis, and management*. St. Louis, MO: Mosby.

Goodglass, H. (1993). *Understanding aphasia*. San Diego, CA: Academic Press.

Heilman, K. M., & Valenstein, E. (Eds.). (1993). *Clinical neuropsychology* (3rd ed.). New York: Oxford University Press.

Hillis, A. E. (Ed.). (2002). *Handbook on adult language disorders: Integrating cognitive neuropsychology, neurology, and rehabilitation*. Philadelphia: Psychology Press.

Kertesz, A. (Ed.). (1994). *Localization and neuroimaging in neuropsychology*. San Diego, CA: Academic Press.

Rothi, L. J. G., Crosson, B., & Nadeau, S. (Eds.). (2000). *Aphasia and language: Theory and practice*. New York: Guilford Press.

PART IV

NEUROLOGICAL SYNDROMES

CHAPTER 19

Margaret G. O'Connor and Ginette Lafleche

Amnesic Syndromes

This chapter addresses neuroanatomical and neuropsychological aspects of memory disorders. We begin by examining memory deficits in terms of localization of function. We then consider memory deficits in terms of etiology and behavioral outcomes. The neuropsychological assessment of memory and various clinical instruments are reviewed.

I. CLINICAL MANIFESTATIONS OF AMNESIA

A. Definitions

The purest form of amnesia is a circumscribed and dense memory deficit in which there is preserved intelligence and reasoning. Amnesic patients are unable to encode and consolidate verbal and nonverbal information regardless of the modality of presentation (auditory or visual) or the nature of the material (verbal or nonverbal). In contrast, attention span, language functions, and reasoning are relatively preserved. Amnesic patients show the greatest deficits on tasks of **declarative memory** in that they are unable to demonstrate awareness of prior learning experiences, whereas **procedural memory** (skills, habits, and classically conditioned responses) remains intact. A wide variety of studies have shown that **semantic memory** (knowledge of facts and other general information) is intact in amnesia, whereas **episodic memory** (experiential knowledge involving the recall of temporal or spatial aspects of events) is impaired (Tulving, 1983). Amnesic patients are capable of normal (or near-normal) performance on tasks of **implicit memory** in that they may show learning on tasks of perceptual and conceptual memory even though they do not recall detailed information regarding the learning event. However, patients with amnesia are not capable of normal performance on tasks of **explicit memory** in that they have no awareness of the learning episode.

The examination of an amnesic patient should focus on **anterograde** and **retrograde** aspects of the memory disturbance (see Figure 19.1 for a flow chart describing the evaluation process). **Anterograde amnesia** (AA) refers to an inability to learn new information after the onset of amnesia. AA is present in most cases of amnesia and is typically associated with bilateral brain lesions. **Retrograde amnesia** (RA) refers to deficient recall of events preceding the onset of amnesia. Patients demonstrate various profiles of RA. In some instances, RA is limited to days, weeks, or months before the onset of memory loss; in others, it encompasses events and memories that extend back to the distant past. The RA exhibited by patients with Wernicke–Korsakoff syndrome (WKS) has been described as "temporally graded" because remote memories are better preserved than are memories closer in time to the onset of amnesia. Cases of RA consisting of a loss of a great deal of information over an extended time period usually involve extensive neural damage in neocortical brain regions (Rempel-Clower, Zola, Squire, & Amaral, 1996). Cases of RA in the absence of significant AA are rare but have been described (Kapur, 1993a; O'Connor, Butters, Miliotis, Eslinger, & Cermak, 1992).

B. Stability of the Clinical Presentation

In most instances, the term **amnesic** is restricted to patients with isolated and stable memory impairment that presents acutely and that is permanent. However, some patients experience memory disorders that change over time. For example, patients with amnesia secondary to rupture and surgical repair of anterior communicating artery (ACoA) aneurysms may show improvement in memory and other cognitive functions in the months following surgery (D'Esposito et al., 1994). Other patients present with isolated memory problems that progress to dementia with deficits in multiple cognitive domains.

Figure 19.1. Evaluation of amnesia. TIAs = transient ischemic attacks.

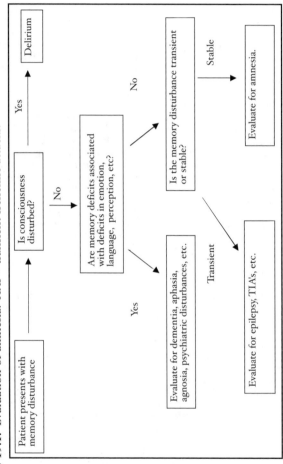

Transient global amnesia (TGA) is a condition involving the acute onset of memory loss for a period of hours to days. TGA may occur as a result of decreased perfusion to medial temporal or diencephalic brain regions. Patients with TGA demonstrate profound AA and variable profiles of RA. There is often complete resolution of TGA when testing is conducted weeks or months after the episode; however, some TGA patients demonstrate residual deficits on challenging tests of verbal long-term memory (Mazzucchi, Moretti, Caffarra, & Parma, 1980) and time estimation. Semantic memory, procedural learning, and implicit memory have been described as intact during the TGA episode (Hodges, 1994).

Transient forms of amnesia have also been described in conjunction with epilepsy. Some patients with temporal lobe epilepsy experience temporary episodes of amnesia referred to as **epileptic amnesic syndrome** (Gallassi, Morreale, Sarro, & Lugaresi, 1992). These episodes may occur frequently and are usually associated with subtle behavioral disturbances. It is interesting that performance on formal neuropsychological tests is often normal despite patients' subjective memory complaints. Some patients with temporal lobe epilepsy have demonstrated significant RA in comparison to mild or moderate disturbances of anterograde memory (Kapur, 1993b; O'Connor, Sieggrreen, Ahem, Schomer, & Mesulam, 1996).

C. Subtypes of Amnesia

Amnesic patients present with a variety of medical conditions and psychosocial issues that influence their patterns of memory loss and residual learning skills. One way of reducing this variability is to group amnesic patients according to neuroanatomical differences (see Table 19.1).

Medial temporal lobe (MTL) amnesia occurs as a consequence of hypoxic-ischemic brain damage, limbic encephalitis, cerebrovascular accidents, and Alzheimer's disease. Historically, patients with MTL amnesia have been described as having (a) preserved insight, (b) increased rate of forgetting, (c) limited RA, and (d) lack of confabulation. However, more recent studies demonstrated that accelerated forgetting does not differentiate MTL patients from other patients with amnesia (McKee & Squire, 1992). Further questions have arisen regarding the notion that MTL amnesic patients have a restricted RA: Neuropathological investigations have underscored an association between severity of RA and extent of pathology in the hippocampus and adjacent cortices (Rempel-Clower et al., 1996).

Table 19.1. Neuroanatomic Distinctions in Memory Impairment

Profile	Location		
	Medial temporal lobe	Diencephalic	Frontal
Cause	Anoxia, limbic encephalitis, cerebrovascular accident, Alzheimer's disease	Infarction of thalamic arteries, trauma, diencephalic tumor, Wernicke–Korsakoff	Cerebrovascular accident, tumor, surgery, anterior aneurysm
Insight	Present	Absent	Often
Confabulation	Absent	Present	Often present
Deficits	Retrograde[a] Declarative memory[b]	Retrograde[c]	Retrograde[d] Contextual memory[e]

[a]Extent depends on the extent of the damage to the lateral temporal neocortex. [b]Deficits in the conscious recall of facts. [c]Often caused by deficits in the initial processing stages of memory and sensitivity to proactive interference. [d]The degree of retrograde amnesia is variable and is often attributable to attentional deficits that adversely affect encoding and retrieval. Recognition of previously learned material is often normal, suggesting that consolidation is relatively intact. [e]Memory for temporal and spatial aspects of events.

Diencephalic amnesia results from infarction of thalamic arteries, trauma, diencephalic tumors, and WKS (Butters & Stuss, 1989). Patients with diencephalic amnesia demonstrate deficits in the initial processing stages of memory, confabulation, sensitivity to **proactive interference** (prior learning interferes with the acquisition of new material), and lack of insight into the memory disturbance. Most patients with diencephalic pathology forget information at a normal rate. The range of remote memory deficits in these patients varies from minimal to severe. Confabulation and diminished insight often occur in this group as a result of the disruption of frontal networks. The memory deficits in diencephalic amnesia have been attributed to damage in the medial thalamic structures, the mammillary bodies, or both of these regions (Markowitsch, 1982). It is interesting that material-specific deficits (i.e., disproportionate impairment for either verbal or nonverbal–spatial information) may occur as a result of unilateral thalamic damage (Speedie & Heilman, 1983).

A third group includes amnesic patients with memory impairments secondary to damage in frontal brain regions, stroke, tumors, surgical intervention, and rupture and surgical repair of ACoA aneurysms. These patients exhibit attention difficulties that adversely affect encoding and retrieval. Under some circumstances recognition is normal, suggesting that consolidation is relatively intact. Patients with frontal amnesia often lack insight into their memory problems and tend to confabulate. Deficits are also seen on tasks of proactive interference, **contextual memory** (memory for temporal and spatial aspects of events), and semantic categorization. Some frontal amnesic patients present with RA due to impaired retrieval of previously stored information.

A number of investigators have argued that anatomically based classification systems are reductionistic and fail to consider the interplay of processing deficits that affect the memory profiles of patients with amnesia (Weiskrantz, 1985). Others have raised questions regarding whether patients in different subgroups have sustained neuroanatomically discrete lesions. For example, MTL and diencephalic amnesia may be based on common neuropathological substrates. Finally, comparisons across subtypes may be influenced by extraneous factors such as baseline intelligence and education. For instance, diencephalic amnesia studies are often restricted to WKS patients, who have limited education and extensive histories of alcohol abuse. These patients differ from MTL amnesic patients, who tend to have higher intelligence and socioeconomic status. It may be that these extraneous differences affect memory differentially, thereby confounding subtype comparisons.

II. NEURAL SUBSTRATES OF AMNESIA

A. The Neuroanatomy of Memory

Current information regarding brain systems involved in memory is based on neuroimaging and lesion studies. Declarative memory deficits have been associated with damage in bilateral and medial temporal regions (Scoville & Milner, 1957). Initial investigation with nonhuman primates supported the idea that new learning was dependent on two neural systems: the **hippocampal pathway** (the hippocampus, fornix, mammillary bodies, mammillothalamic tract [MTT], and cingulate cortex) and the **amygdaloid pathway** (amygdala, dorsal medial thalamus, and dorsomedial cortex). Damage to either system was thought to result in moderate-level memory loss, whereas damage to both was associated with severe amnesia (Mishkin & Appenzeller, 1987). More recent work has challenged the importance of the amygdala, mammillary bodies, and fornix in the etiology of amnesia. Converging data from studies with patients and with nonhuman primates have suggested that damage restricted to the hippocampus proper is associated with mild to moderate memory deficits, whereas damage to the hippocampus and adjacent parahippocampal, entorhinal, and perirhinal cortices increases severity of amnesia (Zola-Morgan, Squire, Amaral, & Suzuki, 1989).

In all likelihood, medial temporal lobe and medial thalamic structures work together in establishing new memories. Studies of patients with damage in the region of the third ventricle have highlighted the contribution of diencephalic structures to memory. Postmortem analyses have shown that damage to midline thalamic (the internal medullary lamina and interomedial or dorsomedial nuclei) and mammillary nuclei is associated with amnesia (Cramon, Hebel, & Schuri, 1985; Markowitsch, 1988). The basal forebrain, including the medial septal nucleus, the diagonal band of Broca, and the nucleus basalis of Meynert, has also been studied extensively in human and animal models of amnesia. Some investigators have emphasized that damage restricted to the basal forebrain produces mild memory loss, whereas basal forebrain damage combined with lesions in striatal and frontal brain areas produces severe amnesia (Cramon et al., 1985; Markowitsch, 1988). Other investigators have emphasized that septal damage is the cause of amnesia in basal forebrain damage as a result of the destruction of anatomic connections to the hippocampus (Zola-Morgan & Squire, 1993).

There is a great deal of support for the idea that medial temporal lobe and medial diencephalic structures play critical, but temporary, roles in new learning. Observations of intact remote memory in the context of severe amnesia suggest that information eventually becomes independent of hippocampal and diencephalic circuitry (Squire & Alvarez, 1995). However, it may be the case that more complex autobiographical memories are dependent on hippocampal input MTT for an extended period of time (Nadel & Moscovitch, 1997). Memory researchers have shown that extent of neocortical damage influences severity of remote memory loss: Limited damage to core hippocampal structures is associated with an attenuated RA, whereas more severe damage in neocortical damage may result in more severe RA.

B. Diseases That Give Rise to Amnesia

Amnesia occurs in conjunction with a variety of psychiatric and neurological disorders. In light of space limitations, psychiatric causes of amnesia are not discussed in this chapter. Closed head injury and Alzheimer's disease are not elaborated on because these disorders are reviewed elsewhere in this volume. What follows is a summary of neurological conditions that give rise to amnesia (see Table 19.2).

1. SURGICAL ABLATION

Over the last 40 years, there have been many investigations of H.M., a patient who underwent bilateral temporal lobe resection for treatment of refractory seizures (Milner, 1966; Scoville & Milner, 1957). Findings from studies with H.M. have greatly influenced theories regarding the neuroanatomical underpinnings and psychological parameters of memory. H.M.'s clinical profile is considered the prototypical amnesic syndrome. His profound amnesia underscored the critical roles of hippocampal and surrounding cortical regions in new learning. Initial studies with H.M. validated the distinction between short- and long-term memory. More recent work with H.M. supported theories suggesting that distinct brain systems mediate implicit versus explicit memory processes.

Surgical intervention remains a treatment option for patients with intractable epilepsy. However, knowledge gained

Table 19.2. Neurological Illnesses Associated With Amnesia

Illness	Lesion	Disturbance	Reference
Anterior communicating artery aneurysms	Basal forebrain (restricted damage)	Mild memory problems	Irle et al. (1992)
	Basal forebrain, striatum (extensive damage)	Severe amnesia	
Herpes simplex encephalitis	Lateral and medial temporal cortices (left or right) Lateral temporal cortex	Verbal learning, nonverbal learning, severe retrograde	Kapur et al. (1994); Utley et al. (1997)
Anoxic encephalopathy	Medial temporal lobe	Anterograde; variable effects on remote memory	Zola-Morgan et al. (1989)
Posterior cerebral artery infarction	Medial temporal lobes	Material-specific memory loss in association with laterality of lesion	Benson et al. (1974); Ott and Saver (1993)
Wernicke–Korsakoff syndrome	Anteromedial, dorsomedial, and intralaminar thalamic nuclei; mammillary bodies and frontal network systems	Anterograde and temporally graded retrograde amnesia	Cramon et al. (1985); Victor et al. (1989)

from H.M.'s unfortunate outcome has resulted in a number of modifications in epilepsy surgery programs. Surgery is now limited to unilateral temporal lobe removal and is typically performed after careful neuropsychological evaluation that includes intracarotid amobarbital studies to minimize the risk of postoperative amnesia.

2. HERPES SIMPLEX ENCEPHALITIS

Herpes simplex encephalitis (HSE) is the most common cause of nonepidemic, sporadic viral encephalitis in the United States. The diagnosis of HSE depends on identification of the herpes simplex virus within the cerebrospinal fluid or within brain tissue by means of brain biopsy. Other neurodiagnostic methods of diagnosis include electroencephalography (EEG) and brain imaging studies. Characteristic EEG findings include spike and slow wave activity in temporal lobe regions. Computed tomography (CT) scans show edema in the temporal lobe early on and hemorrhagic necrotic lesions later. Magnetic resonance imaging (MRI), the preferred imaging diagnostic method, often shows edema very early in the onset of the viral infection. The brain involvement is typically diffuse, with petechial hemorrhages and necrosis distributed in an asymmetric fashion throughout the medial temporal and inferior frontal lobes. Kapur and colleagues (Kapur, Barker, Burrows, Ellison, & Brice, 1994) examined imaging studies of 10 patients with HSE. In their group, lesions always involved brain regions beyond the hippocampus, including the parahippocampus, the insula, basal forebrain, mammillary bodies, and the fornix. Anterior and inferior temporal cortices were invariably damaged more extensively than superior and posterior temporal gyri. Less common was damage in frontal brain regions and thalamic nuclei.

HSE patients initially present with confusion, impaired memory, aphasia, and agnosia that may gradually resolve to a circumscribed amnesic syndrome. There is a great deal of variability in the type and extent of preserved and impaired memory skills in HSE (Utley, Ogden, Gibb, McGrath, & Anderson, 1997). Specific patterns of memory loss vary in conjunction with the location of the lesion; disproportionate verbal learning difficulties are associated with greater left-hemisphere involvement, whereas nonverbal deficits are associated with more extensive lesions in the right hemisphere (Eslinger, Damasio, Damasio, & Butters, 1993). Patients with HSE may demonstrate extensive RA in association with lateral temporal brain damage (O'Connor et al., 1992). Semantic memory problems have also been described in this patient group. Circumscribed semantic memory deficits can occur, such as preservation of memory for concepts pertaining to living versus nonliving things (Sartori, Remo, Miozzo, Zago, & Marchiori, 1993) and being able to remember people's names but nothing about major events related to the same people (McCarthy & Warrington, 1992). A significantly better outcome was seen in HSE survivors who were given acyclovir earlier in the course of their illness (Utley et al., 1997).

3. HYPOXIC ISCHEMIC BRAIN DAMAGE

Anoxic encephalopathy occurs as a result of cardiac arrest, respiratory distress, strangulation, and carbon monoxide poisoning. When oxygen saturation is depleted for 5 minutes or more, permanent brain damage occurs as a result of the accumulation of pathological excitatory neurotransmitters or lactic acid. A sustained hypoxic episode can result in extensive cerebral and cerebellar brain damage and in a variety of cognitive, perceptual, and motor abnormalities. However, because the medial temporal lobes are particularly sensitive to oxygen deprivation, hypoxia may result in circumscribed amnesia. Area CA1 of the hippocampus has been identified as particularly sensitive to the effect of hypoxic ischemic damage. An isolated lesion in this area can result in a moderately severe amnesia with minimal effect on remote memory (Zola-Morgan, Squire, & Amaral, 1986). More commonly, however, the memory impairment following an anoxic event is similar to that of frontal amnesia in which the deficit is one of retrieval, rather than encoding, as a result of impaired systematic search initiation processes. Anoxic patients typically benefit from cued and recognition formats. This type of memory disorder can be accounted for by the fact that the sustained oxygen deprivation preferentially damages the watershed zones of the cerebral cortex, including that of the frontal watershed cortex and basal ganglia structures. In addition to amnesia, patients with anoxic encephalopathy may suffer from a number of other cognitive difficulties, including perceptual and executive deficits as well as motor problems.

4. CEBREBRAL VASCULAR ACCIDENTS

Amnesia secondary to bilateral **posterior cerebral artery** (PCA) **infarction** has been well described in the literature. In addition, some investigators have described patients with memory deficits in the wake of unilateral (primary left) PCA infarction (Benson, Marsden, & Meadows, 1974; Ott & Saver, 1993). Unfortunately, many investigators have failed to include measures of nonverbal memory and rate of forgetting in their description of

PCA-related amnesia. Consequently, it is difficult to determine whether the memory deficit of patients with unilateral PCA infarction are qualitatively or quantitatively different from those of other patients with amnesia. It is important to note that deficits beyond memory loss, including visual deficits, hemianopic alexia, pure alexia, color agnosia, and object agnosia, often occur in association with PCA strokes. The latter difficulties are more likely when the lesion extends posteriorly to include occipitotemporal cortices. Lesions in the posterior parahippocampus or collateral isthmus (a pathway connecting the posterior hippocampus to association cortices) are viewed as critical to the memory disturbance in this patient group (Cramon et al., 1985).

Another vascular event associated with memory loss is infarction of thalamic arteries, particularly the tuberothalamic and paramedian vessels. There is some variability in neuropsychological profiles related to lesion location. Again, a number of cases have been described with memory loss secondary to unilateral damage.

5. WERNICKE–KORSAKOFF SYNDROME

Patients with WKS develop amnesia as a result of chronic alcohol abuse and thiamine deficiency (Victor, Adams, & Collins, 1989). The diagnosis of WKS is clinical and based on the classic triad of oculomotor palsies, gait ataxia, and encephalopathy that signals the acute phase of the Wernicke phase. MRI can inform diagnosis in that, in the early phase, lesions appear within the diencephalon and periaqueductal gray on T2 and diffusion-weighted images. Acute treatment with thiamine results in rapid improvement in ataxia and confusion within days to weeks. The signal abnormalities documented on MRI diminish following thiamine treatment. Many patients are left with the Korsakoffs amnesic syndrome and personality changes, in addition to other residual neurological deficits. Patients with WKS are prone to irritability and apathy, problems that often undermine performance on tasks of new learning (Butters & Cermak, 1980). The neuropathology of WKS involves damage in anteromedial, dorsomedial, and intralaminar thalamic nuclei; mammillary bodies; and frontal network systems (Victor et al., 1989). The extent to which these areas separately or convergently result in amnesia is controversial. Frontal (i.e., executive) deficits also undermine WKS patients' ability to learn new information. The memory impairment also consists of an extensive and temporally graded remote memory deficit. It is important to understand that the severe alcohol abuse associated with

WKS is often accompanied by long-standing social isolation and a general lack of interest in world events. These premorbid psychosocial patterns adversely affect WKS patients' performance on tests measuring knowledge of public events.

6. ANTERIOR COMMUNICATING ARTERY ANEURYSMS

Approximately 40% of patients who suffer rupture and undergo repair of ACoA aneurysms present with impairments in memory and personality changes. Descriptions of patients with ACoA emphasize amnesia, apathy, disorientation, and confabulation, symptoms that may occur secondary to vasospasm, hematoma formation, herniation of the medial temporal lobes, hydrocephalus, and surgical intervention. Heterogeneity in the neuropsychological presentations of these patients is due to the fact that there is variability in the site of neural damage. Brain lesions are seen in basal forebrain, striatal, and frontal regions. It is widely assumed that basal forebrain damage is the critical underpinning of the memory deficits in this patient group, although some investigators have suggested that combined basal forebrain and striatal lesions may be necessary for severe memory problems (Irle, Wowra, Kunert, Hampi, & Kunze, 1992).

Patients with ACoA aneurysms are often described as experiencing attentionally based memory problems. They tend to benefit from recognition cues, perhaps as a consequence of deficient strategic retrieval. Performance on tasks of RA varies. In a recent study, we found that ACoA patients demonstrated RA on tasks of public events knowledge but their RA was less severe than that seen in the temporal lesion patients. Patients with ACoA aneurysms are also prone to confabulation (Diamond, DeLuca, & Fisher, 2000), which may vary in tandem with poor source monitoring because of frontal systems involvement (D'Esposito, Alexander, Fischer, McGlinchey-Berroth, & O'Connor, 1996).

III. NEUROPSYCHOLOGICAL EVALUATION

Evaluation of amnesia takes place in the context of a comprehensive assessment of intelligence, attention, language, perception, reasoning, and emotional status. Information regarding performance across a broad array of neuropsychological tasks is important for diagnostic and therapeutic purposes. A diagnosis of focal amnesia cannot be made unless it is firmly established that the individual is relatively intact in other cognitive domains. Information regarding baseline IQ and other cognitive functions facilitates the determination of the extent of severity of the memory impairment. In addition, a comprehensive neuropsychological evaluation may identify other factors that adversely affect memory, such as coexisting comorbid depression. Furthermore, cognitive strengths are highlighted that inform the remediation plan.

The clinical assessment of memory has been greatly influenced by cognitive research with amnesic patients. Previous cognitive models of amnesia emphasized disruptions in various stages of learning. On the basis of their work with WKS patients, Butters and Cermak (1980) identified **encoding** deficits as the critical problem in amnesia. Investigations of patient H.M. led Milner (1966) to speculate that amnesia was due to the interruption of information from short- to long- term memory, thereby highlighting **consolidation** deficits in amnesia. Warrington and Weiskrantz (1968, 1970) proposed that amnesia was due to faulty **retrieval**. Despite the fact that researchers no longer view amnesia as a unitary deficit in a specific stage of learning, the clinical assessment of amnesia still involves discrimination between encoding, consolidation, and retrieval deficits.

Persistent use of the stage model approach in the clinical assessment of amnesia is based on the fact that this framework is both parsimonious and clinically meaningful. Information regarding disruption in various stages of memory can be obtained from standard clinical tests of memory. Encoding and retrieval abilities are inferred from performance on tasks of immediate recall: If the individual fails to recall a normal amount of information, the examiner may assume the presence of either encoding or retrieval problems. More information regarding the relative contribution of encoding versus retrieval is gained from multiple comparisons across tasks. Retrieval abilities are judged from a comparison of recognition versus free recall: A large disparity favoring recognition over recall suggests that retrieval is deficient; however, normal immediate recall or recognition implies that encoding is intact. Information regarding consolidation (or retention) is based on a comparison of immediate versus delayed memory: The relative preservation of immediate memory versus poor performance on delayed memory tasks implicates a consolidation deficit.

As noted, over the last three decades there have been major advances in our conceptualization of memory processes so that we now are able to make distinctions between declarative and procedural forms of memory. Declarative (i.e., episodic and semantic) memory is a core part of most clinical assessments, whereas procedural memory (knowledge for skills and routines) is only examined when there is a specific clinical need. Episodic memory (knowledge for contextually integrated events) is probed using tests of new learning as well as tasks focusing on recollection of remote events. Semantic memory (memory for facts and generic information) is assessed with tasks of vocabulary and various measures of world knowledge. In the clinical examination, material-specific aspects of memory are also examined; previous investigations have shown that verbal information is mediated by left temporal regions and nonverbal information is mediated by right temporal regions.

A. Assessment of Anterograde Memory

There are many good tests of memory. Because of space limitations, we only focus on tests that are part of the amnesia battery at the Memory Disorders Research Center at the Boston University School of Medicine. These tests include the following (see Table 19.3).

1. THE WECHSLER MEMORY SCALE—III

The Wechsler Memory Scale—III (WMS–III; Wechsler, 1997) is perhaps the most widely used instrument to assess new learning. The WMS–III consists of a variety of subtests that focus on different aspects of memory. Eight primary indexes provide information on general memory functions (paragraph recall, paired-associate learning, face recognition, picture recall, and auditory recognition), working memory (letter–number sequencing and spatial span), auditory immediate memory (paragraph recall and paired-associate learning), auditory delayed memory (paragraph recall and paired-associate learning), visual immediate memory (face recognition and picture recall), and visual delayed memory (face recognition and picture recall). Discrepancy analyses of specific subtests allow for comparisons of immediate versus delayed memory that bear on the issue of consolidation and that may shed light on the extent of hippocampal damage. Functional information regarding modality-specific (auditory vs. visual) deficits is also available. Discrepancies between memory performance on the WMS–III and overall IQ are also made that are particularly useful when assessing the severity of memory impairment (Bornstein, Chelune, & Prifitera, 1988).

2. REY AUDITORY VERBAL LEARNING TEST

The Rey Auditory Verbal Learning Test (RAVLT; Rey, 1964) involves the presentation of a list of 15 words across five trials followed by a second (interference) list, with testing under

Table 19.3. Clinical Evaluation of Memory

Test	Focus of assessment	Reference
Rey Auditory Verbal Learning Test	Learning curve, recency and primacy effects, proactive and retroactive interference	Osterreith (1944); Rey (1941)
Rey-Osterrieth Complex figure	Nonverbal (visual) memory	Osterreith (1944); Rey (1941)
California Verbal Learning Test—II	Learning curve, proactive and retroactive interference, semantic memory, forced-choice recognition	Delis et al. (2000)
Wechsler Memory Scale—III	Working memory, single-trial learning, learning slope, retention, retrieval	Wechsler (1997)
Biber Figure Learning Test	Nonverbal (visual) memory that parallels verbally based list learning tasks; learning curve recall and recognition, proactive and retroactive interference	Glosser et al. (1989)
Warrington Recognition Memory Test	Verbal and nonverbal recognition memory	Warrington (1984)
Doors and People Test	Overall score; visual–verbal discrepancies; Recall–recognition discrepancies, forgetting score	Baddeley et al. (1994)
Brief Visuospatial Memory Test—Revised	Visuospatial memory; learning curve; immediate and delayed recall; recognition, alternative forms	Benedict (1997)
Autobiographical Memory Interview	Remote autobiographical memory	Kopelman et al. (1989)
Crovitz procedure	Remote memory	Crovitz and Schiffman (1974)
Famous Faces Test	Remote memory for public figures	Albert et al. (1979)
Transient News Events Test	Remote memory for public events, recognition and recall	O'Connor et al. (2000)

delayed recall and delayed recognition conditions. A comparison of performance on immediate versus delayed recall provides information regarding retention, whereas a comparison of free recall versus recognition highlights retrieval efficiency. Serial presentation of a supra-span list (one that exceeds attention span limitation) provides information regarding the learning curve, thus elucidating the extent to which repetition enhances learning. The RAVLT also provides a measure of primacy (first few items on the list) and recency (last few words) effects. This task also provides information regarding proactive (intrusions of the first list on recall of the second list) and retroactive (intrusions of the second list on recall of the first list) interference. The RAVLT is a well-normed and widely used memory test. It provides useful information regarding the density and nature of memory problems in amnesic patients. It is often the case that patients with memory loss secondary to medial temporal damage perform poorly on delayed recognition testing (compatible with a consolidation deficit), whereas patients with frontal dysfunction preferentially benefit from recognition probes (compatible with a retrieval deficit).

3. THE CALIFORNIA VERBAL LEARNING TEST

The second edition of the California Verbal Learning Test (CVLT–II) represents a major revision of the CVLT (Delis, Kramer, Kaplan, & Ober, 2000). Additions to the test include an Alternate Form that is statistically equated to the standard form, a Short Form (9 words instead of 16 words) that can be used for screening or with more severely impaired patients, and an optional forced-choice recognition trial that is administered approximately 10 minutes after the traditional yes-no recognition testing, to detect lack of effort and malingering. Finally, various scores have been added, including those used for the early detection of the memory deficits that characterize Alzheimer's disease and used to identify memory disorders arising from subcortical-frontal damage versus those arising from mesial-temporal damage. The manner in which the test is administered is essentially unchanged, except that there is now no reference to a "shopping list" in the instructions given to patients. As with the original CVLT, a first list (List A) is presented with 16 words from four categories (furniture, vegetables, means of transportation, and animals). The words are presented over five learning trials. Subsequently, a one-trial second list (List B) is presented; this list has two overlapping categories with the first list (vegetables and animals) and two nonoverlapping categories (musical instruments and parts of a house). Following the free recall of List B, both free and cued recall of List A are tested then and 20 minutes later. Delayed recall is followed by a delayed recognition condition. Two significant changes have been incorporated in this revision aimed at making the test more difficult and better suited for the calculation of various memory scores: The recognition task no longer includes phonemically similar items, and all 16 items of List B are now included as distractors on the recognition list. Studies have shown that the use of categories at encoding and retrieval can point to the deficits that underlie some memory deficits. For instance, patients with Alzheimer's disease may make many intrusive and perseverative errors, perhaps because of degradation of semantic memory (Kramer et al., 1988), whereas patients with memory problems secondary to impaired organization may benefit from the structure afforded by the test. This test has been used with a wide range of neurologically impaired and psychiatric patients. In general, patients perform similarly on the CVLT–II as the RAVLT. There is also a nine-item version of the CVLT–II available for older patients who are cognitively impaired (Libon et al., 1996).

4. THE REY OSTERRIETH COMPLEX FIGURE

The Rey Osterrieth Complex Figure Test (CFT; Osterreith, 1944; Rey, 1941) is a test of complex visual organization and visual memory. Individuals are asked to copy a two-dimensional figure without time restrictions. Scoring focuses on the accuracy of details rendered. The strategy used in copying the figure may be clinically informative: Some individuals are very organized and use a "gestalt" approach to the figure, whereas others copy the CFT figure in a segmented, disorganized manner. Memory for the CFT figure depends on the extent to which the individual can encode complex information that exceeds normal attention span limitations. Initial copying is done without the knowledge that memory will be examined; hence, initial recall is a measure of incidental learning. Delayed recall performance is examined relevant to rate of forgetting. A recognition condition can be added to the test whereby the individual components of the figure are presented along with foils. If the individual is able to discriminate the elements of the figure from distractors, it is thought that consolidation has been preserved. Patients with organizational problems often demonstrate poor recall of the CFT figure because they fail to use an organized approach when copying the figure.

5. THE BIBER FIGURE LEARNING TEST

The Biber Figure Learning Test (BFLT; Glosser, Goodglass, & Biber, 1989) is a test of nonverbal memory designed to measure recall and recognition of information that exceeds attention span limitations. The task is designed to complement many of the verbally based list learning tasks previously described. As a result of parallel design features, a comparison of the BFLT and the verbal tasks can be used to provide information regarding material-specific aspects of memory. A series of 15 geometric figures is presented one at a time. Following the presentation of the entire series, the patient is asked to draw the designs from memory. The same series of designs is presented four more times, and recall is tested after each presentation. Following the fifth trial, a distractor set is presented. Recall for distractor items may be relatively impaired as a result of proactive interference. Following recall of the distractor list, recall of the original list is tested. Delayed recall is examined 15 to 30 minutes later. Subsequently, delayed recognition of the original designs, which are embedded in a group of foil items, is examined. Information obtained from this test may help determine laterality of brain damage. In at least one study (Glosser et al., 1989), delayed recognition problems were associated with relative deficits in patients with right-hemisphere disease.

6. THE WARRINGTON RECOGNITION MEMORY TEST

The Warrington Recognition Memory Test (Warrington, 1984) involves recognition of 50 verbal stimuli (words) and 50 nonverbal stimuli (faces). In the first subtest, patients are shown 50 words (one at a time) at a rate of 3 seconds per stimulus. They are then asked to select the previously viewed words that are presented in a forced-choice list (one foil paired with each target). In the second subtest, 50 black-and-white photographs of male faces are presented. The patient is then shown two faces (one previously seen and one distractor) and asked to point to the target stimulus.

The Warrington Recognition Memory Test provides useful information regarding material-specific aspects of memory. Patients with right-hemisphere lesions demonstrate deficits on the facial memory subtest, whereas their word recognition abilities may be intact. Patients who underwent right temporal lobectomy perform significantly worse than left lobectomy patients on the faces subtest. Conversely, left temporal lobectomy patients perform significantly worse than right lobectomy patients on the word subtest.

7. THE DOORS AND PEOPLE TEST

The Doors and People Test (D&P; Baddeley, Emslie, & Nimmo-Smith, 1994) provides a means of assessing verbal and visual memory using subtests of recall and recognition that have been equated for degree of difficulty. The recall section of the D&P has both verbal (Person Test) and visual (Shapes Test) conditions. In the Person Test, the individual is shown the picture of each of four people and asked to remember their names and surnames. To stimulate learning, the occupation of each individual is provided (i.e., "This is the doctor, his name is Jim Green"). Immediate recall and delayed recall are tested in a paired-associate format: The examinee is asked to provide the name linked with each occupation. In the Shapes Test, four simple drawings are presented. Immediate and delayed recall are tested by asking the examinee to draw the shapes from memory.

The recognition portion of D&P comprises verbal (the Names Test) and visual (the Doors Test) conditions. Both subtests have two forms, Sets A and B, with the latter being more difficult than the former. The examinee reads 12 names aloud; immediate recognition is then tested with the target name among three distractors. Target and distractors share the same forename. For visual recognition, the examinee is shown colored photographs of doors from different kinds of buildings (i.e., houses, sheds, garages, churches, etc.). The doors illustrate various historical periods. Immediate recognition of the target door among three foils is tested. Data from this test include an overall score, visual–verbal discrepancies, recall–recognition discrepancies, and forgetting indices. The overall score is thought to provide the most sensitive and reliable measure of episodic memory performance.

8. THE BRIEF VISUOSPATIAL MEMORY TEST—REVISED

The Brief Visuospatial Memory Test—Revised (BVMT–R; Benedict, 1997) provides measures of immediate recall, rate of acquisition, delayed recall, and recognition of nonverbal line drawings. In this test, six simple figures are presented for study for 10 seconds over three trials on an 8×11 display. Recall is tested after each trial and after a 25-minute delay. Recalled figures are scored according to accuracy and position criteria. Recognition testing follows delayed recall and is done using a yes–no format with 12 designs (6 targets and 6 foils) presented one at a time. The BVMT–R allows the efficient assessment (approximately 15 minutes to administer) of learning, delayed recall, and recognition. The availability of six equivalent forms makes this a good test for use in clinical trials or other situations in which practice effects could confound performance.

B. Assessment of Retrograde Memory

There are many factors that make formal assessment of RA difficult (see Table 19.3). Personal memories from the remote past are difficult to verify, and it is not possible to determine whether errors are due to inadequate storage at the time of initial exposure or disruption of the retrieval process. One method of assessing RA involves recall of public events. The problem with this approach is that there is a great deal of variability in individuals' premorbid fund of knowledge; variations in performance may be due to differences in baseline intelligence or interest in world events. With these caveats in mind, we recommend that the assessment of RA encompass different types and classes of memories (i.e., personal history, world history, and popular culture) that may be disrupted differentially in the context of neurological disease.

1. AUTOBIOGRAPHICAL MEMORY INTERVIEW

The Autobiographical Memory Interview (AMI; Kopelman, Wilson, & Baddeley, 1989) is a semistructured interview that focuses on events from three time periods throughout the life span. Both semantic and episodic aspects of events are probed. Each memory is scored according to the amount of detail and vividness of the recollection. It is important to note that, in general, memory for autobiographical information is selective; even individuals with normal memory functions may fail to remember wedding dates, birth dates, and other events of this nature. Any assessment of autobiographical memory should be accompanied by an interview with someone who can provide a collateral source of information.

2. THE CROVITZ PROCEDURE

The Crovitz procedure (Crovitz & Schiffman, 1974) also provides information regarding autobiographical memory. The individual is asked to generate personal recollections in response to a list of cue words (e.g., a specific memory involving a book). Unique memories with details receive high scores, whereas vague and generic recollections do not. It is particularly difficult to verify the accuracy of memories that are retrieved during the Crovitz test. One way of increasing possible accuracy is to present the same list during two sessions. In the first session, an estimate of the date of each recalled episode is asked to establish a baseline. During the second session, this date and cue word are provided to determine whether the same memory is evoked.

3. THE FAMOUS FACES TEST

The Famous Faces Test (FFT; Albert, Butters, & Levin, 1979) from the Boston Remote Memory Battery requires the individual to identify photographs of famous individuals from the 1920s through the 1990s. The FFT provides useful information regarding the individual's knowledge and recall of public figures. However, the examiner should be aware that the early items (i.e., the face of Charlie Chaplin) are overexposed; hence, not all items are representative of specific temporal epochs.

4. THE TRANSIENT NEWS EVENTS TEST

The Transient News Events Test (TNET; O'Connor et al., 2000) focuses on recall of information that was in the news for a discrete period of time. The TNET was constructed to control for the amount of exposure of news events. Transient events were selected according to objective criteria: Each event had been in *The New York Times* 60 times on a particular year, with a rapid decline in the 2 subsequent years. Free recall and recognition are probed. Recall questions are worded in such a way as to circumvent naming problems. Recognition questions are administered in a forced-choice format in which the correct answer is paired with a distractor item.

IV. CONCLUSION

Over the past four decades, clinical and research investigations of amnesic patients have yielded fascinating insights regarding the psychological parameters and biological substrates of memory. Neuropsychologists have attempted to identify conditions that facilitate learning for memory-impaired patients, including environmental supports, pharmacological intervention, and cognitive remediation. The neuropsychological evaluation provides the framework for remediation. Information derived from clinical assessment highlights residual learning abilities as well as learning deficits. This may influence whether pharmacological intervention is warranted: Severely amnesic patients do not derive a great deal of benefit from medications, whereas patients with mild attentionally based difficulties may respond to some medications. Pragmatic recommendations should be individually tailored to each patient's cognitive and emotional needs.

BIBLIOGRAPHY

Albert, M., Butters, N., & Levin, J. (1979). Temporal gradients in the retrograde amnesia of patients with alcoholic Korsakoffs disease. *Archives of Neurology, 36,* 211–216.

Baddeley, A., Emslie, H., & Nimmo-Smith, I. (1994). *Doors and people.* Bury St. Edmunds, England: Thames Valley Test Company.

Benedict, R. (1997). *Brief Visuospatial Memory Test—Revised.* Odessa, FL: Psychological Assessment Resources.

Benson, D., Marsden, C., & Meadows, J. (1974). The amnesic syndrome of posterior cerebral artery occlusion. *Acta Neurologica Scandinavia, 50,* 133–145.

Bornstein, R., Chelune, G., & Prifitera, A. (1988). IQ–memory discrepancies in normal and clinical samples. *Journal of Consulting and Clinical Psychology, 1,* 203–206.

Butters, N., & Cermak, L. S. (1980). *Alcoholic Korsakoffs syndrome: An information processing approach.* New York: Academic Press.

Butters, N., & Stuss, D. T. (1989). Diencephalic amnesia. In F. Boiler & J. Grafman (Eds.), *Handbook of neuropsychology* (Vol. 3, pp. 107–148). Amsterdam: Elsevier Science.

Cramon, D. Y. V., Hebel, N., & Schuri, U. (1985). A contribution to the anatomical basis of thalamic amnesia. *Brain, 108,* 993–1008.

Crovitz, H. F., & Schiffman, H. (1974). Frequency of episodic memories as a function of their age. *Bulletin of the Psychonomic Society, 4,* 517–518.

D'Esposito, M., Alexander, M. P., Fischer, R., McGlinchey-Berroth, R., & O'Connor, M. (1996). Recovery of memory and executive function following anterior communicating artery rupture. *Journal of the International Neuropsychological Society, 2,* 565–570.

D'Esposito, M., McGlinchey-Berroth, R., Alexander, M. P., Fisher, R., O'Connor, M. G., & Walbridge, M. (1994, February). *Cognitive recovery following anterior communicating artery rupture and repair.* Paper presented at the meeting of the International Neuropsychological Society, Cleveland, OH.

Delis, D., Kramer, J., Kaplan, E., & Ober, B. (2000). *California Verbal Learning Test—II.* San Antonio, TX: Psychological Corporation.

Diamond B. J., DeLuca J., & Fisher, C. (2000). Confabulation and memory in anterior community artery aneurysm. *Archives of Clinical Neuropsychology, 15,* 721–722.

Eslinger, P. J., Damasio, H., Damasio, A. R., & Butters, N. (1993). Nonverbal amnesia and asymmetric cerebral lesions following encephalitis. *Brain and Cognition, 21,* 140–152.

Gallassi, R., Morreale, A., Sarro, D., & Lugaresi, E. (1992). Epileptic amnesic syndrome. *Epilepsia, 33,* S21–S25.

Glosser, G., Goodglass, H., & Biber, C. (1989). Assessing visual memory disorders. *Journal of Consulting and Clinical Psychology, 1,* 82–91.

Hodges, J. R. (1994). Semantic memory and frontal executive function during transient global amnesia. *Journal of Neurology, Neurosurgery, and Psychiatry, 57,* 605–608.

Irle, E., Wowra, B., Kunert, H. J., Hampi, J., & Kunze, S. (1992). Memory disturbance following anterior communicating artery rupture. *Annals of Neurology, 31,* 473–480.

Kapur, N. (1993a). Focal retrograde amnesia in neurological disease: A critical review. *Cortex, 29,* 217–234.

Kapur, N. (1993b). Transient epileptic amnesia: A clinical update and a reformulation. *Journal of Neurology, Neurosurgery, and Psychiatry, 56,* 1184–1190.

Kapur, N., Barker, S., Burrows, E. H., Ellison, D., & Brice, J. (1994). Herpes simplex encephalitis: Long term magnetic resonance imaging and neuropsychological profile. *Journal of Neurology, Neurosurgery, and Psychiatry, 57,* 1334–1342.

Kopelman, M. D., Wilson, B. A., & Baddeley, A. D. (1989). The autobiographical memory interview: A new assessment of autobiographical and personal semantic memory in amnesic patients. *Journal of Clinical and Experimental Neuropsychology, 11,* 724–744.

Kramer, J., Delis, D., Blusewicsz, M., Brandt, J., Ober, B., & Strauss, M. (1988). Verbal memory errors in Alzheimer's and Huntington's dementias. *Developmental Neuropsychology, 4*(1), 1–15.

Libon, D., Mattson, R., Glosser, G., Kaplan, E., Malamut, B., Sands, L., et al. (1996). A nine-word dementia version of the California Verbal Learning Test. *The Clinical Neuropsychologist, 10,* 237–244.

Markowitsch, H. J. (1982). Thalamic mediodorsal nucleus and memory: A critical evaluation of studies in animals and man. *Neuroscience and Biobehavioral Reviews, 6,* 351–380.

Markowitsch, H. J. (1988). Diencephalic amnesia: A reorientation towards tracts? *Brain Research Review, 13,* 351–370.

Mazzucchi, A., Moretti, G., Caffarra, P., & Parma, M. (1980). Neuropsychological functions in the follow-up of transient global amnesia. *Brain, 103,* 161–178.

McCarthy, R. A., & Warrington, E. K. (1992). Actors but not scripts: The dissociation of people and events in retrograde amnesia. *Neuropsychologia, 30,* 633–644.

McKee, R. D., & Squire, L. R. (1992). Equivalent forgetting rates in long-term memory in diencephalic and medial temporal lobe amnesia. *Journal of Neuroscience, 12,* 3765–3772.

Milner, B. (1966). Amnesia following operation on the temporal lobes. In C. W. M. Whitty & O. L. Zangwill (Eds.), *Amnesia* (pp. 109–133). London: Butterworths.

Mishkin, M., & Appenzeller, T. (1987). The anatomy of memory. *Scientific American, 256,* 80–89.

Nadel, L., & Moscovitch, M. M. (1997). Memory consolidation, retrograde amnesia and the hippocampal complex. *Current Opinion in Neurobiology, 7,* 217–227.

O'Connor, M. G., Butters, N., Miliotis, P., Eslinger, P. J., & Cermak, L. (1992). The dissociation of anterograde and retrograde amnesia in a patient with herpes encephalitis. *Journal of Clinical and Experimental Neuropsychology, 14,* 159–178.

O'Connor, M. G., Sieggrreen, M. A., Ahem, G., Schomer, D. L., & Mesulam, M. M. (1996). Accelerated forgetting in association with temporal lobe epilepsy and paraneoplastic limbic encephalitis. *Brain and Cognition, 35,* 71–84.

O'Connor, M. G., Sieggreen, M., Bachna, K., Kaplan, B., Cermak, L., & Ransil, B. (2000). Long-term retention of transient news events. *Journal of International Neuropsychological Society, 6,* 44–51.

Osterreith, P. (1944). Le test de copie d'une figure complexe [The test of copying a complex figure]. *Archives de Psychologic, 30,* 206–356.

Ott, B. R., & Saver, J. L. (1993). Unilateral amnesic stroke: Six new cases and a review of the literature. *Stroke, 24,* 1033–1042.

Rempel-Clower, N. L., Zola, S. M., Squire, L. R., & Amaral, D. G. (1996). Three cases of enduring memory impairment after bilateral damage limited to the hippocampal formation. *Journal of Neuroscience, 16,* 5233–5255.

Rey, A. (1941). L'examen pscyhologique dans les cas d'encephalopathie traumatique [The psychological examination in cases of traumatic encephalopathy]. *Archives de Psychologic, 28,* 286–340.

Rey, A. (1964). *L'examen clinique en psychologic* [The clinical exam in psychology]. Paris: Presses Universitaires de France.

Sartori, F., Remo, J., Miozzo, M., Zago, S., & Marchiori, G. (1993). Category-specific form-knowledge deficit in a patient with herpes simplex virus encephalitis. *Journal of Clinical and Experimental Neuropsychology, 15,* 280–299.

Scoville, W. B., & Milner, B. (1957). Loss of recent memory after bilateral hippocampal lesions. *Journal of Neurology, Neurosurgery, and Psychiatry, 20,* 11–12.

Speedie, L. J., & Heilman, K. M. (1983). Anterograde memory deficits for visuospatial material after infarction of the right thalamus. *Archives of Neurology, 40,* 183–186.

Squire, L. R., & Alvarez, P. (1995). Retrograde amnesia and memory consolidation: A neurobiological perspective. *Current Opinion in Neurobiology, 5,* 169–177.

Tulving, E. (1983). *Elements of episodic memory.* Oxford, England: Oxford University Press.

Utley T. F., Ogden J. A., Gibb, A., McGrath, N., & Anderson, N. E. (1997). The long-term behavioral outcome of herpes simplex encephalitis in a series of unselected survivors. *Neuropsychiatry, Neuropsychology, and Behavioral Neurology, 10,* 180–189.

Victor, M., Adams, R. D., & Collins, G. H. (1989). *The Wernicke–Korsakoff syndrome and related neurologic disorders due to alcoholism and malnutrition* (2nd ed.). Philadelphia: Davis.

Warrington, E. K. (1984). *Recognition Memory Test.* London: NFER-Nelson.

Warrington, E. K., & Weiskrantz, L. (1968, March 9). A new method of testing long-term retention with special reference to amnesic patients. *Nature, 217,* 972–974.

Warrington, E. K., & Weiskrantz, L. (1970). Amnesic syndrome: Consolidation or retrieval? *Nature, 228,* 628–630

Wechsler, D. (1997). *The Wechsler Memory Scale, Third Edition.* San Antonio, TX: Psychological Corporation.

Weiskrantz, L. (1985). On issues and theories of the human amnesic syndrome. In N. Weinberger, J. McGaugh, & G. Lynch (Eds.), *Memory systems of the brain* (pp. 380–415). New York: Guilford Press.

Zola-Morgan, S., & Squire, L. R. (1993). Neuroanatomy of memory. *Annual Review of Neurosciences, 16,* 547–563.

Zola-Morgan, S., Squire, L., & Amaral, D. (1986). Human amnesia and the medial temporal region: Enduring memory impairment following a bilateral lesion limited to field CA1 of the hippocampus. *Journal of Neuroscience, 6,* 2950–2967.

Zola-Morgan, S., Squire, L. R., Amaral, D. G., & Suzuki, W. A. (1989). Lesions of the perirhinal and parahippocampal cortex that spare the amygdala and hippocampal formation produce severe memory impairment. *Journal of Neuroscience, 9,* 4355–4370.

CHAPTER 20
Mieke Verfaellie and Kenneth M. Heilman

Neglect Syndromes

Unilateral neglect is an acquired disorder that affects an individual's ability to be aware of or respond to stimuli on the side contralateral to a lesion. A diagnosis of neglect is made only when the disorder cannot be attributed to elementary sensory or motor deficits (Heilman, Watson, & Valenstein, 2003). Neglect can be manifested in a variety of ways, and it is now generally acknowledged that the subtypes of the disorder may have different mechanisms or pathophysiology. Although some of the acute signs of neglect may remit spontaneously, many patients continue to manifest signs of neglect for months or even years after onset. These manifestations can have devastating consequences for daily living and significantly influence the prognosis for functional recovery. Efficient remediation of neglect requires accurate diagnosis of its different forms and the ability to link these manifestations to underlying processing deficits (see Table 20.1 for overview).

I. SUBTYPES OF NEGLECT

A. Sensory Neglect or Inattention

Sensory neglect is a failure to detect stimuli presented on the side contralateral to a central nervous system lesion

Table 20.1. Varieties of Neglect

Type of neglect	Manifestations	Sectors of space
Sensory neglect	Unawareness of contralateral stimuli; allesthesia; extinction	Personal; peripersonal; far extrapersonal
Motor neglect	Akinesia; hypokinesia; motor impersistence; motor extinction	Personal; peripersonal; far extrapersonal

(contralesional). This deficit is not due to a sensory disturbance but rather to a disruption of the mechanisms responsible for attending to the contralateral side of space. Because attention modulates perception of incoming information, this form of neglect is also referred to as **perceptual neglect**. Sensory neglect may manifest in the following ways.

1. INATTENTION OR UNAWARENESS OF CONTRALATERAL STIMULI

Patients with sensory neglect or inattention might be unaware of visual, tactile, or auditory stimuli presented to the contralesional side. These patients might also be unaware of stimuli presented in ipsilateral space, but the contralesional inattention is usually more severe than the ipsilesional inattention.

2. EXTINCTION TO DOUBLE SIMULTANEOUS STIMULATION

In less severe cases, inattention might not be apparent with the presentation of single unilateral stimuli, but when two stimuli are presented simultaneously, one to each side of the body, to each ear, or to each visual field, patients who can detect isolated contralesional stimuli might fail to report the stimulus on the contralesional side when the stimulus is paired with an ipsilesional stimulus. Although extinction is most obvious when a contralesional stimulus is presented simultaneously with an ipsilesional stimulus, it can also occur when two stimuli are presented on one side of the body or in one visual field. In this testing condition, it is the more contralateral of the two stimuli that the patient might not perceive. Multimodal extinction is commonly seen during the course of recovery from unilateral inattention. Unimodal extinction, in contrast, may occur in the absence of other manifestations of neglect and may be the result of different neuropathological mechanisms.

B. Motor or Intentional Neglect

Motor neglect is a failure to respond appropriately to stimuli in the contralateral side of space in the absence of obvious weakness and when this failure cannot be attributed to a sensory deficit or inattention. This response failure is striking because it occurs despite patients' awareness of the presence of a stimulus. It can affect movement of the head and eyes as well as movements of the limbs bilaterally, but testing of the contralateral limbs is often impossible owing to the co-occurrence of hemiparesis. In the acute phase, patients may show a marked deviation of the head, eyes, and trunk to the ipsilesional side. This motor bias can also be seen during examination of eye movements, with scanning saccades restricted to the ipsilateral side of space, even though patients may be capable of making full extraocular movements to command (Halligan & Marshall, 1993). Impairments in intention or response preparation can be manifested in the following ways.

1. AKINESIA

Akinesia is a failure to initiate movements. This failure can be in the arm, neck, or eyes. This akinesia is most often contralesional, such that even in the absence of weakness the patient fails to move the contralesional arm or cannot turn the head or eyes toward contralesional hemispace. This akinesia can also be associated with a motor bias, such that the patient's eyes and head might deviate toward ipsilateral hemispace. Although this limb and directional akinesia is primarily contralateral, many patients with this disorder following right-hemisphere injury have reduced spontaneous movements on even their ipsilesional side. Also, when asked to point straight ahead with their ipsilesional arm with eyes closed, patients with a directional akinesia might point toward ipsilateral hemispace.

2. HYPOKINESIA

Hypokinesia refers to a delay in the initiation of a movement, even when the stimuli that are a signal for initiation are presented on the ipsilesional side. This delay in initiation can be seen even in the ipsilesional forelimb but is often more severe in the contralesional forelimb. This hypokinesia can also be directional (movements toward contralesional hemispace) or hemispatial (movements in contralesional hemispace).

3. MOTOR IMPERSISTENCE

Motor impersistence is a failure to sustain a movement or posture. This impersistence can be for movements that are directed toward or in contralateral space (e.g., sustained left-ward gaze).

4. MOTOR EXTINCTION

Motor extinction is a failure to move or maintain movement of the contralateral limb when the ipsilateral limb is moved simultaneously. Like sensory extinction, motor extinction often occurs during the course of recovery and represents a mild form of motor neglect.

C. Hemispatial or Unilateral Spatial Neglect

In addition to classifying neglect as afferent (sensory neglect or inattention), efferent (motor or intentional neglect), or a combination of sensory and motor, neglect can be classified by location. Therefore, the sensory, motor, or sensorimotor neglect discussed earlier can affect extrapersonal space (hemispatial neglect), personal space (personal neglect), or both.

Findings from human studies have suggested that extrapersonal space can be parsed in a number of different ways. One distinction concerns **close extrapersonal space** (also called **peripersonal**) and **far extrapersonal space**. Neglect can differentially affect one or both of these spatial domains. For example, patients with peripersonal neglect show attentional disturbances within reaching or grasping space. They may perform poorly when line bisection or search tasks are presented 30 to 60 cm away from their body but not when the stimuli are presented further away. The opposite pattern occurs in patients with far extrapersonal neglect, in whom attentional disturbances may be detected only when stimuli are presented out of reach and responses are made by means of a light pointer.

Another way in which space can be parsed is with respect to the frame of reference used. Clinical evidence demonstrates that hemispace is not rigidly defined by an absolute egocentric midline. **Hemispace** is a dynamic construct that is defined not only by the position of the trunk but also by the position of the head and eyes. Thus, as the head and eyes move, the right and left hemispace move accordingly. As a consequence, neglect commonly affects the side contralateral to a viewer's focus of attention. When attention operates on a global environmental spatial array, independent of the orientation of the patient's body, one side of the environment is ignored (environmental neglect). When attention operates within segregated figures, as defined by the patient's viewpoint, the portion of the stimulus that is on the contralesional side of the patient might be ignored (viewer-centered neglect). Finally, when the spatial coordinates intrinsic to an object form the frame of reference within which attention operates (regardless of the position of the object in the environment and its relationship to the viewer), the contralateral portion of this object might be unattended (object-centered neglect).

Under most ordinary circumstances, the environmentally centered, object-centered, and viewer-centered frames of reference coincide with each other. Methods aimed at disentangling these frames of reference, however, have demonstrated that some patients' neglect is primarily in one of these spatial domains.

D. Personal Neglect

Patients with **personal neglect** show attentional disturbances for the contralateral side of their body. They may fail to discriminate the position of their contralateral limb or neglect to use objects such as a comb or razor on the contralateral side of their own body. They often also have an impairment in the representation of the contralateral side of their body (see next section). For instance, when asked to identify pictures of the left or right hand seen from the palm or from the back, they perform poorly, which suggests that they are unable to match perceptual information to body representations.

E. Representational Neglect

When some patients are asked to imagine a scene or a part of their body, they may fail to report portions on the side opposite to their lesion. Although **representational neglect** is often associated with hemispatial or personal neglect, these disorders might be dissociable. Some patients with neglect might also have difficulty recalling perceived contralateral stimuli.

II. NEUROPATHOLOGICAL MECHANISMS UNDERLYING NEGLECT

Neglect is most commonly seen in patients with vascular disease (thrombotic infarction, embolic infarction, and hemorrhage), but it is occasionally seen with tumors as well as with degenerative diseases. It also can be an ictal or postictal manifestation in patients with seizures. Although neglect can occur following lesions of either the left or the right hemisphere, its frequency of occurrence and severity are greater following right- than left-

Table 20.2. Anatomical Substrates of Neglect

Anatomical substrate	Putative contribution
Parietal lobe	Orienting of attention, spatial representation
Prefrontal lobe	Motor intention
Basal ganglia	Motor control
Reticular formation, intralaminar thalamic nuclei	Arousal
Anterior cingulate	Motivation for action
Posterior cingulate	Stimulus significance

hemisphere dysfunction. Persistent right-sided neglect is unusual, and when present it should raise the suspicion of bilateral lesions. The association between neglect and right-hemisphere lesions has led to theories of right-hemispheric dominance in the mediation of different components of attention (Heilman & Van den Abell, 1980; Rainville, Giroire, Periot, Cuny, & Mazaux, 2003).

Neglect can be caused by a variety of cortical and subcortical lesions (see Table 20.2). The most common site of damage is the inferior parietal lobe, but lesions of frontal cortex, cingulate gyrus, basal ganglia, thalamus, and reticular formation may also cause neglect (Heilman et al., 2003; Vallar, Bottini, & Paulesu, 2003). Electrophysiological studies have suggested that the inferior parietal lobe is critical for directing attention to information that is coded in a spatial framework, whereas the frontal lobes, including the frontal eye fields, are critical for coordinating the motor programs for exploration, scanning, and navigation in space. The contribution of the cingulate gyrus lies primarily in the evaluation of the motivational significance of stimuli, whereas the thalamus and mesencephalic reticular formation are critical for the modulation of the overall level of arousal and vigilance. In light of these findings, it has been suggested that sensory neglect or inattention results from a disruption in the parietal and limbic (posterior cingulate) components of this attentional network and that motor or intentional neglect results from a disruption in the prefrontal, basal ganglionic, and limbic (anterior cingulate) components. Given their role in arousal, the thalamus and reticular formation are thought to be important for both sensory and motor components of attention. In agreement with this framework, several researchers have reported motor neglect following frontal lesions and sensory neglect following parietal lesions (e.g., Coslett, Bowers, Fitzpatrick, Haws, & Heilman, 1990), but sometimes it is difficult to isolate the intentional and attentional components, and many patients have both components. This may be due to limitations in the assessment techniques, but it also may reflect the tight connectivity between the areas that mediate these components.

The neuroanatomic fractionation of subtypes of neglect that affect different sectors of space is even less clear. Whereas dorsal (parietal) lesions can induce neglect of lower space, ventral lesions might be associated with neglect of upper space. Animal studies have shown that lesions of discrete cerebral areas may cause isolated neglect for far or for near extrapersonal space (Rizzolatti & Camarda, 1987), but a clear neuroanatomic counterpart in humans has not been found.

III. COGNITIVE MECHANISMS UNDERLYING NEGLECT

Humans have a limited ability to simultaneously process all the stimuli to which they are exposed. In addition, people often attend to internally generated stimuli. Humans also must select from an almost infinite number of actions that they can perform. Thus, we must have systems for allocating limited resources. The means by which organisms select stimuli is called **attention**, and the means by which they select and prepare for actions is called **intention**. The most commonly accepted class of theories concerning neglect are those that propose some form of allocation (attentional or intentional) deficit (for reviews, see Heilman et al., 2003; Robertson & Marshall, 1993). These theories are based on the notion that each hemisphere mediates attention as well as intention, in and toward the contralateral side of space. In humans, however, because neglect is more commonly associated with right- than left-hemisphere lesions, the right hemisphere appears more capable of allocating attention as well as intention to ipsilateral space. Thus, a unilateral lesion in the right hemisphere that damages these attentional or intentional control networks results in a contralateral orienting deficit to novel stimuli, an unawareness or a failure to fully process meaningful stimuli that are presented on the contralesional side, and a failure to explore or act in or toward contralateral space. A unilateral lesion in the left hemisphere has less severe consequences, as the right hemisphere can still allocate attention to the ipsilateral side.

Cognitive theories of attention distinguish between a reflexive form of orienting (bottom-up) that is automatically evoked by salient stimuli and an internally controlled form of orienting that is under voluntary control (top-down). Spatial neglect is thought to be due primarily to a deficit in bottom-up or reflexive orienting, such that novel or significant stimuli do not automatically attract attention when they are presented in the contralesional side of space. This deficit can be overcome to some extent when cues are provided that help patients voluntarily redirect attention to the contralesional portion of space. In contrast, representational neglect may be an example of a failure in top-down processing.

A contralateral orienting deficit disrupts the attentional balance between the two hemispheres, and consequently it also manifests itself as an orienting or attentional bias to the ipsilateral side of space. This bias has also been described as **attentional capture**, or **hyperattention**. This ipsilateral attentional bias might be related to disinhibition of the uninjured hemisphere induced by injury to the opposite hemisphere (Kinsbourne, 1993). Consistent with this hypothesis is the observation that some patients with neglect might more rapidly detect and respond to ipsilesional stimuli that do normal subjects. An alternative hypothesis suggests that right-hemisphere lesions induce bilateral but asymmetrical inattention, and asymmetrical attention to hemispace induces an ipsilateral attentional bias. Support for this hypothesis comes from the observation that on some tasks, such as cancellation tests, patients with right-hemisphere injury and left sided neglect will fail to be aware of some ipsilesional (right) targets, but these ipsilesional errors will be less severe than those in contralesional (left) hemispace. A third explanation for the attentional bias is that patients with neglect cannot disengage their attention from ipsilateral stimuli. Support for this hypothesis comes from the observation that having patients erase rather than cancel targets reduces the severity of their neglect.

Independent of the cause of the ipsilesional attentional bias, patients with neglect often also demonstrate an intentional and exploratory bias, such that they fail to move their eyes, head, and limbs toward and in contralesional hemispace. Studies have revealed that although this intentional bias is often associated with an attentional bias, they are dissociable.

A striking feature in some patients with neglect is that they ignore the contralateral side, not only of externally presented information but also of internally generated images. This deficit cannot be caused by a loss of information because when these patients mentally view the same scene from the opposite perspective, they demonstrate knowledge of those parts of the scene that they initially neglected. Findings such as these have led some theorists to suggest that neglect reflects a representational deficit, that is, an inability to construct the contralateral side of mental representations (Bisiach, 1993). Such a view need not be seen as contradicting an attentional viewpoint, however, because attentional networks are critical in the creation and scanning of internal representations.

The attentional–intentional account of neglect might also explain why some perceptual and even meaning-based processes remain preserved in the face of severe neglect. At a perceptual level, the visual field is rapidly parsed on the basis of primitive features such as colors, shape, and orientation to define regions of interest for subsequent analysis. This early level of analysis, which includes processes for figure-ground segregation and symmetry analysis, occurs preattentively and is largely intact in patients with neglect. Likewise, activation of meaning-based representations may occur automatically and preattentively, a finding that may account for a variety of recent reports of preserved processing of neglected information (e.g., McGlinchey-Berroth, Milberg, Verfaellie, Alexander, & Kilduff, 1993).

IV. DIFFERENTIAL DIAGNOSIS

When diagnosing inattention, it is important to demonstrate that primary sensory disorders such as hemianesthesia or hemianopia are not the cause of a patient's behavioral deficits. In contrast to attentional deficits, primary sensory deficits are not ameliorated by attentional cues or by conditions that limit the number of distracting stimuli. Thus, patients with hemianopia fail to identify stimuli in the contralateral field even when tested in the dark, without conflicting stimuli. True hemianopia is retinotopic, but visual inattention is often body or viewer centered. Thus, having a patient gaze toward ipsilesional hemispace might alleviate the unawareness in the contralesional visual field. Patients with visual inattention often perform poorly on tests for spatial neglect (see below), but patients with hemianopia often learn to compensate for their disability and perform normally on these tests. When evaluating auditory processing, it is important to consider that because each ear projects to both hemispheres, contralesional unawareness of auditory stimuli cannot be attributed to deafferentation. Structural imaging might also help distinguish deafferentation from inattention, because in the latter condition the brain injury does not involve

Exhibit 20.1. Evaluation of Neglect

Neglect rather than primary sensory deficit

Auditory inattention
Effects of position of the eye or limb in space
Normal sensory evoked potentials

Bedside evaluation

Extrapersonal neglect
    Single stimulation; verbal and nonverbal responses, crossed
      responses
    Double simultaneous stimulation

Personal neglect
    Orienting to contralateral body parts
    Movement of contralateral body parts
    Matching body parts to external representations

Tests of spatial neglect

Cancellation
Line bisection
Drawing
Reading and writing

---

a sensory area. Sensory inattention might also be reversed with cold water caloric stimulation ipsilateral to the unattended side. Evoked potentials and skin conductance responses can also be used to dissociate hemi-inattention from deafferentation.

V. ASSESSMENT FOR NEGLECT

In many cases of acute neglect, observation of spontaneous behavior when the patient is interacting with an examiner or interacting with objects in the environment, grooming, or even using a wheelchair may reveal the presence of contralateral attentional or intentional deficits. Simple bedside testing may allow the examiner to specify more clearly the nature of these disorders. In milder cases, deficits may be detected only with more taxing cognitive tasks. Regardless of severity, however, a thorough assessment of different manifestations of neglect is necessary for an adequate understanding of the nature of a patient's deficits (see Exhibit 20.1).

Patients with neglect may perform well on some tasks and poorly on others because the tasks are sensitive to different components of neglect (e.g., disorders of attention vs. intention vs. representation). It is the pattern of performance across different tasks that commonly leads to the diagnosis of a particular subtype of neglect. Some patients, however, may also show high variability in their performance on a single task across repeated observations (or on different tasks thought to measure the same component of neglect). Such variability may be due to fluctuations in a patient's state of arousal, distractibility, or fatigue. Performance is also commonly influenced by the attentional load of a task, with patients performing more poorly as the attentional demands of a task increase (Rapscak, Fleet, Verfaellie, & Heilman, 1989). Finally, stimuli in the environment that function as distractors or as spatial cues may affect performance and should be avoided as much as possible. For this reason, testing should take place in a quiet room with the examiner positioned directly in front of (or behind) the patient to avoid lateral orienting biases.

A. Sensory Neglect or Inattention

An examination for sensory inattention consists of asking the patient to detect the presence and location of auditory stimuli (e.g., while the patient is blindfolded, either making a noise by rubbing or snapping fingers near the patient's left or right ear or not making a noise), visual stimuli (e.g., placing one hand in the patient's left visual field and the other in the right and either moving or not moving the left or right index finger), and tactile stimuli (e.g., with the patient blindfolded, touching the ipsilateral and contralateral hand in random order or not touching). Patients with inattention may fail to respond to contralateral stimuli in one or more modalities.

B. Extinction

Following testing for unilateral inattention, if the patient was able to detect stimuli on the side contralateral to his or her lesion, the examiner should also test for extinction to simultaneous stimulation by intermixing unilateral trials with trials on which two stimuli are presented simultaneously to homologous areas of space or body.

C. Personal Neglect

Patients who are unaware of the contralesional side of their body will often fail to groom or dress that part of their body. Thus, it might be important to observe a patient when he or she grooms and dresses.

Different commands that require orienting to or awareness of contralateral body parts can also be used to test for personal neglect. For example, patients can be asked to touch their contralateral side with the ipsilateral extremity. Patients with neglect may interrupt their movement before the target is reached or may fail to initiate a movement to the contralateral limb. Another task consists of asking patients to match parts of their body with external representations, for example, to touch on their own body the body part pointed out on a model or to point to a body part on a model when it is touched on their own body. Finally, they can be shown either their own hand versus the examiner's hand and asked whose hand is indicated. Patients with personal neglect might claim that their own left hand belongs to the examiner.

D. Hemispatial or Unilateral Neglect

Most standardized tests of spatial neglect consist of visual tasks performed in peripersonal space, but several can also be performed in far extrapersonal space or can be easily adapted to the tactile modality. Despite the surface similarity among these tasks, several investigators have demonstrated that these tasks assess more than a single neuropsychological process, and thus patients with spatial neglect might show dissociations in their performance on these tests. For this reason, a broad-based assessment is needed.

1. CANCELLATION TESTS

There are a variety of tasks that require patients to mark or cross out items presented in an array. These tests are commonly scored in terms of the number of omissions, but they also provide valuable information regarding a patient's search strategy. They vary in difficulty from simple tests in which patients are asked to cancel all items, such as Albert's (1973) Line Cancellation task, to more demanding ones in which patients have to find targets embedded in a dense field of distractors, such as the Bells Test (Gauthier, Dehaut, & Joanette, 1989). Another test on which normal individuals rarely make errors and that is highly sensitive to the presence of neglect is the Starr Cancellation test (Wilson, Cockburn, & Halligan, 1987).

Contralateral omissions in a cancellation task can be due either to an attentional deficit causing unawareness of contralesional stimuli or to an intentional failure causing a reluctance to move the eyes and head to the contralateral side (a failure of exploration), to move the arm toward or in contralesional space, or an inability to sustain these movements in contra-lesional hemispace. Consequently, several investigators have tried to disentangle these components by decoupling the direction of movement and the direction of attention so that the patient has to move his or her hand to the left to initiate a movement to the right. This can be done relatively easily by presenting the test on an overhead projector, because this arrangement mirror-reverses the display of visual information (Nico, 1996). Patients cancel the targets on a transparency presented on the overhead projector, but direct view of the transparency is prevented so that the stimuli can be seen only displayed on the opposing wall. If a patient with left neglect on a standard cancellation task omits stimuli on the right side of the transparency, an attentional deficit is inferred because the omitted information is displayed on the left side on the opposing wall. If the patient omits stimuli on the left side of the transparency, an intentional deficit is inferred, because the patient can see this information displayed on the right but fails to move to the left to cancel the stimuli.

2. LINE BISECTION

In this task, patients are asked to cut lines in half by placing a mark in the center of each line. Normal individuals tend to mark lines quite accurately, with small deviations (e.g., 1 or 2 mm) most often occurring to the left of center. Patients with neglect, however, often demonstrate much larger deviations, typically toward the ipsilateral side (neglecting the contralesional side). Some patients, however, especially those with right frontal lesions, systematically deviate toward the contralesional side. This disorder is called **ipsilateral neglect**. In both normal individuals and patients with neglect, deviations from center increase with increasing line length. The position of the line in space also systematically affects the performance of patients with neglect, with performance in ipsilateral space more accurate than that in midline or contralateral space. A version of the test developed by Schenkenberg, Bradford, and Ajax (1980) incorporates the features of both line length and line position.

Although horizontally oriented lines (at the intersection of the transverse and coronal planes) are most often used to assess for contralateral neglect, neglect can also be vertical and radial. By using vertical and radial lines, it is possible to assess these dimensions. To assess the patient for viewer-centered versus environmental neglect, the examiner can ask the patient to perform vertical and horizontal line bisections while the patient is upright and reclining on his or her side.

As previously discussed, an overhead projector can be used to disentangle sensory from motor neglect. An alternative technique (Milner, Harvey, Roberts, & Forster, 1993) is to present patients with lines that are pretransected at the midline and to ask them to point to the end of the line closer to the transection mark. Patients who have sensory neglect point to the contralateral end of the line, because the contralateral extent of the line is perceived as being shorter. In contrast, patients who have motor neglect point to the ipsilateral end of the line, because there is a reluctance to move to the contralateral side.

3. DRAWING

Spatial neglect can be assessed by asking patients to copy or draw spontaneously simple symmetrical figures (e.g., a cross) or figures that contain equally important details bilaterally (e.g., a flower). Patients with right-hemisphere lesions frequently have visuoconstructional deficits that affect their drawings. A test that is less affected by visuoconstructional deficits is the Clock-Drawing Test, in which patients are asked to place numbers on a clock. It should be noted, however, that verbal intelligence may compensate for neglect on this test. Another way to disentangle visuoconstructional from attentional deficits is to compare patients' standard figure copy with a hidden figure copy (McGlinchey-Berroth et al., 1996). In this task, patients are asked to copy on a piece of carbon paper placed over a blank sheet of paper using a stylus rather than a pencil. This arrangement does not produce a visible result to the patient, but it does produce a drawing on the underside of the blank sheet of paper that is exposed to the carbon paper, thus allowing the drawing to be evaluated later. In this condition, copy performance is not affected by the appearance of increasing amounts of ipsilateral information that may capture attention. Consequently, patients with neglect often perform much better in this condition. Visuoconstructional deficits, on the other hand, are not ameliorated by this manipulation.

4. READING AND WRITING

Assessment of reading should include both single words and compound words as well as paragraph-length passages that require scanning across the entire page. Two useful reading tests are part of the Behavioral Inattention Battery (Wilson et al., 1987): (a) Menu Reading, in which 10 food items, one or two words long, are presented for reading in two columns, and (b) Article Reading, in which two paragraphs are presented in a columnar arrangement, similar to a newspaper article. In evaluating writing, attention should be paid to the use of the space on a page. Typing on a keyboard may also elicit neglect, as patients may fail to use the keys on the contralesional side.

5. IMAGERY TASKS

Unfortunately, no standardized assessment techniques are available to test imagery. The examiner usually asks the patient to imagine a familiar scene and to tell the examiner what he or she sees in his or her mind eye. If the examiner is not familiar with the scene (such as a patient's home), it is important to get the aid of a person who is able to corroborate the patient's description.

VI. ASSOCIATED DISORDERS

In patients with right-hemisphere lesions, a number of disorders may co-occur with neglect. Whether these disorders are functionally related or are functionally independent but anatomically related currently remains controversial. The most commonly associated deficits follow.

A. Anosognosia

Neglect can be associated with unawareness of illness or disability. Patients may explicitly deny their hemiparesis or sensory loss, or they may avoid responding to questions that make reference to their impairments. These phenomena are most often seen during the acute phase of illness and might be related to a failure of feedback induced by sensory deficits or inattention, a deficit in body image (asomatognosia), an intentional disorder in which there is a failure to develop an expectation, or an interhemispheric disconnection such that the left hemisphere confabulates a response.

B. Anosodiaphoria

After a few days or weeks, patients with anosognosia will usually acknowledge their illness, but they may appear unconcerned about their illness and disabilities or may even joke about their disabilities. This aberrant behavior might be related to emotional disorders associated with right-hemisphere damage or the fact that patients have only a partial awareness of disability.

C. Other Visuospatial Deficits

Patients with right-hemisphere lesions often have deficits in the processing of global information and, consequently, show a bias toward processing of local objects. In contrast, patients with left-hemisphere lesions have difficulty processing local information and, consequently, show a bias toward processing global scenes. These visuospatial deficits may exacerbate neglect, especially in patients with right-hemisphere lesions. Typically, a visual display contains more local than global information. Because patients with right-hemisphere lesions are biased toward local information, it becomes even more difficult for them to move their attention away from local objects in ipsilesional space.

D. Allesthesia and Allokinesia

When stimulated on the contralesional (e.g., left) side and asked where they were stimulated, some patients with neglect indicate that they were stimulated on the ipsilateral (e.g., right) side. This phenomenon is called **allesthesia**, and although some investigators have proposed that this disorder might be related to a hemispatial and hemibody representational deficit, the cognitive mechanism underlying this disorder is not completely understood.

Patients with **allokinesia** have a similar deficit at the output stage. Thus, when stimulated on the contralesional side (e.g., left) and asked to move the ipsilesional limb in the direction of the stimulation, the patient moves in an ipsilesional (e.g., rightward) direction. Similarly, when asked to move the stimulated (contralesional) limb, the patient moves the ipsilesional (e.g., right) limb. Unlike patients who have allesthesia, patients with allokinesia can correctly localize the position of the stimulus verbally. Although allokinesia is often associated with directional or limb akinesia, the mechanisms of this disorder are also incompletely understood.

VII. TREATMENT

Because patients with neglect might be unaware of portions of their environment or body, they should not be permitted to engage in any activity that could hurt themselves or others (e.g., driving a car). There are now several forms of behavioral and pharmacological treatments that appear to reduce the signs and symptoms of neglect. Inducing the illusion of environmental movement by vestibular stimulation (e.g., cold water caloric stimulation) or by moving the background can reduce the signs of neglect, but only temporarily. Behavioral treatments that might improve neglect include training patients to orient to the left side of space, having them learn to move the left side of their body, or having them wear prism glasses while providing midline training. There are some reports that patching the ipsilesional eye might improve some patients, but others improve with patching of the contralesional eye. Thus, with eye patching, both eyes should be assessed. Dopamine agonists have also been reported to improve neglect, but if a patient's lesion extends into the basal ganglia, this treatment might make their neglect more severe. Thus, patients will need to be assessed before treatment and during treatment to learn if these medications induce an improvement.

VIII. CONCLUSION

Neglect refers to a class of disorders in which patients fail to attend or respond to stimuli presented in the contralateral part of space. Attentional disturbances can affect the processing of incoming information (sensory neglect or inattention) as well as responses to these stimuli (motor or intentional neglect), and it can selectively affect one or more sectors of space as well as the patient's body. Because there are multiple neural circuits that mediate the distribution of attention in space and the preparation for action, neglect can be caused by a variety of lesions, including the right hemisphere's parietal and frontal lobes, the cingulate gyrus, and the thalamus. In diagnosing the disorder, care should be taken to rule out sensory disorders as the cause of a patient's deficits. Bedside evaluation in the acute phase and standardized testing once a patient's condition has stabilized are required to document the nature and severity of the disorder and to devise an appropriate management and rehabilitation plan.

BIBLIOGRAPHY

Albert, M. L. (1973). A simple test of visual neglect. *Neurology, 23,* 658–664.

Bisiach, E. (1993). The Twentieth Bartlett Memorial Lecture: Mental representation in unilateral neglect and related disorders. *Quarterly Journal of Experimental Psychology, 46A,* 435–461.

Coslett, H. B., Bowers, D., Fitzpatrick, E., Haws, B., & Heilman, K. M. (1990). Dissociated neglect hypokinesia and hemispatial inattention in neglect. *Brain, 113,* 475–486.

Gauthier, L., Dehaut, F., & Joanette, Y. (1989). The Bells Test: A quantitative and qualitative test for visual neglect. *International Journal of Clinical Neuropsychology, 11,* 49–54.

Halligan, P. W., & Marshall, J. C. (1993). The history and clinical presentation of neglect. In I. H. Robertson & J. C. Marshall (Eds.), *Unilateral neglect: Clinical and experimental studies* (pp. 3–25). Hillsdale, NJ: Erlbaum.

Heilman, K. M., & Van den Abell, R. (1980). Right hemisphere dominance for attention: The mechanism underlying hemispheric asymmetries of inattention. *Neurology, 30,* 327–330.

Heilman K. M., Watson, R. T., & Valenstein, E. (2003). Neglect and related disorders. In K. M. Heilman & E. Valenstein (Eds.), *Clinical neuropsychology* (4th ed., pp. 296–346). New York: Oxford University Press.

Kinsbourne, M. (1993). Orientational bias model of unilateral neglect: Evidence from attentional gradients within hemispace—Mechanisms of unilateral neglect. In I. H. Robertson & J. C. Marshall (Eds.), *Unilateral neglect: Clinical and experimental studies* (pp. 63–86). Hillsdale, NJ: Erlbaum.

McGlinchey-Berroth, R., Bullis, D. P., Milberg, W. P., Verfaellie, M., Alexander, M., & D'Esposito, M. (1996). Assessment of neglect reveals dissociable behavioral but not neuroanatomical subtypes. *Journal of the International Neuropsychological Society, 2,* 441–451.

McGlinchey-Berroth, R., Milberg, W., Verfaellie, M., Alexander, M., & Kilduff, P. (1993). Semantic processing in the neglected field: Evidence from a lexical decision task. *Cognitive Neuropsychology, 10,* 79–108.

Milner, A. D., Harvey, M., Roberts, R. C., & Forster, S. V. (1993). Line bisection errors in visual neglect: Misguided action or size distortion? *Neuropsychologia, 31,* 39–49.

Nico, D. (1996). Detecting directional hypokinesia: The epidiascope technique. *Neuropsychologia, 34,* 471–474.

Rainville, C., Giroire, J. M., Periot, M., Cuny, E., & Mazaux, J. M. (2003). The impact of right subcortical lesions on executive functions and spatio-cognitive abilities: A case study. *Neurocase, 9,* 356–367.

Rapscak, S. Z., Fleet, W. S., Verfaellie, M., & Heilman, K. M. (1989). Selective attention in hemispatial neglect. *Archives of Neurology, 46,* 178–182.

Rizzolatti, G., & Camarda, R. (1987). Neural circuits for spatial attention and unilateral neglect. In M. Jeannerod (Ed.), *Neurophysiological and neuropsychological aspects of spatial neglect* (pp. 289–313). Amsterdam: North-Holland.

Robertson, I. H., & Marshall, J. C. (1993). *Unilateral neglect: Clinical and experimental studies.* Hillsdale, NJ: Erlbaum.

Schenkenberg, T., Bradford, D. C., & Ajax, E. T. (1980). Line bisection and unilateral visual neglect in patients with neurologic impairment. *Neurology, 30,* 509–517.

Vallar, G., Bottini, G., & Paulesu, E. (2003). Neglect syndromes: The role of the parietal cortex. *Advances in Neurology, 93,* 293–319.

Wilson, B., Cockburn, J., & Halligan, P. (1987). *Behavioral Inattention Test.* Titchfield, England: Thames Valley Test Company.

CHAPTER 21

Russell M. Bauer

The Agnosias

The **agnosias** are rare disorders in which a patient with brain damage becomes unable to recognize or appreciate the identity or nature of sensory stimuli. Clinical examination of the patient reveals a profound, modality-specific recognition impairment that cannot be fully explained by problems in elementary sensory processing, mental deterioration, attentional disturbances, aphasic misnaming, or unfamiliarity with the stimuli used to assess recognition abilities. Classically, a distinction between apperceptive and associative forms of agnosia has been made whereby the patient with **apperceptive** agnosia is said to have deficits in early stages of perceptual processing, whereas the patient with **associative** agnosia either does not display such problems or does so to a degree not sufficient to substantially impair the ability to perform perceptual operations. The associative agnosic patient can typically draw, copy, or match unidentified objects, whereas the apperceptive agnosic patient cannot. This distinction has been clinically useful, although it is clear that nearly all agnosic patients have *some* degree of perceptual ("apperceptive") disturbance. It should be remembered that adequate copying or matching *by itself* does not indicate normal perceptual processing (see Bauer & Demery, 2003; Farah, 1990).

Clinical assessment of the putative agnosic patient has two fundamental goals. First, the possibility that the recognition disturbance exists because of elementary sensory disturbance, dementia, aphasia, or unfamiliarity with the stimulus should be ruled out with standardized neuropsychological testing instruments. Second, the scope and nature of the patient's recognition disturbance should be determined. Does the recognition disturbance exist only for certain stimuli or classes of stimuli? Is it restricted to a particular sensory modality? Under what conditions (if any) can the patient recognize stimuli? This phase of the evaluation often requires detailed testing using specially formulated testing materials and should be conducted from the point of view of cognitive models of recognition disturbance (see next section). Appropriate referrals for neurological, neuroradiological, and basic sensory–perceptual (e.g., ophthalmologic, audiological) testing are often important in formulating a clinical diagnosis.

I. BASIC DEFINITIONS

Several types of agnosia have been identified in the literature. References summarizing the basic subtypes, clinicoanatomic correlations, and neurobehavioral mechanisms producing disturbances in recognition include Bauer and Demery (2003) and Farah (1990). Humphreys and Riddoch (1987) provided an excellent book-length description of a visual agnosic patient written from a cognitive neuropsychology perspective. "Pure" forms of these disorders are quite rare, and the etiology of the patient's disorder (e.g., whether from focal stroke vs. a more diffuse cause such as carbon monoxide poisoning) or the stage of recovery (if acute onset) will determine the observed pattern of deficits. Defining characteristics of the basic subtypes of agnosia are given in the following section and in Table 21.1. The remainder of this section provides basic characteristics of agnosia in outline form. This method of presentation is intended to stimulate attempts at differential diagnosis but should not discourage attempts at more in-depth analysis of presenting syndromes.

A. Visual Agnosias

1. VISUAL OBJECT AGNOSIA

a. Key features

1. Patients cannot recognize the meaning of visually presented objects.
2. Disorder is not restricted to naming (e.g., patient cannot point to the object when named or describe or demonstrate its use).

Table 21.1. Subtypes of Agnosia: Defining Characteristics and Key References

Subtype	Affected stimulus category	Varieties	Basis for distinction	Suggested reference
Visual agnosias				
Visual object agnosia	Objects	a. Apperceptive b. Associative	a. Drawing, matching – b. Drawing, matching +	Farah (1990) Benson and Greenberg (1969) Rubens and Benson (1971)
Simultanagnosia	Multiple objects or pictures	a. Dorsal b. Ventral	a. Cannot see multiple items b. Can see multiple items	Hecaen and Ajuriaguerra (1954) Kinsbourne and Warrington (1962)
Prosopagnosia	Faces	a. Apperceptive b. Associative	a. Match, categorize faces – b. Match, categorize faces +	DeRenzi et al. (1991) Pallis (1955)
Color agnosia	Colors	a. Achromatopsia b. Color anomia c. Color aphasia d. Color agnosia	a. Failure of color vision b. Can succeed at nonverbal color tasks c. Disproportionate deficit with color names d. Residual category	Damasio et al. (1980) Geschwind and Fusillo (1966) Kinsbourne and Warrington (1964)
Auditory agnosias				
Cortical deafness and cortical auditory disorder	All sounds	a. Cortical deafness b. Agnosia	a. Subjective deafness? b. Patient claims not to be deaf	Vignolo (1969) Michel et al. (1980) Kanshepolsky et al. (1973)

Pure word deafness	Speech sounds	a. b. Phonemic	a. Auditory acuity generally impaired b. Disorder of phonemic discrimination	Buchman et al. (1986)
Nonverbal auditory agnosia	Nonspeech sounds	a. Perceptual b. Associative	a. Misidentifications primarily acoustic b. Misidentifications primarily semantic	Spreen et al. (1965)
Sensory (receptive) amusia	Musical sounds			Bauer and McDonald (2003)
Tactile agnosias				Delay (1935) Caselli (1991)
Cortical tactile disorder	Tactually presented objects and object qualities	a. Object-based? b. Spatial?	a. Fail on object discrimination tasks b. Fail on tasks requiring spatial discrimination	Corkin (1978) Semmes (1965)
Tactile agnosia	Tactually presented objects	a. Disconnection b. Agnosic	a. Unilateral; can demonstrate object use b. Bimanual, cannot demonstrate object knowledge	Geschwind and Kaplan (1962) Hecaen and David (1945)

Note. + = function is spared; – = function is impaired.

3. Recognition sometimes is better for real objects than for pictures or line drawings.
4. Patient can recognize objects when presented in other modalities.

b. Varieties

1. *Apperceptive:* Patient cannot demonstrate adequate perception of object through drawing, copying, or matching tasks.
2. *Associative:* Drawing, copying, or matching tasks bring more success, although performance is sometimes "slavish"; patients demonstrate that they can perceive but not recognize.

c. Sometimes recognition disturbance is worse for certain categories of objects (e.g., living things, tools); recognition testing should use various categories of objects.

2. SIMULTANAGNOSIA

a. Key features

Patient cannot apprehend the overall meaning of a picture or stimulus but may be able to appreciate and describe isolated elements.

b. Varieties

1. *"Dorsal (bilateral occipitoparietal lesions):* Patients cannot see more than one object at a time.
2. *"Ventral" (left inferior occipital lesions):* Patients may be able to "see" more than one object at a time but cannot appreciate entire stimulus array.

c. Often considered a variant of apperceptive agnosia

3. PROSOPAGNOSIA

a. Key features

1. Patient is unable to recognize the identity of viewed faces.
2. Patient often can appreciate aspects of faces such as age, gender, or emotional expression.

b. Varieties

Apperceptive and associative forms have been identified on the basis of matching tasks.

c. Associated features

Within-class recognition of other types of visually similar objects (e.g., recognition of individual chairs, cars, animals) may be impaired.

4. COLOR AGNOSIA

Because colors can only be appreciated visually, the status of color agnosia as a true agnosic deficit has been difficult to establish. Nonetheless, four classes of patients have been identified with disproportional impairment in recognizing, naming, or otherwise using color information.

a. Central achromatopsia

Patient has acquired deficit in color vision due to central nervous system (CNS) disease and cannot match, discriminate, or name colors. There likely are bilateral occipital lesions but may be unilateral.

b. Color anomia

Patient has specific difficulty in naming colors, usually found in the context of right homonymous hemianopia and pure alexia (Geschwind, 1965). Other aphasic signs are generally absent; there is likely a posterior left-hemisphere lesion.

c. Specific color aphasia

Seen in the context of aphasia, this represents a disproportionate difficulty in linguistic processing (including naming) of colors; there is suspect left (dominant) parietal lobe damage.

d. Color agnosia

This is a residual category of patients who have difficulty appreciating the nature or name of color they see but who do not fall within the previously discussed categories.

5. OPTIC APHASIA

a. Key features

1. Patient cannot name a visually presented object but can name when the object is heard in use–action or when placed in the hand (i.e., naming deficit is *modality specific to vision*).
2. Patient can demonstrate its use by gesture or can point to it when named.

b. Condition is not regarded as a true agnosia.

c. It may represent a visual–verbal disconnection.

B. Auditory Agnosias

Subtypes of auditory agnosia have been distinguished on the basis of the type of auditory stimulus the patient has difficulty recognizing (Bauer & McDonald, 2003). Although much remains to be understood about these disorders (which have not been studied as exhaustively as cases of visual agnosia), four general classes of deficits have been described.

1. CORTICAL AUDITORY DISORDER AND CORTICAL DEAFNESS

a. Key features

1. Patient has difficulty recognizing auditory stimuli of many kinds, verbal and nonverbal.
2. Basic audiological testing results are abnormal.

b. Varieties

1. *Cortical deafness:* Patient complains of a subjective sense of deafness.
2. *Cortical auditory disorder:* There is no subjective sense of deafness.

c. Conditions may evolve to one of the more selective types of auditory agnosia described below; longitudinal assessment is important.

2. PURE WORD DEAFNESS

a. Key features

1. Patient is unable to comprehend spoken language but can read, write, and speak in a *relatively* normal manner.
2. Comprehension of nonverbal sounds is relatively spared.
3. Patient is relatively free of aphasic symptoms found with other disorders affecting language comprehension (Buchman, Garron, Trost-Cardamone, Wichter, & Schwartz, 1986).

3. AUDITORY SOUND AGNOSIA (AUDITORY AGNOSIA FOR NONSPEECH SOUNDS)

a. Key features

1. Patient is unable to comprehend meaning of common environmental sounds, with relative sparing of speech comprehension.
2. Condition is far rarer than pure word deafness.

b. Varieties (Vignolo, 1969)

1. *Perceptual-discriminative form:* Patient makes predominantly acoustic errors (e.g., "whistling" for birdsong).
2. *Semantic-associative form:* Patient makes predominantly semantic errors (e.g., "train" for automobile engine).

4. SENSORY (RECEPTIVE) AMUSIA

a. Key features

1. Patient is unable to appreciate various characteristics of heard music.
2. Impairment in perceptual versus conceptual aspects of music should be evaluated.

b. **Impaired music perception occurs to some extent in all cases of auditory sound agnosia and in most cases of aphasia and pure word deafness; exact prevalence unknown**

c. **Condition is probably underreported because a specific musical disorder rarely interferes with everyday life.**

d. **Perception of pitch, harmony, timbre, intensity, and rhythm may be affected to different degrees or in various combinations**

C. Tactile Agnosias

Compared with visual agnosias, somatosensory (tactile) agnosias have received scant attention and are poorly understood. Several distinct disorders have been identified, and many classifications of tactile agnosia have been offered. Delay (1935) distinguished three disorders: (a) **amorphognosia**, impaired recognition of the size and shape of objects; (b) **ahylognosia**, impaired recognition of the distinctive qualities of objects such as weight, density, texture, and thermal properties; and (c) **tactile asymbolia**, impaired recognition of tactile objects in the absence of amorphognosia or ahylognosia. Although only tentative, a clinically useful distinction can be made between cortical tactile disorders (which probably encompass the first two of Delay's deficit classes) and tactile agnosia (which represents an inability to appreciate the nature of tactually manipulated objects).

1. CORTICAL TACTILE DISORDERS

a. Key features

Deficits are in appreciating distinct object qualities such as size, shape, weight, or spatial configuration of tactually presented objects.

b. Varieties

Some patients have especially obvious defects of size discrimination, whereas others fail in tasks that emphasize the spatial character of tactually manipulated objects.

c. No hemispheric specialization exists in elementary somatosensory function, but patients with right-hemisphere disease may have difficulty in performing the spatial component of many tactile discrimination tasks.

2. TACTILE AGNOSIA

a. Key features

1. Patient cannot identify objects placed in the hand.
2. Elementary sensory function is intact.

b. Varieties

1. Deficit exists in both hands: patient has an "agnosic" deficit (an inability to appreciate the nature of stimuli because of a central defect in processing the nature of a stimulus) and cannot demonstrate use of object through gesture.
2. Deficit exists in one (usually left) hand: patient has a "visual–verbal disconnection," can demonstrate use of the object, and can name the object if placed in the other hand.

II. NEUROANATOMIC CORRELATES

Lesion localization that is based on individual case studies and recent reviews of the agnosic syndromes previously described is presented in Table 21.2. In general, apperceptive agnosias involve more extensive damage to sensory association cortex, whereas associative agnosias result from lesions of corticocortical pathways or from impairment in those areas in which semantic representations of objects are stored. In most published cases, lesions are caused by ischemic stroke, although cases of carbon

Table 21.2. Lesion Localization for Various Forms of Agnosia

Disorder	Lesion localization	Reference
Visual agnosias		
1. Apperceptive visual object agnosia	Diffuse, posterior damage to occipital lobes and surrounding regions	Benson and Greenberg (1969)
2. Associative visual object agnosia	Bilateral; inferior occipitotemporal	Rubens and Benson (1971)
3. Simultanagnosia		
a. Dorsal	Bilateral parietal and superior occipital	Farah (1990)
	Localized bilaterally to either superior occipital or inferior parietal lobes	Hecaen and Ajuriaguerra (1954)
b. Ventral	Dominant occipitotemporal junction	Kinsbourne and Warrington (1962)
4. Prosopagnosia		
a. Apperceptive	Traditionally seen as bilateral in all or nearly all cases; cortex and white matter in occipitotemporal gyrus or projection system, typically including fusiform face area	Bauer and Demery (2003) Barton et al. (2002) Rossion et al. (2003)
	More recently a few cases of what appears to be unilateral damage to right visual association cortices within occipital and parietal lobes	Damasio et al. (1990) DeRenzi (1986)
b. Associative	Bilateral anterior temporal regions compromising hippocampal and other regions	Damasio et al. (1990)

(Continued)

Table 21.2. Lesion Localization for Various Forms of Agnosia *(Continued)*

Disorder	Lesion localization	Reference
5. Color agnosia		
a. Achromatopsia	Unilateral or bilateral inferior ventromedial region of occipital lobe—involves lingual and fusiform gyri—superior field defects	Damasio et al. (1980)
b. Color anomia	Dominant occipital infarction with corpus callosum involvement	Geschwind and Fusillo (1966)
c. Specific color aphasia	Dominant parietal damage coincident with posterior aphasia	Kinsbourne and Warrington (1964)
d. Color agnosia	Bilateral lesion of ventral visual stream	DeVreese (1991)
6. Optic aphasia	Unilateral; dominant occipital lobe and splenium	Riddoch and Humphreys (1987) Geschwind (1965)
Auditory agnosias		
1. Cortical auditory disorder	Variable; can involve superior temporal gyrus and efferent connections of Heschl's gyrus or bilateral subcortical lesions	Kazui et al. (1990) Oppenheimer and Newcombe (1978)
2. Pure word deafness	Bilateral; symmetrical lesions of anterior section of superior temporal gyri; most often bilateral disconnections of Wernicke's area from auditory input	Buchman et al. (1986)

	Unilateral (rare); deep subcortical in dominant superior temporal region damaging primarily auditory cortex or pathways to and from medial geniculate gyrus	Weisenburg and McBride (1935/1964)
3. Auditory sound agnosia		
a. Perceptual-discrimination type	Nondominant hemisphere	Vignolo (1969)
b. Semantic-associative type	Dominant hemisphere; linked with posterior aphasia	Vignolo (1969)
4. Sensory (receptive) amusia	Unilateral temporal lobe; if comorbid with aphasia, lesion is on dominant side	Bauer and McDonald (2003)
Tactile agnosias		
1. Cortical tactile disorders	Severe and long-lasting; contralateral postcentral gyrus Less severe, bilateral lesions of secondary somatosensory area	Corkin (1978)
2. Unilateral tactile anomia	Corpus callosum (affecting crossing somatosensory fibers (minimally; actual lesion may be more extensive)	Geschwind and Kaplan (1962)
3. Tactile agnosia	Contralateral primary somatosensory projection area in postcentral gyrus	Caselli (1991)

monoxide poisoning, posttraumatic hematoma, and neoplasm have been reported (Bauer & Demery, 2003; Farah, 1990). It is becoming increasingly recognized (most prominently in the visual domain) that apperceptive agnosia can result from degenerative disease, with particular attention being devoted to dementia syndromes presenting with predominant visuoperceptual disturbance (Biran & Coslett, 2003; Caselli, 2000; Jackson & Owsley, 2003; Mendez, Mendez, Martin, Smyth, & Whitehouse, 1990).

III. DIFFERENTIAL DIAGNOSIS OF AGNOSIA

A. Basic Decision-Making Process in Differential Diagnosis

Diagnosis of the agnosias begins with identification of the basic characteristics of the patient's recognition defect. The process of reaching a tentative initial diagnosis is outlined in flowchart form in Figure 21.1. In applying the flowchart, clinicians should remember that "pure" forms of agnosia are not commonly encountered. The first part of the flowchart (Figure 21.1a) presents three "streams" representing visual, auditory, and tactile agnosias and outlines basic questions that should be asked in making a tentative initial diagnosis. The second part of the flowchart (Figure 21.1b) deals specifically with visual agnosias, which are more common and are better understood than their auditory and tactile counterparts.

The flowchart assumes that simple materials for bedside testing are available (or can be manufactured) and that the clinician consults other disciplines to further document the extent of neuroanatomical damage and to better characterize sensory–perceptual function. In many cases, the physician or the treatment team makes such referrals, but it should be remembered that the informed neuropsychologist can serve as a valuable advisor in ensuring that appropriate referrals are made. In addition to an extended behaviorally oriented neurological examination, potentially useful referrals include neuroimaging consults (computed tomography [CT] or magnetic resonance imaging [MRI]), evoked potential studies, and referrals to ophthalmologists, speech pathologists, audiologists, or other professionals for more detailed evaluation of sensory–perceptual and neurobehavioral status. Referral decisions should not be made automatically but should depend on the likely cost-effectiveness of obtaining the requested information.

Figure 21.1a. Flowchart for clinical decision-making differential diagnosis of agnosia.

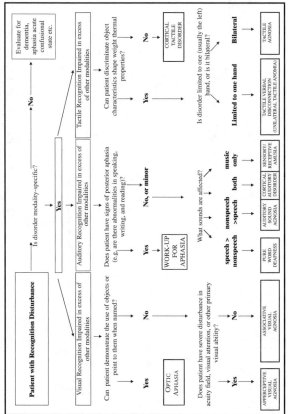

Figure 21.1b. Differential diagnosis of visual agnosia.

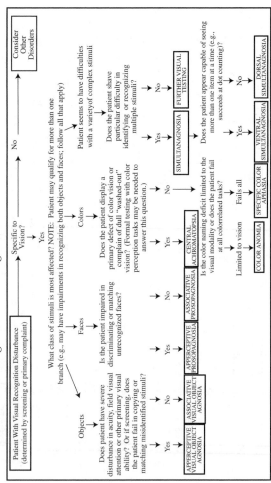

B. Neuropsychological Assessment in Differential Diagnosis

Once a tentative diagnosis has been reached (or once the clinician has narrowed the differential diagnosis to a subset of possible disorders on the basis of clinical presentation), formal assessment of neuropsychological skills is indicated. As discussed earlier, neuropsychological assessment of the putative agnosic patient seeks to (a) rule out alternative explanations of the patient's deficit and (b) characterize in more precise terms the nature of the patient's deficit so that its underlying mechanism and it relationship to pathological anatomy can be understood.

1. RULING OUT ALTERNATIVE EXPLANATIONS

As suggested earlier, disturbances of "recognition" can occur in a variety of neurological conditions but are considered agnosic only if they exist in the relative absence of aphasia, generalized dementia, impaired attentional capacity, or other defect that nonspecifically impairs some or all of the information-processing steps involved in object recognition. Therefore, one critical aspect of the assessment of the agnosic patient involves assessment of these "bracketing" conditions to rule them out as explanations for the recognition defect. A review of available case reports reveals considerable variability in the methods used for this portion of the assessment. Table 21.3 presents a reasonable strategy for achieving this goal, although it is recognized that many other tests are available for achieving this purpose.

In general, patients should receive a basic neuropsychological examination designed to determine and assess general intellectual status, memory function, linguistic competence, and sensory–perceptual processing. The clinician may wish to perform a comprehensive neuropsychological battery to better understand the patient's cognitive strengths and weaknesses, to document baseline functioning, or to assist in treatment planning. Assessment of language ability (naming, auditory comprehension, fluency, repetition, reading, writing, and praxis) is especially important in understanding the possible role that linguistic factors might play in the patient's recognition defect. A comprehensive aphasia battery (e.g., Boston Diagnostic Aphasia Examination [Goodglass & Kaplan, 1983]; Multilingual Aphasia Examination [Benton & Hamsher, 1989]; Western Aphasia Battery [Kertesz, 1982]) is useful for this purpose, although it may be necessary to perform supplementary tests to ensure that naming and recognition are tested in all sensory modalities.

Table 21.3. Ruling Out Alternative Causes of Recognition Disturbance

Condition or problem	Assessment instruments	Domains tested	Reference
Generalized dementia	Dementia Rating Scale—2	Memory, attention/ concentration, construction, initiation/perseveration	Jurica et al. (2001)
Aphasia	Boston Diagnostic Aphasia Exam Multilingual Aphasia Exam Western Aphasia Battery	Fluency, comprehension, naming, repetition, reading, writing, praxis	Goodglass and Kaplan (1983) Benton and Hamsher (1989) Kertesz (1982)
Disturbances of attention/ orientation (e.g., delirium)	Temporal Orientation Test Visual Search and Attention Test WAIS–R Digit Span Sentence Repetition WMS–R Mental Control Line Bisection	Time orientation Visual search and selectivity Focused attention span Focused attention span (sentences) Mental tracking, sustained attention Spatial attention, hemispatial neglect	Benton et al. (1994) Trenerry et al. (1990) Benton and Hamsher (1989) Schenkenberg et al. (1980)

| Unfamiliarity with stimuli | Determined subjectively; the examiner needs to ensure that failures of naming/identification are not based on experiential, cultural, or other factors that lead to the patient's unfamiliarity with stimuli tested; use of common or frequently encountered items typically circumvents this problem. | Visual, auditory, and tactile object identification with common objects should be tested in each patient to determine familiarity statistics and to determine modality specificity; subjects who cannot name objects should be encouraged to divulge anything they know about them or to group items into familiar and unfamiliar categories. | Familiarity must be determined, even informally, on an individual-subject basis. If creating in-house stimulus sets, general references containing relevant statistics on item frequency, imageability, and so on should be consulted to construct a balanced set of items. |

Note. WAIS–R = Wechsler Adult Intelligence Scale—Revised; WMS–R = Wechsler Memory Scale—Revised.

2. CHARACTERIZING THE NATURE OF THE AGNOSIC DEFICIT

Once the patient's general neuropsychological status has been determined, the clinician will want to perform further testing to more precisely characterize the nature of the patient's recognition deficit. At this stage, cognitive neuropsychological models of the perceptual-recognition process become helpful in guiding the approach to assessment. A representative model, adapted from Ellis and Young (1988), is presented in Figure 21.2. Consulting individual case reports contained in Tables 21.1 and 21.2 will also assist in planning an appropriate assessment.

Figure 21.2 draws on a diverse literature in perceptual psychology and neuropsychology (Ellis & Young, 1988) and is presented to the clinician because such models have succeeded in parsing the process of object recognition into distinct information-processing components or stages. The left side of the figure represents dissociable stages of the object recognition process suggested by clinical and experimental research. The right side of the figure presents the most important implications of the model for clinical assessment and suggests some commonly available tests that can be used in "localizing" the defect at a particular processing level. Defects before the level of the "object recognition unit" can be roughly considered apperceptive in nature, whereas subsequent deficits correspond to associative forms of agnosia. The model presented in Figure 21.2 is obviously best suited to evaluating a visual recognition disturbance but should provide guidance in assessing auditory and tactile agnosia as well. A comprehensive evaluation proceeds by evaluating all levels of the model, even in situations in which "early" deficits are found.

IV. RELEVANT LABORATORY, EEG, AND NEUROIMAGING CORRELATES

As a general neuropsychological classification, agnosia is not associated with any definitive pattern of abnormality in laboratory tests. Electroencephalography (EEG) and neuroimaging findings vary with the type of agnosia, as might be anticipated from lesion localization data presented in Table 21.2. The most common etiologies of agnosia include cerebrovascular accident, tumor, carbon monoxide poisoning, closed head injury, and CNS infection, although as indicated earlier, it is becoming increasingly recognized that some cases of degenerative dementia

Figure 21.2. Clinical application of cognitive neuropsychological model.

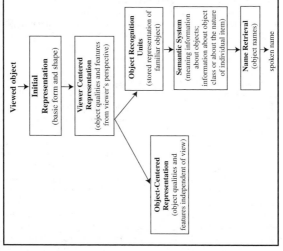

Assessment Notes for Each Level

Key issue: Can subject appreciate basic object form and shape qualities? Object and shape discriminations (e.g., Warrington & James, 1991), Visual Closure (e.g., Street, 1931), Visual Form Discrimination (Benton et al., 1994)

Key issue: Can subject match identical objects or discriminate between same and different items? Birmingham Object Recognition Battery (Riddoch & Humphreys, 1993), Benton Face Recognition, Items 1–6 (Benton et al., 1994)

Key issue: Can subject match objects presented in different views? Birmingham Object Recognition Battery (Riddoch & Humphreys, 1993); Benton Face Recognition, Items 7–22 (Benton et al.,1994)

Key issue: Is the item familiar or not? Birmingham Object Recognition Battery (Riddoch & Humphreys, 1993); familiarity discriminations; famous face recognition from Albert Remote Memory Battery (Albert et al., and subsequent modifications)

Key issue: Can subject recognize the general class to which item belongs? Have subject group like objects together (e.g., tools, office items) on the basis of semantic similarity; Birmingham Object Recognition Battery (Riddoch & Humphreys, 1993)

Key issue: Can subject derive the specific name for the presented item? Confrontation naming tests (Benton & Hamsher, 1989; Kaplan et al., 1983)

Viewed object

Initial Representation (basic form and shape)

Viewer Centered Representation (object qualities and features from viewer's perspective)

Object Recognition Units (stored representation of familiar object)

Semantic System (meaning information about objects; information about object class or about the nature of individual item)

Name Retrieval (object names)

spoken name

Object-Centered Representation (object qualities and features independent of view) with primary involvement of posterior cortex can present with prominent signs of (primarily apperceptive) agnosia. Medical findings vary with etiology and localization. Because of these considerations, it can be said that laboratory, EEG, and neuroradiological findings per se do not typically play an integral role in differential diagnosis. One exception to this rule is the occasional utility of auditory or visual evoked potentials as a way of determining whether a defect exists in the sensory projection areas as opposed to the primary sensory or association cortex. Instead, the clinician should rely on behavioral factors and should consider the physical findings as confirmatory.

V. PSYCHOLOGICAL AND PSYCHIATRIC COMORBIDITY

The lesions most likely to produce agnosic defects often spare limbic, paralimbic, or frontal regions that, when damaged, produce primary affective or personality changes. For this reason, specific forms of psychopathology are not obligatory accompaniments of agnosic syndromes. However, secondary emotional reactions to the real-life consequences of agnosia are common. Factors such as unemployment, changes in social life, dependency on others for help in everyday activities (i.e., dressing, transportation, eating), and boredom are seen. These major lifestyle changes may lead to depression or adjustment disorders in some individuals, whereas others may find adaptive ways to cope. As an excellent example, Humphreys and Riddoch (1987) described in detail how their patient, John, and his wife both cope with John's visual agnosia. Their description contains evidence of both adaptive and maladaptive compensations. Although epidemiological studies have yet to be conducted, auditory and tactile agnosias seem less likely to produce major life changes so that it may be that such disorders have less deleterious consequences. Such speculations await definitive research.

Another trait sometimes seen in patients with agnosia is sensory compensation. This is an interesting and as yet unresearched phenomenon reported in the animal literature (Horel & Keating, 1969), in which the agnosic patient comes to rely on intact sensory modalities (e.g., audition and touch in the case of visual agnosia) in exploratory activity. Whether this represents an attempt to achieve an optimal arousal level through sensory stimulation or an attempt to gain understanding of the world through an intact modality remains to be seen. For example, Bauer's (1984) patient with severe visual agnosia listens to music constantly to lessen the boredom of living with the disorder. In my experience, substance abuse is a risk in the chronic period, possibly in response to the reduced stimulation that results from an agnosic deficit, and possibly a result of premorbid factors. It should be emphasized that one problem in understanding psychiatric comorbidity in agnosia is that the relative rarity of these syndromes complicates an analysis of whether such problems are caused or exacerbated by the underlying neurological impairment or whether the appearance of such problems reflects preinjury factors that would have exerted themselves in any event. Such issues await systematic research.

VI. CONCLUSION

Agnosia refers to an acquired impairment in the ability to recognize the identity or nature of sensory stimuli. It is a relatively rare disorder that can produce significant everyday impairment. No specific laboratory or neuroradiological marker exists, although orderly anatomical findings have been reported in the literature on visual, auditory, and tactile agnosia that should serve, if present, to raise suspicion about the diagnosis in the individual case. Key symptoms, characteristic neuroradiological findings, and a general assessment approach based on cognitive neuropsychological models of object recognition were summarized in this chapter. Although significant progress has recently been made, much remains to be learned about these complex disorders, and clinicians are encouraged to take a hypothesis-oriented approach to enlarge the available knowledge base.

BIBLIOGRAPHY

Albert, M. S., Butters, N., & Levin, J. (1979). Temporal gradients in the retrograde amnesia of patients with alcoholic Korsakoff's disease. *Neurology, 36,* 211–216.

Barton, J. J., Press, D. Z., Keenan, J. P., & O'Connor, M. (2002). Lesions of the fusiform face area impair perception of facial configuration in prosopagnosia. *Neurology, 58,* 71–78.

Bauer, R. M. (1984). Autonomic recognition of names and faces in prosopagnosia: A neuropsychological application of the Guilty Knowledge Test. *Neuropsychologia, 22,* 457–469.

Bauer, R. M., & Demery, J. A. (2003). Agnosia. In K. M. Heilman & E. Valenstein (Eds.), *Clinical neuropsychology* (4th ed., pp. 236–295). New York: Oxford University Press.

Bauer, R. M., & McDonald, C. R. (2003). Auditory agnosia and amusia. In T. Feinberg & M. J. Farah (Eds.), *Behavioral neurology and neuropsychology* (2nd ed., pp. 257–270). New York: McGraw-Hill.

Benson, D. F., & Greenberg, J. P. (1969). Visual form agnosia. *Archives of Neurology, 20,* 82–89.

Benton, A. L., & Hamsher, K. deS. (1989). *Multilingual Aphasia Examination.* Iowa City, IA: AJA Associates.

Benton, A. L., Sivan, A. B., Hamsher, K. deS., Varney, N. R., & Spreen, O. (1994). *Contributions to neuropsychological assessment* (2nd ed.). New York: Oxford University Press.

Biran, I., & Coslett, H. B. (2003). Visual agnosia. *Current Neurological and Neuroscience Reports, 3,* 508–512.

Buchman, A. S., Garron, D. C., Trost-Cardamone, J. E., Wichter, M. D., & Schwartz, M. (1986). Word deafness: One hundred years later. *Journal of Neurology, Neurosurgery, and Psychiatry, 49,* 489–499.

Caselli, R. J. (1991). Rediscovering tactile agnosia. *Mayo Clinic Proceedings, 66,* 129–142.

Caselli, R. J. (2000). Visual syndromes as the presenting feature of degenerative brain disease. *Seminars in Neurology, 20,* 139–144.

Corkin, S. (1978). The role of different cerebral structures in somesthetic perception. In C. E. Cartarette & M. P. Friedman (Eds.), *Handbook of perception* (pp. 105–155). New York: Academic Press.

Damasio, A. R., Damasio, H., & Tranel, D. (1990). Impairments of visual recognition as clues to the processes of memory. In G. M. Edelman, W. E. Gall, & W. M. Cowan (Eds.), *Signal and sense: Local and global order in perceptual maps* (pp. 451–473). New York: Wiley.

Damasio, A. R., Yamada, T., Damasio, H., Corbett, J., & McKee, J. (1980). Central achromatopsia: Behavioral, anatomic, and physiologic aspects. *Neurology, 30,* 1064–1071.

Delay, J. (1935). *Les astereognosies. Pathologie due toucher: Clinique, physiologie, topographie* [Astereognosia. Pathology of touch: Clinical features, physiology, and topography]. Paris: Masson.

DeRenzi, E. (1986). Prosopagnosia in two patients with CT scan evidence of damage confined to the right hemisphere. *Neuropsychologia, 24,* 385–389.

DeRenzi, E., Faglioni, P., Grossi, D., & Nichelli, P. (1991). Apperceptive and associative forms of prosopagnosia. *Cortex, 27,* 213–221.

DeVreese, L. P. (1991). Two systems for colour-naming defects: Verbal disconnection vs. colour imagery disorder. *Neuropsychologia, 29*, 1–18.

Ellis, A. W., & Young, A. W. (1988). *Human cognitive neuropsychology*. Hillsdale, NJ: Erlbaum.

Farah, M. J. (1990). *Visual agnosia: Disorders of object recognition and what they tell us about normal vision*. Cambridge, MA: MIT Press.

Geschwind, N. (1965). Disconnexion syndromes in animals and man. *Brain, 88*, 237–294, 585–644.

Geschwind, N., & Fusillo, M. (1966). Color-naming defects in association with alexia. *Archives of Neurology, 15*, 137–156.

Geschwind, N., & Kaplan, E. F. (1962). A human disconnection syndrome. *Neurology, 12*, 675–685.

Goodglass, H., & Kaplan, E. (1983). *Boston Diagnostic Aphasia Examination (BDAE)*. Philadelphia: Lea & Febiger. (Distributed by Psychological Assessment Resources, Odessa, FL)

Hecaen, H., & Ajuriaguerra, J. (1954). Balint's syndrome (psychic paralysis of visual fixation) and its minor forms. *Brain, 77*, 373–400.

Hecaen, H., & David, M. (1945). Syndrome parietale traumatique: Asymbolie tactile et hemiasomatognosie paroxystique et douloureuse [Traumatic parietal syndrome: Tactile asymbolia and paroxystic and painful hemisomatognosia]. *Revue Neurologique, 77*, 113–123.

Horel, J. A., & Keating, E. G. (1969). Partial Kluver–Bucy syndrome produced by cortical disconnection. *Brain Research, 16*, 281–284.

Humphreys, G. W., & Riddoch, M. J. (1987). *To see but not to see: A case study of visual agnosia*. London: Erlbaum.

Jackson, G. R., & Owsley, C. (2003). Visual dysfunction, neuro-degenerative diseases, and aging. *Neurological Clinics, 21*, 709–728.

Jurica, S. J., Leitten, C. L., & Mattis, S. (2001). *Dementia Rating Scale–2: Professional manual*. Odessa, FL: Psychological Assessment Resources.

Kanshepolsky, J., Kelley, J., & Waggener, J. (1973). A cortical auditory disorder. *Neurology, 23*, 699–705.

Kaplan, E. F., Goodglass, H., & Weintraub, S. (1983). *Boston Naming Test*. Philadelphia: Lea & Febiger.

Kazui, S., Naritomi, H., Sawada, T., & Inque, N. (1990). Subcortical auditory agnosia. *Brain and Language, 38*, 476–487.

Kertesz, A. (1982). *Western Aphasia Battery*. San Antonio, TX: Psychological Corporation.

Kinsbourne, M., & Warrington, E. K. (1962). A disorder of simultaneous form perception. *Brain, 85,* 461–486.

Kinsbourne, M., & Warrington, E. K. (1964). Observations on color agnosia. *Journal of Neurology, Neurosurgery, and Psychiatry, 27,* 296–299.

Mendez, M. F., Mendez, M. A., Martin, R., Smyth, K. A., & Whitehouse, P. J. (1990). Complex visual disturbances in Alzheimer's disease. *Neurology, 40,* 439–443.

Michel, J., Peronnet, F., & Schott, B. (1980). A case of cortical deafness: Clinical and electrophysiological data. *Brain and Language, 10,* 367–377.

Oppenheimer, D. R., & Newcombe, F. (1978). Clinical and anatomic findings in a case of auditory agnosia. *Archives of Neurology, 35,* 712–719.

Pallis, C. A. (1955). Impaired identification of faces and places with agnosia for colors. *Journal of Neurology, Neurosurgery, and Psychiatry, 18,* 218–224.

Riddoch, M. J., & Humphreys, G. W. (1987). Visual object processing in optic aphasia: A case of semantic access agnosia. *Cognitive Neuropsychology, 4,* 131–185.

Riddoch, M. J., & Humphreys, G. W. (1993). *Birmingham Object Recognition Battery.* Mahwah, NJ: Psychology Press.

Rossion, B., Caldara, R., Seghier, M., Schuller, A. M., Lazeyras, F., & Mayer, E. (2003). A network of occipito-temporal face sensitive areas besides the right middle fusiform gyrus is necessary for normal face processing. *Brain, 126,* 2381–2395.

Rubens, A. B., & Benson, D. F. (1971). Associative visual agnosia. *Archives of Neurology, 24,* 304–316.

Schenkenberg, T., Bradford, D. C., & Ajax, E. T. (1980). Line bisection and unilateral visual neglect in patients with neurological impairment. *Neurology, 30,* 509–517.

Semmes, J. (1965). A non-tactual factor in astereognosis. *Neuropsychologia, 3,* 295–314.

Spreen, O., Benton, A. L., & Fincham, R. (1965). Auditory agnosia without aphasia. *Archives of Neurology, 13,* 84–92.

Street, R. F. (1931). *A Gestalt Completion Test* (Contributions to Education Report No. 481). New York: Teachers College, Columbia University, Bureau of Publications.

Trenerry, M. R., Crosson, B., DeBoe, J., & Leber, W. R. (1990). *Visual Search and Attention Test.* Odessa, FL: Psychological Assessment Resources.

Vignolo, L. A. (1969). Auditory agnosia: A review and report of recent evidence. In A. L. Benton (Ed.), *Contributions to clinical neuropsychology* (pp. 172–208). Chicago: Aldine Press.

Warrington, E. K., & James, M. (1991). *Visual Object and Space Perception Battery.* Bury St. Edmunds, Suffolk, England: Thames Valley Test Co. (Distributed by National Rehabilitation Services, Gaylord, MI)

Weisenburg, T. S., & McBride, K. L. (1964). *Aphasia.* New York: Hafner. (Original work published 1935)

CHAPTER 22

Kenneth M. Heilman, Robert T. Watson, and
Leslie J. Gonzalez-Rothi

Limb Apraxias

Limb apraxia is defined as an inability to correctly perform purposeful, skilled movements with the forelimbs (Heilman & Rothi, 1993). Limb apraxia may be developmental or induced by neurological dysfunction. In addition to apraxia, there are many other disorders that might interfere with the production of skilled movements. Thus, the diagnosis of apraxia is typically made by excluding other causative factors. To be classified as a patient with apraxia, a person's inability to perform learned movements cannot be directly secondary to (a) sensory loss or more elemental motor disorders such as weakness, tremors, dystonia, chorea, ballismus, athetosis, myoclonus, ataxia, or seizures or (b) severe cognitive, memory, motivational, or attentional disorders. Although the presence of these disorders does not preclude apraxia, before making this diagnosis the clinician should be certain that these behavioral disorders do not fully account for the patient's inability to perform skilled acts.

Although limb apraxia is a common, disabling, and enduring sequela of brain damage, it may be the least recognized neuropsychological disorder associated with cerebral disease. It is most commonly associated with strokes and degenerative dementia of the Alzheimer type, but it may be seen with many other diseases of the central nervous system. For example, apraxia may be associated with cerebral trauma and tumors. It may be the presenting symptom in corticobasal degeneration and focal atrophies.

There are several reasons that apraxia often goes unrecognized. When apraxia is associated with hemispheric injury such as stroke or trauma, patients often also have a right hemiparesis. When these patients attempt to perform skilled acts with their nonpreferred arm and find that they are impaired, they often attribute their difficulty to premorbid clumsiness of the nonpreferred arm. In addition, apraxic patients are often anosognosic for their apraxia (Rothi, Mack, & Heilman, 1990). Finally, many health professionals do not test for limb apraxia, are not fully aware of the nature of errors associated with apraxia, and do not know what these errors imply.

I. TYPES OF LIMB APRAXIA

In this chapter we discuss six types of limb apraxia: limb kinetic, ideomotor, disassociation, conduction, ideational, and conceptual. Each of these disorders is defined by the nature of errors made by the patient. The most common errors associated with each of the apraxic syndromes described here are summarized in Table 22.1. Although constructional apraxia and dressing apraxia also involve the limbs, these disorders are strongly associated with visuoperceptual and visuospatial disorders as well as neglect (Walker, Sunderland, Sharma, & Walker, 2004); therefore these two disorders are not discussed here.

A. Limb Kinetic, or Melokinetic, Apraxia

1. CLINICAL PRESENTATION

Patients with limb kinetic apraxia demonstrate a loss of deftness including the ability to make finely graded, precise, individual, but coordinated finger movements. The patient may have difficulty picking up a straight pin from the top of a desk using a pincher grasp of the thumb and forefinger. Limb kinetic apraxia usually affects the hand that is contralateral to a hemispheric lesion. Recommended tasks include (a) the Rapid Finger Oscillation Test, (b) the Grooved Pegboard Test, and (c) timed coin rotation between thumb, index, and middle fingers (Hanna-Pladdy, Mendoza, Apostolos, & Heilman, 2002).

2. PATHOPHYSIOLOGY

Animal models have shown that lesions confined to the corticospinal system result in similar errors. In humans, lesions

Table 22.1. Errors Associated With Each of the Apraxic Syndromes

Syndrome	Error type				
	Gesture to command	Discrimination–comprehension	Imitation	Series	Mechanical knowledge
Ideomotor					
Anterior	+++	O	++	O	O
Posterior	+++	+++	++	O	O
Conduction	+	O	+++	O	O
Disassociation	+++	O	O	O	O
Ideational	O	O	O	++	O
Conceptual	O	O	O	O	+++

Note. This table lists the error types that define each syndrome. However, patients often have more than one apraxic disorder. O indicates no presence of errors; + indicates presence of errors; ++ indicates greater errors; +++ indicates the greatest number or most serious errors.

in the corticospinal system and convexity premotor cortex may also produce this disorder. In right-handed people, injury to the left hemisphere often induces limb kinetic apraxia of the ipsilateral (left) hand (Hanna-Pladdy, Mendoza, Apostolos, & Heilman, 2002; Heilman, Meador, & Loring, 2000).

B. Ideomotor Apraxia

1. CLINICAL PRESENTATION

Patients with ideomotor apraxia (IMA) make the most errors when asked to pantomime transitive acts to verbal command, and their performance typically improves with imitation. When they use tools or implements, their performance may improve even further, but it often remains impaired. Patients with IMA make primarily spatial and temporal production errors. Spatial errors include errors of posture (or internal configuration), spatial movement, and spatial orientation. Goodglass and Kaplan (1963) noted that when apraxic patients were asked to pantomime, they often used a body part as the tool (a form of postural error). For example, when asked to pantomime using a pair of scissors, they may use their fingers as if they were the blades. Because many normal individuals make similar errors, it is important that the patient be instructed not to use a body part as a tool. Unlike normal individuals, in spite of these instructions, patients with IMA may continue using their body parts as tools. When not using their body parts as tools, patients with IMA often fail to position their hands as if they were holding the tool or object.

When normal individuals are asked to use a tool, they orient that tool to an imaginary target of the tool's action. Patients with IMA often fail to orient their forelimbs to an imaginary target. For example, when they are asked to pantomime cutting a piece of paper in half with a pair of scissors, rather than keeping the scissors oriented in the sagittal plane, these patients either may orient them laterally (Rothi, Mack, Verfaellie, Brown, & Heilman, 1988) or may not maintain the scissors in any consistent plane.

When patients with IMA attempt to make a learned skilled movement, they often make the correct core movement (e.g., twisting, pounding, cutting), but their limb movements through space are often incorrect (Poizner, Mack, Verfaellie, Rothi, & Heilman, 1990; Rothi et al., 1988). These spatial trajectory errors are caused by incorrect joint movements. Patients with apraxia often stabilize a joint that they should be moving and move joints that should not be moving. For example, when pantomiming the use of a screwdriver, a patient with IMA may rotate his or her arm at the shoulder and fix his or her elbow. Shoulder rotation moves the hand in arcs when the hand should be rotating on a fixed axis. The patient with apraxia may be unable to coordinate multiple joint movements to get the desired spatial trajectory. For example, for a person to pantomime slicing bread with a knife, the shoulder and elbow joints must be alternately flexed and extended. When the shoulder joint is being flexed, it also needs to be adducted, and when the shoulder joint is being extended, it also needs to be abducted. If joint movements are not well coordinated, the patient may make primarily chopping or stabbing movements.

Poizner et al. (1990) noted that patients with IMA may also make timing errors, including a long delay before initiating a movement and brief multiple stops (stuttering movements). When normal individuals make a curved movement, they reduce their speed of movement, and when they move in a straight line, they increase their speed of movement. Patients with IMA, however, do not demonstrate a smooth sinusoidal hand speed when performing cyclic movements such as cutting with a knife. Recommended tests include (a) performing transitive movements to verbal command (pantomime to command), (b) imitating the examiner performing transitive movements, (c) performing transitive movements with actual tools or implements, and (d) discriminating between well-performed and incorrectly performed transitive gestures.

2. PATHOPHYSIOLOGY

In right-handed individuals, IMA is almost always associated with left-hemisphere lesions, but in left-handed individuals, IMA is usually associated with right-hemisphere lesions. IMA is associated with lesions in a variety of structures, including the corpus callosum (Watson & Heilman, 1983), the inferior parietal lobe (Heilman, Rothi, & Valenstein, 1982; Rothi, Heilman, & Watson, 1985), and the supplementary motor area (Watson, Fleet, Rothi, & Heilman, 1986). IMA has also been reported with subcortical lesions that involve the basal ganglia (Hanna-Pladdy, Heilman, & Foundas, 2001) and the hemispheric white matter (Hanna-Pladdy et al., 2001). Patients with apraxia from callosal lesions usually have unilateral apraxia (the nonpreferred hand). Patients with apraxia from premotor or callosal lesions can discriminate well from incorrectly performed gestures, whereas patients with parietal lesions often cannot correctly make these discriminations.

C. Conduction Apraxia

1. CLINICAL PRESENTATION

Patients with IMA perform better when imitating the examiner than when pantomiming to verbal command. Ochipa, Rothi, and Heilman (1990) reported a patient who was more severely apraxic when imitating than when pantomiming to command. Because this patient was similar to patients with conduction aphasia who repeat poorly, Ochipa et al. (1990) termed this disorder **conduction apraxia**. The recommended test is imitation to command.

2. PATHOPHYSIOLOGY

The patient of Ochipa et al. (1990) with conduction apraxia could comprehend the examiner's pantomimes and gestures. Thus, this patient's visual system could access movement representations, also termed **praxicons**, and these activated movement representations could access semantic–conceptual representations. Decoding a gesture might require accessing different movement representations (input praxicon) than those important in programming an action (output praxicon). In the verbal domain, a disconnection of the hypothetical input and output lexicons induces conduction aphasia, and in the praxis domain a disconnection between the input and output praxicons could induce conduction apraxia. The lesions that induce conduction aphasia are usually in the supramarginal gyrus or Wernicke's area, but the location of lesions that induce conduction apraxia is unknown.

D. Disassociation Apraxia

1. CLINICAL PRESENTATION

Heilman (1973) described patients who, when asked to pantomime, looked at their hand but did not perform recognizable gestures. Unlike the patients with IMA and conduction apraxia, these patients' imitations and use of objects were flawless. De Renzi, Faglioni, and Sorgato (1982) reported patients similar to those reported on by Heilman (1973) but also described patients who had a similar defect in other modalities. For example, they may have been unable to pantomime in response to visual or tactile stimuli but able to correctly pantomime with verbal commands. The recommended tasks are (a) pantomime to visual or tactile stimuli, (b) pantomime to verbal commands, (c) imitation, and (d) use of actual objects.

2. PATHOPHYSIOLOGY

Right-handed patients present differently from left-handed patients. Right-handed patients with callosal lesions might demonstrate an IMA of their left but not right forelimb. It is important to look for comorbidity with IMA, given that patients who develop an IMA probably have unilateral left-hemisphere movement representations. Other patients with callosal lesions might develop a disassociation apraxia in which they fail to use their left arm correctly to verbal commands but perform normally with imitation and actual objects. Patients with dissociation apraxia probably have movement representations bilaterally represented. Thus, a callosal lesion induces disassociation apraxia only of the left hand because the verbal command cannot get access to the right hemisphere's movement representations, but these patients can perform imitation and use of actual objects correctly because these do not need verbal mediation and the movement representations stored in their right hemisphere can be activated by visual input.

Left-handed patients may demonstrate IMA without aphasia from a right-hemisphere lesion. These patients are apraxic because their movement representations are stored in their right hemisphere, and their lesions have destroyed these representations (Valenstein & Heilman, 1979). These patients are not aphasic because language is mediated by their left hemisphere (as in 70% of left-handed people). If these patients had a callosal lesion, they might demonstrate disassociation apraxia of their left arm and IMA of their right arm.

The patients with dissociation apraxia reported on by Heilman (1973) and by De Renzi et al. (1982) probably have intrahemispheric language-movement formula, visual-movement formula, or somesthetic-movement formula disassociations. The locations of the lesions that cause these intrahemispheric disassociation apraxias are not known.

E. Ideational Apraxia

1. CLINICAL PRESENTATION

The inability to carry out a series of acts or formulate an ideational plan has been called **ideational apraxia** (Pick, 1905). When performing a task that requires a series of acts, these patients have difficulty sequencing the acts in the proper order. Unfortunately, use of the term ideational apraxia has been confusing; the term has been used erroneously to label other disorders. For example, Heilman (1973) used this term when he first described disassociation apraxia. Patients with IMA usually improve when using tools and objects, but De Renzi, Pieczuro, and Vignolo (1968) reported patients who made errors with the use of tools and objects and they called this disorder ideational apraxia. Although the inability to use actual tools and objects may be associated with a conceptual disorder, a severe production disorder (IMA) may also impair object use. The term ideational apraxia has also been used to describe patients who make conceptual errors. We, however, term this problem **conceptual apraxia**, and we discuss the disorder in the next section. The recommended task is assessment of ability to perform multistep tasks (as described earlier).

2. PATHOPHYSIOLOGY

Frontal lobe dysfunction is often associated with temporal order processing deficits. Pick (1905) noted that most patients with this type of ideational apraxia have a degenerative dementia.

F. Conceptual Apraxia

1. CLINICAL PRESENTATION

To perform a skilled act, a person needs two types of knowledge: conceptual knowledge and production knowledge. Whereas dysfunction of the praxis production system induces IMA, defects in mechanical knowledge needed to select tools and objects is termed **conceptual apraxia** (CA). Therefore, patients with IMA make production errors (e.g., spatial and temporal errors), and patients with CA make content and tool selection errors. Patients with CA may also not recall the types of actions associated with specific tools, utensils, or objects (tool–object action associative knowledge) and therefore make content errors (De Renzi & Lucchelli, 1988; Ochipa, Rothi, & Heilman, 1989). For example, when asked to demonstrate the use of a screwdriver by either pantomiming or using the actual tool, the patient with the loss of tool–object action knowledge may pantomime a hammering movement or use the screwdriver as if it were a hammer.

Patients with CA may be unable to recall which specific tool is associated with a specific object (tool–object association knowledge). For example, when shown a partially driven nail, they may select a screwdriver rather than a hammer from an array of tools. This conceptual defect may also be in the verbal domain: When a tool is shown to a patient, the patient may be able to name it, but when asked to name or point to a tool when its function is described, he or she might be unable to perform correctly. Patients with CA may also be unable to describe the functions of tools.

Patients with CA might also have other forms of impaired mechanical knowledge. For example, if they are attempting to drive a nail into a piece of wood and there is no hammer available, they may select a screwdriver rather than a wrench or pliers (which are hard, heavy, and good for pounding; Ochipa, Rothi, & Heilman, 1992). Mechanical knowledge is also important for tool development, and patients with CA may be unable to create simple tools correctly (Heilman, Maher, Greenwald, & Rothi, 1997; Ochipa et al., 1992).

2. PATHOPHYSIOLOGY

De Renzi and Lucchelli (1988) argued that the temporoparietal junction is integral to the mediation of conceptual knowledge. The patient reported on by Ochipa et al. (1989) was left handed and rendered conceptually apraxic by a lesion in the right hemisphere, which suggests that both production and conceptual knowledge have lateralized representations and that such representations are contralateral to the preferred hand. Further evidence that these conceptual representations are lateralized contralateral to the preferred hand comes from the observation of a patient who had a callosal disconnection and demonstrated conceptual apraxia of the nonpreferred (left) hand (Watson & Heilman, 1983) and a study demonstrating that strokes in the hemisphere contralateral to the preferred hand induce conceptual apraxia (Heilman et al., 1997). CA, however, is perhaps most commonly associated with degenerative dementia of the Alzheimer type (Ochipa et al., 1992). Ochipa et al. also noted that the severity of CA and IMA did not always correspond. The observation that patients with IMA may not demonstrate CA and patients with CA may not demonstrate IMA provides support for the postulate that the praxis production and praxis conceptual systems are independent. Normal function, however, requires that these two systems interact. Recommended tasks include (a) gesture to holding and seeing tools, (b) association tools with objects, and (c) demonstration of mechanical knowledge.

II. THE EXAMINATION FOR LIMB APRAXIA

To diagnose the specific forms of apraxia that we have discussed, one must perform a series of diagnostic tests. The examiner should determine whether the patient performs these tests correctly or incorrectly as well as note the type of errors made by the patient.

A. Perform a Neurological Examination

Because the diagnosis of apraxia is in part a diagnosis of exclusion, the clinician must perform a neurological examination to determine whether the abnormal motor performance can be completely accounted for by any of the nonapraxic motor, sensory, or cognitive disorders listed in the introduction to this chapter. The presence of elemental motor defects does not prohibit or preclude praxis testing, but the examiner must interpret the results of praxis testing with the knowledge gained from the neurological examination. **Whenever possible, both the right and left arms and hands should be tested.** When one arm is weak or is the site of another motor disorder that would preclude testing, the nonparetic limb should be tested.

B. Tests

1. **Gesture to command:** Testing praxis involves selectively varying input and task demands. When possible, the same items should be used for all subtests. First, patients should be requested to pantomime to verbal commands (e.g., "Show me how you would use a bread knife to cut a slice of bread"). Both transitive (i.e., using tools and instruments) and intransitive (i.e., communicative gestures such as waving good-bye) gestures should be tested.
2. **Gesture imitation:** Patients should be asked to imitate the examiner performing both meaningful and meaningless gestures.
3. **Gesture in response to seeing and holding tools and objects:** Regardless of the results of the pantomime to command and imitation tests, the patient should be asked to hold tools or objects and to demonstrate how to use these implements. In addition to having the patient pantomime to verbal command, the examiner may want to show the patient pictures of tools or objects and ask him or her to pantomime their use. The examiner may also want to show the patient real tools or the objects on which tools work (e.g., nail) and, without having the patient hold the tool or object, request that the patient pantomime the action associated with the tool or object.

4. **Pantomime recognition and discrimination:** It may be valuable to see if the patient can name or recognize transitive and intransitive pantomimes made by the examiner and discriminate between well-performed and poorly performed pantomimes done by the examiner.
5. **Sequential acts:** The patient should be asked to perform a task that requires several sequential motor acts (e.g., making a sandwich).
6. **Associative tool–object knowledge and mechanical knowledge:** The patient may be asked to match tools with the objects on which they operate (e.g., given a partially driven nail, will the patient select a hammer from an array of tools?) and to fabricate tools or select alternative tools to solve mechanical problems.

III. TYPES OF ERRORS

The types of errors made by patients with apraxia often define the nature of their praxis defect; therefore, it is important to qualify errors. We use a scoring system in which we first classify praxis errors as either production or content errors. Content errors include semantically related productions (e.g., pantomiming playing a trumpet rather than a trombone) and unrelated productions (e.g., making hammering movements rather than those associated with playing a trombone). Production errors include assuming the wrong posture, incorrect orientation of the limb, timing errors, moving the incorrect joints, or improperly coordinating multijoint movements. Each gesture produced by the patient may contain one or more praxis errors. For details concerning this scoring system, see Rothi et al. (1988) and Poizner et al. (1990).

IV. CONCLUSION

Apraxia is defined as an inability to perform purposeful skilled movements. In this chapter we have discussed the clinical presentations and pathophysiology of six forms of apraxia. These forms of apraxia are distinguished by the profile of praxis tests that patients fail to perform correctly and by the type of praxis errors the patients exhibit.

BIBLIOGRAPHY

De Renzi, E., Faglioni, P., & Sorgato, P. (1982). Modality-specific and supramodal mechanisms of apraxia. *Brain, 105*, 301–312.

De Renzi, E., & Lucchelli, F. (1988). Ideational apraxia. *Brain, 113*, 1173–1188.

De Renzi, E., Pieczuro, A., & Vignolo, L. (1968). Ideational apraxia: A quantitative study. *Neuropsychologia, 6*, 41–52.

Goodglass, H., & Kaplan, E. (1963). Disturbance of gesture and pantomime in aphasia. *Brain, 86*, 703–720.

Hanna-Pladdy, B., Heilman, K. M., & Foundas, A. L. (2001). Cortical and subcortical contributions to ideomotor apraxia. *Brain, 124*, 2513–2527.

Hanna-Pladdy, B., Mendoza, J. E., Apostolos, G. T., & Heilman, K. M. (2002). Lateralized motor control: Hemispheric damage and the loss of deftness. *Journal of Neurology, Neurosurgery, and Psychiatry, 73*, 574–577.

Heilman, K. M. (1973). Ideational apraxia: A re-definition. *Brain, 96*, 861–864.

Heilman, K. M., Maher, L. M., Greenwald, M. L., & Rothi, L. J. R. (1997). Conceptual apraxia from lateralized lesions. *Neurology, 49*, 457–464.

Heilman, K. M., Meador, K. J., & Loring, D. W. (2000). Hemispheric asymmetries of limb-kinetic apraxia: A loss of deftness. *Neurology, 55*, 523–526.

Heilman, K. M., & Rothi, L. J. G. (1993). Apraxia. In K. M. Heilman & E. Valenstein (Eds.), *Clinical neuropsychology* (pp. 141–163). New York: Oxford University Press.

Heilman, K. M., Rothi, L. J., & Valenstein, E. (1982). Two forms of ideomotor apraxia. *Neurology, 32*, 342–346.

Ochipa, C., Rothi, L. J. G., & Heilman, K. M. (1989). Ideational apraxia: A deficit in tool selection and use. *Annals of Neurology, 25*, 190–193.

Ochipa, C., Rothi, L. J. G., & Heilman, K. M. (1990). Conduction apraxia. *Journal of Clinical and Experimental Neuropsychology, 12*, 89.

Ochipa, C., Rothi, L. J. G., & Heilman, K. M. (1992). Conceptual apraxia in Alzheimer's disease. *Brain, 114*, 2593–2603.

Pick, A. (1905). *Sudien uber Motorische Apraxia und ihre Mahestenhende Erscheinungen* [Studies of motor apraxia]. Leipzig, Germany: Deuticke.

Poizner, H., Mack, L., Verfaellie, M., Rothi, L. J. G., & Heilman, K. M. (1990). Three dimensional computer graphic analysis of apraxia. *Brain, 113*, 85–101.

Rothi, L. J. G., Heilman, K. M., & Watson, R. T. (1985). Pantomime comprehension and ideomotor apraxia. *Journal of Neurology, Neurosurgery, and Psychiatry, 48*, 207–210.

Rothi, L. J. G., Mack, L., & Heilman, K. M. (1990). Unawareness of apraxic errors. *Neurology, 40*, 202.

Rothi, L. J. G., Mack. L., Verfaellie, M., Brown, P., & Heilman, K. M. (1988). Ideomotor apraxia: Error pattern analysis. *Aphasiology, 2,* 381–387.

Valenstein, E., & Heilman, K. M. (1979). Apraxic agraphia with neglect induced paragraphia. *Archives of Neurology, 36,* 506–508.

Walker, C. M., Sunderland, A., Sharma, J., & Walker, M. F. (2004). The impact of cognitive impairment on upper body dressing difficulties after stroke: A video analysis of patterns of recovery. *Journal of Neurology, Neurosurgery, and Psychiatry, 75,* 43–48.

Watson, R. T., Fleet, W. S., Rothi, L. J. G., & Heilman, K. M. (1986). Apraxia and the supplementary motor area. *Archives of Neurology, 43,* 787–792.

Watson, R. T., & Heilman, K. M. (1983). Callosal apraxia. *Brain, 106,* 391–404.

CHAPTER 23

Daniel X. Capruso, Kerry deS. Hamsher, and
Arthur L. Benton

Clinical Evaluation of Visual Perception and Constructional Ability

The evaluation of visual perception and constructional ability is a necessary component of the comprehensive neuropsychological examination. A focal lesion or incipient dementia may cause a profound deficit of visuoperceptual discrimination, visuospatial judgment, or constructional ability in an otherwise articulate patient with normal verbal functioning and normal visual acuity. This chapter outlines the major visual perceptual deficit syndromes and their neuroanatomical correlates. Practical methods of measuring visual perception and constructional ability are described, and examples of the error types commonly observed in patients with constructional deficits are provided.

I. DEFINITION OF DISORDERS IN VISUAL PERCEPTION AND CONSTRUCTIONAL ABILITY

A. Definition of Terms

1. VISUAL PERCEPTION

Visual perception is the process through which sensory information derived from light is interpreted for object

We gratefully acknowledge Sherry Card, a registered and licensed occupational therapist, for her contribution of selected clinical examples of constructional deficit.

recognition or spatial orientation. Visual perception consists of visuoperceptual and visuospatial ability, two functionally independent processes that have separate neuroanatomical substrates. This functional distinction is commonly referred to as "what" (visuoperceptual) verses "where" (visuospatial).

a. Visuoperceptual ability

Visuoperceptual ability subsumes form or pattern discrimination. Color, shape, and other intrinsic features are processed by the visuoperceptual system, regardless of the spatial dimensions of an object or environment.

b. Visuospatial ability

Visuospatial ability is the processing of visual orientation or location in space, regardless of the intrinsic features of that object or environment. Depth and motion are subsumed by this system.

2. CONSTRUCTIONAL ABILITY

Synonymous with constructional praxis, **constructional ability** is the capacity to draw or assemble an object from component parts, either on command or to copy a model. The concept measures the integrative aspect of construction. Patients with a constructional deficit may be able to reproduce component parts of a design, but they will be unable to produce a design that represents an accurate and integrated whole.

B. Etiology

Posterior right-hemisphere lesions produced by cerebrovascular accidents, head trauma with hematoma or contusion, or neoplastic disease are the most frequent cause of focal deficit syndromes in visual perception and constructional ability. Left-hemisphere lesions and conditions producing bilateral multifocal or diffuse disease may also cause deficits on tests of visual perception, although careful evaluation will typically show that these visual deficits are subsumed under overarching neurobehavioral syndromes such as aphasia, dementia or confusion. See the following "Competing Diagnoses" section for differential diagnosis of those conditions. In rare cases, childhood cerebral diseases such as seizure disorder or the presence of a mass lesion in the left hemisphere can cause language functions to be pathologically localized in an intact right hemisphere. A resulting "crowding effect" can lead to weakness or deficit in visual perception, as the functional capacity of the right hemisphere may be strained by specialization for both language and visual perception.

C. Specific Disorders

1. VISUOPERCEPTUAL DEFICIT

a. Visual agnosia

Visual agnosia is a deficit in recognition of common objects or familiar faces. Intact naming in the tactile mode differentiates visually agnosic from aphasic patients. The apperceptive versus associative basis for the disorder can be determined using the methods described in the following sections for evaluating the intactness of visual perception and constructional ability. Visual agnosia as a syndrome independent of dementia is uncommon. Bilateral temporo-occipital lesions damaging the visual association cortices of both hemispheres are usually necessary for the manifestation of visual agnosia.

b. Deficits in form or pattern discrimination

Deficits of form discrimination may be found on a variety of tasks, including the following:

- matching of complex patterns;
- discrimination of unfamiliar human faces;
- visual analysis, which involves the identification of overlapping or hidden figures;
- visual synthesis, which involves the ability to mentally combine disparate parts into an integrated whole; and
- identification or matching of objects obscured by excessive shadowing or by presentation at unusual angles

The typical neuroanatomical substrate for these deficits is a lesion in the right temporo-occipital area. A left superior quadrantanopia is frequently seen as a correlated sign.

c. Acquired deficits in color vision

Congenital color blindness is relatively common and is secondary to abnormalities in the photopigments or photoreceptors of the retina. Achromatopsia, an acquired deficit in color vision, is rare and is caused by a lesion in the inferior temporo-occipital junction, with sparing of the underlying optic radiations and the adjacent primary visual cortex of the fusiform gyrus. A bilateral lesion of this type will produce a "full" achromatopsia in both visual fields, whereas a unilateral lesion may produce a "hemiachromatopsia" affecting only the contralateral visual field. Right hemiachromatopsia is often accompanied by color anomia or alexia.

2. VISUOSPATIAL DEFICITS

a. Balint–Holmes syndrome

Balint–Holmes syndrome comprises the following symptom tetrad:
- impaired visual attention (simultanagnosia),
- defective judgment of distances,
- oculomotor apraxia, and
- misreaching (optic ataxia or visuomotor apraxia).

The spatial disturbance in patients with Balint–Holmes syndrome can be so severe that despite adequate visual acuity, the patients may collide with large objects in their path and may be unable to grasp objects placed within their reach. Balint–Holmes syndrome is associated with bilateral lesions of the superior parietal lobule and occurs when that region no longer performs its normal function of preparation and guidance of visual attention to specific points in space, along with the coordination of arm movements toward specific objects.

b. Visual neglect

Visual neglect is pathological inattention to objects or events in the visual space contralateral to a brain lesion. Visual neglect is a disorder of the integrated functioning of vision and attention. Neglect is often correlated with, but is functionally unrelated to, the presence of visual field defects or hemianopia. Neglect may be seen in the context of completely full visual fields. Visual neglect is most often apparent in the acute stage of recovery from a cerebral insult. Neglect occurs more frequently and with greater severity following right-hemisphere lesions than left-hemisphere lesions. Visual neglect has been observed following unilateral lesions of the parietal lobe, dorsolateral frontal lobe, putamen, cingulate gyrus, thalamus, and mesencephalic reticular formation.

c. Deficit in visuospatial judgment

Deficits in judging the position and orientation of objects are frequently observed in the context of posterior right-hemisphere disease. Relatively low frequencies of defective performance are observed in patients with right-anterior or left-hemisphere lesions.

d. Topographic disorientation

Topographic disorientation, or the inability to find one's way in the environment, may be caused by a number of mechanisms, including the following:

- visual neglect, causing a patient to always turn in one direction;
- deficits in landmark recognition; and
- a memory disorder specific to spatial schema such as cognitive maps.

Difficulties on navigational tasks may be seen with lesions of either parietal lobe, although posterior right-hemisphere disease is strongly suggested. The "amnestic" form of topographic disorientation has particular association with lesions of the right hippocampus and its overlying temporal neocortex.

3. CONSTRUCTIONAL DEFICITS

Constructional deficits are typically measured using graphomotor tasks, two-dimensional (2-D) mosaic block designs, or three-dimensional (3-D) block designs. Graphomotor copying has a low correlation with the other constructional tasks, whereas 2-D and 3-D block designs are modestly correlated. Right parietal disease is the most frequent etiology for constructional apraxia, although both right frontal disease and aphasia with comprehension deficit may also lead to constructional deficits.

a. Graphomotor copying

Reproduction of a design with a writing implement is not a preferred method of measuring constructional ability in many patients with neurological disease because of the confounding demands on fine motor coordination. In particular, the performance of right-handed patients with left-hemisphere lesions may be affected by poor motor control in the preferred right hand, or because use of the nonpreferred left hand may be forced by an acquired hemiparesis. Qualitative aspects of performance on graphomotor copying tasks may differ depending on the laterality and anterior versus posterior locus of lesion.

1. **Left-hemisphere lesions**: Patients with left-hemisphere lesions may reproduce the spatial elements or outer configuration of a figure successfully, but their reproductions tend to be oversimplified and with significant omission of internal details.
2. **Right-hemisphere lesions**: Patients with right-hemisphere lesions often neglect to draw the left side of the figure, or they may crowd details from the left side of the figure into the right side. They may reproduce individual details accurately but with distortion of the spatial relations of design elements. Misplacement of design features is also frequently seen.

Figure 23.1. Mosaic block design error. The external 2 × 2 configuration of the stimulus model (A) is reproduced in the patient's solution (B), but with errors of internal detail apparent.

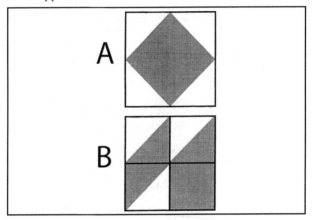

3. **Dementia**: Patients with dementia often show both simplification and spatial distortion of designs. A tendency to copy their production directly onto the stimulus model is often apparent.

b. **Two-dimensional block designs**

The Wechsler Adult Intelligence Scale—III (WAIS–III; Wechsler, 1997) Block Design subtest is the most frequently used version of the 2-D, or mosaic block, task. Performance on this task is sensitive to lesions of either hemisphere, as the task is complex and demands diverse cognitive resources such as visual analysis, visual synthesis, planning ability, intelligence, and psychomotor speed. In the easiest designs, each block corresponds to a specific feature of the stimulus model. In contrast, the features of the more difficult designs transcend individual blocks and must be assembled from combinations of blocks (Walsh, 1985).

1. **Focal left-hemisphere lesions**: Patients with left-hemisphere lesions may construct block designs with the correct 2 × 2 or 3 × 3 configuration, but they often make errors concerning the internal details of the design (see Figure 23.1). Correct placement of the center block of

Figure 23.2. Mosaic block design error. The stimulus model (A) demands that nine blocks be assembled into a 3 × 3 design with an internal diagonal band. The patient's solution (B) maintains the diagonal concept but creates an incorrect 1 × 4 external configuration.

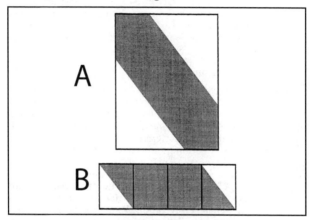

the 3 × 3 designs often presents particular difficulty. Patients with left- as opposed to right-hemisphere lesions are more likely to demonstrate insight that their reproductions are incorrect.

2. **Focal right-hemisphere lesions**: Patients with right-hemisphere lesions often construct designs that preserve internal features of the design, but they may "break" the external 2 × 2 or 3 × 3 configuration of their solution (see Figure 23.2). When blocks are disproportionately skewed into right hemispace, this may be an artifact of visual neglect. Patients with right-hemisphere lesions often demonstrate a dramatic lack of insight into the fact that their reproductions may be incorrect and grossly distorted and incorrect. At times they may think that they have not been given a sufficient number of blocks to attain the solution.

Because relative weakness on the WAIS–III Block Design subtest will be present as a normal variant in the intellectual profiles of many patients, the presence of a low score on Block Design should not be interpreted in isolation as a sign of brain disease or as a rationale for the presence of cerebral dysfunction.

c. Three-dimensional block construction

This task makes little demand on intellectual capacity and has the advantage of face validity, task familiarity, and the use of real depth that is present neither in graphomotor tasks nor in 2-D block designs. Deficits in 3-D block construction are most frequently seen with posterior right-hemisphere lesions. Frontal lobe lesions may also produce constructional deficits that are related to perseveration and deficits in planning and self-monitoring.

d. Error types on constructional tasks

A number of clinically informative error types may be apparent on constructional tasks. Some error types have already been discussed, such as the internal detail versus configural errors commonly seen on 2-D mosaic block designs. It is difficult to attribute a reliable clinical significance to any particular error type, as the type of solution produced is often confounded with the overall severity of constructional deficit. The type of error produced will also result from an interaction between the patient's pathology and the features of the particular stimulus item. For example, a stimulus item with considerable internal redundancy may elicit perseveration. A stimulus item with internal oblique features may elicit rotational errors. A complex stimulus with many design elements may elicit a recognizable but simplified solution in a patient with dementia. Many of the following error types may be observed in graphomotor, 2-D, or 3-D block designs.

   1. **Attentional error:** This is the only error type frequently seen in normal patients and that may be a product of impulsivity or carelessness. Design elements may be overlooked and omitted on graphomotor copying. On 2-D block designs, one or two blocks may be oriented incorrectly. On 3-D block designs, one or more blocks may be omitted or rotated, or a minor substitution of an incorrect block may be apparent. The patient may produce a completely accurate solution that is rotated 180°. Although this rotational error may represent a deficit in visuospatial judgment in some patients, the careless patient will usually correct the rotational error when the examiner asks the patient to check if his or her solution is correct. These error types typically represent attentional lapses and do not reflect true constructional apraxia, which is better represented by the following error types.

2. **Neglect:** Half of the design may be constructed, or elements from both halves of the design may be crowded into unilateral hemispace (see Figure 23.3). On 3-D constructions, designs may be produced in which blocks repeatedly fall off into the neglected hemispace.

3. **Spatial compression:** The design may be dramatically shortened in one spatial dimension (see Figure 23.4). At times, this may be the result of visual neglect as previously described, but it may also be the result of a failure to accurately perceive the proper size of an object (i.e., micropsia).

4. **Spatial expansion:** The design may be dramatically expanded in one spatial dimension (see Figure 23.5). As with spatial compression, this may result from a misperception of design elements (i.e., macropsia).

5. **Simplification:** All three spatial dimensions of the design may be represented, but the solution does not reflect the complexity of the stimulus model (see Figure 23.6).

Figure 23.3. Left-sided neglect. The patient's solution (at left) shows crowding of design elements into right hemispace.

Figure 23.4. Spatial compression. The patient's solution (in foreground) reproduces all three dimensions of the stimulus model (in background) with sufficient complexity, but with an overall reduction in size of the design elements.

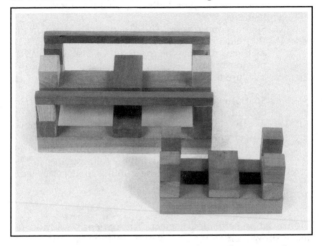

6. **Fragmentation:** Recognizable but separate design elements may not be integrated into a whole design (see Figure 23.7).
7. **Closing-in:** An attempt is made to construct the solution directly onto, or integrated with, the stimulus model (see Figure 23.8). This error type is often consistent with dementia.
8. **Vertical "piling-up":** Only the vertical dimension of the design is recognized or reproduced (see Figure 23.9). Blocks are piled straight up in the vertical dimension, and the design often collapses of its own instability. The patient may then react with bewilderment.
9. **Horizontal "stringing-out":** Only the horizontal dimension of the design is recognized or reproduced (see Figure 23.10). Blocks are strung out in one plane while the depth of the design is generally ignored.
10. **Dismantling:** An attempt is made to deconstruct the stimulus model rather than to construct a solution.
11. **Nonpurposeful activity:** Seemingly random behavior, such as repeatedly moving blocks around without

Figure 23.5. Spatial expansion. The patient's solution (in background) reproduces all three dimensions of the stimulus model (in foreground), but with a magnification of the design into right hemispace.

assembling any substantive object, is frequently observed in severely demented or globally aphasic patients. The patient either fails to grasp the task to be performed despite repeated demonstration or fails to execute purposeful behavior toward a goal.

Two frequently observed error types, described next, often reflect executive or "frontal lobe systems" deficits in self-monitoring and self-correction.

12. **Perseveration of design elements.** A correct component of the solution may be repeated as the patient fails to terminate what may initially have been appropriate behavior (see Figure 23.11). The vertical piling-up error and horizontal stringing-out error may represent variant types of perseveration, as the patient becomes mentally fixed on building within a single dimension.

13. **Failure to self-correct.** A patient may commit a serious error early in the construction, which, unless corrected, will prevent him or her from achieving an accurate solution. These patients will often be observed to puzzle over the problem, realizing that they are not

Figure 23.6. Simplification error. All three dimensions of the stimulus model (at left) are reproduced in the patient's solution (at right) but in a grossly simplified manner.

reaching their goal, yet it does not occur to them to go backward and correct their initial error. Instead they produce a solution that is an approximation of the stimulus model with the solution built around the initial error.

4. POSITIVE VISUAL PHENOMENA

Neuropsychologists are typically concerned with areas of deficit that represent "negative" symptoms of disease or areas of reduced function. Occasionally, patients will present with **positive visual phenomena**, which represent new onset of experiences that were not present premorbidly and which often have diagnostic significance.

a. Visual hallucinations

1. **Simple hallucinations:** These phenomena range from simple flashes of light (photisms, photopsias, or phosphenes) to complex and scintillating geometric patterns and may be caused by lesions located anywhere from the retina to the primary visual cortex. Ischemia in the occipital lobe, such as found in migraine, is an especially common etiology.

Figure 23.7. Fragmentation error. The patient's solution (in foreground) reproduces elements of the stimulus model without integrating the solution into a whole.

2. **Complex (formed) hallucinations:** The content of these phenomena is usually of people or animals, often of a lilliputian, or reduced, size. Common etiologies are described in the following list.
    - **Toxicometabolic confusion:** The most common etiology for complex visual hallucinations is toxicometabolic confusion, frequently induced by drug intoxication or withdrawal.
    - **Focal vascular lesions:** Strategically placed lesions of the mesencephalon, cerebral peduncles, diencephalon, occipitotemporal, and occipitoparietal regions may cause Lhermitte's hallucinosis, in which vividly colored and animated formed hallucinations occur in an otherwise clear sensorium.
    - **Dementia:** Patients with dementia often suffer from complex hallucinations, particularly during episodes of nocturnal confusion. They often regard the hallucinations as a nuisance to which they react with a mild annoyance.
    - **Psychiatric disorders:** Visual hallucinations are rare in patients with psychiatric disorders, whereas they are commonly reported by malingering patients.

Figure 23.8. Closing-in error. The patient's solution (in the foreground at left) is built directly onto the stimulus model.

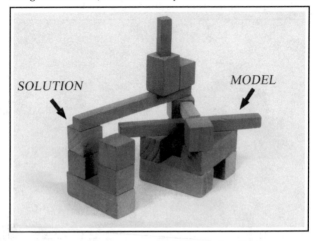

b. Visual illusions

Visual illusions represent either distortions or misinterpretations of actually seen objects; these occur in normal persons and in patients with psychopathology. Most of these phenomena are rare. These positive symptoms are usually caused by areas of neuronal irritation (e.g., subclinical electrical abnormalities) or partial deafferentation (Jacobs, 1989). The locus of dysfunction is typically in the parieto-occipital region, and the phenomenon usually occurs in a visual field defect created by the lesion.

1. **Metamorphopsia:** This phenomenon subsumes alteration in the size (micropsia or macropsia), form (dysmorphopsia), or color of objects. A viewed object may also be perceived as a different object or as a more complex version of the viewed object.
2. **Spatial illusions:** Illusions of depth may occur through experience of distorted perspectival cues. Lesions of the tegmentum or brainstem involving the vestibular pathways are frequently responsible.
3. **Palinopsia:** The phenomenon represents the persistence or reappearance of a recently viewed object. Development or resolution of a visual field defect is usually in

Figure 23.9. Vertical "piling-up" error. Cubes rise in the vertical dimension from the patient's simplified and rotated solution (at right).

progress. Neoplastic or vascular lesions of the posterior cerebrum are usually present.

4. **Polyopia:** This is the perception of multiple, simultaneous visual images while viewing a single object. Parieto-occipital lesions are usually present, although ocular, cerebellar, and vestibular dysfunction may also cause the phenomenon.

5. **Visual allesthesia:** A visual image is transposed from one visual half-field to the opposite, usually defective, half-field. The etiology is unknown, although bilateral cerebral lesions, dementing conditions, and severe psychiatric disorders are common etiologies. Hallucinogenic drugs may produce this effect in some patients.

6. **Oscillopsia:** This is the perception of back-and-forth movement in a stationary object. Nystagmus is the typical cause.

7. **Visual synesthesia:** This is the experience of a visual sensation in response to a stimulus in another sensory modality and most typically occurs during an auditory startle response. Visual synesthesia can occur in otherwise normal persons, and it may also occur in a visual

Figure 23.10. Horizontal "stringing-out" error. The patient's solution (in foreground) has essentially no depth and is "closed-in" through a bridging block built onto the stimulus model.

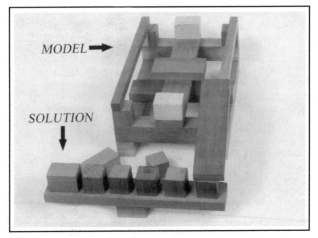

field defect caused by a lesion of the optic nerve or chiasm. It also occurs with the use of hallucinogens.

c. Nonpathological hallucinations and illusions

Hallucinations occurring while falling asleep (hypnagogic) or awakening (hypnopompic) may be seen in otherwise normal people. The experience of an illusory moving object, such as a small fleeting animal, in the visual periphery ("grand runners") is normal. These visual false alarms occur because of the high concentration of motion-sensitive photoreceptors in the retinal periphery where acuity is limited. Catching a fleeting glimpse of a deceased relative may be experienced during bereavement.

II. FUNCTIONAL NEUROANATOMIC CORRELATES

The visual discernment of an object's form and spatial attributes is mediated by two functionally and anatomically distinct systems within the human brain (Kandel, Schwartz, & Jessell, 2000). The visuoperceptual system (form perception) and visuo-

Figure 23.11. Perseveration of design elements. The stimulus model (at left) was successfully reproduced by the patient, who then continued the pyramidal scheme until she ran out of cubes. After that, she began piling up larger blocks in the vertical dimension.

spatial systems both derive their input from the photoreceptors, but they exhibit segregation as early as the ganglion cell level of the retina. These dual visual systems project to many of the same thalamic and occipital areas, but they remain separate by synapsing in separate cell layers, are represented in different retinotopic maps in the same areas of the occipital lobes, then ultimately project to different areas of the association cortex. The action of focal lesions on these two visual systems may produce the distinct syndromes previously described.

A. The Visuoperceptual System

The visuoperceptual system derives its input from the "Type P" retinal ganglion cells, projects to the dorsal layers of the lateral geniculate nucleus, then projects to the inferior occipital and temporal cortices.

B. The Visuospatial System

The visuospatial system derives its input from the "Type M" retinal ganglion cells, projects to the ventral layers of the lateral geniculate nucleus, then projects to the superior occipital and parietal cortices.

III. COMPETING DIAGNOSES

In differential diagnosis of a visual perception or constructional deficit syndrome, a number of competing diagnostic possibilities should be considered.

A. Psychiatric Disorder

As part of the attentional disturbance often seen in psychiatric patients, numerous minor or careless errors may be apparent on tests of visual perception and constructional ability. A pattern of deficits on other tasks demanding focused concentration, sustained effort, and cognitive efficiency may help to differentiate psychiatric disorder from neurological disease.

B. Dementia

In keeping with the multifocal or diffuse nature of the syndrome, dementia will often be accompanied by deficits in visual perception and constructional ability. Occasionally, the initial presentation of an incipient degenerative disease process may take the form of an isolated deficit in visual perception or constructional ability. This clinical situation is relatively rare, as Alzheimer's disease is the most common etiology, and typically memory is the cognitive domain that is first and most seriously affected. With that knowledge, evaluation of visual perception and constructional ability can aid in the clinical staging of a progressive dementia such as Alzheimer's, as the development of additional perceptual and constructional deficits will imply that the disease has passed its initial amnestic phase.

C. Confusional States

Confusion or delirium, whether acute or subacute, is likely to cause deficits on tests of visual perception and constructional ability (Lee & Hamsher, 1988). History of a recent toxicometabolic disturbance and fluctuating level of alertness indicate that confusion should be considered in the differential diagnosis. In confusion, as with psychiatric disorder, deficits on the neuropsychological battery as a whole will be more contingent on attentional demands and on task complexity than on the type of cognitive domain tested.

D. Aphasia With Comprehension Deficit

Defective performances on tests of visual perception and constructional ability are frequently observed in aphasic patients with comprehension deficit. Globally aphasic patients are frequently unable to perform purposeful or conceptual activities in nonverbal imitation of the examiner.

IV. RELEVANT MEDICAL HISTORY

In the absence of a wider dementia syndrome, a history of right-hemisphere disease whether from cerebrovascular accident, head trauma with mass lesion or contusion, or neoplastic disease is the most frequent cause of a focal deficit in visual perception. As described earlier, seizure disorder or other cerebral disease during childhood may cause weakness or deficit in visual perception if developing language functions and visual perception are crowded into a single hemisphere. The developmental history should also be reviewed for the possible contributing factors of nonverbal learning disability. In older patients, inquiry should be made regarding any episodes of disorientation in which they have become lost in a previously familiar setting.

V. SENSORY AND MOTOR CORRELATES

A. Visual Acuity

Adequate visual acuity is necessary but not sufficient for performance on tasks of visual perception and constructional ability. Profound deficits on tasks of visual perception and constructional ability may occur in patients with normal visual acuity.

B. Visual Field Defects

Left-sided visual field defects often accompany deficits in visual perception and constructional ability. This relationship is correlative rather than causative. A posterior right-hemisphere lesion will frequently result in both left-sided visual field defects and perceptual deficits. Unless the patient has visual neglect, they will typically make eye and head movements to compensate for the visual field defect. There is no relationship between right-sided visual field defects and disorders of complex visual perception.

C. Left Hemiparesis

Constructional deficits are frequently associated with left hemiparesis, but as with visual field defects, the association is correlative rather than causative. As noted earlier, left-hemisphere lesions can cause particular difficulty on graphomotor construction tasks for right-handed individuals. The fine motor control demanded by graphomotor tasks is often compromised in the preferred hand and may be limited when forced use of the nonpreferred hand occurs. The 2-D and 3-D constructional tasks make lesser demands on fine motor control.

VI. LABORATORY DATA

Because deficits in visual perception typically result from acquired lesions or degenerative disease of the brain, laboratory results are usually noncontributory.

VII. NEUROIMAGING CORRELATES

For people with focal cerebral disease, neuroimaging typically identifies the location and extent of neuropathology before neuropsychological examination takes place. The more powerful magnetic resonance imaging (MRI) sometimes produces signal anomalies of unclear clinical significance. The presence of a visual perception deficit syndrome may provide clinical correlation for interpretation of those signals as lesions if they are concentrated in the posterior right hemisphere. Likewise, the coincidence of a new onset of deficit in visual perception with the dilatation of a ventricular horn, enlargement of sulci, or nonsymmetrical atrophy of gyri in the posterior right hemisphere may suggest a locus of incipient neurodegenerative disease.

VIII. THE NEUROPSYCHOLOGICAL EXAMINATION

There are three clinical situations in which evaluation of visual perception and constructional ability is essential: (a) in the context of known or suspected posterior right-hemisphere disease, (b) in the presence of aphasia with comprehension deficit, and (c) during dementia evaluations when a sampling of all major cognitive domains is sought.

A. Posterior Right-Hemisphere Disease

It has been emphasized that patients with known or suspected posterior right-hemisphere disease are most likely to have deficits in visual perception or constructional ability. For these patients, the core neuropsychological examination should be supplemented by a complete examination of complex visual functioning.

1. VISUAL ACUITY SCREENING

A pocket chart such as the widely used Rosenbaum Visual Screener will determine whether a valid examination of visual perception can be obtained. As a convention, corrected near-point visual acuity of 20/70 or better is considered adequate for the purposes of neuropsychological evaluation.

2. VISUAL NEGLECT

The presence of hemispatial neglect is easily assessed by cancellation tasks, which demand that the patient visually scan an array and cross-out designated targets. Line bisection tasks, in which patients are asked to draw a mark through the midpoint of a horizontal line, may also be used. A variety of these tasks are illustrated in Lezak (1995), or they can be easily improvised on a sheet of unlined paper if they are not readily available to the examiner. The patient with neglect will fail to cross out target stimuli on one side of the cancellation task, and on line bisection tasks his or her center mark will grossly deviate from the actual midpoint of the line. If the patient has a motor limitation that does not permit administration of these tasks, then two-syllable words may be used. For example, the patient with a left-sided neglect may read *football* as *ball*. If visual neglect is apparent, the examiner may attempt to help the patient compensate by placing stimuli eccentrically in the intact hemiattentional space, with frequent demonstrations to the patient of the necessity of scanning the entire stimulus field. Admittedly, this approach will often be of limited value as the patient may ignore everything to one side of his or her center of visual attention no matter where an object is situated. Yet, to place all stimuli directly to the center of a patient will convert every test into a measure of visual neglect.

3. VISUOPERCEPTUAL DISCRIMINATION

Benton, Sivan, Hamsher, Varney, and Spreen's (1994) Test of Facial Recognition is a clinically useful test of visuoperceptual discrimination. A reliable and valid short form of the test is available.

4. VISUOSPATIAL JUDGMENT

Benton's et al.'s (1994) Judgment of Line Orientation task is a clinically useful test of visuospatial judgment, although it also tends to be relatively sensitive to attentional disturbance. A reliable and valid short form of the test is available.

5. CONSTRUCTIONAL ABILITY

a. Graphomotor tasks

A number of standardized approaches to measure graphomotor performances are described in the following.

1. **Developmental Test of Visual–Motor Integration** (Beery, Buktenica, & Beery, 2004): This is a useful test for both pediatric and adult patients in whom severe deficit is suspected. The test has a wide range of stimuli, which vary from single lines that demand no integrative constructional ability to complex two-dimensional figures such as a Necker cube and interlocking triangles.

2. **Benton Visual Retention Test** (Sivan, 1992): The copy trial of this task provides a range of stimuli of varying size and difficulty. This test is especially practical when normative data corrected for premorbid intellectual status are needed.

3. **Rey–Osterreith Complex Figure**: The complexity of this task makes it effective for patients in whom subtle constructional deficits are suspected. The stimulus model (Lezak, 1995) has both a geometric spatial framework and a variety of internal details that makes it sensitive to both right- and left-hemisphere disease. Numerous scoring systems and normative samples exist (e.g., Lezak, 1995; Loring, Martin, Meador, & Lee, 1990; Spreen & Strauss, 1998), and a subsequent recall trial measures visual memory.

b. WAIS–III Block Design or Object Assembly

Age-corrected scaled scores should always be used on the WAIS–III Block Design subtest (Wechsler, 1997) as performance on this task plummets with age. Motor deficit or slowing of thought processes may substantially affect performance because of the timed nature of the test. The Object Assembly subtest also purportedly measures constructional ability, although there is a recognition component as well as a constructional component. Object Assembly would ordinarily have a low priority in the neuropsychological examination as it has the lowest reliability and validity of any WAIS–III subtest, and its administration is not necessary for derivation of the Perceptual–Organization Index Score.

c. Three-Dimensional Block Construction

The first design of this Benton et al. (1994) test is actually two-dimensional, having only width and height but not depth. The other two designs measure constructional ability in all three dimensions. An advantage of the test is its simplicity and lack of intellectual demand, allowing evaluation of constructional ability even in poorly educated or low-functioning patients. The relatively large size of the blocks and generous time limits allow evaluation of patients who are slow or who have difficulty with motor dexterity.

6. COLOR VISION

The Ishihara Pseudoisochromatic plates are the standard for evaluation of color deficits, although most of the plates measure red/green vision, with only two of the plates measuring blue/yellow vision. The test is also confounded with form discrimination as the patient must fuse an array of isochromatic circles together to perceive a target number. Administration of plates that have been rendered monochromatic by photocopying can help determine whether a deficit in form discrimination is confounding the test. Ordinary crayons or common objects can be used to examine for gross color vision deficits if color plates are not readily available.

B. Aphasia With Comprehension Deficit

Examination of visual perception and constructional ability is useful in the aphasic patient to measure the intactness of nonverbal performance. Because of its simple task demands, the Three-Dimensional Block Construction task can be informative. If the patient fails to comprehend verbal instruction, the examiner may resort to building the first design in view of the patient, then having the patient imitate this performance. If the patient cannot construct even these simple designs, then it is clear that the patient's aphasia has caused a pervasive cognitive deficit such that the patient is incapable of performance even on tasks that make no overt demands on verbal comprehension.

C. Dementia

Evaluation of memory should be given priority in this clinical situation, but poor performance on a visual memory task should not be interpreted in the absence of data from tests of visual perception and constructional ability. A wider syndrome of visual deficit will often be seen, and as described earlier, will have implications for staging the course and classifying the severity of certain progressive dementias.

IX. CONCLUSION

The neuropsychological constructs of visuoperceptual ability and visual–constructional ability are defined in this chapter, as are the subtypes of deficits in visuoperceptual and visuoconstructive functions. The range of disorders that lead to deficits in these areas and their functional neuroanatomical correlates are described. Finally, the neuropsychological methods used to characterize such deficits are reviewed.

BIBLIOGRAPHY

Beery, K. E., Buktenica, N. A., & Beery, N. A. (2004). *Beery–Buktenica Developmental Test of Visual–Motor Integration* (5th ed.). Columbus, OH: Modern Curriculum Press.

Bender, M. B., Rudolph, S. H., & Stacy, C. B. (1982). The neurology of the visual and oculomotor systems. In R. J. Joynt (Ed.), *Clinical neurology* (Vol. 1, pp. 1–132). Philadelphia: Lippincott-Raven.

Benton, A. L., Sivan, A. B., Hamsher, K. deS., Varney, N. R., & Spreen, O. (1994). *Contributions to neuropsychological assessment* (2nd ed.). New York: Oxford University Press.

Benton, A. L., & Tranel, D. (1993). Visuoperceptual, visuospatial, and visuoconstructive disorders. In K. M. Heilman & E. Valenstein (Eds.), *Clinical neuropsychology* (3rd ed., pp. 165–213). New York: Oxford University Press.

Capruso, D. X., Hamsher, K. deS., & Benton, A. L. (1995). Assessment of visuocognitive processes. In R. L. Mapou & J. Spector (Eds.), *Clinical neuropsychological assessment: A cognitive approach* (pp. 137–183). New York: Plenum Press.

Gainotti, G. (1985). Constructional apraxia. In J. A. M. Frederiks (Ed.), *Handbook of clinical neurology: Vol. 1. Clinical neuropsychology* (pp. 491–506). Amsterdam: North Holland/Elsevier.

Jacobs, L. (1989). Comments on some positive visual phenomena caused by diseases of the brain. In J. Brown (Ed.), *Neurophysiology of visual perception* (pp. 165–182). Hillside, NJ: Erlbaum.

Kandel, E., Schwartz, J., & Jessell, T. (2000). *Principles of neural science* (3rd ed.). New York: McGraw-Hill/Appleton & Lange.

Kaplan, E. (1990). The process approach to neuropsychological assessment of psychiatric patients. *Neuropsychiatry, 2,* 72–87.

Kirk, A., & Kertesz, A. (1989). Hemispheric contributions to drawing. *Neuropsychologia, 27,* 881–886.

Lee, G. P., & Hamsher, K. deS. (1988). Neuropsychological findings in toxicometabolic confusional states. *Journal of Clinical and Experimental Neuropsychology, 10,* 769–778.

Lezak, M. D. (1995). *Neuropsychological assessment* (3rd ed.). New York: Oxford University Press.

Loring, D. W., Martin, R. C., Meador, K. J., & Lee, G. P. (1990). Psychometric construction of the Rey–Osterreith Complex Figure: Methodological considerations and interrater reliability. *Archives of Clinical Neuropsychology, 5,* 1–14.

Sivan, A. B. (1992). *Benton Visual Retention Test* (5th ed.). San Antonio, TX: Psychological Corporation.

Spreen, O., & Strauss, E. (1998). *A compendium of neuropsychological tests: Administration, norms, and commentary.* New York: Oxford University Press.

Walsh, K. W. (1985). *Understanding brain damage: A primer of neuropsychological evaluation.* Edinburgh, Scotland: Churchill Livingstone.

Wechsler, D. (1997). *Wechsler Adult Intelligence Scale—Third Edition.* San Antonio, TX: Psychological Corporation.

Chapter 24

Ronald A. Cohen, Paul F. Malloy, Melissa A.
Jenkins, and Robert H. Paul

Disorders of Attention

Impairments of attention are among the most common manifestations of brain damage. Many neuropsychological syndromes that result from highly circumscribed focal brain lesions
are relatively rare in clinical practice (e.g., visual agnosia). In
contrast, disorders of attention are quite common, occurring
following damage to a variety of different cortical and subcortical brain systems. Attention dysfunction also occurs as a nonspecific effect of neurophysiological factors that affect arousal and
metabolic state. Alterations in level of consciousness associated
with acute brain dysfunction invariably have a direct impact
on attention. It is essential, therefore, that attention be assessed
as a standard part of a neuropsychological evaluation.

Patients with attentional dysfunction are usually unable
to allocate cognitive resources effectively to the task at hand.
Clinical examination reveals that the patient fails to perform
at optimal levels even though primary cognitive resources, such
as sensory registration, perception, memory, and associative
functions, are intact. Patients with primary attentional disorders
are able to perceive sensory input, comprehend language, form
and retrieve memories, and perform other cognitive functions,
yet they fail to do so consistently. The performance inconsistency that is a hallmark feature of attentional disturbances stems
from the fact that attention consists of a set of dynamic processes
that influence the interaction between other core cognitive

functions, such as perception and memory, and the external environment.

Whereas perception, language, and memory consist of processes that form the substrates of cognition, attention governs the information flow and processing within each of these cognitive domains. Attentional processes facilitate, enhance, or inhibit other cognitive processes. Attention enables people to respond to particular information while either consciously or unconsciously ignoring other potential stimuli. Attention implies cognitive or behavioral withdrawal from some things so that others can be effectively dealt with. Attention results in behavioral orientation toward particular stimuli or response demands associated with the task at hand. Therefore, a primary function of attention is to facilitate selection of salient sensory information for further processing (**sensory selective attention**). Attentional processes also serve to facilitate responding by influencing the tendency to respond in particular ways to task demands (i.e., response bias). Through the processes of **response intention, selection,** and **control**, attentional selectivity relative to available response alternatives is possible.

In addition to being selective, attention governs the intensity of cognitive allocation directed toward a particular stimulus or task. This intensity of attentional allocation is often conceptualized as focus, and subjectively it is experienced as the ability to concentrate. Attentional focus is a direct function of capacity limitations, influenced by both energetic (e.g., arousal) and structural (e.g., processing speed) factors. When attention capacity is reduced, either by structural brain damage or neurophysiological disturbance, people become less able to focus and concentrate. Attention also has a strong temporal dynamic. Whereas the content of associations, language, and percepts can be considered to be independent of the variable of time, what is attended to is usually a direct function of the time period that one examines. Furthermore, the ability of people to attend and focus selectively changes over time. Variations in attention over time is a function of the individual's capacity for **sustained attention**.

Attention was once conceptualized as a single process, similar to a filter or bottleneck, that restricted the flow of sensory input subject to higher cognitive operations, thereby limiting the amount of information to be processed to manageable levels. Although this model has intuitive appeal, compelling evidence now exists that attention is not a unitary process but a function of the interaction of at least four component processes under the influence of multiple brain systems. A variety of attentional disorders exist that differentially affect the underlying component processes of sensory selective attention, response selection and control, capacity and focus, and sustained attention (Cohen, 1993; Mirsky et al., 1991). Figure 24.1 depicts the primary factors underlying attention.

I. COMPONENTS OF ATTENTION

A. Sensory Selective Attention

Sensory selective attention refers to the processes by which sensory input is chosen for additional cognitive processing and focus. Perceptual processes are engaged relative to target stimuli and are disengaged from nontargets. It occurs at a very early stage of processing, often before a clear task demand is present. The orienting response, the most elementary behavioral response identified during classical conditioning, is a simple form of automatic sensory selection. Stimuli that are novel, salient, or potentially significant elicit an orienting response, whereas nonsalient "old" stimuli fail to do so. Salience may reflect perceptual factors, such as figure–ground contrast, or informational value derived from past experience. Sensory selection is contingent on the integration of the following elementary operations:

1. **Filtering:** At early stages of perceptual processing, selection occurs on the basis of sensitivities to or preferences for certain types of sensory features. Input that has these features receives additional processing, whereas input that does not is filtered.

2. **Enhancement:** Prior to the presentation of a stimulus to a particular spatial location, cortical neuronal sensitivity to that location is increased by information that creates an expectancy that an event will occur there. Attentional readiness and expectancy to spatial position form the basis of spatial selective attention. The neuronal substrates of enhancement have been demonstrated in primates (e.g., Goldberg & Bushnell, 1981).

3. **Disengagement:** Once attention has been focused on a particular stimulus, it remains fixed until another stimulus or internal event signals a shift of attention to another spatial location or perceptual feature. This attentional shift requires disengagement from the initial stimulus, before attention can be allocated to new stimuli. Attentional disengagement requires processing resources, and it takes time.

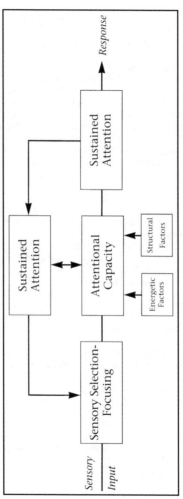

Figure 24.1. Primary factors underlying attention. Flow of information is shown through the four major components of attention: sensory selection and focusing, response selection and control, capacity, and sustained attention. Attentional capacity is influenced by energetic and structural components. Sustained attention is a product of the information flow through the system and the resulting feedback that affects each factor.

B. Response Selection and Control (Intention)

Attentional processes also serve to facilitate action through the selection and control of behavioral responding. **Intention** refers to allocation of attentional resources for response selection and control.

1. Although sensory selective attention is sometimes viewed as an antecedent to responding, in many cases response intention and selection precede sensory selection. For instance, if one loses one's keys, an intent to search and a search strategy may be generated before the perceptual act of selectively attending to a particular spatial location is initiated.

2. Intention depends on the individual being prepared to make a response. The following functional states influence the generation of intention as well as sensory selective attention:
   a. **Readiness:** The individual must be ready to make a response for optimal performance to occur. Readiness is mediated by arousal and reinforcement associated with a task.
   b. **Expectancy:** In addition to being ready to respond, one has the expectation that a response will need to be made at a particular time.
   c. **Anticipatory response:** Preparatory responses in anticipation of the need to respond often serve to facilitate intentional response selection and control.

3. Response selection and control are usually controlled and effortful, in contrast to sensory selective attention, which often is performed more automatically.

4. Conscious awareness usually occurs with response selection and control, whereas sensory selection often occurs without awareness.

5. Sequential processing is usually associated with response selection and control, whereas sensory selection often occurs as a result of parallel processing.

6. Executive functions are strongly linked to response selection and control. Specific executive functions that have direct attentional underpinnings include the following:
   a. intention: processes by which response set and preparation are established,
   b. initiation: processes by which the response is started,
   c. generative capacity: processes that facilitate production of the response,

    d. persistence: processes that enable sustained responding,

    e. inhibition: processes that prevent or enable cessation of the response, and

    f. switching: processes that enable a shift from one response to another.

C. Attentional Capacity and Focus

Once a stimulus has been selected for further processing, attention is allocated in accordance with the demands of the task at hand. For many cognitive operations, quality of performance is a function of the intensity of directed attention.

1. Focused attention controls the intensity and scope of attentional allocation and, consequently, the cognitive resources directed to a particular task or cognitive operation.

2. Conversely, focus is a function of processing capacity limitations (Kahneman, 1973).

3. Attentional capacity is governed by both structural and energetic limitations (Cohen, 1993). Energetic capacity limitations tend to be state dependent, composed of factors such as arousal and motivational state. Structural capacity tends to be less state dependent, is determined by factors intrinsic to the individual, and varies greatly across people.

4. Structural factors that provide attentional capacity limitations include the following:

    a. neural transmission and processing speed,

    b. working memory capacity,

    c. temporal processing constraints, and

    d. spatial processing constraints.

D. Automatic Versus Controlled Processing

An important distinction exists between automatic and controlled attention. In many instances, attention is elicited automatically when particular environmental signals occur. Furthermore, some tasks can be performed without the need for much attentional capacity (e.g., typing).

1. **Automaticity** refers to the capacity to attend to and perform particular cognitive operations with minimal effort and without the need for controlled intensive serial processing (Hasher & Zacks, 1979; Schneider & Shiffrin, 1977).

2. Increasing attentional focus relative to the task at hand usually results in a reduction in automaticity.
3. With automaticity, there is usually relatively little demand placed on attentional capacity, and often attention can occur without much awareness or subjective effort (e.g., attending to other cars while driving on a highway with light traffic).
4. Once a task is learned, less working memory is required, and demands for controlled effortful processing are reduced.
5. Automaticity occurs most commonly in the context of sensory selective attention, particularly when involving single-frame parallel processing, in which rapid selection of relevant targets from the larger set of potential stimuli in the environmental field can be accomplished at a very early stage of processing (single frame). Visual selective attention is particularly well suited for single-frame parallel processing. Visual information typically occurs in parallel with a vast array of information reaching the brain almost instantaneously. Automaticity is more difficult to achieve for tasks that require sequential cognitive operations, although greater automaticity is often attainable through practice.
6. Selective response attention (intention) is less likely to occur with automaticity than is sensory selective attention. One reason is that motor responding often requires the sequencing of complex responses. The development of well-learned motor programs (e.g., typing, musical performance) often enables attentional automaticity. Increasing memory demands usually decrease the capacity for attentional automaticity (Schneider & Shiffrin, 1977).
7. Sustained attention often can be performed with automaticity. Yet when long durations of sustained attention or vigilance are required, automaticity decreases and greater demand for controlled attentional processing results. Demands for concurrent attention on more than one task or unit of information often cause a rapid decrease in automaticity.

E. Sustained Attention

The maintenance of optimal performance over time requires sustained attention. When one considers most other cognitive processes, a consistent level of performance is usually assumed.

For instance, in a neurologically healthy person, visual perception always occurs when certain psychophysical parameters are met. Similarly, language competence usually implies that once individuals have achieved comprehension, they will always comprehend particular information. In contrast, temporal inconsistency is a defining characteristic of attention, because the ability to attend and focus selectively varies over time.

1. The variability of performance over extended time periods illustrates an important feature of attention that distinguishes it from other cognitive processes.
2. Vigilance is a special form of sustained attention in which there is a demand for a high level of anticipatory readiness for low-probability targets or stimulus events (Parasuraman & Davies, 1984).
3. Sustained attention is a direct function of the task duration. Any task can be extended to the point that a failure of sustained attention will occur.
4. Sustained attention is dependent on the target–distractor ratio. Generally, sustained performance is most difficult in situations in which target stimuli are rare.
5. Tasks that demand high levels of attentional focus and capacity are usually more difficult to sustain.
6. Energetic capacity, including arousal, is a strong determinant of sustained attention performance.
7. Reinforcement greatly influences sustained attention. Incentive and internal motivational state are important determinants of how attention is maintained over time.

II. FUNCTIONAL NEUROANATOMY OF ATTENTION

Attention cannot be localized to one discrete brain system; rather, multiple brain systems interact in a network to control attention (Cohen, 1993; Heilman, Watson, & Valenstein, 1993; Mesulam, 1981). However, the specific attentional processes are controlled by different brain systems within this network (see Figure 24.2).

The **inferior parietal cortex** plays a central role in spatial selective attention (Heilman et al., 1993; Heilman, Watson, Valenstein, & Goldberg, 1988; Mattingley, Bradshaw, Bradshaw, & Nettleton, 1994; Mesulam, 1981; Posner, Walker, Friedrich, & Rafal, 1987). In primates, area PG of the nondominant hemisphere contains neurons that enhance attentional responses to particular spatial positions. Damage to this area results in

Figure 24.2. Functional neuroanatomy of attention. Multiple brain systems interact in a network to control attention.

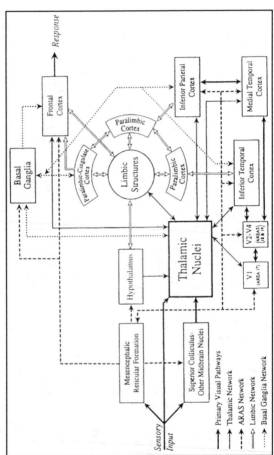

impaired spatial attention (e.g., hemineglect). Other posterior cortical areas also appear to be involved in selective attention. For example, the inferior temporal lobes exhibit attentional enhancement, which facilitates higher order sensory analysis such as object recognition. Attentional enhancement enables selective focus on relevant visual features.

The **frontal cortex** appears to be important for all four of the attention component processes and therefore is an essential brain region for attention. The most obvious function of the frontal cortex occurs with respect to executive functions relating to response selection and control. However, it also influences most other aspects of attention, including focused and sustained attention and capacity. Even sensory selection seems to be influenced by the frontal cortex, as evidenced by findings of spatial hemi-inattention following unilateral nondominant hemisphere damage. The frontal cortex plays an integral role in switching and search for sensory selective attention.

The **orbital frontal region** plays a major role in response initiation and inhibition. Damage to this area causes go/no-go impairments, which have direct implications for attention (Fuster, 1989). The medial frontal lobe, including the paralimbic cingulate cortex, plays an important role in the formation of intent to respond, the temporal consistency of responding, and focused attention (Cohen, 1993). The dorsolateral frontal cortex also appears to play a role in attention, although this is less well understood. This region seems to influence response sequencing, persistence, switching, and focus, particularly with respect to integration and responding in relation to semantic representations. The frontal eye fields control saccadic eye movements and are important for visual search and looking. Neuronal response of this region is influenced by attention neurons in the parietal cortex. The premotor cortex facilitates planned movements; although it is not in its own right an attentional system, it influences response automaticity.

Limbic system structures, such as the amygdala and septal nuclei, affect attention by influencing motivational and affective processing and establishing salience, which in turn determines the priority given new information as well as existing associations. The limbic system plays an essential role in defining the limits of attentional capacity and focus, and it also is instrumental in determining response biases and propensity (Cohen, 1993; Pribram & McGuinness, 1975). Memory encoding and retrieval functions of the hippocampus constrain attentional capacity. The rate at which short-term memories are encoded into long-term representations influences the ease with which attentional operations can be performed (Schneider & Shiffrin, 1977). Interactions of the amygdaloid, septal, and hypothalamic nuclei are responsible for the creation and experience of motivation and emotions, and ultimately they govern the salience associated with information.

Subcortical systems play a critical role in attention. Thalamic nuclei are involved in both sensory and response selective attention, and they have a gating function as sensory input is relayed through the thalamus to cortical areas. Furthermore, motor control signals sequenced within the basal ganglia are processed through the thalamus and then relayed to supplementary motor and frontal areas prior to motor output, with the thalamus serving as a gatekeeper. The caudate nucleus of the basal ganglia is important not only for the selection of motor responses but also for the selection and coordination of sensory information in relation to these responses. There is now considerable evidence that basal ganglia dysfunction plays a significant role in attention deficit disorder (ADD).

Midbrain systems, particularly the mesencephalic reticular system, are essential for production of arousal and activation (Cohen, 1993; Pribram & McGuinness, 1975). Arousal establishes a tonic energetic level, which in turn influences the responsiveness and attentional bias of the system. The reticular system activates the thalamus, limbic system, and cortical areas and is therefore critical for maintaining consciousness. Midbrain nuclei are also involved in the control of saccadic movements for visual search.

III. NEUROLOGICAL AND NEUROPSYCHIATRIC DISORDERS OF ATTENTION

A. Stroke

Focal lesions associated with embolic or hemorrhagic cerebrovascular infarction often produce the most dramatic form of attentional disturbance. **Hemineglect, extinction,** and **hemi-inattention** syndromes are among the disorders of attention that are common after stroke. These syndromes are discussed in considerable detail elsewhere in this text and are not extensively reviewed here. However, several key summary points regarding these syndromes are in order.

1. Hemi-inattention and neglect are manifestations of unilateral brain lesions. Striking spatial asymmetry in attentional performance is a central feature of these syndromes.

2. Neglect usually occurs relative to the left side of space, which illustrates the importance of the nondominant cortical hemisphere in spatial attention.

3. Although most patients with neglect have a number of common symptoms, the specific attentional disturbance depends on the exact location of the lesion.

   a. Lesions affecting the reticular system that produce neglect also involve significant arousal and activation impairments.

   b. Unilateral basal ganglia damage often results in both hemi-attention and intention impairments, reflecting the importance of this system to sensorimotor integration.

   c. Cingulate lesions are more likely to affect intention than sensory selective attention.

Although hemineglect syndrome is one of the most dramatic forms of attentional disturbance, focal lesions secondary to stroke commonly produce disorders that do not involve hemineglect.

4. Focal frontal lesions may produce impairments of focused attention in addition to the common finding of attentional impairments of response selection and control.

5. Thalamic lesions may result in problems with informational gating and selection regardless of whether unilateral neglect is present.

6. Subcortical lesions often produce impairments of arousal, activation, and information-processing speed, which in turn may limit attentional capacity.

7. Subcortical small vessel disease secondary to cerebral hypoperfusion may result in dementia; this type of dementia seems to affect attention and information-processing efficiency most dramatically.

B. Dementia

Alzheimer's disease and other neurological diseases that result in diffuse global cortical dysfunction often have significant associated attentional impairments. Yet patients with dementia are often able to sit and sustain a general attentional orientation toward the examiner, and automatic attention is usually preserved until relatively late stages of the illness. Therefore, clinicians often conclude erroneously that attention is preserved in these patients.

1. Attentional capacity and focusing ability are almost always impaired early in the disease course, although sensory selective attention tends to be intact.
2. Simple response selection and control are affected to varying degrees in early stages of dementia.
3. Executive functions often fail relatively early.
4. Sustained attention may appear adequate with respect to a patient's ability to sit and respond to the examiner. Yet sustained performance on structured tasks is usually quite impaired, and there may be problems with impersistence.

C. Multiple Sclerosis

Of the cognitive impairments that often accompany multiple sclerosis (MS), the most common disorders involve attention (Cohen, 1993).

1. Fatigue is the most common of all symptoms in MS. Fatigue is associated not only with motor effort but also with attending to and performing cognitive tasks.
2. Subcortical lesions secondary to demyelination may disrupt attentional control.
3. Subcortical white matter lesions also reduce neural transmission speed. Slowed processing time reduces attentional capacity and creates processing bottlenecks.

D. Hydrocephalus

Hydrocephalus often creates pressure on periventricular white matter subcortical systems, and attention and information-processing problems are quite common. Because ventricular pressure often fluctuates, attentional difficulties frequently exhibit a fluctuating course with this disorder.

E. Head Trauma

Whereas diffuse neuronal injury often results from moderate or severe head trauma, the most common areas of bilateral damage are the frontal lobes, basal temporal lobes, and subcortical brain systems. Brain damage to these areas occurs not only as a by-product of an object hitting the cranium but also as a result of shearing forces, especially when an accident has involved rapid acceleration–deceleration.

1. Attentional impairments of the type described previously for patients with focal frontal lesions are often observed.

2. The shearing effects that damage subcortical white matter often result in arousal and activation deficits.
3. Slowing of information processing is also common.

F. Schizophrenia

Severe attention impairments are common.
1. Problems with informational filtering or gating often exist.
2. Selective attention is often impaired with increased information load.
3. Problems distinguishing relevant from irrelevant input are quite common and seem to belie a problem with the tagging of semantic value of informational input or associations that are attended to.
4. Sustained and focused attention are often poor, and capacity is often limited, particularly for divided attention (concurrent task performance).

G. Affective Disorder

Attentional disturbance is the most common cognitive symptom associated with major affective disorders.
1. Subjective complaints of problems with concentration and focus are among the symptoms that are considered in a diagnosis of depression.
2. Problems with reduced energetic capacity (focused attention) and sustained attention are most common. Response selection and control is often more moderately impaired. Sensory selective attention is usually less affected.
3. Attentional performance is often quite variable over time.
4. The quality of attentional impairments varies as a function of affective state. Manic patients tend to make more errors of commission and fail to inhibit responding, whereas depressed patients make more errors of omission and are likely to show low levels of arousal with psychomotor slowing. Great effort is often required for attention.
5. Given the strong likelihood of attentional disturbance in patients with affective disorders, it is essential that depression be ruled out or factored in when one is assessing attention associated with other brain disorders.

H. Attention Deficit Disorder

The most commonly diagnosed disorder of attention, ADD has become one of the most frequently diagnosed disorders in the United States. Although a diagnosis of ADD is now sometimes made on the basis of patient self-reported symptoms, there is considerable evidence that self-reported symptoms do not always correspond well with evidence of attentional impairments observed on assessment. This is particularly true for adults presenting with new concerns about possible ADD but without a history of childhood ADD.

1. Attention impairment is usually milder than in patients with neurological disorders affecting strategic brain regions that control attention.
2. High comorbidity with depression, other psychiatric disorders, substance abuse, and learning disabilities exists.
3. Thorough attentional assessment ADD is strongly suggested. Data from the attentional assessment should be reconciled with medical, psychiatric, and educational history data (including childhood school records or behavioral reports) and behavioral observations from the clinical interview and during the course of the evaluation.

IV. ASSESSING DISORDERS OF ATTENTION

Although it is an essential cognitive process, attention is difficult to observe directly or to measure. Attention fluctuates in accordance with changes in task demands and the processing capacity of the patient over time. Unlike other cognitive functions, performance may differ greatly at different points in time; it is this variability that in fact defines attention. Attention is often situation specific. For example, many children with ADD are capable of sustaining their attention and regulating their behavior for hours while playing videogames despite reports of gross problems of inattention in school or during other less personally salient activities at home. Attention primarily serves to facilitate other cognitive functions; it enhances or inhibits perception, memory, motor output, and executive functions, including problem solving. Yet attentional performance is measured as a function of performance on tasks that also load on one or more other domains. Therefore, a number of methodological issues need to be considered when attention is assessed.

A. Methodological Issues

1. Pure tests of attention do not exist.
2. Attention usually must be assessed within the context of performance on tasks that measure performance in other functionally separable cognitive domains.
3. Attentional performance is often a function of a derived measure obtained by comparing performance across tasks that each contribute in an additive manner with respect to key attentional parameters (e.g., target–distractor ratio).
4. Absolute performance often proves less informative than measures of performance inconsistencies in the assessment of attention. For example, how performance varies as a function of time, spatial characteristics, or memory load provides more information about attentional dynamics than does the total number of errors on a visual detection task.
5. Because attention is not the by-product of a unitary process, it cannot be adequately assessed on the basis of findings from one specific test. For example, conclusions about attention based solely on digit span performance are misguided.
6. Attentional assessment requires a multifactorial approach.

The specific measures used in an evaluation depend on the overall level of functioning of the patient.

1. For patients with global cognitive dysfunction, it may be difficult to use tasks that require complex responses.
2. For patients with relatively high overall cognitive abilities, tasks should be chosen that require multiple component processes. If the patient is able to perform well on these tasks, severe attentional disturbance involving specific attentional component processes can be ruled out. The Stroop and Trail Making tests are examples of tasks that require multiple attentional processes.
3. If impairments are found on such tasks, more extensive testing of specific component processes can be conducted.
4. Whenever possible, efforts should be made to use tasks that incorporate signal detection methods, even when one is not evaluating sensory selective attention per se. These methods provide the best means of accurately summarizing performance relative to all possible types of errors. Also, tasks using a signal detection approach

can often be easily integrated with response time measures.

B. Attentional Parameters That Should Be Considered

A thorough assessment of attention should be based on analysis of data from a comprehensive battery of attentional tests (Cohen, 1993) that sample the various component processes of attention (see Table 24.1). These tasks should enable evaluation of performance as a function of different stimulus, response, and task parameters. Tasks should be differentially sensitive to the following attentional parameters:

- spatial characteristics;
- temporal dynamics;
- memory demands;
- processing speed requirements;
- perceptual complexity;
- demand for different levels of control and sequencing;
- demand for various types and complexity of cognitive operation;
- effortful demands;
- task salience, relevance, and reward value; and
- demand for single-frame parallel and multiframe serial processing.

C. Levels of Assessment

Although multifactor neuropsychological assessment provides the best means of evaluating attentional impairments, a comprehensive attentional evaluation may not be feasible in everyday clinical practice because (a) the patient is too ill to participate for long time periods, (b) other functions in addition to attention must be assessed, or (c) there are time constraints in the clinical context. Consequently, clinicians should be aware of the information that can be obtained from different levels of attentional assessment.

1. CLINICAL INTERVIEW

The most common source of information regarding a possible attentional disorder is the clinical interview. A number of structured interview procedures exist for assessing subjective reports of attention deficit (e.g., the Wender Utah Rating Scale, or WURS). Although the clinical interview often provides useful information, the following key problems arise if one relies only on this source of information:

Table 24.1. Component Processes of Attention-Associated Neuropsychological Tests

Component	Tests
Sensory Selective Attention	Letter and symbol cancellation Line bisection Cued spatial detection (Posner task) Spatial search tasks (span of apprehension) Dichotic listening CPT (D′) Line orientation
Response selection and control	Go/no-go Complex motor programs Rampart figures Trail Making CPT (F+) Porteus Mazes—breaks Sorting tasks—failure to maintain response set Fluency measures (COWAT, design fluency)
Capacity and focus	Digit symbol (Stroop) Paced Serial Addition Test (PASAT) Stroop tests (interference) Reaction time measures Levels of processing (working memory tasks) Timing tasks (motor continuation, duration discrimination) Spatial rotation tasks Dichotic listening (divided attention paradigms)
Sustained Attention	CPT vigilance decrement Motor persistence tasks (sustained finger tapping) Variation across session on repeated administration of task

a. Subjective complaints of attentional problems often do not correlate well with actual impairments on attentional tests. Patients may present to neuropsychological clinics having amassed significant information from the Internet, in which numerous behavioral checklists and descriptions of attentional difficulties have been publicized. Patients may describe, in some cases quite eloquently, the nature and severity of their deficits in attention, yet the complaints may not be corroborated by external sources.

b. Patients with the most severe attentional problems often have little awareness of their impairments.

c. Family members frame their experience of symptoms on the basis of their own tolerance for certain types of behavior, which results in questionable validity for this source of data.

d. Because of the preceding problems, interview and even questionnaire data should be treated with caution, as a starting point in the assessment of attention.

2. BEHAVIORAL OBSERVATION

Observation of the patient's behavior during the clinical interview and subsequent testing provides useful information. Use of a behavior symptom checklist for some of the key symptoms of attention disturbance described previously may facilitate such observation and improve validity.

a. Behavioral observation methods enable systematic recording during the examination of behavioral events that reflect attentional problems. These methods include **event recording** of behavioral frequency, **interval recording** of the presence of an event at certain times, and **scan sampling** of duration of events per unit of time. In the less structured environment of clinical interviews, rich information regarding attentional function can be ascertained. Can the patient sustain attention throughout the course of the interview? Is the patient easily distracted by noises (e.g., paper shuffling, competing conversation) or movement? How well can the patient complete a line of communication, or does the patient shift his or her attention from one topic to the next? Although all of these observations are vulnerable to disturbances in other cognitive domains, the processing capacity imposed by attentional resources significantly influences the ability to execute this aspect of the evaluation. The importance of the behavioral observation might be most applicable during the bedside evaluation. A bedside assessment of attention requires some mental flexibility from the clinician, as the testing environment and process are dynamic and the clinician will likely need to overcome a variety of obstacles (e.g., interruptions by house staff, frequent external noises, presence of individuals in the room). As much as these factors place some limits on the testing process, they can also serve as useful sources of information. Behavioral observations can be especially helpful in these contexts, as the clinician has the opportunity to examine the patient's ability to filter information and focus on relevant stimuli.

b. Behavioral observation methods often provide the most ecologically valid measures of attention. However, the following limitations exist in relation to their use:

1. Behavioral observation methods can be quite labor intensive.
2. The methods require long recording periods to detect low-frequency events.
3. Behavioral observation does not directly measure or provide much information regarding the cognitive processes underlying inattention symptoms.

3. TRADITIONAL PSYCHOMETRIC APPROACHES

Many psychological tests that were not designed specifically to assess attention have been used for this purpose. For instance, the Wechsler Adult Intelligence Scale—III (WAIS–III), originally developed as an intelligence test, is widely used to provide information about specific cognitive functions, including attention.

a. The Working Memory Index (WMI) of the WAIS–III provides a qualitative assessment of attentional functions. The WMI is composed of three subtests from the WAIS–III: Digit Span, Arithmetic, and Letter-Number Sequencing. This index correlates strongly with other measures of attention, including the Attention-Concentration index of the WAIS–III ($r = .66$), Trail Making ($r = -.37$), and the Attention/Mental Control Index of the MicroCog ($r = .65$).

b. Additional information regarding speeded attentional function can be derived from the Processing Speed Index (PSI) of the WAIS–III. This index is composed of two additional subtests of the WAIS–III, the Digit Symbol Coding and Symbol Search, and the index correlates strongly with Trail Making ($r = -.49$) and the Attention/ Mental Control Index of the MicroCog ($r = .60$). It is important to note that the WMI and the PSI have been identified as independent factors in exploratory factory analysis studies of the WAIS–III.

c. Independent subtests of the WAIS–III that are not included in the WMI or the PSI also yield useful information regarding attention function. For example, the Picture Completion subtest may be helpful for detecting visual selective attentional problems in some cases, although evidence of impairment needs to be interpreted with caution because task performance is influenced by various factors, including perceptual and inferential ability and cultural knowledge.

d. On the Wechsler Memory Scale—III (WMS–III), the Letter-Number Sequencing test and the Spatial Span test constitute a Working Memory factor. These tasks require short-term memory retention (i.e., working memory) and cognitive operations that demand attentional focus.

e. On the WAIS–III and WMS–III, attentional problems may also be identified on the basis of the patients' response characteristics, as follows:

1. Excessive interitem variability may reflect fluctuations in attentional focus and problems with sustained attention.

2. Intertest variability, particularly when inconsistencies are noted among subtests measuring the same cognitive function, may also suggest impaired attention.

3. Caution should be used when interpreting attentional impairments on the basis of performance variability, because variability may also reflect the standard error of measurement and subtle psychometric factors associated with test construction.

4. NEUROPSYCHOLOGICAL ASSESSMENT OF ATTENTION

Ideally, the assessment of attention should include neuropsychological tests that have been developed to be sensitive to the different component processes of attention. With the use of these tests, impairments of attention can be more easily dissociated from other cognitive problems. Norms exist for many of these tests.

a. Sensory selective attention

Tests used in the assessment of neglect syndromes provide a foundation for the assessment of sensory selective attention.

1. Letter and symbol cancellation tasks are useful for detecting abnormalities in both the spatial distribution of visual attention and general signal detection capacity.

2. Line bisection may also provide evidence for a hemispatial attentional disturbance.

3. The paradigm of double simultaneous stimulation (DSS) provides a method for detecting extinction and neglect of stimuli in impaired hemispace.

4. The analysis of the spontaneous drawings of objects and copying of figures may point to lateral differences in attention to detail or spatial quality.

5. Although paper-and-pencil tests and simple behavioral tasks such as DSS provide the best method for initial assessment, computerized tests based on experimental paradigms provide for a more thorough evaluation of sensory selective attention.

   a. Dichotic listening paradigms, which involve the presentation of different information to the two ears, provide a way of assessing auditory attentional selection under different conditions of discriminability and response bias. However, this paradigm also involves divided attention and reflects capacity limitations as well. Dichotic listening has been used in shadowing paradigms, which require the participant to repeat material being presented auditorily in one ear while processing a competing message in the other ear. Participants have great difficulty extracting information from the nonshadowed ear during dichotic listening, but they can detect physical changes in the stimuli to that ear. Participants also show little memory of material presented to the nonshadowed ear, although they attend better to the nonshadowed channel when different modalities are used and after they have learned to attend to the nonshadowed channel.

   b. Spatial search tasks provide an excellent means of assessing the spatial distribution for visual attention. Tachistoscopic or computerized presentation of an array of visual stimuli enables attentional search to be evaluated as a function of the time taken to scan the visual array for a particular target (visual spatial search tasks). By mapping this spatial distribution as a function of attentional parameters, it is possible to determine what factors influence search. Search accuracy tends to be best above the fixation point, whereas extreme points in the vertical dimension are the least likely to be accurately searched. Selection has also been shown to vary greatly along the horizontal axis, and search times are greatest when there is high similarity between targets and distractors. The accuracy of visual search depends on the attentional demands of the task. Accurate detection should occur at an almost perfect rate when the location of the target is obvious and not difficult to discriminate. Reduced speed and accuracy occur when targets are shifted in the visual field and the location is uncertain.

c. Spatial cue paradigms, which measure the influence of attentional bias in anticipation of spatial position, provide another important method for assessing visual selective attention (Posner et al., 1987). Although a variety of spatial cue paradigms exist, the principles underlying these tasks are generally the same. A neutral cue is presented at some spatial location prior to the onset of a target. On some trials, the cue correctly signals the future position of a target stimulus, whereas on other trials the information provided by the cue is incorrect. The accuracy of detection and reaction times can then be measured as a function of the anticipatory cue to either correct or incorrect spatial position.

b. Response selection and control

A large number of tasks are available for use in assessing response selection and control. Many of these tasks fall within the rubric of tests of executive functions. These tests are differentially sensitive to the executive functions of intention, initiation, generation, persistence, inhibition, and switching that were described previously. Simple motoric response control may be assessed by tasks such as double alternating movements, alternating graphic sequences (e.g., Rampart Figures), motor impersistence, and the go/no-go paradigm. Tests such as Trail Making, the Stroop tasks, the Wisconsin Card Sorting Test (WCST), and the Porteus Mazes provide a means for assessing higher order executive functions such as goal-directed behavior, response planning, and active switching of response set.

c. Intention

1. Response selection and control is predicated on the formation of intent to act. Although intent is often inferred rather than measured directly, there are ways of assessing intentional impairments.

    a. A failure to initiate a search or goal-directed behaviors despite motivational feedback that provides incen-

tive for such action suggests an intention impairment.
    b. Failure to persist in a search strategy (impersistence) may also reflect impaired intention.
    c. The quantity and quality of spontaneously initiated behaviors, including the ability to generate alternative creative solutions to problems, may provide the best intention index.
2. Capacity for initiation, generation, and persistence can be measured in a number of different ways.
    a. Verbal and design fluency not only indicate the total quantity of response output for a circumscribed time period but also can point to problems with initiation and persistence.
    b. Simple and choice reaction time may help to characterize response initiation problems.
    c. Tests of motor functioning such as the Grooved Pegboard Test measure generation of and persistence in fine motor response production.
    d. Motor system deficits need to be considered when one is assessing whether a response generation deficit relates to attentional-executive impairments; occasionally, problems in the motor domain may present a confounding variable in the interpretation of neuropsychological results. Deficits in the ability to persist on motor tasks may also reflect problems with attention and executive functioning. For instance, patients with MS show fatigue that extends beyond their motor deficits. This fatigue has been shown to be related to attentional deficits in these patients.
3. **Response inhibition:** The ability to inhibit responses can be measured through a number of different tasks. Interference tasks such as the Stroop test determine the ability to inhibit attentional response to one stimulus characteristic while responding to another characteristic. The go/no-go paradigm and continuous-performance tests (CPTs) also provide information regarding the patient's ability to inhibit false-positive responses. Intrusion errors on these tests point to failed response inhibition.
4. **Response alternation and switching:** Several of the tasks described previously (alternating graphic sequences, go/no-go) require the alternation of response pattern and therefore provide information about this capacity. The Trail Making Test is one of the most

commonly used tests of response-switching ability and mental control. Errors occur when the patient fails to alternate between letters and numbers or when there is a break in the sequence and a particular item is omitted.

d. Attentional capacity and focus

Many paradigms are available for assessing attentional capacity and focus. Although these tasks are similar in that they require attentional focus, the cognitive operation that is necessary to perform the task may vary. Therefore, patients may exhibit performance inconsistencies across tasks according to their ability to perform certain cognitive operations.

1. There are several tests of focused attention, including the following:
    a. Among the standard measures used to assess attentional focus are tests that require mental arithmetic and control. Digit Span Backwards, Backwards Spelling, the Arithmetic subtest of the WAIS–III, and serial addition and subtraction tests are examples of such tasks. All of these tasks are also quite sensitive to brain dysfunction.
    b. The Paced Auditory Serial Addition Test (PASAT) is an example of a highly controlled test of attention that requires both focused and sustained attention. The PASAT is quite sensitive to subtle attentional impairments. Because considerable effort is required for adequate performance, however, the PASAT cannot be used with patients with severe brain dysfunction. Also, poor motivation or reduced arousal greatly affects performance on the PASAT.
    c. The Symbol Digit Modality Test (SDMT) and Digit Symbol subtest of the WAIS–III are also excellent measures of focused attentional capacity. Because these tasks require rapid processing of symbolic information and the coding of symbol–number pairs, they collectively can be considered symbol coding tests. Focused attention is required because the symbol–number pairs to be coded are not familiar to the patient. Therefore, attentional capacity is taxed in accordance with the memory demands of the task and the requirements of visual tracking, perceptual-motor integration, and time pressure.
2. Some tasks place demands on attentional capacity and focus because of the requirement for divided attention. Dichotic listening is the best example of such a task.

a. The ability to inhibit interfering stimulus characteristics while responding to a target feature is another example of divided attention that taxes capacity limitations. The Stroop test fits this category, because the patient is required to inhibit responses to words that are presented but to name the color that the word is printed in. Interference is created by the fact that the color of the printed word conflicts with the color denoted by the word itself.

b. Concurrent production tasks (e.g., finger tapping while demonstrating verbal fluency) provide a vehicle for assessing capacity limitations associated with divided attention. Such tasks are extremely effortful and require controlled focused attention. The task of finger tapping with fluency is useful for assessing response to the demands associated with two forms of response production. Alternatively, dichotic listening paradigms provide a way of assessing focused attention in the context of sensory selective attention.

c. Focused attention associated with demand for specific cognitive operations can be assessed through a number of different paradigms. For example, levels of processing memory paradigms create semantic activation with an associated level of attentional activation and effort. In principle, most cognitive tasks can be modified such that the fundamental cognitive operation remains constant but the demand for focused attention is controlled. For instance, by comparing digit–symbol with symbol–symbol coding performance, the effects of different levels of attentional focus can be assessed.

3. Tests of brief attention span provide a means of assessing capacity limitations associated with short-term or working memory. Digit Span Forwards is an example of such a test that also illustrates a problem associated with the traditional interpretation of attentional deficits. Digit Span Forwards has often been used as a general index of attention, yet strong performance is usually possible with minimal demand for attentional focus.

a. Performance on this test is most strongly associated with short-term memory (STM), working memory, and the language requirement of repetition. Performance depends on the ability to hold a string of items for a brief interval until a response is required.

b. Encoding of this information into more permanent memory storage is not necessary for task completion, and typically people are unable to retain the material soon after initial recall. Tests of brief attention span, therefore, bridge attention and STM.

c. Weak performance on Digit Span Forwards is not very informative in its own right, although when analyzed in relation to other findings, it may provide clinical information about working memory as well as the motivation of the patient.

d. Considerable interitem variability, such as missing some short sequences but correctly repeating longer sequences, is significant, because it suggests a lapse of attention.

e. Other tests, such as the Corsi Blocks and the Knox Cube Test, provide an opportunity to measure brief span in the visual–spatial modality. However, poor performance on spatial span tests may reflect spatial selective attentional deficits as well.

e. Sustained attention and vigilance

Tests that measure performance over time provide a means of assessing sustained attention and vigilance.

1. The continuous-performance test (CPT) paradigm measures signal detection performance over blocks of trials and provides one of the most widely used approaches for assessment of sustained attention. Many versions of the CPT exist, all consisting of the same basic paradigm. Either visual or auditory stimuli (usually letters) are presented sequentially. Intermixed among distractor stimuli are particular target stimuli, such as the letter *A*. The task is to respond to the target and the distractors. The attentional demands of the task can be modified on many CPT tests by changing the ratio of targets to distractors, total number of stimuli, total time of the test, perceptual complexity of the stimuli and background, interstimulus interval, and use of anticipatory stimuli. A variety of signal detection measures, such as misses, false positives, inconsistency, and vigilance decrement, can be determined that help to quantify impairments of sustained attention. Among the many CPT-based tests currently available, the most widely used is the Connors CPT (Conners et al., 2003; Connors & MHS Staff, 2005). Other versions of the CPT also may be useful. The Adaptive Rate Continuous Performance (Cohen, 1993) is of

shorter duration than the Conner's CPT, which makes it more practical for many testing situations. The ARCPT also adjusts the interstimulus interval over time, so that vigilance and signal detection performance can be dissociated from processing speed problems.

2. Information about sustained attention can also be derived from other neuropsychological measures. For instance, symbol cancellation tests require the patient to scan a sheet of paper to detect a particular stimulus or sequence of stimuli and to mark all target stimuli with a pencil. Performance is measured as a function of total time for task completion and of target stimuli missed. Failure to detect stimuli is considered to be an indicator of inattention. This type of task also provides information about sensory selective attention, including the presence of neglect.

3. Symbol coding tasks such as the Digit Symbol subtest may also be used to assess sustained attention by comparing performance during the early and late stages of the task. Similar modifications can also be made on tasks that involve more complex cognitive operations to make them more sensitive to impairments of sustained attention.

4. Tests of sustained attention, such as CPTs and symbol cancellation tests, can be modified to increase the demand for focused attention and effort. On the CPT, this can be done by increasing the complexity of rules governing target selection (e.g., respond to x only when preceded by A). Also, by adjusting parameters such as memory load, interstimulus times, or the presence of more than one stimulus in a target field on a trial, other attentional factors besides sustained attention can be examined. This is particularly useful in experimental studies, although it is somewhat problematic for clinical use because modifying task demands invalidates comparison to standardized, normative performance.

D. Assessment Strategy

The primary disadvantage of most traditional neuropsychological tests of attention stems from their reliance on a paper-and-pencil format. Although such methods typically provide useful data about error characteristics, they are not well suited for response time measurement, and they do not provide adequate information about interitem variability or change in performance across the task duration. For these reasons, it is recommended that efforts be made to use some computerized tests of attention that enable greater experimental control over stimulus and response parameters, such as the rate of stimulus presentation, the spatial characteristics of visual stimuli, and response times. Among the methods that enhance the assessment of attention are the following.

1. SIGNAL DETECTION METHODS

Error types associated with attentional processing can be best assessed using signal detection methods. Besides providing information about the relationship between errors caused by missing targets and false-positive errors caused by responding to nontargets (ß) and discriminability (d'), these methods enable a determination of expected response characteristics given the ratio of targets to distractors. Other attentional indices such as vigilance decrement and response inconsistency are also easily derived using signal detection methods.

2. CHRONOMETRIC ANALYSIS

Reaction time (RT) provides a useful index of the processing time involved in an attentional selection or response on particular tasks. Greater processing demands relative to capacity limitations tend to be associated with increased RTs. The costs and benefits of attentional allocation and disengagement (e.g., spatial cuing) can be determined through RT methods as well.

3. PHYSIOLOGICAL METHODS

Psychophysiological measurement provides a potentially rich source of information regarding the neurobiological substrates of attention. Although these methods have not yet been well integrated into standard neuropsychological practice, physiological findings can help to confirm clinical hypotheses by providing an independent index of attentional allocation.

    a. Autonomic measures are particularly useful in characterizing elicitation and habituation of the orienting response. These measures can also provide an index of the intensity of attentional focus and effort.

    b. Measures of central nervous system activity, such as electroencephalography (EEG), also provide indices of attentional processes.

    c. Event-related potentials yield waveforms that correspond to specific attentional processes, such as initial registration, attentional allocation, and response to stimulus salience.

d. Recently developed functional imaging techniques, such as positron emission tomography (PET), single photon emission computed tomography (SPECT), and functional magnetic resonance imaging (fMRI), enable dissociation of component processes of attention and undoubtedly will be clinically useful in the future.

4. COMPREHENSIVE ASSESSMENT BATTERIES

Several test batteries have been developed over the past decade that provide a standardized approach to assessment of attention. These include the Test of Everyday Attention (TEA), d2 Test of Attention, Behavioral Inattention Test (BIT), and Integrated Visual and Auditory Continuous Performance Test (IVA). The d2 Test of Attention and the IVA provide measures of several aspects of attention including vigilance and impulsivity and are similar to the CPT in format. These measures can be completed in fewer than 20 minutes.

The TEA and BIT require more time to administer, but both provide information regarding attention function using tests with high face validity and ecological relevance. For example, subtests of the TEA include visual search of a geographic map, vigilance on a simulated lottery game, and focused attention tests using a simulated elevator. The BIT was initially developed to identify neglect following stroke, and as such the battery is heavily weighted toward assessment of attention allocation across visual space. Additional clinical information can be obtained from subtests that provide information regarding the real-world impact of visual neglect on tasks such as map navigation, coin sorting, and use of clocks. Clinicians desiring to assess attention in a structured and comprehensive manner with tasks specifically designed to assess attention may benefit from the use of such batteries.

E. Recommended Measures for Initial Assessment

The demands of the clinical environment and important patient considerations will largely determine the breadth and nature of assessment aimed at attentional function. For example, use of a computer to administer a sustained vigilance task may not be feasible; alternatively, the patient's stamina may limit the total scope of a comprehensive neuropsychological assessment. Whenever the testing conditions allow, however, it is important to administer measures that will provide some information about each attentional component process.

The demands of the clinical environment and important patient considerations will largely determine the breadth and nature of assessment aimed at attentional function. For example, use of a computer to administer a sustained vigilance task may not be feasible; alternatively the patient's stamina may limit the total scope of a comprehensive neuropsychological assessment. Whenever the testing conditions allow, however, it is important to administer measures that will provide some information about each attentional component process.

An example of a core mini battery includes the Digit Symbol subtest, Trail Making, a letter cancellation task, and a CPT. The Digit Symbol subtest provides information about focused attention, working memory, and processing speed. Trail Making provides information about spatial search and response-switching ability. Letter cancellation provides information about visual search and sensory selective attention. The CPT is the best available means of assessing sustained attention. Expansion of this battery for a more comprehensive clinical assessment could include the following: the PASAT, Letter Number Sequencing, and Symbol Coding (for focused attention); Stroop, WCST, and Categories Test (for response selection); Line Bisection and Clock Drawing (for sensory selective attention); and Adaptive Rate CPT, Degraded Stimulus CPT, and the Sustained Attention to Response Task (for sustained attention).

F. Steps in Decision Making When Assessing Attention

Regardless of the battery that is chosen, the assessment of attention depends on a logical, stepwise decision process. A decision tree for evaluation of attention disorders is provided in Figure 24.3.

Step 1: Level of consciousness. Is the patient fully alert? Is lethargy or fatigue evident?

Step 2: Arousal. Is activity level within normal limits, or is the patient slowed or agitated?

Step 3: Motivation. Does the patient seem to exert adequate effort?

Step 4: Are sensory, perceptual, and motor functions intact? If not, it is essential to factor in the contribution of these impairments.

Step 5: Is attentional capacity reduced? Do impairments consistently appear on tasks requiring high levels of focus, working memory, or effort?

Step 6: Is reduced capacity general or limited to specific operations or modalities? If it is operation specific, attentional

Figure 24.3 Interrelated functions to be evaluated systematically according to the recommended steps and decision making during an examination of attention.

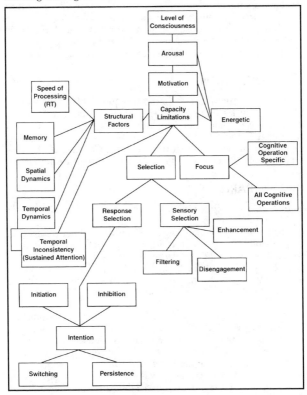

effects may be secondary to the greater effort required for tasks that are more difficult cognitively for the patient.

Step 7: If a general capacity problem is present, limiting factors should be examined in detail. This involves assessing factors such as processing speed and memory influence.

Step 8: Is attentional performance temporally inconsistent? Is there a performance decrement? If so, a more thorough assessment of sustained attention is in order.

Step 9: Is the attention problem limited to sensory selection or to response selection and control?

Step 10: If sensory selective attention impairment is suggested, is spatial distribution of attention abnormal? Is attention also impaired in nonspatial visual or auditory tasks?

Step 11: Are response selection problems related to specific problems with intention, initiation, inhibition, persistence, switching, or other executive functions?

V. CONCLUSION

Disorders of attention are common sequelae of a wide variety of brain injuries or diseases. The components of attentional control are complex and are mediated by an elaborate and highly integrated series of neural systems. The proper evaluation of attentional dysfunction forms an integral, routine, and necessary portion of a complete bedside or outpatient examination.

BIBLIOGRAPHY

Cohen, R. A. (1993). *Neuropsychology of attention.* New York: Plenum.

Colquhoun, W. P., & Baddeley, A. D. (1967). Influence of signal probability during pretraining on vigilance decrement. *Journal of Experimental Psychology, 73,* 153–155.

Conners, C. K., Epstein, J. N, Angold, A., & Klaric, J. (2003). Continuous performance test performance in a normative epidemiological sample. *Journal of Abnormal Child Psychology, 31*(5), 555–562.

Conners, C. K., & MHS Staff. (2005). Conners' Continuous Performance Test II (CPT II) (Version 5 for Windows) [computer software]. Lutz, FL: Psychological Assessment Resources.

Desimone, R., & Gross, C. G. (1979). Visual areas in the temporal cortex of the macaque. *Brain Research, 178,* 363–380.

Fuster, J. M. (1989). *The prefrontal cortex: Anatomy, physiology, and neuropsychology of the frontal lobe.* New York: Raven Press.

Gibbon, J., & Allan, L. (Eds.). (1984). Timing and time perception. *Annals of the New York Academy of Sciences, 423.*

Goldberg, M. E., & Bushnell, M. D. (1981). Behavioral enhancement of visual response in monkey cerebral cortex: II. Modulation in frontal eye fields specifically related to saccades. *Journal of Neurophysiology, 46,* 783–787.

Hasher, L., & Zacks, R. T. (1979). Automatic and effortful processes in memory. *Journal of Experimental Psychology: General, 108,* 356–388.

Heilman, K. M., Watson, R. T., & Valenstein, E. (1993). Neglect and related disorders. In K. M. Heilman & E. Valenstein (Eds.), *Clinical neuropsychology* (3rd ed., pp. 279–336). New York: Oxford University Press.

Heilman, K. M., Watson, R. T., Valenstein, E., & Goldberg, M. E. (1988). Attention: Behavior and neural mechanisms. *Attention, 11*, 461–481.

Kahneman, D. (1973). *Attention and effort.* Englewood Cliffs, NJ: Prentice-Hall.

Kahneman, D., & Treisman, A. (1984). Changing views of attention and automaticity. In R. Parasuraman & D. R. Davies (Eds.), *Varieties of attention* (pp. 29–61). New York: Academic Press.

Kaplan, R. F., Verfaellie, M., DeWitt, L. D., & Caplan, L. R. (1990). Effects of changes in stimulus contingency on visual extinction. *Neurology, 40*, 1299–1301.

Mattingley, J. B., Bradshaw, J. L., Bradshaw, J. A., & Nettleton, N. C. (1994). Residual rightward attentional bias after apparent recovery from right hemisphere damage: Implications for a multi-component model of neglect. *Journal of Neurology, Neurosurgery, and Psychiatry, 57*, 597–604.

Mesulam, M. A. (1981). A cortical network for directed attention and unilateral neglect. *Archives of Neurology, 10*, 304–325.

Mirsky, A. F. (1989). The neuropsychology of attention: Elements of a complex behavior. In E. Perecman (Ed.), *Integrating theory and practice in neuropsychology* (pp. 75–91). Hillsdale, NJ: Erlbaum.

Mirsky, A. F., Anthony, B. J., Duncan, C. C., Ahearn, M. B., & Kellam, S. G. (1991). Analysis of the elements of attention: A neuropsychological approach. *Neuropsychology Review, 2*(2), 109–145.

Parasuraman, R., & Davies, R. B. (1984). *Varieties of attention.* New York: Academic Press.

Pardo, J. V., Fox, P. T., & Raichle, M. E. (1991, January 3). Localization of a human system for sustained attention by positron emission tomography. *Nature, 349*, 61–64.

Posner, M. I., & Cohen, Y. (1984). Components of visual orienting. In H. Bouma & D. Bowhuis (Eds.), *Attention and performance X* (pp. 531–556). Hillsdale, NJ: Erlbaum.

Posner, M. I., Walker, J. A., Friedrich, F. A., & Rafal, R. D. (1987). How do the parietal lobes direct covert attention? *Neuropsychologia, 25*, 135–145.

Pribram, K. H., & McGuinness, D. (1975). Arousal, activation, and effort in the control of attention. *Psychological Review, 82*, 116–149.

CHAPTER 25

Paul F. Malloy, Ronald A. Cohen, Melissa A.
Jenkins, and Robert H. Paul

Frontal Lobe Function and Dysfunction

Historically, frontal lobe functions have been poorly understood. Although their role in emotion and psychopathology
was recognized early on (Moniz, 1940), the prefrontal cortex
was not thought to play a major role in cognition. For many
years, clinicians persisted in referring to the prefrontal lobes as
silent areas, because sensorimotor signs were often absent after
prefrontal damage. The lack of a thorough understanding of the
functioning of the frontal lobes was also due to the functional
diversity of this phylogenetically recent area and the resultant
variety of clinical syndromes that emerge following damage to
the frontal lobes.

From a biological perspective, the frontal lobes are quite
remarkable in humans.

1. Compared with other animal species, the frontal cortex
   encompasses by far the greatest quantity of cortical volume in humans.
2. From an evolutionary perspective, the phylogenetic progression of neural development involves increased frontal lobe size and complexity.
3. Frontal lobe function in humans reflects the evolutionary development of speech and expressive language and
   fine motor ability involving the hands.
4. Control over the execution of movement and, more
   broadly, behavioral responding is the defining feature

of frontal lobe function. All higher cognitive functions attributed to the frontal cortex can ultimately be viewed as an outgrowth of the intention, planning, and control of responding.

5. The organization of the frontal lobes reflects increasing levels of functional complexity from the motor strip to more anterior prefrontal areas. This increased functional complexity plays an important role in the planning and modulation of responding, which contributes greatly to humans' advantage in problem solving and adaptability.

6. Frontal lobe ontogeny follows a similar developmental path. Frontal lobe function is among the last cognitive functions to fully develop as people mature. Optimal frontal functioning does not occur in humans until after adolescence.

The extensive connections to and from the frontal lobes have become clearer through animal studies (Goldman-Rakic, 1987; Nauta, 1972; Pandya & Barnes, 1987). Clinical syndromes have been better described following observation of patients with disease or injury affecting the frontal lobes (Luria, 1980; Malloy, Webster, & Russell, 1985) and study of patients undergoing psychosurgery (Stuss et al., 1983; Valenstein, 1990). Recent advances in structural and functional neuroimaging have also been important in advancing the understanding of frontal functions in normal people (Marenco, Coppola, Daniel, Zigun, & Weinberger, 1993; Martin, Friston, Colebatch, & Frackowiak, 1991) and in patients (Andreasen et al., 1986; Weinberger, Berman, & Zec, 1986).

I. FRONTAL LOBE FUNCTIONS

A. General Functions

The frontal lobes subserve pyramidal motor functions, sensorimotor integration in complex volitional movement, and executive and self-regulatory abilities. Self-regulation is essential for modulation of affect and socially appropriate conduct. The term **executive** refers to the role of these systems in response choice and execution. While the motor strip controls primary motor response, premotor areas anterior to the motor strip enable the planning and execution of more complex motor sequences. Prefrontal cortical areas can be thought of as systems that facilitate "pre" premotor functions, which essentially involve the formation of intent to respond, planning of responses, and higher level control of behavior. Broadly, the term **executive functioning** is used to refer to these capacities. Executive functions include the following abilities:

- formulating goals with regard for long-term consequences,
- generating multiple response alternatives,
- choosing and initiating goal-directed behaviors,
- self-monitoring the adequacy and correctness of the behavior,
- correcting and modifying behaviors when conditions change, and
- persisting in the face of distraction.

Patterns of limbic activation, along with sensory association signals, are processed by the frontal regions and sequenced with regard to the anticipated response possibilities. This system has an important function in regulating the flow of behavior into a "stream" of continuous behavior and cognition. The course of this stream is dictated by changes in the environment on the basis of affective–motivational data perceived by the sequencing system. The organism selects from the available response alternatives; broadens or narrows environmental search and monitoring parameters; and sustains, discontinues, or adjusts ongoing behaviors in relation to environmental demands. Thus, the monitoring of the junction between organism and environment, with ensuing self-regulation, is crucial to the executive control of behavior.

B. Frontal Systems

In humans the frontal lobes constitute about one third of the cerebral cortex (Goldman-Rakic, 1987). They lie anterior to the central sulcus and may be divided into a number of anatomic-functional subsystems. Functional frontal subdivisions include the following:

1. primary motor area,
2. premotor area,
3. frontal eye fields,
4. dorsolateral area,
5. orbital and basal areas, and
6. supplementary motor and anterior cingulate gyros areas.

Each of these frontal zones has extensive connections with specific posterior cortical structures, thalamic nuclei, and basal ganglia (see Table 25.1). Frontal zones act in concert with these other structures to form frontal lobe systems. Only a few of the

Table 25.1. Functions and Primary Connections of the Frontal Subsystems

Subsystem	Major functions	Afferent connections
Primary motor	Fine motor movement	Primary somatosensory area of parietal lobe Ventrolateral thalamic nucleus
Premotor	Praxis (complex volitional movement) Sensorimotor integration	Secondary somatosensory area of parietal lobe Extrapyramidal motor system Primary motor area Ventroanterior thalamic nucleus
Frontal eye fields	Voluntary gaze Visual search Directing complex attention	Dorsomedial thalamic nucleus
Dorsolateral prefrontal	Executive functions	Posterior association cortex Angular and supramarginal gyri Dorsomedial thalamic nucleus
Orbital prefrontal area	Smell discrimination Behavioral inhibition	Cingulate Anterior temporal lobes Limbic system Dorsomedial and intralaminar thalamic nuclei
Supplementary motor and anterior cingulate	Initiation and inhibition of exploratory search	

major pathways are listed in Table 25.1; the frontal cortex has a multitude of interconnections that allow communication with most other areas of the brain.

II. FRONTAL LOBE DYSFUNCTION

A. General Dysfunctions

Primary motor area lesions result in flaccid hemiplegia in the contralateral side of the body, which typically resolves into spastic hemiplegia. Less severe lesions to this area or its connections result in hemiparesis and incoordination of the contralateral side.

Premotor area lesions result in apraxia (difficulty programming complex volitional movements) and the inability to make use of sensory feedback to modify movements smoothly. Disruption of connections with sensory areas of the parietal lobe to this area can also result in difficulty in integrating sensory information into ongoing motor plans.

Frontal eye field damage can result in the inability to control volitional eye movements in the contralateral visual field, inability to direct complex attention during defensive behaviors, and problems guiding eye movements during goal-directed behavior involving memory.

Prefrontal damage impairs more complex behaviors and metacognition. These higher prefrontal functions are generally of greater concern to the neuropsychologist. Conceptually, deficits caused by prefrontal lobe damage can be divided into disorders of executive control, behavioral excess, and diminished response.

B. Specific Syndromes

Three prefrontal syndromes have been associated with damage to these anterior subsystems: (a) a dysexecutive syndrome in the dorsolateral convexity, (b) a disinhibited syndrome in the orbital area, and (c) an akinetic syndrome in the medial area.

1. DYSEXECUTIVE SYNDROME

Lesions of the dorsolateral prefrontal area can result in an inability to integrate disparate sensory elements into a coherent whole, a stereotyped or limited response repertoire, easy loss of task set, perseverative or inflexible behavior, and lack of self-monitoring of errors. In the realm of memory, executive problems result in decreased working memory, inefficient learning, failure to make use of active learning strategies, reduced memory for temporal or situational context information, and inefficient free recall despite normal recognition of newly learned information. Problems with behavioral switching cause a lack of response flexibility, such that the patient becomes "stuck in set."

2. DISINHIBITED SYNDROME

Anosmia, disinhibited personality change, amnesia with confabulation, and failure on neuropsychological tests of inhibition are signs of orbitofrontal damage (Malloy, Bihrle, Duffy, & Cimino, 1993). Lesions of this subsystem result in disruption of inhibitory and emotional mechanisms, with impulsive and socially inappropriate behavior resulting. A patient may be aware that a particular behavior is inappropriate but unable to inhibit the behavior. Disorders of emotional reactivity can include emotional incontinence, affective lability, and situationally inappropriate emotional reactions. Perseveration may also result from a failure of inhibition, as can the inability to release from the current stimulus despite a change in its salience (stimulus-bound behavior). Related cognitive problems include difficulties with attention, most commonly, increased distractibility by irrelevant stimuli and diminished sustained and divided attention.

3. APATHETIC–AKINETIC SYNDROME

Lesions to the anterior cingulate gyrus can result in **akinetic mutism**, in which the patient fails to respond to environmental stimuli and remains inert. When the lesion is unilateral, akinesia is typically transient, whereas persistent akinesia usually results from bilateral lesions. Conversely, lesions to the supplementary motor area and corpus callosum result in "alien hand syndrome," in which the patient may grab objects, throw things, and otherwise explore the environment in a disinhibited way (Goldberg & Bloom, 1990). The patient feels that he or she has no control over movements of the left hand. In reality, these movements are probably attributable to the actions of the right hemisphere in initiating behaviors while disconnected from the verbal left hemisphere.

Diminished responsiveness can manifest itself in problems with initiating or persisting in behavior. Patients may have lowered responsiveness to environmental triggers or a preserved motivation to act but be unable to organize these impulses into directed drives, action plans, or response sequences. **Impersistence** refers to the failure to maintain a particular response despite reinforcement, feedback, cues, or other signals indicating that additional responding is necessary. Flat or diminished affect may be seen. Some patients become docile, apathetic, or even akinetic. Social changes (divorce, job loss, difficulty initiating or maintaining friendships) often occur in the wake of a frontal lobe injury. Personality changes are commonly reported. Inability to follow through with tasks at work is a typical problem.

C. Nonlocalized Frontal Deficits

The frontal lobes normally inhibit a number of primitive reflexes (e.g., grasp, snout, glabellar). The presence of these **frontal release signs** may be another indication that frontal damage has occurred. However, frontal release reflexes are also seen in elderly people without neurological disease and in patients with generalized neurological conditions such as degenerative dementias.

Environmental dependency is a syndrome in which the patient responds in a habitual way to stimuli in the surrounding area without regard for the current necessity or appropriateness of the response (Hoffmann & Bill, 1992). A subtype is **utilization behavior**, in which the patient uses objects without a specific goal or need (e.g., sipping from an empty cup when satiated; Lhermitte, 1983). Environmental dependency has been conceptualized as the release of parietal exploratory behavior owing to absence of frontal inhibition (Lhermitte, Pillon, & Serdaru, 1986).

A variety of neuropsychiatric disorders have also been linked to frontal lesions, including **reduplicative paramnesia** (the delusion that a place has been duplicated; Benson, Gardner, & Meadows, 1976), **Capgras syndrome** (the delusion that a person has been duplicated; Malloy, Cimino, & Westlake, 1992), and **secondary depression** and **secondary mania** (Cummings & Mendez, 1984).

III. DISEASES THAT COMMONLY AFFECT FRONTAL FUNCTIONS

Conceptualizing brain–behavior relationships in terms of systems rather than discrete centers is nowhere more important than in executive and self-regulatory functions, occupying as they do the apex of the behavioral hierarchy. It follows that "frontal lobe" dysfunction can occur with lesions to any part of these systems (Cummings, 1993), including (a) cortical frontal areas, (b) subcortical nuclei having connections with the frontal lobes, and (c) white matter lesions disrupting the connections.

Traumatic brain injury (TBI), for example, may cause dysfunction because of damage to the frontal lobes themselves or to white matter connections. The orbital surface and frontal poles are particularly vulnerable to focal damage from TBI because of their close proximity to the bony prominences of the skull (Mattson & Levin, 1990), but patients with TBI often suffer damage to multiple frontal zones. Diffuse axonal injury can also result in dysexecutive syndromes owing to disruption of white matter connections affecting widely distributed frontal systems.

Neoplasms can cause gradual or abrupt changes in mood and personality that may or may not be accompanied by dramatic cognitive complaints (depending on size, location, and rate of progression). Intrinsic tumors such as gliomas are most common; they often begin unilaterally in frontal white matter but can spread bilaterally by invading the corpus callosum. Extrinsic tumors, such as meningiomas, are frequently located subfrontally or in the falx cerebri, where they compress mesial frontal lobes bilaterally.

Vascular lesions can occur secondary to stroke, aneurysm, or microvascular disease. Large vessel strokes commonly cause unilateral damage. Left frontal damage may be accompanied by speech and language deficits (Broca's or transcortical motor aphasia), right-sided sensory and motor deficits, and secondary depression. Right-hemisphere damage may result in diminished performance on spatial tasks as well as elevated mood, pressured or disorganized speech, and grandiosity. Another major category of vascular lesion affecting the frontal lobes results from ruptured aneurysms of the anterior communicating artery (ACoA), producing personality changes and a characteristic amnesic syndrome with prominent confabulation. Microvascular disease involves damage to the small blood vessels found in subcortical brain regions. These small changes may appear as hyperintense areas on T2- or proton-density-weighted magnetic resonance imaging (MRI) scans. Risk factors for microvascular disease include advancing age (it is found in many normal elderly people), hypertension, cardiovascular disease, and possibly smoking and diabetes. Microvascular disease can occur in the frontal lobes themselves and also can disrupt major cortical and subcortical connections to the frontal lobes. Subcortical ischemic vascular disease is believed to represent the most common subtype of vascular dementia (Chui & Gontheir, 1999).

Certain **dementing illnesses** (Pick's disease, Lewy body disease, dementia of the frontal type) cause gradual deterioration of frontal lobe functioning. Early in the course of these frontal dementias, there is typically disturbance to personality and social behavior out of proportion to deficits in memory (Neary, Snowden, Northen, & Goulding, 1988). This pattern is in contrast to the usual impairment in Alzheimer's disease, in which dramatic memory loss typically precedes change in personality and emotional function.

Subcortical dementing processes also commonly cause executive dysfunction along with changes in motor functioning (Gotham, Brown, & Marsden, 1988). Examples of these diseases include Huntington's disease, Parkinson's disease, multiple sclerosis, HIV, and progressive supranuclear palsy (for a review, see Cummings, 1993). The neuropathology differs between these diseases, with prominent involvement in specific subcortical nuclei in some cases (e.g., the caudate in Huntington's disease and HIV) and the white matter in other cases (e.g., multiple sclerosis). However, in each of these diseases the common clinical manifestation of executive dysfunction is believed to result from disruption of functional circuits that connect frontal regions to the underlying white matter, basal ganglia, and related nuclei (Mega & Cummings, 1994).

IV. ASSESSMENT OF FRONTAL LOBE FUNCTIONING

Both informal and psychometric methods of assessing frontal deficits can be useful. Delis, Kaplan, and Kramer (2001) introduced the Delis–Kaplan Executive Function System (D-KEFS), a standardized battery of frontal measures that examines cognitive flexibility, problem solving, concept formation, and planning. The battery includes nine tests that represent adaptations of traditional frontal measures (e.g., the Trail Making Test, Verbal Fluency Test, Tower Test). The battery was normed on a large number of individuals ranging in age from 8 to 89 years. In addition to comprehensive batteries, highly valuable clinical information can be obtained using common bedside maneuvers and individual formal tests for assessment of each frontal system (see Table 25.2).

A. Primary Motor Functions

The clinician can test basic motor functions at bedside using the familiar maneuvers of the elementary neurological examination. Motor strength can be tested by having the patient squeeze the examiner's fingers and attempting to extricate the fingers from the patient. This maneuver allows the comparison of the relative strengths of the two hands, which should

Table 25.2. Bedside and Neuropsychological Tests of Frontal System Dysfunction

Subsystem	Bedside maneuvers	Neuropsychological tests
Primary motor	Patient squeezes the examiner's fingers; compare relative strength of the two hands.	Retain Grip Strength Test and Finger Tapping Test
	Patient performs rapid movements with the hands and feet.	
Premotor	Patient touches each finger to the thumb sequentially; observe for clumsiness, slowing, or inaccuracies.	Grooved Pegboard Boston Diagnostic Aphasia Examination tests of praxis
	Patient commanded to perform single and serial limb movements, whole body postures, and buccofacial movements.	
	Luria reciprocal motor tasks and alternating graphic sequences (Luria, 1980, No. 26).	
Frontal eye fields	Observe patient in direct gaze to command versus passive following of a moving stimulus.	Visual search tasks
Dorsolateral prefrontal	EXIT (Royall et al., 1992, No. 20).	Word Fluency Figural Fluency Wisconsin Card Sorting Test
Orbital prefrontal	Go/No-Go Tasks (Malloy, 1985, No. 5). Informal tests of smell discrimination.	University of Pennsylvania Smell Identification test Stroop Color–Word Test Frontal Lobe Personality Scale (FLOPS)

Note. EXIT = Executive Interview.

be approximately equal. Motor speed and dexterity can be assessed by having the patient perform rapid movements with the hands and feet. Neuropsychological tests of simple motor abilities include the Reitan **Grip Strength Test** and the **Finger Tapping Test** (Reitan & Wolfson, 1985).

B. Premotor System Functions

Deficits in this subsystem can be tested at bedside by having the patient touch each finger to the thumb sequentially and observing for clumsiness, slowing, or inaccuracies. Callosal connections between premotor systems can be assessed by placing the fingers of one of the patient's hands in certain positions and requiring the patient to reproduce the positions using the other hand with eyes closed (Luria, 1980). Psychometric tests for evaluating complex movement and its disturbances include the **Purdue Pegboard** (Purdue Research Foundation, 1948) and the **Grooved Pegboard** (Lafayette Instrument Company, n.d.), which require the patient to place as many pegs into holes on a board as possible within a time limit. Praxis can be assessed by requiring the patient to perform single and serial limb movements, whole body postures, and buccofacial movements. Examples of such tasks can be found in the Boston Diagnostic Aphasia Examination manual (Goodglass & Kaplan, 1972).

C. Frontal Eye Fields Functions

Lesions in the frontal eye fields (FEF) result in transient ipsilateral eye deviation and more persistent contralateral gaze paresis. Secondary to these deficits in eye movement, the patient is unable to pursue a target or search visual space efficiently. Patients with FEF lesions are unable to search actively the side of the page contralateral to their lesion, although they are capable of passive eye movements in the same visual field. The intactness of passive gaze distinguishes such patients from those with hemispatial neglect.

D. Dorsolateral Prefrontal Functions

Dorsolateral functions encompass a variety of aspects of behavior, and numerous assessment methods are available for examining this domain. For example, Royall, Mahurin, and Gray (1992) developed a brief bedside test for measuring a variety of these functions, called the **Executive Interview** (EXIT). The EXIT includes tasks derived from a number of sources, including so-called frontal release signs from the neurological examination, abbreviated versions of neuropsychological tests such as word fluency, and Luria's complex motor tasks.

Generation of multiple response alternatives can be measured by word and figure fluency tasks. The most widely used word fluency task is the **Controlled Oral Word Fluency Test** (COWA; Benton, 1968). Other categorical fluency tasks (e.g., naming animals, fruits, and vegetables) have been shown to be more sensitive and specific than COWA in detecting dementia, but they may not tap executive functions to the same extent as the COWA. The COWA requires not only multiple response generation but also maintenance of a complex task set: The words must not include proper names and must not consist of previously used words with a suffix. In addition, there is the opportunity to observe perseverative intrusion errors and the use of vulgar or socially inappropriate words by patients with disinhibitory deficits. A nonverbal, or figural, fluency task was developed by Jones-Gotman and Milner (1977), who demonstrated that whereas patients with left frontal lobe dysfunction failed in verbal fluency tasks, those with right frontal lobe dysfunction differentially failed in figural fluency tasks. Ruff and colleagues developed a figural fluency task incorporating some constraints to enhance reliability. The **Ruff Figural Fluency Test** has been shown to be sensitive to right versus left frontal lesions, and large-scale norms are available for adults (Ruff, 1988).

Luria (1980; Malloy et al., 1985) described a number of bilateral hand movements and alternating graphic sequences that theoretically require intact motor, premotor, and executive functions, particularly the ability to produce alternating response sets. In administering these tasks, it is important to ensure that a response set is established and then changed and that the task is sustained long enough to allow observation of subtle executive dysfunction (within-task perseverations, cross-task perseverations, simplification of the movements, and intrusions of habitual responses such as writing letters rather than drawing the required shapes).

The **Wisconsin Card Sorting Test** (WCST; Heaton, 1981) has been considered the premiere test of executive functions for many years. It taps a variety of executive abilities, including maintenance of task set, flexibility in response to feedback or changing circumstances, and perseverative tendencies. The WCST has been shown to be sensitive to effects of frontal lobe lesions in a number of studies, but negative findings have also been reported regarding the frontal specificity of the test (van den Broek, Bradshaw, & Szabadi, 1993).

The **Category Test** and **Trail Making Test** have generally been considered measures of abstraction, set maintenance, and cognitive flexibility. Hence, clinicians frequently use these tests as measures of dorsolateral frontal functions. However, research has indicated that these tests are failed by patients with nonfrontal as well as frontal lesions (e.g., Pendleton & Heaton, 1982).

E. Orbital Prefrontal Functions

Relatively few measures of orbital frontal functions in humans exist. Clinicians may therefore have difficulty detecting common behavioral sequelae of orbital frontal damage.

Anosmia can be assessed clinically by having the patient identify common aromatic substances such as coffee, tobacco, or cocoa. Psychometric assessment of smell discrimination is possible using the University of Pennsylvania **Smell Identification Test** (Doty, 1983), which provides age-corrected norms (major declines in smell thresholds are seen with normal aging). There are many other medical causes of reduced smell discrimination, however, such as infections of the nasal passages, smoking, and medication use.

Go/no-go tasks require the patient to make a response to a go signal and withhold or inhibit response to a no-go signal. The task can be made more difficult by changing the habitual meaning of the signals (e.g., go to a red light, no-go to a green light). A bedside example of this task can involve asking the patient to tap his or her fist when the examiner says stop and not tap when the examiner says go (Malloy et al., 1985). The **Stroop Color–Word Test** (Stroop, 1935) is another task that places demands on inhibitory abilities. Orbital frontal zones are activated in normal people during this task (Bench et al., 1993), but patients with orbital lesions have particular difficulty with the inhibitory portion (i.e., naming the color and ignoring the word during the color–word trial).

Disinhibited or socially inappropriate behavior can be observed informally on the treatment unit, and family reports should always be sought. Patients with orbital frontal dysfunction may display such behaviors as facetious humor, inappropriate sexual behavior, and labile emotionality. The Frontal Systems Behavior Scale (FrSBe) provides a psychometric means of assessing patient, staff, and family ratings of behavioral change caused by frontal lesions. The measure consists of a 46-item rating scale that assesses three behavioral domains: apathy/akinesia, disinhibition/emotional dysregulation, and executive dysfunction. Informants rate each behavior twice, once describing the patient's behavior prior to injury/disease onset, and again to describe the patient's behavior over the preceding 2 weeks. Scores can be compared with age-, education-, and gender-corrected norms. The individual scales of the FrSBe are sensitive to behavioral changes associated with dementia and psychiatric disorders (Stout, Ready, Grace, Malloy, & Paulsen, 2003; Velligan, Ritch, Sui, DiCocco, & Huntzinger, 2002).

F. Cingulate and Supplementary Motor Area Functions

Lesions to the anterior cingulate gyrus and supplementary motor area (SMA) can result in akinetic mutism and alien hand syndrome, respectively (Goldberg & Bloom, 1990). Utilization behavior and the more general class of behavior called environmental dependency have been commonly reported with large bilateral frontal lesions and in unilateral mesial frontal lesions, although the precise localization remains unclear. These dramatic syndromes require no special assessment techniques beyond the ability of the examiner to make the appropriate anatomic–clinical correlations.

G. General Observations

Most neuropsychological tests are fairly well structured and call for a limited sample of behavior. Much of the planning and organization of the task are performed by the examiner in presenting instructions and rules. This may limit the opportunity to observe dysexecutive problems. A number of abnormal behaviors may be more apparent during the relatively unstructured interview, including reduced initiative and drive, poor insight into deficits, inappropriate social behavior, environmental dependency, poor self-monitoring of errors, easy agitation, and hypomaniclike state. The examiner should pay particular attention to discrepancies between patient and caregiver reports of problems.

The qualitative or process aspects of performance may nonetheless be informative in a patient with frontal dysfunction. On memory testing, for example, patients often display impoverished learning strategies, intrusions and perseverations, poor retrieval strategies, and difficulty with temporal tagging of learned information. The **California Verbal Learning Test** (CVLT; Delis, Freeland, Kramer, & Kaplan, 1988; Delis, Kramer, Kaplan, & Ober, 1987) is an excellent tool for examining these process dimensions. By using the CVLT, it is possible to observe patients with frontal lobe dysfunction producing a shallow learning curve across the five trials (owing to inefficient encoding strategies), mixing up the first and second lists (owing to problems in temporal tagging), showing inordinate gains from cued or recognition recall in comparison with free recall (owing to inability to formulate a retrieval strategy), and producing large numbers of perseverations and intrusions. This is a markedly different pattern from that of Alzheimer's disease, for example, in which patients typically do not benefit from cuing or recognition to a significant degree.

Patients with frontal lobe dysfunction often perform well on simple attentional tasks such as digits forward but display characteristic errors on complex attentional tasks requiring active manipulation of information. This deficit is often most apparent when the patient is required to overcome overlearned or habitual behavioral patterns (e.g., saying the days of the week backward rather than forward).

Dysexecutive and disinhibitory problems may affect the performance of these patients throughout the assessment session. Poor organization may lead the patient to fail to plan number placement on clock drawings. Perseverative tendencies may cause him or her to reuse an earlier item during a confrontational naming test. The examiner must be aware of the underlying frontal deficit lest these errors be mistaken for primary difficulties in visuospatial or language functions. Hence, it is usually desirable to assess frontal functions early in the assessment session.

V. CAUTIONS IN EVALUATING FRONTAL FUNCTIONS

First, the examiner must remember that most complex behaviors require that various frontal subsystems act in concert to produce adaptive functioning. Sustained and directed attention is an example of an ability involving multiple frontal zones (including dorsolateral, orbital, and cingulate areas). Second, many patients show combinations of the frontal syndromes described because naturally occurring lesions damage multiple subsystems.

Some deficits may be the result of either frontal or nonfrontal lesions. For example, abstract reasoning can be viewed as a measure of ability to shift mental set from the specific (i.e., more concrete or tangible) to the general (i.e., abstract) principle. It is often measured through proverb interpretation or similarities tests at bedside. However, abstract reasoning is strongly dependent on innate intelligence and education as well as general intactness of the brain. Although abstraction is quite susceptible to the effects of injury involving frontal systems, poor ability to abstract is not specific to frontal injury.

VI. CONCLUSION

The skilled clinician must be guided by a knowledge of frontal lobe subsystems and their roles in determining specific types of abnormal behavior. Bedside maneuvers can then be designed to discriminate dysfunction, and the clinician will be alerted to changes in incidental behavior that indicate frontal impairment. Neuropsychological assessment can provide an invaluable tool for testing frontal lobe functions, taking into account the complexity of these behaviors and the profound effects of maturation and aging on frontal functions.

BIBLIOGRAPHY

Andreasen, N., Nasrallah, H. A., Dunn, V., Olson, S. C., Grove, W. M., Ehrhardt, J. C., et al. (1986). Structural abnormalities in the frontal system in schizophrenia: A magnetic resonance imaging study. *Archives of General Psychiatry, 43,* 136–144.

Bench, C. J., Frith, C. D., Grasby, P. M., Friston, K. J., Paulesu, E., Frackowiak, R. S., & Dolan, R. J. (1993). Investigations of the functional anatomy of attention using the Stroop test. *Neuropsychologia, 31,* 907–922.

Benson, D. F., Gardner, H., & Meadows, J. C. (1976). Reduplicative paramnesia. *Neurology, 26,* 147–161.

Benton, A. L. (1968). Differential behavioral effects in frontal lobe disease. *Neuropsychologia, 6,* 53–60.

Chui, H., & Gontheir, R. (1999). Natural history of vascular dementia. *Alzheimer Disease and Associated Disorders, 13,* S124–S130.

Cummings, J. L. (1993). Frontal–subcortical circuits and human behavior. *Archives of Neurology, 50,* 873–880.

Cummings, J. L., & Mendez, M. F. (1984). Secondary mania associated with focal cerebrovascular lesions. *American Journal of Psychiatry, 14,* 1084–1087.

Delis, D. C., Freeland, J., Kramer, J. H., & Kaplan, E. (1988). Integrating clinical assessment with cognitive neuroscience: Construct validation of the California Verbal Learning Test. *Journal of Consulting and Clinical Psychology, 56,* 123–130.

Delis, D. C., Kaplan, E., & Kramer, J. H. (2001). *Delis–Kaplan Executive Function System: Examiner's manual*. San Antonio, TX: Psychological Corporation.

Delis, D. C., Kramer, J. H., Kaplan, E., & Ober, B. A. (1987). *The California Verbal Learning Test: Research edition*. New York: Psychological Corporation.

Doty, R. L. (1983). *The University of Pennsylvania Smell Identification Test administration manual*. Philadelphia: Sensonics.

Goldberg, G., & Bloom, K. K. (1990). The alien hand sign: Localization, lateralization and recovery. *American Journal of Physical Medicine and Rehabilitation, 69*, 228–238.

Goldman-Rakic, P. S. (1987). Circuitry of the primate prefrontal cortex and regulation of behavior by representational memory. In F. Plum & V. Mountcastle (Eds.), *Handbook of physiology, the nervous system, and higher functions of the brain* (Sec. 1, Vol. 5, pp. 373–417). Bethesda, MD: American Physiological Society.

Goodglass, H., & Kaplan, E. (1972). *The assessment of aphasia and related disorders*. Philadelphia: Lea & Febiger.

Gotham, A. M., Brown, R. G., & Marsden, C. D. (1988). "Frontal" cognitive function in patients with Parkinson's disease "on" and "off" levodopa. *Brain, 111*, 2.

Heaton, R. K. (1981). *Wisconsin Card Sorting Test manual*. Odessa, FL: Psychological Assessment Resources.

Hoffmann, M. W., & Bill, P. L. (1992). The environmental dependency syndrome, imitation behaviour and utilisation behaviour as presenting symptoms of bilateral frontal lobe infarction due to moyamoya disease. *South African Medical Journal, 81*, 271–273.

Jones-Gotman, M., & Milner, B. (1977). Design fluency: The invention of nonsense drawings after focal cortical lesions. *Neuropsychologia, 15*, 653–674.

Lafayette Instrument Company. (n.d.). *Instructions for the Grooved Pegboard*. Lafayette, IN: Author.

Lhermitte, F. (1983). "Utilization behavior" and its relation to lesions of the frontal lobes. *Brain, 106*, 237–255.

Lhermitte, F., Pillon, B., & Serdaru, M. (1986). Human autonomy and the frontal lobes: Part I. Imitation and utilization behavior. A neuropsychological study of 75 patients. *Annals of Neurology, 19*, 326–334.

Luria, A. R. (1980). *Higher cortical functions in man*. New York: Basic Books.

Malloy, P. F., Bihrle, A., Duffy, J., & Cimino, C. (1993). The orbitomedial frontal syndrome. *Archives of Clinical Neuropsychology, 8*, 185–202.

Malloy, P. F., Cimino, C., & Westlake, R. (1992). Differential diagnosis of primary and secondary Capgras delusions. *Neuropsychiatry, Neuropsychology, and Behavioral Neurology, 5,* 83–96.

Malloy, P. F., Webster, J. S., & Russell, W. (1985). Tests of Luria's frontal lobe syndrome. *International Journal of Clinical Neuropsychology, 7,* 88–94.

Marenco, S., Coppola, R., Daniel, D. G., Zigun, J. R., & Weinberger, D. R. (1993). Regional cerebral blood flow during the Wisconsin Card Sorting Test in normal subjects studied by xenon-133 dynamic SPECT: Comparison of absolute values, percent distribution values, and covariance analysis. *Psychiatry Research, 50,* 177–192.

Martin, A. J., Friston, K. J., Colebatch, J. G., & Frackowiak, R. S. (1991). Decreases in regional cerebral blood flow with normal aging. *Journal of Cerebral Blood Flow and Metabolism, 11,* 684–689.

Mattson, A. J., & Levin, H. S. (1990). Frontal lobe dysfunction following closed head injury: A review of the literature. *Journal of Nervous and Mental Disease, 178,* 282–291.

Mega, M. S., & Cummings, J. L. (1994). Frontal–subcortical circuits and neuropsychiatric disorders. *Journal of Neuropsychiatry and Clinical Neurosciences, 6,* 358–370.

Moniz, E. (1940). Prefrontal leucotomy in treatment of mental disorders. *American Journal of Psychiatry, 93,* 1379–1385.

Nauta, W. J. H. (1972). Neural associations of the frontal cortex. *Acta Neurobiologiae Experimentalis, 32,* 125–140.

Neary, D., Snowden, J. S., Northen, B., & Goulding, P. (1988). Dementia of frontal lobe type. *Journal of Neurology, Neurosurgery, and Psychiatry, 51,* 353–361.

Pandya, D. N., & Barnes, C. L. (1987). Architecture and connections of the frontal lobe. In E. Perecman (Ed.), *The frontal lobes revisited* (pp. 41–72). New York: IRBN Press.

Pendleton, M. G., & Heaton, R. K. (1982). A comparison of the Wisconsin Card Sorting Test and the Category Test. *Journal of Clinical Psychology, 38,* 392–396.

Purdue Research Foundation. (1948). *Examiner's manual for the Purdue Pegboard.* Chicago: Science Research Associates.

Reitan, R. M., & Wolfson, D. (1985). *The Halstead–Reitan Neuropsychological Test Battery.* Tucson, AZ: Neuropsychology Press.

Royall, D. R., Mahurin, R. K., & Gray, K. F. (1992). Bedside assessment of executive cognitive impairment: The executive interview. *Journal of the American Geriatric Society, 40,* 1221–1226.

Ruff, R. M. (1988). *Ruff Figural Fluency Test administration manual*. San Diego, CA: Neuropsychological Resources.

Stout, J. C., Ready, R. E., Grace, J., Malloy, P. F., & Paulsen, J. S. (2003). Factor analysis of the frontal systems behavior scale (FrSBe). *Assessment, 10,* 79–85.

Stroop, J. R. (1935). Studies of interference in serial verbal reactions. *Journal of Experimental Psychology, 18,* 643–662.

Stuss, D. T., Benson, D. F., Kaplan, E. F., Weir, W. S., Naeser, M. A., Lieberman, I., & Ferrill, D. (1983). The involvement of orbitofrontal cerebrum in cognitive tasks. *Neuropsychologia, 21,* 235–248.

Valenstein, E. S. (1990). The prefrontal area and psychosurgery. *Progress in Brain Research, 85,* 539–553.

van den Broek, M. D., Bradshaw, C. M., & Szabadi, E. (1993). Utility of the Modified Wisconsin Card Sorting Test in neuropsychological assessment. *British Journal of Clinical Psychology, 32,* 333–343.

Velligan, D. I., Ritch, J. L., Sui, D., DiCocco, M., & Huntzinger, C. D. (2002). Frontal Systems Behavior Scale in schizophrenia: Relationships with psychiatric symptomatology, cognition and adaptive function. *Psychiatry Research, 113,* 227–236.

Weinberger, D. R., Berman, K. F., & Zec, R. F. (1986). Physiologic dysfunction of dorsolateral prefrontal cortex in schizophrenia: I. Regional cerebral blood flow evidence. *Archives of General Psychiatry, 43,* 114–124.

Adult Attention-Deficit/ Hyperactivity Disorder

Attention-deficit/hyperactivity disorder (ADHD) is a developmental disorder characterized by symptoms of inattention, impulsivity, and hyperactivity. The fourth edition of the *Diagnostic and Statistical Manual of Mental Disorders* (4th ed., text revision [*DSM–IV–TR*]; American Psychiatric Association, 2000) lists specific criteria that are used to diagnose ADHD (see Exhibit 26.1). However, for adults, it is necessary to reword some criteria, to reflect problems that they experience at work and at home. These include difficulties with initiation and sustained effort in work-related tasks or household chores, problems with time management, and problems with physical organization of paperwork and personal belongings. Symptoms of hyperactivity tend to remit over time and are more likely to be reflected in adults as fidgetiness, the need to be active and constantly engaged with something, or a sense of "cognitive restlessness." They may also be reflected in enjoyment of recreational activities that are fast-paced or involve some risk. Barkley and colleagues (Barkley, 1998; DuPaul, Power, Anastopoulos, & Reid, 1998; Murphy & Barkley, 1996) have reported that fewer symptoms are needed to diagnose ADHD at older ages. That is, although at least six symptoms are necessary to diagnose the disorder in children, adults may meet diagnostic criteria with only four or five symptoms. They have also noted that although the *DSM–IV* (American Psychiatric Association, 1994) criteria

Exhibit 26.1. *DSM–IV–TR* Diagnostic Criteria for
Attention-Deficit/Hyperactivity Disorder

A.   Either (1) or (2)

(1) Six (or more) of the following symptoms of **inattention** have
persisted for at least 6 months to a degree that is maladaptive
and inconsistent with developmental level:

Inattention
   (a) often fails to give close attention to details or makes
        careless mistakes in schoolwork, work, or other
        activities
   (b) often has difficulty sustaining attention in tasks or play
        activities
   (c) often does not seem to listen when spoken to directly
   (d) often does not follow through on instructions and fails
        to finish schoolwork, chores, or duties in the workplace
        (not due to oppositional behavior or failure to under-
        stand instructions)
   (e) often has difficulty organizing tasks and activities
   (f) often avoids, dislikes, or is reluctant to engage in tasks
        that require sustained mental effort (such as school-
        work or homework)
   (g) often loses things necessary for tasks or activities
        (e.g., toys, school assignments, pencils, books or tools)
   (h) is often easily distracted by extraneous stimuli
   (i) is often forgetful in daily activities

(2) Six (or more) of the following symptoms of **hyperactivity–
impulsivity** have persisted for at least 6 months to a degree that
is maladaptive and inconsistent with developmental level:

Hyperactivity
   (a) often fidgets with hands or feet or squirms in seat
   (b) often leaves seat in classroom or in other situations in
        which remaining seated is expected
   (c) often runs about or climbs excessively in situations in
        which it is inappropriate (in adolescents or adults, may
        be limited to subjective feelings of restlessness)
   (d) often has difficulty playing or engaging in leisure activi-
        ties quietly
   (e) is often "on the go" or often acts as if "driven by a
        motor"
   (f) often talks excessively

Impulsivity
   (g) often blurts out answers before questions have been
        completed
   (h) often has difficulty awaiting turn
   (i) often interrupts or intrudes on others (e.g., butts into
        conversations or games)

(Continued)

Exhibit 26.1. *DSM–IV–TR* Diagnostic Criteria for
Attention-Deficit/Hyperactivity Disorder *(Continued)*

B.   Some hyperactive-impulsive or inattentive symptoms that
      caused impairment were present before age 7 years.
C.   Some impairment from the symptoms is present in two or
      more settings (e.g., school [or work] and at home).
D.   There must be clear evidence of clinically significant im-
      pairment in social, academic, or occupational functioning.
E.   The symptoms do not occur exclusively during the course
      of a pervasive developmental disorder, schizophrenia, or
      other psychotic disorder and are not better accounted for
      by another mental disorder (e.g., mood disorder, anxiety
      disorder, dissociative disorder, or a personality disorder).

Code based on type:
      **314.01 Attention-deficit/hyperactivity disorder, com-
      bined type:** if both Criteria A1 and A2 are met for the
      past 6 months
      **314.00 Attention-deficit/hyperactivity disorder, pre-
      dominantly inattentive type:** if Criterion A1 is met but
      Criterion A2 is not met for the past 6 months
      **314.01 Attention-deficit/hyperactivity disorder, pre-
      dominantly hyperactive-impulsive type:** if Criterion
      A2 is met, but Criterion A1 is not met for the past 6
      months

Coding note: For individuals (especially adolescents and adults)
who currently have symptoms that no longer meet full criteria,
"In partial remission" should be specified.

Note. From the *Diagnostic and Statistical Manual of Mental Disorders* (4th Edition, Text Revision; *DSM–IV–TR*). Copyright 2000 by
the American Psychiatric Association. Reprinted with permission.

state that impairment must be evident by age 7, some individuals do not manifest problems until early adolescence, when
greater demands are placed on executive functioning.

I. ALTERNATIVE CRITERIA FOR DIAGNOSING ADHD IN ADULTS

As an alternative to the *DSM* criteria, Wender and colleagues
(Ward, Wender, & Reimherr, 1993; Wender, 1995) established
the Utah Criteria specifically for diagnosing ADHD in adults (see
Exhibit 26.2). These empirically based criteria were developed to
address the problem of a childhood focus of the *DSM* criteria.
Unlike the *DSM–IV–TR* criteria, the Utah Criteria require the
presence of *both* hyperactivity (in some form) and inattentive-

Exhibit 26.2. Utah Criteria for Adult ADHD

I. CHILDHOOD CHARACTERISTICS

Childhood history consistent with ADHD in childhood. Obtaining reliable historical data usually requires input from the individual's parents or older siblings. The following are our diagnostic criteria for ADHD in childhood:

A. Narrow Criteria (*DSM–III*)
That the individual met *DSM–III–R* criteria (now *DSM–IV* criteria) for ADHD in childhood.

B. Broad Criteria
Both characteristics 1 and 2, and at least one characteristic from 3 through 6.

1. *Hyperactivity:* More active than other children, unable to sit still, fidgetiness, restlessness, always on the go, talking excessively.
2. *Attention deficits:* Sometimes described as having a "short attention span," distractibility, unable to finish school work.
3. *Behavior problems in school*
4. *Impulsivity*
5. *Overexcitability*
6. *Temper outbursts*

II. ADULT CHARACTERISTICS

A. The presence in adulthood of both characteristics 1 and 2—which the patient observes or says others observe in him—together with two of characteristics 3 through 7.

1. *Persistent motor hyperactivity:* Manifested by restlessness, inability to relax, "nervousness," (meaning inability to settle down–not anticipatory anxiety), inability to persist in sedentary activities (e.g., watching movies, TV, reading the newspaper), being always on the go, dysphoric when inactive.
2. *Attentional difficulties:* Manifested by an inability to keep mind on conversations, distractibility (being aware of other stimuli when attempts are made to filter them out); difficulty keeping mind on reading materials or task; frequent "forgetfulness"; often losing or misplacing things, forgetting plans, car keys, purse, etc.; "mind frequently somewhere else."
3. *Affective lability:* Usually described as antedating adolescence and in some instances beginning as far back as the patient can remember. Manifested by definite shifts from a normal mood to depression or mild euphoria or—more often—excitement; depression described as being

(Continued)

Exhibit 26.2. Utah Criteria for Adult ADHD *(Continued)*

"down," "bored," or "discontented"; mood shifts usually last hours to at most a few days and are present without significant physiological concomitants; mood shifts may occur spontaneously or be reactive.

4. *Disorganization, inability to complete tasks:* The subject reports lack of organization in job, running household, or performing school work; tasks frequently not completed; subject switches from one task to another in haphazard fashion; disorganization in activities, problem solving, organizing time, lack of "stick-to-it-tiveness."

5. *Hot temper, explosive short-lived outbursts:* Subject reports he may have transient loss of control and be frightened by his own behavior. Easily provoked or constant irritability. Temper problems interfere with personal relationships.

6. *Emotional overreactivity:* Subject cannot take ordinary stresses in stride and reacts excessively or inappropriately with depression, confusion, uncertainty, anxiety, or anger. Emotional responses interfere with appropriate problem solving. Subject experiences repeated crises in dealing with routine life stresses. Describes self as easily "hassled" or "stressed out."

7. *Impulsivity:* Minor manifestations include talking before thinking things through; interrupting others' conversations; impatience (e.g., while driving); impulse buying. Major manifestations may be similar to those seen in mania and Antisocial Personality Disorder and include, to varying degrees, poor occupational performance; abrupt initiation or termination of relationships (e.g., multiple marriages, separations, divorces); antisocial behavior such as joy-riding, shop-lifting; excessive involvement in pleasurable activities without recognizing risks of painful consequences (e.g., buying sprees, foolish business investments, reckless driving). Subject makes decisions quickly and easily without reflection, often on the basis of insufficient information, to his own disadvantage; inability to delay acting without experiencing discomfort.

B. Absence of the following disorders:

1. Antisocial Personality Disorder
2. Major Affective Disorder

C. Absence of signs and symptoms of the following disorders:

1. Schizophrenia
2. Schizo-affective Disorder

D. Absence of Schizotypal or Borderline Personality Disorders or traits

(Continued)

Exhibit 26.2. Utah Criteria for Adult ADHD *(Continued)*

> E. Associated features:
> Marital instability; academic and vocational success less than expected on the basis of intelligence and education; alcohol or drug abuse; atypical responses to psychoactive medications; family histories of ADHD in childhood, alcoholism, drug abuse, Antisocial Personality Disorder and Briquet's syndrome.
>
> F. Child Temperament Questionnaire
> (Conners Abbreviated Rating Scale.) Although not necessary for diagnosis, a score of 12 or greater as rated by the patient's mother is helpful for diagnostic purposes and may be predictive of treatment response.

Note. From *Adult Attention-Deficit Hyperactivity Disorder*, by P. H. Wender, 1995. Reprinted with permission of the author. The Wender–Reimherr Adult Attention Deficit Disorder Scale is used to assess the severity of the seven adult characteristics. It can be obtained from Fred Reimherr, MD, Mood Disorder Clinic, Department of Psychiatry, University of Utah School of Medicine, 50 North Medical Drive, Salt Lake City, UT 84132.

ness. The Utah Criteria include additional symptoms related to emotional control and describe associated characteristics that are typical of adults with ADHD and important to assess. Although the Utah Criteria in Exhibit 26.2 require the absence of major affective disorder and antisocial personality disorder to diagnose ADHD, Wender noted that this was done to create a more homogeneous and purer sample for research (Wender, Wolf, & Wasserstein, 2001). Therefore, the presence of these two disorders should not be used to rule out ADHD when the Utah Criteria are used clinically (P. H. Wender, October 2003, personal communication). The severity of the seven adult characteristics can be assessed with a structured interview, the Wender–Reimherr Attention Deficit Disorder Scale, which is a revision of an interview that originally appeared in Wender (1995).

Another approach has been taken by Brown (1996), who refers to a group of attention-deficit disorders. His diagnostic system is broader than the *DSM–IV* or the Utah Criteria. In addition to problems with attention, he includes symptoms related to working memory, activation for work, and affective interference, which he believes are more characteristic of adults than are the *DSM–IV* symptoms. His system places less emphasis on hyperactivity and impulsivity. However, Brown's system has been criticized by others as lacking empirical support and as reflecting a disorder different from ADHD as defined by the *DSM–IV* (Barkley & Murphy, 1998).

The exact prevalence of ADHD in adults is not known. Summarizing a series of studies using *DSM* or the International Classification of Disease criteria, Barkley (1998) reported ADHD prevalence from 2% to 29% of school-age children, although most prevalence rates were under 10%. Wender et al. (2001) reported childhood prevalence of 3% to 10%. Follow-up studies in adults, many of which have been methodologically flawed owing to attrition and to differing methods of symptom assessment (e.g., self-report vs. observer report), have estimated that from one third to two thirds of children with ADHD continue to experience symptoms as adults (Wender et al., 2001). It is interesting to note that Barkley, Fischer, Smallish, and Fletcher (2002) have shown that symptom persistence is strongly related to who is reporting the symptoms. In a longitudinal study of young adults diagnosed with ADHD in childhood, prevalence was low for self-reports (12%) but was much higher for parent reports (66%). Taken together, these data indicate that from 1% to 6% of adults will meet criteria for diagnosis of ADHD (Wender et al., 2001).

II. FUNCTIONAL NEUROANATOMY

Structural and functional neuroimaging studies have implicated dysfunction in the frontal and subcortical regions of the brain (Barkley, 1997; Giedd, Blumenthal, Molloy, & Castellanos, 2001). This is especially true of individuals displaying symptoms of hyperactivity and impulsivity. Similarly, results of neuropsychological and behavioral studies of ADHD in adults have been interpreted as implicating dysfunction of the dorsolateral prefrontal cortex and the orbitofrontal limbic circuit (Woods, Lovejoy, & Ball, 2002). Although there is general agreement regarding the involvement of the frontal lobes and associated systems, Stefanatos and Wasserstein (2001), from a selective literature review, have proposed the involvement of right-hemisphere regions, both anterior and posterior, in the etiology of ADHD. However, they described their data as speculative rather than conclusive. Nonetheless, they and others (Wolf & Wasserstein, 2001) have cautioned against a simplistic neuroanatomic conceptualization of ADHD until further research is done.

There is also a question of whether frontal system involvement applies to all forms of ADHD. Barkley (1997) argued that his theory of ADHD, which is linked to frontal system functioning and which identifies impaired inhibition as the primary deficit, applies only to the hyperactive-impulsive or combined type of ADHD. He believes that the inattentive type is a very different disorder, with different behavioral features, cognitive characteristics, and outcome. Others, however (e.g., Mirsky & Duncan, 2001), believe that this theory is too limiting to account for all individuals diagnosed with ADHD. Many speculate that this debate will be reflected in the characterization of ADHD in the next edition of the *DSM* (i.e., the *DSM–V*).

III. COMPETING DIAGNOSES TO BE RULED OUT

Many adults seek evaluation for ADHD because they experience problems with attention, organization, and time management. Yet, attentional disorders are the most frequent disorders encountered in clinical practice. In that regard, reports of attention problems have about the same diagnostic value as does a fever. That is, although a fever indicates that there is something wrong, it does not tell the physician *what* is wrong, without further assessment. Similarly, an attentional problem indicates to the neuropsychologist that something is wrong but does not indicate what that something is, without further assessment.

In addition, attention is not a unitary function. It is composed of several different cognitive components, each of which can be selectively impaired. Each component can be tied to different regions of the brain (Mirsky & Duncan, 2001; Mirsky, Fantie, & Tatman, 1995). Consequently, most disorders that affect the brain are going to affect one or more components of attention. The pathways that mediate attention are widespread, originating in the brainstem, passing through the subcortical regions, and connecting to the cortex, especially the frontal and parietal lobes. Furthermore, because the frontal lobes are connected to most other areas of the brain, disorders that disrupt the frontal lobes, either directly or indirectly, are likely to affect attention. Finally, there is much overlap between the executive functions and attention. In fact, Barkley (1997) characterized the problem in ADHD as not so much one of attention but, rather, as an inability to inhibit one's attention from gravitating to activities that are more reinforcing than the task at hand. For adults with ADHD, then, issues of executive functioning also play a role.

Consequently, many disorders that affect attention and executive functioning must be considered as competing diagnoses. A list of these is shown in Table 26.1. Although these are the most common competing diagnoses, the list is not exhaustive. Furthermore, many of these co-occur with ADHD, and their

Table 26.1. Competing Diagnoses to be Ruled Out During Evaluation

Psychiatric disorders	Neurological disorders	Medical disorders
Major depression	Traumatic brain	Thyroid
Bipolar disorder	injury	dysfunction
Anxiety disorders	Seizure disorders	Metabolic disorders
Adjustment	Brain tumors	Systemic lupus
disorders	Multiple sclerosis	erythematosus
Dysthymia	Exposure to	Diabetes
Alcohol abuse	neurotoxic agents	Liver or kidney
Substance abuse	Cerebrovascular	disease
	disorders	Hypertension
	Dementia	HIV disease/AIDS

presence does not rule out an ADHD diagnosis. Both Katz, Goldstein, and Beers (2001) and Barkley (1998) have stated that ADHD in its "pure" form is rare in adults. An additional complication is that children and adolescents who are impulsive because of ADHD are at risk for traumatic brain injury and substance abuse. When several disorders co-occur, it can be a challenge to determine whether ADHD is present and the extent to which it is contributing to the patient's difficulties.

Learning disabilities, and especially those that affect spoken language, can often mimic problems with attention. For example, a problem with spoken language comprehension may lead an adult to report difficulty paying attention when listening. In addition, individuals with learning disabilities frequently have associated problems with executive functioning (e.g., Niemi, Gundersen, Leppäsaari, & Hugdahl, 2003). Finally, learning disabilities frequently co-occur with ADHD (Barkley, 1998).

IV. DIAGNOSTIC CLUES FROM PAST HISTORY

Having been diagnosed with ADHD in childhood can be the first indication that persisting symptoms are affecting functioning as an adult. However, for many individuals, the diagnosis is not made until they are adults. Unfortunately, the high level of media coverage of adult ADHD since the publication of *Driven to Distraction* (Hallowell & Ratey, 1994b) has led many adults to self-diagnose, on the basis of media reports and Internet sites, and to seek treatment. However, many are basing their diagnosis on current symptoms rather than on their past history. Consequently, collecting key historical information from several

Exhibit 26.3. Useful Questions for Eliciting Historical Information Relevant to ADHD

- As a younger student in school, did you have problems paying attention or concentrating in class? Did you daydream frequently? Were you hyperactive? Did you get into trouble with your teachers for these behaviors? Did your teachers make comments about these behaviors to your parents or in your report cards?
- Did you have problems completing your homework on time?
- Were you in any special classes? Were you tutored? Did you receive special education services? If yes, describe.
- Did you repeat any grades?
- Were you given any accommodations in school? What were they? Were they helpful?

For those completing or who have completed postsecondary education, the following questions are helpful:

- Do you have trouble paying attention or concentrating in large lectures?
- Is taking notes difficult for you? Do you get behind in what is being presented?
- Do you have difficulty completing tests in the allotted time?
- Do you have problems with time management? Do you procrastinate? Do you have difficulty handing in your assignments on time? Do you complete work at the last minute? Do you pull all-nighters?
- Have you failed courses or taken incompletes? In which courses?
- Have you received any accommodations in college? Were these helpful? On what basis did you receive the accommodations—informally, provisionally pending evaluation, or previous diagnosis of ADHD?

sources (patient, significant other, parents) is a crucial part of assessment.

Exhibit 26.3 lists questions that can elicit historical information for diagnosis. The Wender–Reimherr Attention Deficit Disorder Scale, mentioned earlier, can also be used for this purpose. In addition, whenever possible, report cards from primary and secondary school and transcripts from postsecondary education should be obtained and reviewed. In the absence of a childhood ADHD diagnosis, comments from primary school teachers can be very helpful in obtaining a snapshot of childhood difficulties. This also eliminates the difficulties inherent in retrospective recollection of difficulties, which can be biased by current perception of problems (e.g., Conners, Ehrhardt, & Sparrow, 1998; McCann, Scheele, Ward, & Roy-Byrne, 2000).

V. EEG AND NEUROIMAGING CORRELATES

Abnormalities in children and adults with ADHD have been reported using quantitative electroencephalography (EEG) and event-related potentials (Barkley, 1998; Monastra, Lubar, & Linden, 2001). However, the research is not sufficiently well developed as to allow these methods to be used diagnostically. Similarly, neuroimaging research has helped elucidate the neuroanatomical basis of ADHD (see section II of this chap., Functional Neuroanatomy). Although some have advocated the use of neuroimaging as a tool to diagnose ADHD (Amen, 2001), most researchers believe that neuroimaging in and of itself should not be used to diagnose ADHD. However, neuroimaging can be helpful during diagnosis if there is concern about neurological abnormalities, if there is co-occurring psychosis, if the symptom presentation is atypical, or if the patient has not responded to conventional treatment (Giedd et al., 2001).

VI. EMPHASIS ON NEUROPSYCHOLOGICAL ASSESSMENT

Neuropsychological research has shown deficits in adults that are similar to those that have been reported in children. A review by Woods et al. (2002) summarizing studies of adult ADHD since 1979 (all but three published since 1993) concluded that impairments were evident in divided and sustained attention, timed word generation, auditory–verbal list learning, planning, organization, impulsivity, cognitive flexibility, and information-processing speed. Yet, impairment was selective rather than global, showing the need for multiple measures of attention and executive functioning during evaluation. Hervey, Epstein, and Curry (2004), in a meta-analysis of 33 studies, 76% of which were published after 1996, reported similar results. Deficits, again, were not global and were most evident in attention, response inhibition, word generation, and memory. In addition, adults with ADHD performed more poorly on tests that used verbal rather than visual presentation. Finally, adults with ADHD showed increasingly impaired performance as task complexity increased.

These findings imply that neuropsychological assessment can contribute to diagnosis of ADHD. Specifically, assessment should be broad and should include measures with a range of complexity. Nonetheless, there is debate over whether neuropsychological assessment plays a necessary role in adult ADHD diagnosis. According to the "gold standard" of ADHD assessment, diagnosis does not require cognitive testing. Rather, only a good interview, preferably with both the patient and significant others, completion of rating scales, and a record review are necessary (American Academy of Child and Adolescent Psychiatry, 1997; Goldman, Genel, Bezman, & Slanetz, 1998). The gold standard states that psychological testing can be helpful but is not essential. Barkley (1998), in particular, views neuropsychological testing as not helpful and not necessary. In part, this is an issue of specificity; a negative test result does not mean the absence of ADHD. Failure to identify ADHD based on the results of neuropsychological testing has been reported in both children (Grodzinsky & Barkley, 1999) and adults (Woods et al., 2002). P. H. Wender (personal communication, October 2003) noted that psychological testing does not adequately assess the seven adult characteristics (see Exhibit 26.2) and that the diagnostic interview remains the gold standard.

Yet, in their review of neuropsychological studies of adult ADHD, Woods et al. (2002, p. 29) concluded that neuropsychological dysfunction is an "integral component of the constellation of symptoms experienced by adults with ADHD" and stated that "the potential contribution of comprehensive neuropsychological assessment should not be overlooked in the assessment and diagnosis of adults with ADHD." They went on to note that because ADHD is a diagnosis of exclusion, neuropsychological measures can contribute to differential diagnosis. Furthermore, by delineating the patient's cognitive strengths and weaknesses, the clinician can (a) establish the presence of a co-occurring learning disability, (b) determine whether a learning disability or other disorder better explains symptoms, and (c) provide information for developing interventions and compensatory strategies. In fact, special educators and college counselors have noted that an ADHD diagnosis alone is insufficient for designing intervention programs for students. This is because interviews and rating scales alone cannot provide the information necessary to inform treatment planning.

It is my premise that neuropsychological assessment is an important component when evaluating an adult for ADHD. Given what is known about ADHD, the emphasis on testing should be on sampling multiple aspects of attention, executive functions, problem-solving skills, learning, and memory. However, because of differential diagnostic issues and because many

Exhibit 26.4. Topics Covered in a Semistructured Interview for Current ADHD Symptoms

Physical or cognitive restlessness
Attention and concentration when listening to others
Remembering things told to you
Attention and concentration when reading or studying
Comprehending and remembering written material
Forgetfulness
Organization (home, school, and, work)
Time management and procrastination
Initiation and follow-through on tasks
Thinking before speaking or acting (impulsivity)
Risk-taking
Emotional lability, temper control, and handling stress

adults seeking assessment have not been evaluated before, a broad approach is recommended. That is, measures of intellectual functioning from which more specific cognitive information can be derived, academic skills, language, and visuospatial skills are also recommended.

VII. KEY TESTS AND MEASURES

As noted, historical information is key in making a diagnosis of ADHD. Hence, collecting a thorough history is crucial. Current symptoms can be elicited through a semistructured interview, based on the *DSM–IV–TR* and the Utah Criteria and covering the issues outlined in Exhibit 26.4. The same questions should be asked of a significant other, preferably in the absence of the patient.

Interviews should be supplemented with behavioral rating scales. All of the recommended instruments use Likert scales, with most ratings ranging from 0 to 3. Retrospective data can be collected using the Wender Utah Rating Scale (WURS) for the patient and the associated Parents' Rating Scale (PRS; referred to as the Child Temperament Questionnaire in Exhibit 26.2) for the individual's primary caregiver (mother, father, or close relative if neither parent is available). Key items are totaled on the WURS, and all items are totaled on the PRS, with comparisons made with empirically established cutoff scores (for the questionnaires and normative data, see Ward et al., 1993; Wender, 1995). The ADHD Rating Scale–IV–Retrospective (Du-Paul et al., 1998; Murphy & Barkley, 1996) can be used to obtain retrospective information on *DSM–IV* symptoms and the impact of symptoms on past functioning across different settings. Scores are provided for inattentive symptoms, hyperactive-impulsive symptoms, and total symptoms. Normative data are stratified by age and gender. Current data can be collected using the Self-Report and Observer forms of the Conners' Adult ADHD Rating Scales (Conners et al., 1998). The Long Form of each provides *T* scores on four empirically derived factor scales (Inattention/Memory Problems, Hyperactivity/Restlessness, Impulsivity/Emotional Lability, and Problems With Self-Concept), three *DSM–IV* symptom scales (Inattentive Symptoms, Hyperactive-Impulsive Symptoms, ADHD Symptoms Total), and an empirically derived ADHD Index. There is also an Inconsistency Index that can be used as a validity check. Normative data are stratified by age and gender. Finally, the ADHD Rating Scale–IV–Current is a parallel version of the Retrospective Questionnaire that provides data on current *DSM–IV* ADHD symptoms and their impact on current functioning in several settings. Data are stratified by age only (DuPaul et al., 1998; Murphy & Barkley, 1996).

According to Woods et al. (2002), neuropsychological measures that best discriminate between ADHD adults and normal controls include Stroop tasks, word generation tasks, auditory–verbal list learning, and continuous performance tests. However, for the reasons noted earlier, a broader battery is recommended. The battery I currently use is shown in Table 26.2 (please see Mapou, in press-a & in press-b for a more detailed battery that includes tests used to assess learning disorders in more depth). Normative data for most tests are widely available. Normative data for the Porteus Mazes can be found in Krikorian and Bartok (1998).

VIII. PSYCHOLOGICAL AND PSYCHIATRIC CO-OCCURRING DISORDERS

ADHD frequently co-occurs with mood, anxiety, personality, and substance abuse disorders (Faraone et al., 2000; Marks, Newcorn, & Halperin, 2001). However, the reported prevalence of these disorders can vary, depending on the research design and the acquisition source. Because co-occurring disorders are so common, neuropsychological evaluation should always include measures of personality and emotional functioning. The Minnesota Multiphasic Personality Inventory—2 (MMPI–2) can be particularly useful, as the scales and subscales can inform the clinician about ADHD-related problems, in addition to providing information on co-occurring depression or anxiety. For example, Scales 4 and 9 of the MMPI–2 can provide information relevant to impulsivity and hyperactivity. Scales 2 and 8 can

Table 26.2. Neuropsychological Test Battery

Component	Measures used
Intellectual functioning	Wechsler Adult Intelligence Scale—III (WAIS-III)
Academic skills	Selected sections of the Woodcock-Johnson Tests—III Tests of Achievement (WJ3ACH). Comparing the Academic Skills and Academic Fluency cluster scores can be useful if speed is an issue. Sections of the Wechsler Individual Achievement Test—II can also be used. Nelson–Denny Reading Test (Form G or H): Comprehension (compare the Standard and Extended time versions)
Attention deployment	
Arousal	Behavioral observation
Focused attention	WAIS-III Digit Symbol-Coding, Symbol Search, and Processing Speed Index Trail Making Test Digit Vigilance Test
Sustained attention	Integrated Visual and Auditory (IVA) Continuous Performance Test or Test of Variables of Attention (TOVA)
Attention encoding	
Span of attention	WAIS-III Digit Span, Forwards California Verbal Learning Test—II, Trial 1 Woodcock-Johnson—Revised Tests of Cognitive Ability: Memory for Sentences Wechsler Memory Scale—III (WMS-III) Logical Memory I 1st Recall
Resistance to interference	Consonant Trigrams

Mental manipulation/ divided attention	WAIS–III Digit Span, Backwards; Arithmetic; Letter-Number Sequencing; and Working Memory Index
Executive functions, problem-solving skills, and reasoning abilities	
Planning	Porteus Maze Test Delis-Kaplan Executive Functioning System (D-KEFS): Tower Test
Flexibility of thinking	Wisconsin Card Sorting Test
Organization	California Verbal Learning Test—II, Semantic Versus Serial Clustering Rey-Osterrieth Complex Figure Test, Copy
Reasoning	WAIS–III Similarities, Comprehension, Picture Completion, Picture Arrangement, and Matrix Reasoning D-KEFS: Twenty Questions Test
Language comprehension	
Single word	WAIS–III Vocabulary
Complex	WJ3ACH Oral Comprehension, Understanding Directions, Listening Comprehension Cluster
Language production	
Naming	Boston Naming Test
Single word	Controlled Oral Word Association Test (letters F, A, S, and categories)

(Continued)

Table 26.2. Neuropsychological Test Battery (*Continued*)

Component	Measures used
Language production (*continued*)	
Complex	Observation of speech and language production in conversation and in response to test items
Visuospatial skills	
Perception	Visual errors on the Boston Naming Test Rey–Osterrieth Complex Figure Test
Construction	WAIS–III Block Design Rey–Osterrieth Complex Figure Test, Copy
Learning/memory	
Verbal	California Verbal Learning Test—II WMS–III Logical Memory
Visual	Rey–Osterrieth Complex Figure Test, Immediate and Delayed Recall WMS–III Faces or Family Pictures WAIS–III Digit Symbol–Incidental Learning

provide information about cognitive efficiency, lack of clarity in thinking, and initiation.

Longitudinal studies of children and studies of adults diagnosed with ADHD as children show lower academic achievement, greater cognitive impairment, and lower occupational attainment (Barkley, 1998; Barkley, Fischer, et al., 2002) among adults with ADHD. These issues can contribute to co-occurring emotional and psychiatric problems. Of additional interest is a study in which young adults with ADHD were found to be at higher risk for driving difficulties, including traffic citations for speeding, crashes, and license suspensions (Barkley, Murphy, DuPaul, & Bush, 2002). They also had lower scores than controls on a test of driving rules and decision making but performed equally well on a driving simulator. Modest relationships were found between measures of executive functioning and accident frequency and total traffic violations, even after severity of ADHD was controlled. Yet, there was no relationship between driving difficulties and co-occurring emotional problems or substance abuse. Thus, driving is another area of functioning that can be seriously affected by ADHD.

IX. PSYCHOPHARMACOLOGIC AND NONPHARMACOLOGIC TREATMENTS

Psychostimulants are the most effective treatment for adults with ADHD. Compared with treatment in children, treatment in adults is about 10% less effective, although about 60% of adults with ADHD will respond to medication (Barkley & Murphy, 1998; Wender et al., 2001). Furthermore, if one psychostimulant is not effective or has too many side effects, another one should be tried. This points to the need for a thorough medication trial completed by a physician familiar with ADHD in adults. Pemoline, although effective, is no longer considered safe for treating ADHD because of hepatotoxicity (Wender et al., 2001). Atomoxetine, which affects the noradrenergic system and does not have the addiction potential of the psychostimulants, has also shown effectiveness in adults (Spencer et al., 1998). It came on the market in winter 2002. However, my own experience is that clients have not found this medication to be very helpful. Recent studies have shown efficacy of other medications, including buproprion (Wilens et al., 2001), guanfacine (Taylor & Russo, 2000), and modafinil (Taylor & Russo, 2000). Some researchers have reported good efficacy of tricyclic antidepressants (Higgins, 1999; Wilens, Biederman, Mick, & Spencer, 1995), although a recent review reported that others have not replicated this finding (Wender et al., 2001).

This same review noted that earlier studies have shown the effectiveness of monoamine oxidase inhibitors, pargyline, selegeline, and buproprion, but that selective serotonin reuptake inhibitor antidepressants have failed to demonstrate adequate efficacy.

Unfortunately, medication does not address educational issues, problematic social interactions, or ways to compensate for difficulties. Although models and methods for treating these problems in adults have been described in scholarly (e.g., Nadeau, 1995; Wasserstein, Wolf, & Le Fever, 2001) and more popular (e.g., Hallowell & Ratey, 1994a, 1994b; Kelly & Ramundo, 1993) texts, there is essentially no research demonstrating efficacy. However, methods developed from research on improving and managing attention problems in individuals following traumatic brain injury can be adapted to adults with ADHD (Sohlberg & Mateer, 2001). Extended time on tests has been a common accommodation offered to college students with ADHD. Leadbetter, Petros, Yeager, Zevenbergen, and Smith (2001) found that extended time on reading comprehension tests improved performances of adults with ADHD combined with depression or with a reading disability but resulted in far less improvement for those with ADHD alone. This may be because adults with ADHD tend to rush through tests because of impulsivity.

A final issue is documentation of ADHD. Those writing reports for colleges, testing agencies, and professional licensing boards should always follow guidelines for documenting ADHD in adolescents and adults that have been established by the Educational Testing Service (1998). These can be found on the organization's Web site (www.ets.org). These guidelines mandate the use of *DSM–IV* diagnostic criteria and the use of neuropsychological (or cognitive) testing to document the underlying cognitive impairment. Moreover, they state that ADHD must cause a significant limitation in a person's functioning to qualify as a disability under the 1990 Americans With Disabilities Act. Because almost all colleges and all testing agencies and professional licensing boards adhere to these guidelines, neuropsychologists writing these types of reports should be sure that their reports are consistent with the guidelines. They should also check the Web sites of these organizations for guideline changes because they are frequently evolving.

X. CONCLUSION

This chapter reviewed the diagnostic criteria for clinical evaluation of adult-onset attention deficit/hyperactivity disorder. Key neuropsychological measures for making this diagnosis were described. In addition, common co-occurring psychological and learning disorders were discussed. Finally, both the treatment options for these patients and the medicolegal implications for making this diagnosis were reviewed.

BIBLIOGRAPHY

Amen, D. C. (2001). *Healing ADD: The breakthrough program that allows you to see and heal the 6 types of ADD*. New York: Putnam.

American Academy of Child and Adolescent Psychiatry. (1997). Practice parameters for the assessment and treatment of children, adolescents, and adults with attention-deficit hyperactivity disorder. *Journal of the American Academy of Child and Adolescent Psychiatry, 36*(Suppl.), 85S–121S.

American Psychiatric Association. (1994). *Diagnostic and statistical manual of mental disorders* (4th ed.). Washington, DC: Author.

American Psychiatric Association. (2000). *Diagnostic and statistical manual of mental disorders* (4th ed., text revision). Washington, DC: Author.

Americans With Disabilities Act of 1990, 42 U.S.C.A. §12101 *et seq.* (West 1993).

Barkley, R. A. (1997). *ADHD and the nature of self-control*. New York: Guilford Press.

Barkley, R. A. (1998). *Attention deficit hyperactivity disorder: A handbook for diagnosis and treatment* (2nd ed.). New York: Guilford Press.

Barkley, R. A., Fischer, M., Smallish, L., & Fletcher, K. (2002). The persistence of attention-deficit/hyperactivity disorder into young adulthood as a function of reporting source and definition of disorder. *Journal of Abnormal Psychology, 111*, 279–289.

Barkley, R. A., & Murphy, K. R. (1998). *Attention deficit hyperactivity disorder: A clinical workbook* (2nd ed.). New York: Guilford Press.

Barkley, R. A., Murphy, K. R., DuPaul, G. J., & Bush, T. (2002). Driving in young adults with attention deficit hyperactivity disorder: Knowledge, performance, adverse outcomes, and the role of executive functioning. *Journal of the International Neuropsychological Society, 8*, 655–672.

Brown, T. E. (1996). *Brown Attention-Deficit Disorder Scales manual*. San Antonio, TX: Psychological Corporation.

Conners, C. K., Ehrhardt, D., & Sparrow, E. S. (1998). *Conners' Adult ADHD Rating Scales (CAARS)*. North Tonawanda, NY: Multi-Health Systems.

DuPaul, G. J., Power, T. J., Anastopoulos, A. D., & Reid, R. (1998). *ADHD Rating Scale–IV: Checklists, norms, and clinical interpretation.* New York: Guilford Press.

Educational Testing Service. (1998). *Policy statement for documentation of attention-deficit/hyperactivity disorder in adolescents and adults.* Princeton, NJ: Author.

Faraone, S. V., Biederman, J., Spencer, T., Wilens, T., Seidman, L. J., Mick, E., & Doyle, A. E. (2000). Attention-deficit/hyperactivity disorder in adults: An overview. *Biological Psychiatry, 48,* 9–20.

Giedd, J. N., Blumenthal, J., Molloy, E., & Castellanos, F. X. (2001). Brain imaging of attention deficit/hyperactivity disorder. In J. Wasserstein, L. Wolf, & F. L. Fever (Eds.), *Adult attention deficit disorder: Biological mechanisms and life outcomes* (pp. 33–49). New York: New York Academy of Sciences.

Goldman, L. S., Genel, M., Bezman, R. J., & Slanetz, P. J. (1998). Diagnosis and treatment of attention-deficit hyperactivity disorder in children and adolescents. *Journal of the American Medical Association, 279,* 1100–1107.

Grodzinsky, G. M., & Barkley, R. A. (1999). Predictive power of frontal lobe tests in the diagnosis of attention deficit hyperactivity disorder. *The Clinical Neuropsychologist, 13,* 12–21.

Hallowell, E. M., & Ratey, J. J. (1994a). *Answers to distraction.* New York: Pantheon Books.

Hallowell, E. M., & Ratey, J. J. (1994b). *Driven to distraction.* New York: Pantheon Books.

Hervey, A. S., Epstein, J. N., & Curry, J. F. (2004). Neuropsychology of adults with attention-deficit/hyperactivity disorder: A meta-analytic review. *Neuropsychology, 18,* 485–503.

Higgins, E. S. (1999). A comparative analysis of antidepressants and stimulants for treatment of adults with attention-deficit hyperactivity disorder. *Journal of Family Practice, 48,* 15–20.

Katz, L. J., Goldstein, G., & Beers, S. S. (2001). *Learning disabilities in older adolescents and adults.* New York: Kluwer Academic/Plenum.

Kelly, K., & Ramundo, P. (1993). *You mean I'm not lazy, stupid, or crazy?* New York: Simon & Schuster.

Krikorian, R., & Bartok, J. A. (1998). Developmental data for the Porteus Maze Test. *The Clinical Neuropsychologist, 12,* 305–310.

Leadbetter, L., Petros, T., Yeager, C., Zevenbergen, A., & Smith, J. (2001). The impact of extended time on reading comprehension in adults with disabilities. *Journal of the International Neuropsychological Society, 7,* 160.

Mapou, R. L. (in press-a). Learning disabilities in adults. In J. E. Morgan & J. H. Ricker (Eds.), *Comprehensive textbook of clinical neuropsychology.* New York: Psychology Press.

Mapou, R. L. (in press-b). Comprehensive evaluation of adults with learning disabilities. In L. E. Wolf, H. Schreiber, & J. Wasserstein (Eds.), *Adult learning disorders: Contemporary issues*. New York: Psychology Press.

Marks, D. J., Newcorn, J. H., & Halperin, J. M. (2001). Comorbidity in adults with attention-deficit/hyperactivity disorder. In J. Wasserstein, L. Wolf, & F. L. Fever (Eds.), *Adult attention deficit disorder: Biological mechanisms and life outcomes* (pp. 216–238). New York: New York Academy of Sciences.

McCann, B. S., Scheele, L., Ward, N., & Roy-Byrne, P. (2000). Discriminant validity of the Wender Utah Rating Scale for attention-deficit/hyperactivity disorder in adults. *Journal of Neuropsychiatry and Clinical Neurosciences, 12,* 240–245.

Mirsky, A. F., & Duncan, C. C. (2001). A nosology of disorders of attention. In J. Wasserstein, L. Wolf, & F. L. Fever (Eds.), *Adult attention deficit disorder: Biological mechanisms and life outcomes* (pp. 17–32). New York: New York Academy of Sciences.

Mirsky, A. F., Fantie, B. D., & Tatman, J. E. (1995). Assessment of attention across the lifespan. In R. L. Mapou & J. Spector (Eds.), *Clinical neuropsychological assessment: A cognitive approach* (pp. 17–48). New York: Plenum Press.

Monastra, V. J., Lubar, J., & Linden, M. (2001). The development of a quantitative electroencephalographic scanning process for attention deficit-hyperactivity disorder: Reliability and validity studies. *Neuropsychology, 15,* 136–144.

Murphy, K., & Barkley, R. A. (1996). Prevalence of *DSM–IV* symptoms of ADHD in adult licensed drivers: Implications for clinical diagnosis. *Journal of Attention Disorders, 1,* 147–161.

Nadeau, K. G. (Ed.). (1995). *A comprehensive guide to attention deficit disorder in adults*. New York: Brunner/Mazel.

Niemi, J., Gundersen, J., Leppäsaari, T., & Hugdahl, K. (2003). Speech lateralization and attention/executive functions in a Finnish family with specific language impairment (SLI). *Journal of Clinical and Experimental Neuropsychology, 25,* 457–464.

Sohlberg, M. M., & Mateer, C. A. (2001). Improving attention and managing attentional problems: Adapting rehabilitation techniques to adults with ADD. In J. Wasserstein, L. Wolf, & F. L. Fever (Eds.), *Adult attention deficit disorder: Biological mechanisms and life outcomes* (pp. 359–375). New York: New York Academy of Sciences.

Spencer, T. J., Biederman, J., Wilens, T. E., Prince, J., Hatch, M., Jones, J., et al. (1998). Effectiveness and tolerability of tomoxetine in adults with attention deficit hyperactivity disorder. *American Journal of Psychiatry, 155,* 693–695.

Stefanatos, G. E., & Wasserstein, J. (2001). Attention deficit/hyperactivity disorder as a right hemisphere syndrome. In J. Wasserstein, L. Wolf, & F. L. Fever (Eds.), *Adult attention deficit disorder: Biological mechanisms and life outcomes* (pp. 172–195). New York: New York Academy of Sciences.

Taylor, F. B., & Russo, J. (2000). Efficacy of modafinil compared to dextroamphetamine for the treatment of attention deficit hyperactivity disorder in adults. *Journal of Child and Adolescent Psychopharmacology, 10,* 311–320.

Ward, M. F., Wender, P. H., & Reimherr, F. W. (1993). The Wender Utah Rating Scale: An aid in the retrospective diagnosis of childhood attention deficit hyperactivity disorder. *American Journal of Psychiatry, 150,* 885–890.

Wasserstein, J., Wolf, L., & Fever, F. L. (2001). *Adult attention deficit disorder: Biological mechanisms and life outcomes.* New York: New York Academy of Sciences.

Wender, P. H. (1995). *Attention-deficit hyperactivity disorder in adults.* New York: Oxford University Press.

Wender, P. H., Wolf, L. E., & Wasserstein, J. (2001). Adults with ADHD: An overview. In J. Wasserstein, L. Wolf, & F. L. Fever (Eds.), *Adult attention deficit disorder: Biological mechanisms and life outcomes* (pp. 1–16). New York: New York Academy of Sciences.

Wilens, T. E., Biederman, J., Mick, E., & Spencer, T. J. (1995). A systematic assessment of tricyclic antidepressants in the treatment of adult attention-deficit hyperactivity disorder. *Journal of Nervous and Mental Disease, 183,* 48–50.

Wilens, T. E., Spencer, T. J., Biederman, J., Girard, K., Doyle, R., Prince, J., et al. (2001). A controlled clinical trial of buproprion for attention deficit hyperactivity disorder in adults. *American Journal of Psychiatry, 158,* 282–288.

Wolf, L. E., & Wasserstein, J. (2001). Adult ADHD: Concluding comments. In J. Wasserstein, L. Wolf, & F. L. Fever (Eds.), *Adult attention deficit disorder: Biological mechanisms and life outcomes* (pp. 396–408). New York: New York Academy of Sciences.

Woods, S. P., Lovejoy, D. W., & Ball, J. D. (2002). Neuropsychological characteristics of adults with ADHD: A comprehensive review of initial studies. *The Clinical Neuropsychologist, 16,* 12–34.

CHAPTER 27

Daniel N. Allen, Linda V. Frantom, Teri J. Forrest, and Gregory P. Strauss

Neuropsychology of Substance Use Disorders

The lifetime prevalence rates for alcohol and drug use disorders are 18.2% and 6.1%, respectively. Males are two to three times more likely to be diagnosed with a substance use disorder than females. Substance use disorders are often chronic, debilitating, and associated with increased mortality rates, homelessness, and utilization of health care systems. As a result, substance use disorders are enormously costly, with estimates of yearly costs reaching $300 billion. Neuropsychological testing has been used extensively to evaluate individuals with substance use disorders because substances can cause a wide range of neurocognitive deficits. These deficits are associated with treatment outcomes and also provide insight into brain regions that are susceptible to the effects of various substances.

I. GENERAL ISSUES

A. Diagnostic Categories

The American Psychiatric Association's (2000) *Diagnostic and Statistical Manual of Mental Disorders* (4th ed., text revision; *DSM–IV–TR*) lists two substance-related disorders: substance use disorders and substance-induced disorders.

    1. **Substance use disorders** include the subcategories of substance abuse and substance dependence. These are

the most commonly diagnosed substance-related disorders.

    a. **Substance abuse** is indicated when maladaptive substance use leads to significant problems in one of four domains (legal, interpersonal, work or school, or hazardous behaviors). Problems must occur repeatedly within the same 12-month period. In contrast to substance dependence, there is no withdrawal, tolerance, or compulsive use. A diagnosis of substance dependence preempts that of substance abuse.

    b. **Substance dependence** is diagnosed when there is persistent substance use resulting in three or more cognitive, behavioral, or physiological symptoms occurring within the same 12-month period. Symptoms include, among others, persistent or unsuccessful attempts to cut down, tolerance, withdrawal, and curtailment of social, occupational, or recreational activities to use or obtain the substance. Increased tolerance or withdrawal symptoms are not required for diagnosis. Substance dependence can be diagnosed for all substances except caffeine.

2. **Substance-induced disorders** include substance intoxication, substance withdrawal, substance-induced delirium, substance-induced persisting dementia, substance-induced persisting amnestic disorder, substance-induced psychotic disorder, substance-induced mood disorder, substance-induced anxiety disorder, substance-induced sexual dysfunction, and substance-induced sleep disorder.

B. Not All Substances Cause All Substance-Related Disorders

Cannabis use, for example, can cause substance abuse, substance dependence, and substance intoxication but not substance withdrawal, substance-induced persisting dementia, or substance-induced persisting amnestic disorder.

C. *DSM–IV–TR* Substance Classifications

The *DSM–IV–TR* substance classifications include 11 categories: alcohol, cannabis, cocaine, opioids, amphetamines, hallucinogens, caffeine, inhalants, nicotine, phencyclidine, and sedatives, anxiolytics, or hypnotics. Neurocognitive effects associated with chronic use vary depending on the unique pharmacokinetics of the substance.

D. Accurate Diagnosis of Substance Use Disorders

An accurate history is needed for a diagnosis of substance use disorders. However, this may be difficult to obtain for the following reasons.

1. **Obstacles to obtaining an accurate substance use history**
   a. Individuals who have substance use disorders often deny or underreport the extent and consequences of their substance use.
   b. Individuals who are intoxicated or delirious are unable to provide accurate histories.
   c. Individuals with persisting substance-induced cognitive impairment may be unable to provide information on recent or remote substance use.
   d. Clinicians unaware of possible substance use will fail to take adequate histories.
2. **Methods to increase accuracy of the substance use history**
   a. Always inquire about substance use when taking medical and psychosocial histories.
   b. In cases of suspected substance use, obtain historical information from significant others when possible.
   c. Recommend alcohol and drug screening when there is suspicion of substance use.
   d. Consult medical records for patterns of physical problems consistent with substance abuse, prescription medications with high potential for abuse (e.g., benzodiazepines, narcotics), and history of substance use disorders (see chap. 1, this volume).
3. **Psychometric assessment and screening**. In addition to an accurate history and routine laboratory tests, self-report measures may assist in identifying individuals at risk for substance use disorders. The Michigan Alcohol Screening Test (MAST), Rapid Alcohol Problems Screen (RAPS; Cherpitel, 2002), and Substance Abuse Subtle Screening Inventory—3 (SASSI) are brief and assess a range of alcohol use (MAST, RAPS) or alcohol and drug use (SASSI) behaviors. They have established cutoff scores indicating risk for substance use disorders. However, before a final diagnosis is made, further evaluation

of symptomatology is necessary for individuals identified as at risk.

4. **Concurrent abuse or dependence diagnoses**. When one substance use diagnosis is made, it significantly increases the risk that another substance is being used (e.g., cocaine and alcohol abuse often occur concurrently). Thus, when one substance use diagnosis is made, careful consideration of additional substance use diagnoses is warranted.

E. Age Effects

By the year 2020, it is projected that 18% of the United States population (approximately 52 million people) will be over the age of 65. Because of this general aging trend, the number of elderly individuals with substance use disorders will increase substantially (for a review, see Allen & Landis, 1998). With regard to substance use, these older individuals differ from younger individuals in significant ways.

1. **Risk factors for substance abuse or dependence**: Unique factors place elderly individuals at risk for developing substance use disorders.
   a. Elderly individuals are the largest consumers of prescribed medication, receiving approximately 30% of all prescribed drugs and almost 40% of benzodiazepine prescriptions, which have a high potential for abuse and addiction. Increased access increases potential for prescription drug abuse or dependence.
   b. Age-related changes in physiology cause drugs to be more potent and less predictable in the elderly, which increases the potential for negative substance-related outcomes.
   c. Other risk factors include poor understanding of medication effects and interactions, inadequate education or misconceptions regarding proper use of medications, and decreased cognitive abilities.
2. **Prevalence rates of substance use disorders**: Despite these risk factors, substance use disorders are typically less prevalent in older individuals.
   a. For males 18 to 24 years old, the 1-year prevalence rate of alcohol use disorders is 22.1%, compared with 1.2% for men 65 years of age and older. Comparable rates for females are 9.8% and 0.3%, respectively.
   b. One-year drug use disorders prevalence rates are 4.0% for individuals 18 to 29 years old and 0.7% for indi-

viduals 30 years of age or older. The one-year prevalence rate is less than one tenth of 1.0% for individuals older than 65.

c. Decreased prevalence rates have been explained by the "maturing out" theory, which suggests that decreased prevalence is accounted for by passing from one developmental stage to the next, or by increased mortality rates in those with substance use disorders. However, three other factors relating to underdetection of substance use disorders may also play a role in reports of decreased prevalence.

- **Inadequate or inappropriate diagnostic criteria.** Because physical health, age-appropriate life tasks, and socioeconomic resources vary with age, elderly individuals with substance use disorders may go undiagnosed because they meet fewer diagnostic criteria than younger individuals. For example, because older adults are often unemployed, live alone, and have decreased social activities, one would expect to observe fewer instances of adverse consequences in these domains when compared with younger individuals.

- **Abuse of prescription medications.** Underdetection of elderly prescription substance abusers may occur because health care providers do not seriously consider potential for abuse and dependence by those who are prescribed drugs.

- **Late-life onset of substance abuse.** Health care providers may be less likely to detect substance abuse in elderly individuals because many elders have no history of substance abuse. However, between 15% and 68% of elderly individuals treated for alcohol problems are late-onset drinkers.

d. Note that the incidence of alcohol abuse appears significantly more prevalent in elderly hospitalized patients, with incidence of alcohol abuse as high as 50%.

3. **"Maturing in" theory.** The decrease in older substance users caused by "maturing out" could be countered by a "maturing in" process, whereby the unique and novel challenges of late life, combined with increased access to prescription medications and increased potency secondary to age-related physiological changes, cause the onset of substance use disorders in an otherwise low-risk elderly population.

F. Treatment

Neurocognitive deficits can interfere with treatment. Deficits in the areas of memory may limit the individual's ability to learn and retain psychoeducational information that is often present as a component of substance use treatment, whereas executive function deficits may hinder the application of this information to avoid relapse, retain employment, and attain better psychosocial adjustment. The relationship between treatment outcome and neurocognitive deficits is complex. It is likely that neurocognitive impairment exerts both mediating and moderating effects, depending on the outcome domains, risk factors, and neurocognitive abilities under consideration (Bates, Bowden, & Barry, 2002). Despite this complexity, neurocognitive deficits are important to consider when planning treatment for individuals with substance use disorders. When deficits are present, cognitive rehabilitation procedures may help to remediate deficits and thereby increase treatment efficacy. Bates et al. (2002) provided specific suggestions for remediating substance-induced deficits.

G. Assessment of Substance-Induced Neurocognitive Deficits

1. **Stability of deficits:** Neurocognitive deficits may vary in severity over time and from one individual to the next. Factors influencing the severity of deficits include the acute versus chronic effects of substances, comorbid psychiatric disorders, limited education, and substance-related medical conditions. Prior to attributing cognitive deficits to neurotoxic effects of any particular substance, the potential influence of these factors must be considered, with special attention given to comorbid medical and psychiatric disorders.

   a. **Diagnosis of comorbid medical disorders**: In all patients who have substance use disorders, thorough physical examination is necessary to rule out comorbid disorders that could affect neurocognitive functioning, including the following:
      - disorders resulting from malnutrition such as Wernicke–Korsakoff disorder,
      - cirrhosis of the liver leading to hepatic encephalopathy,
      - subdural hematoma, contusions, and diffuse axonal injury secondary to head injury,

- epileptic seizures (alcohol withdrawal is a common cause of adult onset seizures), and
- infectious diseases associated with substance use (e.g., HIV resulting from intravenous drug use).

b. **Diagnosis of comorbid psychiatric disorders.** Some psychiatric disorders have high comorbidity with substance abuse and dependence. Also, in disorders such as schizophrenia, substance abuse occurs at a very high rate and may produce compounding effects with regard to neurocognitive deficits (Allen, Goldstein, & Aldarondo, 1998). The following psychiatric disorders occur at increased rates in substance users and can cause neurocognitive deficits:

- Major depression occurs with greater prevalence in alcohol, cannabis, cocaine, and polysubstance use disorders.
- Attention-deficit/hyperactivity disorder has increased incidence in alcohol and heroin use disorders and in early-onset (adolescent) substance use disorders.
- Anxiety disorders occur with greater frequency in alcohol use disorders.
- Antisocial personality disorder has increased incidence in alcohol, cannabis, cocaine, and polysubstance use disorders.

2. **Choice of neuropsychological tests:** In this section, we briefly describe cognitive screening instruments and address issues relevant to neuropsychological evaluation of individuals with substance use disorders. Because this is a summary, specific tools are not discussed in depth. Clinicians who are unfamiliar with the assessment instruments or wish to learn more about specific tests can consult one of the standard texts.

a. **Cognitive screening**: Because many clinicians do not have the time or expertise to administer and interpret full neuropsychological batteries, cognitive screening instruments have been developed, such as the Cognistat and the Repeatable Battery for the Assessment of Neuropsychological Status (RBANS). In addition, screening batteries have been proposed, such as the Neuropsychological Screening Battery (NSB; Heaton, Thompson, Nelson, Filley, & Franklin, 1990). Each screening method has advantages and disadvantages. Advantages of Cognistat and RBANS are that they do not require extensive training and take 30 minutes or less to administer. Neither has been extensively validated with individuals who have substance use disorders. However, the NSB takes longer to administer but reliably discriminates individuals with substance use disorders from control participants.

- Cognistat's subtests assess orientation, attention, language comprehension, language repetition, confrontational naming, construction, memory, calculation, verbal abstraction, and judgment. Some studies suggest that it overdiagnoses cognitive dysfunction in elderly individuals.
- The RBANS's 12 subtests evaluate immediate and delayed memory, visuospatial–constructional abilities, attention, and language.
- The NSB consists of six commonly used neuropsychological tests. It provides assessment of attention, visual and verbal learning and memory, psychomotor speed, language and reading comprehension, verbal fluency, and visuoconstructional ability.

b. **Full neuropsychological evaluation**. For discussions of approaches to comprehensive neuropsychological assessment, see Lezak (1995) or Reitan and Wolfson (1993). The subsequent sections focus on describing the typical neuropsychological deficits of individuals who abuse specific substances. It should be noted that of all substances, neurocognitive effects of alcohol are by far the most thoroughly investigated. Also, alcohol is the most widely abused substance. Because of this, much of the review focuses on alcohol-related neurocognitive deficits. The review also covers cannabis, cocaine, amphetamines and club drugs, opiates, benzodiazepines, and polysubstance use, because effects of these substances have been investigated.

II. ALCOHOL

Alcohol is a central nervous system depressant. In the United States, over 90% of individuals over the age of 18 have used alcohol at some time in their lives.

A. Intoxication and Withdrawal

Common neurological symptoms of alcohol intoxication are slurred speech, ataxia, incoordination, and nystagmus. Behavioral symptoms include increased aggression. Psychological symptoms such as fluctuations in mood state and impaired cognitive abilities (memory, attention, and judgment) are also present. Physiological dependence develops after heavy prolonged consumption. Withdrawal usually occurs within 4 to 12 hours of drinking cessation, and almost always within 48 hours. Withdrawal symptoms vary in severity, and most resolve within 1 week. Common mild symptoms include anxiety, irritability, increased heart rate, perspiration, and insomnia. Severe symptoms include grand mal seizures, delirium, and hallucinations.

B. Neuropsychological Findings

In the following sections, neurocognitive deficits in individuals without dementia or Wernicke–Korsakoff syndrome are discussed first. This discussion is divided into three time periods following cessation of alcohol use and the deficits that occur during these time periods: acute deficits (first week of abstinence), short-term deficits (2–5 weeks after abstinence), and long-term deficits (13 months or more after abstinence; for a review, see Allen, Goldstein, & Seaton, 1997). Alcohol-induced persisting dementia, Wernicke–Korsakoff syndrome, and hepatic encephalopathy are then discussed.

1. **Acute deficits**: Neurocognition is most significantly impaired immediately after cessation of alcohol use. In younger alcoholics, this impairment gradually improves over 3 to 4 weeks. Older alcoholics exhibit slower recovery. During the first week of sobriety, performance on tasks assessing intellectual functioning, memory, and visual motor skills often shows marked improvement. This spontaneous improvement probably results not only from abstinence but also from other factors, such as improved nutrition. Spontaneous improvement in neurocognition is diminished or reversed with relapse.

2. **Short-term deficits**: Studies of recently detoxified alcoholics (2–5 weeks) indicate presence of impairment across a number of cognitive and motor domains, although there does appear to be an age effect. For younger individuals (less than 35 years old) with relatively short drinking histories (5–10 years), those who consume more alcohol over the course of their lives exhibit poorer performance on neuropsychological measures. However, when younger individuals are abstinent an average of 4 to 6 weeks, cognitive functioning appears to return to expected or "normal" levels. Neuro-

cognitive deficits that do persist after drinking cessation may be a result of the cumulative effects of a lifetime pattern of alcohol abuse. Deficits in the following areas are most prominent: (a) abstraction ability and problem solving, (b) perceptual–motor ability, (c) short-term and long-term verbal and nonverbal memory with nonverbal memory relatively more impaired, (d) visuospatial abilities, and (e) gait and balance.

3. **Long-term deficits**: Studies examining alcoholics abstinent for longer periods of time are less conclusive regarding the nature and severity of impairment. In general, it appears that verbal abilities recover more quickly, whereas nonverbal learning and memory recover more slowly. Improvement in some cognitive domains is related to age, length of abstinence, and interim drinking. Complex memory deficits found in some individuals with chronic alcoholism may be due to use of inefficient organization strategies during encoding and may actually represent a learning strategy formation deficit. Other deficits that may persist after long-term abstinence, particularly in older individuals, include (a) problem solving, (b) perceptuomotor abilities, (c) visual learning and memory, and (d) contextual memory deficits.

4. **Wernicke–Korsakoff syndrome**: Wernicke–Korsakoff (WK) syndrome is caused by a deficiency in thiamin to which some alcoholics are particularly susceptible because of poor dietary practices. Thiamin deficiency causes hemorrhages in the third ventricle (antero- and dorsomedial thalamic nuclei) and mammillary bodies, which cause ataxic gait, nystagmus, opthalmoplegia, and confusion during the acute phase of the disorder (Wernicke's encephalopathy). With large doses of thiamin, these symptoms typically resolve within 4 weeks. Most patients then go on to develop Korsakoff's syndrome, which is characterized by severe anterograde amnesia, as well as temporally graded retrograde amnesia. Impairment in other areas of cognitive functioning may be present, including executive functions. General intellectual functioning and semantic memory are typically preserved. Some have suggested that milder forms of WK may account for much of the persisting neurocognitive deficits in chronic alcoholics, although this suggestion remains controversial. Because cognitive deficits

due to thiamin deficiency are severe and debilitating, clinicians should always evaluate the patient's nutritional status and consider giving thiamin prophylactically.

5. **Alcohol-induced persisting dementia.** Controversy exists regarding the etiology of alcohol-induced persisting dementia. Some reports indicate that as many as 25% of elderly alcoholic patients and 24% of institutionalized elderly people have alcohol dementia (see chap. 10, this volume, for information on dementia).

   a. **Characteristics of alcohol-related dementia**
      ▪ onset of alcohol-induced persisting dementia is insidious;
      ▪ neurocognitive dysfunction is present for general intellectual abilities as well as memory, visuospatial abilities, and abstraction and problem solving;
      ▪ neurocognitive impairment is permanent, persisting long after alcohol consumption has ceased; and
      ▪ neurocognitive deficits significantly interfere with daily functioning.

   b. **Differential diagnosis**
      ▪ Orientation to time and place, as well as language abilities such as fluency and confrontational naming, remains relatively well preserved in alcohol dementia, which may help clinicians distinguish it from Alzheimer's dementia, in which disorientation and prominent aphasic language disturbances are present.
      ▪ Individuals with alcohol dementia may be on average 10 years younger than those with other dementias and have twice the average length of institutionalization.
      ▪ Neurocognitive deficits in alcohol dementia are consistent with both subcortical dementia (intact recognition memory with impaired recall) and cortical dementia (intact procedural learning; Munro, Saxton, & Butters, 2001).

6. **Hepatic encephalopathy.** Approximately 30% of individuals with alcohol use disorders develop cirrhosis of the liver, which can cause hepatic encephalopathy. Studies by Tarter and colleagues provide the following conclusions (Tarter & Butters, 2001):

   a. Individuals with cirrhosis resulting from alcohol use disorders perform worse on tests of short-term

> memory, eye tracking, and hand–eye coordination when compared with individuals with non-alcohol-induced cirrhosis.
>
> b. Although many cognitive deficits improve following liver transplantation in alcoholic cirrhotic patients, memory capacity does not.
>
> c. Subclinical hepatic encephalopathy (i.e., typical alterations in mood, cognition, and consciousness are *not* present) can produce significant memory impairment and motor slowing, although intellectual functioning and abstraction abilities remain intact.

C. Neuroimaging Findings

1. Computed tomography (CT) and magnetic resonance imaging (MRI) results indicate that in recently detoxified alcoholics, cerebral atrophy and white and gray matter volume loss are present. Loss is most pronounced in older alcoholics. The prefrontal cortex appears especially sensitive to combined effects of aging and alcohol. Prolonged abstinence (3–6 months) may cause white matter volume increases, decreased third ventricle diameter, and cerebral spinal fluid volume reductions (for a review, see Sullivan, Rosenbloom, & Pfefferbaum, 2000).

2. Positron emission tomography (PET) studies suggest neuropsychological impairment is associated with overall decreased glucose metabolism and hypoperfusion in the frontal cortex and subcortical structures (hypometabolism is significantly associated with performance on "frontal lobe" tests).

3. Single photon emission computed tomography (SPECT) indicates reductions in regional cerebral blood flow (rCBF) in multiple brain regions, as well as reduced benzodiazepine binding sites in chronic alcoholism (see Kaufman, 2001).

III. CANNABIS

Of the illicit substances, cannabinoids are the most widely used, with 30% of the U.S. population reporting marijuana use, 10% using it at least once a year, and 1% using it monthly. Cannabinoids are obtained from the cannabis plant, and psychoactive effects are caused by delta-9-tetrahydrocannabinol, or THC.

A. Intoxication and Withdrawal

Common physiological symptoms of cannabis intoxication include increase in appetite, blood-shot eyes, and dry mouth. Psychological symptoms include fluctuations in mood state (euphoria or anxiety), thought disorder (grandiosity, paranoia, or hallucinations), and impaired cognitive abilities (e.g., memory, sensory perception, and judgment). It is not clear whether cessation of cannabis use leads to withdrawal, so the *DSM–IV–TR* does not include a diagnostic category for cannabis withdrawal. After cessation of heavy prolonged use, withdrawal may occur and include psychological (anxiety and irritability) as well as physiological (insomnia, nausea, and tremor) symptoms. Cannabis abuse and dependence are associated with negative psychosocial outcomes, including poor motivation, social relationships, and work records; lower employment status; higher incidence of legal problems, affective blunting, and apathy; and decreased libido.

B. Neuropsychological Findings

Researchers have examined cognitive deficits caused by cannabis during intoxication as well as acute (24 hours after cessation) and long-term deficits.

1. **Cannabis intoxication**: Cannabis intoxication produces significant and widespread cognitive deficits in the areas of (a) problem solving, (b) abstraction, (c) attention, (d) expressive and receptive language, and (e) memory.
2. **Acute deficits**: During the 24 hours following cessation of cannabis use, impairment has been reported in the areas of (a) attention, (b) executive functions, (c) mental arithmetic, (d) immediate recall of verbal information, and (e) complex reaction times.
3. **Long-term deficits**: For chronic heavy users, subtle deficits in the ability to learn and recall new information may persist long after cessation of use (Grant, Gonzalez, Carey, Natarajan, & Wolfson, 2003). It is not clear whether these deficits reflect neurological damage caused by cannabis or if they are premorbid in nature. However, it appears that cannabis use disorders do not lead to marked long-term neurocognitive deficits.

C. Neuroimaging Findings

The effects of cannabis on structure and function of the cerebrum have not been extensively investigated using neuroimaging techniques.

1. CT studies indicate no consistent differences between users and nonusers after neurological and medical risk factors are controlled. Structural MRI studies are lacking.
2. Functional MRI (fMRI) studies of chronic users after short-term and long-term abstinence demonstrate abnormal dorsolateral prefrontal cortex activation during a working memory task (for a review, see Kaufman, 2001).
3. PET studies following acute administration demonstrate increased rCBF in the cerebellum, consistent with a high concentration of cannabinoid C1 receptors. Increased rCBF has also been reported in the orbitofrontal cortex, insula, and cingulate gyrus following acute intoxication (Kaufman, 2001). Chronic users demonstrate reduced baseline levels of cerebral blood flow, which improve with abstinence.

IV. COCAINE

Cocaine is a stimulant. It causes cerebral vasoconstriction and hypertension, which can cause ischemic stroke; cerebral vasculitis; cerebral, subarachnoid, and parenchymal brain hemorrhage; and seizures. Use of cocaine can also lead to death from respiratory or cardiac failure (see chap. 12, this volume, for information on cerebrovascular accidents).

A. Intoxication and Withdrawal

Cocaine intoxication is accompanied by physiological, behavioral, and psychological symptoms. Physiological symptoms of intoxication include pupil dilation, increased blood pressure, tachycardia, and perspiration, among others. Behavioral changes induced by cocaine include restlessness, hyperactivity, and stereotyped behavior. Psychological symptoms induced by cocaine include euphoria, increased alertness, anxiety, depression, and grandiosity. Physiological dependence typically develops after heavy chronic use. Withdrawal begins within hours after cessation and almost always within 2 to 3 days. During withdrawal, individuals typically experience feelings of sadness, depression, and anxiety. This dysphoria is accompanied by disrupted sleep, appetite, and psychomotor functioning. Symptoms typically abate after physiological withdrawal is complete (1–5 days), although some symptoms may last much longer. Anhedonic symptoms have been reported to last up to 10 weeks in some individuals.

B. Neuropsychological Findings

Current users of cocaine demonstrate deficits in verbal and visual recall, working memory, and attention. Moderate to heavy cocaine users who are drug free and no longer in cocaine withdrawal may exhibit impairment in the following areas: (a) mental flexibility and control, (b) attention and concentration, (c) visuomotor ability, and (d) verbal and visual learning and memory (Strickland et al., 1993). In most cases, gross intellectual abilities remain intact.

C. Neuroimaging Findings

1. Cocaine users who develop seizures have been found to have brain atrophy on CT scans. MRI reveals decreased volumes in the frontal lobes. There is a strong correlation between amount of cortical atrophy and length of cocaine use, suggesting that increased and lengthier use causes increased cerebral damage.
2. During cocaine intoxication, fMRI indicates activation of the lateral prefrontal cortex, anterior cingulate gyrus, nucleus accumbens, and the hippocampal gyri, as well as decreased signal intensity in the medial prefrontal cortex, amygdala, and temporal pole.
3. SPECT studies indicate that during acute use, cocaine causes widespread hypoperfusion in periventricular areas. Long-term cocaine users exhibited cerebral hypoperfusion in the frontal, temporal/parietal, and periventricular regions. SPECT also indicated that women tend to have fewer cerebral abnormalities than men and often appear normal.
4. With acute intoxication, PET studies indicate decreased glucose metabolism throughout the brain. For patients abstinent from cocaine for several months, PET indicates decreased glucose metabolism in the frontal cortex. These abnormalities appear to be related to dose and length of cocaine use.

V. AMPHETAMINES AND METHYLENDIOXYMETHAMPHETAMINE (MDMA)

Amphetamines and related substances such as methamphetamine and dextroamphetamines are stimulants with properties similar to cocaine. Unlike cocaine, amphetamines do not produce a local anesthetic effect, making them less apt to induce medically related problems. The psychostimulant actions tend to be longer lasting, and the symphathomimetic effects are generally more potent than cocaine. MDMA (3,4-methylendioxymethamphetamine), also known as "Ecstasy," is a member of the amphetamine family with hallucinogenic properties. Although other "club" drugs, such as gamma-hydroxybutyrate (GHB, liquid ecstasy), Rohypnol, Ketamine, and methamphetamine, are popular, MDMA use in youths ages 13 through 17 increased substantially from the early 1980s to late 1990s in the United States, with prevalence rates increasing from 2.7% to 4.3% in 8th graders and from 8% to 11% in 12th graders (Landry, 2002). Long-term damage of serotonergic function at axon terminals and neuroanatomic changes in terms of neuronal pruning have been documented in animals treated with typical doses of MDMA, and similar effects are now being reported in humans. Neuronal damage appears proportional to the amount and duration of use. Because serotonin regulates various functions such as behavior, mood, and sleep, chronic MDMA use may lead to significant changes in these areas.

A. Intoxication and Withdrawal

Common physiological symptoms of MDMA and amphetamine intoxication include increased heart rate, blood pressure, and body temperature; tachycardia; cardiac arrhythmias; and pupillary dilation. Psychological symptoms include elevated mood, perceptual alterations, impaired judgment, and decreased concentration. Some individuals (about 25%) have strong negative reactions to MDMA during intoxication, including severe anxiety. For chronic heavy amphetamine users, cessation of use causes withdrawal symptoms to occur within a few hours or few days. Dysphoria is common during withdrawal, as is disrupted sleep, fatigue, increased appetite, psychomotor agitation or retardation, and anhedonia.

B. Neuropsychological Findings

1. **Amphetamines:** Few studies have been conducted on the neuropsychological effects of amphetamines, but findings are similar to those with cocaine abuse, which reveal deficits primarily in attention and memory. During intoxication, amphetamines produce general cognitive arousal and increased vigilance without a corresponding improvement in cognition or memory. Following acute methamphetamine use, deficits in at-

tention, psychomotor speed, verbal fluency, and verbal learning and memory have been found (Kalechstein, Newton, & Green, 2003). Long-term deficits have been noted in attentional and motor skills in heavy stimulant users with a minimum of 1 year of abstinence (Toomey et al., 2003), as well as deficits in verbal memory and attention in chronic amphetamine-dependent users.

2. **MDMA**

   a. **Acute deficits:** Verbal memory impairments have been demonstrated in MDMA users who have been abstinent for relatively short periods of time (at least 3 weeks). Additionally, impairments in working memory and attentional tasks have been found several days following acute ingestion. Impairments in verbal fluency and immediate and delayed prose recall have been found in occasional, chronic, and abstinent users.

   b. **Long-term deficits:** Long-term cognitive deficits have been reported in individuals with both occasional and heavy MDMA use, with deficits persisting up to 1 year postabstinence (for a review, see Parrot, 2001). The most consistent deficits were found in the areas of learning and memory, particularly verbal memory. Additional deficits have been found in the areas of executive function and planning, attention and vigilance, verbal fluency, and visual scanning.

C. Neuroimaging Findings

SPECT and PET studies have examined the neurotoxicity of MDMA, although fMRI studies are lacking.

1. PET studies indicate that a single dose of MDMA causes increased rCBF in the ventromedial and occipital cortex, inferior temporal lobe, and the cerebellum, with corresponding decreases in the motor and somatosensory cortex, temporal lobe, cingulate cortex, insula, and thalamus. For heavy MDMA users, global decreases in serotonin (5-HT) transporter densities are present primarily in the parieto-occipital, occipital, and sensory cortex, indicating serotonin neuronal injury.

2. SPECT studies also demonstrate decreases in 5-HT transporter densities, as well as changes in postsynaptic 5-HT receptors indicative of down-regulation in most cortical regions, except for up-regulation in the occipital cortex.

Female MDMA users may be more susceptible to its neurotoxic effects.

VI. OPIOIDS

The *DSM–IV–TR* category of opioids includes naturally occurring substances, such as opium and morphine, semisynthetic substances such as heroin, and synthetic substances such as methadone and codeine. Heroin is the most commonly abused opioid. Medical and psychosocial factors associated with heroin use disorder include history of head trauma, poor school or occupational performance, and hyperactivity or attention problems. Opioid use disorders are much less common than substance use disorders associated with alcohol or cannabis, although some evidence suggests that heroin use is increasing.

A. Intoxication and Withdrawal

Opioid intoxication is characterized by feelings of euphoria, impaired attention and judgment, lethargy, slurred speech, and constriction of the pupils. Dysphoria often follows the initial euphoria. Less common symptoms include hallucinations and delirium. Withdrawal symptoms from opioids such as heroin typically occur within 24 hours of cessation. During withdrawal, dysphoric feelings of anxiety and depression are common, as are physical symptoms such as malaise, nausea, dilation of pupils, sweating, insomnia, and muscle aches. Most withdrawal symptoms resolve within a week, but some can continue for several months (e.g., dysphoria).

B. Neuropsychological Findings

Studies evaluating residual cognitive deficits in long-term opioid abusers have reported conflicting results. Some studies have found significant differences between heroin abusers and control participants, whereas others report negligible differences. As with other drugs, cognitive effects of long-term heroin use are difficult to evaluate because heroin is infrequently the only substance used. Studies of cognitive abilities during acute administration of opioids are less equivocal and suggest that heroin impairs delayed verbal and visual recall, as well as some measures of attention and concentration. Some studies of current users also suggest impairment of fine motor speed, visuospatial and visuomotor abilities, attention, verbal fluency, memory, as well as diffuse cognitive impairment. Again, conclusions about severity of cognitive impairment are highly tentative because of methodological limitations. Deficits that persist following cessation of heroin use in chronic users may include impairment of executive functions and nonverbal reasoning. However, cognitive deficits noted in individuals with histories of chronic heroin use may reflect the influence of other drug use (such as cocaine and alcohol), childhood factors (attention-deficit/ hyperactivity disorder, poor education, etc.), or comorbid medical and psychiatric disorders.

C. Neuroimaging Findings

Neuroimaging studies of individuals who use opiods are limited.

1. No CT scan differences were present between abstinent heroin addicts and control participants. MRI studies of polysubstance abusers, primarily heroin and cocaine, indicate decreased volumes in prefrontal cortex bilaterally, with specific reductions in gray but not white matter (Kaufman, 2001).
2. Preliminary fMRI findings suggest global decreases in cerebral activation following acute heroin administration.
3. SPECT studies demonstrate diffuse decreases in cerebral blood flow in opioid-dependent individuals, particularly in the prefrontal cerebral cortex. These perfusion abnormalities persist during withdrawal. A right greater than left cerebral blood flow asymmetry appears reversed in opioid-dependent individuals. Individuals who use heroin and cocaine concurrently exhibit more perfusion abnormalities than individuals who abuse cocaine only. Perfusion abnormalities may be partially reversible with abstinence.
4. PET indicates decreased glucose metabolism in the whole brain after morphine administration.

D. HIV and Intravenous Drug Use

Because many individuals who use heroin or cocaine administer it intravenously, these individuals are at significantly higher risk for contracting HIV. Individuals with HIV exhibit a number of neurocognitive symptoms that range from mild to severe. As a result, it is important to consider the role HIV could play in the cognitive deficits of individuals with heroin or other intravenous drug use disorders.

VII. BENZODIAZEPINES

Benzodiazepines are classified as sedative/hypnotics. They are one of the most widely prescribed medications in the world and have a high potential for abuse because of their calming and sometimes euphoric effects. Benzodiazepines are more often abused by elderly individuals because they receive almost 40% of benzodiazepine prescriptions and benzodiazepines are often used to treat disorders that increase with age (e.g., insomnia). In addition to increased potential for abuse, benzodiazepines can produce more adverse reactions in elderly individuals. For some of these individuals, delirium can be induced by even small doses. Also, sudden discontinuance of benzodiazepines can cause confusion. Therefore, it is recommended that clinicians pay special attention to the assessment of benzodiazepine use disorders in the elderly.

A. Intoxication and Withdrawal

Physiological side effects of benzodiazepine use include ataxia, dysarthria, incoordination, diplopia, vertigo, and dizziness. Benzodiazepines also induce relaxation, calmness, euphoria, and, less frequently, feelings of hostility and depression. Long-term use of benzodiazepines can lead to development of tolerance to their therapeutic effects. Physiological dependence can appear after only a few days or weeks of use. Symptoms of withdrawal can include anxiety, irritability, insomnia, muscle twitching or aching, sweating, concentration difficulties, depression, and derealization. More severe withdrawal symptoms include seizures, delirium, and confusion. Withdrawal symptoms may be more intense when shorter acting benzodiazepines are discontinued. However, abrupt discontinuance of benzodiazepines with long half-lives (e.g., diazepam) can cause seizures within 3 days of discontinuation.

B. Neuropsychological Findings

Investigators have examined changes in cognitive function during benzodiazepine use. Short and long half-life benzodiazepines have been examined. Also, young and elderly samples have been compared. These studies suggest that elderly individuals tend to be more sensitive to the negative effects benzodiazepines can have on cognition. The acute cognitive effects of low-dose benzodiazepine administration appear negligible in younger individuals. For older individuals, even low doses can impair cognitive abilities. In addition, cognitive impairment increases as dose increases, and cognitive deficits become less pronounced with chronic administration. Few studies have examined residual cognitive deficits after benzodiazepine cessation.

1. **Acute effects**
   a. **Long-acting benzodiazepines** can cause impaired immediate and delayed verbal recall, impaired delayed visual recall, slowed reaction time and psychomotor performance, and increased intrusion errors on list-learning tasks.
   b. **Short-acting benzodiazepines** can cause impairment of attention and a variety of memory functions including explicit, implicit, working, and semantic memory.
2. **Benzodiazepine discontinuance.** Individuals with suspected or actual cognitive impairment exhibit improved cognitive functioning after discontinuing benzodiazepines.
3. **Long-term use.** Cognitive deficits noted in chronic long-term benzodiazepine users may not improve even after 6 months of abstinence. Deficient cognitive performance has been noted in middle-aged patients withdrawn from diazepam on tasks requiring verbal memory, visuospatial abilities, and psychomotor abilities (Tata, Rollings, Collins, Pickering, & Jacobson, 1994).

C. Neuroimaging Findings

1. CT studies suggest no structural differences between long-term users and control participants.
2. PET studies reveal benzodiazepine administration decreases regional cerebral glucose metabolism, with dose-dependent global and regional cerebral blood flow reductions in prefrontal, insular, cingulate, and thalamic regions. Acute alprazolam administration reduces whole brain cerebral blood flow by 25% to 30%.
3. fMRI studies reveal reduced cerebral blood volume in left caudate nucleus and inferior prefrontal cortex following acute administration of alprazolam in subjects with a family history of alcoholism and reduced cerebral blood volume in right inferior prefrontal and anterior cingulate in control participants (Kaufman, 2001).

VIII. POLYSUBSTANCE USE

The *DSM–IV–TR* includes a diagnosis of polysubstance dependence. To be assigned this diagnosis, the individual must have been repeatedly using three substances (excluding caffeine and nicotine) over a 1-year period and the combined symptomatology produced by this multiple substance use must meet criteria for substance dependence. However, to make this diagnosis, *none of the substances used can meet criteria for substance dependence in and of themselves.* A broader definition of polysubstance abuse would be abuse of or dependence on more than one substance. Using *DSM–IV–TR* nomenclature, multiple diagnoses of abuse and dependence would be given, rather than a single diagnosis of polysubstance dependence. Most studies examining neuropsychological concomitants of polysubstance use have used the broader (non-*DSM–IV–TR*) definition.

A. Intoxication and Withdrawal

Symptoms of intoxication and withdrawal reflect the specific symptoms associated with each substance. However, some substances can potentiate the effects of others. For example, using alcohol and benzodiazepines together will produce greater sedation and euphoria than use of either one. In assessing individuals who abuse multiple substances, consideration of substance interactions is warranted.

B. Neuropsychological Findings

Up to 50% of current polysubstance users exhibit cognitive deficits (Grant & Judd, 1976). However, because of the varying effects of different substances on cognitive function, it is difficult to make any definitive statements regarding the whole category of polysubstance users. In this group, cognitive deficits will represent not only the combined neurotoxic effects of the substances use disorders but also the unique comorbid factors associated with each substance (e.g., medical and psychiatric disorders). With this in mind, the literature examining individuals who have multiple substance use disorders suggests that the most consistently impaired cognitive abilities are (a) perceptuo-motor skills, (b) motor ability, (c) visuospatial abilities, (d) problem solving, and (e) visual and verbal memory.

C. Neuroimaging Findings

Neuroimaging abnormalities among individuals who abuse multiple substances are largely dependent on the substances they abuse. Multiple substance use can create a host of neurological abnormalities or, conversely, have relatively benign effects. When examining the neuroimaging studies of individuals with polysubstance use, the previous sections on imaging results may be helpful in determining the types of abnormalities that are likely to be present.

IX. CONCLUSION

There is growing recognition of the importance of evaluating cognitive deficits in individuals who have substance use disorders. At this time, most information is available on cognitive deficits associated with prolonged and excessive alcohol consumption. This literature suggests that some cognitive deficits do improve with abstinence while others do not. Also, the cognitive deficits associated with alcoholism are not always the result of the neurotoxic effects of alcohol; they are often produced by comorbid medical or psychiatric conditions or may reflect premorbid differences. It is also apparent that the neurocognitive deficits associated with other substances are also multiply determined. Because multiple factors produce neurocognitive deficits, determining the etiology of specific deficits in individuals with substance use disorders requires thorough physical, psychiatric, and psychosocial evaluation. Also, more information is needed before firm conclusions can be drawn about long-term cognitive effects of many illicit substances, although functional neuroimaging procedures are providing new insights into brain regions that are adversely affected. Finally, further investigation is necessary to determine how neurocognitive deficits interact with substance abuse treatments to produce positive or negative outcomes.

BIBLIOGRAPHY

Allen, D. N., Goldstein, G., & Aldarondo, F. (1999). Neurocognitive dysfunction in patients diagnosed with schizophrenia and alcoholism. *Neuropsychology, 13*S, 62–68.

Allen, D. N., Goldstein, G., & Seaton, B. E. (1997). Cognitive rehabilitation of chronic alcohol abusers. *Neuropsychology Review, 7*, 21–39.

Allen, D. N., & Landis, R. K. B. (1998). Substance abuse in elderly individuals. In P. D. Nussbaum (Ed.), *Handbook of neuropsychology and aging* (pp. 111–137). New York: Plenum.

American Psychiatric Association. (2000). *Diagnostic and statistical manual of mental disorders* (4th ed., text revision). Washington, DC: Author.

Bates, M. E., Bowden, S. C., & Barry, D. (2002). Neurocognitive impairment associated with alcohol use disorders:

Implications for treatment. *Experimental and Clinical Psychopharmacology, 10*, 193–212.

Cherpitel, C. J. (2002). Screening for alcohol problems in the U.S. general population: Comparison of the CAGE, RAPS4, and RAPS4-QF by gender, ethnicity, and service utilization—Rapid Alcohol Problems Screen. *Alcoholism: Clinical and Experimental Research, 26*, 1686–1691.

Grant, I., Gonzalez, R., Carey, C. L., Natarajan, L., & Wolfson, T. (2003). Non-acute (residual) neurocognitive effects of cannabis use: A meta-analytic study. *Journal of the International Neuropsychological Society, 9*, 679–689.

Grant, I., & Judd, L. (1976). Neuropsychological and EEG disturbances in polydrug users. *American Journal of Psychiatry, 133*, 1039–1042.

Heaton, R. K., Thompson, L. L., Nelson, L. M., Filley, C. M., & Franklin, G. M. (1990). Brief and intermediate length screening of neuropsychological impairment in multiple sclerosis. In S. M. Rao (Ed.), *Multiple sclerosis: A neuropsychological perspective* (pp. 149–160). New York: Oxford University Press.

Kalechstein, A. D., Newton, T. F., & Green, M. (2003). Methamphetamine dependence is associated with neurocognitive impairment in the initial phases of abstinence. *Journal of Neuropsychiatry and Clinical Neuroscience, 15*, 215–220.

Kaufman, M. J. (Ed.). (2001). *Brain imaging in substance abuse: Research, clinical, and forensic applications*. Totowa, NJ: Humana Press.

Landry, M. J. (2002). MDMA: A review of epidemiologic data. *Journal of Psychoactive Drugs, 34*, 163–169.

Lezak, M. D. (1995). *Neuropsychological assessment* (3rd ed.). New York: Oxford Press.

Munro, C. A., Saxton, J., & Butters, M. E. (2001). Alcohol dementia: "Cortical" or "subcortical" dementia. *Archives of Clinical Neuropsychology, 16*, 523–533.

Parrot, A. C. (2001). Human psychopharmacology of Ecstasy (MDMA): A review of 15 years of empirical research. *Human Psychopharmacology, 16*, 557–577.

Reitan, R. M., & Wolfson, D. (1993). *The Halstead–Reitan Neuropsychological Test Battery: Theory and clinical interpretation* (2nd ed.). Tucson, AZ: Neuropsychology Press.

Strickland, T. L., Mena, I., Villanueva-Meyer, J., Miller, B. L., Cummings, J., Mehringer, C. M., et al. (1993). Cerebral perfusion and neuropsychological consequences of chronic cocaine use. *Journal of Neuropsychiatry and Clinical Neurosciences, 5*, 419–427.

Sullivan, E. V., Rosenbloom, M. J., & Pfefferbaum, A. (2000). Pattern of motor and cognitive deficits in detoxified alcoholic men. *Alcoholism: Clinical and Experimental Research, 24,* 611–621.

Tarter, R. E., & Butters, M. (2001). Neuropsychological dysfunction due to liver disease. In R. E. Tarter, M. Butters, & S. R. Beers (Eds.), *Medical neuropsychology* (2nd ed., pp. 85–105). Dordrecht, the Netherlands: Kluwer Academic.

Tata, P. R., Rollings, J., Collins, M., Pickering, A., & Jacobson, R. R. (1994). Lack of cognitive recovery following withdrawal from long-term benzodiazepine use. *Psychological Medicine, 24,* 203–213.

Toomey, R., Lyons, M. J., Eisen, S. A., Hong, X., Sunanta, C., Seidman, L. J., et al. (2003). A twin study of the neuropsychological consequences of stimulant abuse. *Archives of General Psychiatry, 60,* 303–310.

Emotional Disorders Associated With Neurological Diseases

The assessment of emotional status in a patient with possible brain dysfunction is essential because of the potential influence that emotional status might have on the performance of tasks that are used to assess other functional strengths and limits. In addition, a patient's emotional status, in and of itself, may be of neurodiagnostic significance. There has been a tremendous increase in the basic and clinical research on the neuroscience of emotion since the first edition of this book was published in 1997. Despite this research proliferation, we still do not have a completely adequate arsenal of reliable, valid, commercially available instruments at our disposal to test the various aspects of emotion that are of potential neuropsychological significance. However, options for neuropsychologists are more favorable now than in the past. In fact, Borod (2000) has edited an excellent book on the neuropsychology of emotion. One chapter is particularly relevant to the goal of this book in that it critically evaluates many of the currently available instruments intended to evaluate the various aspects of emotional processing (Borod, Tabert, Santschi, & Strauss, 2000). The reader interested in exploring the issue of the neuropsychology of emotion, in general, and assessment issues, in particular, in greater depth than is possible in a pocket handbook would do well to read Borod's text.

Because emotional alterations can be associated with a wide range of neurological disorders, only neurological disorders for which a component of emotion is a particularly striking feature of symptom presentation are discussed here. Reference is made to those investigators who have developed or described methods of emotion evaluation that have been applied specifically to well-defined neurological groups.

I. DEFINITION OF THE EMOTIONAL PROBLEM

A. Is It a Problem of Affect, Emotion, or Mood?

The first challenge one faces in an attempt to assess emotions is related to the issue of complexity of the construct itself. Theorists and researchers have parsed the general construct of emotion in a number of ways. At the most molar level, a potentially useful heuristic would be to consider whether the problem one is observing (or the patient is reporting) is a matter of an alteration in affect, emotion, or mood.

Affect is considered to be a fundamental, irreducible emotional feeling state. The experience of affect is, by definition, subjective. At the most basic level, affect is experienced as either a pleasant or an unpleasant feeling state. Affect is generally regarded as temporally limited, that is, as a fleeting or momentary emotional state.

Emotion lends itself to more definitional variability. Despite disagreements about the range and types of experiences that should be included in a definition of emotion, most investigators are in general agreement that emotions are object focused. That is, the experience and expression of an emotion are related to some specific environmental event or cognitive representation of an event. Emotions function to signal the presence of a personally relevant environmental situation and to prepare the person for some specific action. Whereas an affective experience is always a private event, an emotion is an observable, "public" event (although behavioral expression can be suppressed or masked). It is generally accepted that there is a limited, finite number of core or basic emotions. A representative listing of basic emotions, each of which has unique behavioral qualities such as characteristic facial expressions, include **happiness–joy, sadness, fear, anger, disgust,** and more equivocally, **surprise.** There is strong empirical evidence that these are universally experienced and recognized emotions. More complex emotions, such as jealousy or guilt, are thought to be based on differing combinations of basic emotions. A relatively prolonged sequence of transactions between an individual and an environmental event of particular salience or relevance is described as an **emotional sequence.** Regardless of the complexity of the feeling state or environmental condition, the essential, defining feature of an emotion is rooted in its properties as a signal of a specific event that requires a specific action.

Mood is defined as a more generalized, diffuse, feeling state that has no specific object or referent associated with its experience. Whereas individuals can generally identify the object of their emotional state (e.g., one feels angry at someone or happy about something), they are hard-pressed to identify the specific reason for a mood state (why one is in an angry mood or a happy mood). In addition, a mood state is generally considered more enduring than either an affective or an emotional state. There is much less empirical investigation reported on mood states, especially compared with the literature on emotions. Some research indicates that moods can function to moderate either an emotional experience or an affective appraisal of specific environmental events. For example, a person may be more likely to experience anger if his or her mood is depressed. Similarly, a person is more likely to attend to the more unpleasant aspects of the environment during a depressed mood.

B. Is It a Problem of Perception, Expression, or Experience?

This characterization, called **mode of processing**, also refers to the nature of the demand placed on the patient during a structured interaction with the examiner. That is, what is required of the patient during a particular task? The majority of clinical research has focused on the perception and expression of emotion. A somewhat separate body of literature has focused on the experience of emotion, which includes the experience of basic emotions as well as of mood states.

C. What Is the Channel of Communication?

Channel of communication refers to the sensorimotor system used to display the target emotion. The preponderance of clinical investigation has focused on four communication channels:
- facial display of emotion,
- vocal intonation of emotion (emotional prosody),
- gestures of emotion, and
- speech content (lexicon of emotion words).

II. DEVELOPMENT OF DISRUPTIONS IN EMOTIONAL FUNCTIONING

The disruption of emotional functioning is not specific to a particular neurological disorder. Emotional dysfunction can occur in association with acute focal conditions such as cerebrovascular accidents (CVAs), acute diffuse disorders such as traumatic brain injury (TBI), progressive focal disorders such as localized tumors, or progressive neural degenerative disorders such as senile dementia of the Alzheimer's type (SDAT) or Huntington's disease (HD).

In contrast to the extensive literature on cognitive functioning, there is much less information regarding the course of emotion symptoms associated with the onset of neurological disorders. The literature that does exist, however, suggests that symptom course may be related to mode of emotional processing. For example, alterations in the perception of emotion may follow a course more similar to that seen for cognitive processing such as perceptual processing of nonemotional stimuli or language processing. Expression and experience of emotion, however, may exhibit a more complex pattern of presentation. Because environmental conditions play a larger role in the elicitation of emotional expression and probably emotional experience, there is more variability in their manifestation. The relative contribution of neurological and environmental factors in the expression and experience of emotions remains an unresolved issue.

III. VARIANTS OF EMOTIONAL DYSFUNCTION

Emotional valence (i.e., positive emotions vs. negative emotions) may be of lateralizing significance, although there is no clear consensus on this issue at present. The right hemisphere may be specialized for the expression and experience of negative emotion, whereas the left hemisphere may be specialized for the expression and experience of positive emotion. Models of contralateral neural inhibition have been proposed to account for the expression of specific emotions in the presence of lateralized neurological dysfunction. Thus, a left-hemisphere lesion may lead to the expression or experience of a negative emotional state such as depression through the release of contralateral inhibition of right-hemisphere (i.e., negative emotion) processes. An alternative view of hemisphere-specific emotional expression suggests that lateralized emotional valence can best be understood from the perspective of disruptions in ipsilateral,

Table 28.1. Emphasis of Research on Emotional Dysfunction

Disorder	Perception	Expression	Experience
Alzheimer's disease	+++	+	+
Cerebrovascular accident	+++	+++	+++
HIV	0	+	+++
Huntington's disease	++	+	0
Parkinson's disease	+++	++	++
Traumatic brain injury	+	+++	++

Note. 0 = none; + = minor emphasis; ++ = moderate emphasis; +++ = major emphasis.

cortical–subcortical neural processes. Still others have suggested that hemispheric asymmetries in emotional expression may be associated with motivational factors such as approach or withdrawal motives. Interested readers are referred to Gainotti (2000) for a more thorough discussion of this issue. Finally, some researchers suggest that these asymmetries in emotional valence may extend to *perception* of emotions as well, although there is even more debate about the lateralized specialization for emotional valence for this mode of processing.

IV. NEUROPATHOLOGICAL CORRELATES OF DYSFUNCTION IN THE PERCEPTION, EXPRESSION, AND EXPERIENCE OF EMOTION

This section is organized by mode of processing. For each mode of processing (perception, expression, and experience), the most commonly reported site(s) of neuroanatomical dysfunction is presented. Each subsection concludes with a list of the neurodiagnostic groups that have reportedly demonstrated impairment within that mode of processing. Diagnostic groups that have not been reported in the literature to have been specifically evaluated for performance on that particular dimension of emotion are not included. The purpose of offering a brief listing of neurodiagnostic groups is to emphasize the range of neurological disorders that can present with symptoms of emotional disruption, not to provide an exhaustive list of all possible neurological disorders that might exhibit a particular emotional symptom. Table 28.1 represents an overview of the research that has been published since 1999 that included at least one empirical measure of the perception, expression, or experience of emotion. Although not exhaustive, the table provides a reasonable view of the relative emphasis of the emotion research for different diagnostic groups. For example, one can find numerous studies on the perception, expression, and experience of emotion among CVA patients. The research with HIV patients, in contrast, has focused on the experience of emotion with virtually no reported research on the effect of HIV on the perception of emotion. Regardless of diagnostic group, few studies have measured perception, expression, and experience in the same patients. This remains a limitation of the clinical research on emotion.

A. Perception of Emotion

Focal lesions of the right hemisphere, particularly the right posterior region, have been most consistently associated with deficits in the perception of emotion for facial, prosodic, and lexical stimuli. However, mode of response may interact with side of lesion. For example, facial emotion **matching** deficits have been associated with right-hemisphere lesions, whereas facial emotion **naming** deficits have been associated with both right- and left-hemisphere focal lesions.

Patients with nonfocal or multifocal lesions can also be impaired in the perception of emotion with less association with side or site of lesion. For example, among TBI patients with bilateral lesions, the anterior–posterior axis does not appear to be related to performance, although this dimension has been shown to be related to performance among TBI patients without bilateral damage.

Individuals with the following diagnoses have demonstrated impaired performance on a variety of emotion perception tasks:

- cerebrovascular accidents (right and, less commonly, left),
- traumatic brain injury,
- senile dementia of the Alzheimer type,
- Parkinson's disease,
- Huntington's disease, and
- complex-partial seizures (temporal lobe epilepsy).

B. Expression of Emotion

1. STRUCTURED CONDITIONS

Lesions of the right hemisphere, particularly the right anterior region, have been associated with impaired expression of basic emotions under both posed (e.g., requiring the patient to demonstrate a target emotion) and spontaneous but structured (e.g., during a structured or semistructured interview) conditions. Expressions are usually diminished in intensity, frequency, or accuracy.

The following neurological disorders have been reported to display disruptions in the expression of emotion under structured or posed conditions:

- cerebrovascular accidents,
- traumatic brain injury, and
- Parkinson's disease (impaired facial expression but not prosody).

2. UNSTRUCTURED CONDITIONS

Disruptions in the spontaneous expression of emotion under unstructured conditions have been identified with greater variety in site of neuropathology, although lesions along the frontolimbic pathways are most frequently reported.

- Diminished emotional expression (e.g., apathy and indifference) are most commonly associated with dorsolateral frontal lesions.
- Excessive emotional expression (e.g., affective lability, impulsiveness, irritability) have been associated with orbitofrontal lesions.
- Spontaneous, unprovoked, intense emotional expression (specifically pathological laughing or crying) has been associated with subcortical lesions, particularly those that encroach the corticobulbar tracts. Such states have also been reported among individuals with lesions in virtually any brain region. The particular emotion expressed may be of lateralizing significance as there have been reports of "silent" lesions of the right hemisphere eliciting pathological laughing and "silent" lesions of the left hemisphere eliciting pathological crying. This should not be considered pathognomic, however.
- Unprovoked expression of fear or intense anxiety, with or without the concomitant subjective experience, has also been reported among some individuals with temporal lobe epilepsy. However, positive emotional expressions (gelastic seizures) are rarely reported as part of the ictus of a temporal lobe seizure.

Disruption in the expression of emotion under unstructured or spontaneous conditions has been reported for the disorders in the list that follows. A brief description of the most frequently reported manifestations of emotional expression is included.

- focal lesions (e.g., CVA, tumor): diminished expression, dorsolateral frontal lesions and exaggerated expression, orbitofrontal lesions;
- traumatic brain injury: irritability or anger;
- Parkinson's disease: masked facies is a hallmark of this disorder;
- Huntington's disease: apathy, indifference, outbursts of anger;
- senile dementia of the Alzheimer type: coarseness and shallowness of emotional expression; and
- temporal lobe epilepsy: ictal fear or anxiety and, more rarely, ictal laughter.

C. Experience of Emotion

Disruption in mood state is the most commonly reported aspect of dysfunction in emotional experience among brain-injured individuals. Psychiatric classification of affective disorders and self-report measures of specific mood states (e.g., depression, anxiety, anger inventories) generally do not distinguish specifically between affective, emotional, and mood states. These approaches, nonetheless, form the basis of the understanding of disruptions in emotional experience following brain injury. An overview of such states is provided in this section.

1. DEPRESSION

Depression is the most frequently cited disruption in mood state following any type of brain insult. Usually the depression is associated with left anterior or right posterior lesions, the latter being more frequently reported among patients with a family history of affective illness. The specific symptoms present in clinical depression may vary by hemisphere of lesion; however, this is an extremely complex issue that is not yet clearly resolved. The following is a partial list of neurodiagnostic groups that have been reported to experience depressed mood:

- cerebrovascular accidents,
- tumors,
- traumatic brain injury,
- senile dementia of the Alzheimer type,
- Parkinson's disease,
- Huntington's disease,
- progressive supranuclear palsy, and
- multiple sclerosis.

2. EUPHORIA

Excessively positive emotional experiences, ranging from mild euphoria to frank mania, have been reported following brain insult. Disruptions in right-hemisphere processing, particularly within the right orbitofrontal or basotemporal regions, have been associated with euphoric and manic states. Indifference to one's medical condition and associated life circumstances can be a concomitant feature. Euphoric reactions have been reported in the following diagnostic groups:

- cerebrovascular accidents (right hemisphere),
- traumatic brain injury,
- Huntington's disease, and
- multiple sclerosis.

3. ANXIETY

Ranging from mild apprehension to major fear reaction and panic episodes, anxiety has also been reported as a sequelae of brain insult. Both cortical and subcortical structures have been implicated, including lesions in the left dorsolateral cortical regions and discharging lesions (i.e., seizures) in the amygdala and anterior cingulate cortex. The amygdala is purported to be a particularly critical structure in the process of fear conditioning. Anxiety reactions have been reported for the following diagnostic groups:

- cerebrovascular accidents,
- traumatic brain injury,
- seizure disorders, and
- senile dementia of the Alzheimer type.

V. COMPETING DIAGNOSES THAT MUST BE RULED OUT

In the case of emotional disruption following brain injury, the most obvious competing diagnoses are associated with psychiatric disorders. Without entering into the fray of the neurobiological basis of psychiatric disorders, neuropsychologists are often faced with the task of determining if the patient is experiencing a primary psychiatric disorder or is experiencing psychiatric symptoms that are the direct result, or an associated feature, of an acquired brain disorder. This becomes particularly important because characteristic patterns of cognitive deficit can be associated with psychiatric disorders in and of themselves, such as a dementia-like presentation among some clinically depressed elderly patients (see chap. 9, this volume). In addition, comorbid psychiatric and neurological disorders can yield more pronounced cognitive deficits, and perhaps different patterns of cognitive deficit, than would be expected on the basis of the presence of a given neurological disorder by itself. This can result in errors in diagnosis as well as overestimation of the severity of cognitive sequelae associated with neurological insult.

Both depression and schizophrenia (per criteria of the American Psychiatric Association's [2000] *Diagnostic and Statistical Manual of Mental Disorder, Fourth Edition, Text Revision* [*DSM–IV–TR*]) have also been associated with impairment on direct measures of emotion perception. Patients with schizophrenia have been reported to be more broadly and severely impaired, whereas depressed patients reportedly have greater difficulty with emotion naming as opposed to emotion matching. In addition, depressed groups may overidentify emotional stimuli as representing a sad emotion and be less likely to correctly identify happy emotional stimuli.

VI. THE NEUROPSYCHOLOGICAL EVALUATION OF EMOTIONAL DYSFUNCTION

A. Areas of Emphasis

The logic of examining a patient for evidence of disruptions in emotional functioning should follow the logic of any good neuropsychological examination. A clinical screening of the perception, expression, and experience of emotion can be incorporated into any neuropsychological exam with minimal additional time burden. Specifically, in the clinical interview, the examiner should directly inquire about changes in emotion. Third-party report of alterations in general mood, as well as emotional reactions to specific events, should be pursued.

Systematic evaluation of all aspects of emotional functioning is particularly important in any situation in which there has been an abrupt change in mood or behavior, especially if there is no prior history of such behavior. Similarly, uncooperative or oppositional patients who are referred for evaluation warrant particular attention, because such behavior may reflect impaired functioning in one or more of the emotional domains. Systematic evaluation is critical because emotional processes are interrelated in complex ways. For example, without careful assessment, it is impossible to know if an individual with intermittent angry outbursts is having difficulty with the modulation of emotional expression, is responding appropriately to a misperception of the emotional context of the situation, or is manifesting features of a dysfunctional mood state (e.g., depression).

B. Methods of Assessment: Response and Stimulus Alternatives

The following is an overview of the various methods that have been used in the clinical and clinical research literature to evaluate the perception, expression, and experience of emotion, with a focus first on the types of responses typically required of the patient, followed by the kinds of stimuli that are most often used. Table 28.2 provides a listing of the more frequently cited instruments that use standardized stimuli to tap one or more of the emotion domains.

1. PERCEPTION OF EMOTION

a. Response alternatives

When choosing the method of response, it is important to keep in mind that there have been some clinical research reports indicating that response mode can influence performance at least for different focal lesion groups. For example, both right- and left-hemisphere focal lesion groups have been reported to be equally impaired when naming the emotion of a facial display, whereas right focal lesion groups have been reported to perform more poorly than left focal lesion groups when matching facial displays (e.g., Blonder, Bowers, & Heilman, 1991).

Naming emotional stimuli. Emotion naming is generally conducted using a multiple-choice format in which several, if not all, of the names of the basic emotions are printed in a vertical array on a cue card. The patient is asked to either state or point to the name that corresponds to a displayed emotional stimulus. Given the obvious language demands associated with this response mode, it is recommended that the examiner confirm that the patient can read, name, and point to the response options prior to presenting any emotion stimuli.

Identifying named emotions. An array depicting several different emotions is presented either simultaneously (e.g., a vertical array of four faces, each depicting a different emotion) or sequentially (e.g., the repetition of a sentence expressing the prosody associated with different emotions). The patient is asked to identify a target emotion that has been specified by the examiner (e.g., "Point to the happy face"; "Raise your hand when you hear the sentence spoken in a sad tone of voice").

Table 28.2. Selected Measures of Emotional Perception, Expression, or Experience

Instrument and Author(s)	Perception		Expression			
	Face	Voice	Face	Voice	Behavior	Experience
Aprosodia Battery (Ross, 1981)	+			+		
Battery of Emotional Expression and Comprehension (Chancelliere & Kertesz, 1990)		+	+			
Carolina Older Adults Test of Nonverbal Communication (Spell & Frank, 2000)	+	+				
Courtauld Emotional Control Scales (Watson & Greer, 1983)					+	+
Diagnostic Analysis of Nonverbal Accuracy 2 (Nowicki & Duke, 1994)	+	+				
DANVA FACES 2 (Nowicki & Carton, 1993)	+					
Florida Affect Battery (Bowers et al., 1999)	+	+				
New York Emotion Battery (Borod, 2000)	+	+		+		+
Neurobehavioral Rating Scale—Revised (McCauley et al., 2001)					+	+
Neuropsychological Behavior and Affect Profile (Nelson et al., 1989)					+	+
Pictures of Facial Affect (Ekman & Friesen, 1976)	+					
Toronto Alexithymia Scale (Bagby et al., 1994)					+	+

Matching emotion stimuli. This task is loosely analogous to a discrimination procedure in which pairs of emotion stimuli are presented either simultaneously or sequentially and the patient is asked to indicate only if the pair represents the same emotion or different emotions. This procedure has been most often reported for use with facial and prosodic stimuli. Some cross-modality studies have also been reported (e.g., a face depicting anger is displayed along with an audiotape of a sentence spoken in a fearful tone).

b. Types of stimuli

Facial display. Slides of adult men and women depicting basic emotions (happy, sad, fear, anger, surprise, disgust, neutral) are presented to the patient, who is expected to provide a response that identifies the depicted emotion. Slides are commercially available (e.g., Ekman & Friesen, 1976) with norms for each slide. Given the large number of slides per emotion, it is fairly easy to select slides that have been accurately identified by at least 80% of non-brain-damaged individuals.

Videos of adult men and women displaying basic emotions have also been developed. These are usually developed for use within specific research laboratories. An advantage of video stimuli is its ecological validity, allowing the patient to observe an emotion as it unfolds. Equipment constraints and relative difficulty obtaining stimulus tapes reduce the clinical utility of video stimuli.

Bedside examination can be conducted by a clinician displaying the facial expression associated with each of the basic emotions. This approach requires practice on the part of the clinician. It is useful to obtain independent ratings of facial displays by colleagues before use with patients.

Regardless of the type of stimulus used, multiple trials (at least five) of several different emotions are generally presented to the patient to obtain sufficient sampling of patient performance for meaningful interpretation. O'Sullivan (1982) has reviewed a number of tests, both static and video, that have been developed to measure perception of facial emotion.

Vocal intonation. Audiotapes of adult men and women reciting sentences that are neutral in emotional content (e.g., "The book is on the desk") using the emotional expression, or prosody, associated with basic emotions (happy, sad, fear, anger, surprise, disgust, neutral) are used to assess a patient's ability to comprehend vocal intonation.

Bedside examination can be accomplished using the same procedure. Ross (1981) provided an excellent description of how to conduct a bedside examination of emotion prosody. As recommended with facial stimuli, multiple trials per emotion should be presented.

Gestures. Bedside examination is the most typical procedure reported for the evaluation of emotional gesturing. The clinician pantomimes basic emotions (happiness, sadness, fear, anger, surprise, disgust) in the presence of the patient. Ross (1981) provided a description of this procedure and specifically recommended that emotional gesturing be evaluated separately from emotional prosody.

Examination of emotional gestures has been incorporated into videos of emotional communication. For example, the Profile of Nonverbal Sensitivity (PONS; Rosenthal, Hall, DiMatteo, Rogers, & Archer, 1979) includes gestures as a separate dimension of emotional communication. However, the PONS was not initially developed for use with neurological patients and can be difficult for some patients to complete as the segments are relatively short (about 2 seconds) and are not intended to display single, basic emotions.

Speech content (lexicon). Emotion words that are semantically related to the basic emotions (e.g., *terror* and *dread* for the basic emotion fear) are presented to the patient. Emotion words and nonemotion words of similar frequency of use in the language of examination are typical stimuli for evaluating emotion lexicon. Words are often selected from a general word source that also provides information about frequency of use, such as the Thorndike and Lorge (1944) list. Any of the emotion responses previously described could be used to assess emotion lexicon integrity.

Short emotion sentences are presented to the patient that infer a basic emotion either by the use of an emotion word in the sentence (e.g., "He was elated by his victory") or by context alone (e.g., "His eyes were full of tears as he left the funeral"). In the assessment of lexicon, stimuli can be presented in a written format, by audiotape, or by using a combination of the two methods. Borod, Andelman, Obler, Tweedy, and Welkowitz (1992) have provided a detailed description of the methodologies associated with the evaluation of emotion words and emotion sentences. In addition, Ross, Thompson, and Yenkosky (1997) have described a more structured aprosody battery.

2. EXPRESSION OF EMOTION

a. Response alternatives

Posed responses are the channel-specific actions produced by the patient in response to a specific direction by the examiner (e.g., "Make a happy face"; "Make a face that looks like the one I am making"). Posed responses are judged primarily for accuracy. Spontaneous responses are generally multichannel actions produced by the patient that have been elicited by either a structured or an unstructured stimulus condition. Spontaneous responses to structured stimuli are judged for both accuracy and frequency, whereas spontaneous responses to unstructured stimuli are often judged for accuracy, frequency, and appropriateness to the situation.

Regardless of the type of stimulus condition or response alternative used, it is optimal to videotape the patient's responses and to have independent judges rate the dimensions of interest. However, for clinical purposes, the examiner can (with practice) conduct clinically useful ratings during the examination. Questionnaires have also been developed to examine a broader range of behavioral disruptions often associated with brain dysfunction, such as the Neurobehavioral Rating Scale (McCauley, Levin, & Vanier, 2001) and the Brief Neuropsychological Rating Scale (Nelson et al., 1989). Often the measures created specifically for use with brain-injured patients include both self-report and informant rating versions.

b. Stimulus conditions

In general, the examiner attempts to create a condition that will elicit an emotional response from the patient. This can be accomplished using a relatively structured or unstructured format. Structured conditions include direct commands (e.g., "Show me an angry face"), displays of basic emotions (e.g., "Make a face like the person in the picture"), or emotion-eliciting stimuli (e.g., a picture or video of a surgical procedure). An array of emotion-eliciting pictures has been developed and normed by the University of Florida emotion and attention research group (Center for the Psychophysiological Study of Emotion and Attention, 1994). In contrast to structured stimulus conditions, unstructured conditions are not intended to directly or discretely elicit a particular emotion. Clinical observations during an interview or during a patient activity not directed by the examiner are most representative of this approach.

3. EXPERIENCE OF EMOTION

There is considerably less systematic information in the neuropsychological literature on the experience of emotion as compared with the literature on the perception and expression of emotion. The concept of being unable to identify or describe one's feeling has been reported primarily in the psychiatric literature as **alexithymia**. This concept is gaining increased attention in the neurological and neuropsychological literature, and its usefulness for elucidating neurologically relevant problems in the experience of emotion is beginning to be established (Berthoz et al., 2002). There are valid and reliable measures of alexithymia (e.g., Bagby, Parker, & Taylor, 1994).

Although there are specific assessment instruments that have been developed to assess the experience of emotion, few have been used with neurological groups. For example, Lang (1980) described a procedure using a series of manikin drawings that depict affective valence (pleasant to unpleasant) and affective arousal (calm to intensely aroused). Similarly, visual analog scales have been applied to the self-rating of mood states (Cowdrey, Gardner, O'Leary, Leibenluft, & Rubinow, 1991). Such scales can be either bipolar or unipolar. Bipolar scales include opposing mood states represented pictorially at the anchor points of a line. A vertical display is typically used to reduce the potential biasing effects of visual neglect or visual field cuts on self-ratings of mood. The patient indicates, by pointing or marking with a pencil, the position along the line that best represents his or her current mood state. Conversely, single mood state scales use a "thermometer" approach of measurement. A single mood is represented pictorially at the base with a vertical line extending up the page. The patient represents the degree or magnitude of that feeling state along the vertical line. Responses can be quantified by measuring the distance from the center (neutral response) of bipolar scales or from the base of unipolar scales. Such instruments are particularly useful when assessing individuals with language disorders.

Mood states also continue to be evaluated using the self-report and clinical rating instruments commonly used with non-neurologically impaired groups (e.g., Beck Depression Inventory, Hamilton Rating Scale, and State–Trait Anxiety Inventory). At best, they are imperfect measures of the putative mood state when used with neurologically impaired groups and should be interpreted with caution.

Despite the limited research in this area, the experience of emotion is an important dimension to include in a comprehensive evaluation of the emotional status of a neurological patient. Anecdotal reports have indicated that dissociation can occur between the expression and experience of emotion among some clinical groups. For example, a patient may not display an emotion such as anger when provoked but may report an intense feeling of anger associated with the situation. Conversely, a clinician may observe an intense expression of emotion with no concomitant report of subjective emotional experience, as has been described in cases of pathological laughter or pathological crying. Such dissociations may be of diagnostic significance.

VII. CONCLUSION

It is difficult to convey within a guidebook format the full richness and complexity of the construct of emotion as it applies to neuropsychological assessment and its relevance to central nervous system disease. This chapter is intended to provide an introduction to this topic, and the interested reader will easily find a rich literature of additional readings on this topic. The assessment of emotional perception and expression is an important component of any comprehensive neuropsychological examination, and this chapter has described the methods by which this is accomplished.

BIBLIOGRAPHY

American Psychiatric Association. (2000). *Diagnostic and statistical manual of mental disorders* (4th ed., text revision). Washington, DC: Author.

Bagby, R. M., Parker, J. D. A., & Taylor, G. J. (1994). The twenty-item Toronto Alexithymia Scale—I: Item selection and cross-validation of the factor structure. *Journal of Psychosomatic Research, 38*, 23–32.

Berthoz, S., Artiges, E., Van de Moortele, P.-F., Poline, J.-B., Rouquette, S., Consoli, S. M., & Martinot, J.-L. (2002). Effect of impaired recognition and expression of emotions on fronto-cingulate cortices: An fMRI study of men with alexithymia. *American Journal of Psychiatry, 159*, 961–967.

Blonder, L. X., Bowers, D., & Heilman, K. M. (1991). The role of the right hemisphere in emotional communication. *Brain, 114*, 1115–1127.

Borod, J. C. (2000). *The neuropsychology of emotion.* New York: Oxford University Press.

Borod, J. C., Andelman, F., Obler, L. K., Tweedy, J. R., & Welkowitz, J. (1992). Right hemisphere specialization for the identification of emotional words and sentences: Evidence from stroke patients. *Neuropsychologia, 30*, 827–844.

Borod, J. C., Tabert, M. H., Santschi, C., & Strauss, E. H. (2000). Neuropsychological assessment of emotional processing in brain-damaged patients. In J. C. Borod (Ed.), *The neuropsychology of emotion* (pp. 80–105). New York: Oxford University Press.

Bowers, D., Blonder, L. X., & Heilman, K. M. (1999). *Florida Affect Battery: A manual.* Gainesville: University of Florida Press.

Center for the Psychophysiological Study of Emotion and Attention. (1994). *The International Affective Picture System* [Photographic slides]. Gainesville: University of Florida, Center for Research in Psychophysiology.

Chancelliere, A. E. B., & Kertesz, A. (1990). Lesion localization in acquired deficits of emotional expression and comprehension. *Brain and Cognition, 13*, 133–147.

Cowdry, R. W., Gardner, D. L., O'Leary, K. M., Leibenluft, E., & Rubinow, D. R. (1991). Mood variability: A study of four groups. *American Journal of Psychiatry, 148*, 1505–1511.

Ekman, P., & Friesen, W. V. (1976). *Pictures of facial affect.* Palo Alto, CA: Consulting Psychologists Press.

Gainotti, G. (2000). Neuropsychological theories of emotion. In J. C. Borod (Ed.), *The neuropsychology of emotion* (pp. 214–236). New York: Oxford University Press.

Lang, P. J. (1980). Behavioral treatment and bio-behavioral assessment: Computer applications. In J. B. Sidowski, J. H. Johnson, & T. A. Williams (Eds.), *Technology in mental health care delivery systems* (pp. 119–137). Norwood, NJ: Ablex.

McCauley, S. R., Levin, H. S., & Vanier, M. (2001). The Neurobehavioral Rating Scale—Revised: Sensitivity and validity in closed head injury. *Journal of Neurology, Neurosurgery and Psychiatry, 71*, 643–651.

Nelson, L. D., Satz, P., Mitrushina, M., van Gorp, W., Cichetti, D., Lewis, R., & Van Lancker, D. (1989). Development and validation of the Neuropsychology Behavior and Affect Profile. *Psychological Assessment, 1*, 266–272.

Nowicki, S., Jr., & Carton, J. (1993). The measurement of emotional intensity from facial expressions: The DANVA FACES 2. *Journal of Social Psychology, 133*, 749–750.

Nowicki, S., Jr., & Duke, M. P. (1994). Individual differences in the nonverbal communication of affect: The Diagnostic Analysis of Nonverbal Accuracy Scale. *Journal of Nonverbal Behavior, 18*, 9–35.

O'Sullivan, M. (1982). Measuring the ability to recognize facial expressions of emotion. In P. Ekman (Ed.), *Emotion in the human face* (2nd ed., pp. 281–317). New York: Cambridge University Press.

Rosenthal, R., Hall, J. A., DiMatteo, M. R., Rogers, P. L., & Archer, D. (1979). *Sensitivity to nonverbal communication: The PONS test.* Baltimore: Johns Hopkins University Press.

Ross, E. D. (1981). The aprosodias: Functional–anatomic organization of the affective components of language in the right hemisphere. *Archives of Neurology, 38*, 561–569.

Ross, E. D., Thompson, R. D., & Yenkosky, J. (1997). Lateralization of affective prosody in brain and the callosal integration of hemispheric language functions. *Brain and Language, 56*, 27–54.

Spell, L. H., & Frank, E. (2000). Recognition of nonverbal communication of affect following traumatic brain injury. *Journal of Nonverbal Behavior, 24*, 285–300.

Thorndike, E. L., & Lorge, I. (1944). *The teacher's word book of 30,000 words*. New York: Bureau of Publications, Teachers College.

Watson, M., & Greer, S. (1983). Development of a questionnaire measure of emotional control. *Journal of Psychosomatic Research, 27*, 299–305.

Selective Listing of Medical Record Abbreviations

a	arterial
Aa	alveolar/arterial
a̅a̅	of each
abd	abdomen
ABG	arterial blood gas
abn	abnormal
ac	before meals
A/C	assist control
ACE	angiotensin-converting enzyme; adrenocortical extract
ACLS	advanced cardiovascular life support
ACT	activated clotting time
ACTH	adrenocorticotropic hormone
ADH	antidiuretic hormone
ADL	activities of daily living
ad lib	as desired, freely
adm	admission
AF	atrial fibrillation
AIDS	acquired immunodeficiency syndrome
AJ	ankle jerk
AKA	above-knee amputation
AL	arterial line
alb	albumin
ALL	acute lymphoblasic leukemia

ALS	amyotrophic lateral sclerosis
AM	morning
AMA	against medical advice
AMI	acute myocardial infarction
AML	acute myelogenous leukemia
amp	ampule
AMP	adenosine monophosphate
amt	amount
amy	amylase
ANA	antinuclear antibody
ANLL	acute nonlymphocytic leukemia
AODM	adult-onset diabetes mellitus
AOP	aortic pressure
AP	anteroposterior
appt	appointment
aq	water
ARC	AIDS-related complex
ARDS	acute respiratory distress syndrome
ARF	acute renal failure
ARM	arterial rupture of membranes
ART	assessment, review, and treatment
AS	atriosystolic; aortic stenosis
asa	aspirin
ASHD	arteriosclerotic heart disease
at fib	atrial fibrillation
ATC	around the clock
ATN	acute tubular necrosis
AV	arteriovenous; atrioventricular
AVM	arteriovenous malformation
B	black
ba	barium
BBB	blood-brain barrier; bundle branch block
BC	blood culture
BCP	birth control pill
BE	barium enema
BEE	basal energy expenditure
bid	two times per day
bilat	bilateral
bili	bilirubin
BKA	below-knee amputation
Bl s	blood sugar
BM	bowel movement
BMR	basal metabolic rate
BP	blood pressure
BPH	benign prostatic hypertrophy
bpm	beats per minute

BR	bed rest
BRP	bathroom privileges
BS or bs	breath sounds
BSA	body surface area
BSO	bilateral salpingo-oophorectomy
BTL	bilateral tubal ligation
BUN	blood urea nitrogen
BW	body weight
Bx	biopsy
$\bar{c}$	with
C	centigrade
Ca	cancer
Ca^{+2}	calcium
CAB	coronary artery bypass
CABG	coronary artery bypass graft
CAD	coronary artery disease
cal	calorie
cap	capsule
CAT	computerized axial tomography
cath	catheterization
CBC	complete blood cell count
CBD	common bile duct
cc	cubic centimeter
CC	chief complaint
CCr	creatine clearance
CCU	coronary care unit
CD4	helper-inducer T cells
CD8	suppressor-cytotoxic T cells
CEA	carcinoembryonic antigen
CF	complement fixation; conversion factor
CHD	congenital heart disease
CHF	congestive heart failure
cho	carbohydrate
CI	cardiac index
CK	creatine kinase
CK-MB	creatine kinase, myocardial band
cl	clear
Cl^-	chloride
CLL	chronic lymphocytic leukemia
cm	centimeter
CM	costal margin
CNS	central nervous system
CO	cardiac output; carbon monoxide
c/o	complains of
CO_2	carbon dioxide
CoA	coenzyme A

conc	concentrate
COPD	chronic obstructive pulmonary disease
CPAP	continuous positive airway pressure
CPK	creatine phosphokinase
CPR	cardiopulmonary resuscitation
cps	cycles per second
Cr	creatinine
CR	cardiorespiratory
CRH	corticotropin-releasing hormone
C/S	culture and sensitivity
CSF	cerebrospinal fluid
C/sec	cesarean section
CT	computed tomography
Cu	copper
CV	cardiovascular
cva	costovertebral angle
CVA	cerebrovascular accident
CVP	central venous pressure
CXR	chest X-ray
cysto	cystoscopy
D&C	dilation and curettage
D/C	discontinue
D&S	dilation and suction
DAT	diet as tolerated
Dial	dialysis
dil	dilute
dl	deciliter
DLE	drug-related lupus erythematosus
DM	diabetes mellitus
DNA	deoxyribonucleic acid
DOA	dead on arrival
DP	dorsalis pedis
DPT	diphtheria, pertussis, tetanus
DFR	delivery room
ds	double strand
DSD	dry sterile dressing
FS	frozen section
FSH	follicle-stimulating hormone
FWB	full weight bearing
fx	fracture
g	gram
Ga	gallium
GA	general anesthesia
GB	gallbladder
Gc	gonoccocus
GERD	gastroesophageal reflux disease

GI	gastrointestinal
glu	glucose
gr	grain
GSW	gunshot wound
gtt	drop
GTT	glucose tolerance test
GU	genitourinary
GVHD	graft-versus-host disease
Gyn	gynecology
H/A	headache
HAV	hepatitis A virus
Hb	hemoglobin
HBP	high blood pressure
HBV	hepatitis B virus
hct	hematocrit
HCV	hepatitis C virus
HD	hospital discharge
HDL	high-density lipoprotein
HDV	hepatitis D virus
HEENT	head, eyes, ears, nose, and throat
Hg	hemoglobin
H/H	hemoglobin/hematocrit
HIV	human immunodeficiency virus
H&L	heart and lungs
HLA	human leukocyte antigen
H_2O	water
H_2O_2	hydrogen peroxide
H&P	history and physical examination
HPI	history of present illness
HR	heart rate
HRS	hepatorenal syndrome
hs	hour of sleep (at bedtime)
HSV	herpes simplex virus
ht	height
HTN	hypertension
hx	history
I&D	incision and drainage
IABP	intraaortic balloon pump
IBC	iron-binding capacity
IBD	inflammatory bowel disease
IBS	irritable bowel syndrome
ICP	intracranial pressure
ICU	intensive care unit
ID	intradermal
IDDM	insulin-dependent diabetes mellitus
Ig	immunoglobulin

ILD	interstitial lung disease
IM	intramuscular
Imp	impression
inf	infusion
inh	inhalation
inj	injection
I&O	intake and output
IOP	intraocular pressure
IQ	intelligence quotient
IUD	intrauterine device
IV	intravenous
IVC	inferior vena cava
J	joule
JVP	jugular vein pulse
K⁺	potassium
Kj	knee jerk
kg	kilogram
KUB	kidney, ureter, and bladder
l	left
L	liter
LA	left atrium
lab	laboratory
lac	laceration
LAD	left axis deviation
lap	laparotomy
lb	pound
LBP	low back pain
LBBB	left bundle branch block
LDL	low-density lipoprotein
LFT	liver function test
LH	luteinizing hormone
LHRH	luteinizing hormone-releasing hormone
Li	lithium
Lip	lipid
liq	liquid
LLL	left lower lobe
LLQ	left lower quadrant
LMD	local medical doctor
LMP	last menstrual period
LNMP	last normal menstrual period
LOC	level of consciousness
LP	lumbar puncture
LPN	licensed practical nurse
LSk	liver, spleen, and kidney
LUL	left upper lobe
LUQ	left upper quadrant

LVH	left ventricular hypertrophy
L&W	living and well
m	murmur
M	midnight; monoclonal
MAO	monoamine oxidase
MAP	mean arterial pressure
MAT	multifocal atrial tachycardia
MCA	middle cerebral artery
MCV	mean cell volume
med	medication
MED	medical
mets	metastases
MF	maturation factor
mg	milligram
Mg^{2+}	magnesium
MI	myocardial infarction
min	minute
mixt	mixture
ml	milliliter
ML	malignant lymphoma
μmol	micromole
mm	millimeter
mM, mmol	millimole
mod	moderate
MOM	milk of magnesia
MRI	magnetic resonance imaging
MS	mitral stenosis; mental status; multiple sclerosis
MVA	motor vehicle accident
MVP	mitral valve prolapse; mitomycin; vinblastien, cisplatin (Platinol)
N	normal
NA	not applicable
Na^+	sodium
NAS	no added sodium
NB	newborn
NCP	nursing care plan
ng	nanogram
NG	nasogastric
NH^3	ammonia
NHL	non-Hodgkin's lymphoma
NIDDM	non-insulin-dependent diabetes mellitus
NIH	National Institutes of Health
NKA	no known allergies
NKDA	no known drug allergies
NM	neuromuscular

no	number
noc	night
NPH	normal pressure hydrocephalus; neutral protamine Hagedorn (insulin)
NPO	nothing by mouth
NS	normal saline
NSAID	nonsteroidal antiinflammatory drug
NSR	normal sinus rhythm
NTG	nitroglycerin
OA	oral airway
OB	obstetrics
OD	overdose
OD	right eye
OETT	oral endotracheal tube
oint	ointment
OOB	out of bed
OOP	out on pass
OPD	outpatient department
opt	optimum
ophth	ophthalmology
OR	operating room
Oral	oral surgery
Orth or ortho	orthopedics
OS	left eye
osm	osmolality
OT	occupational therapy
OU	each eye
oz	ounce
P	after pulse
PAP	pulmonary artery pressure
para	number of pregnancies
PASP	pulmonary artery systolic pressure
PAT	paroxysmal atrial tachycardia
PAWP	pulmonary artery wedge pressure
pc	after meals
Pco_2	carbon dioxide tension
PE	physical examination; pulmonary embolism
PEARL	pupils equal and reactive to light
ped	pediatric
PEEP	positive end-expiratory pressure
PEFR	peak expiratory flow rate
per	by
PERRLA	pupils equal, round, reactive to light and accommodation
PFT	pulmonary function test
pg	picogram

PGE	prostaglandin E
PH	past history
phos	phosphorus
PHR	peak heart rate
PI	present illness
PKU	phenylketonuria
PM	afternoon
PMP	previous menstrual period
PM&R	physical medicine and rehabilitation
PO	by mouth
postop	postoperative
Po_2	oxygen tension
PP	postpartum
preop	preoperative
prep	preparation
prn	as needed
psi	pounds per square inch
Psych	psychiatry
pt	patient
PT	prothrombin time; physical therapy; posterior tibia
PTA	prior to admission
Pth	pathology
PUD	peptic ulcer disease
PX	physical
q	every
qd	every day
qh	every hour
qhs	every bedtime
qid	four times a day
qns	quantity not sufficient
qod	every other day
qs	quantity sufficient
r	right
R	respiratory rate (per minute)
RA	rheumatoid arthritis; right atrium
RAI	radioactive iodine
RAN	resident's admission note
RAP	right atrial pressure
RBC	red blood cells
RDW	red cell distribution width
R&E	round and equal
readm	readmission
REM	rapid eye movement
RF	rheumatoid factor
Rh	Rhesus blood factor

RIA	radioimmunoassay
RL	Ringer's lactate
RIND	reversible ischemic neurological deficit
RLL	right lower lobe
RLQ	right lower quadrant
RML	right middle lobe
RN	registered nurse
RNA	ribonucleic acid
R/O	rule out
ROM	range of motion
ROS	review of systems
rpt	repeat
RPT	registered physical therapist
RR	recovery room
RSR	regular sinus rhythm
rt-PA	recombinant tissue plasminogen activator
R/T	related to
RTC	return to clinic
RUL	right upper lobe
RUQ	right upper quadrant
RV	right ventricle; residual volume
RVH	renovascular hypertension; right ventribular hypertrophy
Rx	therapy; treatment; prescription
S/A	sugar and acetone
SA	sinoatrial
SAH	subarachnoid hemorrhage
sat	saturated
SB	stillbirth
SC	subcutaneous
SCP	standard care plan
SGA	small for gestational age
SL	sublingual
SLE	systemic lupus erythematosus
SLR	straight leg raising
SMI	suggested minimum increment
SMS	somatostatin
SNF	skilled nursing facility
SO_2	oxygen saturation
SOB	shortness of breath
SOC	state of consciousness
sol	solution
S/P	status post
SQ	subcutaneous
SR	slow release
SRM	spontaneous rupture membranes

ss	half
S/S	signs and symptoms
SS	Sjögren's syndrome
stat	immediately
STD	sexually transmitted disease
STS	serologic test for syphilis
subcu, SC	subcutaneous
supp\	suppository
Surg	surgery
susp	suspension
SVC	superior vena cava
SVR	systemic vascular resistance
SVT	supraventricular tachycardia
Sx	symptoms
syr	syrup
T&A	tonsillectomy and adenoidectomy
tab	tablet
TAH	total abdominal hysterectomy
TB	tuberculosis
TBIL	total bilirubin
TBNa	total body sodium
Tbsp	tablespoon
TBW	total body water
T/C	throat culture
temp	temperature
TENS	transcutaneous electrical nerve stimulation
TIA	transient ischemic attack
tid	three times daily
tinc	tincture
TLC	total lung capacity
TM	tympanic membrane
TNM	tumor-nodes-metastases
TO	telephone order
top	topical
tPA	tissue plasminogen activator
TP	total protein
TPN	total parenteral nutrition
TPR	temperature, pulse, and respiration
TRIG	triglycerides
tsp	teaspoon
TTS	transdermal therapeutic system
Tx	therapy
U	unit
UA	umbilical artery
U/A	urinalysis
UGI	upper gastrointestinal

ung	ointment
U/P	urine: plasma ratio (concentration)
URAC	uric acid
URI	upper respiratory tract infection
UTI	urinary tract infection
UV	ultraviolet
v	mixed venous
V	volume
vag hyst	vaginal hysterectomy
VD	venereal disease
VER	visual evoked response
VF	ventribular fibrillation
VO	verbal order
vs	visit
VS	vital signs
VSD	ventricular septal defect
VT/VF	ventricular tachycardia-fibrillation
W	white
WBC	white blood cell count
w/c	wheelchair
WD	well developed
WF	white female
WHO	World Health Organization
WN	well nourished
WNL	within normal limits
wt	weight
y/o	years old
X	times

SYMBOLS

@	at	>	greater than
++	moderate amount	<	less than
+++	large amount	µ or µm	micron (micrometer)
0	zero, none	+	positive
°	degree	″	minute
♀	female	′	second
♂	male	∅	absence of
#	number	✔	check
↑	increased	−	negative, absence
↓	decreased	Δ	changes

Index

About the Editors

Peter J. Snyder, PhD, graduated with high honors from The University of Michigan in 1986, after completing an undergraduate major in psychology. His PhD in clinical psychology, with an emphasis in behavioral neuroscience, was awarded by Michigan State University in 1992, following an internship in clinical neuropsychology at the Long Island Jewish Medical Center (Albert Einstein College of Medicine). Dr. Snyder received a Wilder Penfield Research Fellowship in 1992 from the Epilepsy Foundation of America, and he served as a Clinical Neurosciences Fellow in the National Institute of Mental Health Clinical Research Center for the Study of Schizophrenia at Hillside Hospital (Albert Einstein College of Medicine) in 1992 and 1993. He also served as a visiting scientist at the National Institutes of Health in 1991.

Dr. Snyder publishes regularly and maintains numerous scientific collaborations. He serves as an associate editor of *Brain and Cognition*, and he has delivered over 100 presentations at international scientific conferences. His academic interests range from the evolutionary bases of functional neuroanatomical specialization to the neurobiological substrates of emotion and prosodic speech. Dr. Snyder's clinical interests bridge a wide variety of neurological and neuropsychiatric conditions. As a director and early clinical leader at Pfizer Global R & D—Groton Laboratories (Connecticut), he has led the early clinical development of novel compounds for the treatment of schizophrenia and Alzheimer's disease, at the central research laboratories for Pfizer Inc.

As a professor in the Department of Psychology at the University of Connecticut (Storrs), Dr. Snyder teaches graduate courses in cognitive neuroscience and neuropsychology, maintains an active laboratory, and serves as the major professor for several graduate and postdoctoral students.

Dr. Snyder is a fellow of the American Psychological Association (Division 40, Clinical Neuropsychology), and he is the recipient of the 2001 Early Career Contributions Award from the National Academy of Neuropsychology.

Paul D. Nussbaum, PhD, graduated with high honors from the University of Arizona in 1985, after completing an undergraduate major in psychology. His PhD in clinical psychology, with an emphasis in clinical neuropsychology and minor in gerontology, was awarded in 1991 following an internship in clinical neuropsychology at the Highland Drive Veterans Administration Medical Center (Pittsburgh, Pennsylvania). Dr. Nussbaum then completed a 1-year postdoctoral fellowship in geriatric neuropsychology in the Department of Psychiatry, University of Pittsburgh School of Medicine. He is an adjunct associate professor in neurosurgery at the University of Pittsburgh School of Medicine.

Dr. Nussbaum has over 15 years experience in the care of older people with dementia and related disorders, and he has worked in all sectors of the continuum of care. Dr. Nussbaum has published over 50 peer-reviewed articles, books, and chapters, and he lectures internationally on the topics of aging and health promotion. Much of his writing and speaking is geared to the nonacademic, with a clear intention of educating the general public about the aging process. Dr. Nussbaum also writes a monthly article on healthy aging for the *Pittsburgh Post Gazette-South* that is read across the United States.

Diana L. Robins, PhD, graduated with high honors from Oberlin College, after completing undergraduate majors in psychology and neuroscience. Her doctoral degree in clinical psychology, with a concentration in neuropsychology, was awarded by the University of Connecticut in 2002 following an internship in clinical neuropsychology at the University of Florida Health Sciences Center. Dr. Robins completed a postdoctoral fellowship at the Yale University School of Medicine Child Study Center in 2004. Her first year at Yale was supported by the Marie Bristol-Power Postdoctoral Fellowship from the National Alliance for Autism Research, and her second year was supported by a competitive fellowship award from the Yale School of Medicine and by a training grant in neuropsychiatric disorders from the National Institute of Mental Health.

Dr. Robins has developed an active research program with a primary focus on social deficits in autism spectrum disorders, and her research and clinical interests also include many areas of child and adult neuropsychology. Dr. Robins is assistant professor of psychology at Georgia State University, working in the divisions of clinical psychology and neuropsychology and behavioral neuroscience.